An Introduction to

INTERCULTURAL COMMUNICATION

seventh edition

An Introduction to

INTERCULTURAL
COMMUNICATION

Identities in a Global Community

seventh edition

FRED E. JANDT
California State University, San Bernardino

Los Angeles | London | New Delhi
Singapore | Washington DC

Los Angeles | London | New Delhi
Singapore | Washington DC

FOR INFORMATION:

SAGE Publications, Inc.
2455 Teller Road
Thousand Oaks, California 91320
E-mail: order@sagepub.com

SAGE Publications Ltd.
1 Oliver's Yard
55 City Road
London EC1Y 1SP
United Kingdom

SAGE Publications India Pvt. Ltd.
B 1/I 1 Mohan Cooperative Industrial Area
Mathura Road, New Delhi 110 044
India

SAGE Publications Asia-Pacific Pte. Ltd.
33 Pekin Street #02-01
Far East Square
Singapore 048763

Acquisitions Editor: Matthew Byrnie
Associate Editor: Nathan Davidson
Production Editor: Eric Garner
Copy Editor: Trey Thoelke
Typesetter: C&M Digitals (P) Ltd.
Proofreader: Jennifer Gritt
Cover Designer: Bryan Fishman
Marketing Manager: Liz Thornton
Permissions Editor: Karen Ehrmann

Copyright © 2013 by SAGE Publications, Inc.

Printed in the United States of America

Library of Congress Cataloging-in-Publication Data

Jandt, Fred Edmund.

An introduction to intercultural communication : identities in a global community / Fred E. Jandt.—7th ed.

p. cm.
Includes bibliographical references and index.

ISBN 978-1-4129-9287-9 (pbk.)

1. Intercultural communication. 2. Intercultural communication—United States. 3. Communication, International. I. Title.

GN345.J43 2013
303.48'2—dc23   2011049041

This book is printed on acid-free paper.

12 13 14 15 16 10 9 8 7 6 5 4 3 2 1

BRIEF CONTENTS

About the Author   xii

Preface   xiii

Acknowledgments   xvii

PART 1: CULTURE AS CONTEXT
FOR COMMUNICATION   1

Chapter 1. Defining Culture and
Identities   4

Chapter 2. Understanding Face-to-Face
and Mediated Communication   34

Chapter 3. Culture's Influence on
Perception   58

PART 2: COMMUNICATION
VARIABLES   77

Chapter 4. Barriers to Intercultural
Communication   80

Chapter 5. Nonverbal
Communication   106

Chapter 6. Language as a Barrier   132

PART 3: CULTURAL VALUES   165

Chapter 7. Dimensions of Culture   168

Chapter 8. Dominant U.S. Cultural
Patterns: Using Value Orientation
Theory   196

Chapter 9. Comparative Cultural
Patterns: Arab Culture   224

Chapter 10. Culture and Gender   248

Chapter 11. Contact Between
Cultures   278

PART 4: CULTURES WITHIN
CULTURES   305

Chapter 12. Immigration and
Acculturation   308

Chapter 13. Cultures Within
Cultures   336

Chapter 14. Identity and
Subgroups   366

Glossary   G-1

References   R-1

Credits   C-1

Index   I-1

DETAILED CONTENTS

About the Author   xii

Preface   xiii

Acknowledgments   xvii

PART 1: CULTURE AS CONTEXT FOR COMMUNICATION   1

Chapter 1. Defining Culture and Identities   4

Regulators of Human Life and Identity   5
  Culture   5
    Nineteenth-Century Definition   6
    Today's Definition   6
  Cultures Within Cultures   8
  Subculture   8
    Economic or Social Class   12
    Ethnicity   12
  Co-Culture   13
  Case Study: American Indians   17
  Subgroup   17
    Definition   18
    Deviant Label   18
    Temporality   18
    "Wannabe" Behavior   18
Race and Skin Color   19
  The Concept of Race   19
  Identity and Race   20

The Contact Zone   22
  Today's Contact Zone Challenges   23
    Ethnic and Religious Conflict   24
    Role of Women   25
    Technology   26
    Migration   27
    Environmental Sustainability   31
Summary   32
Discussion Questions   32
Key Terms   33
Readings   33

Chapter 2. Understanding Face-to-Face and Mediated Communication   34

Intercultural Communication Competence   35
  Personality Strength   35
  Communication Skills   36
  Psychological Adjustment   36
  Cultural Awareness   36
Intercultural Communication Ethics   37
Cultural Definitions of Communication   39
  Confucian Perspectives on
    Communication   39
  Western Perspectives on Communication   41
  Twentieth-Century Theory   42
  Components of Communication   42
The Media of Intercultural Communication   45
  Human Couriers and Intermediaries   45
  Letter Writing   46
  Telephone   46
  Internet   48
    Language Use   48
    Design Elements   50
    Social Network Sites   50
The Special Case of Prejudice and Racism   52
Summary   55
Discussion Questions   56
Key Terms   56
Readings   56

Chapter 3. Culture's Influence on Perception 58

Sensing 60
  Effect of Culture on Sensing 61
Perceiving 62
  Selection 62
    Japanese/English Difficulties
      With Speech Sounds 63
  Organization 64
    Grouping Like Objects
      Together 64
  Interpretation 66
    Dogs as Pets or as Food 66
    Weather Vane as Christian
      Cross 67
High Versus Low Context 69
The Concept of Face 72
A Case Study of Perception and Food 72
Summary 74
Discussion Questions 75
Key Terms 75
Readings 76

PART 2: COMMUNICATION VARIABLES 77

Chapter 4. Barriers to Intercultural Communication 80

Anxiety 82
Assuming Similarity Instead of Difference 82
Ethnocentrism 83
  Negative Effects on Communication 85

Stereotypes and Prejudice 85
  Stereotypes 85
  Negative Effects on
    Communication 88
  Case Study: Asian-Americans 89
  Prejudice 90
  Case Studies 90
    The Roma 91
    Japan and Korea 92
    United States 92
Case Study of Intercultural Communication
  Barriers: China and the United States 93
    Population 93
    History 93
    Regional Differences 95
    China's International Relationship
      Issues 97
    Status of Taiwan 98
    Tibet 99
    Human Rights and Free Speech 100
    Broadcast Media and the Internet 101
    Energy and Sustainability 102
      Economic Issues 103
Summary 104
Discussion Questions 104
Key Terms 105
Readings 105

Chapter 5. Nonverbal Communication 106

Nonverbal Behaviors as Cues 107
Nonverbal Communication as Intentional
  Communication 109
    Functions 109
Knowing Culture Through Nonverbal
  Messages 113
Nonverbal Misinterpretations as a Barrier 113
Nonverbal Message Codes 114
    Proxemics 114
    Kinesics 115
    Chronemics 121
    Paralanguage 122
    Silence 123

Haptics   124
Clothing and Physical
 Appearance   125
Territoriality   126
Olfactics   126
Case Study: The Wai in Thailand   128
Case Study: Korean-American Neighborhood
 Businesses   129
Summary   129
Discussion Questions   130
Key Terms   130

Chapter 6. Language as a Barrier   132

Study of Language Origins   134
Sapir-Whorf Hypothesis   136
 Development of the Hypothesis   136
  Linguistic Determinism   137
  Linguistic Relativity   138
 Applications   138
  Vocabulary   138
  Grammar and Syntax   140
  Case Study: Arabic and the Arab
   Culture   140
Translation Problems   141
 Vocabulary Equivalence   141
 Idiomatic Equivalence   142
 Grammatical-Syntactical
  Equivalence   143
 Experiential Equivalence   143
 Conceptual Equivalence   143
Pidgins, Creoles, and Universal
 Languages   146
 Pidgins   146
 Creoles   146
 Esperanto   147
Language as Nationalism   147
 English: A History of Borrowed
  Words   148
 The Spread of English   149
 India   150
 South Africa   152
 Australia and New Zealand   152
 Canada   153
 United States   154

The Situation in Hawai'i   159
Loss of American Indian
 Languages   160
Puerto Rico and Statehood   161
Summary   161
Discussion Questions   162
Key Terms   162
Readings   163

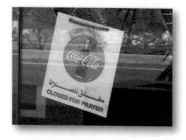

PART 3: CULTURAL VALUES   165

Chapter 7. Dimensions of Culture   168

Individualism Versus Collectivism   169
 Case Study: Japan as a Homogeneous
  Culture   172
  History   173
  Religion   174
  Cultural Patterns   176
Masculinity Versus Femininity   180
Power Distance   182
Uncertainty Avoidance   186
Long-Term Versus Short-Term Orientation   188
 Case Study: Singapore   188
Environmental Sustainability   190
Summary   192
Discussion Questions   193
Key Terms   193
Readings   194

Chapter 8. Dominant U.S. Cultural Patterns: Using Value Orientation Theory   196

Origins of U.S. Cultural Patterns   198
 Pre-16th-Century Indigenous
  Americans   198

European Enlightenment   198
Regional Differences Resulting From
   Immigration   198
     Communication Markers of
      Regions   200
Forces Toward the Development of a Dominant
  Culture   200
Value Orientation Theory   202
What Is a Human Being's Relation to
  Nature?   202
   The Individual-and-Nature
    Relationship   203
   Science and Technology   205
   Materialism   207
What Is the Modality of Human Activity?   209
   Activity and Work   210
   Efficiency and Practicality   210
   Progress and Change   210
What Is the Temporal Focus of Human
  Life?   211
What Is the Character of Innate Human
  Nature?   212
   Goodness   212
   Rationality   212
   Mutability   213
What Is the Relationship of the Individual to
  Others?   213
   Individualism   213
   Self-Motivation   214
   Social Organization   216
    Equality   216
    Conformity   217
Forces Toward the Development of Regional
  Cultures   218
   The New Regions   220
Summary   222
Discussion Questions   222
Key Terms   223
Readings   223

**Chapter 9. Comparative
Cultural Patterns: Arab Culture   224**

The Arab States   225
The Islamic Faith   225

Muhammad, the Prophet   228
The Koran   230
Religious Practices   230
Saudi Arabia   232
  Geography   232
  Discovery of Oil   233
  Ruling Saud Family and Conservative
    Wahhabism   233
  Media   233
  Matawain   234
    Contact With the United
     States   234
Dubai   236
Dominant Cultural Patterns   238
  Worldview   238
  Activity Orientation   238
  Time Orientation   239
  Human Nature Orientation   240
  Relational Orientation   240
    Role of Women   240
Communication Barriers   242
  Political Unrest and Terrorism   242
  Political Unrest and Social
    Media   243
  Westernization Versus Cultural
    Norms   245
  Stereotypes   245
Summary   246
Discussion Questions   247
Key Terms   247

Chapter 10. Culture and Gender   248

Gender and Communication   249
Status of Women   251
   United Nations Studies   251
World Economic Forum Study   254
    Health   255
    Education   256
    Economics   256
    Political Participation   258
Comparison of Individual Countries   261
   Nordic Countries   261
   Mexico   265
   China   265

Japan   268
South Korea   269
India   270
Sub-Saharan Africa   271
Arab States   272
Family Units   274
Marriage   275
Summary   276
Discussion Questions   277
Key Terms   277

Chapter 11. Contact Between Cultures   278

Colonialism   279
Hawai'i   280
Australia   281
Cultural Imperialism   282
Cultural Icons   285
Cultural Hegemony   286
Japanese Icon in Mexico   286
U.S. Cultural Icons   287
Coca-Cola and Pepsi   287
Euro Disney and Hong Kong
Disneyland   288
McDonald's   291
Kentucky Fried
Chicken   295
Budweiser   296
SPAM®   296
Barbie   296
Marlboro   296
Diffusion Model   298
Roles in the Diffusion Process   298
Opinion Leadership and Change
Agents   298
Adopters   299
Change Agent Ethics   299
Case Study: Quality Circles   300
Convergence Model   301
Adapting the Message   301
Case Study: Marketing Gerber Baby Foods
Worldwide   301
Case Study: Religious Missionary Work in
New Guinea   302

Summary   302
Discussion Questions   303
Key Terms   303
Readings   303

PART 4: CULTURES WITHIN CULTURES   305

Chapter 12. Immigration and Acculturation   308

Culture Shock   309
Stages of Culture Shock   309
Reverse Culture Shock   311
Symptoms   311
Third-Culture Kids   311
Migration Within One Country   312
Citizenship Policies   313
Germany   313
Israel   315
Japan   316
Immigration   316
Migration From Japan to Brazil and
Peru   317
Migration From Korea to Brazil and
Argentina   317
Migration From Europe to Argentina   317
Migration From the United States to
Brazil   318
Recent Immigration to Western
Europe   319
Immigration to the United States   320
Colonial Policies on
Immigration   320
U.S. Policies on Immigration   320
Contributing Countries Prior
to 1800   322

Contributing Countries
Since 1800 323
Predictors of Acculturation 329
Similarity of Culture 329
Personal Characteristics and Experiences 329
Effect of Media and Transportation
Advances 329
Categories of Acculturation 331
Summary 334
Discussion Questions 335
Key Terms 335
Reading 335

Chapter 13. Cultures Within Cultures 336

Marginalization: The Hmong 337
History 338
Cultural Patterns 339
Separation: Koreans in Russia 340
Separation: The Amish 340
History 340
Values 341
Religion 341
Controlled Use of Technology 341
Accepting Amish Identity 342
Education 342
Work 342
Change 343
Diversity Among the Amish 344
Indigenous Cultures 345
Assimilation: United States 347
Melting Pot Concept 348
Integration: United States 349
From Melting Pot to Symphony and
Stew 349
Hispanic Cultures 350
Terminology 350
Spanish-Language Use 354
Values 354
Cultural Identity and Media 356
Print 356
Radio 358
Television 359
Spanish-Language Internet and
Social Media 360
Cultural Identity and Marketing 360

Postethnic Cultures 362
Summary 363
Discussion Questions 363
Key Terms 364
Readings 364

Chapter 14. Identity and Subgroups 366

Argot 367
Specialized Vocabulary 367
Argot and Subgroup Identity 367
Argot and Subgroup Boundaries 368
Argot and Meaning 368
Subgroup Media and Values 368
Examples of Subgroups 369
The Working Class 369
British Punk 370
Corporate Cultures 372
Case Study: Southwest
Airlines 373
Southwest Airlines former CEO
Herb Kelleher 374
Case Study: Google 376
Sexual Orientation as a Basis for
Subgroups 376
Sexual Orientation and Othering 377
Rejecting All Labels 377
Attitudes Toward Sexual Orientation 378
Cultural Bases for Attitudes 380
Consequences of Othering 381
Homophobia 381
Traditional and Social Media 383
From Separation to Assimilation 384
Evidence of Separate Status 385
Integration or Assimilation of Subgroups 385
A Final Word 386
Summary 388
Discussion Questions 388
Key Terms 388
Readings 389

Glossary G-1

References R-1

Credits C-1

Index I-1

ABOUT THE AUTHOR

Fred E. Jandt was born of second-generation German immigrants in the multicultural south-central region of Texas. His doctorate in communication is from Bowling Green State University. He has taught and been a student of intercultural communication for more than 35 years, developing his experience through travel and international training and research projects.

While Professor of Communication at State University of New York at Brockport, his reputation as a teacher led to his appointment as SUNY's first director of faculty development. He is currently Dean of the Palm Desert Campus and Professor of Communication at California State University, San Bernardino, and has been a visiting professor at Victoria University of Wellington in New Zealand.

He has extensive experience in the areas of intercultural and international communication, negotiation and mediation, and computer-mediated communication.

He is known for his book *Win-Win Negotiating* (1985), which has been translated into eight languages. The focus of his interest is on the overlap of conflict and culture studies. He edited with Paul B. Pedersen *Constructive Conflict Management: Asia-Pacific Cases* (1996).

PREFACE

I started teaching intercultural communication out of the belief that so many misunderstandings between individuals, groups, and even nations resulted from a lack of an appreciation of culture—both one's own and another's. Over the years I became increasingly involved in international intercultural communication training programs and student exchange programs, and I developed an appreciation of the genuine efforts students made to become more competent communicators.

OVERCOMING BARRIERS THROUGH INTERCULTURAL COMPETENCE

I felt that my life experiences seeing prejudice from the unclouded eyes of a child had provided me with a perspective that could be of value to others striving to overcome cultural barriers. My agenda is to facilitate students' development of self-concepts that value their histories and appreciate diversities. My approach is to promote the skills of intercultural competence by developing an understanding of how individuals perceive and react to cultural rules. I believe that understandings of the pull to join and the push to make separate are critical for developing intercultural communication competence. These motivations led me to write the first edition of this introductory intercultural communication textbook, published in 1995. Looking back at the first edition today I see that while many of the examples and statistics have changed, my goal for the textbook remains the same: to help students develop an understanding of cultures to better appreciate the opportunities and challenges each culture presents to its people.

This text will aid students in becoming competent in communication with others of diverse cultural backgrounds by helping them to develop the following skills and understandings.

Expanding Your Range of Verbal and Nonverbal Communication Skills

Effective communicators have the ability to select and perform communication behaviors appropriate to various settings.

Becoming Able to Communicate Effectively in Unfamiliar Settings

We all experience stress in unfamiliar settings. More effective communicators recognize and handle that stress.

Recognizing the Influence Your Own Culture Has Had on the Way in Which You View Yourself

More effective communicators understand how they became who they are and are less threatened by those of different backgrounds.

Expanding Your Knowledge of the Ways of Other Cultures

More effective communicators know more about the norms and values of other cultures.

UPDATED CONTENT

This edition is probably the most extensive revision of any previous edition. The chapter sequence and each chapter's focus have been retained so that current users of the text can easily adapt to this new edition. But within the chapters the reader will find extensive updating of facts and statistics and extensive updating and expansion of references. Many new examples have been added from recent international events, such as the Japanese earthquake in March of 2011, many more examples from Africa, more recent material on immigration and attitudes toward immigration, more recent material on the Arab states, and a recasting of the material on subgroups into an international, rather than U.S., perspective. I have always encouraged feedback from students and instructors, and I have used their comments to make corrections, eliminate some material, and add new material.

Perhaps the most significant change in this edition is a new focus on social media. Rather than include a new chapter on social media, I have taken the effort to incorporate material on social media into each chapter in ways that make social media part of the content of the subject matter rather than an "add on." I've included new research that illustrates how people use social media based on the reality of their culture.

MEANINGFUL FEATURES

It has been my hope since the very first edition that students using this book will find it interesting and readable. So, in this new edition I've included up-to-date examples throughout the text that will help make the concepts come alive and relate to everyday experience. I have also given special attention to the visual elements of the photographs, figures, and tables in order to offer vivid illustrations of intercultural communication skills, practices, and concepts. Finally, I have updated and added the following pedagogical features that will help guide students through important concepts and connect intercultural competence to their own life experiences in order to increase understanding.

- *Updated* Focus on Theory boxes call students' attention to communication theories, and they have been updated to offer additional insights into theoretical concepts.
- *New* Focus on Culture boxes help students understand cultural norms and practices within other cultures and within their own.

- *Updated* Focus on the Environment boxes connect intercultural communication skills and practices to the challenges of the global environment.
- *New* Global Voices boxes use brief, provocative quotes to introduce students to a diverse range of perspectives on global intercultural communication.
- *Updated* Photo Essays introduce each of the book's four parts, engaging students visually in critical thinking about key topics discussed in each part of the text.
- *New* chapter-opening Focus Questions guide students through the goals of the chapter with critical thinking questions that call attention to key topics and concepts.
- *Updated* end-of-chapter Discussion Questions encourage students to reflect critically on what they have learned in each chapter.
- *Updated* Glossary with Key Terms highlighted in each chapter.
- Readings at the end of each chapter connect the chapters to resources in *Intercultural Communication: A Global Reader,* which may be used alongside this text.

TEACHING AND LEARNING ANCILLARIES

Additional ancillary materials further support and enhance the learning goals of this edition of *Introduction to Intercultural Communication.* These ancillary materials include the following.

Instructor Teaching Site: www.sagepub.com/jandt7e

The new instructor teaching site provides one integrated source for all instructor materials, including the following key components:

- An updated electronic test bank, available to PCs and Macs through Diploma software, offers a diverse set of test questions and answers to aid instructors in assessing students' progress and understanding. The software allows for test creation and customization, and each chapter includes multiple choice, true/false, short-answer, and essay questions. The test bank is also available in Microsoft Word.
- PowerPoint presentations designed to assist with lecture and review, highlighting essential content, features, and artwork from the book.
- Chapter outlines for each chapter can be used to structure daily lesson plans.
- Course syllabi are designed to help instructors structure a quarter or semester-long course.
- Classroom assignments are provided to reinforce active learning.
- Informative websites and media links provide students with another source of enrichment material related to each chapter's content.
- Internet activities encourage students to use the Web to enhance their understanding of important topics.
- Carefully selected, Web-based video resources feature relevant content for use in independent and classroom-based exploration of key topics.
- A "Learning from SAGE Journal Articles" feature provides access to recent, relevant full-text articles from SAGE's leading research journals. Each article supports and expands on the concepts presented in the chapter.

Student Study Site: www.sagepub.com/jandt7e

This open-access student study site provides a variety of additional resources to build on students' understanding of the book content and extend their learning beyond the classroom.

- Web quizzes with 10 to 15 multiple-choice and true/false questions for every chapter allow students to independently assess their progress in learning course material.
- Flashcards reinforce student understanding and learning of key terms and concepts in the book.
- Web resources and media links to various sites on the Web for further research and for real-life stories and situations related to the chapter topic.
- A "Learning from SAGE Journal Articles" feature provides access to recent, relevant full-text articles from SAGE's leading research journals. Each article supports and expands on the concepts presented in the chapter. Discussion questions are also provided to focus and guide student interpretation.
- Carefully selected, Web-based video resources feature relevant content for use in independent and classroom-based exploration of key topics.
- Web exercises direct students to various websites and ask them to apply their knowledge to a particular topic.
- Sample essays provide students with excellent examples for use in crafting their own written work.

ACKNOWLEDGMENTS

Through the years many people have reviewed previous editions and I have thanked them in each and every edition. That list has grown so that I can only thank previous reviewers collectively and list the new reviewers for this edition. This group of reviewers has provided extensive critical comments that have made this the best possible edition. They include:

A. M. Mason (Pittsburg State University)

Bosah Ebo (Rider University)

Carolyn M. Hale (Missouri Southern State University)

Dana Janbek (Lasell College)

Elenie Opffer (Texas A & M, Corpus Christi)

Jianglong Wang (Western Washington University)

Jin Xu (Winona State University)

Kay L. Colley (Texas Wesleyan University)

Milan Andrejevich (Ivy Tech Community College)

Richard Fiordo (University of North Dakota)

Roxanna M. Senyshyn (Abington College, Pennsylvania State University)

Galina Sinekopova (Eastern Washington University)

Yuxia Qian (Albion College)

Over the years, the professional staff at Sage has done so much to make this book such a success. My previous editor, Todd Armstrong, helped start the thinking for this edition. My new editor, Matthew Byrnie, quickly grew to understand and appreciate the book and has provided the guidance to make it better. Special thanks to Eric J. Garner, Senior Project Editor at Sage, who oversaw the production of this edition and gave it its exciting new look. And thanks to Trey Thoelcke, copyeditor for this new edition. Thanks, as well, to Theresa Accomazzo, who supervised the development of the book's website. And special thanks to associate editor Nathan Davidson who has been a joy to work with in the day-to-day development of the project. The team at Sage has done so much to make this edition the best and I am deeply appreciative.

PART 1

Culture as Context for Communication

Billions of us live on this planet and each one of us is unique. Height, hair texture, facial features, clothing, food preferences, language, and so many other variables distinguish each of us. And all of those variables have become the basis for categorization, separation, communication barriers, and hate.

For a class project and later independent study, a 22-year-old undergraduate anthropology student at the University of Missouri at St. Louis collected 30 paint samples from a local hardware store that ranged in color from dark brown to pale cream. She asked other students to identify the lines separating Blacks, Whites, Asians, and American Indians. She found that about 75% of non-White students overlapped the categories while about two thirds of the White students said that the categories were mutually exclusive. Her research project received national press coverage and was selected to appear in Conrad Phillip Kottaks's textbooks *Cultural Anthropology* (11th ed.) and *Anthropology: The Exploration of Human Diversity* (11th ed.).

Consider skin color. How conscious are you of your own skin color? How conscious are you of the skin color of your classmates? How conscious are you of how conscious your classmates are of your skin color?

Why are we more aware of skin color than of other variables that distinguish each of us? For example, how aware are you of having detached or attached ear lobes?

In Part 1 of this book, you will examine what constitutes the basis of a culture, co-culture, and subgroup. Each of us has cultural identifications, and associated with those cultural identifications are shared perceptions, experiences, values, and patterns of behavior.

Can there be a single human culture? Or will there always be multiple cultures? Can we more consciously choose cultural identities? Will multiple cultural identifications facilitate communication? Consider these questions as you read through Part 1.

CHAPTER

1

FOCUS QUESTIONS

- In general, how does culture provide for humans?

- What are the meanings of the terms culture, subculture, ethnicity, co-culture, subculture, subgroup, and race?

- What are some of the major issues in today's cultural contact zones?

Defining Culture and Identities

Regulators of Human Life And Identity
    Culture
        Nineteenth-Century Definition
        Today's Definition
    Cultures Within Cultures
    Subculture
        Economic or Social Class
        Ethnicity
    Co-Culture
    Case Study: American Indians
    Subgroup
        Definition
        Deviant Label
        Temporality
        "Wannabe" Behavior
Race and Skin Color
    The Concept of Race
    Identity and Race
The Contact Zone
    Today's Contact Zone Challenges
        Ethnic and Religious Conflict
        Role of Women
        Technology
        Migration
        Environmental Sustainability
Summary
Discussion Questions
Key Terms
Note
Readings
Student Study Site

Today about 7 billion people live on Earth, and no two of them alike. People can be small and large and in many colors. We wear different clothes and have different ideas of beauty. Many of us believe in one God,[1] others believe in many, and still others believe in none. Some people are rich and many are desperately poor. Have you ever considered why there's not one human culture rather than many cultures? Biologists Rebecca Cann, Mark Stoneking, and Allan C. Wilson (1987) studied genetic material from women around the world and contend that all humans alive today share genetic material from a woman who lived some 200,000 years ago in sub-Saharan Africa. Their African "Eve" conclusion may be supported by linguistic observations. Cavalli-Sforza, Piazza, Menozzi, and Mountain (1988) have shown that considerable similarity exists between Cann's tree of genetic relationships and the tree of language groups, which hypothesizes that all the world's languages can be traced to Africa.

Languages that are the most different from other languages today can be found in Africa. This may suggest that they are older. Africa's Khoisan languages, such as that of the !Kung San, use a clicking sound, which is denoted in writing with an exclamation point. Such evidence, along with genetic evidence, suggests that all of us alive today share ancestry from one group in Africa. How then did diverse cultures develop?

Climate changes or some other pressure led to migrations out of Africa. The first may have been along the coastline of southern Asia through southern India into Australia. The second wave may have traveled to the Middle East, and from there, one branch went to India and a second to China. Those who left the Middle East for Europe may have actually traveled first through Central Asia and then throughout the world to other parts of Asia, Russia, the Americas, and Europe (Wells, 2002).

Centuries of geographical separation were concurrent with the development of diverse ways of interpreting the world and the environment and relating to other peoples. Neuroscientist Antonio Damasio (2010) contends that our world, our environment, is so complex and so varied on the planet that social networks and cultures developed to regulate life so that we could survive. For much of the latter part of the 20th century, the dominant worldview was us versus them. Failures of political leadership led to two world wars and many regional wars. Today's challenges in the contact zone where cultures interact are identified as ethnic and religious conflict, the changing role of women, technology, migration, and environmental sustainability.

REGULATORS OF HUMAN LIFE AND IDENTITY

As Damasio suggests, culture is a regulator of human life and identity. That regulatory function extends to cultures within cultures, which we will study as subcultures, co-cultures, and subgroups.

Culture

Cultures provide diverse ways of interpreting the environment and the world, as well as relating to other peoples. To recognize that other peoples can see the world differently is one thing. To view their interpretations as less perfect that ours is another.

This can be seen in the evolution of the connotative meaning of the word *barbarian* from its initial use in the Greek of Herodotus to its meaning in contemporary English (Cole, 1996). To better understand the origins of hostilities between the Greeks and the Persians, Herodotus visited neighboring non-Greek societies to learn their belief systems, arts, and everyday practices. He called these non-Greek societies "barbarian," a word in Greek in his time that meant people whose language, religion, ways of life, and customs differed from those of the Greeks. Initially, *barbarian* meant different from what was Greek.

Later, the Greeks began to use the word to mean "outlandish, rude, or brutal." When the word was incorporated into Latin, it came to mean "uncivilized" or "uncultured." The Oxford English Dictionary gives the contemporary definition as "a rude, wild, uncivilized person," but acknowledges the original meaning was "one whose language and customs differ from the speaker's."

Nineteenth-Century Definition

In the 19th century, the term *culture* was commonly used as a synonym for *Western civilization*. The British anthropologist Sir Edward B. Tylor (1871) popularized the idea that all societies pass through developmental stages, beginning with "savagery," progressing to "barbarism," and culminating in Western "civilization." It's easy to see that such a definition assumes that Western cultures were considered superior. Both Western cultures, beginning with ancient Greece, and Eastern cultures, most notably imperial China, believed that their own way of life was superior. The study of multiple cultures without imposing the belief that Western culture was the ultimate goal was slow to develop.

Today's Definition

Cultures are not synonymous with countries. Cultures do not respect political boundaries. Border cities such as Juárez, El Paso, Tijuana, and San Diego can develop cultures that in some ways are not like Mexico or the United States. For example, major stores in U.S. border cities routinely accept Mexican currency.

In this text, **culture** refers to the following:

- A community or population sufficiently large enough to be self-sustaining; that is, large enough to produce new generations of members without relying on outside people.
- The totality of that group's thought, experiences, and patterns of behavior and its concepts, values, and assumptions about life that guide behavior and how those evolve with contact with other cultures. Hofstede (1994) classified these elements of culture into four categories: symbols, rituals, values, and heroes. **Symbols** refer to verbal and nonverbal language. **Rituals** are the socially essential collective activities within a culture. **Values** are the feelings not open for discussion within a culture about what is good or bad, beautiful or ugly, normal or abnormal, which are present in a majority of the members of a culture, or at least in those who occupy pivotal positions. **Heroes** are the real or imaginary people who serve as behavior models within a culture. A culture's heroes are expressed in the culture's myths, which can be the subject of novels and other forms of literature (Rushing & Frentz, 1978). Janice Hocker Rushing (1983) has argued, for example, that an enduring myth in U.S. culture, as seen in films, is the rugged individualist cowboy of the American West.

FOCUS ON CULTURE 1.1

Personalizing the Concept

 Let's try to develop a personal feeling for what is meant by the term *culture*. I will assume you have a sister, brother, or very close childhood friend. I would like you to think back to your relationship with that sibling or friend. Probably, you remember how natural and spontaneous your relationship was. Your worlds of experience were so similar; you shared problems and pleasures; you disagreed and even fought, but that didn't mean you couldn't put that behind you because you both knew in some way that you belonged together.

Now let's imagine that your sibling or friend had to leave you for an extended period. Perhaps your sister studied abroad for a year or your brother entered the military and served overseas. For some time, you were separated. Time brought you back together again, but you recognized that your relationship had forever changed because of the different experiences you had had during that separation. You still had years of common experiences and memories to reinforce your relationship, but sometimes differences cropped up from your time apart—small differences, but differences nonetheless—that led you both to know that you were more separate than you had been before.

During the time your sister studied abroad, she likely acquired new vocabulary, new tastes, and new ideas about values. She uses a foreign-sounding word in casual conversation; she now enjoys fast food or hates packaged food; she now has strong feelings about politics. Of course, these are small things, but they somehow remind you that you don't share as much as you had in the past. During the time of your separation, each of you had different experiences and challenges and had somehow been changed by those experiences and challenges. In a very simple way, this experience can be the beginning point of understanding what is meant today by the term *culture*. Even so, it illustrates only one aspect of the word's definition—shared experiences.

- The process of social transmission of these thoughts and behaviors from birth in the family and schools over the course of generations.
- Members who consciously identify themselves with that group. Collier and Thomas (1988) describe this as **cultural identity**, or the identification with and perceived acceptance into a group that has a shared system of symbols and meanings as well as norms for conduct. What does knowing an individual's cultural identity tell you about that individual? If you assume that the individual is like everyone else in that culture, you have stereotyped all the many, various people in that culture into one mold. You know that you are different from others in your culture. Other cultures are as diverse. The diversity within cultures probably exceeds the differences between cultures. So just knowing one person's cultural identity doesn't provide complete or reliable information about that person. Knowing another's cultural identity does, however, help you understand the opportunities and challenges that each individual in that culture had to deal with.

As Collier and Thomas suggest each of us has a cultural identity. That identity may or may not be the same as citizenship in one of the world's 200-some countries. Consider for a moment where you learned your symbols, rituals, values, and myths.

We can have no direct knowledge of a culture other than our own. Our experience with and knowledge of other cultures are limited by the perceptual bias of our own culture. An adult Canadian will never fully understand the experience of growing up an Australian. To begin to understand a culture, you need to understand all the experiences that guide its individual members through life. That includes language and gestures; personal appearance and social relationships; religion, philosophy, and values; courtship, marriage, and family customs; food and recreation; work and government; education and communication systems; health, transportation, and government systems; and economic systems. Think of culture as everything you would need to know and do so as not to stand out as a "stranger" in a foreign land. Culture is not a genetic trait. All these cultural elements are learned through interaction with others in the culture (see Focus on Culture 1.1).

Can there be a more critical time to study intercultural communication? Intercultural communication refers not only to the communication between individuals of diverse cultural identities but also to the communication between diverse groups. This text focuses on two equally important aspects of improving intercultural communication: first, that your effectiveness as an intercultural communicator is in part a function of your knowledge of other peoples and their cultures and, second, that as you learn more about other people from various cultures, you also discover more about yourself. This results in an appreciation and tolerance of diversity among people and makes you a more competent communicator in multicultural settings.

Cultures Within Cultures

Just as culture is a regulator of human life and identity, so can cultures within cultures be. Now let's look at the definitions of the terms *subculture, ethnicity,* and *co-culture* as attempts to identify groups that are cultures but that exist within another culture.

Subculture

Complex societies such as the United States are made up of a large number of groups with which people identify and from which are derived distinctive values and norms and rules for behavior. These groups have been labeled *subcultures.* A subculture resembles a culture in that it usually encompasses a relatively large number of people and represents the accumulation of generations of human striving. However, subcultures have some important differences. They exist within dominant cultures and are often based on economic or social class, ethnicity, or geographic region.

FOCUS ON CULTURE 1.2

Superstitions

Some cultural customs are often labeled as *superstitions*. They are the practices believed to influence the course of events. Whether it is rubbing a rabbit's foot for luck or not numbering the 13th floor in a building, these practices are part of one's cultural identification. We may not follow them, but we recognize them. For example, in Mexican *pulquerias,* saloons where people gather to drink *pulque,* a distillate of cactus, it's considered good fortune to get the worm in your cup.

Beckoning cat

In Japan, you may see a *maneki neko,* or "beckoning cat" figurine, with its front paw raised. The beckoning gesture brings customers into stores and good luck and fortune into homes.

In China, sounds and figures reflect good fortune. The phonetic sound of eight, *baat* in Cantonese and between *pa* and *ba* in Mandarin, is similar to *faat,* meaning prosperity. The number 8, then, is the most fortuitous of numbers, portending prosperity. The date and time of the 2008 Olympics' opening ceremony on August 8 had as many eights as possible (8:08:08 p.m., August 8, 2008). In Hong Kong, a license plate with the number 8 is quite valuable. But the number 4 can be read as *shi,* which is a homophone for death, so hospitals may not have a Room 4. Some Chinese would avoid buying a house with a street address with the number 4.

Superstitions are only a small part of culture but certainly an interesting part. Culture, then, refers to the totality of a people's socially transmitted products of work and thought. All these elements are interrelated like a tangled root system. Pull on one, the others move. Change one, the others must change.

FOCUS ON THEORY 1.1

Read the following court transcript (Liberman, 1981) and assess how successful you think the communication was.

Magistrate: Can you read and write?

Defendant: Yes.

Magistrate: Can you sign your name?

Defendant: Yes.

Magistrate: Did you say you cannot read?

Defendant: Hm.

Magistrate: Can you read or not?

Defendant: No.

Magistrate: [Reads statement.] Do you recall making that statement?

Defendant: Yes.

Magistrate: Is there anything else you want to add to the statement?

Defendant: [No answer.]

Magistrate: Did you want to say anything else?

Defendant: No.

Magistrate: Is there anything in the statement you want to change?

Defendant: No.

Magistrate: [Reads a second statement.] Do you recall making that statement?

Defendant: Yes.

Magistrate: Do you wish to add to the statement?

Defendant: No.

Magistrate: Do you want to alter the statement in any way?

Defendant: [Slight nod.]

Magistrate: What do you want to alter?

Defendant: [No answer.]

Magistrate: Do you want to change the statement?

Defendant: No.

Of course, it is doubtful that the defendant understands the proceedings. On the basis of this exchange, we also could raise doubts about the defendant's "statement." If I told you the defendant was an **Aboriginal** in Australia, could you say more about the interaction? How you attempt to answer that question illustrates two major approaches to intercultural communication.

If you examined the transcript in detail to locate the problems the defendant and the magistrate had in their exchange, your approach was *ethnographic.* If you asked for information about Aboriginals and the Australian legal system, your analysis would be called a *cultural studies approach.*

Ethnography is the direct observation, reporting, and evaluation of the customary behavior of a culture. Ideally, ethnography requires an extended period of residence and study in a community. The ethnographer knows the language of the group, participates in some of the group's activities, and uses a variety of observational and recording techniques. In a sense, the accounts of 15th-century explorers of the unfamiliar cultural practices they encountered were primitive ethnographies.

Modern ethnography tries to avoid questionnaires and formal interviews in artificial settings; observation in natural settings is preferred. The objective is an analysis of cultural patterns to develop a grammar or theory of the rules for appropriate cultural behaviors.

An ethnographic approach to understanding the dialogue between the magistrate and the defendant would use the perspective of the parties themselves to analyze the problems that each faces in the attempt to communicate. Thus, it appears that the Aboriginal defendant is engaged in a strategy of giving the answers "Yes," "No," or "Hm" that will best placate the magistrate (Liberman, 1990a).

A **cultural studies** approach attempts to develop an ideal personification of the culture, and then that ideal is used to explain the actions of individuals in the culture. For example, using the cultural approach, it would be important to know that the Aboriginal people began arriving on the Australian continent from Southeast Asia 40,000 years before North and South America were inhabited and that it wasn't until 1788 that 11 ships arrived carrying a cargo of human prisoners to begin a new British colony by taking control of the land. Liberman (1990b) describes the unique form of public discourse that evolved among the isolated Aboriginal people of central Australia: Consensus must be preserved through such strategies as unassertiveness, avoidance of direct argumentation, deferral of topics that would produce disharmony, and serial summaries so that the people think together and "speak with one voice." If any dissension is sensed, there are no attempts to force a decision, and the discussion is abandoned. Western European discourse style is direct, confrontational, and individualistic. Thus, it can be said that the Aboriginal defendant in the example finds it difficult to communicate a defense by opposing what has been said and rather frequently concurs with any statement made to him (Liberman, 1990b). The ethnographic and cultural approaches are complementary and together can help our understanding of breakdowns in intercultural communication.

Economic or Social Class

It can be argued that socioeconomic status or social class can be the basis for a subculture (Brislin, 1988). *Social class* has traditionally been defined as a position in a society's hierarchy based on income, education, occupation, and neighborhood. Gilbert and Kahl (1982) argue that in the United States, the basis of social class is income and that other markers of social class follow from income level. For example, income determines to some extent who you marry or choose as a lover, your career, and the neighborhood in which you are likely to live.

Melvin Kohn (1977) has shown that middle-class and working-class parents emphasize different values when raising children. Middle-class parents emphasize self-control, intellectual curiosity, and consideration for others. The desired outcomes of self-direction and empathic understanding transfer easily to professional and managerial jobs that require intellectual curiosity and good social skills. Working-class parents emphasize obedience, neatness, and good manners. Gilbert and Kahl (1982) argue that these lead to a concern with external standards, such as obedience to authority, acceptance of what other people think, and hesitancy in expressing desires to authority figures. These working-class concerns can be a detriment in schools, with their emphasis on verbal skills. The resulting learned behaviors transfer more directly to supervised wage labor jobs. Though these observations are based on large numbers of students, they should not be interpreted to apply to any one family. Working-class parents who encourage verbal skills through reading and conversation have children who are as successful in school. Although the United States does have social classes that have been shown to have different values, many people in the United States believe that these barriers of social class are easier to transcend in the United States than in other countries.

Ethnicity

Another basis for subcultures is ethnicity. The term *ethnicity* is like the term *race* in that its definition has changed over time. Its different definitions reflect a continuing social debate. Ethnicity can refer to a group of people of the same descent and heritage who share a common and distinctive culture passed on through generations (Zenner, 1996). For some, *tribes* would be a more understood term. In Afghanistan, for example, people identify by tribes—Tajiks and Pashtuns. According to some estimates, there are 5,000 ethnic groups in the world (Stavenhagen, 1986). Ethnic groups can exhibit such distinguishing features as language or accent, physical features, family names, customs, and religion.

Ethnic identity refers to identification with and perceived acceptance into a group with shared heritage and culture (Collier & Thomas, 1988).

Sometimes, the word *minority* is used by some. Technically, of course, the word *minority* is used to describe numerical designations. A group might be a minority, then, if it has a smaller number of people than a majority group with a larger number. In the United States, the word *majority* has political associations, as in the *majority rules,* a term used so commonly in the

United States that the two words have almost become synonymous. According to the *Oxford English Dictionary,* the term *minority* was first used to describe ethnic groups in 1921. Since that time, advantage has been associated with the majority and disadvantage has been associated with the minority.

Just as definitions of words such as *culture* have changed, the way words are written has changed. In U.S. English, ethnic groups are usually referred to in hyphenated terms, such as *Italian-American.* The hyphen gives the term a meaning of a separate group of people. Most style manuals today have dropped the use of the hyphen, as in *Italian American,* using *Italian* as an adjective, giving the meaning of "Americans of Italian descent"—a change that puts the emphasis on what Americans share rather than on what makes groups different from one another. This text uses the hyphen to communicate the meaning of a culture within a culture.

What about ethnic groups, such as German-Americans, who are not commonly referred to by a hyphenated term? Does this mean these groups have lost ethnic identities in an assimilated U.S. nationality? Does this imply that the U.S. national identity is composed only of those assimilated groups? To determine what labels to use in its job statistics, the U.S. Labor Department asked people how they prefer to be identified. The results for those people who did not identify as Asian-American, American Indian, Black, Hispanic, or multiracial are shown in Table 1.1A. Very few people chose to use the term *European-American,* which would indicate a culturally based identification.

Most chose *White* or *Caucasian,* which at best is a sociohistorical racial label. This text uses the word *White* in this same sense. The same survey noted that the label preferred by native tribes is *American Indian* (see Table 1.1B).

In a 1977 resolution, the National Congress of American Indians and the National Tribal Chairmen's Association stated that in the absence of a specific tribal designation, the preferred term is *American Indian* and/or *Alaska Native.* This text uses that label as it is important to use the label the group itself prefers.

See Focus on Culture 1.3 for the experience of the Māori of New Zealand. In New Zealand, for voting and land claims, one elects to be Māori.

That ethnic identity can be the basis of a cultural identity and affect communication with others outside that group has been demonstrated by Taylor, Dubé, and Bellerose (1986). In one study of English and French speakers in Quebec, they found that though interactions between ethnically dissimilar people were perceived to be as agreeable as those between similar people, those same encounters were judged less important and less intimate. The researchers concluded that to ensure that interethnic contacts were harmonious, the communicators in their study limited the interactions to relatively superficial encounters.

Co-Culture

Whereas some define *subculture* as meaning "a part of the whole," in the same sense that a subdivision is part of—but no less important than—the whole city, other scholars reject

Table 1.1   U.S. Department of Labor's Race and Ethnic Categories

As part of a review of which race and ethnic categories to use in its job statistics, the U.S. Labor Department asked people nationwide in approximately 60,000 households how they prefer to be identified.

A. Percentage responses by people not identifying as Asian-American, American Indian, Black, Hispanic, or multiracial	
White	61.7
Caucasian	16.5
European-American	2.4
Anglo	1.0
Some other term	2.0
No preference	16.5
B. Percentage responses by native tribespeople	
American Indian	49.8
Native American	37.4
Alaskan Native	3.5
Some other term	3.7
No preference	5.7

Source: From U.S. Labor Department, reported in *U.S. News & World Report,* ("People labels," 1995, p. 28).

the use of the prefix *sub* as applied to the term *culture* because it seems to imply being under or beneath and being inferior or secondary. As an alternative, the word co-culture is suggested to convey the idea that no one culture is inherently superior to other coexisting cultures (Orbe, 1998).

However, mutuality may not be easily established. Assume the case of a homogeneous culture. One of the many elements of a culture is its system of laws. The system of laws in our hypothetical homogeneous culture, then, was derived from and reflects the values of that culture. Now assume immigration of another cultural group into the hypothetical culture. New immigrants may have different understandings of legal theory and the rights and responsibilities that individuals should have in a legal system. In the case of a true co-culture, both understandings of the law would be recognized.

FOCUS ON CULTURE 1.3

The Māori of New Zealand

New Zealand Māori dance.

The original inhabitants of what is today known as New Zealand were Polynesians who arrived in a series of migrations more than 1,000 years ago. They named the land Aotearoa, or land of the long white cloud. The original inhabitants' societies revolved around the *iwi* (tribe) or *hapu* (subtribe), which served to differentiate the many tribes of peoples. In 1642, the Dutch explorer Abel Janszoon Tasman sailed up the west coast and christened the land Niuew Zeeland after the Netherlands' province of Zeeland. Later, in 1769, Captain James Cook sailed around the islands and claimed the entire land for the British crown. It was only after the arrival of the Europeans that the term Māori was used to describe all the tribes on the land. Those labeled Māori do not necessarily regard themselves as a single people.

The history of the Māori parallels the decline of other indigenous peoples in colonized lands, except for the signing of the Treaty of Waitangi in 1840 by more than 500 chiefs. The treaty was recorded in Māori and in English. Differences between the two versions caused considerable misunderstandings in later years. The Māori and the English may have had different understandings of the terms *governance* and *sovereignty*. In exchange for granting sovereignty to Great Britain, the Māori were promised full exclusive and undisturbed possession of their lands, forests, fisheries, and other properties and the same rights and privileges enjoyed by British subjects. The terms of the treaty were largely ignored as Māori land was appropriated as settlers arrived.

Activism in the late 1960s brought a renaissance of Māori languages, literature, arts, and culture, and calls to address Māori land claims as the Treaty of Waitangi became the focus of grievances. In 1975, the government introduced the Waitangi Tribunal to investigate Māori land claims, which

(Continued)

(Continued)

resulted in some return of Māori land. In 1994, the government proposed to settle all Māori land claims for $1 billion—a very small percentage of current value.

Today, New Zealand's population by descent is approximately 13% Māori and 78% Pakeha (European). New Zealand is governed under a parliamentary democracy system loosely modeled on that of Great Britain, except that there are two separate electoral rolls: one for the election of general members of parliament and one for the election of a small number of Māori members of parliament. Pakeha can enroll on the general roll only; people who consider themselves Māori must choose which one of the two rolls they wish to be on. The following article appeared in an August 1999 edition of the newspaper *The Dominion*.

What Makes a Māori?

The definition of "Māori" for voting purposes . . . is entirely one of self-definition. The 1956 Electoral Act defined a Māori as "a person belonging to the aboriginal race of New Zealand, and includes a half-caste and a person intermediate in blood between half-castes and persons of pure descent from that race."

In 1975, the Labour government, prompted by then Māori affairs minister Matiu Rata, rewrote the act to define a Māori as "a person of the Māori race of New Zealand, and includes any descendant of such a person who elects to be considered as a Māori for the purposes of this act." Such a person could choose either the Māori roll or the general roll. So, if you are descended from a Māori, then you are Māori and can choose to vote on the Māori roll. Nigel Roberts, head of Victoria University's School of Political Science and International Relations, says such self-identification is appropriate: "I think that ethnicity is very largely, in the late 20th century, a matter of identification—it is a cultural matter. The world has moved on from classifying people by blood, which was a meaningless definition."

What about Treaty of Waitangi settlements? How does one prove entitlement to the land, fisheries quota, shares, and cash that are being returned to Māori in compensation for successive Crown breaches?

The definition is different again—and more stringently enforced. The South Island's Ngai Tahu iwi was awarded $170 million compensation [in 1998] after a gruelling process of Waitangi Tribunal hearings, mandating, and negotiations. Ngai Tahu *whakapapa* (genealogy) unit spokeswoman Tarlin Prendergast says the iwi is in the fortunate position of having good records from an 1848 census of Ngai Tahu members, just before the Crown's purchase of South Island land. And in 1920, a group of *kaumatua* had travelled around Ngai Tahu settlements recording the whakapapa of families. "Anyone who is Ngai Tahu must be able to show their lines of descent from a kaumatua alive in 1848.

"That is the basis of our tribal membership," she says. "It is up to the individuals to align themselves with the *runanga* (area council) that they say they come from and to keep alive their connections. We call it *ahi kaa*—keeping the home fires burning."

Source: Milne (1999, p. 9). Reprinted with permission.

Case Study: American Indians

Can one nation have two legal systems? Can two legal systems coexist equally? Some 309 distinct nations exist by treaty within the territorial limits of the United States. One is the government in Washington, DC. The remaining 308 are American Indian nations that enjoy some areas of complete sovereignty and some areas of limited sovereignty. By treaty, the American Indian nations have their own territory, governmental structure, and laws; collect their own taxes; and are protected by U.S. federal law in the practice of their culture and religion (Dudley & Agard, 1993). The American Indian Religious Freedom Act of 1978 proclaimed "to protect and preserve for American Indians their inherent right to believe, express and exercise the traditional religions."

Recent Supreme Court decisions, however, have negated this law. In 1988, in *Lyng v. Northwest Indian Cemetery Protection Association,* the Supreme Court held that the U.S. Forest Service could build a road through an area sacred to three Indian tribes. And in 1990, in *Employment Division of Oregon v. Smith,* the Court held that the state could deny unemployment benefits to two men fired from their jobs because they ingested peyote as part of their religion. The *Smith* decision has now been cited in cases involving a Sikh's wearing a turban on the job, a Hmong couple's protesting their son's autopsy, and an Amish man's refusal to post traffic signs. The Religious Freedom Restoration Act of 1993 attempts to restore those rights; however, the point being made here is that the U.S. government exercises ultimate dominance over all indigenous peoples within its boundaries.

When nations adopt one system of laws, that system reflects the cultural values of one culture. But when one is surrounded by a more powerful culture or exists within the culture of the other, the less powerful culture must accept the laws and legal system of the other, thus subordinating any other understanding of legal systems. At least in this one way, the groups are not mutually powerful. The case of American Indians supports the argument that the term *co-culture* does not accurately reflect reality in the United States. Just as the term *subculture* has undesired consequences, so too does *co-culture*. In an attempt to avoid misunderstandings, this text avoids using either word. Instead, as much as possible, the phrase "cultures within cultures" is used throughout to more accurately represent the reality of contemporary U.S. life.

Just as each of us has a cultural identity, we may have a one or more subcultural identities based on social class, ethnicity, or geographical region. Consider for a moment if you learned any symbols, rituals, values, and myths that you acknowledge and share with others. If you were born and reared in the U.S. South, do you acknowledge that subculture as part of your identity? Did your parents or your country of birth provide you with an important part of your identity?

Subgroup

Just as cultures and subcultures are regulators of human life and identity, so can subgroups. Let's look at the definition of the term subgroup and look at how subgroups can function in a similar manner to cultures and subcultures.

Definition

Psychologists have long recognized that subgroups, or membership groups, have an important influence on the values and attitudes you hold. Like cultures, subgroups provide members with relatively complete sets of values and patterns of behavior, and in many ways pose similar communication problems as cultures. Subgroups exist within a dominant culture and are dependent on that culture. One important subgroup category is occupation. Think of large organizations and of occupations in which most people dress alike, share a common vocabulary and similar values, and are in frequent communication, as through magazines and newsletters. These subgroups include nurses and doctors, police officers, and employees of large organizations such as Microsoft.

Subgroups usually do not involve the same large number of people as cultures and are not necessarily thought of as accumulating values and patterns of behavior over generations in the same way cultures do.

Deviant Label

The term *subgroup* has at times been unfortunately linked to the word *deviant*. Actually, however, *deviant* simply means differing from the cultural norm, such as vegetarians in a meat-eating society. Unfortunately, in normal discourse, most people associate deviance with undesirable activities. To understand what is meant by subgroups, you must recognize that vegetarians are as deviant as prostitutes—both groups deviate from the norm, and both are considered subgroups.

Temporality

Membership in some subgroups is temporary; that is, members may participate for a time and later become inactive or separate from it altogether. For example, there are organizations devoted to Ford cars and trucks. Some people are preoccupied with that for a while and then lose interest and relinquish membership in the group. Membership in other subgroups may be longer lasting. One person may be a firefighter for life and another gay.

However, it is a mistake to think of membership in a culture or subgroup as being so exclusive that it precludes participation in other groups. All of us are and have been members of a variety of subgroups. Think of times in your life when you were preoccupied with the concerns of a certain group. At those times, you were a subgroup member. Examples range from Girl Scouts to Alcoholics Anonymous to youth gangs to religious cults to the military.

"Wannabe" Behavior

Recognize, too, that individuals can adhere to values and attitudes and behaviors of groups of which they are not members. The term **reference group** refers to any group to which one aspires to attain membership (Sherif & Sherif, 1953). This behavior is identified in contemporary slang as the *wannabe*, an individual who imitates the behavior of a group he or she desires to belong to. Some people dress like and talk like gang members but are not members of any gang.

Just as each of us has a cultural identity and one or more subcultural identities, we may, as well, have a subgroup identity. While that group membership may be short-lived, it can, for awhile, provide some symbols, rituals, values, and myths that you acknowledge and share with others. Identity for yourself past and present subgroup memberships.

RACE AND SKIN COLOR

Can race or skin color be the basis of cultural or subcultural identification? One important factor would be the Collier and Thomas (1988) criteria for cultural identity of identification with and perceived acceptance into a group that has a shared system of symbols and meanings as well as norms for conduct.

The Concept of Race

It was popularly believed that differences between peoples were biological or racial. From the popular biological perspective, race refers to a large body of people characterized by similarity of descent (Campbell, 1976). From this biologically based definition, your race is the result of the mating behavior of your ancestors. Some physical traits and genes do occur more frequently in certain human populations than in others, such as some skull and dental features, differences in the processing of alcohol, and inherited diseases such as sickle-cell anemia and cystic fibrosis.

The biologically based definition is said to derive from Carolus Linnaeus, a Swedish botanist, physician, and taxonomist, who said in 1735 that humans are classified into four types: *Africanus, Americanus, Asiaticus,* and *Europeaeus.* Race became seen as biologically natural and based on visible physical characteristics such as skin color and other facial and bodily features. In the 19th century, scientists thought that the races had different kinds of blood, so hospitals segregated blood supplies.

Twentieth-century scientists studying genetics found no single race-defining gene. Popular indicators of race such as skin color and hair texture were caused by recent adaptations to climate and diet. Jablonski and Chaplin (2000) took global ultraviolet measurements from NASA's Total Ozone Mapping Spectrometer and compared them with published data on skin color in indigenous populations from more than 50 countries. There was an unmistakable correlation: The weaker the ultraviolet light, the fairer the skin. Most scientists today have abandoned the concept of biological race as a meaningful scientific concept (Cavalli-Sforza, Menozzi, & Piazza, 1994; Owens & King, 1999; Paabo, 2001).

Another way to define race is as a sociohistorical concept, which explains how racial categories have varied over time and between cultures. Worldwide, skin color alone does not define race. The meaning of race has been debated in societies, and as a consequence, new categories have been formed and others transformed. Dark-skinned natives of India have been classified as Caucasian. People with moderately dark skins in Egypt are identified as White. Brazil has a history of intermarriage among native peoples, descendants of African slaves, and immigrants from Europe, the Middle East, and Asia, but no history of explicit segregation policies. So in Brazil, with the world's largest Black population after Nigeria, and where half of the population is Black, there are hundreds of words for skin colors (Robinson, 1999), including a census category *parda* for mixed ancestry. The biologically based definition establishes race as something fixed; the sociohistorically based definition sees race as unstable and socially determined through constant debate (Omi & Winant, 1986). People may be of the same race but of diverse cultures: Australia and South Africa have very different cultures that include individuals of the same ancestries. Then, too, people can be of the same culture but of different ancestries: The United States, for example, is a culture of people of many ancestries (see Focus on Culture 1.4).

FOCUS ON CULTURE 1.4

U.S. Census Bureau Definitions of Race

 Information on race has been collected in every U.S. census beginning with the first in 1790, but what the U.S. Census bureau considered as a racial category has changed in almost every census.

For example, according to Gibson and Jung (2002) from 1790 to 1850, the only categories used were "White and Black (Negro), with Black designated as free and slave" In 1860, American Indians (excluding those living on reservations) and Chinese were identified separately. Japanese were identified separately starting in 1870.

During decades of high immigration, Irish, Italians, and many central European ethnic groups were considered distinct races. "Armenians were classified as white in some decades, but not in others" (Hotz, 1995, p. A14).

In the 1930 census, there was a separate race category for Mexican; later people of Mexican ancestry were classified as White and today as Hispanic but who could be of any race.

Immigrants from India have gone from Hindu, a religious designation used as a racial category, to Caucasian, to non-White, to White, to Asian Indian.

Michael Omi, an ethnic studies expert at UC Berkeley, described the resulting confusion, "You can born one race and die another" (Hotz, 1995, p. A14).

Identity and Race

To be a co-culture or subculture, individuals must identify with one another as a group. Racial categories were created by power-holding Europeans who constructed the cultural and behavioral characteristics associated with each racial category, linking superior traits with Europeans and inferior traits with Blacks and Indians. Scholars from a variety of disciplines have argued that White people in the United States are observed by other groups to be distinct, superior, and unapproachable, whereas Whites themselves are relatively unaware of their racial identity compared to people of color (Dyer, 1997; Hayman & Levit, 1997; Katz & Ivey, 1977).

Peggy McIntosh (1994) uses a comparison to being right-handed. Pick up a pair of scissors, grasp a door handle, and sit at a student's desk. They are all designed for right-handed people. Yet right-handed people do not tend to recognize how the world favors right-handedness. White culture resulted from a synthesis of ideas, values, and beliefs inherited from European ethnic groups in the United States. As the dominant culture in the United States, White culture is the foundation of social norms and organizations.

McIntosh has written about White privilege, which describes how a dominant culture empowers some:

> As a white person, I have realized I had been taught about racism as something which puts others at a disadvantage, but had been taught not to see one of its corollary aspects, white privilege, which puts me at an advantage. I think whites are carefully taught not to recognize white privilege, as males are taught not to recognize male privilege. So I have begun in an untutored way to ask what it is like to have white privilege. I have come to see white privilege as an invisible package of unearned assets which I can count on cashing in on each and every day, but about which I was "meant" to remain oblivious. White privilege is like an invisible weightless knapsack of special provisions, maps, passports, code books, visas, clothes, tools and blank checks. (p. 12)

People of color are likely to be more aware of a racial identity and associate inferior traits with skin color. Racial categorization is prevalent especially among people who live in a "multiracial" society. When given a list of racial categories, most people can identify their own racial group and those of others (Montepare & Opeyo, 2002). This perception of racial disparity can lead to socially constructed stereotypes and prejudice to influence interracial communication.

According to Jackson, Shin, and Wilson (2000), through acknowledging the superiority and privilege of Whites in U.S. society, people of color can come to internalize their status as inferior and believe White interaction partners regard them as mediocre, unprivileged, and subordinate. In one study conducted by Maddox and Gray (2002), participants were presented with photographs of Black discussants and statements made by the discussants. The skin tone (lightness and darkness) of discussants was varied in the photographs. The participants were asked to match each of the statements with the photograph of the discussant who they believed made the statement. The study found that both Black and White participants used race as an organizing principle in their perceptions—participants tended to associate positive traits with light-skinned Blacks and negative traits with dark-skinned Blacks.

It's important to note that both Whites and people of color are both participants in this process. All people must challenge negative perceptions of race. Race scholars such as McPhail (2002) argue that such perceptions must be engaged openly to remedy the communication patterns between racial groups.

Are race and skin color an identifying factor determining a co-cultural or subculture identity? The answer is not simple. Race and skin color can be an identifying factor, but they don't necessarily define co-cultural or subculture identity.

THE CONTACT ZONE

Mary Pratt coined the term *contact zone* to refer to "the space in which peoples geographically and historically separated come into contact with each other and establish ongoing relations, usually involving conditions of coercion, radical inequality, and intractable conflict" (1992, p. 6). What characterizes the contact zone where cultures, subcultures, and subgroups come into contact? Is it the relationship characterized by Herodotus' sense of the word *barbarian* or by the later sense of the word, involving as Pratt suggests "coercion, inequality, and intractable conflict?"

The 1904 World's Fair in St. Louis included an exhibit of living "foreign people." The head anthropologist at the fair wrote in an essay "The Trend of Human Progress" that humans "are conveniently grouped in the four culture grades of savagery, barbarism, civilization, and enlightenment. . . . The two higher culture-grades [are]—especially the Caucasian race, and . . . the budded enlightenment of Britain and full-blown enlightenment of America" (quoted in Wexler, 2008, p. 204). The human "exhibits" at the fair were grouped to illustrate this progression.

Othering refers to the labeling and degrading of cultures and groups outside of one's own (Riggins, 1997). Indigenous peoples, women, lesbians and gay men, and ethnic groups have been "othered" by other groups in language. One common way is to represent the Other as the binary opposite. For example, "Colonists were hard-working; natives were lazy" (Jandt & Tanno, 2001).

It seems as people create a category called "us," another category of "not us" or "them" is created. The collective pronouns *us* and *them* become powerful influences on perception. The names given to "them" can be used to justify suppression and even extermination. Bosmajian (1983) calls this "the language of oppression." The Nazis labeled Jews "bacilli," "parasites," "disease," "demon," and "plague." Why do the words used to refer to "them" matter? It's because although killing another human being may be unthinkable, "exterminating a disease" is not. Segregation was justified when Blacks were considered "chattel" or property. The subjugation of American Indians was defensible when the word *savage* was used. And the words *chicks* and *babes* labeled women as inferior.

Some would argue that the forced categorization of national censuses is a form of othering. The first U.S. census was supervised by Thomas Jefferson in 1790. People were counted as free Whites, slaves, or "others," which included American Indians and free Blacks.

By the early 1800s, people who were one quarter Black (i.e., had one Black grandparent) were counted by the census as mulatto. Later, that became the "one-drop rule," a racist device to ensure that slaveholders' multiracial children remained slaves.

In 1911, a congressional commission developed the "Dictionary of Races of People" with 45 non-White racial subgroups. After opposition, the government discarded that category system. Yet other categories were used. After the Mexican-American War in 1848, the census counted people with Spanish surnames as White. By 1930, a separate "Mexican" category was created. By 1940, it was eliminated. Since 1980, Hispanicity has been treated as an ethnicity apart from race and asked in a separate question.

The census categories in use today were drafted to help agencies enforce civil rights laws. People have been asked to choose one racial classification from White, Black, American Indian or Alaska Native, Asian or Pacific Islander, and Other. In a separate question, people were asked whether they were of Hispanic origin. In the 1980 census, the Census Bureau for the first time asked U.S. residents to volunteer their ethnic origin. Ten percent did not answer. Of the remaining 90%, 83% identified with an ethnic group. Only 6% refused ethnic labeling by using the term *American*. In this book, you will find no reference to any group as "they" or "them," for it is my belief that doing so encourages you to continue thinking of "them" as different from and, in some way, not as good as "we."

FOCUS ON CULTURE 1.5

We and They

Father, Mother, and Me,

Sister and Auntie say

All the people like us are We,

And everyone else is They.

And They live over the sea

While we live over the way,

But—would you believe it?—They look upon We

As only a sort of They!

We eat pork and beef

With cow-horn-handled knives.

They who gobble

Their rice off a leaf

Are horrified out of Their lives;

While They who live up a tree,

Feast on grubs and clay,

(Isn't it scandalous?) look upon We

As a simple disgusting They!

We eat kitcheny food.

We have doors that latch.

They drink milk and blood

Under an open thatch.

We have doctors to fee.

They have wizards to pay.

And (impudent heathen!) They look upon We

As a quite impossible They!

All good people agree,

And all good people say,

All nice people, like us, are We

And everyone else is They:

But if you cross over the sea,

Instead of over the way,

You may end by (think of it!) looking on We

As only a sort of They!

—Rudyard Kipling

Today's Contact Zone Challenges

Several issues are particularly conflict prone in today's contact zone: ethnic and religious conflict, role of women, technology, migration, and environmental sustainability. A recent Pew Research Center (2007) worldwide survey finds that there are increasing concerns about inequality, threats to culture, threats to the environment, and threats posed by immigration. In nearly every country surveyed, people express concerns about losing their traditional culture and national identities and feel their way of life needs protection against foreign influences.

Ethnic and Religious Conflict

With the end of the Cold War and ideological conflict, the world has seen in increase in ethnic and religious conflict. These conflicts have largely been based on conflicts in cultural values and have seen hatred, fear, and violence. Consider just these examples:

- *Basque Separatist Conflict in Spain* (beginning in 1958). The rebel group Basque Fatherland and Liberty guerrilla group (ETA) has waged an urban guerrilla movement for independence for the Basque region of northern Spain.
- *Northern Ireland Conflict* (beginning in 1969). The Irish Catholic minority sought to break away and join the Irish Republic. The IRA conducted an urban guerrilla campaign and Protestant groups waged a largely underground war against the Catholic population.
- *Sri Lankan Civil War* (beginning in 1983). Sri Lanka's civil war was due to problems between the Tamil minority and the Sinhalese majority. In the 1980s, India intervened on the government's side, but later withdrew its troops (L. R. Kohn, 1986).
- *Rwandan Civil War* (beginning in 1994). The Rwandan government, dominated by the Tutsi tribe, overthrew the old government dominated by the Hutu tribe. Before losing power, the Hutu militia massacred over half a million people.

Rows of the skulls of victims of the Rwanda genocide of 1994

- *Roma.* In 2010, France deported 1,000 Roma to Romania and Bulgaria, and bulldozed some 300 Roma camps. France's actions were called a "disgrace" by the European Commission, and have been likened to ethnic cleansing (Bennhold & Castle, 2010).

Add to this list Kosovo, Chechnya, Indonesia, Bosnia, India, the Middle East, and Nigeria and the deaths could total a million. Add then to the list the major terrorist attacks around the world, as well as ethnic and religious attacks within a country, and the challenge is obvious.

While some would content that history, politics, and economics are motivators for some of these conflicts, it cannot be denied that differing perceptions and value systems along with coercive actions to gain other's compliance with one's perception and value system contributed to these conflicts.

In Chapter 3 you will read about culture and perception and in Chapters 7, 8, and 9 you will read about cultural values. One objective is to develop a better understanding of these as critical factors in intercultural communication.

Role of Women

In 1979, the UN General Assembly adopted the Convention on the Elimination of All Forms of Discrimination Against Women. According to the convention, discrimination against women is:

> . . . any distinction, exclusion or restriction made on the basis of sex which has the effect or purpose of impairing or nullifying the recognition, enjoyment or exercise by women, irrespective of their marital status, on a basis of equality of men and women, of human rights and fundamental freedoms in the political, economic, social, cultural, civil or any other field.

The measures to end discrimination included:

- to incorporate the principle of equality of men and women in their legal systems, abolish all discriminatory laws and adopt appropriate ones prohibiting discrimination against women;
- to establish tribunals and other public institutions to ensure the effective protection of women against discrimination; and
- to ensure elimination of all acts of discrimination against women by persons, organizations or enterprises.

In July 2010, the UN General Assembly voted unanimously to create a single UN body tasked with accelerating progress in achieving gender equality and women's empowerment. The objectives that were raised included:

- Promoting gender equality and empowering women is essential to the achievement of development goals.
- The need to strengthen the full integration of women into the formal economy.
- Boost national and international efforts to prevent and eliminate all forms of violence against women and girls.

- Improve access to health systems for women and girls.
- Creating a new vision for conserving earth's biological diversity that must encompass gender. ("In historic move," 2010)

In Chapter 10, you will read about the status of women and how that relates to cultural values.

Technology

Opponents of technology argue that it has made "the corporation the most powerful institution on earth" (Frank, 2000). Global corporations such as Monsanto, Time Warner, and McDonald's are seen as undermining local cultures. Technology has made it possible for Mexico to have frappuccinos at Starbucks and the United States to have the novels of Carlos Fuentes (Cowen, 2002). Because the United States has promoted both free markets and democracy throughout the world, technology is perceived as reinforcing U.S. wealth and dominance. Between July and October 2002, the Pew Research Center for the People and the Press surveyed some 38,000 people speaking 46 languages around the world. In country after country where people like U.S. technology and popular culture, they are displeased with the spread of U.S. ideas and cultural values (see Table 1.2), which are seen as embedded in U.S. technology.

Table 1.2 What the World Thinks			
Country	Spread of U.S. Ideas a "Good Thing" (%)	Like U.S. Music, Movies, TV (%)	Like U.S. Science and Technology (%)
Canada	37	77	76
Britain	39	76	77
Russia	16	42	41
Mexico	22	60	69
South Korea	30	53	81
South Africa	43	71	79
Turkey	11	44	67
Egypt	6	33	51
Jordan	13	30	59
Pakistan	2	4	42

Source: Pew Research Center (2002).

On January 1, 2002, 300 million people in 12 Western European nations adopted the euro, the first common currency since the Roman Empire two millennia ago. New bills and coins replaced German marks, French francs, and other national moneys. No images of people or specific buildings appear in the designs for the new bank notes. Rather, anonymous architecture was designed to represent the countries' shared culture. Today the European Union (EU) has grown to 27 member nations. Its population is larger than that of the United States and its economy roughly equal to it. While the euro does symbolize European unity, the recent economic crisis saw two or three countries consider leaving the EU.

Chapter 11 addresses the issues of spread of products and practices from one culture to another made possible by advanced technology, as well as how some peoples view that as the influence one country can have on another.

Migration

In both poor and rich countries, people are concerned about immigration. Large majorities in nearly every country express the view that there should be greater restriction of immigration and tighter control of their country's borders. Table 1.3 shows the percentage of citizens in selected countries who favor restricting immigration.

FOCUS ON CULTURE 1.6

 It's not only U.S. ideas that are spread by technology. Japan and Korea have a two-thousand-year history of contact. In modern times, relations have been bitter, largely resulting from the Japanese occupation of Korea from 1910 to 1945, which included Japan conscripting Koreans into forced labor in Japan and conscripting some 200,000 Korean and Chinese young women to serve as "comfort women" at military instillations.

Against this backdrop, in 2002 came the South Korean television miniseries *Winter Sonata*, starring Choi Ji-woo and Bae Yong Joon, about first love, lost memory, and unknown family ties. In 2009 the series was adapted into an anime series. The series was broadcast on Japan's NHK and has had a major following in Japan and throughout Asia.

Bae Yong Joon became the most popular man in Japan. The actor was nicknamed "Yonsama" by the Japanese. *Sama* is an honorific usually reserved for royalty. In the series he plays "a sensitive, bespectacled architect with hair dyed brown and a scarf tied in a different way in each scene" (Onishi, 2004, para. 11). Older Japanese women said it reminded them of "simpler times at home." Yonsama represented qualities Japanese women found lacking in Japanese men. He was "sincere, pure, giving, passionate and soothing" (para. 16).

After the series aired, Japanese tourism to South Korea grew by 40% in 2004. Japanese women took tours of the location where the series was filmed, others enrolled at his alma mater, others enrolled in Korean conversation classes. Total increased economic activity attributed to the series and Yonsama was estimated as $2.3 billion.

Media scholars have labeled Yonsama as one of the first *kkonminam* icons, young boyish male pop idols with style and fashion. Jung (2011) describes Bae Yong Joon's popularity with Japanese middle-aged women as an attraction to constructed "soft masculinity."

Yonsama's popularity in Japan continued long after the series. His 2009 book on Korean culture sold 50,000 copies in its first day of release in Japan. In the past, Koreans were discriminated against in Japan. *Winter Sonata* and Yonsama have changed that prejudice.

Immigration issues in Europe and the United States are quite distinct. In Europe, the issues focus more on concerns over Islam and cultural differences. Historically, Europe is a continent of nations with aging populations and falling birthrates. European population may drop by 2.5 million a year by the middle of the century. In contrast, the Muslim population has doubled to about 15 million since the 1980s and has become its largest minority. Some see the religious head scarves, the arranged marriages, and conservative imams as challenges to equality and democracy.

Table 1.3 Global Attitudes Toward Immigration

Country	Percentage Agreement With Restricting Immigration
Côte d'Ivoire	94
Indonesia	89
South Africa	89
Italy	87
United States	75
Israel	74
Mexico	71
France	68
Germany	66
China	52
Japan	47

Source: Pew Research Center (2007).

Consider the challenge Sweden, a country of 9 million, is facing: More than 2 million Iraqis have fled their homeland since the U.S.-led invasion in 2003. Most are living in Syria, Jordan, and other Middle Eastern nations where they are not allowed to work and are denied visas, but they are unwilling to go home. Now a growing number are heading toward Europe, especially Sweden, which for decades has offered refugees and asylum seekers government aid and generous family reunification plans. As of 2011, Sweden had 82,629 refugees and another 18,635 asylum seekers.

Some of the refugees pay smugglers up to $15,000 for passage to Sweden. Refugees must then apply for asylum and learn Swedish with its many sounds for the letter *g*, adapt to Swedish culture without the familiar calls to prayer, eat meat that was not slaughtered according to Islamic tradition, and drink hot tea in a land of lattes and espressos.

Consider France: For more than 200 years since the French Revolution, France has declared that distinctions of race or creed must be submerged for the good of La France. Everyone is French, so no politician campaigns for the votes of ethnic groups. The French are so committed to the idea of equality that it is against the law to survey the population by race, ethnicity, or religion.

Despite the burgeoning population of immigrants from North African and Muslim countries, France has no Black or Arab mayors and no minorities representing mainland France in the National Assembly. Philippe Maniere, director of the Montaigne Institute, a nonpartisan think tank, said, "In France, we still believe in this completely idealistic principle born during our revolution that you should not talk about your community [of origin] because it gives the impression you will favor it, which is unacceptable" (quoted in Baum, 2008, p. A3).

North Americans are generally more welcoming to immigrants than Western Europeans are. The issues in the United States focus more on Hispanic immigrants and employment.

Consider the United States: Immigration accounts for more than 40% of the U.S. growth since 2000. The challenge that migration presents has been identified by Robert Putnam (2007) in a new study based on 30,000 interviews in the United States. The greater the diversity in a community, the less civic engagement it shows: Fewer people vote, fewer volunteer, less is given to charities, and less cooperative work is done on community projects. In addition, the greater the diversity in a community, the less people trust each other, not only across ethnic lines but also within the lines. In other words, people in the most ethnically mixed neighborhoods show the least trust not only of other ethnicities but also of people of their own ethnicity.

Putnam was concerned that his research would be used to argue against immigration, affirmative action, and multiculturalism, and that has occurred. Putnam's research, in total, does argue the following:

- Increased immigration and diversity are not only inevitable in modern societies but over the long term are desirable. The history of the United States demonstrates that over the long run, ethnic diversity is an important social asset.
- In the short to medium run, immigration and ethnic diversity challenge social solidarity and inhibit the strength of relationships that bond people similar people together and bridge people of diversity.
- In the medium to long run, successful immigrant societies create new forms of social solidarity and dampen the negative effects of diversity by constructing new, more encompassing identities.

Putnam's research findings are consistent with conflict studies that show that the challenge of modern immigrant societies is to create new broader definitions of the sense of "we"—that is, to create a larger, more inclusive sense of identity.

Consider India's approach. On August 15, 1947, the new independent state of India was born on a subcontinent with a history of bloody divisions. Its very survival was in doubt. No other national state has ever had the diversity of ethnic groups, mutually incomprehensible language (35 languages spoken by more than a million people each), a variety of topography and climate, and a diversity of religions and cultural practices. Six decades later, India is the world's largest democracy, with years of rapid economic growth.

In stark contrast to the U.S. motto of *e pluribus unum,* India embraced *e pluribus pluribum.* The idea India has embraced is one land embracing many. If the United States is a melting pot, India is a *thali,* a selection of dishes in different bowls on one plate to make one meal. Instead of suppressing diversity in the name of a single national identity, India acknowledges pluralism. All groups, faiths, tastes, and ideologies were to participate in the new system. It wasn't easy. India suffered caste conflicts, clashes over the rights of different linguistic groups, religious riots between Hindus and Muslims, and threats of separation from various ethnicities.

India permits all religions to flourish while ensuring none is privileged by the state. Muslims have their own "personal law" to govern their marriages, divorces, and deaths distinct from the common civil code. No one identity has triumphed in India: India saw a Roman Catholic political leader replaced by a Sihk sworn in as prime minister by a Muslim in a country that is 81% Hindu (Tharoor, 2006, 2007).

Chapters 12 deals directly with immigration. Chapters 13 and 14 deal with groups within cultures, subcultures and subgroups, and their relationships with the dominant culture.

Environmental Sustainability

Easter Island in the Pacific Ocean is one of the most remote locations on Earth. The gigantic stone statues located in the Rono Raraku volcanic crater are all that remain of what was a complex civilization. The civilization disappeared because of the overexploitation of environmental resources. Competition between rival clans led to rapid deforestation, soil erosion, and the destruction of bird populations, undermining the food and agricultural systems that sustained human life (Diamond, 2005). The Easter Island story is a case study of the consequences of failure to manage shared ecological resources.

The World Commission on Environment and Development (1987), also known as the Brundtland Commission, defined sustainable development as development that "meets the needs of the present without compromising the ability of the future generations to meet their own needs."

One revision of this definition is attributed to the state of Oregon: Sustainability means "using, developing and protecting resources at a rate and in a manner that enables people to meet their current needs and also provides that future generations can meet their own needs" (Oregon Department of Transportation, 2007, para. 1) and "Sustainability requires simultaneously meeting environmental, economic and community needs" ("Sustainability," 2008). Such definitions have become the basis of significant international policy.

People fill every ecological niche on the planet, from icy tundra to rainforests to deserts. In some locations, societies have outstripped the carrying capacity of the land, resulting in chronic hunger, environmental degradation, and a large-scale exodus of desperate populations.

Climate change is now a scientifically established fact. Just a few years ago, the world was debating whether climate change was taking place and whether it was human induced. Today the debate is over, and climate skepticism is an increasingly fringe activity. Nonetheless, the exact impact of greenhouse gas emission is not easy to forecast. In 2004, the United States, with 4.6% of the world's population, accounted for 20.9% of the world's carbon emissions. China with 20% of the world's population, accounted for 17.3% of carbon emissions. Russia, India, and Japan accounted for about 5% each.

People have unequal incomes and wealth across the world. Climate change will affect regions very differently.

Global Voices

Twenty years ago, Chico Mendes, the Brazilian environmentalist, died attempting to defend the Amazon rainforest against destruction. Before his death, he spoke of the ties that bound his local struggle to a global movement for social justice: "At first I thought I was fighting to save rubber trees, then I thought I was fighting to save the Amazon rainforest. Now I am fighting for humanity."

Source: United Nations Development Programme (2008, p. 6).

Climate change is already starting to affect some of the poorest and most vulnerable communities around the world, threatening food supplies, coastlines, health, and the survival of countless species.

Throughout this text, you will find Focus on the Environment boxes that will help you apply the concepts of intercultural communication to this global issue.

SUMMARY

Our culture provides regulation for life and provides individual identities. Today the term *culture* refers to the totality of a large group's thoughts, behaviors, and values that are socially transmitted, as well as to members who consciously identity with the group. The term *subculture* refers to a group that exists within a culture, usually based on social class, ethnicity, or geographic region. As the prefix *sub* can mean "less than," some scholars prefer the term *co-culture* to indicate that no one culture is inherently superior to other coexisting cultures. Finally, the term *subgroup* refers to groups that provide members with relatively complete sets of values and patterns of behavior and in many ways pose similar communication problems as cultures

Twentieth-century scientists have found no single race-defining gene. The sociohistorical concept of defining race explains that racial categories have varied over time and between cultures. Worldwide, skin color alone does not define race. Scholars from a variety of disciplines have argued that White people in the United States are observed by other groups to be distinct, superior, and unapproachable, whereas Whites themselves are relatively unaware of their racial identity compared to people of color.

The term *contact zone* refer to the space in which cultures come into contact and establish ongoing relations, usually involving coercion, inequality, and conflict. The term *othering* refers to the labeling and degrading of cultures and groups outside of one's own. Indigenous peoples, women, lesbians and gay men, and ethnic groups have been othered by other groups in language. One common way is to represent the Other is as the binary opposite, for example, "Colonists were hardworking; natives were lazy."

Finally, today's challenges in the contact zone are identified as ethnic and religious conflict, the changing role of women, technology, migration, and environmental sustainability. Each of these is addressed in subsequent chapters.

DISCUSSION QUESTIONS

1. Expand on Damasio's thesis that culture is a regulator of human life and identity. What does culture provide to its members?

2. How does one acquire cultural, subcultural, and subgroup identities?

3. Why do you believe social class differences, ethnic identity, and skin color are difficult for most people in the United States to discuss?

4. Can it be said that ethnic and religious conflicts were less prominent during the Cold War era?

5. Why do some people in the world admire the United States? Why do others feel differently?

6. Will environmental issues divide or unite the world?

KEY TERMS

Aboriginal   11

co-culture   14

cultural identity   7

cultural studies   11

culture   6

ethnic identity   12

ethnicity   12

ethnography   11

heroes   6

myths   6

othering   22

race   19

reference group   18

rituals   6

subculture   8

subgroup   17

symbols   6

values   6

White privilege   21

NOTE

1. The word *God* is capped through this text, but no endorsement of any religion is implied. The intent is to honor all religions.

READINGS

All readings are from *Intercultural Communication: A Global Reader* (Jandt, 2004).

Claude Lévi-Strauss, "Race, History, and Culture" (p. 1)
M. Gene Aldridge, "What Is the Basis of American Culture?" (p. 84)
Ashis Nandy, "Consumerism: Its Hidden Beauties and Politics" (p. 400)
Randy Kluver, "Globalization, Informatization, and Intercultural Communication" (p. 425)

STUDENT STUDY SITE

Visit the student study site at www.sagepub.com/jandt7e for these additional learning tools:

- Web Resources
- Audio and Video Links
- SAGE journal articles
- eFlashcards
- Web Quizzes
- Sample Essays

CHAPTER

2

Understanding Face-To-Face and Mediated Communication

FOCUS QUESTIONS

- What skills make you competent in intercultural communication?
- What ethical considerations could guide intercultural interactions?
- How do definitions of communication reflect culture?
- How do telephone and Internet use reflect culture?
- What are the consequences of racism and prejudice in intercultural communication?

Intercultural Communication Competence
    Personality Strength
    Communication Skills
    Psychological Adjustment
    Cultural Awareness
Intercultural Communication Ethics
Cultural Definitions of Communication
    Confucian Perspectives on Communication
    Western Perspectives on Communication
    Twentieth-Century Theory
    Components of Communication
The Media of Intercultural Communication
    Human Couriers and Intermediaries
    Letter Writing
    Telephone
    Internet
        Language Use
        Design Elements
        Social Network Sites
The Special Case of Prejudice and Racism
Summary
Discussion Questions
Key Terms
Note
Readings
Student Study Site

Intercultural communication generally refers to interactions among people of diverse cultures. The formal study of intercultural communication in the United States originated in 1946 when Congress passed the Foreign Service Act, which established the Foreign Service Institute to provide language and anthropological cultural training for foreign diplomats. Outside the Foreign Service Institute, the study of intercultural communication is generally associated with the publication of Edward T. Hall's book, *The Silent Language,* in 1959. While associated with the Foreign Service Institute, Hall applied abstract anthropological concepts to the practical world of foreign service and extended the anthropological view of culture to include communication. Later in his popular book, Hall defined culture as basically a communication process (Leeds-Hurwitz, 1990). President John F. Kennedy's creation of the Peace Corps in the early 1960s increased interest in knowing more about how people of diverse cultures could communicate more effectively.

In this chapter you will first read about the skills required to be a competent intercultural communicator. Closely related to intercultural communication competence is the question of intercultural ethics. Are there ethics that transcend all cultures or are all ethics specific to culture? Then, you will read about how communication itself is defined can vary by culture, so what is competence in one culture may not be in another. We give special attention to today's use of social media. Finally, we turn to the special case of prejudice and racism in intercultural communication.

INTERCULTURAL COMMUNICATION COMPETENCE

Intercultural communication competence refers to one's skill in facilitating successful intercultural communication outcomes in terms of satisfaction and other positive assessments of the interaction and the interaction partner (Y. Y. Kim, 2005). There have been many attempts to identify the skills needed to be more effective in intercultural communication.

Definitions of intercultural competence grounded in communication have tended to stress the development of skills that transform one from a monocultural person into a multicultural person. The multicultural person is one who respects cultures and has tolerance for differences (Belay, 1993; Chen & Starosta, 1996). Chen (1989, 1990), for example, identifies four skill areas: personality strength, communication skills, psychological adjustment, and cultural awareness.

Personality Strength

The main personal traits that affect intercultural communication are self-concept, self-disclosure, self-monitoring, and social relaxation. *Self-concept* refers to the way in which a person views the self. *Self-disclosure* refers to the willingness of individuals to openly and appropriately reveal information about themselves to their counterparts. *Self-monitoring* refers to using social comparison information to control and modify one's self-presentation and expressive behavior. *Social relaxation* is the ability to reveal little anxiety in communication. Effective communicators must know themselves well and, through their self-awareness, initiate positive attitudes. Individuals must express a friendly personality to be competent in intercultural communication.

Communication Skills

Individuals must be competent in verbal and nonverbal behaviors. Intercultural communication skills require message skills, behavioral flexibility, interaction management, and social skills. *Message skills* refers to the ability to understand and use language and feedback. *Behavioral flexibility* is the ability to select an appropriate behavior in diverse contexts. *Interaction management* means handling the procedural aspects of conversation, such as the ability to initiate a conversation. Interaction management emphasizes a person's other-oriented ability to interaction, such as attentiveness and responsiveness. *Social skills* are empathy and identity maintenance. Empathy is the ability to think the same thoughts and feel the same emotions as the other person. Identity maintenance is the ability to maintain a counterpart's identity by communicating back an accurate understanding of that person's identity. In other words, a competent communicator must be able to deal with diverse people in different situations.

Psychological Adjustment

Effective communicators must be able to acclimate to new environments. They must be able to handle the feelings of "culture shock," such as frustration, stress, and alienation in ambiguous situations caused by new environments.

Cultural Awareness

To be competent in intercultural communication, individuals must understand the social customs and social system of the host culture. Understanding how a people think and behave is essential for effective communication with them.

Guo-Ming Chen and William J. Starosta (1996) define intercultural communication competence as "the ability to negotiate cultural meanings and to execute appropriately effective communication behaviors that recognize the interactants' multiple identities in a specific environment" (pp. 358–359). This means that competent intercultural communicators interact effectively and appropriately to achieve their own goals and respect and affirm the cultural identities of those with whom they interact.

Chen and Starosta's model includes three perspectives:

- *Affective or intercultural sensitivity*—to acknowledge and respect cultural differences
- *Cognitive or intercultural awareness*—self-awareness of one's own personal cultural identity and understanding how cultures vary
- *Behavioral or intercultural adroitness*—message skills, knowledge of appropriate self-disclosure, behavioral flexibility, interaction management, and social skills

At a bazaar in Iran you can find food, clothing, jewelry, electronics, currency exchange, and more. The experienced bargainer with effective use of spoken language and nonverbal communication can purchase items for half the original price.

INTERCULTURAL COMMUNICATION ETHICS

Closely related to intercultural communication competence is ethics. As a branch of philosophy, ethics addresses the question of how we ought to lead our lives. Kenneth E. Andersen (1991) makes clear that ethical theories tend to reflect the culture in which they were produced and, therefore, present challenges in intercultural communication.

What, though, guides the interactions of people from cultures with diverse ethical perspectives? Are there global values to guide intercultural interactions? Kale (1997) argues that peace is the fundamental human value. The use of peace applies not only to relationships among countries but to "the right of all people to live at peace with themselves and their surroundings" (p. 450). From this fundamental value, he developed four ethical principles to guide intercultural interactions:

- Ethical communicators address people of other cultures with the same respect that they would like to receive themselves. Intercultural communicators should not demean or belittle the cultural identity of others through verbal or nonverbal communication.

- Ethical communicators seek to describe the world as they perceive it as accurately as possible. What is perceived to be the truth may vary from one culture to another; truth is socially constructed. This principle means that ethical communicators do not deliberately mislead or deceive.
- Ethical communicators encourage people of other cultures to express themselves in their uniqueness. This principle respects the right of people to expression regardless of how popular or unpopular their ideas may be.
- Ethical communicators strive for identification with people of other cultures. Intercultural communicators should emphasize the commonalities of cultural beliefs and values rather than their differences.

Developing ethical principles to guide intercultural interactions is a difficult task. Even though Kale's principles may be more acceptable in some cultures than in others, they are certainly a beginning step.

FOCUS ON THE ENVIRONMENT 2.1

The field of environmental ethics concerns human beings' ethical relationship with the natural environment. While numerous philosophers have written on this topic throughout history, environmental ethics in the United States only developed into a specific philosophical discipline in the 1970s. This emergence was no doubt due to the increasing awareness in the 1960s of the effects that technology, industry, economic expansion, and population growth were having on the environment. The development of such awareness was aided by the publication of two important books at this time. Rachel Carson's *Silent Spring,* first published in 1962, alerted readers to how the widespread use of chemical pesticides was posing a serious threat to public health and leading to the destruction of wildlife. Of similar significance was Paul Ehrlich's 1968 book, *The Population Bomb,* which warned of the devastating effects the spiraling human population has on the planet's resources. Of course, pollution and the depletion of natural resources have not been the only environmental concerns since that time: Dwindling plant and animal biodiversity, the loss of wilderness, the degradation of ecosystems, and climate change are all part of a raft of "green" issues that have implanted themselves into both public consciousness and public policy over subsequent years. The job of environmental ethics is to outline our moral obligations in the face of such concerns. In a nutshell, the two fundamental questions that environmental ethics must address are as follows: What duties do humans have with respect to the environment, and why? The latter question usually needs to be considered prior to the former. In order to tackle just what our obligations are, it is usually thought necessary to consider first *why* we have them. For example, do we have environmental obligations for the sake of human beings living in the world today, for humans living in the future, or for the sake of entities within the environment itself, irrespective of any human benefits?

Source: Cochrane (2007, para. 1).

CULTURAL DEFINITIONS OF COMMUNICATION

It has often been said that communication and culture are inseparable. As Alfred G. Smith (1966) wrote in his preface to *Communication and Culture,* culture is a code we learn and share, and learning and sharing require communication. Communication requires coding and symbols that must be learned and shared. Godwin C. Chu (1977) observed that every cultural pattern and every single act of social behavior involve communication. To be understood, the two must be studied together. Culture cannot be known without a study of communication, and communication can only be understood with an understanding of the culture it supports.

FOCUS ON THEORY 2.1

Robert T. Craig (1999) argued that theories are forms of communication that communicate about communication. Communication theories, then, also reflect a culture's understanding of communication. Craig identified seven traditions that reflect how theorists in the United States think about communication and, by extension, think about culture: (1) the rhetorical tradition, which is the extension of Aristotle; (2) the semiotic tradition, which focuses on signs and symbols; (3) the phenomenological tradition, which deals with how individuals experience one another by sharing personal experience through dialogue; (4) the cybernetic tradition, which often focuses on information processing and systems; (5) the sociopsychological tradition, which has focused primarily on behavior; (6) the sociocultural tradition, which has focused on society and culture; and (7) the critical tradition, which has focused on power and oppression.

Confucian Perspectives on Communication

That cultures define communication in diverse ways demonstrates that communication is an element of culture (Krippendorff, 1993). Definitions of communication from many Asian countries stress harmony (Chen & Starosta, 1996). This is most notable in cultures with a Confucian tradition.

The Chinese scholar K'ung-Fu-tzu, a title the Jesuits later Latinized as Confucius (550–478 BCE[1]), lived in a time when the feudal system in China was collapsing. Confucius proposed a government based less on heredity than on morality and merit.

Societies heavily influenced today by Confucian history or tradition are China, North and South Korea, Singapore, and many East Asian countries with large Chinese communities.

Confucius set up an ethical-moral system intended ideally to govern all relationships in the family, community, and state. Confucius taught that society was made up of five relationships: those between ruler and subjects (the relation of righteousness), husband and wife (chaste conduct), father and son (love), elder brother and younger brother (order), and friend and friend (faithfulness). Three of these five bases of relations occur within the family. The regulating factors in family relationships are extended to the whole community and state. The chief virtue is filial piety, a combination of loyalty and reverence, which demands that the son honor and respect his father and fulfill the demands of his elders.

Confucianism emphasizes virtue, selflessness, duty, patriotism, hard work, and respect for hierarchy, both familial and societal. Just as George Washington and the story of the cherry tree is used in the United States to teach the value of honesty, Confucianism reinforces its lessons with stories about people who represent particular virtues. For example, Chinese children learn about such heroes as Mu Lan, a woman of the 6th century who disguised herself as a man and served 12 years as a soldier so that her ill father would not be disgraced or punished because he could not report for military duty. Mu Lan teaches courage and filial devotion.

Confucianism guides social relationships: "To live in harmony with the universe and with your fellow man through proper behavior." Confucianism considers balance and harmony in human relationships to be the basis of society. June Yum (1988) describes five effects that Confucianism has on interpersonal communication:

1. *Particularism.* There is no universal pattern of rules governing relationships: No rules govern interaction with someone whose status is unknown. Instead of applying the same rule to everyone, such factors as status, intimacy, and context create different communication rules for diverse people. In fact, there are several patterns guiding interaction with others whose status is known. In the Confucian country of Korea, it's quite common for strangers to find out each other's age in the first few minutes of conversation and adjust their language to show respect. Koreans are friends (*chingu*) only with those whose age is within a few years of their own. If a male acquaintance is older than this "friendship age range," he must be addressed as *adjussi* and, if female, as *adjumoni*—terms that equate roughly to "uncle" and "aunt," respectively.

2. *Role of intermediaries.* Rituals should be followed in establishing relationships. In China, it's not unusual to use a third party to negotiate with future in-laws about wedding plans and, in general, to use a third party to avoid direct confrontations and resolve disputes (Gao & Ting-Toomey, 1998).

3. *Reciprocity.* Complementary obligations are the base of relationships. Gratitude and indebtedness are important parts of Chinese culture. For example, a person feels uneasy to be indebted to someone, and payback is necessary to achieve balance in the relationship. Reciprocity is the basic rule of interpersonal relationships (Gao & Ting-Toomey, 1998). Obligations in relationships are contrary to Western ideas of individualism.

4. *In-Group/Out-Group Distinction.* Scollon and Scollon (1991) argue that the distinction between inside and outside influences every aspect of Chinese culture. In-group members engage in freer and deeper talk and may find it difficult to develop personal relationships with out-group members (Gao & Ting-Toomey, 1998). There can even be different language codes for in-group members.

5. *Overlap of Personal and Public Relationships.* Business and pleasure are mixed. Frequent contacts lead to common experiences. This contrasts with Western patterns of keeping public and private lives separate. There are several Chinese terms for the English word *communication,* including *jiao liu* (to exchange), *chuan bo* (to disseminate), and *gou tong* (to connect among people). The Chinese term *he* denotes harmony, peace, unity, and kindness. Seeking harmony with family and others is the goal of communication in Chinese culture (Gao & Ting-Toomey, 1998).

As a consequence of the value placed on balance and social harmony, Chang and Holt (1991) explain how the Chinese have developed many verbal strategies such as compliments, greeting rituals, and so on to maintain good interpersonal relations. Fong (2000), for example, has described the "luck talk" (speech acts related to luck) during the celebration of the Chinese New Year.

Korea adopted Confucianism as a state religion for six centuries. Yum (1987) explains how the Korean language easily accommodates the Confucian rules of relationships. A grammatical form of direct address, called an honorific, for example, shows respect. English speakers might vary in how they ask a child, a friend, or a grandparent "to sit" by using a sentence, whereas Korean speakers would use different forms of the root *ahnta,* meaning "to sit or to take a seat:"

- To a child, younger person, or person of lower rank, *ahnjo* or *ahnjara* (informal)
- To a friend or person of equal rank, *ahnjuseyo* (polite)
- To an elder, person of higher rank, or honored person, *ahnjushipshio* (more polite)

Korean has special vocabularies for each sex, for different degrees of social status and degrees of intimacy, and for formal occasions. When two people are introduced, they first engage in small talk to determine each other's social position so they know who should use common language and who should use honorific language. And ironically, because Confucianism does not consider relationships with strangers, Koreans are said to ignore—often to the point that some in other cultures would consider rude—anyone to whom they have not been introduced.

In modern Korea, a generation gap exists: Junior business associates may address seniors with familiar rather than honorific language. The collectivist values of Confucianism mandate a style of communication in which respecting the relationship through communication is more important than the information exchanged. Group harmony, avoidance of loss of face to others and oneself, and a modest presentation of oneself are means of respecting the relationship. One does not say what one actually thinks when it might hurt others in the group.

In some sense, the same ethic can be found in business dealings. Much of commercial life in China is lubricated by *guanxi,* a concept best translated as "connections" or "personal relationships." *Guanxi* is an alternative to the legal trappings of Western capitalism in that business is cemented by the informal relationships of trust and mutual obligation. Sometimes viewed as bribery, *guanxi* is less like using professional lobbyists than relying on mutual friends among whom trust can be maintained.

A Confucian perspective on communication would define it as an infinite interpretive process where all parties are searching to develop and maintain a social relationship. Carey (1989) describes this as a ritual model of communication that "is directed not toward the extension of messages in space but toward the maintenance of society in time; not the act of imparting information but the representation of shared beliefs" (p. 18).

Western Perspectives on Communication

The study of communication in Western culture has a recorded history of some 2,500 years and is said to have begun in Greece with Aristotle's *Rhetoric and Poetics,* which described the process of communication as involving a speaker, the speech act, an audience, and a purpose.

Twentieth-Century Theory

To demonstrate how a communication theory reflects a culture, let's review one well-known theory made popular by David Berlo's (1960) *The Process of Communication.* Berlo was interested in using communication to solve problems such as finding more effective ways of communicating new agricultural technologies to farmers and communicating health information to the peoples of developing countries. Berlo drew from engineering to conceptualize communication as a process of transmitting ideas to influence others to achieve their goals. Even though Berlo emphasized that communication is a dynamic process, as the variables in the process are interrelated and influence each other, overall his conceptualization of communication can be labeled machinelike or mechanistic. Communication was conceptualized as one-way, top-down, and suited for the transmission media of print, telephones, radio, and television.

Components of Communication

Because the transmission models of communication clearly identified components in the communication process, they are particularly useful in beginning a study of communication. You are better able to understand communication when you understand the components of the process (DeVito, 1986). The components of communication, shown in Figure 2.1, are source, encoding, message, channel, noise, receiver, decoding, receiver response, feedback, and context.

Figure 2.1   Ten Components of Communication

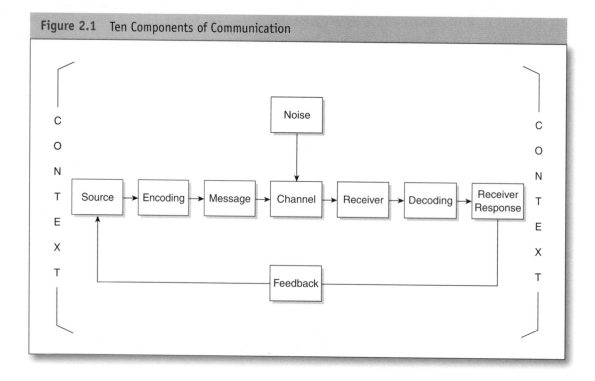

Source. The **source** is the person with an idea he or she desires to communicate. Examples are CBS, the White House, your instructor, and your mother.

Encoding. Unfortunately (or perhaps fortunately), humans cannot share thoughts directly. Your communication is in the form of a symbol representing the idea you desire to communicate. **Encoding** is the process of putting an idea into a symbol. The symbols into which you encode your thoughts vary. You can encode thoughts into words, and you also can encode thoughts into nonspoken symbols. Tobin and Dobard (1999), for example, have shown how messages were encoded in quilts made by slaves.

Message. The term **message** identifies the encoded thought. Encoding is the process, the verb; the message is the resulting object.

Channel. The term **channel** is used technically to refer to the means by which the encoded message is transmitted. Today, you might feel more comfortable using the word media. The channel or medium, then, may be print, electronic, or the light and sound waves of face-to-face communication.

Noise. The term **noise** technically refers to anything that distorts the message the source encodes. Noise can be of many forms:

- External noise can be the sights, sounds, and other stimuli that draw your attention away from the message. Listening to an iPod while reading is an example of external noise.
- Internal noise refers to your thoughts and feelings that can interfere with the message. For example, being tired or hungry can distract you from paying complete attention to the message.
- Semantic noise refers to how alternative meanings of the source's message symbols can be distracting. For example, a speaker's use of uncalled for profanity can cause us to wonder why the speaker used profanity and draw attention away from the message itself.

Receiver. The **receiver** is the person who attends to the message. Receivers may be intentional— that is, they may be the people the source desired to communicate with—or they may be any person who comes upon and attends to the message.

Decoding. **Decoding** is the opposite process of encoding and just as much an active process. The receiver is actively involved in the communication process by assigning meaning to the symbols received.

Receiver Response. **Receiver response** refers to anything the receiver does after having attended to and decoded the message. That response can range from doing nothing to taking some action or actions that may or may not be the action desired by the source.

Feedback. **Feedback** refers to that portion of the receiver response of which the source has knowledge and to which the source attends and assigns meaning. You as a reader of this text may have many responses, but only when you respond to a survey or write a letter to the author does feedback occur. When a radio interview show host receives enthusiastic telephone calls and invites a guest back, feedback has occurred. Feedback makes communication a two-way or interactive process. Linear and interactive models seem to suggest that communication is an isolated single discrete act independent of events that preceded or might follow it.

Context. The final component of communication is context. Generally, context can be defined as the environment in which the communication takes place and helps define the communication. If you know the physical context, you can predict with a high degree of accuracy much of the communication. For example, you have certain knowledge and expectations of the communication that occurs within synagogues, mosques, and churches. At times, you intentionally plan a certain physical environment for your communication: You may want to locate your romantic communications in a quiet, dimly lit restaurant or on a secluded beach. The choice of the environment, the context, helps assign the desired meaning to the communicated words.

In social relationships as well, the relationship between the source and receiver may help define much of the meaning of the communication. Again, if you know the context, you can predict with a high degree of accuracy much of the communication. For example, knowing that a person is being stopped by a police officer for speeding is enough to predict much of the communication. Certain things are likely to be said and done; other things are very unlikely. Culture is also context. Every culture has its own worldview; its own way of thinking of activity, time, and human nature; its own way of perceiving self; and its own system of social organization. Knowing each of these helps you assign meaning to the symbols.

The component of context helps you recognize that the extent to which the source and receiver have similar meanings for the communicated symbols and similar understandings of the culture in which the communication takes place are critical to the success of the communication. From this perspective, communication is intentional, is symbolic, and involves at least two people. You might say that communication occurs when symbols are manipulated by one person to stimulate meaning in another person (Infante, Rancer, & Womack, 1993).

Not everyone agreed with the Berlo model. For example, semanticist S. I. Hayakawa (1978) noted that decoding—or listening—seems to give the receiver a subordinate role to the source. When someone speaks, others stop what they are doing to listen. Therefore, it would seem that the source is viewed as more active and as more important in the process. Hayakawa's observation makes it clear that cultural beliefs affect how the process of communication is defined.

The Berlo model can lead you to think of communication as consisting of an active source and a passive receiver. Speaking may be considered a more noble activity and may demand that others cease other activities to listen. Indeed, in many cultures, listening does place one in a subordinate role to that of the source. In other cultures, where the group's history and knowledge is told and retold verbally, the role of the listener who accurately remembers is critical. The story is told that the Puritans, believing themselves to have been called to save heathens, preached to the American Indians. The Indians affirmed conversions to Christianity to the delight of the early settlers. Then the Indians told the Puritans the Indian story of creation and asked the settlers to affirm it. The Indian communication style was not to disagree but to listen and affirm. The Puritans were disappointed that communication, in the Western understanding of communication, had failed. In the American Indian understanding of communication, it had not.

THE MEDIA OF INTERCULTURAL COMMUNICATION

One component of the communication process is the channel, or medium, by which the encoded message is transmitted. In past centuries, human couriers and letters were the dominant media. Today's dominant media are electronic. Our focus is not on the extent of new media use but rather on how culture is reflected in new media use.

Human Couriers and Intermediaries

One early form of intercultural communication still in widespread use today is human couriers. Another person can be used as a medium. You can easily imagine messages being entrusted to a courier to deliver to a faraway village.

In some cultures, intermediaries are used instead of face-to-face confrontation to reduce the risk of losing face or the value or standing one has in the eyes of others. Ting-Toomey (1985) has proposed that cultures like the United States with a greater concern for privacy and autonomy tend to use direct-face negotiation and express more self-face maintenance, whereas cultures such as China with a greater concern for interdependence and inclusion tend to use indirect-face negotiation and express more mutual-face and other-face maintenance. In a study conducted in Central China, Ma (1992) confirmed that a friend or respected elder intervenes in interpersonal conflict situations serving as a message carrier.

Letter Writing

Since 3800 BCE, when King Sargon of Babylon established a postal service over the roads and footpaths between the Tigris and Euphrates Rivers, we have written letters. As public postal services were established, letter writing became a commonly used medium for intercultural communication. Letters written to others in various other cultures faced the same barriers that effected face-to-face spoken communication. Diverse perception, language, and values obviously were challenges then as they are now.

Telephone

It is estimated that as of 2008 there were 1.3 billion landlines in use. Alexander Graham Bell expected the telephone to be more of a broadcasting medium, more like what radio would become. Well into the 20th century, telephone executives believed the telephone was primarily a medium for business and actually discouraged "socializing" by telephone. The estimated number of cell phones in 2010 was 5.3 billion. Because the United States relied heavily on land lines, cell phone adoption was slower in the United States than in other countries. There were more than 2 million pay phones in the United States in 1997. That number dropped to about 1 million in 2006 as cell phone use became more common. In Africa and Asia where land lines were not as common and in Europe where cell phone service is less expensive than land lines, cell phone adoption was faster (Ling, 2005). In 2005, for example, 95% of European teenagers had cell phones while 45% of U.S. teenagers did (Ling & Baron, 2007). (See Table 2.1.)

There are approximately 400 million cell phone subscribers in Africa. Africans are leading a global trend to mobile Internet use. Studies show that when Africans go online with their mobile

Table 2.1   Land Line and Cell Phones in Use

Landline		Cell Phones	
Country	Number In Millions	County	Number In Millions
1. China	313,680	1. China	747,000
2. United States	141,000	2. India	670,000
3. Germany	48,700	3. United States	286,000
4. Russia	44,802	4. Russia	230,500
5. Japan	41,364	5. Brazil	173,959
6. Brazil	41,497	6. Indonesia	159,248
7. France	36,441	7. Japan	114,917
8. India	35,770	8. Germany	105,000
9. Indonesia	33,958	9. Pakistan	103,000
10. United Kingdom	32,117	10. Vietnam	98,224

Source: CIA World Factbook (2011).

phones they spend much of their time on social media platforms such as Facebook, Twitter, and YouTube. Facebook is the most visited website in most of Africa. The Facebook fan base of Côte d'Ivoire's football star and UN goodwill ambassador Didier Drogba is more than 1 million people. Zambian best-selling author and economist Dambisa Moyo has more than 26,000 followers on Twitter. African companies are launching local social media platforms. In South Africa, MXit, a free instant messaging application, has an estimated 7 million users (Essoungou, 2010).

Using the telephone in intercultural interactions has the barriers of the lack of contextual cues other than those related to voice. For this reason it may be the conversation openings that are significant in establishing the first impression from which the relationship develops. An opening sequence that violates a cultural expectation may lead the parties to develop negative views and attitudes toward each other (Pavlidou, 2006). Later language misunderstandings, for example, the meanings of certain words, idioms, and humor, can exacerbate the problem.

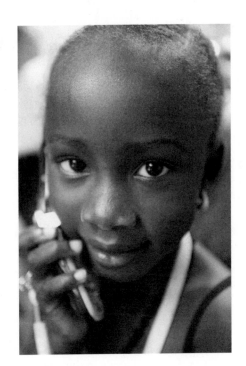

FOCUS ON CULTURE 2.1

How We Answer The Telephone

France	"Allo" The French often add their name and the phrase "Qui est a l'appareil?" That is, "Who is on the phone?"
Italy	"Pronto" or "Ready." The caller may the ask, "Chi parla?" or "Who's speaking?"
Germany	Last name, such as "Schmidt" or "Mueller."
Spain	"Diga" or "Speak."
Mexico	"Diga" or "Bueno," meaning "Good" or "Well."
Southeast Asia	Most commonly a version of "Hello" Hong Kong Chinese say "Wei."
Japan	"Moshi moshi," the equivalent of "Hello, " or perhaps "Hai," which is, "Yes."

Source: Los Angeles Times, quoted in TELCOM DIGEST, quoted in Martin (2000).

FOCUS ON CULTURE 2.2

In 2008, Kenya's controversial presidential election results lead to clashes that left more than 1,000 people dead and 500,000 displaced. The internal security minister announced a ban of live broadcasts. Kenyans turned to short message services (SMS) from mobile phones. Use of social media tools such as wikis, web logs, Facebook, Flickr, YouTube, and Twitter increased.

Because social media serve as channels of expression that could not be easily controlled by the ruling power, they made it possible for "a diversity of voices to be heard and connect with each other."

Source: Mäkinen & Wangu Kuira (2008, p. 328).

Text messaging is the more commonly used term in North America, the United Kingdom, and the Philippines for what other countries are more likely to refer to as Short Message Service (SMS). Shuter and Chattopadhyay (2010) compared texting in the United States and India and found a definite relationship to each culture's norms. For example, consider where texting is done. In the United States in public settings, people still maintain private areas. Consistently, people in the United States are more likely to send and read messages in public social settings like restaurants, shops, and movie theaters. Perhaps because of the area where texting is done, people in the United States text when they are with strangers and acquaintances or friends but much less than with family members. Indians text when they are with family members or boyfriends or girlfriends. People in the United States are more likely to consider it impolite to text in a classroom, movie theater, at dinner, and while conversing with others, especially with loud text alerts. Indians are more likely to find as impolite swearing in texts. Shuter and Chattopadhyay conclude that the social use of texting is guided by forces deeply imbedded in each culture.

Internet

When the World Wide Web became available in the early 1990s, there were about 2.6 million Internet users. By 2000 there were some 385 million users. Communication became instant with e-mail, instant messaging, Voice over Internet Protocol (VoIP), two-way video, discussion forums, blogs, and social networking. Let's look at both language use on the Internet and design elements of websites.

Language Use

As shown in Table 2.2, there are more Internet users in China than in the United States. Whether the result of the origin of the Internet, of the extent of English use worldwide, or that

FOCUS ON THE ENVIRONMENT 2.2

How long will you use your current cell phone? How will you dispose of it when you get a new one? One estimate is that four cell phones per second end up in landfills.

Since cell phones first came on the market, there have been at least 5 billion in existence. While the ecological impact of one cell phone may be small, the cumulative effect is a major problem. Mobile phones contain heavy metals such as mercury, lead, and cadmium, as well as brominated flame retardants in the printed circuit boards and casings. These substances can have a devastating impact if they are released into the environment.

The UN Environment Programme (UNEP) estimates that up to 50 million tons of waste from discarded electronic goods is generated annually. The majority is shipped from the West to Asian countries such as China and India, but tighter regulations means more and more is ending up in Africa where there are few facilities to safely deal with it.

The EU law, the Waste Electrical and Electronic Equipment (WEEE) Directive, requires producers to bear the cost of the collection, recovery, and disposal of "e-waste." NEC has developed a handset that uses plant-derived bioplastics and emits 50% less carbon dioxide than conventional approaches.

Source: Kinver (2006).

Table 2.2   Internet and Facebook Users, 2009/2011

Country	Internet Users	Facebook Users
China	389,000,000	391,200
United States	245,000,000	154,971,340
Japan	99,182,000	3,059,000
Brazil	75,982,000	15,929,000
Germany	65,125,000	17,929,680
India	61,338,000	23,042,800
United Kingdom	51,444,000	30,257,300
France	45,262,000	21,819,200
Nigeria	43,989,000	2,991,200
Russia	40,853,000	4,422,880

Sources: CIA World Factbook (2011) and Internet World Stats (2011a).

early computer systems were limited to the characters in the American Standard Code for Information Interchange (ASCII), a subset of the Latin alphabet, English has been the dominant language of the Internet. In the mid-1990s, an estimated 80% of international websites were in English. While Indonesian and Korean newspapers may have been available on the Internet, they were only viewed and read by those language speakers.

A study first reported in 2000 examined the language use of young Egyptian professionals. For the reasons stated above, the dominant language use online was English, but a previously little used written form of Romanized Egyptian Arabic also was used for expressing personal thoughts and feelings. This group used Romanized Egyptian Arabic as a reinforcement of their local identity (Warschauer, El Said, & Zohry, 2002).

Will Chinese, then, become the dominant language on the Internet? With the development of Unicode, the computing industry standard for the consistent encoding, representation, and handling of text, most of the world's writing systems can be displayed reliably. Translation technology will make it possible for everyone to use any preferred language and be understood by anyone. Google Translate provides text translations for 57 languages, including Chinese characters. Translations are built into the Chrome Web browser.

Design Elements

As you have seen in the model of communication presented earlier, communication symbols can be verbal and nonverbal. While translation technology may deal to some extent with the verbal symbols, there remain the nonverbal. Research has demonstrated that culture is reflected in the nonverbal aspects of the Internet. Singh, Zhao and Hu (2003) assert that "the web is not a culturally neutral medium," because websites contain unique design elements that give "country-specific websites a look and feel unique to the local culture" (p. 63). Design elements include different icons, colors, and site structures (Barber & Badre, 1998). Schmid-Isler (2000) compared Western and Chinese Internet news sites and found that their layout is different. They contend that this difference is related to culturally influenced perceptions of information storage and display.

Even beyond symbol use, Internet sites also reflect deep-seated cultural values. Singh and Baak (2004) compared Mexican and United States e-commerce sites for cultural values. You will read more about cultural values in Chapter 7, but for now let's generalize their results to say that the Mexican websites showed more content related to cultural values of collectivism, masculinity, and power distance. Studies of cultural values detailed in Chapter 7 show that these three cultural values are characteristic of the Mexican culture. Pfeil, Zaphiris, and Ang (2006) studied contributions to French, German, Japanese, and Dutch Wikipedia websites and found cultural differences in the style of the contributions. The researchers conclude that "cultural differences that are observed in the physical world also exist in the virtual world."

Social Network Sites

As mentioned above, countries may differ in how social network sites (SNS) are accessed. However accessed, SNS continue to grow in popularity throughout the world. While Facebook and Myspace both originated in the United States and both have worldwide use, local SNS

The layout of a website can reveal cultural elements.

are growing as well. Cyworld, a Korea-based SNS, enjoyed 23 million members in 2009 (Goh, 2009)—more than a third of the entire Korean population—while Japan's Mixi has 26.8 million members in 2010 ("Profiling the Facebooks," 2010).

Kim, Sohn, and Choi (2011) compared U.S. and Korean college student SNS use and found clear cultural connections. In both countries the reasons for using SNS were the same: seeking friends, social support, information, entertainment, and convenience. The difference was that, for students in the United States, socially close others (e.g., families and close friends) were only a minor part of their online social networks, while families and close friends were 70% of the Koreans' networks. The researchers conclude that students in the United States tend to focus more on entertaining themselves by making new friends through SNS, while Korean students tend to focus more on existing relationships with socially close others from whom they can acquire useful information and social support" Abeele and Roe (2011) found a similar pattern comparing Flemish and U.S. new college students. Flemish students were more likely to text and instant message precollege friends, while U.S. students were more likely to text and instance message new friends.

THE SPECIAL CASE OF PREJUDICE AND RACISM

Communication can play a role in either spreading prejudice and racism or stopping their spread. Prejudice and racism are commonly viewed as being rooted in the child's early socialization and fostered in communication with other people who are prejudiced or racist (Adorno, Frenkel-Brunswick, Levinson, & Sanford, 1950). Just overhearing racist comments has been shown to negatively affect the listener's evaluation of the person being spoken about. Research studies have demonstrated this effect (Greenberg & Pyszczynski, 1985; Kirkland, Greenberg, & Pyszczynski, 1987). In the study conducted by Jeff Greenberg and Tom Pyszczynski (1985), groups of White college students observed a debate between a White and an African-American student and were asked to evaluate the skill of the debaters. The debates were staged so that the African-American debater won half the time and lost half the time. Immediately after the debate and before the evaluations, a confederate made a derogatory ethnic slur against the African-American debater, criticized the African-American debater in a nonracist manner, or made no comment. Ethnic slurs did cue prejudiced behavior. The study's results showed that when the audience overheard the derogatory ethnic slur, the rating given the African-American debater who lost was significantly lower but not so when the African-American debater won. The researchers' comment that evaluations of individual minority group members can be biased by overheard derogatory ethnic labels when the person's behavior is less than perfect.

Out of realizations that speech can cue prejudiced behavior in others, some have attempted to restrict that type of speech, often referred to as *hate speech*. Hate speech includes threats or verbal slurs directed against specific groups or physical acts such as burning crosses or spray-painting swastikas on public or private property (Walker, 1994). Some cities and colleges in the United States have adopted policies attempting to ban hate speech. Strong arguments have been raised that such prohibitions are in violation of the First Amendment, the right from government abridgment of freedom of expression other than libel and obscenity. Others counter that hate speech is less like political expression and more like an action, such as a slap in the face (see Haiman, 1994), and that such regulations are necessary to protect equality. Internationally, the trend since World War II has been to protect individuals and groups from expressions of hatred, hostility, discrimination, and violence. In fact, Australia, Austria, Canada, France, Germany, Great Britain, Italy, the Netherlands, New Zealand, Norway, and Sweden all have statutes or constitutional provisions prohibiting forms of hate speech. The International Covenant on Civil and Political Rights, in Article 20(2), expressly provides that "any advocacy of national, racial, or religious hatred that constitutes incitement to discrimination, hostility, or violence shall be prohibited by law." In 1992, when the U.S. Senate ratified this treaty, it stipulated that the United States would not be bound by this provision but would adhere to its own constitution.

In 1996, the U.S. Congress passed the Communications Decency Act, which made it a federal crime to put obscene and indecent words or images on the Internet. The concern was to protect children from pornographic material. The next year, the U.S. Supreme Court invalidated a key provision of the law. The Court ruled that in seeking to protect children, the law violated the rights of adults. In that same year (1997), the Wiesenthal Center identified more than 500 hate sites. Its 1999 report identified 1,426 sites, including an online video

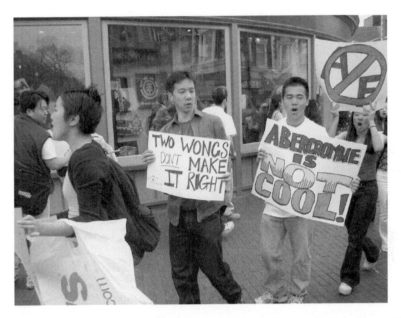

In 2002, Abercrombie & Fitch (A&F) pulled a line of T-shirts after complaints. The T-shirts show Asian cartoon characters. Printed on the shirts were ads for hypothetical businesses: "Rick Shaw's Hoagies and Grinders. Order by the foot. Good meat. Quick feet" and "Wong Brothers Laundry Service—Two Wongs Can Make It White." A senior manager at A&F said, "These graphic T-shirts were designed with the sole purpose of adding humor and levity to our fashion line."

game with the objective to lynch a Black man. The first federal prosecution of an Internet hate crime occurred in 1996. A 19-year-old male former student at the University of California, Irvine, sent an e-mail message signed "Asian hater" to about 60 Asian students, accusing Asians of being responsible for all crimes on campus and ordering the students to leave the campus or be killed by him. He was convicted in 1998 of interfering with students' civil rights to attend a public university.

In 1997, Germany passed a law under which online providers can be prosecuted for offering a venue for content illegal in Germany, such as Nazi propaganda, if they do so knowingly and if it's technically possible to prevent it. The First Amendment would not permit such a restriction in the United States. Because laws banning hate speech may not be constitutional in the United States, there are other, more positive approaches to dealing with

> ## Global Voices
>
> The point is that racism has come out of the closet and people are beginning to not be afraid of declaring blatantly racist views and getting away with it.
>
> —South African Archbishop Desmond Tutu, December 1991

Global Voices

We cannot overlook the fact . . . that much linguistic expression serves a dual communicative function: it conveys not only ideas capable of relatively precise, detached explication, but otherwise inexpressible emotions as well. In fact, words are often chosen as much for their emotive as their cognitive force. We cannot sanction the view that the Constitution, while solicitous of the cognitive content of individual speech, has little or no regard for that emotive function which, practically speaking, may often be the more important element of the overall message sought to be communicated.

—Justice Harlan, in *Cohen v. California* (1971)

Source: U.S. Supreme Court Reports (1972, p. 294)

prejudice and racism. Establishing cultural norms against such behaviors may be more effective.

Social media add an immediacy and range to prejudice and racism not known before. In 2011, the day after the Japan earthquake, a UCLA student posted a video on YouTube in which she complained about and mocked Asian students. She did take it down a few hours after posting it, but in that short time it had been reposted and remixed, taking on a life of its own. Asian student groups responded with calls for increased diversity requirements in the curriculum. Greg Lukianoff, president of the Foundation for Individual Rights in Education, an advocacy group for freedom of expression on college campuses, responded to the controversy by saying that the student's video was protected by the First Amendment and observing that "social media is teaching us, habituating us, to respond to speech with more speech." UCLA's chancellor recorded a statement condemning the student's video that was also posted on YouTube (Rojas, 2011).

One research project demonstrated that hearing other people express strongly antiracist opinions influences both public and private expressions of racist opinions. In their study, Blanchard, Lilly, & Vaughn (1991) interviewed students on the way to classes. In each interview, three people were involved: the White interviewer, a White confederate, and a naive White respondent. The interviewer asked the confederate and respondent questions about how their college should respond to anonymous racist notes. The confederate always answered first. The study compared how the respondents answered the questions when the confederate answered with the most antiracist statements to how they answered when the confederate answered with the least antiracist statements. The results showed that hearing the confederate express strongly antiracist opinions produced dramatically stronger antiracist opinions than hearing opinions more accepting of racism. In a second study, Blanchard and colleagues showed the same results when the respondents expressed their answers privately on paper. On the basis of this research, it can be argued that cultural norms can minimize the public expression of discriminatory or otherwise interracially insensitive behavior. Yum and Park (1990), however, argue that for well-established stereotypes to change, more frequent information and stronger content are needed. What each of us says about racial discrimination really does matter. Your vocal opinions affect what others think and say.

FOCUS ON THE ENVIRONMENT 2.3

University of Rochester researchers Netta Weinstein, Andrew K. Przybylski, and Richard M. Ryan (2009). showed computer images of either urban settings of buildings and roads or natural settings of landscapes and lakes. Study participants were asked to study the computer images and note colors and textures and imagine the sounds and smells associated with the images. They then ask the participants to complete questionnaires about various values including wealth, fame, connectedness to community, relationships, and the betterment of society. Participants who studied the computer images of natural settings rated close relationships and community values higher than they had after observing the images of urban environments. Participants who studied the computer images of urban settings rated fame and wealth higher.

SUMMARY

The formal study of intercultural communication in the United States originated with the 1946 Foreign Service Act, which provided for language and anthropological cultural training for foreign diplomats. Outside the Foreign Service Institute, the study of intercultural communication is generally associated with the publication of Edward T. Hall's book, *The Silent Language,* in 1959. Since that time, the emphasis has been on improving intercultural communication competence through personality strength, communication skills, psychological adjustment, and cultural awareness. Kale (1997) developed four ethical principles to guide intercultural interactions.

Culture cannot be known without a study of communication, and communication can only be understood with an understanding of the culture it supports. A Confucian perspective on communication would define it as an infinite interpretive process in which all parties are searching to develop and maintain a social relationship. A Western perspective would define it as a process involving a speaker, the speech act, an audience, and a purpose. Components of communication can include source, encoding, message, channel, noise, receiver, decoding, receiver response, feedback, and context.

One component of the communication process is the channel or media by which the encoded message is transmitted. Today's new media use reflects significant aspects of culture. For example, people in the Unites States are more likely to send and read text messages in public social settings like restaurants, shops, and movie theaters; Indians text when they are with family members or boyfriends and girlfriends. And Western and Chinese Internet news sites have different layouts, which is related to culturally influenced perceptions of information storage and display.

Hate speech includes threats or verbal slurs directed against specific groups or physical acts such as burning crosses or spray-painting swastikas on public or private property. Hate speech is spread in new media. Communication can play a role in either spreading prejudice and racism or stopping their spread. Countries differ in restrictions placed on hate speech.

DISCUSSION QUESTIONS

1. What are the most critical elements of intercultural communication competence?

2. Kale (1997) suggests that peace is a fundamental human value that could guide intercultural interactions. Evaluate this proposition.

3. This chapter contrasts Western and Confucian understandings of communication. What might characterize Hindu or Islamic understandings of communication?

4. Is social media changing culture or does culture determine social media use?

5. Who should be responsible for prejudice and racism on Internet sites?

KEY TERMS

channel 43	feedback 43	noise 43
communication 35	hate speech 52	Peace Corps 35
Confucianism 40	honorific 41	receiver 43
context 44	in-group 40	receiver response 43
decoding 43	intercultural communication 35	source 43
encoding 43	message 43	

NOTE

1. Recently, BCE (before the common era) and CE (common era) have been used to avoid the more culturally limited BC (before Christ) and AD (*anno Domini,* in the year of the Lord).

READINGS

All readings are from *Intercultural Communication: A Global Reader* (Jandt, 2004).

Peter Mühlhäusler, "Babel Revisited" (p. 103)
He-Soo Kim, Greg Hearn, Caroline Hatcher, and Ian Weber, "Online Communication Between Australians and Koreans: Learning to Manage Differences That Matter" (p. 143)

Fred E. Jandt and Dolores V. Tanno, "Decoding Domination, Encoding Self-Determination: Intercultural Communication Research Processes" (p. 205)

Becky Michele Mulvaney, "Gender Differences in Communication: An Intercultural Experience" (p. 221)

Akira Miyahara, "Toward Theorizing Japanese Interpersonal Communication Competence From a Non-Western Perspective" (p. 279)

Randy Kluver, "Globalization, Informatization, and Intercultural Communication" (p. 425)

STUDENT STUDY SITE

Visit the student study site at www.sagepub.com/jandt7e for these additional learning tools:

- Web Resources
- Audio and Video Links
- SAGE journal articles
- eFlashcards
- Web Quizzes
- Sample Essays

CHAPTER

3

Culture's Influence on Perception

FOCUS QUESTIONS

- What is the relationship between culture and sensation?

- What is the relationship between culture and each step of the perception process?

- What is the distinction between high-context and low-context cultures?

- What is meant by the concept of face?

- How can cultural interpretations placed on perceptions, such as food, reflect other elements of culture?

Sensing
    Effect of Culture on Sensing
Perceiving
    Selection
        Japanese/English Difficulties With
           Speech Sounds
    Organization
        Grouping Like Objects Together
    Interpretation
        Dogs as Pets or as Food
        Weather Vane as Christian Cross
High Versus Low Context
The Concept of Face
A Case Study of Perception and Food
Summary
Discussion Questions
Key Terms
Readings
Student Study Site

This chapter is about the effect of culture on our perception of the world external to our minds. Can we say that there is a world external to our minds; that is, independent of our awareness of it? Wexler (2008) states it dramatically by stating "the relationship between the individual and the environment is so extensive that it almost overstates the distinction between the two to speak of a relationship at all" (p. 39). Sensory input is a physical interaction; for example, cells in our mouths and noses have receptor molecules that combine with molecules from the environment to initiate electrical impulses. Our perception and thought processes are not independent of the cultural environment.

If our perception and thought processes are such a part of "what is out there," what then is the relationship between changes in the cultural environment and who we are? Wexler points out that we humans shape our environment and, hence, it could be said that the human brain shapes itself to a human-made environment. Our brain both is shaped by the external world and shapes our perception of the external world.

In this chapter we first examine the effects of culture on the sensation process. Then we examine the perception process. While the effect of culture on perception is independent of language, language (as we examine in a later chapter), influences thought. Some of the examples in this chapter illustrate the interrelationships of perception, language and thought. Later in the chapter, you will read about the concept of high-context and low-context cultures and the concept of face. And as food choices are examples of the perceptional step of interpretation, you will read about food in China.

FOCUS ON CULTURE 3.1

The Greeks Had Aristotle and the Chinese Had Confucius

Much of the research in this area and most of the examples in this chapter contrast Eastern and Western cultures. Nisbett (2003) and others contend that Eastern and Western cultures literally perceive different worlds. Modern Eastern cultures are inclined to see a world of substances—continuous masses of matter. Modern Westerners see a world of objects—discrete and unconnected things. There is substantial evidence that Easterners have a holistic view, focusing on continuities in substances and relationships in the environment, while Westerners have an analytic view, focusing on objects and their attributes.

FOCUS ON THEORY 3.1

Phenomenological theories assume that humans come to understand the world through direct personal experience with it. The basic principles are as follows:

- Knowledge is found directly in conscious experience.
- How you relate to an experience determines its meaning for you.
- Language is the vehicle of meaning (Deetz, 1973).

Central to phenomenological theories is the process of interpretation, or assigning meaning to experiences. In phenomenology, interpretation forms what is real for the person. Reality cannot be separate from interpretation. For Heidegger (1959/1972), words assign meaning to experience. Experience, words, and social interaction are linked.

Fritz Heider (1958) developed attribution theory to focus on the ways people infer the causes of behavior; that is, we attribute causes to behavior. We see a person act and draw conclusions that go beyond sensory information. We see a person act, make a judgment as to whether the behavior was intentionally performed, and finally determine whether we believe the person was forced to perform the behavior (attribute cause to the situation) or not (attribute cause to the person).

SENSING

Sensation is the neurological process by which we become aware of our environment. Of the human senses, sight, hearing, smell, taste, and touch, including pain, temperature, and pressure, are the most studied (Gordon, 1971). The world appears quite different to other forms of life with different sensory ranges: A bat, for example, senses the world through ultrasound; a snake does so through infrared light; some fish sense distortions of electrical fields through receptors on the surface of their bodies—none of these directly sensed by humans. But is there significant variation in sensation among individual humans? You need to remember that sensation is a neurological process. You are not directly aware of what is in the physical world but, rather, of your own internal sensations. When you report "seeing" a tree, what you are aware of is actually an electrochemical event. Much neural processing takes place between the receipt of a stimulus and your awareness of a sensation (Cherry, 1957). Is variation in human sensation attributable to culture?

Nisbett (2003) has demonstrated that humans sense and perceive the world in ways unique to their environments by contrasting Eastern and Western cultures.

Ancient Greeks had a strong sense of individual identity with a sense of personal agency, the sense that they were in charge of their own destinies. Greeks considered human and non-human objects as discrete and separate. And the Greeks made a clear distinction between the external world and our internal worlds. Thus, two individuals could have two different perceptions of the world because the world itself was static, unchanging, and independent of perception. It was through rhetorical persuasion that one could attempt to change another's perception. The attributes of individual objects are the basis of categorization of objects and categories are subject to behavioral rules that could be discovered and understood by the human mind. Thus rocks and other objects are in the category of objects that have the property of gravity.

The Chinese counterpart to the Greek sense of personal agency was harmony. Every Chinese was a member of a family and a village. The Chinese were less concerned with controlling their own destinies but more concerned with self-control so as to minimize conflict with others in the family and village. For the Chinese, the world is constantly changing and every event is related to every other event. The Chinese understood the world as continuously interacting substances, so perception focused on the entire context or environment. Chinese thought is to see things in their context in which all the elements are constantly changing and rearranging themselves.

Effect of Culture on Sensing

How much alike, then, are two persons' sensations? Individuals raised in diverse cultures can actually sense the world differently. For example, Marshall Segall and his associates (Segall, Campbell, & Herskovits, 1966) found that people who live in forests or in rural areas can sense crooked and slanted lines more accurately than can people who live in urban areas. This demonstrates that the rural and urban groups sense the same event differently as a result of their diverse cultural learnings.

The term field dependence refers to the degree to which perception of an object is influenced by the background or environment in which it appears. Some people are less likely than others to separate an object from its surrounding environment. When adults in Japan and the United States are shown an animated underwater scene in which one large fish swims among small fish and other marine life, the Japanese describe the scene and comment more about the relationships among the objects in the scene. The Americans were more likely to begin with a description of the big fish and make only half as many comments about the relationships among the objects. Not surprisingly, when showed a second scene with the same big fish, the Americans were more likely to recognize the big fish as the same one as in the first scene (Nisbett, 2003).

More recently, Kitayama, Duffy, Kawamura, and Larsen (2003) showed Japanese and European Americans a picture of a square with a line inside it (see Figure 3.1). They were then given an empty square of a different size and asked to either draw a line the same length as the one they had seen or a line of the same relative length to the one they had seen. The European Americans were significantly more accurate in drawing the line of the same length while the Japanese were significantly more accurate in drawing the line of relative length. Differences in the environment and culture affected sensation.

The researchers then compared Americans who had been living in Japan and Japanese who had been living in the United States. The time for both was a few years. Given the same picture and task, the Americans who had been living in Japan were close to the Japanese in the original study while the Japanese who had been living in the United States were virtually the same as the native-born Americans. While other explanations are possible, one strong suggestion is that even living for an extended time in new culture can modify sensation and cognitive processes.

Figure 3.1   Stimulus for Culture's Effect on Sensation

Source: Ishii and Kitayama (2003).

PERCEIVING

Culture also has a great effect on the **perception** process (Tajfel, 1969; Triandis, 1964). Human perception is usually thought of as a three-step process of selection, organization, and interpretation. Each of these steps is affected by culture.

Selection

The first step in the perception process is **selection**. Within your physiological limitations, you are exposed to more stimuli than you could possibly manage. To use sight as an example, you may feel that you are aware of all stimuli on your retinas, but most of the data from the retinas are handled on a subconscious level by a variety of specialized systems. Parts of our brains produce output from the retinas that we cannot "see." No amount of introspection can make us aware of those processes.

In an interesting study by Simons and Chabris (1999), participants viewed videotape of a basketball game. They were told to count the number of passes one team made. In the video, a woman dressed as a gorilla walks into the game, turns to face the camera, and beats her fists on her chest. Fifty percent of all people who watch the video don't see the gorilla. Mack and Rock (1998) argue that we don't consciously see any object unless we are paying direct, focused attention on that object. When we need something, have an interest in it, or want it, we are more likely to sense it out of competing stimuli. When we're hungry, we're more likely to attend to food advertisements.

Being in a busy airport terminal is another example. While there, you are confronted with many competing stimuli. You simply cannot attend to everything. However, if in the airport terminal an announcement is made asking you by name to report to the ticketing counter, you would probably hear your name even in that environment of competing stimuli. Just as you've learned to attend to the sound of your name, you've learned from your culture to select out other stimuli from the environment. A newborn child is a potential speaker of any language. Having heard only those sounds of one's own language and having learned to listen to and make only those differentiations necessary, anyone would find it difficult to hear crucial differences in speech sounds in another language.

Japanese/English Difficulties With Speech Sounds

If you grew up speaking English, certain aspects of the Japanese language are difficult for you to perceive. These aspects do not occur in English, so you never learned to listen for them and you literally do not hear them. For example, vowel length does not matter in English. You can say "Alabama" or "Alabaaama," and others would know you're referring to a southern U.S. state. Vowel length is important in Japanese. Japanese has short-duration vowels and long-duration vowels. Vowel length in the following pairs of Japanese words actually determines their meanings:

obasan	aunt
obaasan	grandmother
kita	came
kiita	heard

Because vowel length is not a critical attribute in English, perceiving the difference in sounds is a problem for those attempting to understand Japanese.

Other sounds that present difficulties for English speakers are the following:

Doubled consonants:

shita	did
shitta	new

Accent:

kaki	oyster
kaki	persimmon

Pitch:

hashi	bridge
hashi	chopsticks
hashi	edge of a table

If you grew up speaking Japanese, some aspects of the English language are difficult for you to perceive. English has some consonant sounds that do not exist in Japanese. If you grew up speaking Japanese, you didn't learn to listen for those consonant sounds. English uses the consonant sounds *f, v, th* as in *think, th* as in *breathe, z, zh* as in *treasure, j* as in the *dge* of *judge, r,* and 1. Thus, if you grew up speaking Japanese, it is difficult to distinguish between the sounds *b* and *v, s* and *sh, r* and 1, and so forth, with the result that *lice* and *rice* or *glamour* and *grammar* are frequently pronounced the same way.

Japanese has borrowed thousands of English words. But if you grew up speaking English, you would have difficulty recognizing them. In Japanese, syllables are basically a consonant sound followed by a vowel. Syllables can end only with a vowel sound or an *n*. For example, the Japanese word *iiau* (quarrel) has four syllables—each vowel is pronounced as a separate syllable. A native-born English speaker would not know to do that and would try to pronounce the word as an unsegmented single sound. An English speaker pronounces the word *thrill* as one syllable. In Japanese, consonant sounds do not exist without vowels, so a Japanese speaker would pronounce all three syllables, something like *sooriroo*. The Japanese *r*, by the way, is difficult for English speakers. It's similar to the Spanish *r* in *pero* or *Roberto*. From our first language, we learned what sounds are critical to listen for. Because languages can have different critical sounds, learning a new language means learning to attend to new sounds.

Organization

The second step in the perception process is **organization**. Along with selecting stimuli from the environment, you must organize them in some meaningful way. When you look at a building, you do not focus on the thousands of possible individual pieces; you focus on the unified whole, a building. Turning a picture upside down, for example, can trick you into focusing on individual components rather than your unified concept of the object in the picture.

How are perceptions categorized? One argument is that you somehow grasp some set of attributes that things have in common. On that basis they are grouped together in a category provided by language that gives the conceptual categories that influence how its speakers' perceptions are encoded and stored. The philosopher Ludwig Wittgenstein (1889–1951), however, concluded that there needs be no such set of shared characteristics. Your language provides the symbol to group perceptions of any kind together.

Grouping Like Objects Together

"One of These Things" is a song used on *Sesame Street* when children are shown a group of four items, one of which is different from the other three. Children are asked to identify the item that does not belong with the others. Look at the three objects in Figure 3.2.

In this case, which two objects would you place together? The chicken and the grass? The chicken and the cow? Or the grass and the cow? Chiu showed such figures to children from China and the United States. American children grouped objects because they belonged to the same taxonomic category; that is, the same categorization term could be applied to both. The Americans would more likely group the chicken and cow together as "animals." The Chinese children preferred to group objects on the basis of relationships. The Chinese children would more likely group the cow and grass together because "cows eat grass" (Chiu, 1972).

Figure 3.2 Stimulus for Culture's Effect on Organization

a.

b.

c.

Source: Adapted from Nisbett (2003), p. 141.

In a similar study Mutsumi Imae and Dedre Gentner (1994) showed objects to Japanese and Americans of various ages and asked them to group them together. For example, one object was a pyramid made of cork, which they called a *dax*, a word that had no meaning to the participants. Then they showed them a pyramid made of white plastic and a different object made of cork. They then asked the participants to point to a dax. To which would you point?

Americans in the study chose the same shape, indicating that the Americans were coding what they saw as an object. The Japanese were more likely to choose the same material, indicating that they were coding what they saw as a substance.

Global Voices

Language plays a large and significant role in the totality of culture. Far from being simply a technique of communication, it is itself a way of directing the perception of its speakers and it promotes for them habitual modes of analyzing experience into significant categories. And to the extent that languages differ markedly from each other, so should we expect to find significant and formidable barriers to cross-cultural communication and understanding.

—Harry Hoijer, *Language in Culture* (1954, p. 94)

Interpretation

The third step in the perception process is **interpretation**. This refers to attaching meaning to sense data and is synonymous with decoding. The same situation can be interpreted quite differently by diverse people. A police officer arriving at a crime scene can be experienced by the victim as calming and relief giving but by the criminal as fearsome and threatening.

Here, too, the effect of culture is great. As you encounter people of your own culture, you constantly make judgments as to age, social status, educational background, and the like. The cues you use to make these decisions are so subtle that it's often difficult to explain how and why you reach a particular conclusion. Do people in the United States, for example, perceive tall men as more credible? Perhaps.

Applying these same cues to someone from another culture may not work. People in the United States, for example, frequently err in guessing the age of Japanese individuals, such as judging a Japanese college student in her mid-20s to be only 14 or 15.

Dogs as Pets or as Food

The meanings you attach to your perceptions are greatly determined by your cultural background. Think of how speakers of English categorize life. Most probably use the categories of human life and animal life. Now think of how you typically categorize animal life—probably into wild animals and domesticated animals. Now think of how you typically categorize domesticated animal life—probably into animals used for food, animals used for sport and recreation, and pets. Look at the picture of the puppy and capture your feelings.

Most of us see this puppy in the category of pet, for which we have learned to relate warm, loving feelings. Puppies are cute, cuddly, warm, loving creatures. Now look at the next picture

Many consider dogs as pets. (The author's first dog, Smokey.)

of a man holding up a dog, read the caption, and capture your feelings. Most of us who love dogs find this picture uncomfortable and disgusting. How can people eat dogs? They are pets, not food! It all depends on where you categorize them. Dogs are pets in some cultures and food in others. In the Arab world, dogs are acceptable as watchdogs and as hunting dogs but are not kept in the home as pets because they are seen as unclean and a low form of life. To call someone a dog is an insult among Arabs. People in most cultures have strong ideas about which foods are acceptable for human consumption and which are not. People in some countries think the custom in the United States of eating corn on the cob is disgusting because that food is fit only for pigs. Some Ukrainians like to eat *salo*, raw pig fat with black bread and vodka, which might cause nausea in some, as would knowing that horse meat from California is served in restaurants in Belgium, France, and Japan.

Can you explain your feelings about this photograph? As China's economy boomed and affluence spread, attitudes toward dogs changed. Traditional Chinese may have eaten dog meat because it was thought to improve blood circulation. Urban Chinese today are more likely to have dogs as pampered companions.

Your reaction of disgust to the picture is a culturally learned interpretation—and that interpretation can be quite strong. In 1989, California made it a misdemeanor for any person to sell, buy, or accept any animal traditionally kept as a pet with the intent of killing the animal for food. More recently, animal rights groups have protested the sale of live animals, such as turtles, frogs, lobsters, crabs, fish, and chicken, for food at Asian-American markets. Asian tradition is that fresh meat is tastier and more healthful, that the best meat "enters your house still breathing." Animal rights activists contend that the animals are treated inhumanely in the shops and are killed in ways that cause them unnecessary pain. Asian-American groups argue that eating dogs and cats is an extreme rarity among Southeast Asian immigrants and call the law and the animal rights activists racist.

In some cultures, parts of some animals are categorized as medicine. In other cultures, certain animals are considered sacred and certainly would not be eaten. The Hindu elephant-headed God Ganesh is accompanied by a rat whenever he travels. Rats, like cows, are deified in India. No Hindu worship is complete without an offering to Ganesh and his companion, the rat. Rats are fed and rarely killed in India.

Weather Vane as Christian Cross

The examples so far have been of practices that could offend some English speakers. Let's turn that around with an example of what speakers of English do that could be offensive to others. Johnston Pump Company, a U.S. company now based in Brookshire, Texas, has been doing business with Saudi Arabia for more than 70 years. By the 1930s, Johnston Pump was well established in California, its pumps having helped change California's arid lands into a leading agricultural area. Johnston's general manager at the time was a world traveler. During a trip to Saudi Arabia, he noted how similar the climate was to areas of California and convinced the Saudi government that vast wastelands could be turned into fertile farmland through the use of Johnston pumps. The first pump was installed in the king's palace.

Over the years, Johnston's success in the kingdom largely has been due to its respect for the country's strict religious customs. All personnel in its international division receive cultural training.

"Making the deserts bloom for 50 years" was Johnston's advertising campaign in 1986. Ads in English and Arabic began appearing in various Middle East publications early in the year. With the success of the campaign, Johnston made large posters of the ads to be distributed throughout the kingdom.

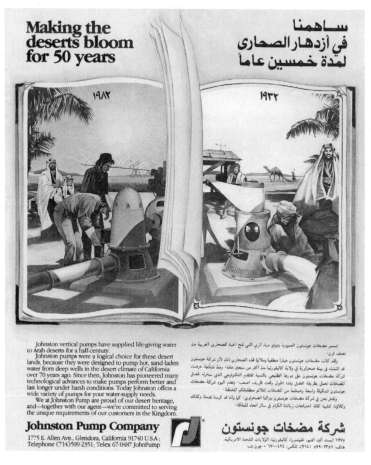

Johnston Pump poster.

Study the Johnston Pump poster and see if you can tell why a Saudi customs inspector would not allow it into the country. Saudi Arabia allows no public worship of any religion other than Islam. No churches, temples, or any symbols of other religions are permitted. To the customs inspector, the weather vane in the poster looked like a Christian cross and would therefore be prohibited from being displayed. It took intervention by the Minister of Customs to allow the posters into the country.

Years later, 10 million bags of potato chips from Thailand were confiscated by the Saudi Ministry of Commerce because toys inside each bag were adorned with crossed triangles that were perceived to be the Star of David. With the perception step of categorization comes a culture's values, and it is those differing categorizations that can so often impede communication, particularly when one group believes its perceptions are right and any other's wrong.

FOCUS ON THE ENVIRONMENT 3.1

According to C. G. Jung, there are different levels to the psyche: conscious awareness, personal unconscious, and the collective unconscious. The collective unconscious contains basic, instinctive patterns of behavior, emotion, and imagery that are common to all humans, often referred to as archetypes, which guide and give meaning to our interactions with other people and the world.

Jungian psychologists often turn to mythology for symbolic portrayals of archetypes. For example, the moon goddess Artemis, who is associated with forests and hunting, has been nominated as the "Goddess of Conservation." And ecologists and others have adopted the earth goddess, Gaia, as the personification of the whole-earth organism.

When archetypes are projected onto nature, the environment can evoke powerful emotions and take on a profound significance for the individual. Trees can evoke awe-inspiring fascination and reverence. A sequoia grove can be perceived as a sacred paradise on earth, a perfection removed from the everyday world.

Source: Schroeder (1991).

HIGH VERSUS LOW CONTEXT

Another way that culture affects perception is whether the culture is high or low context. The concept of high-context and low-context cultures was popularized by Edward T. Hall (1976). Recall that context was defined in Chapter 2 as the environment in which the communication process takes place and that helps define the communication. Table 3.1 shows examples of both types.

In some recent studies, European Americans and Japanese were shown scenes (Miyamoto, Nisbett, & Masuda, 2006). Each had a background scene and foreground objects. In their experiments, they compared perceptions of changes in the foreground with perception of changes in the background. European Americans were significantly better at detecting changes

Table 3.1 Level of Context, by Culture

High	Low
China	Switzerland
Japan	Germany
Korea	North America, including the United States
American Indian	Nordic states
Most Latin American cultures	
Southern and eastern Mediterranean cultures, such as Greece, Turkey, and the Arab states	

in the foreground, while the Japanese were significantly better at detecting changes in the background. These studies have argued that Europeans (low context) focus attention on objects independent of context (i.e., perceive analytically), whereas East Asians focus on the context (i.e., perceive holistically).

Cultures in which little of the meaning is determined by the context because the message is encoded in the explicit code are labeled **low context**. Cultures in which less has to be said or written because more of the meaning is in the physical environment or already shared by people are labeled **high context**.

Earlier, Hall (1976) had focused attention on the communication of high-context and low-context cultures. Think of the difference this way. On meeting a stranger, your verbal communication with that person is highly explicit—or low context—simply because you have no shared experiences. You cannot assume anything. However, when you communicate with your sister or brother with whom you have shared a lifetime, your verbal communication is less explicit because you make use of your shared context. For example, the mention of a certain name can lead to laughter. With the stranger, you would have to explain in language the story that that name represented. Also, with your sister or brother, a certain facial expression can have a shared meaning, such as "There Mom goes again," but the stranger would have no idea what your facial expression communicated. Again, you would have to explain in words that your mother's specific behavior was characteristic, somewhat irritating, but so uniquely her.

In low-context cultures, verbal messages are elaborate and highly specific, they and tend to be highly detailed and redundant as well. Verbal abilities are highly valued. Logic and reasoning are expressed in verbal messages. In high-context cultures, most of the information is either in the physical context or internalized in the person. Very little is in the coded, explicit, transmitted part of the message. High-context cultures decrease the perception of self as separate from the group. High-context cultures are more sensitive to nonverbal messages; hence, they are more likely to provide a context and setting and let the point evolve.

It has been said that language separates people. When understood from the perspective of high and low context, that statement makes sense. In high-context cultures, people are brought closer by the importance of their shared context. Those meanings are often lost in low-context cultures. I have often shown films of the traditional Japanese tea ceremony to classes in the United States. The tea ceremony reflects the Zen and Taoist traditions celebrating the beauty in the mundane, the superiority of spirit over matter, and tranquility with busy lives. The ceremony united the host and guest in a concert of harmony. Though not as commonly practiced as in the past, the tea ceremony is an excellent example of a high-context experience. Nothing is spoken; all the meanings are in the context of shared experience, the teahouse, the flower arrangement, the calligraphy scroll, and the ceramics. A typical response from a low-context observer is, "Hurry up and drink the tea!" Your social experiences over coffee take little meaning from the context and more from the conversation—the words.

The Japanese tea ceremony, or *chanoyu,* is a revered tradition derived from Zen Buddhism and is approached with great respect and concentration. Adherence to time-honored rules is essential, both during the ceremony itself and in the construction of the tea house, or *cha-shitsu,* which should appear rustic, simple, and tranquil.

The concept of high and low context also applies to self-understanding. In low-context cultures, one speaks of a person as having attributes independent of circumstances or of personal relations. This self is a free agent who can move from group to group, from setting to setting, without significant changes. But in high-context cultures, the person is connected, fluid, and conditional. Participation in relationships makes it possible to act; completely independent behavior usually isn't possible, nor even desirable (Nisbett, 2003).

Global Voices

High-context cultures make greater distinction between the insiders and outsiders than low-context cultures do. People raised in high-context systems expect more of others than do the participants in low-context systems. When talking about something they have on their minds, a high-context individual will expect his interlocutor to know what's bothering him, so that he does not have to be specific. The result is that he will talk around and around the point, in effect putting all the pieces in place except the crucial one. Placing it properly—this keystone—is the role of his interlocutor.

—Edward T. Hall, *Beyond Culture* (1976, p. 98)

THE CONCEPT OF FACE

In Chinese culture, face is conceptualized in two ways: *lien* (face) and *mien* or *mien-tzd* (image). While these are often used interchangeably, they have different meanings. Hu (1944) defines *lien* as something that "represents the confidence of society in the integrity of ego's moral character, the loss of which makes it impossible to function properly with the community" (p. 45). *Mien* "stands for the kind of prestige that is emphasized in this country, a reputation achieved through getting on in life, through success and ostentation" (p. 45). Ting-Toomey (1985) has proposed that low-context cultures, such as the United States, with a greater concern for privacy and autonomy, tend to use direct-face negotiation and express more self-face maintenance, whereas high-context cultures, such as China, with a greater concern for interdependence and inclusion, tend to use indirect-face negotiation and express more mutual-face or other-face maintenance.

Communication in high-context cultures such as China is hence more indirect or implicit and is more likely to use intermediaries. Because social harmony and face maintenance are crucial, communication through intermediaries is especially functional because using intermediaries eliminates face-to-face confrontation and reduces the risk of losing face.

In interviews conducted in central China, Ma (1992) confirmed that unofficial mediation is common in situations involving interpersonal conflict. The mediator is usually a friend of the two parties in conflict or an elderly person respected by both. Intervention by the friend or respected elder is either self-initiated or in response to a request by a person not connected with the competing parties. Impartiality and face maintenance are considered the two key factors in successful mediation.

A CASE STUDY OF PERCEPTION AND FOOD

Perception interpretations provided by a culture can reveal much about that culture. Cultures use food to reinforce and express identities. One book's title expresses the importance of cultural identity to food: *You Eat What You Are: People, Culture, and Food Traditions* (Barer-Stein, 1999). In the following case study of food in China, identify the elements of culture that are reflected in food preparation.

FOCUS ON THE CULTURE 3.2

Americans eat oysters but not snails. The French eat snails but not locusts. The Zulus eat locusts but not fish. The Jews eat fish but not pork. The Hindus eat pork but not beef. The Russians eat beef but not snakes. The Chinese eat snakes but not people. The Jali of New Guinea find people delicious.

Source: Robertson (1987, p. 63).

China has the oldest continuing culture of any nation in the world. About 500 BCE, the philosophies of Confucianism and **Taoism** became the prime motivating forces in the development of the cuisine. The counterbalance of these two major philosophies became the basis of Chinese cuisine as an art.

Confucius encouraged a sense of balance and harmony. For example, when meats were used as ingredients, they could not overpower the rice included in the same meal. He also emphasized the aesthetic aspects of cooking and eating. He said a proper dish should appeal to the eye as well as to the palate. For example, intricately carved vegetables are a common decoration.

The distinctive process of preparing Chinese cuisine is based on Confucius and his philosophy of balance. There is a division between *fan,* Chinese for grains and other starch foods, and *chai,* vegetable and meat dishes. A balanced meal, then, must have an appropriate amount of fan and chai.

The main principle of Tao is a life in perfect accord with nature. Taoism as a religion arose from the philosophy of Lao-Tzu. Lao-Tzu means "old philosopher" or even "old child"—and may have been a Chinese philosopher who lived around the 6th century BCE, or it may refer to a line of thought. The basic assumption of Taoism is that there is an underlying pattern or direction of the universe that cannot be explained verbally or intellectually. Lao-Tzu cautioned against naming things, for doing so subjugates reality through abstraction and analysis. The Tao is this underlying pattern, commonly known as "the Way," which can never be captured in words. The Taoist ideal is a person who leads a simple, spontaneous, and meditative life close to nature. Taoists are encouraged to explore roots, fungi, herbs, marine vegetation, and other natural foods to discover their life-giving elements.

There is also a belief in a balance that governs all of life and nature—the **yin** and the **yang**. Originally, *yin* meant the shady side of a hill and *yang* the sunny side. Yin is the dark, moist, cool aspect of the cosmos. Females have more yin quality. Yang is the bright, dry, warm aspect. Males have more yang quality. Foods also have yin and yang qualities. Most water plants, crustaceans, and certain beans are cooling yin foods. Oily and fried foods, pepper-hot flavoring, fatty meat, and oil plant foods such as peanuts are warm yang foods. The kind of food eaten is related to one's health. When yin and yang forces in the body are not balanced, problems result. Proper amounts of food of one kind or the other must then be eaten to correct this imbalance. For example, a body sore or fever could be due to overeating "warm" foods.

Remember, all elements of a culture interrelate. Half of China is mountainous or unsuited to cultivation. China cannot depend on large animals like cattle that are land intensive. Through necessity, the Chinese have used all forms of edible ingredients—from lotus roots, birds' nests, and sea cucumbers to pig brains and fish lips. Because of a scarcity of fuel and raw materials, stir-frying was developed. Small pieces of meat, poultry, fish, or vegetables take only a few minutes to cook and thus save fuel.

For at least 5,000 years, rice has been grown in China. Its importance has made it synonymous with food and life. Rice is the symbol of well-being and fertility. Leaving one's job is called breaking one's rice bowl. It's considered bad luck to upset a rice bowl. And the worst of all insults is to take another's bowl of rice and empty it onto the ground. At the Chinese table, it's the unspoken words that matter. The meal is the message. *Chi fan!*—Dinner is served!

SUMMARY

Perception and thought are not independent of the cultural environment; therefore, our brains are both shaped by the external world and shape our perception of the external world. Sensation is the neurological process of becoming aware of our environment and is affected by our cultures.

The Greek idea of a strong individual identity and the Chinese idea of harmony affected both the sensation and perception process in each culture. Perception is usually thought of as having three steps—selection, organization, and interpretation—each affected by culture.

The concept of high-context and low-context cultures was popularized by Edward T. Hall (1976). Cultures in which little of the meaning is determined by the context because the message is encoded in the explicit code are labeled low context. Cultures in which less has to be said or written because more of the meaning is in the physical environment or already shared by people are labeled high context. Low-context cultures, such as the United States, with a greater concern for privacy and autonomy, tend to use direct-face negotiation and express more self-face maintenance, whereas high-context cultures, such as China, with a greater concern for interdependence and inclusion, tend to use indirect-face negotiation and express more mutual face or other-face maintenance.

Perception interpretations can even be revealed in how cultures use food to reinforce and express identities. For example, in China, rice is the symbol of well-being and fertility. Leaving one's job is called breaking one's rice bowl.

DISCUSSION QUESTIONS

1. My veterinarian once said that he wished he could be a cat just for a few minutes to experience how a cat senses the world. He speculated, though, that such an experience would forever change him. How would the experience of "two realities" be so disconcerting?

2. Even within one culture, subgroups may have diverse perceptions. Consider the diverse perceptions of a moose by hunters, vegetarians, and even political parties.

3. Consider specific countries that have diverse populations and those with fairly homogeneous populations. How does the concept of high and low context help explain political debate, dispute resolution processes, and other forms of public communication?

4. Describe how the concept of face can help explain dispute resolution. How should a student confront an instructor over a grading error?

5. Speculate (and research) how one's cultural background affects the experience of listening to music.

KEY TERMS

face 72	low context 70	sensation 60
field dependence 61	organization 64	Taoism 73
high context 70	perception 62	yang 73
interpretation 66	selection 62	yin 73

READINGS

All readings are from *Intercultural Communication: A Global Reader* (Jandt, 2004).

Kil-Ho Kang, "Korean's Politeness Strategies" (p. 131)
Kiyoko Suedo, "Differences in the Perception of Face: Chinese Mien-Tzu and Japanese Metsu" (p. 292)

STUDENT STUDY SITE

Visit the student study site at www.sagepub.com/jandt7e for these additional learning tools:

- Web Resources
- Audio and Video Links
- SAGE journal articles
- eFlashcards
- Web Quizzes
- Sample Essays

PART 2

Communication Variables

As you will study in Part 2, when you travel internationally, you are likely to experience anxiety in situations in which you aren't sure what you're expected to do. For example, when visiting someone's home, are you expected to give a gift? Does giving a gift to a potential business associate signal a willingness to work together, or is it seen as ostentatious and inappropriate? What if the gift is a set of four items? Four may be an unlucky number. What if the gift is wrapped in greenpaper? Green may be an unlucky color.

Perhaps more people experience anxiety over nonverbal behaviors than anything else. I'm sure individuals in your class can share experiences they have had when traveling internationally.

Consider what some call the OK gesture, which is popular in the United States. Be prepared elsewhere, it's rude or obscene. It all depends on where you are.

The meaning of other nonverbals may be less obvious.

Perhaps some nonverbals are innate. Babies smile worldwide.

In Part 2, you will read about these and other nonverbals, as well as other barriers to effective intercultural communication. Barriers or not, we have always tried to communicate with one another. Imagine meeting someone from another country who has never had any previous contact with someone from your country.

CHAPTER

4

FOCUS QUESTIONS

- What are commonly considered to be barriers to effective intercultural communication?

- What communication barriers exist between the world's first and second largest economies?

Barriers to Intercultural Communication

Anxiety
Assuming Similarity Instead of Difference
Ethnocentrism
    Negative Effects on Communication
Stereotypes and Prejudice
    Stereotypes
    Negative Effects on Communication
    Case Study: Asian-Americans
    Prejudice
    Case Studies
        The Roma
        Japan and Korea
        United States
Case Study of Intercultural Communication Barriers:
    China and the United States
    Population
    History
    Regional Differences
    China's International Relationship Issues
    Status of Taiwan
    Tibet
    Human Rights and Free Speech
    Broadcast Media and the Internet
    Energy and Sustainability
        Economic Issues
Summary
Discussion Questions
Key Terms
Readings
Student Study Site

This chapter begins a series of three chapters focused on recognizing and avoiding breakdowns in intercultural communication. In Chapter 1, you read that every culture and subgroup provides its members with rules specifying appropriate and inappropriate behavior. Were you to approach intercultural communication from the perspective of attempting to learn the norms of all cultures and subgroups, it certainly would be an impossible task. There is no way that you could learn all the rules governing appropriate and inappropriate behavior for every culture and subgroup with which you came into contact. You would always be doing something wrong; you would always be offending someone. Your communication likely would suffer, as your violation of norms would be a form of noise limiting the effectiveness of your communication.

In fact, you wouldn't even know if you were expected to conform to the other culture's norms or if you were expected to behave according to your own culture's norms while respecting those of the other.

A better approach is to examine on a general level the barriers to intercultural communication. LaRay M. Barna (1997) has developed a list of six such barriers: anxiety, assuming similarity instead of difference, ethnocentrism, stereotypes and prejudice, nonverbal misinterpretations, and language. His categories of barriers are used herein when discussing problems that can arise in intercultural encounters. The first four kinds of barriers are discussed in this chapter. Nonverbal misinterpretations and language are discussed separately in following chapters. Taking these common mistakes into account can help you improve your intercultural communication skills.

This chapter concludes with an extended case study of communication barriers between China and the United States. At this critical time in the relationship between the two countries, misunderstandings have arisen over many issues, including Tibet, human rights, sustainability, and regulation of media and the Internet.

FOCUS ON THEORY 4.1

The German sociologist Georg Simmel's (1858–1918) concepts of "the stranger" and "social distance" were precursors to Berger and Calabrese's (1975) uncertainty reduction theory (Rogers, 1999). This theory assumes that during the initial phase of interaction with another person, your primary communication goal is to reduce your uncertainty about that person. Thus, you are attempting to discover information about the other person and to share information about yourself.

Gudykunst and his colleagues (see, e.g., Gudykunst, 1983, 1985) have applied this theory to intercultural communication by further developing the concept of the "stranger." Strangers are people who are members of other groups who act in ways different from one's own culture. When encountering strangers, one experiences uncertainty and anxiety and is unsure how to behave. Uncertainty means not knowing what the reactions of strangers will be and not knowing how to explain the reactions of strangers. Anxiety arises when a person is apprehensive about initial interactions. When anxiety is high, we tend to avoid interactions, and when it is too low, we tend not to care what happens in the interaction.

ANXIETY

The first barrier is high **anxiety**. When you are anxious due to not knowing what you are expected to do, it's only natural to focus on that feeling and not be totally present in the communication transaction.

For example, you may have experienced anxiety on your very first day on a new college campus or in a new job. You may be so conscious of being new—and out of place—and focus so much of your attention on that feeling that you make common mistakes and appear awkward to others. Sugawara (1993) surveyed 168 Japanese employees of Japanese companies working in the United States and 135 of their U.S. coworkers. Only 8% of the U.S. coworkers felt impatient with the Japanese coworkers' English. While 19% of the Japanese employees felt their spoken English was poor or very poor and 20% reported feeling nervous when speaking English with U.S. coworkers, 30% of the Japanese employees felt the U.S. coworkers were impatient with their accent. Almost 60% believed that language was the problem in communicating with the U.S. coworkers. For some, anxiety over speaking English properly contributed to avoiding interactions with the U.S. coworkers and limiting interactions both on and off the job.

ASSUMING SIMILARITY INSTEAD OF DIFFERENCE

The second barrier is *assuming similarity instead of difference*. A middle-class Angolan teenager may purchase a CD of American music. Does that demonstrate that we all like the same music? The cultural difference may be in how teenagers listen to that music: The Angolan teenager probably will play the music in communal fashion for several people to listen, dance, and sing along. Most probably in the United States, the teenager listens to the music alone. Four Spaniards may meet at a McDonald's in Madrid. They may order Big Macs, french fries, and milkshakes. Does that demonstrate that we all like the same food? The cultural difference may be in the rituals of dining together in Spain. Most probably they will not rush their meal, and the person who invited the others will pay as it is very unlikely each would pay for individual portions. When you assume similarity between cultures, you can be caught unaware of important differences.

When you have no information about a new culture, it might make sense to assume no differences exist, to behave as you would in your home culture. But making that assumption could result in miscommunication. In 1997, a Danish woman left her 14-month-old baby girl in a stroller outside a Manhattan restaurant while she was inside. Other diners at the restaurant became concerned and called New York City police. The woman was charged with endangering a child and was jailed for two nights. Her child was placed in foster care. The woman and the Danish consulate explained that leaving children unattended outside cafés is common in Denmark. Pictures were wired to the police showing numerous strollers parked outside cafés while parents were eating inside. The Danish woman had assumed that Copenhagen is similar to New York and that what is commonly done in Copenhagen is also commonly done in New York.

School districts in the United States have been accused of assuming similarity by groups such as the Council of American-Islamic Relations. Muslims pray five times a day and require space to unfurl a prayer rug, face Mecca, and touch the head to the floor. Muslim parents have asked schools to recognize difference and become more accommodating to Muslim students.

Each culture *is* different and unique to some degree. Boucher (1974), for example, has shown how cultures differ as to whom it is appropriate to display emotions. If you assume that display of emotions is similar to your culture, you might see people of different cultures in certain circumstances as lacking emotion and others in other circumstances as displaying emotions inappropriately.

The inverse can be a barrier as well. Assuming difference instead of similarity can lead to one not recognizing important things that cultures share in common.

It's better to assume nothing. It's better to ask, "What are the customs?" rather than assuming they are the same—or different—everywhere.

FOCUS ON THEORY 4.2

Hamilton and Harwood (1997) note that while cultural differences may be the most visible among people, they may not be the differences most likely to cause conflict. They warn against treating people as members of a cultural group without recognizing their individuality and other identities that might be important to them.

ETHNOCENTRISM

The third barrier to effective intercultural communication is ethnocentrism, or negatively judging aspects of another culture by the standards of one's own culture. To be ethnocentric is to believe in the superiority of one's own culture. Everything in a culture is consistent to that culture and makes sense if you understand that culture. For example, assume that global warming is a fact and, as a result, assume that summers in the United States average 43°C (109°F). It would be logical to make adjustments: Rather than air-condition buildings all day, you might close schools and businesses in the afternoons to conserve energy. Such adjustments would make sense. Why, then, do some people attribute sensible midday siestas in hot climates to laziness?

After reading the comments by Benjamin Franklin (see Focus on Culture 4.1), who do you think was being ethnocentric?

FOCUS ON CULTURE 4.1

Benjamin Franklin's Remarks on American Indians

Savages we call them, because their Manners differ from ours, which we think the Perfection of Civility; they think the same of theirs.

Perhaps, if we could examine the Manners of different Nations with Impartiality, we should find no People so rude, as to be without any Rules of Politeness; nor any so

(Continued)

(Continued)

polite, as not to have some Remains of Rudeness. The Indian Men, when young, are Hunters and Warriors; when old, Counsellors; for all their Government is by Counsel of the Sages; there is no Force, there are no Prisons, no Officers to compel Obedience, or inflict Punishment. Hence they generally study Oratory, the best Speaker having the most influence. The Indian Women till the Ground, dress the Food, nurse and bring up the Children, and preserve and hand down to Posterity the Memory of public Transactions. These Employments of Men and Women are accounted natural and honourable. Having few artificial Wants, they have an abundance of Leisure for Improvement by Conversation. Our laborious Manner of Life, compared with theirs, they esteem slavish and base; and the Learning, on which we value ourselves, they regard as frivolous and useless. An Instance of this occurred at the Treaty of Lancaster, in Pennsylvania, anno 1744, between the Government of Virginia and the Six Nations. After the principal Business was settled, the Commissioners from Virginia acquainted the Indians by a Speech that there was at Williamsburg a College, with a Fund for Educating Indian youth; and that, if the Six Nations would send down half a dozen of their young Lads to that College, the Government would take care that they should be well provided for, and instructed in all the Learning of the White People. It is one of the Indian Rules of Politeness not to answer a public Proposition the same day that it is made; they think it would be treating it as a light manner, and that they show it Respect by taking time to consider it, as of a Matter important. They therefor deferr'd their Answer till the Day following; when their Speaker began, by expressing their deep Sense of the kindness of the Virginia Government, in making them that Offer; "for we know," says he, "that you highly esteem the kind of Learning taught in those Colleges, and that the Maintenance of our young Men, while with you, would be very expensive to you. We are convinc'd, therefore, that you mean to do us Good by your Proposal; and we thank you heartily. But you, who are wise, must know that different Nations have different Conceptions of things; and you will therefore not take it amiss, if our Ideas of this kind of Education happen not to be the same with yours. We have had some Experience of it; Several of our young People were formerly brought up at the Colleges of the Northern Provinces; they were instructed in all your Sciences; but, when they came back to us, they were bad Runners, ignorant of every means of living in the Woods, unable to bear either Cold or Hunger, knew neither how to build a Cabin, take a Deer, or kill an Enemy, spoke our language imperfectly, were therefore neither fit for Hunters, Warriors, nor Counsellors; they were totally good for nothing. We are however not the less oblig'd by your kind Offer, tho' we decline accepting it; and, to show our grateful Sense of it, if the Gentlemen of Virginia will send us a Dozen of their Sons, we will take great Care of their Education, instruct them in all we know, and make Men of them."

Source: Quoted in Mott and Jorgenson (1939).

In contrast to the term ethnocentrism, **cultural relativism** refers to the view that an individual's beliefs and behaviors should only be understood in terms of that person's own culture. It does not mean that everything is equal. It does mean that we must try to understand other people's behavior in the context of their culture. It also means that we recognize the arbitrary nature of our own cultural behaviors and are willing to reexamine them by learning about behaviors in other cultures (Cohen, 1998).

A less extreme form of ethnocentrism can be labeled *cultural nearsightedness,* or taking one's own culture for granted and neglecting other cultures. For example, people in the United States often use the word *Americans* to refer to U.S. citizens, but actually that word is the correct designation of all people in North and South America. Its careless use is a form of ethnocentrism.

Cultural nearsightedness often results in making assumptions that simple things are the same everywhere. Designing forms for something as simple as a person's name is not that simple if you recognize how widely practices vary. For example, in Mexico, people may have two surnames, with the first from the father's first surname and the second from the mother's surname. Often, only the first surname is used and the second abbreviated. When a woman marries, she usually retains both of her surnames and adds her husband's first surname. Or consider China with 1.3 billion people and only about 3,100 surnames, with 90% of the population sharing 100 of them. Based on its 1982 census, China has 87 million people sharing the name Li—the most common surname in the world. The name Smith is shared by 2.4 million people in the United States.

Another example is Eurocentric ethnocentrism. This would include, for example, recognizing only Western holidays in schools or basing curriculum only on Western history, music, and art. The terms *the West* and *the East* themselves have been labeled Eurocentric ethnocentrism. Asia is east of Europe, but to call Asia "the East" makes its identity dependent on Europe.

Negative Effects on Communication

Extreme ethnocentrism leads to a rejection of the richness and knowledge of other cultures. It impedes communication and blocks the exchange of ideas and skills among peoples. Because it excludes other points of view, an ethnocentric orientation is restrictive and limiting.

> **Global Voices**
>
> The easiest idea to sell anyone is that he is better than someone else.
>
> —Gordon Allport, *The Nature of Prejudice* (1954, p. 372)

STEREOTYPES AND PREJUDICE

Stereotypes and prejudice are a pernicious stumbling block to intercultural communication. The term **stereotype** is the broader term and is commonly used to refer to negative or positive judgments made about individuals based on any observable or believed group membership. **Prejudice** refers to the irrational suspicion or hatred of a particular group, race, religion, or sexual orientation. The terms are related in that they both refer to making judgments about individuals based on group membership.

Stereotypes

The word *stereotyping* was first used by journalist Walter Lippmann in 1922 to describe judgments made about others on the basis of their ethnic group membership. Today, the term is more broadly used to refer to judgments made on the basis of any group membership. Psychologists have attempted to explain stereotyping as mistakes our brains make in the perception of other people that are similar to those mistakes our brains make in the perception of visual illusions (Nisbett, 1980). When information is ambiguous, the brain often reaches the wrong conclusion. As illustrated in Figure 4.1, the moon appears to be much larger when it floats just above the horizon than when it shines overhead. The brain's estimation of distance changes, as does the apparent size of the moon.

What we see, the most readily available image, is what we expect to see. We can reject any information that challenges that expectation. In Figure 4.2, a sign appears to read "Paris in the spring," but it actually has an extra *the*. As we don't expect to see a double *the*, we do not

Figure 4.1   Visual Illusions

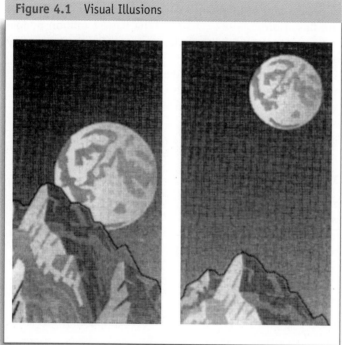

Note: The moon on the right has been made smaller to simulate the illusion.

Figure 4.2

PARIS
IN THE
THE SPRING

Figure 4.3

Figure 4.4

Count the number of times the letter *f* appears in the first sentence and the letter *s* in the second.

1. Finished files are the result of years of scientific study combined with the experience of years.

2. Sunday is shown after Wednesday, isn't it, inside those calendars he has made us paste together for our game days next season?

perceive it. In a like manner, if we expect that heads of corporations are tall, slender, White males, we don't see the disabled, women, and people of color in that group.

In Figure 4.3, a white triangle appears to float in front of three green circles even though no triangle exists. Our brain constructs the triangle; we see something that doesn't exist. We do not so much believe what we see as see what we believe. We tend to discount any perceptions that do not conform to our beliefs.

In Figure 4.4, odds are you missed some of the *f*s that made a *v* sound and *ss* that sound like a *z*. The brain overlooks what it doesn't expect. (There are 6 *f*s in the first sentence and 14 *ss* in the second.)

Who stereotypes? And who is the target of stereotyping? The answer to both questions is that anyone can stereotype and anyone can be the target of stereotyping.

Stereotypes are used by all groups. Until recently, the sign for *Japanese* in American Sign Language was a twist of the little finger at the corner of the eye to denote a slanted eye. The new sign, taken from Japanese Sign Language, is a hand signal to show the shape of the Japanese islands (Costello, 1995). In Japanese Sign Language, the sign for *foreigner* is the index finger making a circular motion around the eye denoting "round eye."

Are Native American logos and mascots stereotypes? In 2001, the U.S. Commission on Civil Rights called for an end to the use of American Indian images and team names by non–American Indian schools. Beginning in 2006, the National Collegiate Athletic Association (NCAA) prohibited 18 colleges and universities from displaying their nicknames, logos, or mascots based on American Indian imagery or references at postseason games. By 2008, the ban also applied to the uniforms of cheerleaders, dance teams, and band members at NCAA championship sites. Central Michigan, Florida State, Midwestern State, Mississippi College, and University of Utah retained their eligibility by receiving support from the eponymous tribe. Schools under this ban include the Florida State Seminoles, the Illinois Fighting Illini, and the Utah Utes.

What is the difference between **cultural sensitivity** and ethnic stereotyping? In 1997, American Airlines was criticized for a flight manual that said Latin American customers like to drink before takeoff. Is that cultural information that makes it possible for the airline to provide better customer service, or is it a stereotype? That same flight manual also said that Latin American customers do not expect flights to depart on time and will even call in bomb threats if they are running late and want the flight to be delayed.

Is the practice of profiling stereotyping? **Profiling** refers to a law enforcement practice of scrutinizing certain individuals based on characteristics thought to indicate a likelihood of criminal behavior. For example, it's believed that a person traveling alone is more likely to engage in terrorist activity. Profiling also refers to, for example, conducting traffic stops based on the vehicle occupant's perceived race, ethnicity, gender, or economic status. The September 11, 2001 attacks on the United States created a climate that gave law enforcement agencies wider latitude to engage in more intensive airport security checks of people who appear to be of Middle Eastern descent. Is profiling a useful and necessary law enforcement tool, or is it a form of stereotyping that unfairly targets minorities?

Although you may think of stereotypes as being negative judgments, they can be positive as well. Some people hold positive stereotypes of other individuals based on their professional group membership. For example, some people assume that all doctors are intelligent and wise.

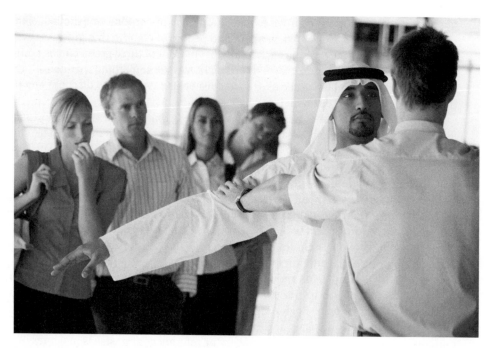

Some contend that ethnic sensitivity should be secondary to homeland security; others argue that increased racial profiling only raises ill-feelings toward the United States.

Negative Effects on Communication

Does it matter who speaks the words? Don Imus lost his nationally distributed morning radio show after referring to the women of the Rutgers University basketball team as "nappy-headed hos." He later said he didn't realize the words would be offensive because he had heard Black rappers use the same language.

Stereotypes are harmful because they impede communication in at least four ways:

- They cause us to assume that a widely held belief is true when it may not be. Research conducted by Gordon Allport (1954) showed, for example, that the prevalent stereotype of Armenians as dishonest was proved false when a credit-reporting association gave the group credit ratings as good as those given others.
- Continued use of the stereotype reinforces the belief. Stereotypes of women as ornaments, people of color as stupid or licentious, or gay men as promiscuous reinforce a belief that places individual women, African-Americans, and gay men at risk. Popular television may reinforce those stereotypes. Shaheen (1984), for example, has cited the four Western myths about Arabs as shown on television: Arabs are wealthy, barbaric, sex maniacs, and terrorist minded.

- Stereotypes also impede communication when they cause us to assume that a widely held belief is true of any one individual. For example, if a group is stereotyped as dishonest, that does not mean that any one individual in that group is dishonest. A classic psychology study in the 1970s had two groups of undergraduates read stories about a woman. The stories were identical, except that one had the sentence "Betty is now a lesbian." On a test one week later, individuals in the group who had read that Betty is a lesbian were much more likely than individuals in the other group to recall having read that Betty never dated men. In fact, the story that both groups had read stated that Betty dated men occasionally. The group's stereotype of a lesbian influenced what they recalled having read (Snyder & Uranowitz, 1978).
- The stereotype can become a "self-fulfilling prophecy" for the person stereotyped. Research by psychologists Steele and Aronson (1995) has shown that a negative stereotype creates a threat that can distract the individual stereotyped and lower performance.

When stereotypes lead us to interpret an individual's behavior from the perceptual screen of the stereotype, they impede communication. Were you to believe that Armenians are dishonest, then if you saw a man you knew to be Armenian taking a package from a car, you would be more likely to assume he was stealing it. In 1994, a young man with cigarette burns and the tattoo of an eagle on his arm was arrested by police, who cited the burns and tattoo as proof that he was in a Chinese gang. The young man had chosen to get the tattoo, which also showed the words "bird without its flock," following his mother's death to speak of his loneliness living in Iowa. The burns on his arm were self-administered at the time of his mother's death. The young man was Vietnamese.

Case Study: Asian-Americans

Asian-American groups in the United States have experienced stereotyping, which, although often positive, has impeded communication. The term *Asian-American* was created by University of California, Los Angeles, historian Yuji Ichioka in the late 1960s to refer to all people of Asian descent in the belief that all Asians shared a common history and struggle in the United States. And up to the 1970s, Asian-Americans were largely born in the United States. The Immigration and Nationality Act amendments of 1965 abandoned the old policy of immigration quotas for each country and established a new system giving preference to relatives of U.S. residents. That change resulted in large numbers of Asians immigrating to the United States between 1981 and 1989. The label *Asian-American* includes more than 30 ethnicities, with family origins extending from East Asia and Southeast Asia to the Indian subcontinent, as well as the Philippines and Indonesia. The continued use of the term *Asian-American* contributes to a stereotype of some 10 million people of Asian ancestry as a single community.

During the civil rights era of the 1960s, Asian-Americans became associated with the stereotype of the "model minority," who achieved success through hard work, perseverance, silent stoicism, strong family ties, and strong support for education. This stereotype seemed to continue the belief that any group can achieve the American Dream if its members "just work hard enough." This stereotype continues in the media. Asian-Americans of all groups are most often portrayed in the press as industrious and intelligent; enterprising and polite, with strong values; and successful in schools and business and in science and engineering. The 2000 census showed that Asian-Americans had the highest percentage of households with annual incomes of $75,000 or more. But the stereotype associated with the label hides that Asian-Americans are also the fastest growing segment on welfare. The rate of households on welfare climbed from 9.7% in 1980 to 12% in 1998. About 40% of Asian-Americans have a college or postgraduate education. And again, the stereotype associated with the label hides that one in seven Asian-Americans lacks a high school diploma. The stereotype is reinforced in news reports that Asian-American students score much higher on math exams than their White counterparts and that the percentage of U.S. scientists who are Asian-American is two to three times the percentage of Asian-Americans in the total population. Asian-American high school students of all backgrounds complain that teachers often counsel Asian-Americans to go into math and sciences. Some teachers respond that this is done so that immigrants will not have to contend with language problems. Asian-Americans argue that some teachers continue to do this even to those who are fluent in English and that the reason why teachers do this is that Asians are perceived as not being free thinking or extroverted.

The model minority stereotype is too narrow and confining. A smaller percentage of Asian-American students are encouraged to enter the creative fields of art and theater or the management field.

Prejudice

Whereas stereotypes can be positive or negative, prejudice refers to the irrational dislike, suspicion, or hatred of a particular group, race, religion, or sexual orientation (Rothenberg, 1992). Persons within the group are viewed not in terms of their individual merit but according to the superficial characteristics that make them part of the group. Psychologists have identified the highly prejudiced individual as having an **authoritarian personality** (Adorno et al., 1950). Such persons tend to overgeneralize and think in bipolar terms; they are highly conventional, moralistic, and uncritical of higher authority. Highly prejudiced people are unlikely to change their attitudes even when presented with new and conflicting information.

Global Voices

In 1913, members of the Pueblo tribe challenged the degree of control that Congress exercised over tribal affairs. In its decision on *United States v. Sandoval*, the Supreme Court ruled, "Always living in separate and isolated communities, adhering to primitive modes of life, largely influenced by superstition and fetishism, and chiefly governed according to crude customs inherited from their ancestors, [the Pueblos] are essentially a simple, uninformed and inferior people....As a superior and civilized nation, [the U.S. government has both] the power and the duty of exercising a fostering care and protection over all dependent Indian communities within its borders."

Case Studies

Like stereotyping, anyone can be prejudiced and anyone can experience prejudice. Prejudice exists in cultures around the world, as can been seen in cases of the Roma, Japan and Korea, and the United States.

The Roma

The Roma are believed to have migrated from India more than a millennium ago, settling first in Persia, then arriving in Europe in the 13th or 14th century. The name "Gypsy" was mistakenly applied by medieval Europeans, who thought all dark-skinned people came from Egypt. Leading a nomadic life, the Roma were often regarded as tramps and accused of thefts and robberies. From the beginning of the 17th century, attempts were made to forcibly assimilate the Roma people by requiring permanent settlement and banning the Romany language. The Roma were particularly persecuted by Nazi Germany. About 500,000 died in Nazi gas chambers and concentration camps. The Roma now number slightly more than 5 million in Eastern Europe, 2 million more in Western Europe, and about 2 million elsewhere, mainly in North and South America and North Africa. Romania has the largest number—about 1 million. For decades, Eastern European communist governments suppressed prejudice against the Roma and banned the nomadic life. As the countries shifted to market economies and many lost jobs, the Roma have again experienced discrimination.

Graffiti have now reappeared on walls: "Gypsies go away" and "Gypsies to the gas." The Roma language and culture, including the remembrance of the Holocaust (known in the Roma language as *porraimos,* or "the devouring"), are central to Roma identity throughout the world. The European Union states have made better treatment of the Roma a condition for new members. Critics charge that these efforts are for the purpose of reducing migration into the more prosperous Western European nations.

Roma in the Serbian town of Bujanovac. Roma fled Kosovo in 1999 after the Serbian administration collapsed there. According to the UN refugee body, UNHCR, 40,000 to 50,000 displaced Roma live in Serbia.

Japan and Korea

Relationships between Japan and Korea reflect deep-seated and longstanding prejudice. Historically, Korea had closer ties to China than did Japan, and both Korea and China tended to view Japan as a "troublemaking" state. This view was reinforced time and again by Japanese incursions into Korean territory and 35 years of Japan's colonial rule. It has only been in recent times that the South Korean and Japanese governments have signed mutual friendship treaties, established normal diplomatic relations, and entered into joint economic development agreements. In an act of historic symbolism, South Korea and Japan cohosted the 2002 World Cup soccer games. Despite economic ties, there remains a sense of *han,* or bitter resentment, that many Koreans feel toward the Japanese.

After Japan's annexation of Korea in 1910, thousands of Koreans migrated into Japan seeking employment. Following the great 1923 Kanto earthquake in Japan, it was rumored that Koreans were poisoning water supplies. Mob violence left some 6,000 Koreans dead. Later, between 1939 and 1945, more Koreans were forced to migrate by the Japanese government to work in mines (Weiner, 1994). During World War II, the Koreans in Japan were forced to become Japanese nationals. Japan's surrender to the Allied Forces brought an end to the annexation of Korea, and the majority of Koreans who had been brought to Japan under forced immigration returned to Korea, but some 500,000 to 600,000 Koreans remained in Japan (Fukuoka, 1996).

When the San Francisco Peace Treaty came into effect in 1952, the government of Japan claimed that the Koreans then in Japan should not be granted Japanese nationality. The descendants of the Koreans who remained in Japan, who may never have been to Korea and who may not speak Korean, were legally foreigners.

As the largest minority group in Japan, Japanese-born Koreans are the victims of social, economic, and political prejudice. Japanese law provides little or no protection against the housing and employment discrimination many Japanese-born Koreans experience. In 1974, the National Council for Combating Discrimination Against Ethnic Minorities (*Mintohren*) was founded by Korean residents and concerned Japanese to fight for the human and civil rights of the Korean residents in Japan.

United States

Ireland got the potato plant from South America, and by the 1840s, one third of Ireland's tilled land was devoted to potato production. A fungus wiped out 90% of the crop by 1847, and by 1850, one fourth of the population had died or migrated. Some went to Australia, and more than 1 million migrated to the United States between 1846 and 1851. Many settled in shantytowns of cities in four states—Illinois, Massachusetts, New York, and Pennsylvania. Many took jobs few other workers would take. The Irish worked in mines and mills, and they constructed canals and railroad lines. Editorial cartoons depicted the Irish as lazy, "fighting," and drunken. Signs seeking workers in the period often included the phrase "No Irish Need Apply." In the largely segregated Irish communities, the moral values of the Catholic Church were important. With a shared language and a physical appearance similar to the dominant English immigrant culture and with improved economic status and political participation, the Irish assimilated into the dominant culture. Surveys continue to show that prejudiced attitudes exist in the United States (Crosby, Bromley, & Saxe, 1980) and that prejudice exists not only between Whites and minority groups but between minority groups as well.

CASE STUDY OF INTERCULTURAL COMMUNICATION BARRIERS: CHINA AND THE UNITED STATES

In the United States, a lack of knowledge about China and its history contributes to communication barriers. As you read this section and become more familiar with China and its history, identify examples of the intercultural communication barriers that exist between the two cultures. When and how has the United States assumed similarity to China? When and how have both displayed ethnocentrism?

Population

In terms of land area, China is slightly smaller than the United States. It's also the most populated country in the world. Its population was estimated to be 1.3 billion, as of July 2011, or about 4.3 times as many people as populate the United States. China's population accounts for about one fifth of the entire human race. Over 90% Chinese are of Han ethnicity. The government officially recognizes 55 other ethnic groups.

A large economic gap exists between China's coastal and urban areas and the less prosperous interior. Overall as the world's second largest economy ($10.1 trillion gross domestic product [GDP] compared to $14.7 GDP for the United States), China has led the world in economic growth. Nonetheless, U.S. GDP per capita is six times that in China. Some estimate that China's GDP may almost double that of the United States by 2030. China is now the world's third largest importer and the second largest exporter. By 2001, Walmart alone bought $14 billion in merchandise from China.

History

Today's China represents 4,000 years of civilization. Its history was first recorded more than 1,500 years before the beginning of Christianity. For about half its history, China had multiple governments—at times both a southern and a northern regime. Until early in the 20th century, China was ruled by a series of dynasties and, through the centuries, was largely indifferent to the outside world.

With support from Chinese communities in Hawai'i and mainland United States, as well as students in Europe and Japan, Dr. Sun Yat-sen's United League victory in Wuchang was the end of the Ch'ing dynasty. He earned the distinction of being the "father" of modern China. After Dr. Sun's 1911 revolution, China became fragmented by warlords. In the 1920s, Chiang Kai-shek attempted to reunify the country and establish a nationalist government. Chiang's U.S. support was partly due to the publicity Henry Luce provided through his *Time* magazine, to the popularity of Pearl S. Buck's novels, and to the images of Chiang as a convert to Methodism and of his Wellesley College–educated wife.

World War II brought communism and Mao Zedong, who in 1949 defeated Chiang Kai-shek. Chiang fled with his followers to the island of **Taiwan**, located about 161 kilometers (100 miles) off the coast of China. Taiwan, which had been occupied by Japan from 1895 until the end of World War II when it was returned to China, is about the size of the states of Massachusetts and Connecticut combined. Only 15% of the island's population were 1949 immigrants, but they dominated Taiwan's government through martial law. The nationalist government of Taiwan (the Republic of China) considered itself the legal government of all China, whereas the mainland Chinese government claimed Taiwan as part of its territory. Chiang maintained an army of 600,000 in hopes of regaining the mainland. In 1955, the United States agreed to protect Taiwan in case of attack from mainland China.

For more than four decades, Mao was the dominant figure in Chinese life. In the 1950s, the country benefited from land redistribution, introduction of compulsory universal education, adoption of simplified Chinese characters that led to greater literacy, and the introduction of health and welfare reforms. In 1958, Mao launched the Great Leap Forward. This program forced farmers into communes, abolished private property, and set up backyard steel mills to speed China's entry into the industrial age. The program was a catastrophic failure and brought widespread starvation and the country to bankruptcy. President Liu Shaoqi and Deng Xiaoping, General Secretary of the Communist Party, took over day-to-day control to restore the economy.

Beginning in 1966, Mao led the country through his infamous **Cultural Revolution**. In an attempt to destroy Liu's government and Deng's party, to purify the culture of all outside influences, and to build a new Marxist-Chinese culture, tens of thousands were executed. Millions were exiled to rural labor brigades. During my stays in China, I have spoken with people who were youths during that period. They angrily said their future was stolen from them by Mao. Their only education was Mao's *Red Book* (*The Thoughts of Chairman Mao*).

In 1971, the People's Republic of China (mainland China) was admitted to the United Nations in Taiwan's place despite U.S. objections. In that year, the U.S. national table tennis team was invited to China. They were among the first from the United States to visit the country since 1949. Later that year, President Nixon hosted the Chinese national team in the White House. What became known as "ping-pong diplomacy" led to a breakthrough in U.S.-China relations in 1972 when President Nixon and his national security adviser, Henry Kissinger, established relations with the Chinese government.

On September 9, 1976, Mao died. Shortly after, the Party officially declared Mao's concept of continuing class struggle an ideological mistake, and his call for cultural revolution was commonly believed to have been a terrible disaster. Post-Mao China was dominated by the leadership of Deng Xiaoping. In 1956, Deng had been fourth in power after Mao. By 1962, he had financial control of the country. Deng's economic approach was reflected in his comment to Mao during an argument over farming policies that became his trademark: "Whether a cat is black or white makes no difference. As long as it catches mice, it is a good cat." Deng replaced Marx and Lenin with a commodity economy and profit incentives, but in 1966, he was denounced as a "capitalist roader" and confined to his compound. At the urging of the dying Chou En-lai, Deng swore loyalty to Mao and was returned to power in 1973. Starting in 1978, Deng removed aging leaders and opponents and replaced them with younger, well-educated supporters. Later, in a highly significant move under President Jimmy Carter, on January 1, 1979, the United States normalized relations with the People's Republic of China and severed diplomatic relations with Taiwan, together with terminating the defense agreement protecting the island.

Deng's **four modernizations**—agriculture, industry, science, and technology—sought to remove the dogmas, irrationality, and inefficiencies of Mao's era and—at a deliberate speed—transformed China into a modern nation. Deng was credited with saying, "To get rich is glorious." The trademark of capitalism, a stock market, was established in 1990 in Shanghai, the most open and cosmopolitan of China's cities. Exporting was promoted as the way to economic growth. In 25 years, China moved from a low-income, state-planned economy to a capitalistic, market-oriented economy with improved living standards for hundreds of millions of its people.

FOCUS ON THE ENVIRONMENT 4.1

Economic development in China is a severe threat to the environment:

- Sixteen of China's cities rank among the 20 most polluted in the world.
- In major cities, much of the water is too toxic to drink; only 1% of the surface water in Shanghai is safe.
- Some 700 million Chinese people drink water contaminated with animal and human waste.
- The Gobi Desert is growing by about 4,900 square kilometers (1,900 square miles) annually, resulting in millions of refugees.
- Within 15 years, almost 130 million cars will be on China's roads.
- In 2009, coal-dependent China emitted 50% more greenhouse gases than the United States.

Source: Zuckerman (2008, p. 94).

Perhaps in the long term, the village democracy program may prove to be the most important of Deng's modernizations. To the extent that democracy requires conflict between ideas, groups, and parties, some Chinese see it in opposition to Confucianism, which values harmony and cooperation. With the disbanding of the commune system, the village democracy program began in 1987 with the Organic Law on Village Committees as a way to make local leaders more accountable. A 1994 amendment to the law allowed secret ballots. By the end of 1997, 95% of China's 900,000 villages had implemented the program, and by 1998, district elections were held in the central province of Hubei. The program varies greatly from county to county, and some critics say it only transfers unpopular tasks such as tax collection and family planning to the local level. Nonetheless, millions of rural Chinese elect their local leadership, but there is no organized push for wholesale political changes.

Regional Differences

Britain's 19th-century conflict with China enabled British traders to continue exchanging Indian opium for Chinese tea and silk, making huge profits while devastating China. Defeated in these wars, China was forced to open ports up and down the coast not only to the opium trade but also ultimately to foreign diplomats, residents, missionaries, and traders of every kind. **Hong Kong** island was ceded to Great Britain in perpetuity in 1841, the Kowloon peninsula in 1860, and another slice of the mainland leased in 1898.

Hong Kong is slightly smaller than Los Angeles and home to about 7 million people. It is one of the world's great cities, with the world's largest containership port, one of the world's largest airports, the best-performing stock exchange in the world, and an impressive trade and financial infrastructure. In 1997, this symbol of free enterprise was returned to China. In a critically important move, in 1990, China promised Hong Kong residents in the Sino-British document known as the Basic Law "one country, two systems." Hong Kong would be a special administrative region of China, with press freedom and continuance of its capitalist economic and social system guaranteed for at least 50 years after the takeover. The Basic Law specified that both Chinese and English would be official languages. By 1998, most public schools had switched from teaching in English to Cantonese.

China has made it clear that Hong Kong was never a democracy under British rule. The colony's governor was appointed by the British government. It wasn't until 1991 that Great Britain allowed the first direct election of a portion of the seats in Hong Kong's legislature. Prior to the return, China wrote a new constitution for Hong Kong, reversing some of the civil and democratic rights legislation that was passed after the Basic Law agreement without China's consent. Hong Kong's first chief executive after the return, Tung Chee-hwa, was selected by Beijing through a process of indirect elections involving a campaign and vote by 400 businesspeople and community leaders selected by Beijing. Hong Kong's elected legislature was replaced by an appointed one. Currently half of the 60-seat legislature is elected.

Some believe Hong Kong's leaders will be unable to maintain political distance from Beijing, as laws were changed in 2001 so that now the chief executive is chosen by an 800-member committee largely composed of Beijing loyalists. So the committee essentially serves at the pleasure of the mainland government. And in 2007, China announced that Hong Kong would have to wait another 10 years before it can directly elect its leader.

Yet, economically, capitalism continues to thrive in Hong Kong. At least economically, China has become more like Hong Kong. In this way, China continues to change while Hong Kong has remained the same.

Macau, the first European settlement in Asia and the last Portuguese-held colony, was returned to China in 1999 after 442 years under Portuguese control. Similar to Hong Kong, Macau is a special administrative district with a chief executive chosen by a 300-member committee. Today with half a million residents, Macau has replaced Las Vegas as the most lucrative gambling destination in the world. China hopes that these colonies' return will be followed by the reunification of Taiwan and the mainland.

China is anything but a monolithic communist country, for it has tried dozens of political and economic experiments. China also has significant regional cultural differences. The north, including Beijing, is traditional and conservative. The ancestors of most Chinese in the south migrated from the north, overwhelming the original inhabitants and driving them into what is now Vietnam.

In much the same way that western migration in the United States shaped the character of the west, China's southern migration shaped a different culture in the south. The south is populated with people seeking a better life by escaping the conservatism and poverty of the rural north. Most of China's emigration has been from the south as people left China for Hong Kong, Southeast Asia, and the United States.

Chinese in the south are said to be more active, live better, and talk louder and are reasserting their business savvy. Recognizing this difference, Beijing in the late 1970s allowed Guangdong and Fujian provinces to go "one step ahead" in economic reforms. By 1985, this was expanded to the whole Pearl River Delta, where tens of thousands of factories manufacture shoes, watches, clothes, electronics, and other consumer goods. Guangdong province alone has more than 60,000 factories producing $300 million worth of goods a day. Recently, China's economic growth has spread to other regions.

China's International Relationship Issues

Beginning with Marco Polo's sojourn in China in the late 13th century, there have been two "Chinas"—China as imaged by Westerners and the real China. U.S.-China relations continue to be strained.

FOCUS ON CULTURE 4.2

"Very Sorry" Proves to Be Key Phrase

 In April 2001, a U.S. spy plane made an unauthorized emergency landing on Hainan island after colliding with a Chinese fighter jet, killing its pilot. China regards spy planes 8,000 kilometers from their home as unwarranted; the United States says it has a legal right to fly over international waters off China. China demanded an apology, which the United States refused to give. The wording of the U.S. letter of regret was thoroughly negotiated, yet each side offers a different Chinese translation.

When the U.S. declared itself not just "sorry" but "very sorry" for the loss of a Chinese fighter pilot, the government in Beijing finally had a phrase it could translate into a linguistically acceptable apology.

The nuance of language apparently paved the way for the release of the 24-member crew of the American spy plane detained since April 1. And it will go a long way toward determining how the Chinese people perceive the United States' intentions, spelled out in a key letter from U.S. Ambassador Joseph W. Prueher to Chinese Foreign Minister Tang Jiaxuan on Wednesday.

After days of diplomatic negotiations over the wording of the letter, the U.S. side agreed to insert the "very," breaking the stalemate that has kept the crew detained on Hainan island, according to a senior Bush administration official. The letter also said the Americans were "very sorry" that the U.S. Navy EP-3 intruded into Chinese airspace without verbal permission when it made an emergency landing after colliding with the Chinese jet.

But complicating matters, each side issued different Chinese translations of the document.

(Continued)

(Continued)

The version prepared by the U.S. Embassy in Beijing offered *feichang baoqian* as a translation of "very sorry." But state-run Chinese media used *shenbiao qianyi*, a phrase that means "to express profound apology" but could suggest that the speaker is apologizing with some reservations.

Shenbiao qianyi is a "flexible fuzzy" phrase, according to a veteran Chinese language expert, speaking on condition of anonymity.

The word the Chinese wanted, but didn't get, was *daoqian*, which means "to apologize." "The American side ought to apologize to the Chinese people," Chinese President Jiang Zemin said last week, using the word *daoqian*. Government officials had dismissed as inadequate earlier official U.S. expressions of regret.

"*Daoqian* would be the word Chinese could accept most easily," the language expert said, but added: "Strictly speaking, there is no real difference between *baoqian* and *daoqian*.

"Anyway, without the character *qian* in there, I don't think there would have been a way out of the situation," he said.

The character *qian* comes from a classical Chinese character that means "bad harvest." The right half of the character means, "to be inadequate" or "to owe something." In Chinese, qian implies that the person delivering the apology is at fault. It also implies that the apology is made sincerely and seriously, not just a casual "Sorry about that." "It's the sort of thing Japanese people would bow their heads when saying," the language expert said.

The political correctness of language has been serious business in China for millenniums, since the days when it was taboo to use the characters in an emperor's name. Lately, Chinese media have been careful to stick to the official description of the plane debacle, rendered as "the incident of an American military reconnaissance plane crashing into and destroying a Chinese military plane." After news of the apology broke, China's official media quickly began reporting that some Chinese citizens were not satisfied.

"I think the U.S. government's way of apologizing can't satisfy people," company manager Su Wei told the official *People's Daily* online edition. Su said U.S. leaders should compensate China for its losses and apologize not in a letter, but in a live, globally televised news conference.

Source: Kuhn (2001, p. A14). Reprinted with permission.

Status of Taiwan

Today, Taiwan is a technologically advanced island of 23 million people with a per capita income of more than $35,700 (China's is $7,600; the U.S., $47,200). In the past, Taiwan and the mainland disputed which was the legitimate government of one China. Taiwan's government has evolved from one-party rule under martial law into a full-fledged democracy. In 1996, Taiwan became the first government in the Chinese-speaking world to have a democratically elected president.

The Potala Palace in Lhasa, winter palace of the Dalai Lama since the 7th century, symbolizes Tibetan Buddhism and its role in the administration of Tibet.

Taiwan has never declared formal independence. Taiwan has argued that China is one country with two governments, much like Germany before reunification. On that basis, Taiwan sought greater international recognition and readmission to the United Nations. Seven U.S. presidents have recognized that Taiwan is part of China, yet the United States has sold jet fighters to the Taiwanese and dispatched aircraft carriers to the waters off Taiwan when China displayed military force near its shores. Under the current president, despite public protests, China and Taiwan have held talks on improved relations, launched regular direct flights between the two, and allowed more mainland tourists to visit the island.

Tibet

Chinese control over **Tibet** dates as far back as the 13th century. In the 1940s and 1950s, British and U.S. agents were seen to have been encouraging independence. Chinese troops occupied Tibet in 1950, waging war on the Dalai Lama and Tibetan Buddhism. In 1959, the Dalai Lama unsuccessfully tried to oust Chinese forces and was forced into exile. The Dalai Lama has

> ### Global Voices
>
> "Such an act has grossly interfered in China's internal affairs, hurt the feelings of the Chinese people, and damaged Sino-American relations."
>
> —Ma Zhaoxu, Chinese Foreign Ministry, on President Obama's meeting with the Dalai Lama, July 2011

FOCUS ON THE ENVIRONMENT 4.2

The Chinese call Tibet Xizang, the Western Treasure House, and . . . have systematically plundered its vast forest reserves and ravaged its earth for uranium, gold, and other precious metals. In Tibetan culture, mining was largely forbidden. Instead, the earth was regularly empowered and enriched by filling sechu, or earth treasures vases, with jewels and other precious substances and burying them underground—a covenant with the landscape in radical contrast to Chinese policies of extraction.

Source: Baker (2004, p. 268).

proposed autonomy—not independence—for Tibet, allowing China to retain control over defense and foreign affairs. The major concern has been the elimination of the Tibetan culture as more Chinese move into the region. The India-based Tibetan government-in-exile claims that Chinese immigrants outnumber Tibetans by at least 40 to 1. No Western country challenges China's sovereignty, but the United States and others have protested the treatment of the people and culture of Tibet. China has responded that the Nobel Prize–winner Dalai Lama is trying to achieve political objectives of independence under the guise of religion. The Dalai Lama has since relinquished his political duties and Lobsang Sangay was elected Prime Minister of the Tibetan government-in-exile. Chinese officials declared the election illegal.

Human Rights and Free Speech

In 1989, the death of former Communist Party General Secretary Hu Yaobang, who many considered a political reformer, resulted in the student-led demonstration for democracy in Tiananmen Square in Beijing that June. The army crushed the protest, killing hundreds, perhaps even thousands, on orders believed to have come from Deng (Black & Munro, 1993). Ever since, the Chinese media have blamed the United States for siding with the protesters. Deng, who saw foreign influence in the uprising, dictated that severe measures, such as martial law, would again be taken in the event of future internal turmoil. Only by these means, he felt, would China's national sovereignty be protected from external interference.

The United States, which has protested the imprisonment without trial of religious and democracy proponents and the use of prison and child labor in manufacturing, has insisted on human rights improvements in China. The United States has attempted repeatedly, but unsuccessfully, to gain censure for Chinese human rights policies at the United Nations Commission on Human Rights. Prior to the return of Hong Kong to China, the U.S. Congress passed legislation affirming the human rights of the people of Hong Kong. China views these demands as attacks on its sovereignty, with the United States acting as a global judge of human rights. China also has charged that the U.S. human rights record includes huge prison populations, low voter turnout, and a history of slavery. Rather than viewing this only as a political clash, some would seek explanations based in cultural values. Chinese leaders place a higher premium on social order and a lesser one on individual expression. China emphasizes collective order, whereas Western cultures stress individual liberties (Wasserstrom, 1991).

Soviet communism tried to reform the Soviet Union by loosening the reins on expression while keeping the economy under control. Chinese leaders try the opposite: They allow the economy, particularly in the south, to experiment while they control political speech.

Broadcast Media and the Internet

All broadcast media are owned by, or affiliated with, the Communist Party of China or a government agency. The Central Propaganda Department lists subjects that are off limits to domestic broadcast media. The government approves all programming; foreign-made TV programs must be approved prior to broadcast (CIA, 2011).

One example is the Internet, which became available in China in 1995. The government encourages the Internet for education and business but blocks material deemed subversive. Internet usage has surged from 40 million in 2002 to 100 million in 2005 to 378 million in 2009—more than any other country in the world. Since 1995, more than 60 laws have been enacted governing Internet activities, and periodically, material deemed harmful or otherwise critical of the state has been blocked. Internet companies that deal with China must sign agreements that their Web manager will censor any content on their websites. In 2004, Internet chat rooms with discussions of sensitive topics were banned, and in the next year, restrictions were placed on websites requiring them to give priority to official news. Prior to the Olympics, the government clamped down again in the name of security. Dissidents, including

Figure 4.5   Google China.

online dissident Hu Jia, were arrested on charges of "subverting state authority." China blocked searches on Sina Weibo, a Chinese version of Twitter, during the time of protests in the Middle East in 2011.

Internet search engine Google was accessible in China but much of its content was censored. Google China was founded in 2005. In the next year in January, Google launched its search page Google.cn with results subject to censorship by the Chinese government. If a search contained any prohibited Chinese keywords from a blocked list maintained by the PRC government, Google.cn displayed this message (translated): *In accordance with local laws, regulations and policies, part of the search result is not shown.*

In early 2009, China blocked access to Google's YouTube and denied access to other Google online services. On early 2010, Google announced that the Gmail accounts of Chinese human rights activists had been breached and that Google would no longer allow censorship on Google.cn. Shortly later, Google redirected all search queries from Google.cn to Google Hong Kong (google.com.hk) bypassing Chinese censorship. Hong Kong, as a Special Administrative Region, is not subject to many Chinese laws including those censoring the Internet. At the same time, using any Google search site was banned in China. Anyone accessing Google received a DNS error. China lifted the ban, but Google ended its redirect to Google Hong Kong and instead placed a link to Google Hong Kong to avoid losing their Internet Content Provider license in China.

U.S. Secretary of State Hillary Clinton, in a major speech, has drawn an analogy between the Berlin Wall and restricted access to the Internet (Clinton, 2010). Chinese reaction to her speech was that the United States uses the Internet as a means to create worldwide hegemony based on Western values. The *People's Daily* newspaper compared Google to the opium traders of the 19th century (Demick, 2011).

> ## Global Voices
>
> The belief that non-Western peoples should adopt Western values, institutions, and culture is immoral because of what would be necessary to bring it about. . . . If non-Western societies are once again to be shaped by Western culture, it will happen only as a result of expansion, deployment, and impact of Western power. . . . As a maturing civilization, the West no longer has the economic or demographic dynamism required to impose its will on other societies and any effort to do so is also contrary to the Western values of self-determination and democracy.
>
> —Samuel P. Huntington (1996, p. 310), conservative professor of political science, Harvard University

Energy and Sustainability

China's proven oil reserves are about 20 billion barrels, equivalent to U.S. proven reserves. China's economic boom, which began in the late 1980s, has led to an increase in energy demand. Before 1993, China was self-sufficient in oil. Since the early 1990s, oil consumption has grown. In 2009, China consumed 8 million barrels a day, the third highest demand after the United States and the European Union. Its imports were 4.4 million barrels a day, fourth greatest after the United States, the European Union, and Japan. By 2025, China may need 13 million barrels of foreign oil a day—more than current U.S. import levels—and by 2030 may be importing 80% of its oil. China has become a major competitor with the United States for the world's supply of oil.

Along with energy consumption, other countries charge that China and its entrepreneurs disdain environmental concerns. China's rapid economic transformation has lead to extensive environmental deterioration. Air pollution, soil erosion, and the steady fall of the water table will be long-term problems. Resolution of the world's global environmental challenges will require China's full commitment and cooperation.

Air quality is a major problem in Chinese cities.

Economic Issues

China's economic development continues at a fast pace. In 1999, the constitution was amended to include private industry as an "important component" of the nation's economy, and constitutional protection was expanded to private property. In 2000, the U.S. Congress granted China permanent normal trade status. And a year later, the Chinese Communist Party invited capitalist entrepreneurs to join its ranks. China was admitted to the World Trade Organization after agreeing to further open its economy.

China's currency remains undervalued. This has the effect of making Chinese products cheap, giving China's exporters an unfair competitive advantage and costing jobs in importing nations, and boosting its trade surpluses with its trading partners. French President Nicholas Sarkozy has urged China's leadership to let its currency rise before its trade imbalances become unmanageable. Growing trade deficits with countries such as the United States and France continue to increase at what some see as an alarming rate.

Of equal or greater concern to many in the United States is the amount of U.S. debt held by China. As of January 2011, about 47% of the U.S. debt held by the public ($9.49 trillion) was held outside the United States. The largest holders were the central banks of China, Japan, and the United Kingdom. By 2011, China held about 11% of U.S. debt held outside the United States. The Chinese government has expressed concerns about the size of U.S. budget deficits, which they contend has lowered the value of the dollar and caused global inflation in food and energy. In August 2011, when Standard & Poor's downgraded the U.S. government's credit rating, the New China News Agency commented: "China . . . has every right now to demand the United States address its structural debt problems and ensure the safety of China's dollar assets." (Olesen, 2011, para. 5).

Henry Kissinger was President Nixon's national security advisor and then Secretary of State to Nixon and Gerald Ford. During that service his efforts contributed to formal diplomatic relations with China. Kissinger has recently pointed out the critical importance of the United States and China remaining engaged even if their interests diverge. Both are "too large to be dominated, too special to be transformed and too necessary to each other to be able to afford isolation" (Kissinger, 2011).

SUMMARY

This chapter begins a series of three chapters focused on recognizing and avoiding breakdowns in intercultural communication. LaRay M. Barna developed a list of six such barriers: anxiety, assuming similarity instead of difference, ethnocentrism, stereotypes and prejudice, nonverbal misinterpretations, and language. The first four are discussed in this chapter. *Anxiety* refers to not being totally present in the communication transaction while focusing on one's feelings when one doesn't know what to do. *Assuming similarity instead of difference* refers to behaving as you would in your home culture. *Ethnocentrism* is negatively judging aspects of another culture by the standards of one's own culture. The term *stereotype* is used to refer to negative or positive judgments made about individuals based on any observable or believed group membership, whereas *prejudice* refers to the irrational suspicion or hatred of a particular group, race, religion, or sexual orientation.

The remainder of the chapter uses as an example of communication barriers contacts between China and the United States. China is a country of 1.3 billion people and the world's second largest economy. Misunderstandings have arisen over Taiwan, Tibet, human rights and free speech, energy and sustainability, and economics. Special attention is given to regulation of the media and the Internet.

DISCUSSION QUESTIONS

1. Identify ways that both assuming cultural differences and assuming cultural similarity can be barriers.

2. What is the source of prejudice?

3. It has been said that China's people both admire and resent the United States. Explain the possible reasons for that belief and its associated communication barriers.

4. China has been criticized for melamine-contaminated pet food and baby milk formula. International media reported the scandal as China's rather than as particular companies.' How does this contribute to communication barriers?

5. Identify how communication barriers have arisen between the United States and China and how they might again in the future. What could be done to improve intercultural communication between the peoples of the two cultures?

6. What are possible consequences to China's continuing control of access to the Internet?

KEY TERMS

anxiety 82

authoritarian personality   90

cultural relativism   84

Cultural Revolution   94

cultural sensitivity   87

ethnocentrism   83

four modernizations   94

Hong Kong   96

Macau   96

prejudice   85

profiling   87

stereotype   85

Taiwan   93

Tibet   99

READINGS

All readings are from *Intercultural Communication: A Global Reader* (Jandt, 2004).

Claude Lévi-Strauss, "Race, History, and Culture" (p. 3)

Crispin Thurlow, "Naming the 'Outsider Within': Homophobic Pejoratives and the Verbal Abuse of Lesbian, Gay, and Bisexual High-School Pupils" (p. 189)

Tarla Rai Peterson, Susan J. Gilbertz, Kathi Groenendyk, Jay Todd, and Gary E. Varner, "Reconfiguring Borders: Health-Care Providers and Practical Environmentalism in Cameron County, Texas" (p. 243)

William J. Starosta, "On Intercultural Rhetoric" (p. 307)

Ram Adhar Mall, "The Concept of an Intercultural Philosophy" (p. 315)

Kjell Skyllstad, "Creating a Culture of Peace: The Performing Arts in Interethnic Negotiations" (p. 376)

William Peterson, "Interculturalism in Singapore: Looking for the Big, Bad Other" (p. 403)

STUDENT STUDY SITE

Visit the student study site at **www.sagepub.com/jandt7e** for these additional learning tools:

- Web Resources
- Audio and Video Links
- SAGE journal articles
- eFlashcards
- Web Quizzes
- Sample Essays

CHAPTER

5

Nonverbal Communication

FOCUS QUESTIONS

- Are all nonverbal behaviors intentional communication behaviors?

- How can nonverbal interpretations be a barrier in intercultural communication?

Nonverbal Behaviors as Cues
Nonverbal Communication
   As Intentional Communication
      Functions
Knowing Culture Through Nonverbal Messages
Nonverbal Misinterpretations as a Barrier
Nonverbal Message Codes
     Proxemics
     Kinesics
     Chronemics
     Paralanguage
     Silence
     Haptics
     Clothing and Physical Appearance
     Territoriality
     Olfactics
Case Study: The Wai In Thailand
Case Study: Korean-American Neighborhood
   Businesses
Summary
Discussion Questions
Key Terms
Student Study Site

In Chapter 2, you read how communication as an element of culture is understood differently by cultures. You read that, in the Western transmission models of communication, sources encode ideas into symbols and that symbols can be words or nonspoken symbols. The messages sent without using words are called nonverbal communication. The study of nonverbal communication in Western cultures conceptualizes nonverbals as a language system. Gestures, for example, are studied as if they function just like verbal symbols in a language.

Keep in mind that not all nonverbal behavior is nonverbal communication. Communication occurs when we intentionally use symbols—words or nonspoken symbols—to create meaning for others. This chapter first looks at the different ways that nonverbal communication has been defined. Then nonverbal message codes that have been shown to significantly affect intercultural communication are identified, as well as how nonverbal misinterpretations can be a barrier in intercultural communication. Finally, the use of nonverbal messages in a culture is shown to relate to other factors in that culture.

NONVERBAL BEHAVIORS AS CUES

Some basic nonverbal behaviors seem to be reliable cues as to a person's state of mind because they seem to be "spoken" internationally. Across cultures, people generally recognize the nonverbal cues of pleasure or displeasure, liking or disliking, tension or relaxation, and high status or low status (Buck, 1984).

Darwin (1872/1969) wrote that our facial expressions, such as smiles and frowns, are not learned but are biologically determined. Studies of children born deaf and blind show that, despite the lack of social learning, they smile, laugh, and cry in ways virtually identical to infants who can hear and see adults. Most people worldwide correctly identify the facial expressions of anger, disgust, happiness, fear, sadness, and surprise (Ekman, Friesen, & Ellsworth, 1972; Ekman et al., 1987). Researchers have since found evidence for a seventh universal expression of contempt (Ekman & Heider, 1988). In every culture the researchers studied, a large majority of people correctly named the facial expression in pictures of people who were entirely foreign to them. However, in a more recent study (Shioiri, Someya, Helmeste, & Tang, 1999) of people in Japan and the United States, the facial expressions of surprise and happiness were well understood by both groups, but those of anger, contempt, disgust, fear, and sadness were not always as well recognized by people in Japan. It was Darwin's idea that these expressions evolved because they allow us to know immediately the difference between strangers who are friendly and those who might attack.

FOCUS ON THEORY 5.1

Burgoon and Saine (1978) describe nonverbal behavior as analogic rather than digital. Whereas digital signals are discrete, like numbers, analogic signals are continuous, like the sound volume. In the same way, gestures and other nonverbal behaviors are continuous. We create an arbitrary meaning of that gesture, which may vary by the context of culture, relationship, or situation.

There have been three major approaches to the study of nonverbal behavior. Researchers from the nurture approach believe that nonverbal communication is learned. Traditionally, anthropologists and sociologists have used this approach. In contrast is the nature approach. In the tradition of Charles Darwin (1872/1969) in his classic book *The Expression of the Emotions in Man and Animals*, some researchers believe that nonverbal behavior is innate; that is, nonverbal behavior is believed to be genetically determined. Finally, the functional approach focuses on the types of nonverbal behaviors and the communication functions they perform. Burgoon (1986); Knapp (1990); McCroskey, Burroughs, Daun, and Richmond (1990); and Mehrabian (1981) are examples of researchers who have studied how nonverbal channels are used to accomplish communication functions.

The smile is the near-universal gesture of friendliness. In parts of Southeast Asia, a person may mask embarrassment by smiling. In some Latin cultures a smile may signal "Excuse me" or "Please."

These innate behaviors can change as we grow and learn our culture. For example, even though a smile is universally recognized as a sign of friendliness, it has other meanings that are specific to a culture. Germans smile less often than people from the United States, but this doesn't mean that Germans are less friendly. It does mean that people from Germany and the United States have different ideas of when a smile is appropriate. In a business meeting of people from Germany and the United States, the people from the United States complained that the Germans were cool and aloof; the Germans complained that the people from the United States were excessively cheerful and hid true feelings (Hall & Hall, 1990).

Japanese tradition favors reserved emotional expressions. In photographs, U.S. wives are usually shown smiling at their husbands; Japanese wives are rarely shown smiling. U.S. clerks greet strangers with a smile; Japanese clerks must learn to do so. On the other hand, to maintain reserve, it is said that the Japanese smile to disguise embarrassment, anger, and other negative emotions because the public display of these emotions is considered rude and incorrect in Japanese culture.

NONVERBAL COMMUNICATION AS INTENTIONAL COMMUNICATION

Exactly what is meant by the term *nonverbal communication* must be specified. Nonverbal communication can be narrowly used to refer to intentional use, as in using a nonspoken symbol to communicate a specific message. From this perspective, nonverbal communication refers to a source's actions and attributes that are not purely verbal. For example, communication scholars Judee Burgoon and her colleagues (Burgoon, Boller, & Woodall, 1988) define nonverbal communication as those actions and attributes of humans that have socially shared meaning, are intentionally sent or interpreted as intentional, are consciously sent or consciously received, and have the potential for feedback from the receiver.

The term can be more broadly defined to refer to elements of the environment that communicate by virtue of people's use of them. The color of the walls in the room in which you are interviewed for a job may in some way affect your performance and how you are perceived. Thus, from this perspective, wall color may legitimately be labeled a nonverbal element of communication (Hickson & Stacks, 1989).

Functions

One way to demonstrate how nonverbals can be used to intentionally communicate messages is to look at the functions typically performed through nonverbal communication:

- *Replacing spoken messages*. In some situations words cannot be used. In a very noisy manufacturing facility, for example, communicators might use hand gestures to replace spoken messages. Communicators who do not share a language may try to make themselves understood with gestures. Nonverbal symbols can communicate utilitarian messages (Knapp, 1990). A police officer directing the flow of traffic uses nonverbal communication for utilitarian purposes.

Signs and symbols can replace spoken messages when they are used to identify and to direct attention to the things they designate. Signs are sometimes arbitrary in character, sometimes based on a real or fancied analogy, and usually simpler than symbols. For example, arrows are used to point direction. Symbols frequently are based on likeness, metaphor, or comparison. In Japan, for example, the cherry blossom is a symbol of the samurai because it is beautiful, blooms early, and dies soon. Still, symbol use is arbitrary. For example, the color red is a symbol for Christian charity and for communism and class conflict.

As symbols are independent of language, they can be used to communicate across language barriers. For example, symbols were used along ancient roadways. More recently, international events such as the Olympics make extensive use of symbols. In fact, Katzumie Masaru, the art director of the Tokyo Olympics, developed many of the symbols in use today (Modley, 1976). World travel is facilitated by symbols known to literate and illiterate people alike on highways; at airports; in hospitals, factories, and schools; and on packages and clothing. Almost anyone can function in any international airport. From the symbols, you can find restaurants, restrooms, and telephones.

Not all symbols, however, are universally accepted. What is commonly called the swastika in the United States and Europe has long been understood with other meanings in other parts of the world. Hindus are protesting Germany's move to ban the use of the swastika in the European Union. The same symbol has been used as a Hindu sign of peace for 5,000 years. The International Committee of the Red Cross faces the same challenge. The red cross symbol was adopted to identify medics and ambulances in war zones in 1863. The Ottoman empire unilaterally declared the use of the red crescent during the Russo-Turkish War of 1876. The international group recognized no other symbols, even though Israel insisted on using the Shield of David. After years of criticism that its official symbols had religious meanings, in 2006 the international group accepted a third symbol—the red crystal, a red square standing on one corner—as an officially recognized humanitarian symbol. One of the three symbols must be used by medical staff in war zones.

Symbols continue to be invented. In 1992, Jeremy Irons was the first celebrity to wear the red AIDS ribbon at that year's televised Tony Awards. It was the idea of a New York group, Visual AIDS, to bring attention to the AIDS epidemic. Later in 1992, during the Emmy Awards telecast, Jamie Lee Curtis explained the meaning of the symbol, and by the next year, the red AIDS ribbon had become one of the most recognized symbols worldwide. It was so successful as a symbol that soon there were pink ribbons for breast cancer, lavender ribbons for abused women, and so on. Its use then declined, but it raised the public's awareness of AIDS.

- *Sending uncomfortable messages.* Some messages are awkward or difficult to express in words, but the meaning can be conveyed with nonverbals without hurt feelings or embarrassment. Imagine being on your way home and being stopped by an acquaintance who wants to talk. The message in your mind that you want to communicate is, "Don't bother me. I don't have time for you now." You may not want to say those words, but you can communicate that meaning by slowly continuing to walk away. Your nonverbal communication, followed by the verbal message of "I really have to go," is received without bad feelings because it's clear you really do have to leave. Likewise, you may find it difficult or awkward to say, "I love you," but eye contact, touch, and close proximity deliver the message.

- *Forming impressions that guide communication.* We all attempt at times to manage the impressions that others have of us. Think about how you would give some thought to what you would wear to a job interview. You intentionally choose to wear certain clothes and groom in a certain way to send a message about who you are to the employer.

- *Making relationships clear.* Communication messages have both content and relationship information. Content refers to the subject matter of the message. Relationship information refers to the relationship between the communicators. As relationship information might be uncomfortable if spoken, nonverbal communication removes the threat. For example, think of the nonverbal messages on the job that replace the spoken words "I am your boss and you do as I say, even though you may not like it." In the United States, most nonverbal

FOCUS ON THE ENVIRONMENT 5.1

1. The Original Recycling Symbol

The original recycling symbol was designed by Gary Anderson. He won a contest in 1970—the year of the first Earth Day—at the International Design Conference in Aspen, Colorado, out of more than 500 entries. Gary's original design had the triangle pointing downwards.

The internationally recognizable recycling symbol design of three chasing arrows is sometimes called a Mobius loop, based on a discovery by August Ferdinand Möbius—a 19th-century German mathematician—that a band of paper joined with a half twist forms a continuous single-edged, one-sided surface.

The contest was sponsored by the Container Corporation of America (CCA), then the largest paper recycler in the United States, to find a design that symbolized the recycling process for its 100% recycled paperboard products.

By the time CCA applied to the U.S. Patent and Trademark Office to register the symbol as a trademark, the symbol was becoming popular due to CCA's promotion of it. The registration was challenged, and CCA allowed the design to remain in the public domain without a fight.

2. Nordic Ecolabel Swan

The swan is the official Nordic Ecolabel, and it demonstrates that a product is a good environmental choice. In 1989, the Nordic Council of Ministers decided to introduce a common, impartial, official environmental label for the Nordic region.

The green swan is a variation on the blue swan logo of the Nordic Council of Ministers. The activities within Nordic Ecolabelling are coordinated by the Nordic Ecolabelling Board.

Some quick statistics:

- 67% of people in the Nordic countries understand the swan.
- 77% of Swedes consider that the swan makes a brand extremely reliable.

Sources: Infomancie (2008a, 2008b) and the Nordic Ecollabeling website (http://www.nordic-ecolabel.org/).

communication at work reinforces power. According to Mehrabian (1981), status manifests itself by a relaxed posture and way of interacting. Those of lower status display more rigidity.

- *Regulating interaction.* Have you ever considered how you know when it's your turn to talk in a conversation? If you didn't know when to start talking, you'd be interrupting others all the time. Directing turn taking is an example of how nonverbal communication regulates people's interaction.

- *Reinforcing and modifying verbal messages.* Nonverbal cues can be metamessages that affect the decoding of the spoken message. Nonverbal messages can reinforce the verbal message. You can use your hands to indicate how close another car came to hitting your car as you say the same message in words. Nonverbal messages also can modify—and even negate—the meaning of the verbal message.

KNOWING CULTURE THROUGH NONVERBAL MESSAGES

Some nonverbal messages can be clearly identified with a culture. Min-Sun Kim (1992), for example, has demonstrated how the nonverbal messages shown in Korean and U.S. print media advertising clearly reflect the culture. Culture can be conceptualized as an interrelated system in which each aspect of culture is related to other aspects of that culture. For example, it is said that in Europe, body language is an important indicator of one's level of education and good manners—a relationship not seen as often in the United States. You'll see that many nonverbal messages used in a culture are related to and consistent with other aspects of the culture. In one sense, then, other aspects of a culture are revealed in the nonverbal code. In the next chapter, you will see how the same is true for language.

In Chapter 2, you read that Alfred G. Smith (1966) wrote that communication and culture are inseparable, that culture is a code we learn and share that requires communication, and that communication coding and symbols must be learned and shared. As some of those symbols are nonverbal, it is partially through the nonverbal messages that we experience the culture.

NONVERBAL MISINTERPRETATIONS AS A BARRIER

Chapter 4 identified *nonverbal misinterpretations* as a barrier in intercultural communication. While we expect languages to be different, we are less likely to expect and recognize how the nonverbal symbols are different. Often, when people don't share the same language, some resort to hand gestures to communicate. In such situations, people discover that the belief that hand signals and bodily expressions are universal is not true. Many nonverbal expressions vary from culture to culture, and it is just those variations that make nonverbal misinterpretation a barrier. Judee Burgoon (1986) has identified two perspectives on nonverbal communication. She writes that nonverbal communication must have consensually recognized meanings and consistent usage within a culture. It forms a vocabulary of nonverbal symbols.

In the United States, for example, many gestures are commonly recognized across the country. Burgoon (1986) also contends that some nonverbal communication, even in the same culture, is so ambiguous that its interpretation is mediated by context. For example, in the United States, the meaning of a touch can often be ambiguous. Comparing observations and interpretations of nonverbal symbols often will reveal their ambiguity. The example is given of a technical instructor from the United States who complained that his students in Iran weren't paying any attention to him. The basis of the instructor's inference was that his Iranian students were passively sitting and staring at him instead of taking notes on the important points of his lecture. On the basis of his experience with students in the United States, who expect lectures to supplement texts, he believed that note taking was a nonverbal cue signaling interest and the lack of note taking was a cue signaling boredom or distraction. He failed to learn that Iranian students expect lectures to correspond exactly to the text so there is no need to take notes.

NONVERBAL MESSAGE CODES

Another way to define nonverbal communication is by category. Perhaps you have experienced that a nonverbal symbol can mean different things depending on where you are. The kinds of nonverbal communication given the most attention by travelers and researchers alike are proxemics, kinesics, chronemics, paralanguage, silence, haptics, clothing and physical appearance, territoriality, and olfactics. Each of these nonverbal message codes is discussed below.

Proxemics

The term given to the study of our use of personal space is **proxemics**. Edward Hall's (1959) work has demonstrated clearly that cultures differ substantially in their use of personal space. His general theory is that we exist inside an invisible "bubble" or personal space. How much space we each want between ourselves and others depends on our cultural learning, our upbringing in our families, the specific situation, and our relationship with the people to whom we're talking. Though the physical distance we want between ourselves and others does vary, Hall reports the range is fairly consistent for most people in North America (see Table 5.1).

Table 5.1 Proxemics

	Distance	*Description*	*Voice*
Intimate	Touching to 18 inches	Private situations with people who are emotionally close. If others invade this space, we feel threatened.	Whisper
Personal	18 inches to 4 feet	The lower end is "handshake" distance—the distance most couples stand in public.	Soft voice
Casual	4 feet to 12 feet	The lower end is the distance between salespeople and customers and between people who work together in business.	Full voice
Public	Greater than 12 feet	Situations such as teaching in a classroom or delivering a speech.	Loud voice

Source: Adapted from E. T. Hall (1959).

We learn how close to stand to another in our culture. Standing too close or too far away from what we learn is appropriate can create an intercultural communication barrier.

Experience shows that these distances vary in diverse cultures. In India, there are elaborate rules about how closely members of each caste may approach other castes, and Arabs of the same sex do stand much closer than North Americans. North Americans in an elevator maintain personal space if the physical space permits it. An Arab entering an elevator may stand right next to another person and be touching even though no one else is in the elevator. Queuing means how you form a line while waiting. The traditional first-come, first-served line was typical in 19th-century France, but today, along with the Italians and Spaniards, the French are among the least queue-conscious in Europe. Until recently, the British were known to stand in queues for taxis, for food, and for tickets. Even in shops and pubs, customers were served in order. The practice may be dying in Great Britain, but people in the United States still stand in line—usually—and have elaborate "rules of queuing" (i.e., "cutting in line," "saving places").

Some explain the absence of queues in Europe and in Mediterranean areas as a sign of feelings against unwarranted regulation and interference. Edward T. Hall (1959) argues that queues are more likely to be found in cultures whose people are treated as equals.

Kinesics

Gestures, body movements, facial expressions, and eye contact are behaviors termed **kinesics**. In his landmark book *Gestures,* Desmond Morris (1979) wrote that communication depends heavily on the actions, postures, movements, and expressions of our bodies. In a later book,

FOCUS ON CULTURE 5.1

You and I Are Close Friends

 Every culture has its own polite fictions. Whenever we want to be polite, we must act out certain fictions, regardless of the facts. For example, when you meet someone, you may or may not like him, but either way, you must politely pretend to like him. In such a case, Americans and Japanese share the same polite fiction that "you and I like each other." But in many cases, Americans and Japanese are acting according to very different polite fictions.

The first time I was asked to appear as a guest speaker before a group of Japanese, the organizing committee very kindly arranged for two of the committee members to pick me up and drive me to the meeting place. They escorted me from my front door to their car, ushered me into the back seat, and then the two of them got into the front seat, leaving me to sit out the whole ride all alone in the back.

My first reaction was to feel rejected and lonely. "Why don't they want to sit next to me? Don't they like me? What's wrong with me?" Even after I realized that this must be their way of being polite to me, I still couldn't help feeling embarrassed and uncomfortable sitting all alone, separated from the others. In America, they would have put me in front with the member who was driving, and the other member would have sat alone in back.

The next time a welcoming committee arranged to pick me up, there were too many of them to fit into the front seat. "Good!" I thought. "Now someone will have to sit in back with me, and it won't be so embarrassing." But it was, if anything, even more embarrassing to have to listen to everyone trying to refuse to share the back seat with me. Once again, my initial reaction was, "Nobody wants to make friends with me; what's wrong with me?"

The same thing happened whenever my English students and I had a class party. All the students would cluster at the far side of the table. No one would sit next to me, or even near me. I felt very unpopular. By this time, of course, I knew that this reluctance to be near the guest of honor did not indicate personal dislike. It was simply an expression of the Japanese polite fiction, "I am in awe of you." Yet I still felt uncomfortable and embarrassed. Why? Because while I understood rationally, I couldn't help reacting emotionally, in terms of the very different American polite fiction, "you and I are close friends."

Source: Nancy Sakamoto and Reiko Naotsuka: *Why Japanese and Americans Seem Rude to Each Other*, Tokyo: Kinseido. 1982, pp. 80–83.

Bodytalk, Morris (1995) explained that gestures can be intentional or unconscious. For example, lower classes in ancient Rome used four fingers and thumb to pick up food; upper classes used two fingers and thumb. The difference may have been unconscious, but it clearly communicated class distinctions. Morris and his colleagues studied the use of 20 of the most familiar European gestures to map their use across national boundaries. For example, they found the thumbs-up gesture commonly used in the United States by hitchhikers to be more widely understood to mean "okay." But in Greece and Sardinia, it more accurately communicates the idea of "get stuffed." And in Australia, Iran, and Nigeria, it has similar obscene connotations.

The forefinger-to-thumb gesture forming a circle can mean "okay" in the United States. In France, it means zero or worthless. In Japan, the same gesture can mean change (coins), but in Brazil it is a symbol many times more offensive than the raised middle finger. Curling the middle three fingers into the palm, extending the thumb and little finger, and then twisting the hand back and forth from the wrist is the Hawaiian greeting "hang loose." To the University of Texas Longhorn fans, the pinkie and index finger raised up with the middle two fingers and thumb folded into the palm means "Hook 'em horns." But in parts of Africa, the same gesture is a curse, and to Italians, it is the *cornuto,* signaling that one's wife is being unfaithful. Extending one hand, palm forward, means "stop!" in the United States, but in Greece, it's the *moutza* or hand push, a sign of confrontation. In West Africa, the same gesture is more insulting than the upraised middle finger (Axtell, 1991).

Morris (1979, 1995) and his colleagues found wide variations even with such universal rituals as nodding agreement and greeting friends. Although most cultures do indicate "yes" by an up-and-down head nod and "no" by shaking the head from side to side, there are variations: In Albania and Bulgaria and parts of Greece, Turkey, Iran, and the former Yugoslavia, the yes-no gestures are reversed. In Ceylon, a yes answer to a specific question is indicated by a nod of the head, whereas general agreement is indicated by a slow sideways swaying of the head. For greetings, in the United States, a firm handshake with direct eye contact is appropriate. In France, where the traditional U.S. handshake is considered too rough and rude, a quick handshake with only slight pressure is preferred. In Southern Europe and Latin America, a hearty embrace is common among women and men alike, and men may follow it with a friendly slap on the back. In Ecuador, to greet a person without a handshake is a sign of special respect. In India, the handshake may be used by Westernized citizens, but the preferred greeting is the *namaste*—placing the palms together and bowing slightly. In Japan, the traditional form of greeting is a bow with the depth and length conveying meanings of status. In Tibet, people sometimes stick their tongues out to greet one another.

Likewise, waving good-bye and beckoning vary among cultures. In Italy, Colombia, and China, people may wave good-bye by moving the palm and fingers back and forth with the palm face up, a gesture that more likely means "come here" in the United States. But in Malaysia, beckoning someone by moving the forefingers back and forth would be taken as an insult. In other regions of the world, the same gesture with the palm down can mean "come here" while in others "get out!" Even seemingly obvious gestures can be misunderstood. Using fingers to indicate numbers can vary. In the United States, most people would indicate "1" by holding up the forefinger. In parts of Europe, "1" is indicated by using the thumb and "2" by the thumb and forefinger.

The "V for victory" sign made popular during World War II by Winston Churchill is appropriately made by showing the palm. In the United States in the late 1960s, the same gesture became a symbol for peace (Dresser, 1996). When former British Prime Minister Margaret Thatcher made a "V for victory" sign during an election campaign, she showed the back of her hand. That gesture signifies at least nine different obscenities!

And the list continues: Some Japanese point a forefinger to the face to indicate referring to self, whereas in the United States, people are more likely to point to the chest. In Brazil, people may add emphasis to statements by snapping the fingers with a whiplike motion of the hands. Scraping the sides of

Figure 5.1 Palm-Out V Gesture

U.S. soldiers were warned against using the "V for victory" or peace sign in Bosnia and Herzegovina. The V sign was widely used by the Bosnians and Croatians as a victory/defiance sign. For Croatians it represents the bravery and hope. Serbs used the three finger solute, which was originally associated with the Christian Trinity of the Father, Son, and Holy Spirit. Serb forces often used it after military operations as a nationalist provocation. Serbian athletes also displayed the gesture as a sign of pride.

the chin with the thumb and forefinger as if stroking a beard is a sign of respect in Saudi Arabia (Armstrong & Wagner, 2003). Indians in Delhi may use hands to grasp the ears as a gesture meaning repentance or sincerity. Fijians may fold the arms as a sign of respect when talking to another person.

Patterns of eye contact learned in childhood seem to be relatively unaffected by later experiences. One study showed that Arabs, Latin Americans, and Southern Europeans gaze on the eyes or face of conversational partners, whereas Asians, Indians and Pakistanis, and Northern Europeans tend to show peripheral gaze or no gaze at all (Harper, Wiens, & Matarazzo, 1978). Duration of eye contact varies in diverse cultures (Shuter, 1979). In the United States, the average length of time that two people gaze at each other is 1.18 seconds (Argyle, 1988; Argyle & Ingham, 1972). Any less than that and we may think the person is shy, uninterested, or preoccupied. Any more than that and we may think the person is communicating unusually high interest. A wink is improper in Australia and impolite in parts of Asia.

People from Asian, Latin American, Caribbean, and American Indian backgrounds may offer respect by avoiding eye contact. Looking someone directly in the eyes may be interpreted as a provocation that can lead to violence. Repeatedly blinking the eyes is considered impolite in Taiwan and Hong Kong (Armstrong & Wagner, 2003). In parts of the United States, such as Appalachia, more people have heard of the belief in the "evil eye"—the power attributed to certain persons of inflicting injury or bad luck by a look. One communication professor new to the area worked hard to maintain eye contact with students during lectures only to be told that some students perceived him as having the evil eye. It is said that Spanish men even today in more rural areas may use eye contact to make "passes" toward women on the street. Returning the stare is accepted as a gesture indicating that the man may attempt conversation. It also is said that Spaniards snap the eyelids when angry or impatient. Psychologist Monica Moore (1995) has studied the nonverbals of heterosexual flirting. She says that in Western cultures, women control the process by making the initial choice of the man. To attract men, Moore has noted that women most often smile, glance, primp, laugh, giggle, toss the head, flip the hair, and whisper.

Gestures continue to be developed. Some recently developed gestures in the United States are the high five, butt pat, raise the roof, loser, whatever, and sizzle.

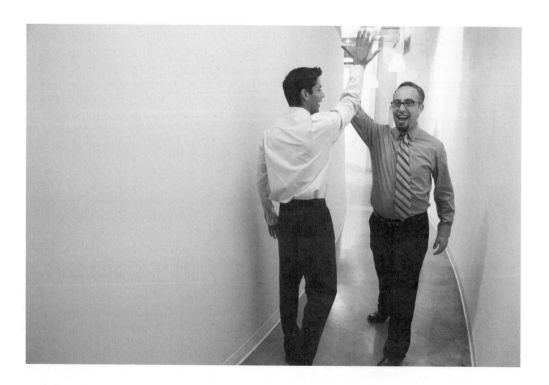

Chronemics

Next is the study of chronemics, or the study of our use of time. Many American Indian peoples understood time to be cyclical, whereas Western cultures think of time in the linear sense of a flow from the past to the present to the future. Yet Western science accepts Einstein's and other physicists' concepts of quantum physics in which there is no definite past, present, or future but only possibilities of position, in which particles can move backward in time as well as forward and in which what happened in the past can be altered by energy events in the future. It is said that the idea of linear time became commonly accepted as we became more aware of change—that is, aware that things were different before change and after change. Acceptance of some religious beliefs necessitates the acceptance of the understanding of time as linear. For example, the Christian belief that Christ's birth and death were unrepeatable events necessitates the acceptance of the understanding of time as linear. It existed in the past of our present, and since it could only occur then, it could not be repeated in our future.

Humans marked time with calendars centuries before Christ. Calendars have been based on the sun or the moon. The ancient Britons may have used Stonehenge as a calendar. Mayan astronomers had determined that a year was precisely 365.24 days long. The Hijrah calendar divided the year into 354 days and 12 lunar months. The Sumerians divided the year into 360 days—12 lunar months of 30 days each. The Egyptians extended this calendar year by adding 5 days at the end of the year.

The original Roman calendar was composed of 10 months and 304 days. Two months and one day were added later. The Julian calendar, devised by Julius Caesar, became the basis for what is used today. Coming at the time of the Reformation, reforms instituted by Pope Gregory XIII in 1582 created the Gregorian calendar year in use today. Pope Gregory's reforms were not immediately adopted in Protestant countries: The Gregorian calendar was adopted in Germany in 1700, in Sweden in 1753, in Britain in 1752, in Russia in 1918, and in China in 1912 but not widely so until the communist victory in 1949 (Duncan, 1998).

The marking of a day also has a long history. In the 11th century, the Chinese scholar Su Sung built an early water clock. In the 13th century, English monasteries had mechanical clocks driven by weights. The bells on these devices were known as "cloks." Precision timekeeping came with the invention of the pendulum clock by Dutch scientist Christian Huygens. The clock introduced a new consciousness—the clock, rather than the sun, became the arbiter of time for everyone. Our technological world demands even more accurate timekeeping. Since 1948, we have used atomic clocks accurate to within 1 second in 300,000 years. Still, we have demanded more accurate marking of time: microsecond (one millionth of a second), nanosecond (one billionth of a second), picosecond (one trillionth of a second), and femtosecond (one thousandth of a picosecond). Consider this: There are more femtoseconds in 1 second than there are seconds in 31 million years.

How we use time varies from culture to culture. That cultures use time differently can be a barrier to intercultural communication. Edward Hall (1983) has provided a useful way of describing how cultures use time. One way is to do one thing at a time, which Hall labels monochronic time; this is characteristic of Northern Europe and the United States. These cultures tend to try to plan the order of their use of time.

Doing many things at once is called **polychronic time** and is characteristic of Latin America and the Middle East. Polychronic time stresses the involvement of people and completion of transactions rather than adherence to schedules. In polychronic cultures, nothing is firm; plans can be changed up to the last minute.

What time you are expected to arrive for an 8 p.m. party varies as to where the party is. How long you should be kept waiting—if at all—for a business appointment varies as well. And once a meeting has begun, it varies how much informal conversation takes place before the actual business discussion begins. Arabs, for example, engage in up to half an hour of informal conversation before turning to business.

Paralanguage

The nonverbal elements of the voice are referred to as **paralanguage** and include the following:

- vocal characterizers, such as laughter and sobs;
- vocal qualifiers, such as intensity (loud/soft), pitch (high/low), and extent (drawl and clipping); and
- vocal segregates, such as "uh," "um," and "uh-huh."

The sounds of "psst" and of whistling are examples of vocal characterizers. "Psst" is an acceptable way of calling a waiter in Spain. In India, whistling is considered offensive.

Thais speak in a very soft and gentle voice and manner. This is based on the cultural belief that speaking in a soft voice is how one shows good manners and an educated character. Voices are raised only to show the emotion of anger or in an argument or confrontation. When first hearing persons in the United States speak, some Thais believe the speakers are rude or angry or even don't like Thais because people from the United States speak so loudly.

Another example is tonal languages. Speakers of English do use tone to some extent but most often to express emotion. Think of how you would say "thank you" to convey a degree of sarcasm. However, in true tonal languages such as Mandarin Chinese and Vietnamese, the denotative meaning of some words depends on the context and how the word is said. Japanese is replete with homophones, where the meanings of many words are distinguished only by stress and intonation, which in turn convey the emotional nuances of anger, surprise, sincerity, and displeasure.

Accent may be considered an aspect of paralanguage. British ears can detect a speaker's educational background in the accent. It can be said that everyone has an accent; it's just that some accents are more accepted than others. Accent may present problems and even lead to charges of racism (Ryan, 1974). One study in San Antonio, Texas (de la Zerda & Hopper, 1979), had employment interviewers listen to taped speech samples of males speaking with varying degrees of accent and make a hiring prediction. Standard speakers were significantly favored for supervisory positions and accented speakers for semiskilled positions. Collier (1988) as well has shown that Whites note Hispanics' inability to speak English as socially inappropriate. In recalling conversations, Whites cite examples of Spanish language use and "broken English" as inappropriate and difficult to understand.

Midlevel Asian-American employees can find promotion to management closed—particularly if spoken English is perceived as nonfluent. In Honolulu, a Filipino man was denied a job as a city clerk. He sued on the basis of racial discrimination. Attorneys for the city argued that his heavy Filipino accent would have kept him from working effectively as a clerk. The case was appealed to the Supreme Court, and in *Fragante v. City and County of Honolulu* (1989), the Court let stand a federal appeals court decision supporting the city.

In Massachusetts, parents petitioned their local school board to ban first-grade and second-grade teachers with pronounced accents. The opposition argued that such a ban would be discrimination based on national origin and would violate the Fourteenth Amendment, which provides equal protection for everyone under the law. In Anaheim (Orange County), California, a radio station contest was based on telephoning convenience store clerks and asking listeners to identify the clerks' nationalities. Some refugee organizations charged the contest was racism disguised as humor.

Silence

We also should consider the use of **silence** in communication. Rather than avoid communication, silence can communicate agreement, apathy, awe, confusion, contemplation, disagreement, embarrassment, obligation, regret, repressed hostility, respect, sadness, thoughtfulness, or any number of meanings. Traditionally, Eastern societies such as India, China, and Japan have valued silence more than Western societies. Oliver (1971) observed that "silence in Asia has commonly been entirely acceptable, whereas in the West silence has generally been considered socially disagreeable" (p. 264). In the Confucian context, silence, not talking, is a virtue.

In India, on the individual level, silence can be viewed as a state of being, allowing you to experience the highest truth and bliss (Jain & Matukumalli, 1993). On the interpersonal level, silence is used to promote harmony, cooperation, and other collectivistic values; it is a sign of interpersonal sensitivity, mutual respect, personal dignity, affirmation, and wisdom. On the level of social movements, silence can be protest, as demonstrated by Mahatma Gandhi in his struggle for India's independence through nonviolence.

To most people in the United States, silence means lack of attention and lack of initiative. A person must speak up to participate. In contrast, to the Chinese, silence means agreement. You should talk only if you have something important to add. One should always let the other talk first.

Silence can mean one is fearful of communicating. This form of silence is associated with the communication variable commonly studied in the United States and known as **communication apprehension** or, more commonly, stage fright. Communication apprehension refers to an individual's fear or anxiety associated with either real or anticipated communication with another person or persons. Studies of communication apprehension by James McCroskey and his colleagues (1990) led them to label that fear the most common handicap that people suffer from today. They also suggest that U.S. society stresses verbal performance so much that U.S. speakers may experience more pressure than those from other cultures. For example, they have shown that Swedish students consider themselves more competent communicators but are less prone to initiate communication than are U.S. students.

Haptics

Less well studied is **haptics**, or the study of our use of touch to communicate. Again, examples support that the use of touch to communicate varies from culture to culture. In Thailand and Laos, it is rude for a stranger or acquaintance to touch a child on the top of the head because the head is regarded as the home of the spirit or soul. It is believed that a child's spirit or soul isn't strong enough to be touched and has a tendency to become ill if patted (Smutkupt & Barna, 1976).

In Iraq, physical contact between adults—particularly between women and men—is governed by strict cultural mores. Postwar security concerns required body searches to help stabilize the country. The United States established the Facilities Protection Service, a security force of some 35,000 Iraqis to provide security checks at thousands of locations too numerous for U.S. soldiers to guard. Women are searched by women and men by men, yet running hands down limbs and patting torsos is an unfamiliar experience.

Compared with other cultures, people in the United States are touch deprived, having one of the lowest rates of casual touch in the world. If you are talking with a friend in a coffee shop in the United States, you might touch each other once or twice an hour. If you were British and in a London coffee shop, you probably won't touch each other at all. But if you were French and in a Parisian café, it is said that you might touch each other a hundred times in an hour.

In many cultures, adult male friends walk hand in hand—a behavior frequently misunderstood by people from the United States who assume the friends are gay. In other cultures, one does not offer anything to another with the left hand, as the left hand is used to clean one's self after using the toilet.

The *hongi,* the traditional greeting of the Māori of New Zealand, is the touching of noses to share the breath of life.

In the United States, more touching may take place in preschool or kindergarten than during any other period. Touching is lowest during the early to mid-teens. The first comprehensive study of communication and touch in the United States was conducted by Jones and Yarbrough (1985). Their study of university students at a western U.S. university showed 12 meanings communicated with touch—affection, announcing a response, appreciation, attention getting, compliance, departures, greetings, inclusion, playful affection, playful aggression, sexual interest or intent, and support—as well as hybrid meanings such as departure/affection and greetings/affection.

In his consulting with businesses, Jones (1993) says that employees are more aware of inappropriate touching and sexual harassment. At least in the United States, most touching has symbolic content, but contextual factors are critical to the meaning. What is appropriate touching in a four-person psychotherapy clinic may not be appropriate in a 200-person insurance office.

Clothing and Physical Appearance

More obvious is the use of **clothing and physical appearance**. What we wear varies so much across the world, as does the meaning conveyed by the clothes. Clothing can reflect cultural heritage. Men in Saudi Arabia may wear a **thawb**, a loose-fitting, ankle-length, usually white shirt; the **ghutrah**, the white or red-and-white check cloth covering the head; and the **iqual** or *agal,* the double ring of black rope or cord used to hold the ghutrah. Muslin women may wear several different types of headscarves and veils. The **burka** covers the entire face and has a mesh screen to see through. The **niqab** does not cover the eyes and is worn with a headscarf. It was estimated that in 2011 about 1,900 women (out of a population of 5 million Muslims) in France wore the niqab. A French parliamentary committee found that women covering their faces was against the French republican principles of secularism and equality. Later that year France imposed a ban on wearing veils that cover the full face in public places such as parks, schools, and theaters. Anyone who violates the ban could be fined and required to take a citizenship course.

Clothing also can reflect subcultural and subgroup identity—medical professionals and military, for example, often wear uniforms outside of work. In Kenya, unlike most of West Africa, attire is generally conservative. In 2003, a legislator entered the nation's parliament dressed in the traditional cap and flowing *agbada* robes of West Africa. The parliament's speaker, dressed in heavy black robes and white wig of the British parliamentary system, described the attire as "pajamas." This dispute over clothing is symbolic of Kenya's struggle to define an African identity.

Territoriality

Territory is the space that an individual claims, whether permanently or temporarily. **Territoriality** refers to how space can be used to communicate messages. Sennett (1999) has described how spaces can encourage democracy. From roughly 600 to 350 BCE, Athens used two very different spaces—the theater and the town square—for its democratic practices. The *Pnyx,* an open-air theater, focused attention on a single speaker at a time, yet it was still possible to gauge others' reactions. The space supported a verbal order, "the unfolding of argument." The *agora* was the town square used for many simultaneous activities. Rather than each group being isolated and segregated, the agora was the place in the city where citizens became accustomed to diversity.

Chinese geomancy, **feng shui** (pronounced fung SCHWAY), is the art of manipulating the physical environment to establish harmony with the natural environment and achieve happiness, prosperity, and health. It is used in site planning and design of buildings for the greatest compatibility with nature. Feng shui also has principles for designing homes and placing furniture. A home with good feng shui has a balance of comfort and style and radiates serenity. Location, room shape, color, plants, artwork, and furniture are arranged for positive energy and balance.

Olfactics

The study of communication via smell is called **olfactics**. Smell remains one of the least understood senses. The amount of the human brain devoted to olfaction is very large. We do know that odor is first detected by the olfactory epithelium in the nose. This starts a chain of events that leads to an information flow to the olfactory bulb and limbic system of the brain, which

Feng shui.

plays a key role in regulating body functions and the emotions. Smell is the only sense linked directly into the limbic system, which may be evidence of its being our most basic, primitive sense. In all cultures, women can detect odors in lower concentrations, identify them more accurately, and remember them longer than men (Doty et al., 1984).

Scientists also have identified a tiny organ in the nasal cavity that responds to chemicals known as pheromones, natural substances believed to play a role in basic human emotions such as fear, hunger, and, most notably, those related to sex. Recently, scientists have uncovered evidence of human pheromones (Weller, 1998).

The ancient Romans were obsessed with roses. They were worn in garlands; used in pillows, medicines, and love potions; and displayed at banquets and orgies. In the 16th century, lovers exchanged "love apples," peeled apples kept in the armpit until they were saturated with sweat and then given to a lover to inhale. In ancient Hawai'i when meeting, traditional Hawaiians inhaled one another's breath. Although many people today consider *haole* (outsider) a derogatory word, in Hawaiian, it originally meant "not of the same breath."

Aromatherapy is the use of oils of flowers, herbs, and plants to make people feel better. Aromatherapy was widely practiced in ancient Chinese, Egyptian, and Indian civilizations and is widely practiced today in Belgium, England, France, Germany, and Switzerland. In Japan, fragrance is used in the workplace. The architectural and construction firm Shimizu has developed computerized techniques to deliver scents through air-conditioning ducts to enhance efficiency and reduce stress among office workers.

Advertisers believe smell is important. Fragrance strips in magazines enable consumers to sample a perfume by pulling open a strip, releasing tiny fragrance capsules glued inside. British stores use smells such as freshly dried linen, chocolate, and musk in the air-conditioning system to put customers in the mood to buy their products.

Smell also refers to body odor. Some cultures are sensitive to any body odor; others mask body odor with perfumes and colognes; others find the odor of perfumes and colognes distasteful. Some say that body odor is affected by the food you eat and that meat eaters have a distinctive body odor.

CASE STUDY: THE WAI IN THAILAND

In Thailand, the wai is a nonverbal gesture used to communicate greeting, bidding farewell, deep and sincere respect, and appreciation (Smutkupt & Barna, 1976). The palms of both hands are placed together and held vertically slightly under the chin followed by a slight head bow, chin toward the fingertips. There is no eye contact because the head is bowed. The wai

is not accompanied by verbal communication. Usually the younger person or subordinate initiates the wai, and the older person or higher ranking person responds with a wai as well (Rojjanaprapayon, 1997).

The wai is consistent with other elements of the Thai culture. Children absorb its nuances along with learning the Thai spoken language, which has a hierarchy of honorific titles and a special language of self-debasement to be used when speaking to royalty. The first nonverbal teaching the Thai child receives is this gesture of obeisance. The mother holds her infant, puts its palms together between her own, and raises the hands to the chin or the forehead—the higher the hands, the greater the degree of deference. Before the child is taken from the house, its hands will be put in the proper position to greet guests. When a mother takes her child to the temple, she raises its palms to pay homage to Buddha. The child is constantly directed to wai on every appropriate occasion until it becomes a regular component of behavior. Children never fail to wai parents and the family's elders before leaving for school in the morning. In the classroom, children stand and perform the wai upon the teacher's arrival. When school ends, the students wai to thank the teacher. On returning home, the children greet all parents and elders with the wai. The day ends with paying homage to Buddha by performing the wai in front of the family's altar. Thus, the wai is a representation of the cultural values, including respect for parents and elders, that the child learns while learning the nonverbal code. By understanding the wai, we also can understand part of the Thai culture.

CASE STUDY: KOREAN-AMERICAN NEIGHBORHOOD BUSINESSES

Communication barriers and racial tension can exist among groups within diverse cultures. One example has been African-American and Korean-American conflict. Today, about 85% of the Korean-American population are immigrants. Some African-Americans have viewed Korean-Americans in business as exploiters. The idea of a neighborhood business with no community commitment was unacceptable. Some Korean-Americans experiencing difficulty with English use words and phrases such as "Go" or "Come back later," which can be viewed as aggressive to customers expecting phrases like "Please come back later." Since the 1992 riots in Los Angeles, Korean-American immigrants have received acculturation and U.S. business practices training to avoid the behaviors that have often been misinterpreted by those unfamiliar with Korean culture. Groups such as the Korean American Management Association advise shopkeepers to greet customers as visiting relatives rather than ignoring customers.

Inappropriate smiles in the Korean culture are interpreted as shallow and thoughtless, so Korean-Americans accustomed to reserving smiles and small talk for friends and families are encouraged to smile and shake hands firmly.

An African-American entering a small store typically expects eye contact and some small talk. If the Korean-American storekeeper, reluctant to develop friendship with a stranger, doesn't engage in those behaviors, the African-American customer may think the store owner is disrespectful or rude. The Korean-American storekeeper, however, raised in a highly structured Confucian culture that stresses formality, sees the outgoing style of the African-American as inappropriate and threatening. Acculturation also involves learning U.S. values, such as the presumption of innocence until proven guilty. In Korea, a person caught shoplifting can be "roughed up" by anyone. Korean-American shopkeepers now learn that that same behavior could result in charges of battery and assault.

SUMMARY

This chapter examines nonverbal as a barrier to effective intercultural communication. Some nonverbals, such as smiles and frowns, are biologically determined. Other nonverbals can be used to intentionally communicate messages. Nonverbals become a barrier because the meaning of many nonverbals vary from culture to culture.

Kinds of nonverbal include:

- *Proxemics*—the use of personal space
- *Kinesics*—gestures, body movements, facial expressions, and eye contact

- *Chronemics*—the use of time
- *Paralanguge*—vocal characterizers, such as laughter; vocal qualifiers, such as pitch; and vocal segregates, such as "uh-huh"
- *Silence*—when not talking can communicate meaning
- *Haptics*—the use of touch to communicate
- *Clothing and Physical Appearance*—when what we wear is used to communicate a message
- *Territoriality*—the use of physical space to communicate messages
- *Olfactics*—the use of smell to communicate messages

In Thailand, for example, the wai gesture is made by placing the palms of both hands together and holding them vertically slightly under the chin. The wai communicates greeting, farewell, sincere respect, and appreciation. Children learn the wai gesture as they learn other elements of the Thai culture. An example of misunderstandings that can arise is interactions between some African-Americans and some Korean-Americans. Eye contact and smiles can have different meanings to each group, resulting in unfortunate misunderstandings.

DISCUSSION QUESTIONS

1. Identify nonverbal symbols throughout history that have incited or otherwise been identified with social change and intercultural communication.

2. Identify nonverbal behaviors, such as crying, that exist in many cultures and have different rules about the behavior, such as who may perform the behavior and when and where it may be performed.

3. Nonverbals on the Internet are known as emoticons, such as the smiley face. Do these represent a form of universal language, or can they also reflect cultural diversity?

4. Create and evaluate the possible arguments in the *Fragante v. City and County of Honolulu* (1989) case.

5. With increasing international travel and media, will nonverbal misinterpretations disappear or become more critical?

KEY TERMS

burka 126	feng shui 126	Hijrah 121
chronemics 121	ghutrah 126	iqal 126
clothing 125		
communication apprehension 123	Gregorian 121	kinesics 115
	haptics 124	monochronic time 121

niqab   126

nonverbal communication   107

olfactics   126

paralanguage   122

physical appearance   125

polychronic time   122

proxemics   114

silence   123

territoriality   126

thawb   125

wai   128

STUDENT STUDY SITE

Visit the student study site at **www.sagepub.com/jandt7e** for these additional learning tools:

- Web Resources
- Audio and Video Links
- SAGE journal articles
- eFlashcards
- Web Quizzes
- Sample Essays

CHAPTER 6

Language as a Barrier

FOCUS QUESTIONS

- What is the relationship between language and culture?

- How do translation problems impede intercultural communication?

- How have humans communicated in language when there is no shared language?

- How can language contribute to nationalism?

Study of Language Origins
Sapir-Whorf Hypothesis
    Development of the Hypothesis
        Linguistic Determinism
        Linguistic Relativity
    Applications
        Vocabulary
        Grammar and Syntax
        Case Study: Arabic and the Arab Culture
Translation Problems
    Vocabulary Equivalence
    Idiomatic Equivalence
    Grammatical-Syntactical Equivalence
    Experiential Equivalence
    Conceptual Equivalence
Pidgins, Creoles, and Universal Languages
    Pidgins
    Creoles
    Esperanto
Language as Nationalism
    English: A History of Borrowed Words
    The Spread of English
    India
    South Africa
    Australia and New Zealand
    Canada
    United States
        The Situation in Hawai'i
        Loss of American Indian Languages
        Puerto Rico and Statehood
Summary
Discussion Questions
Key Terms
Readings
Student Study Site

From Chapter 4, you know that language is a barrier to intercultural communication. What, then, is language? One definition of **language** is that it's a set of symbols shared by a community to communicate meaning and experience. The symbols may be sounds or gestures, as in American Sign Language. What, then, is the relationship between language and culture? Of the thousands of languages spoken today, each has unique sounds, words, and structures. Based on the observation that children learn their native languages so easily and quickly, major linguists, such as Noam Chomsky (1980), argue that all human brains have an innate set of linguistic principles, or Universal Grammar, that underlies the structure of all languages. This approach, known as *generative grammar,* studies grammar as innately possessed. Children need only learn the parochial features of their native languages.

Recent research (Dunn, Greenhill, Levinson, & Gray, 2011) has demonstrated cultural effects in language development. The research employed biological tools to construct evolutionary trees for four language families and demonstrated that each followed its own idiosyncratic structural rules. This is evidence that even our language choices are determined by culture rather than innate rules.

In this chapter, you will first look at how linguists study languages and the development of spoken languages. As was done with nonverbals, language will be shown to relate to other factors in that culture. The Sapir-Whorf hypothesis is discussed. This hypothesis states that the world as we know it is largely predetermined by the language of our culture.

This chapter also deals with two ways in which language affects intercultural communication: translation problems between languages and language as nationalism. Like nonverbals, words as symbols become barriers when their full meaning is not shared. Even speakers of the same language do not share exactly the same meaning for every word. That problem is compounded when you attempt translation between languages. The second way that language becomes a barrier is linguistic imperialism; that is, when the use of a particular language is forced on a people by those with more power.

Language is central to national identity. In 1846, Jacob Grimm, one of the Grimm brothers known for fairytales and a forerunner of modern comparative and historical linguistics, said that "a nation is the totality of people who speak the same language" (King, 1997). When Norway, Ireland, and Israel became independent states, each adopted a largely defunct language (Norse, Gaelic, and Hebrew, respectively) as an official language as necessary for national identity. Even Belgium is experiencing pressures along linguistic lines—the Dutch-speaking north and the French-speaking south. Citizens of the former Yugoslavia spoke roughly the same language, Serbo-Croat, with regional differences. Today, the nationalist regimes that rule Muslim, Serbian, and Croatian parts of Bosnia are adding new words and changing spellings and pronunciations to distinguish their language and national identity. In most post-Soviet countries, instruction at public universities is now almost exclusively in their native ethnic languages.

Hebrew No Parking Truck Sign.

Language, then, has a direct relationship to culture. Language bonds a people together and reflects what people see, eat, and think.

STUDY OF LANGUAGE ORIGINS

Some linguists, particularly scholars in the former Soviet Union, study language from an anthropological or cultural perspective. These scholars are attempting to trace the origins of all the world's languages back to a **mother tongue** or even back to humans' first language. Their study of the origins of languages is based on two assumptions: that languages are dynamic and ever changing and that the relationship between the sound of a word and its meaning is arbitrary. The first assumption, that languages are dynamic and ever changing, can easily be seen from these examples of English:

- Eighth-century Old English: "Hwaet! We Gar-Dena, in geardagum." (Beowulf)
- Fourteenth-century Middle English: "Whan that Aprill with his shoures soote." (Chaucer)
- Sixteenth-century English: "Shall I compare thee to a summer's day?" (Shakespeare)
- Twenty-first-century English: "Don't have a cow, man." (Bart Simpson)

The second assumption, that the relationship between the sound of a word—the symbol—and its meaning is arbitrary, deals with how words mean. With the exception of onomatopoeic words like *sizzle,* the sound of a word has no connection to its meaning. Words represent symbols that a language community uses to refer to other things. In this sense, words are not the thing they refer to, and the use of any word symbol is arbitrary. For example, English uses the word *cat* to refer to a furry domesticated carnivorous mammal having four legs and a tail

Cat, chat, katze, katte, kot.

and noted for its skill at catching mice and rats. Tomorrow, all English speakers could as easily agree to use the word *yahtzee* instead of *cat*.

Linguists study the words in languages and then look for similar-sounding words with similar meanings in different languages. In order to read Hindu legal texts, Sir William Jones, a judge in Calcutta at the end of the 18th century, began to study Sanskrit, the ancient language of northern India. He found similarities between Sanskrit words and ancient Greek and Latin words and argued that the languages were derived from a common mother tongue. Scholars in the 19th century were inspired by this suggestion and began studying languages for their common ancestors. Another important aspect of language is **syntax**, or how words are arranged to convey meaning—the order of subject (S), verb (V), and object (O). Table 6.1 shows the six possible combinations. The first three are overwhelmingly more frequent. In VO languages, prepositions tend to come before nouns, as in English "in class." In OV, prepositions tend to come after, as in Hindi. Basic word order is often reflected in the order of names. In SOV languages, such as Japanese and Korean, the surname comes first, as in *MATSUMOTO Tada*. This also applies to titles, as in *Yamata sensei*—"Professor Yamata."

Table 6.1   Basic Word Order

Word Order	Sample Languages
SVO "cats eat mice"	English, Chinese, Swahili
SOV "cats mice eat"	Japanese, Korean
VSO "eat cats mice"	Classical Arabic, Welsh, Samoan
VOS "eat mice cats"	Tzotzil (a Mayan language)
OSV "mice cats eat"	Kabardian (a language of the northern Caucasus)
OVS "mice eat cats"	Hixkaryana (a language of Brazil)

Source: Matthews, Polinsky, and Comrie (1996).

Note: S = subject; V = verb; O = object.

FOCUS ON THEORY 6.1

In answer to the question "How do we know?" social constructionism answers that reality is a product of symbolic interaction within social groups. Social constructionism remains a controversial theory because it conflicts with the idea that reality is objective. In contrast to social constructionism, the Sapir-Whorf hypothesis contends that reality is embedded in culture's language and, in some sense, then "comes preformed."

Noam Chomsky (1980), however, argues that language structures are universal and that cultural differences in language are superficial. From this perspective, language study should focus on the universals that can explain the human mind.

SAPIR-WHORF HYPOTHESIS

Development of the Hypothesis

Many academic disciplines refer to the **Sapir-Whorf hypothesis** (also known as the Whorfian thesis) when accounting for the differences in languages across cultures (Carroll, 1956). Benjamin L. Whorf (1897–1941), a successful fire prevention engineer at the Hartford Fire Insurance Company, came into contact with the noted linguistic anthropologist Edward Sapir (1884–1939) through a course that Sapir (1921) was teaching at Yale. Largely self-taught, Whorf had studied ancient Hebraic, Aztec, and Mayan cultures, and in the 1930s he went to the U.S. Southwest to study the Hopi's Uto-Aztecan language. Among Whorf's observations were that the Hopi do not:

- Pluralize nouns referring to time, such as *days* and *years*. Instead, time is viewed as a duration.
- Use words denoting phases of a cycle, such as *summer* as a phase of a year, as nouns. Whorf suggested that the Hopi view of time is the perpetual "getting later" of it.
- See time as linear in that there are no tenses in the language. Whorf observed that the Hopi have no words, grammatical forms, constructions, or expressions that refer to time.

Whorf's papers, written in the 1930s on the Hopi language, produced exact and documented expression of the Sapir-Whorf hypothesis that reality for a culture is discoverable in its language.

Nisbett (2003) reports an interesting validation of Sapir-Whorf. Remember the thesis that Westerners favor decontextualization and object emphasis and that Easterners favor integration and relationships in perception. If the Sapir-Whorf hypothesis is true, then it should make a difference which language bilingual speakers are speaking. First, though, *bilingual speakers* should be defined. **Coordinate bilingual** speakers are people who learn a second language later in life and who typically use their second language in a limited number of contexts. **Compound bilingual** speakers are people who learned a second language early in life and use the language in many different contexts. For example, many people from China and Taiwan learn English later in life, while people from Hong Kong and Singapore tend to learn English earlier and use it in many different contexts.

When asked to group objects together, European-Americans tested in English and coordinate Chinese speakers tested in Chinese were twice as likely to group objects on the basis of category than on the basis of relationships. Mainland and Taiwanese Chinese tested in their native language were twice as likely to group on the basis of relationships, whether they were tested in their home countries or in the United States. When tested in English, they were much less likely to group on the basis of relationships. The conclusion is that English served as a different way of representing the world than Chinese for this group.

While compound bilinguals from Hong Kong and Singapore grouped on the basis of relationships, the preference was much weaker than for the coordinate Chinese and Taiwanese speakers. And it made no difference for the compound speakers whether they were tested in Chinese or in English. The researchers concluded that "there is an effect of culture on thought independent of language . . . because both the coordinate Chinese speakers and the compound Chinese speakers group words differently from Americans regardless of language of testing. The differences between coordinate and compound speakers also indicate a culture difference independent of language. The compound speakers from Westernized regions are shifted in a Western direction—and to the same extend regardless of language of testing" (Nisbett, 2003, pp.161–162).

FOCUS ON THE ENVIRONMENT 6.1

Languages evolve and disappear in much the same way as species of plants and animals. In 2003, there were 46 people who were the last remaining speakers of their native language. Population ecologist William Sutherland classified the extinction risk for 6,809 languages using the statistical methods biologists employ to asses species extinction. Areas with high language diversity also have high bird and mammal diversity. All three show similar relationships to area, latitude, area of forest, and, for languages and birds, maximum altitude. Though similar factors explain the diversity of languages and biodiversity, the factors explaining extinction risk for birds and mammals (high altitude, high human densities, and insularity) do not explain the numbers of endangered languages. Languages are more threatened than birds or mammals, but measures to protect biological diversity may help to protect language diversity (Sutherland, 2003).

Linguistic Determinism

After Whorf's studies, scholars divided the hypothesis into the linguistic determinist interpretation and the linguistic relativity interpretation. The linguistic determinist view is that language structure controls thought and cultural norms. Each of us lives not in the midst of the whole world but only in that part of the world that our language permits us to know. Thus, the world as each of us knows it is, to a large extent, predetermined by the language of our culture. And the differences between languages represent basic differences in the worldview of diverse cultures.

Global Voices

When you lose a culture, you're not losing a failed attempt at modernity. You're losing a unique set of answers to the question of what it means to be human.

—Edmund Wade Davis, *Light at the Edge of the World* (Hayden, 2003, para. 5).

Davis is a Canadian anthropologist, ethnobotanist, and photographer whose work has focused on indigenous cultures, particularly in North and South America.

Linguistic Relativity

Subsequent research did not support all the claims made by linguistic determinist researchers (Fishman, 1972; Hoijer, 1954). In 1983, for example, Ekkehart Malotki (1983), a Northern Arizona University professor of languages who standardized a writing system for the Hopi, documented many references to *time* he had found in the Hopi language.

Global Voices

Learn a new language and get a new soul.

—Czech proverb

Human beings do not live in the objective world alone, nor alone in the world of social activity as ordinarily understood, but are very much at the mercy of the particular language which has become the medium of expression for their society.

—Edward Sapir, *Selected Writings in Language, Culture, and Personality* (1949, p. 162)

Even though Whorf's Hopi example might not stand, the Sapir-Whorf hypothesis does offer a useful way of thinking about the relationship between language and culture in the linguistic relativity view. In this interpretation, linguistic characteristics and cultural norms influence each other.

The hypothesis may be expressed, then, as follows: Culture is controlled by *and* controls language.

In this interpretation, language provides the conceptual categories that influence how its speakers' perceptions are encoded and stored. Steinfatt (1989), in an extensive review of the literature, argues that the basis of linguistic relativity is that the difference between languages is not what can be said but what is relatively easy to say.

Applications

Vocabulary

One level of the Sapir-Whorf hypothesis is vocabulary. You can assume that if a language has a particularly rich vocabulary for a thing or activity in comparison to other languages, that thing or activity is important in that culture. The most commonly used example is Eskimo and snow—although this example also has been challenged.

The name *Eskimo* was first applied to the peoples of the Arctic by a Jesuit who heard people using the word *eskimantsik,* which means "eaters of raw meat or fish." Alaska has three native groups: the Aleuts in the Alaska Peninsula and islands beyond; Indians such as the Athapaskan, Haida, and Tlingit; and Eskimo groups such as the Chugach, the Koniag, the Yupik, and the Inupiat, known as the Inuit in Canada and the Inupik in Siberia. It was said that Eskimo languages have many words for different kinds of snow:

qana	falling snow; snowflakes
akilukak	fluffy fallen snow
aput	snow on the ground
kaguklaich	snow drifted in rows

| *piqsirpoq* | drifting snow |
| *qimuqsuq* | snowdrift |

Because the language has many separate single words to refer to different kinds of snow; then snow must be an important part of these groups' lives (Birke-Smith, 1959). Notice, that other languages, such as English, may require several words to describe the same thing. Speakers of diverse languages can perceive all these different conditions of snow—it's just that the Eskimo peoples have more separate single words to refer to these different conditions. The challenge to this example contends that single English words such as *blizzard, dusting,* and *avalanche* exist as equivalents to the Eskimo words.

FOCUS ON THE ENVIRONMENT 6.2

The scientist Will Steger is working to establish the impact of global warming on the indigenous people of the Artic. Hunters he meets on Baffin Island described to him creatures they have no words for in the Inuktitut language—robins, finches, and dolphins.

Source: Duff-Brown, (2007).

In a like way, the Hanunoo tribe of the Philippines has 92 separate single words to refer to rice. In fact, in most of the languages of Asia, one word means both *food* and *rice*. Using the Sapir-Whorf hypothesis, you can assume that rice is important in these cultures.

Speakers of Guguyimadjir in the Australian state of Queensland have no words for "right" or "left" but orient their world by the points of the compass, suggesting seeing things in relation to the world as a whole rather than to ourselves. In a similar way, you might assume that a language with a paucity of terms in comparison to other languages to refer to a thing or activity reflects a culture in which that thing or activity is absent or not important. The Yanomamo of southern Venezuela are one of the few societies in the world with a primitive technology. The Yanomamo language has only three numbers, which correspond to "one," "two," and "more than two" in English. The development of technology requires a language that can symbolize mathematics.

Compared to English, Japanese has a rich vocabulary of words to identify seasons of the year. The four seasons are divided into 24 subseasons according to the traditional lunar calendar. And each subseason is divided into the beginning, middle, and end.

> **Global Voices**
>
> It's said that when a Japanese writes a letter, it always begins with a remark on the weather and the season. It will say things like "It is already mid-May, and the young foliage is fresh and green...."

Grammar and Syntax

The second level of the Sapir-Whorf hypothesis is grammar and syntax. Whorf felt that grammar had an even greater influence than vocabulary. For example, it has been observed that in the Eskimo language, there is a consistent use of the word *if* rather than *when* in reference to the future. Think of the difference between "When I graduate from college . . ." and "If I graduate from college . . ." In this example, *when* seems to indicate more certainty than *if*. Linguists have associated the more common use of *if* in the Eskimo language with the harsh environment that Eskimos live in, where life is fragile and there is little control over nature (Chance, 1966).

English word order is typically SVO (see Table 6.1). English places emphasis on a doer, on an action taker. Only about a third of English sentences lack a subject. In contrast, 75% of Japanese sentences lack a subject. For example, you are more likely to hear, "I brought my textbook with me" in the United States and hear "Brought book" in Japan. The subject is known by context. Similarly, if you have hiked for a day into a deserted canyon you might say to yourself, "I feel lonesome." A Japanese hiker would say only "Samishii," identifying the experience without the need to identify the subject. Yes, in English, we sometimes speak in abbreviated forms, but we're conscious of it being a shortened version of a more detailed statement. The Japanese speaker is not abbreviating; Japanese does not require the specification of a subject.

Case Study: Arabic and the Arab Culture

As a demonstration of the Sapir-Whorf hypothesis, you can use the following case study to learn about Arab culture from the characteristics of the Arabic language that are presented. As you read this section, identify elements of Arab culture that you see in the following description of the language.

Arabic is spoken in one form or another by more than 200 million people. Because Arabic is strongly interconnected with the religion Islam, the Sapir-Whorf hypothesis explains the critical importance of the religion to the culture. The Koran is the ultimate standard for Arabic style and grammar. Islam has had major effects on both written Arabic and the spoken language. Classical Arabic, the language of the Koran, is the accepted standard for the written language (Asuncion-Lande, 1983). As Islam spread throughout the world, so too did spoken Arabic, as all Muslims, regardless of nationality, must use Arabic in their daily prayers.

Like any language, spoken Arabic continues to evolve and does vary from country to country. In classical Arabic, the number 2 is *ithnayn,* but *tween* is used in Lebanon, *itneen* in Egypt, and *ithneen* in Kuwait. Perhaps because of the influences of the Koran, Arabic withstood Turkish-Ottoman occupation and colonial empires and changed less than would have been expected. Advocates of Arab unity continue to work to unify and purify the spoken language. Modern standard Arabic is used, for example, at Arab League meetings, in radio and television news broadcasts, and in books and newspapers. Nonetheless, English or French is still the second language in the region.

Arabic style attempts to go beyond reflecting human experience to transcending the human experience. As Merriam (1974) noted, Al-Sakkaki divided rhetoric into three parts: *al ma'ani* is the part dealing with grammatical forms and kinds of sentences, *al-bayan* refers to modes for achieving lucid style and clarity of expression, and *al-badi* (literally "the science of metaphors") refers to the beautification of style and the embellishment of speech. Skillful use of language commands prestige. Arabic vocabulary is rich. For example, there are 3,000 words for camel, 800 for sword, 500 for lion, and 200 for snake. Translated into English, Arabic statements often sound exaggerated. Instead of "We missed you," the statement may be "You made us desolate with your absence." It's said that because of the love of language, the Arab is swayed more by words than by ideas and more by ideas than by facts.

Arabic emphasizes creative artistry through repetition, metaphor, and simile in part because of the poetic influences of the Koran. The role that formal poetry, prose, and oratory play is missing today in Western culture. Westerners often find it difficult to locate the main idea of an Arabic message; Arabs often fault Westerners for being insensitive to linguistic artistry. Arabic makes more use of paralanguage—pitch, rhythm, intonation, and inflection—than other languages. The language rhythm can be magical and hypnotic. Higher pitch and greater emotional intonation are natural to Arabic speakers. Speakers of Arabic may talk with a lot of noise and emotion. The rhetoric of confrontation—verbal threats and flamboyant language— is common. What may appear to be a heated argument may just be two friends having a chat. A speaker of Arabic uses language as a mode of aggression. Such verbal aggression essentially diffuses and prevents actual violence.

It's said that when an Arab says yes, he means maybe. When he says maybe, he means no. An Arab seldom says no because it may be considered impolite and close off options. Instead of no, an Arab may say *inshallah,* or "if God is willing." *Inshallah* is used when mentioning a future event of any kind as it is considered sacrilegious to presume to control future events. To mean yes, one must be both repetitive and emphatic.

TRANSLATION PROBLEMS

Even when cultures speak the same language—as do Australia and the United States—there can be vocabulary differences. When cultures speak different languages, translation is critical—but always imperfect. When President Jimmy Carter greeted the people of Poland on his 1977 trip there, the translator said, "The President says he is pleased to be here in Poland grasping your secret parts" (Axtell, 1994). Sechrest, Fay, and Zaidi (1972) have identified five translation problems that can become barriers to intercultural communication. Each of these is discussed below.

Vocabulary Equivalence

First is the lack of *vocabulary equivalence.* Recall the discussions of the Sapir-Whorf hypothesis and the example given that Eskimo languages have many different words to refer to snow. Were you to translate on a word-for-word basis, you would translate all those different words into the one English word, *snow.* Much of the meaning of the more specific and more descriptive words—for example, qualities of slushiness or hardness or newness—would be lost in a word-for-word translation. As another example, imagine having to translate all shades of pink,

Global Voices

No one when he uses a word has in mind exactly the same thing that another has, and the difference, however tiny, sends its tremors throughout language.

...All understanding, therefore, is always at the same time a misunderstanding...and all agreement of feelings and thoughts is at the same time a means for growing apart.

—Wilhelm von Humboldt (1767–1835)
(quoted in Cowan, 1963)

burgundy, orange-red, and so on into the one word *red*. As you might imagine, such a limitation would be frustrating to you if you were accustomed to using more descriptive words.

One frequently quoted example of the lack of vocabulary equivalence is from World War II. The Allies had issued the Potsdam Ultimatum, demanding the surrender of the Japanese military to end the war. At a press conference, Prime Minister Suzuki was asked for his opinion. He responded, "The government does not see much value in it. All we have to do is *mokusatsu* it." The Japanese cabinet had carefully chosen that word to convey their intended meaning. Later, Japanese cabinet officials said they intended to convey a bland "no comment" at that time, as there was interest in negotiating a surrender and more time was required for discussions. Unfortunately, the word *mokusatsu* can mean anything from "ignore" to "treat with silent contempt." Western translators used the latter meaning, and the Potsdam Ultimatum was then considered to have been rejected. After-the-fact reasoning argues that that translation led to the continuation of the war and the first use of atomic weapons.

Languages that are different often lack words that are directly translatable. Consider the number of English words with different meanings: A U.S. businessperson might write a letter to be translated into Japanese with the sentence "We wonder if you would prepare an agenda for our meeting." The word *wonder* and the construction of this sentence may have been intended as a polite way of telling the Japanese counterpart to prepare the agenda. The word *wonder* could be translated with the Japanese word *gimon,* which most commonly means doubt. The translated sentence now would read, "We doubt that you would prepare an agenda for our meeting" (Axtell, 1994).

Idiomatic Equivalence

The second barrier to successful translation is the problem of *idiomatic equivalence.* The English language is particularly replete with the idioms. Take the simple example of "the old man kicked the bucket." Native speakers know that this idiom means the old man died. If the sentence is translated word for word, the meaning conveyed would be literally that the old man kicked the bucket—quite different from the intended meaning. You can no doubt think of many other examples. Just think of how the idioms "out to lunch" and "toss your cookies" could cause communication problems!

It's easy to think of many idioms in common use in spoken U.S. English that can be misunderstood: "break a leg," "read between the lines," "hold your horses," and "raining cats and dogs." This is one reason why English is a difficult language to learn as a second language. However, learning the idioms of a language can be an effective way of learning the culture (Lee, 1994).

Grammatical-Syntactical Equivalence

Third is the problem of *grammatical-syntactical equivalence*. This simply means that languages don't necessarily have the same grammar. Often, you need to understand a language's grammar to understand the meaning of words. For example, words in English can be nouns or verbs or adjectives, depending on their position in a sentence. In English, you can say "plan a table" and "table a plan" or "book a place" and "place a book" or "lift a thumb" and "thumb a lift."

Experiential Equivalence

Fourth is the problem of *experiential equivalence*. If an object or experience does not exist in your culture, it's difficult to translate words referring to that object or experience into that language when no words may exist for them. Think of objects or experiences that exist in your culture and not in another. "Department store" and "shopping mall" may be as difficult to translate into some languages as "windsurfing" is into others. The 2000 U.S. census attempted to be sensitive to Vietnamese immigrants' experience with Vietnam's government tracking of individuals. Instead of using the Vietnamese words for *census*, which translates to "investigation of the population," the phrase *Thong ke dan so,* or "survey of population," was used.

Conceptual Equivalence

Fifth, the problem of *conceptual equivalence* refers to abstract ideas that may not exist in the same fashion in different languages. For example, people in the United States have a unique meaning for the word *freedom*. That meaning is not universally shared. Speakers of other languages may say they are free and be correct in their culture, but the freedom they refer to isn't equivalent to what is experienced as freedom in the United States. The English word *corruption* translates as the Korean word *pup'ae,* but the words are not conceptually equivalent. For both people in the United States and Korea, the word connotes negative, bad, improper behavior, but in the United States, corruption is a crime and wrong on moral grounds, whereas in Korea, corruption is not morally wrong. It's wrong in the sense that it interferes with the proper functioning of government and is bad in its social consequences. Even though the word is negative and has similar interpretations, there are sufficient conceptual differences to create intercultural communication misunderstandings (Szalay, Moon, & Bryson, 1971).

A similar misunderstanding can occur with the word *democracy.* To both people in the United States and Korea, democracy means freedom and liberty. In the United States, the meaning of the word places strong emphasis on procedures such as elections, campaigning, and voting, whereas in Korea, the word *democracy* is an abstract ideal. Think of how postcommunist Russians readily embraced the words *democracy, congress,* and *president,* but having just broken with the totalitarian tradition, many had trouble understanding the underlying concepts. In a 1994 interview, former President Jimmy Carter identified conceptual equivalence problems with the term *human rights.* According to Carter, each country defines the term by what it has. In the United States, human rights refers to the Bill of Rights (e.g., freedom of speech, right to a fair trial). In other countries, the term refers to adequate housing or universal health care.

One way to improve translation is to use **back translation**. Back translation involves first translating into the second language, then translating back into the first language, and then comparing the result to the original. Often, the process can prevent amusing translation problems. For example, on a trip to see Hitler's Eagle's Nest, I was given a ticket for my return trip down the mountain. On the back of the ticket, I found this message in English: "The indicated return time must be strictly adhered to. A later return is determined by the disposable bus seats." The misuse of the word *disposable* would probably be caught if the sentence had been translated back into German and then compared to the original German sentence.

Today in Europe and North America, antiterrorism agencies are faced with an acute shortage of Arabic-speaking translators. Can computer-translating programs be effective? In *The Hitchhiker's Guide to the Galaxy,* Douglas Adams envisioned a translation device called the Babel fish, a "small, yellow and leech-like" fish that one stuck in one's ear. One approach to machine translation is to first analyze the syntax of a sentence to identify subject, verb, object, and modifiers. Then, using a dictionary, the words are translated into another language. Finally, the program analyzes the result and generates an intelligible sentence in the new language based on the rules of that language's syntax. Machine translation of the spoken voice is more difficult. One-way handheld voice translators were used by the U.S. military in Afghanistan in 2002. Two-way voice translators involving speech recognition, machine translation, and voice synthesis have been developed for handheld devices for use between English and Iraqi Arabic.

A new approach under development does not rely on linguistic rules but is based on statistical analysis. It generally begins with the analysis of the frequency with which clusters of words appear in close proximity in the same texts in two languages. The development tests have been conducted on United Nations and European Parliament speeches translated by humans. From that analysis, accurate translations of new material have been performed in real time regardless of the subject matter. This approach translates languages based on how they are actually used rather than rigid grammatical rules that are not always observed and often have exceptions.

New software was released in 2010 for instant translation. The VoxOx Universal Translator for instant messages, SMS, e-mail, and social media enables two people to communicate instantly with each other while both typing in their native languages. Trippo VoiceMagix, for iPhone, translates English speech to 14 languages. Speechtrans began testing an iPhone app that makes it possible for two people using two different languages to communicate instantly with each other in English, UK English, German, French, Italian, Spanish, and Japanese. DLP Mobile, released an Android app called Speaking Universal Translator with translation to and from English, Spanish, Italian, and French.

FOCUS ON THE ENVIRONMENT 6.3

In his dissertation, *Managing Nature—Business as Usual: Patterns of Wording and Patterns of Meaning in Corporate Environmental Discourse,* Associate Professor Mark Brown (2008) of the Norwegian School of Management at the University of Oslo examined how environmental organizations and companies use green words. He first downloaded all the texts from homepages of 37 selected nongovernmental environmental organizations and 25 green companies in the United Kingdom. Then, into two databases, he gathered 9 million words: 6 million from the environmental organizations and 3 million from businesses.

After comparing the language of the two databases with the British National Corpus, the standard for average English, Brown (2008) focused on finding the special characteristics of the players' use of the language, identified key words, and discovered patterns in the relationship between the words with a computer program.

The patterns that he found in the use of the language demonstrate that some companies have adopted the environmental movement's terms. Green companies use the environmental movement's language to describe their own environmentally friendly ambitions, but they use the words in new ways to suit their own purpose.

These green businesses do not use words that people normally associate with nature—such as trees, flowers, lakes, and so on—but instead use "executive language," a management language that allows them to manage their relationship with the environment and natural landscape.

Environmentally friendly companies tailor green words to fit their own businesses, such as "emissions per kilowatt-hour" and "biodiversity indicator," giving them a way to control and offset the impact and harm to nature against their own production.

"The consequences of this trend ought to provoke some thoughts also in Norwegians," says Brown, who also states that companies' well-meaning responses to the environmental movement may in fact contribute toward exterminating untouched nature.

"Norway is in the process of becoming a completely controlled landscape—a nature shaped by the green companies' technology, and it is all done in the name of sustainable development," he warns.

PIDGINS, CREOLES, AND UNIVERSAL LANGUAGES

When cultures with no shared language came in contact, such as through international trade or during colonialism, one way to communicate was through the development of pidgins and creoles. Once thought of as crude nonstandard languages, they are now central to the study of linguistic development (Holm, 1989; Romaine, 1988).

Pidgins

A pidgin is the mixture of two or more languages to form a new language, originally used for restricted purposes such as trade. As a contact language between diverse language groups, pidgins have widespread use in West Africa. Cameroon used a pidgin drawn from English, German, French, and local words to facilitate communication among some 285 tribal languages. In the western Pacific, European traders, whalers, and missionaries and the hundreds of tribes there developed a pidgin based on English, German, and a local language with a distinctly Melanesian grammar and sentence structure. Melanesian Pidgin English is a pidgin language based on English. Use of Pidgin English became widespread when colonial European plantations were established in the 19th century in Samoa, Fiji, and other places using laborers from New Guinea and the Solomon Islands, an archipelago of several hundred islands spread over 1,000 miles and more than 50 languages. In the 20th century, Pidgin English died out in the monolingual communities of Samoa and Fiji but continued to be used in the multilingual communities of Papua New Guinea and the Solomons (Keesing, 1988).

The Papua New Guinea constitution recognizes three "national" languages—English, Hiri Motu, and Tok Pisin. English is the major language of education and written communication. Hiri Motu is the language of the southern provinces of the mainland. Its use is declining as the use of Tok Pisin expands. Tok Pisin is used in speeches and reports in the National Parliament and in social interaction among people of diverse language backgrounds. It was spoken when Prince Charles of Great Britain opened Papua New Guinea's National Parliament during independence celebrations in 1975. And in 1984, Pope John Paul II celebrated Mass in New Guinea in pidgin (Romaine, 1992).

The development of a pidgin is not inevitable. One example from East Africa is Swahili, the language used by the coastal tribes that settled in eastern Tanzania. In the 1800s, Arab traders searching for slaves migrated down the coast, spreading Arabic. Over time, 50% of Swahili was derived from Arabic. Later, British colonial rule brought English, but Swahili continued as the unifying language of the country's 120 diverse tribes. African nationalism in the 1960s reinforced the use of Swahili over English. Today, it's not unusual for people to switch back and forth from Swahili to English to communicate ideas.

Creoles

Today, a creole is defined as a new language developed from prolonged contact of two or more languages (Bickerton, 1981). Whereas a pidgin can be thought of as a second language, a creole is acquired by children as their first language. Creoles were largely the product of the colonial era. Creoles are concentrated in areas where slave labor was used—the Caribbean, the Indian Ocean, and Pacific islands. Typically, creoles incorporate the vocabulary of the dominant language with the grammar and some words from the subordinate language to become the new language of the subordinate group. The most well-known creoles are Jamaican Patois, a mixture of English and West African languages, with more than 2 million speakers, and French-based Haitian with some 5 million speakers. These are used increasingly in newspapers and radio.

In Macao, a patois, or **dialect**, developed from Portuguese and Cantonese words in combinations such as *compra som,* meaning to buy groceries from the Portuguese *compra* and the Cantonese *som,* and *avo gong,* which joins together the Portuguese and Cantonese terms for grandfather.

Esperanto

Would communication between individuals of diverse cultures be improved if we all spoke one language? There have been attempts to construct such a universal language. The only moderately successful attempt was **Esperanto**, devised in 1887 by Polish oculist and philologist Lazarus Zamenhof when he was 19 years old. Zamenhof wrote under the name of Doktoro Esperanto, or "one who hopes."

Esperanto is a simplified, regular language with Latin-type grammar and European vocabulary. It is claimed that one can learn the language in 100 hours or less. Estimates of the number of speakers of Esperanto today range from 1 million to 16 million worldwide with some 1,000 native speakers who learned the language as children. Vatican Radio, Cuba, and China broadcast programs in Esperanto, and on its 100th anniversary, an Esperanto version of the play *The Importance of Being Earnest* was presented in London.

When Esperanto was devised, English was the language of commerce, French of diplomacy, and German of science. Today, English, rather than Esperanto, has become the universal language of all three.

Esperanto and other attempts at universal languages are not successful precisely for the reasons described earlier in this chapter as characteristics of language itself. Universal languages are artificial languages; they have no relationship to a culture—hence they are static and don't change and evolve as a culture changes and evolves. Nor do universal languages reflect the worldview of any culture. Any universal first language would probably begin to develop unique regional vocabularies and pronunciations over time and would then again begin to reflect cultural differences as the regional dialects grew further apart.

LANGUAGE AS NATIONALISM

A second way that language can be a barrier relates to the Sapir-Whorf hypothesis. When a group with more power enforces the use of its language on another group, it also is making its culture dominant. The Brazilian Paulo Freire (1992) used the term **cultural invasion** to refer to one group penetrating the culture of another group to impose its own view of the world. Cultural invasion can be physical and overt as in war and political takeover, or it can be indirect or even in the form of assistance. The spread of a language to common use around a region also means the spreading influence of the culture native to that language. (Table 6.2 shows the world's most widely spoken first languages.)

English: A History of Borrowed Words

As the use of English becomes increasingly worldwide, more concerns are voiced that it carries "the baggage" of one culture.

English did not exist when Julius Caesar invaded Britain in 55 BCE. The Celts spoke languages that survive today as Welsh, Gaelic, and Breton. In the mid-5th century, the Jutes (modern Denmark) and the Saxons (Germany) migrated to the south of Britain, and the Angles (Germany) migrated to the north and east of Britain. Pope Gregory's monks brought some Latin and Greek words. The

Table 6.2   Most Widely Spoken First Languages in the World

Language	Percentage
Chinese (Mandarin)	12.65
Spanish	4.93
English	4.91
Arabic	3.31
Hindi	2.73
Bengali	2.71
Portuguese	2.67
Russian	2.16
Japanese	1.83
German	1.35

Source: CIA World Factbook (2011).

Vikings from Scandinavia arrived in the late 8th century and enriched the vocabulary. (*Rear* a child is Anglo-Saxon; *raise* a child is Norse.) The Norman French conquered England in 1066. English kept its relatively simple Germanic structure while adding a huge vocabulary of French words. Even before Columbus, English had borrowed words from 50 languages.

Anglo-Saxon	French	Latin
end	finish	Conclude
fair	beautiful	Attractive
fear	terror	Trepidation

Borrowed words tend to be pronounced the same as in their original language.

The printing press and the European Renaissance added thousands of words to the English vocabulary. In 1780, John Adams moved for the creation of an academy to keep the English language pure. His proposal died in the Continental Congress. The *Oxford English Dictionary* contains more than 600,000 English words. By comparison, German has fewer than one-third that number and French fewer than one sixth. Today, half of the world's published books are in English.

The Spread of English

Even though at one time it could not have been predicted, of particular concern today is the spread of American English. In 449, the Jutes first arrived on the Kent coast. The Germanic dialect of the Jutes, along with those of the Angles and the Saxons, was soon to become known as English. The Germanic invaders took little from the language of the Celts they displaced, but soon they began their characteristic assimilation of words from other languages. First came Latin from Christian missionaries arriving in 597, then Old Norse from Danish invaders, then French from Norman rule (Stevenson, 1999).

> **Global Voices**
>
> The English language hasn't got where it is by being pure.
>
> —Carl Sandburg

In 1582, a scholar observed, "The English tongue is of small reach, stretching no further than this island of ours, nay not there over all" (Mencken, 1935, p. 541). In little more than 25 years, English had spread across the ocean and has not stopped expanding since. In early colonial days, some 5 million people spoke English. By 1930, the number had risen to 200 million. By the mid-1960s, counting those who used English as a second language, the number of people speaking English had doubled to 400 million. By 1990, that number had risen to about 750 million, or one of every seven people.

Today's estimate is that one fifth to one fourth of the world's population is familiar with English (Ostler, 2005). English is the native language in 12 countries and an official or semiofficial language in 33 others. Its study is required or popular in at least 56 other countries. Consider this: An Argentine pilot landing in Turkey speaks to the air traffic controller in English. English is the de facto language of aviation worldwide. A German physicist publishes findings in English-language journals. Japanese executives conduct business in Mexico in English. And in 2009, the Texas-bordering state of Tamaulipas declared itself the first bilingual state in Mexico. Its 320,000 public school students will learn conversational English. It's the most widely studied and most borrowed-from language in the world.

English has grown to dominate in the areas of science, technology, commerce, tourism, diplomacy, and pop culture. CNN International and MTV broadcast in English. Some 80% of the world's electronic databases and communication networks are in English. Western companies today are outsourcing customers to call centers in southern India. The agents are trained in American or British accents and popular culture such as sports teams and television shows. One Indian author and outspoken foe of globalization condemns the adoption of accents for jobs in call centers as showing "how easily an ancient civilization can be made to abase itself completely" (Roy, 2001).

The Internet was developed in the United States, and the overwhelming majority of World Wide Web sites, newsgroups, and chat rooms are based in the United States. Internet search engines are largely in English (see Table 6.3). Even computer keyboards are typically based on the English alphabet. French President Jacques Chirac told la Francophonie, a group formed in France to preserve the use of French in cyberspace, "If in this new medium our language, our programs, our creations don't have a strong presence, our future generations will be economically and culturally marginalized."(Romero, 1996, para. 10). The French government has since decreed that *e-mail* will be pronounced *courriel* from the French words *courier electronique* and chat will be *eblabla*.

Table 6.3   Language Use on the Internet

Language	Users	Percentage
English	536,564,837	27.3
Chinese	444,948,013	22.6
Spanish	153,309,074	7.8
Japanese	99,143,700	5.0
Portuguese	82,548,200	4.2
German	75,158,584	3.8
Arabic	65,365,400	3.3
French	59,779,525	3.0
Russian	59,700,000	3.0
Korean	39,440,000	2.0

Source: Internet World Stats (2011b).

India

A more extreme case of the spread of English is India, the world's second most populated country, with more than 1.2 billion people. India is a country of diversity: a multiplicity of languages as well as religions, castes, and living conditions. Since its independence in 1947, India has struggled to maintain a society that values the country's diverse linguistic, religious, and historic groups.

India's people speak 20 major languages and hundreds of dialects. When India became an independent country in 1947, Hindi was slated to become the national language by 1965. But as 1965 approached, the use of Hindi had not spread Today Hindi is the most widely spoken language, with 41% of the population. Hindi speakers concentrated in the north claim that English is elitist and a holdover from the colonial past. India is slowly eradicating the legacy of British colonial rule by renaming cities and streets. Madras is now Chennai, Bombay is now Mumbai, and Calcutta is now Kolkata. English speakers, largely in the south, argue that Hindi as an official language would exclude those who don't speak it.

From among India's officially recognized languages, individual states are free to adopt their own language of administration and education. Every citizen has the right to petition the government in any of the official languages. Yet, English is India's most important language for national, political, and commercial communication.

India has 61 million Internet users. Currently, as the predominant language on the Internet in India is English, Facebook and Orkut are the top two social networks in India. The extent of social media use in India became known during the terrorist attacks on Mumbai in 2008. An estimated 80 eyewitness tweets were being sent to Twitter.com via SMS every five seconds. Mumbai-based bloggers turned their Metroblog into a news wire service, and the blog MumbaiHelp offered to help users get through to their family and friends in the city, or to get information about them (Busari, 2008).

Indian call center.

South Africa

The first Dutch settlement on the southern tip of Africa dates back to 1652, followed by the arrival of Dutch, German, and French Huguenot immigrants (later known as Afrikaners or as Boers by the British). Dutch became the official language of that colony, but within 150 years, it had been replaced with Afrikaans, perhaps the world's youngest language and the only Germanic language born outside Europe.

Afrikaans was derived from 17th-century Dutch and reflects the influences of Malay, Portuguese, German, French, English, and native African languages. It represents a cultural tradition of self-sufficiency and Calvinist morality. For many years, speakers of Afrikaans were the oppressed under British colonial rule. But in 1925, Afrikaans joined English as one of the country's two official languages. From then on it earned the reputation among Blacks as the language of oppression. The most widely known word in the Afrikaans vocabulary is *apart-heid*—literally *apart-hood* or separateness—government-sanctioned segregation of racial and ethnic groups that ended with Nelson Mandela's election in 1994.

The most commonly spoken languages in South Africa are Zulu (24% of the population) and Xhosa (18%), followed by Afrikaans (13%), Tswana, Northern Sotho, English (perceived as the language of colonial heritage), and Southern Sotho. English is the first language for only 8% of the population, but it is gaining popularity as the second language. The multitude of languages became a major factor in developing a new constitution. English and Afrikaans now will join nine others as official languages.

English may play a role in bridging South Africa's divides, as can be seen with the changes taking place on South Africa's state radio. The English-speaking elite were the audience for the state-owned radio station known as Radio South Africa. Now known as SAfm, the radio of the new South Africa, African-accented English is becoming the norm just as African-accented English is becoming the lingua franca of the country.

Australia and New Zealand

The continent of Australia, along with the island state of Tasmania, is approximately equal in area to the continental United States. The first inhabitants of Australia were the Aboriginals, who migrated there at least 40,000 years ago from Southeast Asia. It's estimated that there may have been a half million to a million Aboriginals at the time of European contact. Today, Aboriginals number about 1% of the total population of 18.7 million.

The first English speakers to arrive in number in Australia were convicts and their guards, who put ashore in 1788 at the penal colony of Botany Bay. (Convicted under the penal code of the day, their offenses would be considered minor today.) The convict argot was known as flash and was so incomprehensible to speakers of Standard English that an interpreter was sometimes needed in the courts. Flash began to die out as former convicts joined new English and Irish immigrants in developing a unique Australian English with some words borrowed from the Aboriginals (Stevenson, 1999).

New Zealand English shares much with Australia's, but each has unique words and idioms. After seal and whale hunters came other European traders and merchants, primarily British, were attracted by flax, forests, and trade with the Māori. Māori, the indigenous language of New Zealand, and English are recognized as official languages in New Zealand. The Māori comprise 7.4% of the nation's 4.3 million population. Māori is an Austronesian language similar to Hawaiian and Samoan and particularly close to the language of the Cook Islands and Tahiti. There were regional dialects, some of which diverged radically, but they have lost influence to a standard dialect. On the South Island, which is dominated by one tribe, the Southern dialect persists.

The final two decades of the 20th century saw an enthusiasm for the survival of the Māori language. Most notable were the efforts of Māori women to establish *kōhanga reo* (language nests) where preschool children are introduced to the language. The first *kōhanga reo* was established in 1982. There are now more than 700, providing immersion education for more than 13,000 children.

> ## Global Voices
>
> *Whänau ana te tamaiti, mauria atu ka whakamau ki te ü, ä, hei reira tonu ka tïmata te körero Mäori atu ki a ia.*
>
> Translation: When a child is born, take it, put it to the breast, and begin speaking Māori at that point.
>
> —Kaumatua Hui, 1980, Te Kōhanga Reo National Trust (www .kohanga.ac.nz)

Canada

The situation in Canada is unique. More than 200 years ago, Canada's French settlers were defeated by the British army on a Quebec field called the Plains of Abraham. New France then became British, but the French settlers were permitted to maintain their language (French) and religion (Roman Catholicism). By itself, Quebec would be the world's 18th largest country in size. Its population is about 7.9 million, about one quarter of Canada's population.

Through the years, Quebec has maintained a vision of itself as a French-speaking society. Several generations chose to keep their language and culture. Canadian French has retained characteristics of the language of the 18th century. To the modern French, Canadian French has a somewhat monotonous intonation and lacks articulation (Stevenson, 1999). Colloquialism, slang, and accents differ widely. Quebec supports French-language artists, newspapers, radio, and television. More than 80% of its population speaks French as the first language. In the 1950s, Quebec began to protest the use of English.

In response, the federal government appointed the Royal Commission on Bilingualism and Biculturalism. The commission first recommended that Canadians of French origin be brought into full participation in Canadian life and later included all other cultural groups. In 1971, the prime minister announced officially that Canada would be bilingual and multicultural. Officially a two-language country, Canada continues to deal with a strong separatist movement in Quebec. Quebec has never ratified the Canadian constitution because it is believed that it fails to protect the province's minority French language and culture. In 1977, Quebec established a French-only policy enforced by 400 "language police." Its inhabitants refer to the rest of Canada as "English Canada" and propose withdrawing from English-speaking Canada. The phrase *nous et les autres* (us and the others) united Quebecers against the English-speaking Canadians and the fast-growing immigrant population that claims neither French nor English as its first language.

Road sign in English and Squamish in British Columbia.

United States

Whereas Canada has two official languages and India many, the United States has none. Nowhere does the U.S. Constitution provide for an official language, although having one was seriously considered. German, French, Greek, and Hebrew were suggested. At the time of independence, the second language in the United States was a form of German known as Pennsylvania Dutch or Pennsylvania German. Half the population of Pennsylvania spoke German. Even an 1863 Pennsylvania law mandated that all official notices appear in German-language newspapers. German was the country's most common second language during the 19th century. Table 6.4 shows the languages spoken at home today.

After independence, there have been times when some have pressed to make English the official language of the United States. In the 1870s, faced with large numbers of Chinese immigrants, California considered English-only laws. Later, with the large number of central and southeastern Europe immigrants at the turn of the 20th century, the United States made oral English literacy a requirement for naturalization in 1906. Still later, during and after World War I, anti-German sentiment led some states to ban German, remove German-language books from libraries, and close German-language theaters (Crawford, 1992). Those laws were declared unconstitutional. During World War II, German-speaking residents of the United States experienced humiliation and insult because of their accents. Since 1950, the requirement for citizenship has been "to read, write, and speak words in ordinary English." Even so, the United States has had a long history of non-English-speaking immigrants. In 1848, Cincinnati, Ohio, had the first bilingual school to serve the German-American community. In the early 1900s,

Table 6.4   Selected Languages Spoken in U.S. Homes

	1980	1990	2000	2007	Percentage change 1980–2007
Total	23,060,040	31,844,979	46,951,595	55,444,485	140.4
Vietnamese	197,588	507,069	1,009,627	1,207,004	510.9
Russian	173,226	241,798	706,242	851,174	391.4
Korean	266,280	626,478	894,063	1,062,337	299.0
Chinese	630,806	1,319,462	2,022,143	2,464,572	290.7
Persia	106,992	201,865	312,085	349,686	226.8
Spanish or Spanish Creole	11,116,194	17,345,064	28,101,052	34,547,077	210.8
German	1,586,593	1,547,987	1,383,442	1,104,354	−30.4
Yiddish	315,953	213,064	178,945	158,991	−49.7
Italian	1,618,344	1,308,648	1,008,370	798,801	−50.6

Source: From the Census Bureau (Shin & Kominski, 2010).

Translated into English: "Quebec separatists want to know what's wrong with dividing a nation along cultural boundaries. . . ."

a dozen states had bilingual education, with at least 4% of students receiving all or part of their instruction in German. At one time, more than 4,100 schools taught German (Grosjean, 1982). By 1920, 75% of the population of some cities were foreign born. Several cities and states printed some official documents in languages other than English (Crawford, 1992).

Before 1980, only two states had official-English laws: Nebraska in 1920 and Illinois in 1923. By the 1950s, Spanish had effectively become the second language. In the 1980s, the official-English movement became active, due in large part to the large numbers of Hispanic immigrants, some of whom had not assimilated as quickly as earlier immigrants. Immigrant children have been taught the Pledge of Allegiance in foreign languages, and the Immigration and Naturalization Service has conducted citizenship ceremonies in Spanish. Residents of southern Florida and southern California could use a 1040 tax return printed in Spanish. (The form was discontinued when only 718 were returned out of a half-million distributed.) A 1992 amendment to the federal Voting Rights Act requires counties to supply voting materials for Hispanic, Asian-American, American Indian, and Alaskan minority groups that number 10,000 or more, speak little or no English, and have a literacy rate below the national average.

Hispanics currently represent 70% or more of the population in 13 U.S. cities, including Santa Ana, Salinas, Oxnard, and Pomona in California; Laredo, Brownsville, McAllen, and El Paso in Texas; and Miami, Florida. It is said that it's possible to live a full life in Miami without ever learning English. Miami has bilingual stores and restaurants, Spanish print and electronic media, and jobs for which only Spanish is required. Miami had an English-only ordinance but has since repealed it. In 2006 an ensemble of Latino pop music stars sang a Spanish-language version of "The Star Spangled Banner" called "Nuestro Himno" on Spanish language radio stations to inspire solidarity for a protest over immigration reform. President Bush voiced his opinion that the national anthem should be English-only.

In 1969, the federal government began providing funds for programs to help children with limited English. In 1974, the Supreme Court ruled in *Lau v. Nichols,* a class-action suit against the San Francisco Unified School District, that schools that don't provide special help for children with limited English are violating these students' civil rights. In the Court's language:

> The failure of the San Francisco school system to provide English language instruction to approximately 1,800 students of Chinese ancestry who do not speak English, or to provide them with other adequate instructional procedures, denies them a meaningful opportunity to participate in the public educational program and thus violates . . . the Civil Rights Act of 1964. (*Lau v. Nichols,* 1974, p. 203)

In effect, the Court held that there is no equality of treatment of students who don't understand English.

As their ruling didn't specify what form this help should take, the Court did not require bilingual education. The Federal Bilingual Education Act of 1978 defined bilingual education as a program of instruction designed for children of limited English proficiency to achieve competence in English and to progress effectively through the education system.

Other arguments to make English the official language point to the millions spent on bilingual education, bilingual ballots, high school equivalency diploma tests, driving tests in foreign languages, and instant translation of court proceedings for defendants who don't speak English. Emergency and health care organizations would face a burden of providing information in all the languages spoken in the United States.

One of the organizations supporting official-English laws was founded with the guidance of former U.S. Senator Hayakawa. U.S. English, a political lobbying organization, argues that because of the influx of Hispanic immigrants, the United States risks becoming divided linguistically and culturally like Canada. Between 1984 and 1988, 12 states passed resolutions making English the official language. During the 1996 election campaign, the U.S. House of Representatives passed the English Language Empowerment Act that would make English the official language. And in 2006, the U.S. Senate voted to declare English the "national language" in an amendment to an immigration bill. By 2010, 31 states had measures making English the official language, and legislation was pending in others. Generally, the laws don't affect what language is spoken in homes or in neighborhoods; the laws do prohibit the states from printing documents, such as voter information pamphlets, in other languages.

So far, courts have shown a tendency to reverse restrictions from official-English ordinances. In 1988, Arizona voters approved by 50.5% an initiative that made English the official language of the state and the language of "all government functions and actions." A lawsuit was filed by a Spanish-speaking state employee saying the measure barred her from speaking Spanish to Spanish-speaking people. In 1990, a federal district court ruled that Arizona's English-only law

Global Voices

U.S. Senator Jim Inhofe (R. Okla.) and U.S. Rep. Steve King (R. Iowa) reintroduced legislation in 2011 to make English the official language of the U.S. government.

"As a nation built by immigrants, it is important that we share one vision and one official language."

—Sen. Inhofe

violated First Amendment guarantees of free speech. The federal judge ruled that the law curtailed government employees' free-speech rights by prohibiting them from using other languages when dealing with the non-English-speaking population. The citizens group that sponsored the initiative appealed the decision to the Ninth Circuit Court of Appeals, which affirmed the district court ruling. The case was then appealed to the Supreme Court, which ruled in 1997 on procedural problems. As the Arizona state employee who had originally sued had long since resigned, the Supreme Court said that the federal district court had no jurisdiction in the case (*Arizonans for Official English v. Arizona,* 1997), which had the effect of returning the issue to the Arizona state courts. Until that case, or another, reaches the Supreme Court, the state laws stand. The next year, the State Supreme Court ruled that the 1988 voter-approved law provision requiring that official state and local business be conducted only in English violates constitutional free-speech rights and the Fourteenth Amendment's equal protection clause (Crawford, 1992).

FOCUS ON CULTURE 6.1

In 1981, California Senator S. I. Hayakawa introduced an amendment to the U.S. Constitution that would make English the official language of the United States. The new article would state the following:

Section 1. The English language shall be the official language of the United States.

Section 2. The Congress shall have the power to enforce this article by appropriate legislation.

The following comments were made by Hayakawa and quoted in a speech by Senator Symms in the *Congressional Record,* January 22, 1985:

Language is a powerful tool. A common language can unify, separate languages can fracture and fragment a society. The American "melting pot" has succeeded in creating a vibrant new culture among peoples of many diverse cultural backgrounds largely because of the widespread use of common language, English.

The ability to force unity from diversity makes our society strong. We need all the elements. Germans, Hispanics, Hellenes, Italians, Chinese, all the cultures that make our Nation unique. Unless we have a common basis for communicating and sharing ideas, we all lose. The purpose of this proposal is to insure that American democracy always strives to include in its mainstream everyone who aspires to citizenship.

In private employment, though, the court has supported English-only job rules. Since 1970, the U.S. Equal Employment Opportunity Commission has told employers they may not enforce English-only rules except in cases of business necessity. This ruling was tested in 1991 when two employees sued their employer, a South San Francisco meat-processing plant, after having been accused of making racist remarks in Spanish about two coworkers. They alleged that their employer's English-only rule violated a federal law barring on-the-job bias based on national origin. A federal appeals court ruled in favor of the employer, and in 1994, the Supreme Court declined to hear the case, thus leaving the appeals court decision as binding law in nine western states. (First Amendment rights do not apply in this case. Remember, the First Amendment applies to the government, not to private employers. For example, a private employer can prohibit union slogans on T-shirts.)

The other side of the issue is the weakening and disappearance of languages. Hawaiian language and culture, for example, are on the verge of extinction. The same can be said of some indigenous American Indian languages.

The Situation in Hawai'i

The Hawaiians had no written language. Centuries of history, genealogies, legends, and religious teachings were passed from generation to generation orally. New England Christian missionaries who first arrived in 1820 devised a written language based on five vowels and seven consonants (*h, k, 1, m, n, p,* and *w*). The glottal stop, the short break between the pronunciation of two vowels, was acknowledged but not denoted. It later became marked with the "backward apostrophe" as in *u'ina,* the word for the glottal stop. The written language that was developed by the missionaries was not Hawaiian as the Hawaiians know it; it reflected what the New England English speakers perceived (Allen, 1982).

After the overthrow of the Hawaiian monarchy in 1893 by U.S. sugar planters and businessmen, Hawai'i became a republic and sought admission to the United States. The Hawaiian language was officially suppressed when the United States annexed the islands. In 1880, there were 150 schools teaching Hawaiian. A decade later, there were none. Public school regulations written at the turn of the 20th century prohibited the use of Hawaiian in the schools.

By 1990, only about 1,000 native Hawaiian speakers remained, and 200 of those lived on Nihau, the privately owned island that is home to the last self-contained community of full-blooded Hawaiians. The language survived primarily through music and a few popular phrases. Nonetheless, at the 1978 constitutional convention, Hawaiian was made an official language of the state along with English and now is the only indigenous language in the United States that is an official state language.

Indigenous Hawaiians number more than 80,000, which is 5.9% of the state's population of 1.36 million. Recognizing that the loss of the language also means the loss of the culture, Hawaiians started a private preschool language immersion program in 1984. Inspired by the Māori of New Zealand and the Mohawks of Canada, a nonprofit foundation, Aha Punano Leo, which means "language nest" in Hawaiian, was established. In 1986, the state legislature lifted the century-old ban on schools teaching only in Hawaiian. The language immersion program then spread to the public school system. Words had to be created for concepts that didn't exist before such as *huna hohoki* for neutron and *wikio* for video.

Hawai'i was an independent kingdom until 1893, a republic from 1893 to 1898, and annexed to the United States in 1898. This statue honors King Kamehameha I.

Now some 1,400 children are enrolled in Hawaiian immersion schools and some 2,000 others in Hawaiian-focused charter schools. Controversy surrounds the program. Some argue that the program is a chance to save the language and recapture a lost cultural identity; others argue that it is the first step toward a separated society like the French in Canada (Dudley & Agard, 1993).

Loss of American Indian Languages

In colonial times, more than 300 indigenous languages were spoken in North America. Today, only about 175 remain, with Navajo having the most speakers, approximately 148,530 (see Table 6.5). From the 1860s until about the 1950s, federal policy and local practice combined to discourage and eliminate American Indian languages from schools and public settings. In the 1920s, students in federal boarding schools were beaten for using their own language. Yet during World War II, U.S. Marines used Navajo "code talkers" at Guadalcanal and Iwo Jima; the Japanese never managed to decipher signals encoded in the Navajo language.

In 1990, the U.S. Congress passed the Native American Language Act, legislation sponsored by Hawai'i Senator Daniel Inouye. The act endorses the preservation of indigenous languages and encourages the use of American Indian languages as languages of instruction.

Table 6.5   Status of American Indian Languages

	Number	*Examples*
Spoken in homes by children	20	Navajo, Western Apache, Hopi, Zuni
Spoken by parents and elders	30	Crow, Cheyenne, Mesquakie
Spoken only by elders	70	Tlingit, Passamaquoddy, Winnebago, Commanche, Nez Percé, Yakima
Spoken by fewer than 10 elders	55	Eyak, Pawnee, Wichita, Omaha, Washoe

The languages remain used in tribal politics and religious ceremonies and on radio stations. It was said that movement to make English the official U.S. language mobilized many tribes in the recognition that linguistic survival is the same as cultural or tribal survival.

Puerto Rico and Statehood

Another story is being played out in Puerto Rico, where the official language has been a part of the argument over statehood. Populated for centuries by aboriginal peoples, The island was claimed by the Spanish Crown after Columbus's second voyage to the Americas. Under colonial rule, the indigenous population was nearly exterminated and African slave labor introduced. The island was made a U.S. territory after Spain ceded it to the United States as a result of the Spanish-American War in 1898. Residents became U.S. citizens in 1917, and in 1952, Puerto Rico became a commonwealth. Residents cannot vote and pay no federal income tax. A 1967 nonbinding plebiscite had 60.4% voting for commonwealth status, 39% for statehood, and 0.6% for independence. A 1993 nonbinding plebiscite had 48.6% voting for commonwealth status, 46.3% for statehood, and 4.4% for independence. A third plebiscite in 1998 had 46.5% voting for statehood and 50.2% voting "none of the above," which was the commonwealth option. Spanish was made the island's official language in 1991 with the backing of statehood opponents. Proponents of statehood were successful in passing a new law in 1993 that made English and Spanish official languages of the territory. Yet, Spanish predominates. U.S. census bureau data shows that for people at least 5 years old, 95% speak a language other than English at home (U.S. Census Bureau, 2009).

SUMMARY

Language is a set of symbols shared by a community to communicate meaning and experience. New research has shown that our language choices are determined by culture rather than innate rules. The Sapir-Whorf hypothesis establishes the relationship between language and culture: Culture is controlled by *and* controls language.

One way that language can be a barrier to effective intercultural communication is translation problems. Five possible translation problems are lack of vocabulary equivalence, idiomatic equivalence, grammatical-syntactical equivalence, experiential equivalence, and conceptual equivalence. Attempts to communicate when there is no shared language are pidgins, creoles, and universal languages such as Esperanto.

While Spanish and Chinese are spoken by more people than English, English has a special role as an international language. However, that widespread use is seen by some as a threat because the language is seen to carry with it elements of U.S. culture. English is the major language on the Internet.

Many countries have official language laws; the United States does not. India and South Africa have several official languages. New Zealand has two: Māori and English. Canada has French and English. While many languages are spoken in the United States, the two most frequently spoken are English and Spanish. Increases in the immigration of Spanish-speaking peoples have lead to calls for official-English language laws.

DISCUSSION QUESTIONS

1. The relationship between language and culture is a fundamental principle of communication studies. While that relationship can seem obvious in examples, explore that relationship more in depth in such areas as identity and conflict.

2. Mandarin Chinese has more primary and secondary speakers worldwide than English. Why has English been labeled as a threat to other cultures?

3. Can a strong nation exist with two cultures each with a unique language?

4. Develop arguments for both sides of the *Lau v. Nichols* (1974) case.

5. What arguments can be raised for and against official language laws?

KEY TERMS

Arabic 140	dialect 147	language 133
back translation 143	Esperanto 147	literacy rate 156
compound bilingual 136	grammar 140	mother tongue 134
coordinate bilingual 136	idiom 142	pidgin 146
creole 146	Islam 140	Sapir-Whorf hypothesis 136
cultural invasion 147	Koran 140	syntax 135

READINGS

All readings are from *Intercultural Communication: A Global Reader* (Jandt, 2004).

Peter Mühlhäusler, "Babel Revisited" (p. 103)
Amadou Hampaté Bâ, "Africa: The Power of Speech" (p. 108)
Eric Aoki, "Mexican American Ethnicity in Biola, CA: An Ethnographic Account of Hard Work, Family, and Religion" (p. 112)
Kil-Ho Kang, "Korean's Politeness Strategies" (p. 131)
Mark Warschauer, Ghada R. El Said, and Ayman Zohry, "Language Choice Online: Globalization and Identity in Egypt" (p. 160)
Wally Penetito, "Research and Context for a Theory of Māori Schooling" (p. 173)

STUDENT STUDY SITE

Visit the student study site at **www.sagepub.com/jandt7e** for these additional learning tools:

- Web Resources
- Audio and Video Links
- SAGE journal articles
- eFlashcards
- Web Quizzes
- Sample Essays

PART 3

Cultural Values

What makes a human a woman?

The term *gender*, which does not easily translate into other languages, is used to distinguish between biological aspects (e.g., giving birth) and cultural aspects (e.g., responsibilities in the home). These cultural aspects tell us more about the culture than about biology.

In India, in Hindu families, marriage is considered almost compulsory and divorce a tragedy. Yet divorce is increasing as more and more women attend college, enter the labor force, and abandon traditional roles.

Likewise, all Muslim women are expected to marry. In the marriage contract, women receive home, food, clothes, and an inheritance from the man and are not expected to work or support the man. In exchange, men receive the authority to be head of the family.

While in the latter half of the 20th century, nearly all Japanese women married, attitudes are changing. As Japan continues to adapt and adopt foreign ideas, changing identities for women surely will result.

The definitions of *woman* are not only products of culture, but they also can and are changed by women. Women can and do redefine traditional roles and redefine what is meant by *family*.

Sub-Saharan Africa comprises many cultures. In East African cultures, ideas are evolving as traditional practices are adapting to contemporary challenges, none the least of which is AIDS and AIDS orphans.

CHAPTER

7

Dimensions of Culture

FOCUS QUESTIONS

- What are ways of describing cultures that go beyond language and customs?

- What characterizes the Japanese culture?

- How do cultures vary in values attached to environmental sustainability?

Individualism Versus Collectivism
　　　Case Study: Japan as a Homogeneous Culture
　　　　　History
　　　　　Religion
　　　　　Cultural Patterns
Masculinity Versus Femininity
Power Distance
Uncertainty Avoidance
Long-Term Versus Short-Term Orientation
　　　Case Study: Singapore
Enviromental Sustainability
Summary
Discussion Questions
Key Terms
Readings
Student Study Site

In 1980, the Dutch management researcher Geert Hofstede first published the results of his study of more than 100,000 employees of the multinational IBM in 40 countries (Hofstede, 1980, 1983, 1984, 1991, 1997, 2001). Hofstede was attempting to locate value dimensions across which cultures vary. His dimensions have been used frequently to describe cultures.

Hofstede identified four dimensions that he labeled individualism, masculinity, power distance, and uncertainty avoidance. His individualism-collectivism dimension describes cultures from loosely structured to tightly integrated. The masculinity-femininity dimension describes how a culture's dominant values are assertive or nurturing. Power distance refers to the distribution of influence within a culture. And uncertainty avoidance reflects a culture's tolerance of ambiguity and acceptance of risk.

Hofstede and Bond (1984; also see Chinese Culture Connection, 1987) identified a fifth dimension, a Confucian work dynamism, also labeled *long-term orientation versus short-term orientation to life*. The Confucian work dynamism dimension describes cultures that range from short-term values with respect for tradition and reciprocity in social relations to long-term values with persistence and ordering relationships by status.

When reading this chapter, and particularly when reading the lists of countries that exhibit or fail to exhibit each dimension, you might think of exceptions: individuals from a culture who do not act as might be implied by these lists. These lists reflect an overall average; no one person should be expected to fit that average exactly. Indeed, to expect so would be stereotyping.

FOCUS ON THEORY 7.1

Young Yun Kim (2005) characterizes individualism-collectivism as top of the list of theories guiding cross-cultural research in communication, psychology, and anthropology. Individualist cultures stress self-direction and self-achievement; collectivist cultures stress in-group loyalty and conformity. This rich area of research has focused on competition and cooperation, conversational constraints, handling disagreements, silence, face work and conflict style, and in-group and out-group communication patterns.

Kim draws a relationship with individualism-collectivism and Edward T. Hall's (1976) theory of high-context and low-context cultures (see Chapter 3). Characterizations of high-context and low-context communication systems are closely associated with the characteristics of individualism and collectivism.

INDIVIDUALISM VERSUS COLLECTIVISM

First is individualism versus collectivism. This dimension refers to how people define themselves and their relationships with others. In an individualist culture, the interest of the individual prevails over the interests of the group. Ties between individuals are loose. People look after themselves and their immediate families. Masakazu (1994) defines modern individualism as "a view of humanity that justifies inner beliefs and unilateral self-assertion, as well as competition based on these" (p. 127). In a collectivist culture, the interest of the group prevails over the interest of the individual. People are integrated into strong, cohesive in-groups that continue throughout a lifetime to protect in exchange for unquestioning loyalty (Hofstede, 1997). One difference is reflected in who is taken into account when you set goals. In individualist cultures, goals are set with minimal consideration given to groups other than perhaps your immediate family. In collectivist cultures, other groups are taken into account in a major way when goals are set. Individualist cultures are loosely integrated; collectivist cultures are tightly integrated.

In individualist cultures such as the United States, for example, when meeting a new person, you want to know what that person does. You tend to define people by what they have done, their accomplishments, what kind of car they drive, or where they live. Individualist cultures are more remote and distant (see Table 7.1).

Cultures characterized by collectivism emphasize relationships among people to a greater degree. Collectivist cultures stress interdependent activities and suppressing individual aims for the group's welfare. Often, it is difficult for individuals from highly individualist cultures to understand collectivist values. This example may help: A student from Colombia may study in the United States and earn a PhD, teach at a distinguished university, and publish important books, but when he returns to visit Colombia, people to whom he is introduced will want to know to whom he is related. Colombians want to know who his family is because that places him in society much more so than any of his accomplishments in the United States.

In the United States, few family names—perhaps only Rockefeller, Kennedy, DuPont, Getty—carry such defining meaning. You are not socially defined by your family name but by your individual accomplishments. A generation or two ago, people were introduced by family name, and a new acquaintance then asked permission to use one's given name. The asking and giving of permission was an important stage in the development of a friendship. Today's introduction by one's given name makes no reference to one's family. Individualism is so strong in the United States that you might even have difficulty appreciating how people might feel content in a collectivist culture. Contentment comes from knowing your place and from knowing you have a place.

In the workplace, in individualist cultures, the employer-employee relationship tends to be established by contract, and hiring and promotion decisions are based on skills and rules; in collectivist cultures, the employer-employee relationship is perceived in moral terms, like a family link, and hiring and promotion decisions take the employee's in-group into account. Hofstede's data revealed several associations with this dimension:

- *Wealth.* There is a strong relationship between a nation's wealth and individualism.
- *Geography.* Countries with moderate and cold climates tend to show more individualism.

Table 7.1 Individualism Rankings for 50 Countries and Three Regions

1	United States	28	Turkey
2	Australia	29	Uruguay
3	Great Britain	30	Greece
4/5	Canada	31	Philippines
4/5	The Netherlands	32	Mexico
6	New Zealand	33/35	East Africa
7	Italy	33/35	Yugoslavia
8	Belgium	33/35	Portugal
9	Denmark	36	Malaysia
10/11	Sweden	37	Hong Kong
10/11	France	38	Chile
12	Ireland	39/41	West Africa
13	Norway	39/41	Singapore
14	Switzerland	39/41	Thailand
15	Germany (F.R.)	42	El Salvador
16	South Africa	43	South Korea
17	Finland	44	Taiwan
18	Austria	45	Peru
19	Israel	46	Costa Rica
20	Spain	47/48	Pakistan
21	India	47/48	Indonesia
22/23	Japan	49	Colombia
22/23	Argentina	50	Venezuela
24	Iran	51	Panama
25	Jamaica	52	Ecuador
26/27	Brazil	53	Guatemala
26/27	Arab countries		

Source: Hofstede (2001, p. 215).

- *Birth Rates.* Countries with higher birth rates tend to be collectivist.
- *History.* Confucian countries are collectivist. Migrants from Europe who populated North America, Australia, and New Zealand tended to be sufficiently individualist to leave their native countries.

Another interesting association with inheritance practices was developed by Knighton (1999). Those cultures that have rules for equal partition of parental property among all offspring tend to be collectivist; those that have rules permitting unequal partition and those that have historically allowed parents to have full freedom in deciding who will inherit tend to be individualist.

Individualism and collectivism have been associated with direct and indirect styles of communication—that is, the extent to which speakers reveal intentions through explicit verbal communication. In the direct style, associated with individualism, the wants, needs, and desires of the speaker are embodied in the spoken message. In the indirect style, associated with collectivism, the wants, needs, and goals of the speaker are not obvious in the spoken message. Rojjanaprapayon (1997), for example, demonstrated specific communication strategies in Thai communication: Thais do not use specific names when they express negative feelings. Thais tend to use words and phrases expressing probability, such as "maybe," "probably," "sometimes," "likely," and "I would say so, but I am not sure." Thais do not show their feelings if doing so would make the other person feel bad. And Thais also use indirect nonverbal communication by having less or avoiding eye contact and keeping greater personal distance.

Case Study: Japan as a Homogeneous Culture

From Hofstede's (1983) research, Japan is placed about in the middle between individualism and collectivism. Yet Japan is popularly stereotyped as a group-oriented culture. In a 1995 study of Japanese students using the original Hofstede questionnaires, Woodring found that students scored higher on individualism and lower on power distance than Hofstede's original sample. Woodring explained that the higher individualism and lower power distance score might be explained by age; that is, Japanese college students may value individualism and equality more than Japanese society does as a whole. Hofstede's longitudinal study did show that national wealth and individualism were related. About 1990, the term *shin jin rui* (literally "new human beings") was applied to youths 25 years old and younger, who were described by older Japanese as "selfish, self-centered, and disrespectful of elders and tradition." Hofstede's study suggested that the Japanese were group-oriented, hierarchical, and formal. There are reasons to suggest that at least younger Japanese prefer moderately egalitarian distribution of power and feel moderately independent of collective thought and action. This demonstrates that we should avoid allowing the Hofstede research to become a stereotype. In 1986, Prime Minister Yasuhiro Nakasone described Japan as being a "homogeneous" country—a widely held view by Japanese society at large. In the following descriptions of Japan's history, religion, and cultural patterns, identify specific ways that homogeneity affects communication.

FOCUS ON THEORY 7.2

Miike (2004) believes that Asian scholars can "paint a number of wonderful portraits about humanity and communication." Miike's own portrait of communication is as "a process in which we remind ourselves of the interdependence and interrelatedness of the universe . . . communication is a process in which we experience the oneness of the universe" (p. 74). In this portrait, we can transcend the illusion of separateness, of fragmentation, and gain a glimpse of the larger relationship of what often appear to be discrete aspects of life (Miike, 2003).

History

Japan is an archipelago formed by four large islands and more than 3,000 small islands covering 377,915 square kilometers, roughly the size of California. Much of the land surface is hilly or mountainous, leaving only 12% arable land. Hence, Japan imports a large amount of its food and relies heavily on the ocean. Seafood is a staple in the Japanese diet, and Japan is the world's leading producer of fish. As an island nation, Japan will never be fully self-sufficient. It has virtually no energy natural resources. It must export in order to import materials it needs to survive.

The population of Japan is approximately 126 million, equivalent to about 40% of the U.S. population, and inhabits only 4% of the land area, which translates to a population density of about 336 people per square kilometer; in the United States, the comparable density is 34. Japan is divided into 47 administrative units or prefectures. More than 67% of Japan's population live in urban areas, with approximately 38% of the population living in the two major metropolitan areas of Tokyo (the largest city in the world) and Osaka-Kobe. More than one in five Japanese are over 65—roughly double that in the United States. In rural areas, the ratio is closer to one in three.

Japan's origins are not clear. It is thought that Chinese culture as it passed through Korea was seminal. Japan is known as the Land of the Rising Sun, as is symbolized on its flag. Founded early in the Christian era, Japan has a parliamentary government with a constitutional monarchy. According to legend, all Japanese are genealogically related to the emperor at some distant point. In pre–World War II Japan, the emperor was worshiped as a living god. Hirohito was the emperor from 1926 until his death in 1989. Tradition dictated that a full year of mourning pass followed by a full season to plant and harvest a crop of sacred rice before his son Akihito could be formally enthroned as a symbolic constitutional monarch in 1990.

Two key points characterize Japanese history: more than 10,000 years of culture continuity and the ability to adapt imported culture and technology to the traditional culture. After Perry's arrival with battleships in 1853, Japan transformed itself from a feudal country into an industrialized nation by adapting Western technology. Later, from the mid-1920s to the mid-1930s, urban Japanese experienced U.S. fashions, movies, and music. Following World War II, Japan

Mount Fuji.

again adopted more Western culture. The postwar constitution drafted by Allied occupation authorities and approved by the Japanese parliament made Japan a constitutional monarchy. The new constitution also renounced war and forbade the use of military forces for offensive purposes. Again because of the U.S.-inspired postwar constitution, Japan maintains only a defense force. Over the period from 1960 to 1988, only 0.8% of its gross national product was spent on defense. (In the same period, the United States spent 6.4%.) Japan now pays about 2 billion dollars annually to subsidize U.S. military bases in Japan. In response to criticism for not providing troops in the 1991 Gulf War, Japan approved providing troops for the United Nations' peacekeeping operations in noncombat roles in East Timor, Cambodia, and Afghanistan, and later in Iraq, and it is becoming more engaged in world security issues.

Even after a decade of poor economic performance, Japan remains the world's third largest economy, with several world-class companies that are technological leaders and household names. Japan is a major foreign investor and a major foreign aid donor. Japanese life and language are Westernized. U.S. popular culture reaches Japan more quickly than it reaches parts of the United States. English loan words in the Japanese language grow at a fast rate. Japan's Westernization has been criticized by some Asian countries.

Religion

Japan is one of the most homogeneous countries in the world: More than 98% of its population is Japanese; Koreans, Chinese, and native Ainu constitute most of the remaining 2%. In 1997, Japan's parliament, or *diet,* voted to replace a century-old law that forced the Ainu to assimilate. The Ainu were recognized by the United Nations as a native people in 1992 and the Japanese Diet called for their recognition as an indigenous people in 2008. The Ainu still face discrimination in Japan.

Except among the older people, religion is not a strong force. Christianity was brought to Japan by Jesuit missionaries in 1549. Though less than 1% of the population is Christian, Christian lifestyles, moral codes, and ethics have become part of Japanese life. The majority of the population traditionally practices a syncretistic combination of Shinto and Buddhism. Shinto is exclusively nationalistic. It was the state religion from the Meiji Restoration of 1868 until the end of World War II. It is not so much a creed as it is a link to ancestors and Gods. Shinto means "the way of the Gods" and has three predominant ideas: worship of the Gods of Japan, loyalty to Japan, and cultivation of a pure Japanese spirit. Almost all Japanese are born Shinto. It is said that to be Japanese and to be a Shintoist are synonymous. There are two types of Shintoism: Popular Shinto, which has its strength in the home, and Sect Shinto, which believes in reincarnation and service to humanity as service to God. A third type, State Shinto, which taught that the Japanese were separate from other races, excelling in virtue, intelligence, and courage, was abolished by order of the Allies in 1945.

Buddhism came to Japan from Korea in the mid-6th century. More than 200 sects of Buddhism exist in Japan, with wide differences in doctrines. Buddhism has been called the "adopted faith of Japan" and centers on the temple and the family altar. Most households observe some ceremonies of both religions, such as a Shinto wedding and a Buddhist funeral. Overall, though, religion is more a social tradition than a conviction. Some charge that due to a lack of religious beliefs, the Japanese have no principles. Meditation, aesthetic appreciation, ritual cleansing, and a respect for nature's beauty and humans' part in it are important cultural beliefs.

FOCUS ON CULTURE 7.1

The Buddhist term for individual is *santana,* or stream. It is intended to capture the idea of interconnectedness between people and their environment and between generations. Buddhist teaching places an emphasis on personal responsibility to achieve change in the world through change in personal behavior.

Source: United Nations Development Programme (2008, p. 61).

A study by Hajime Nakamura (1964) of the National Institute of Science and Technology Policy in Japan asked citizens to name aspects of their country of which they were proudest. Topping that list was Japan's maintenance of social order, followed by its natural beauty, its history and traditions, the diligence and talent of its people, the high level of education, the country's prosperity, and its culture and arts.

In recent years, Japan's performance in education has fallen—in math skills from first to tenth place and in science from second to sixth in an international survey behind Taiwan, Hong Kong, and South Korea. Now India is seen as an educational model—something unheard of just a few years ago.

Cultural Patterns

Critical to understanding the cultural patterns of Japan is the homogeneity of its population, although some would argue that Japan is not all that homogeneous. However, the cultural myth of homogeneity is believed and therefore is an important cultural concept. Because it is an island country and hence borders on no other countries, Japan was little affected by foreign influence until 1853. Japan's isolation means that its history is its own. Everyone shares the same ideas and, lacking outside influences, has no reason to doubt them. In addition, as a small, densely populated country, its ideas and information are easily shared. Even the tradition of rice growing contributes to a society based on cooperation, minimizing conflict, and enhanced cooperation, which, like the rice, are all necessary for survival.

Japan's homogeneity contributes to its people's "communication without language" (Tsujimura, 1968, 1987). It is said that being monolingual and monoracial makes it easy for the Japanese to understand each other with few words. The United States, with its high level of diversity, is verbose—more talking is required to overcome diverse languages, diverse lifestyles, and diverse ways of feeling and thinking. Japanese axioms teach that verbosity is dangerous: "Least said, soonest mended" and "Out of the mouth comes evil." Today, the education system maintains those same cultural values. All schools have the same curriculum. Schools have uniforms and encourage students to take part in after-school group activities.

Japanese worldview is consistent with that of an isolated island. There is no differentiation: People from the United States, Europe, and other parts of Asia are foreigners. The world is divided into Japan and others: *gaikoku,* or outside nation, and gaijin, or outside person.

Japan has often been described as a society in which conflict is avoided by emphasizing homogeneity and dismissing differentness as incidental. The Japanese do not have the same perception of self as an individual that is typical in the United States; instead, the Japanese feel most comfortable with others who empathize. To be completely understood, people have to cooperate in the same context, and in doing so, there can be no differentiation of individuals. In such an extremely homogeneous society, you are not seen as an individual, nor do you regard individualism as a positive trait. It has been said that group life is to the Japanese what individualism is to the United States. Homogeneity is the core value of society that substantially defines other values and permeates all areas of life. This social interdependence has been referred to by Takeo Doi (1956, 1973) as amae (noun that comes from the verb *amaeru,* which means to look to others for support and affection). *Amae* is the feeling of nurturing for and dependence on another. *Amae* is a sense of complete dependence based on a wish to be loved and cared for unconditionally. It develops in the relationship between mother and child and later transfers to the child's teachers and others in positions of authority. *Amae* is a reciprocal relationship. Just as the child is dependent on the mother, the mother is dependent on the child, which arises from the need to be needed. *Amae,* with its emphasis on interdependence, contrasts sharply with individualism. (See Focus on Culture 7.2 for a description of how the game of baseball reflects Japanese cultural patterns.)

Japan is changing. The younger generation is more independent and worldly. Perhaps Japan is beginning to recognize that it is not as homogeneous as the cultural myth suggests. Japan is beginning to identify itself more in terms of nationality rather than ethnicity. Traditional mores

FOCUS ON CULTURE 7.2

Sporty Japanese Import

 Japan began to adopt many modern Western ideas during the Meiji restoration (1867–1912). U. S. professors in Japan may have first organized games with their students in 1872. The game became known as Yakkyu, or "field ball." The Japanese saw the psychology between the pitcher and batter similar to the psychology in sumo and martial arts and appreciated the timing and mental and physical strength the game required (Whiting, 1989). Interest grew when the Giants and the Chicago White Sox came to Japan in 1910, and later Babe Ruth, Lou Gehrig, Jimmy Foxx, and numerous other stars played against Japanese college all-stars. Japan's first professional team, the Great Tokyo baseball club was formed in December 1934.

After World War II, the Allied command official allowed the game to resume as a way to boost morale. By 1950, teams became supported by large corporations. Teams were organized into two leagues, the Central and Pacific, each with six teams.

According to Whiting, a Japanese writer summed up his country's love for the game by saying, "Baseball is perfect for us, if the Americans hadn't invented it, we would have (p. 51).

Yet, there are cultural differences. Jim Allen, author of the 1996 *Jim Allen's Guide To Japanese Baseball,* described one difference: "The rules are essentially the same, even though there are some minor differences in score keeping and such. Ideologically, the purpose of the game is a little different. In America the purpose of the game is to do your best by contributing to the team in every way you

(Continued)

(Continued)

Japan Samurai Bears.

can. In Japan, the purpose of the game is to contribute to the team by not doing certain things: not showing off, or being individualistic. Showing off would be considered a distraction to the team. It is a mirror image of Japanese society." (Jim Allen, interview at http://mcel.pacificu.edu/as/students/baseballjapan/jimall.html) "Everything from the way the players respectfully doff their caps when addressed by their coach to their strategy and philosophy of the game is infused with elements of Japanese culture (Gillette, 1991).

For 20 years, the Yakult Swallows went to Yuma, Arizona, for training. (February is Japan's coldest month.) "To feed baseball frenzy, representatives of six Japanese TV stations, two radio stations, two news agencies, six all-sports dailies, and two general newspapers are on hand to record the Swallows' every move" (Gillette, 1991).

During training, the Swallows do everything as a team. "There is little room for individualism in Japanese baseball, as opposed to American baseball. The Americans like to do their own thing. Some observers say the stifling of initiative hampers Japanese baseball, but others say obedience, discipline, and respect for authority simply reflect their country's culture. American players have traditionally found it difficult to adjust to baseball in Japan. They face a different pitching style, different strike zones, inconsistent umpires, and a different philosophy and strategy (Gillette, 1991).

One difference in strategy is that Japanese coaches believe it is easier to win while their team in ahead, so press for runs in the early innings. But when a team is ahead, the team doesn't go for a big lead to allow the opposing team to save face.

Sources:

Whiting, Robert. *You Gotta Have Wa*. New York: Macmillan Publishing co. 1989.

Gillette (1991). Copyright © 1991, Automobile Club of Southern California. Reprinted by permission, courtesy of Westways.

are becoming less important as Japan becomes more international. Many feel that modern Japan cannot continue to value the communication subtleties that are not easily understood by non-Japanese.

Yet there is evidence that the traditional mores are still deep seated. On March 11, 2011, a 9.0 earthquake and accompanying tsunami hit in northern Japan near Sendai, a city of 1 million people 304 kilometers north of Tokyo. News reports worldwide showed the massive damage to buildings and roadways and loss of life. They also showed people patiently waiting in lines for water and fuel and to enter supermarkets. There was a lack of looting and of egregious price gouging. Researcher Brigitte Steger recorded the daily lives of people displaced by the tsunami. She found that people were driven toward honest behavior by what she called social balance. In fact, by early fall, in Japan's culture of honesty and altruism, citizens had turned over to authorities more than $48 million in found loose cash in the area damaged by the tsunami (Coulton & Glionna, 2011).

The term *Yamato-damashi,* or Japanese spirit, refers to group responsibility and collective consciousness. In that time of crisis, Japanese politesse and an ingrained instinct for orderliness and calm kept hold. In Tokyo, the earthquake temporarily closed the public transportation system. When trains appeared, there was no pushing—the queues were as orderly as on any other day.

The earthquake and tsunami also ravaged the Fukushima nuclear power plant. Fifty workers stayed behind to fight the fires and keep the reactors from melting down. They became

Rather than looting or crowds, after the 2011 earthquake people in Japan waited patiently in line for food and water.

Japan is one of the world's most wired countries: In 2009, Japan had 44 million telephones and 115 million cell phones (seventh among the world's countries). At 99 million users, Internet use ranked third in the world. During the 2011 earthquake crisis, information distribution was constant and widespread. National television networks, newspapers, radio, and Internet sources provided information at local and national levels. The crisis called attention to the special needs of Japan's elderly: Tea kettles with wireless technology warn distant children if a parent doesn't use it every morning.

known as the "Faceless Fifty." It was said that in watching news reports of the Faceless Fifty risking their lives for the common good, the Japanese saw a quiet selflessness and recognized themselves. The group first mentality remains in this essentially ethnically homogeneous society. While some say it is a sensitivity "bred" into the Japanese, it is really cultural learning from parents and teachers (Magnier, 2011).

MASCULINITY VERSUS FEMININITY

The second dimension across which cultures vary is **masculinity versus femininity**. Hofstede (1980) found that women's social role varied less from culture to culture than men's. He labeled as masculine cultures those that strive for maximal distinction between what women and men are expected to do. Cultures that place high values on masculine traits stress assertiveness, competition, and material success. Those labeled as feminine cultures are those that permit more overlapping social roles for the sexes. Cultures that place high value on feminine traits stress quality of life, interpersonal relationships, and concern for the weak. Table 7.2 shows examples of both types.

Table 7.2 Masculinity Rankings for 50 Countries and Three Regions

1	Japan	28	Singapore
2	Austria	29	Israel
3	Venezuela	30/31	Indonesia
4/5	Italy	30/31	West Africa
4/5	Switzerland	32/33	Turkey
6	Mexico	32/33	Taiwan
7/8	Ireland	34	Panama
7/8	Jamaica	35/36	Iran
9/10	Great Britain	35/36	France
9/10	Germany	37/38	Spain
11/12	Philippines	37/38	Peru
11/12	Colombia	39	East Africa
13/14	South Africa	40	El Salvador
13/14	Ecuador	41	South Korea
15	United States	42	Uruguay
16	Australia	43	Guatemala
17	New Zealand	44	Thailand
18/19	Greece	45	Portugal
18/19	Hong Kong	46	Chile
20/21	Argentina	47	Finland
20/21	India	48/49	Yugoslavia
22	Belgium	48/49	Costa Rica
23	Arab countries	50	Denmark
24	Canada	51	The Netherlands
25/26	Malaysia	52	Norway
25/26	Pakistan	53	Sweden
27	Brazil		

Source: Hofstede (2001, p. 286).

It is important to understand that these traits apply to both women and men; that is, both women and men learn to be ambitious and competitive in masculine cultures, and both women and men learn to be modest in feminine cultures. From his study of Thais in the United States, Rojjanaprapayon (1997) notes that masculinity in all cultures is not the same as Hofstede's Western concept of masculinity as assertiveness, aggressiveness, and goal orientation. Thais can be very aggressive and goal-oriented in some situations but are expected to be attentive, supportive, and yielding. Rojjanaprapayon suggests labeling this dimension more appropriately as affection.

In the workplace, in masculine cultures, managers are expected to be decisive and assertive; in feminine cultures, managers use intuition and strive for consensus. Solidarity and quality of life are stressed. Hofstede's data revealed two associations with this dimension:

- *Geography.* Feminine cultures are somewhat more likely in colder climates.
- *Birth Rates.* In feminine cultures, the woman has a stronger say in the number of children. In masculine cultures, the man determines family size.

POWER DISTANCE

The third dimension is **power distance**, or the way the culture deals with inequalities. Hofstede (1997) defines power distance as "the extent to which less powerful members of institutions and organizations within a country expect and accept that power is distributed unequally" (p. 28). Table 7.3 shows countries' rankings on this dimension. Hofstede believes that power distance is learned early in families. In high power distance cultures, children are expected to be obedient toward parents versus being treated more or less as equals. In high power distance cultures, people are expected to display respect for those of higher status. For example, in countries such as Burma (Myanmar), Cambodia, Laos, and Thailand, people are expected to display respect for monks by greeting and taking leave of monks with ritualistic greetings, removing hats in the presence of a monk, dressing modestly, seating monks at a higher level, and using a vocabulary that shows respect.

Mitigated speech is a linguistic term describing deferential or indirect speech in communication between individuals of perceived high power distance (Ng & Bradac, 1993). The term has been popularized in the book, *Outliers* (Gladwell, 2008), where it is defined as "sugarcoating" the meaning of what is being said (p. 194). In a much cited example, Gladwell gives one explanation of why Korean Air Lines (KAL) had one of the worst crash records from the late 1980s to the late 1990s. There was a higher chance for a crash when the most experienced pilots flew. As we saw in an earlier chapter, the Korean language has honorifics and deferential language that separates societal ranks. The culture reinforces power distance. What was happening was that the subordinate or lesser pilot would pay extreme deference to the senior captain and not overtly challenge the senior

Table 7.3 Power Distance Rankings for 50 Countries and Three Regions

1	Malaysia	27/28	South Korea
2/3	Guatemala	29/30	Iran
2/3	Panama	29/30	Taiwan
4	Philippines	31	Spain
5/6	Mexico	32	Pakistan
5/6	Venezuela	33	Japan
7	Arab countries	34	Italy
8/9	Ecuador	35/36	Argentina
8/9	Indonesia	35/36	South Africa
10/11	India	37	Jamaica
10/11	West Africa	38	United States
12	Yugoslavia	39	Canada
13	Singapore	40	The Netherlands
14	Brazil	41	Australia
15/16	France	42/44	Costa Rica
15/16	Hong Kong	42/44	Germany (F.R.)
17	Colombia	42/44	Great Britain
18/19	El Salvador	45	Switzerland
18/19	Turkey	46	Finland
20	Belgium	47/48	Norway
21/23	East Africa	47/48	Sweden
21/23	Peru	49	Ireland
21/23	Thailand	50	New Zealand
24/25	Chile	51	Denmark
24/25	Portugal	52	Israel
26	Uruguay	53	Austria
27/28	Greece		

Source: Hofstede (2001, p. 87).

captain's stewardship of the plane. The subordinate pilot would only use deferential language that never directly challenged the captain nor changed the captain's mind about dangerous situations that should have been obvious. Korean Air instituted a major revision of pilot training. All KAL pilots must be fluent in English and train with U.S. pilots to help break down power distance behaviors. KAL has become one of the safest airlines today.

Power distance also refers to the extent to which power, prestige, and wealth are distributed within a culture. Cultures with high power distance have power and influence concentrated in the hands of a few rather than distributed throughout the population. These countries tend to be more authoritarian and may communicate in a way to limit interaction and reinforce the differences between people.

Two indicators of power distance are income and wealth distributions. The degree of income distribution has been studied in 134 countries on a scale that ranges from zero (everyone in the country has the same income) to 100 (one person in the country has all the income) with what is called the Gini coefficient. Rankings and ratings of selected countries are shown in Table 7.4.

The United States is becoming higher in power distance. The year 2002 was the year of Enron and other corporate scandals. Their chief executive officers (CEOs) had taken excessive

Table 7.4 Income Equality in Selected Countries

Country	Gini Coefficient
1. Sweden	23.0
2. Norway	25.0
17. Denmark	29.0
25. Australia	30.5
35. Canada	32.1
56. India	36.8
61. Japan	38.1
68. Israel	39.2
81. Chin	41.5
90. Iran	44.5
93. United States	45.0
107. Mexico	48.2
125. Brazil	56.7
133. South Africa	65.0

Source: Domhoff (2011).

compensation. In the United States in 1980, the average CEO salary was 42 times as much as the average worker. In 1990, it was 85 times as much. In 2000, it was 525 times as much. (By 2007, it had dropped to 344 times as much.) Japan began to worry when its CEOs were making more than 8 times the factory worker's wage. In 1977, the top 1% in the United States had an after-tax income equal to the bottom 49 million; in 1999, the top 1% had an after-tax income equal to the bottom 100 million. Brazil has one of the largest gaps: One of the 10 richest economies in the world, its poor constitute half the population but earn only 13% of the national income.

The distribution of wealth is not necessarily the same as distribution of income. Table 7.5 shows selected national rankings.

A country can have a highly concentrated wealth distribution and still have a more equal distribution of income, such as is the case in Switzerland and Sweden. Compared to other industrialized democracies, in the United States both wealth and income distributions are highly concentrated (Domhoff, 2011).

In the high power distance workplace, superiors and subordinates consider each other existentially unequal. Power is centralized, and a wide salary gap exists between the top and bottom of the organization. In cultures high in power distance, for example, corporate presidents' offices are more likely to be luxurious, with controlled access. Company bosses are "kings" and employees "loyal subjects" who don't speak out. In the low power distance workplace, subordinates expect to be consulted, and ideal bosses are democratic. In more democratic organizations, leaders are physically more accessible. Marcus and Gould (2000) applied

Table 7.5   Percentage of Wealth Held in 2000 by the Top 10% of the Adult Population in Various Western Countries

Country	Wealth Owned by Top 10%
Switzerland	71.3%
United States	69.8%
Denmark	65.0%
France	61.0%
Sweden	58.6%
United Kingdom	56.0%
Canada	53.0%
Norway	50.5%
Germany	44.4%
Finland	42.3%

Source: Domhoff (2011).

the power distance dimension to website design. They could identify that the prominence given to leaders and the importance given to security and restrictions are related to the power distance of a country. And Robbins and Stylianou (2002) analyzed commercial websites and found a relation between the country of origin's power distance ranking and the frequency of organizational charts on websites.

Hofstede notes four interesting associations with power distance:

- *Geographic Latitude.* Higher latitudes are associated with lower power distance.
- *Population.* Large populations are associated with high power distance.
- *Wealth.* National wealth is associated with lower power distance.
- *History.* Countries with a Romance language (Spanish, Portuguese, Italian, French) score medium to high, as do Confucian cultural inheritance countries. Countries with a Germanic language (German, English, Dutch, Danish, Norwegian, Swedish) score low. Both the Romance language countries and the Confucian cultural inheritance countries were ruled from a single power center, whereas the Germanic language countries remained "barbaric" during Roman days.

UNCERTAINTY AVOIDANCE

Hofstede's (1980) fourth dimension is **uncertainty avoidance**, the extent to which people in a culture feel threatened by uncertain or unknown situations. Hofstede explains that this feeling is expressed through nervous stress and in a need for predictability or a need for written and unwritten rules (Hofstede, 1997). In these cultures, such situations are avoided by maintaining strict codes of behavior and a belief in absolute truths. Cultures strong in uncertainty avoidance are active, aggressive, emotional, compulsive, security seeking, and intolerant. Cultures weak in uncertainty avoidance are contemplative, less aggressive, unemotional, relaxed, accepting of personal risks, and relatively tolerant (see Table 7.6).

Students from high uncertainty avoidance cultures expect their teachers to be experts who have all the answers. And in the workplace, there is an inner need to work hard and a need for rules, precision, and punctuality. Students from low uncertainty avoidance cultures accept teachers who admit to not knowing all the answers. And in the workplace, employees work hard only when needed, there are no more rules than are necessary, and precision and punctuality have to be learned. Hofstede notes two interesting associations with uncertainty avoidance:

- *Religion.* Orthodox and Roman Catholic Christian cultures (except the Philippines and Ireland) score high. Judaic and Muslim cultures tend to score in the middle. Protestant Christian cultures score low. Eastern religions score medium to very low (except Japan).
- *History.* Cultures with a Romance language and history of Roman codified laws score high on uncertainty avoidance. Cultures with Chinese-speaking populations and Confucian tradition tend to score lower.

Table 7.6 Uncertainty Avoidance Rankings for 50 Countries and Three Regions

1	Greece	28	Ecuador
2	Portugal	29	Germany (F.R.)
3	Guatemala	30	Thailand
4	Uruguay	31/32	Iran
5/6	Belgium	31/32	Finland
5/6	El Salvador	33	Switzerland
7	Japan	34	West Africa
8	Yugoslavia	35	The Netherlands
9	Peru	36	East Africa
10/15	France	37	Australia
10/15	Chile	38	Norway
10/15	Spain	39/40	South Africa
10/15	Costa Rica	39/40	New Zealand
10/15	Panama	41/42	Indonesia
10/15	Argentina	41/42	Canada
16/17	Turkey	43	United States
16/17	South Korea	44	Philippines
18	Mexico	45	India
19	Israel	46	Malaysia
20	Colombia	47/48	Great Britain
21/22	Venezuela	47/48	Ireland
21/22	Brazil	49/50	Hong Kong
23	Italy	49/50	Sweden
24/25	Pakistan	51	Denmark
24/25	Austria	52	Jamaica
26	Taiwan	53	Singapore
27	Arab countries		

Source: Hofstede (2001, p. 151).

LONG-TERM VERSUS SHORT-TERM ORIENTATION

In 1987, the "Chinese Culture Connection," composed of Michael H. Bond and others, extended Hofstede's work to include a new dimension they labeled Confucian work dynamism, now more commonly called long-term orientation versus short-term orientation to life. This dimension includes such values as thrift, persistence, having a sense of shame, and ordering relationships. Confucian work dynamism refers to dedicated, motivated, responsible, and educated individuals with a sense of commitment and organizational identity and loyalty.

Countries high in Confucian work dynamism are Hong Kong, Taiwan, Japan, South Korea, and Singapore—popularly referred to as the Five Economic Dragons. Long-term orientation encourages thrift, savings, perseverance toward results, and a willingness to subordinate oneself for a purpose. Short-term orientation is consistent with spending to keep up with social pressure, less savings, preference for quick results, and a concern with face (see Table 7.7).

Case Study: Singapore

Singapore is an island nation of 697 square kilometers, the smallest but one of the most prosperous countries in Southeast Asia. Various groups of people have migrated to Singapore. Its

Table 7.7   Long-Term Orientation Rankings for 23 Countries

1	China	13	Poland
2	Hong Kong	14	Germany (F.R.)
3	Taiwan	15	Australia
4	Japan	16	New Zealand
5	South Korea	17	United States
6	Brazil	18	Great Britain
7	India	19	Zimbabwe
8	Thailand	20	Canada
9	Singapore	21	Philippines
10	The Netherlands	22	Nigeria
11	Bangladesh	23	Pakistan
12	Sweden		

Source: Hofstede (2001, p. 356).

4.7 million population is 77% Chinese. Today, Singapore is a multiracial, multicultural society with a dynamic economy. Its government has been strict and paternalistic, steadily building the country into an economic and trade powerhouse that has education and income levels comparable to those in the United States. The island nation is clean, efficient, and law abiding. While on a trip there in 1987, I came across a newspaper editorial in which Confucianism is considered in juxtaposition to individualism (see Focus on Culture 7.3).

FOCUS ON CULTURE 7.3

Finding the Golden Mean

Confucianism is once again in the news. Its role in Singapore's progress was the theme of the Prime Minister's recent interview with the *New York Times.* And several distinguished scholars are in Singapore this week to discuss the part Confucianism has played in the economic success of East Asian nations. At the heart of this debate is a fundamental question that has exercised the minds of philosophers and kings for ages: How should a society organize itself? The goal has always been to find an effective way to control the passions of people so they can live in harmony among themselves and in peace with their neighbours. The quest is not only for sound political systems but, more importantly, for better social and economic systems.

Whatever the arguments about the State and the individual, the Prime Minister was unequivocal about one of the driving forces behind Singapore's success, namely, the basic Confucian concept of placing the good of society above that of the individual. A related factor was social cohesion. Given Singapore's mix of races, cultures and religions, its fragile harmony cannot withstand what the Prime Minister called the "untrammeled individualism" of the West. There is good reason why these two concepts have been such a constant preoccupation of Singapore's leadership. For while Singaporeans may accept the notion of sacrificing individual interests for a larger common good and to preserve social harmony, several factors make this especially difficult to apply in real life.

One of these stems from the wrenching changes that cultures in Singapore have undergone, all in one generation. In many families now, children who are Western-educated and English-speaking find it difficult to accept the mores of their dialect-speaking and more traditional parents. As families are the basic units of Asian societies, the cultural strains that this imposes are enormous. Unfortunately, the individualist genie, once unloosed, cannot be easily coaxed back into the lamp. But on the other hand, some traditional social norms die hard no matter how badly changes are needed. Witness how even English-educated men in Singapore still have the Eastern preference for submissive wives.

(Continued)

(Continued)

An even bigger paradox arises when trying to preserve Confucian ethics and other Asian traditions within a modern capitalist economy. For capitalism is based essentially on the pursuit of individual gains. The political philosophers of Keynes' day justified capitalism on the grounds that moneymaking was less of an avarice than, and could in fact countervail, other more dangerous passions and vices. Individuals pursuing relentlessly their own interests will, in fact, further the common good. Or so the theory goes. Added to this, of course, is the colonial legacy of a democratic political system in which is enshrined each individual's right to vote.

So the task is to balance Confucian ethics, and its emphasis on the common good, with the individualism inherent in a capitalist economy and in a one-man, one-vote political system. Certainly selfish individualism and abrasive dissent have no place if there is to be order and harmony. Singapore has no margin for error. Still, room must be given for creativity and innovativeness. For Singapore cannot achieve the excellence it seeks as a society if there is no open-mindedness to new, and sometimes opposing, ideas. The government's important role is not so much to deliver the goods but more to inspire the people to accept what it takes to achieve the good life—and for them to work at getting there. Singaporeans must themselves find the golden mean that suits their circumstances for, in the end, they can only be their own selves.

Source: "Finding the Golden Mean" (1987, p. 24). Copyright © 1987 by The Straits Times Press. Reprinted with permission.

ENVIRONMENTAL SUSTAINABILITY

Sustainable development has been defined in many ways. The World Commission on Environment and Development (1987) defined the concept as "development which meets the needs of the present without compromising the ability of future generations to meet their own needs" (p. 8). Sustainability is a multidimensional construct. The World Economic Forum (Global Leaders, 2001) framed the dimensions in terms of the quality of environmental systems, stresses on those systems, the vulnerability of human populations to environmental degradation, the social and institutional capacity to respond to stresses, and global stewardship. Yale University's Center for Environmental Law and Policy, in collaboration with Columbia University's Center for International Earth Science Information Network and the World Economic Forum, publish the Environmental Sustainability Index (ESI). It is a composite index tracking 21 elements of environmental sustainability, covering natural resource endowments, past and present pollution levels, environmental management efforts, contributions to protect the global commons, and the society's capacity to improve its environmental performance over time. Finland, Norway, Uruguay, Sweden, and Iceland rank highest. The United States ranks 45th, a high middle ranking that reflects high performance on issues such as water quality and environmental protection capacity and low performance on other issues such as waste generation and greenhouse gas emissions. The United Arab Emirates, China, Saudi Arabia, and North Korea rank low.

Husted (2005) studied the ESI elements related to Hofstede's dimensions. He concluded that countries with low levels of power distance, high levels of individualism, and low levels of masculinity have higher social and institutional capacity "These egalitarian, individualist, and feminine values appear to constitute 'green' or 'sustainable' values" (p. 363). For example, Costa Rica is low in power distance and also quite low on masculinity. Even though it is quite collectivistic and relatively poor, it has invested considerable resources in its social and institutional capacity for sustainability. He then discusses ways that Hofstede's cultural dimensions can play a role in how sustainability programs can be successfully implemented. A similar study by Park, Russell, and Lee (2007) showed a clear statistical link in a sample of 43 countries between two of Hofstede dimensions and environmental sustainability, again measured by the ESI. Both power distance and masculinity are significantly negatively related to the ESI. They also found that education was positively related to the ESI. Peng and Lin (2009) reported the same relationship: power distance and masculinity are effective and consistent predictors of environmental performance.

Later, a new index, the Environmental Performance Index (EPI), was developed to use outcome-oriented indicators. Table 7.8 shows representative 2010 rankings. The EPI ranks 163 countries on 25 performance indicators to show how close countries are to established environmental policy goals.

Table 7.8 Environmental Performance Index

1.	Iceland	20.	Japan
2.	Switzerland	43.	Mexico
3.	Costa Rica	46.	Canada
4.	Sweden	51.	Australia
5.	Norway	61.	United States
6.	Mauritius	94.	South Korea
7.	France	99.	Saudi Arabia
8.	Austria	121.	China
9.	Cuba	123.	India
10.	Columbia	147.	North Korea
14.	United Kingdom	152.	United Arab Emirates

Source: Yale Center for Environmental Law & Policy (2010).

FOCUS ON THEORY 7.3

Hofstede has not gone without critics (McSweeney, 2002a, 2002b). Typical of the criticisms are the following:

1. Nations are not the best units for studying cultures. Hofstede (2002) himself agrees, arguing that nations are the only kind of units available for comparison.

2. Hofstede's survey data are based on a small sample. Hofstede actually combined the results from two separate surveys from 1968 to 1969 and 1971 to 1973. The total of 117,000 questionnaires is the combined number for both surveys. Of that total, only data from 40 countries were used, and for only six of the included countries did the number of respondents exceed 1,000. In 15 countries, the numbers were fewer than 200.

3. Hofstede's survey data are old and outdated. Hofstede (2002) responds that the dimensions are assumed to have centuries-old roots, that recent replications show no changes, and that the dimensions have been validated against other measures.

4. Hofstede's data are drawn from subsidiaries of only one company that cannot provide information about entire national cultures. Hofstede (2002) responds that the dimensions are based on the differences between nations and that using the IBM data provides unusually well-matched samples from a large number of countries.

5. Four or five dimensions are not enough to define cultures.

And other systems have been proposed; Hampden-Turner & Trompenaars (1997) dimensions: universalism versus particularism, communitarianism versus individualism, neutral versus emotional, defuse versus specific cultures, achievement versus ascription, uman-time relationship, and human-nature relationship. Of these seven value dimensions, two reflect the Hofstede dimensions of collectivism and individualism and power distance. Their other dimensions seem to focus more on underlying value dimensions. Value dimensions are discussed in the next chapter.

Despite such criticisms, Hofstede's work has become the dominant paradigm and framework for subsequent studies (Chapman, 1997).

SUMMARY

Dutch management researcher Geert Hofstede studied more than 100,000 IBM employees in 40 countries to determine the value dimensions across which cultures vary. His work continues to be widely used in a variety of disciplines and has been accepted by many as being helpful in understanding cultural values.

Hofstede identified four dimensions that he labeled individualism, masculinity, power distance, and uncertainty avoidance. The individualism-collectivism dimension describes relationships between the individual and the group. The masculinity-femininity dimension describes how a culture's dominant values are assertive or nurturing. Power distance refers to the distribution of influence within a culture. And uncertainty avoidance reflects a culture's tolerance of ambiguity and acceptance of risk.

Later a fifth dimension was added: long-term orientation versus short-term orientation to life. This dimension describes cultures that range from short-term values with respect for tradition and reciprocity in social relations to long-term values with persistence and ordering relationships by status.

Recently, studies have attempted to correlate the Hofstede dimensions to environmental concerns. A relationship between power distance and masculinity have been shown to be predictors of environmental performance. A new index, the Environmental Performance Index has been developed to use environmental outcome-oriented indicators.

Japan is presented as case study in this chapter. While some assume that Japan is a collectivist culture, it actually ranks near the middle on that dimension. Japan can be better understood as a "homogeneous" country. That belief is reflected in history, religion, and cultural patterns, and communication style. A second case study presents Singapore as a culture that has balanced Confucian values with an individualistic capitalist economy.

DISCUSSION QUESTIONS

1. Compare and contrast cultures exhibiting most and least individualist behaviors.

2. Compare Western individualism with Confucianist thought.

3. What effects does Japan's population homogeneity have on other aspects of its culture?

4. What implications for environmental sustainability do the studies by Husted (2005), Park et al. (2007), and Peng & Lin (2009) suggest?

5. If it is true that the United States is becoming ever more accepting of increased power distance, what changes might be reasonable to expect?

KEY TERMS

amae 177	gaijin 176	power distance 182
collectivism 169	individualism 169	Shinto 175
Confucian work dynamism 188	long-term orientation 188	short-term orientation 188
	masculinity 180	uncertainty avoidance 186
femininity 180	mitigated speech 182	

READINGS

All readings are from *Intercultural Communication: A Global Reader* (Jandt, 2004).

Geert Hofstede, "Business Cultures" (p. 8)

Ashleigh C. Merritt and Robert L. Helmreich, "Human Factors on the Flight Deck: The Influence of National Culture" (p. 13)

Rujira Rojjanaprapayon, Porntipha Chiemprapha, and Achaya Kanchanakul, "Conflict Management in Thai Organizations" (p. 28)

Rueyling Chuang, "An Examination of Taoist and Buddhist Perspectives on Interpersonal Conflicts, Emotions, and Adversities" (p. 38)

Jung-huel Becky Yeh and Ling Chen, "Cultural Values and Argumentative Orientations for Chinese People in Taiwan, Hong Kong, and Mainland China" (p. 51)

Jonathan J. H. Zhu and Zhou He, "Information Accessibility, User Sophistication, and Source Credibility: The Impact of the Internet on Value Orientations in Mainland China" (p. 65)

STUDENT STUDY SITE

Visit the student study site at **www.sagepub.com/jandt7e** for these additional learning tools:

- Web Resources
- Audio and Video Links
- SAGE journal articles
- eFlashcards
- Web Quizzes
- Sample Essays

CHAPTER

8

FOCUS QUESTIONS

- What is value orientation theory?

- Using the value orientation theory, how can dominant U.S. cultural patterns be described?

- How can U.S. cultural patterns affect intercultural communication?

Dominant U.S. Cultural Patterns

Using Value Orientation Theory

Origins of U.S. Cultural Patterns
    Pre-16th-Century Indigenous Americans
    European Enlightenment
    Regional Differences Resulting
        From Immigration
            Communication Markers of Regions
Forces Toward the Development of a
    Dominant Culture
Value Orientation Theory
What Is a Human Being's Relation To Nature?
    The Individual-and-Nature Relationship
    Science and Technology
    Materialism
What Is the Modality of Human Activity?
    Activity and Work
    Efficiency and Practicality
    Progress and Change
What Is the Temporal Focus of Human Life?
What Is the Character of Innate Human Nature?
    Goodness
    Rationality
    Mutability
What Is the Relationship of the Individual to Others?
    Individualism
    Self-Motivation
    Social Organization
        Equality
        Conformity
Forces Toward the Development of Regional Cultures
    The New Regions
Summary
Discussion Questions
Key Terms
Readings
Student Study Site

A 2011 poll (Penn, 2011) showed that since the events of September 11, 2001, more than two thirds of U.S. residents see the past decade as a period of decline for the United States. Some 41% felt that the most important event of the past decade was 9/11 (Obama's election and the economic recession trailed far behind at 9% and 7%). An overwhelming 68% believed that the past decade had been one of decline for the country, and 47% felt that it was one of the worst decades in the past 100 years. The pollsters saw these results as a fundamental change for a country long known for optimism amid adversity. Some argue that the United States has declined; others see it differently. Some other countries have now made significant advances.

> ### Global Voices
>
> "For 500 years the West patented six killer applications that set it apart. The first to download them was Japan. Over the last century, one Asian country after another has downloaded these killer apps—competition, modern science, the rule of law and private property rights, modern medicine, the consumer society and the work ethic. Those six things are the secret sauce of Western civilization."
>
> Niall Ferguson, author of *Civilization: The West and the Rest* (2011; quoted in Zakaria, 2011, para. 5).

We learn values, what is competent, and what is desirable behavior from our culture. This type of learning is called emic knowledge, or knowledge of the culture learned from the inside. Emic knowledge constitutes the rules known from inside the culture and as such are seldom organized or consciously discussed (Stewart, 1982). (When a culture is learned by an outsider, the stranger tends to acquire theoretical and normative information called etic knowledge.) Because culture is widely shared and taken for granted, we have little experience in discussing how cultural values affect our behavior. Of course, not everyone in a culture acts in accordance with the culture's values all the time. Nonetheless, dominant cultural values or patterns of behavior can be identified that make it possible to compare cultures in a meaningful way. Intercultural communication competence requires understanding dominant cultural values and understanding how our own cultural values affect the way we perceive ourselves and others.

This chapter focuses on the United States—the world's most powerful nation, the third largest by size and the third most populous nation in the world. Its economy produces nearly a third of the world's goods and services, and its military is more powerful than the rest of the world's military combined. In this chapter, the origins of U.S. cultural patterns are presented, and the forces that tended to shape a national character from several regional groups are described. Then, what have been labeled the dominant U.S. cultural patterns are described. Finally, the forces that are contributing to new regional groups are described.

ORIGINS OF U.S. CULTURAL PATTERNS

Pre-16th-Century Indigenous Americans

Before Columbus arrived, North America was home to a diverse population of some 10 million people. Indigenous Americans spoke hundreds of languages. Arguably, though, the Iroquois were the most important indigenous group. Like other indigenous groups, their name came from their enemies. The Algonquin called them the Iroqu (Irinakhoiw), or "rattlesnakes." The French added the Gallic suffix *-ois*. The Iroquois call themselves Haudenosaunee meaning "people of the long house." The original homeland of the Iroquois was between the Adirondack Mountains and Niagara Falls, but at one time they controlled most of what is now the northeastern United States and eastern Canada. Surprisingly few in number, the Iroquois had an impact on North American history. Their number has been estimated at 20,000 in 1600. European epidemics and warfare reduced their population to about half that. Unlike other nations, the Iroquois assimilated conquered groups and grew in number.

The Iroquois political system, the Iroquois League (sometimes known as the Five Nations and later the Six Nations), was formed prior to any European contact and hence owed nothing to European influence. The league was founded to maintain peace and resolve disputes between its members. It had a written constitution with a system of checks, balances, and supreme law. Central authority was limited. By 1660, to deal with European powers as an equal, the Iroquois found it necessary to present a united front to Europeans.

Some argue that the Iroquois political organization was an influence on the American Articles of Confederation and Constitution. Others strongly refute that. Nonetheless, in 1988 the U.S. Congress passed a resolution to recognize the influence of the Iroquois League on the Constitution and Bill of Rights (S. Res. 76, 1988).

European Enlightenment

The society that evolved and is dominant today grew from European roots. The scientific method, democracy, and capitalism are institutions of Western cultures (D'Souza, 2002). The dominant language, the system of representative government, the structure of law, and the emphasis on individual liberty all derive from the Enlightenment ideals formulated in England. Other important U.S. ideals, such as the separation of powers, derive from the French philosopher Montesquieu. These values, established early in U.S. history, remain strong.

Regional Differences Resulting From Immigration

The United States is a country of immigrants from all over the world, each person immigrating with his or her own cultural values. Many arrived in groups and tended to remain settled in the same area. Brandeis University historian David Hackett Fischer (1989) argues that the early immigrants from England established distinctive regional cultures that remain today. He further argues that the United States has been a society of diversity—not homogeneity—from its very beginning.

The Puritans came from eastern England to Massachusetts between 1629 and 1641. A small number of Royalist elite and large numbers of indentured servants from southern and western England settled in the Chesapeake region between 1642 and 1675. Quakers from England's

Tocqueville's *Democracy in America* is considered one of the most comprehensive and insightful books ever written about the United States.

north midlands and Wales settled in the Delaware Valley between 1675 and 1725. The final group from Northern Ireland, Scotland, and the border area of northern England settled in Appalachia between 1717 and 1775. Each of these groups had diverse dialects and attitudes, and all retained a degree of separateness. Even Henry Adams's *History of the United States* had separate chapters on the "intellect" of New England, the Middle States, and the South in 1800. Zelinsky (1973) examined regional patterns in language, religion, food habits, architecture, place names, and the culture of the inhabitants who established the first effective settlements. He identified five regions: New England, the Midland, the Middle West, the South, and the West. More recently, Bigelow (1980) examined ethnicity, religion, party affiliation, and dialect and identified these regions: Northeast, Border South, Deep South, Midwest, Mexicano, Southwest, Colorado, Mormondom, Pacific Northwest, Northern California, and Southern California. These analyses clearly show that the United States may never have been a completely homogeneous culture. In 1831, then 26-year-old French aristocrat Alexis de Tocqueville (1805–1859) toured the United States and saw the country as composed of almost separate little nations (Tocqueville, 1835/1945; see also Mayer, 1981).

FOCUS ON CULTURE 8.1

In 1893, Frederick Jackson Turner published *The Frontier in American History* in which he argued that U.S. culture grew from and was nurtured by the ever-present frontier. The frontier provided resources, wildness, a place to test and build character. Survival challenges on the frontier produced a people of strong and durable character. The frontier symbolized economic opportunity, religious freedom, and relief from oppression. The continued promise of "greener pastures" produced a forward-looking people.

Communication Markers of Regions

Variations make each region psychologically and behaviorally distinct. In relation to communication differences, P. A. Andersen, Lustig, and Andersen (1987) suggest regional differences in three areas:

- *Verbal control and dominance.* New Englanders are more likely to be introverts; those in the Mid-Atlantic region are characterized as not particularly talkative or verbally dominant.
- *Affiliativeness and immediacy.* People from Texas, Oklahoma, Arkansas, and Louisiana visit more neighbors and rate friends higher than do people in other regions. Pacific Coast residents report the most isolation from friends, least acquaintance with their neighbors, greatest distance from relatives, and lowest frequency of interactions with confidants.
- *Arousal or activation.* New Englanders employ a nondramatic and reserved communication style. The South and the Northwest are slow and relaxed compared to the fast pace of the urban Northeast.

FORCES TOWARD THE DEVELOPMENT OF A DOMINANT CULTURE

Tocqueville predicted that the United States would be a great power. The reasons he gave were the country's large geographic size, abundant natural resources, a growing population, and a vibrant national character. Historians have charted the series of events that resulted in a dominant national culture:

- Opening of the Erie Canal in 1825 and the emergence of New York as the financial and corporate capital of an integrated industrial complex stretching from the Northeast to the upper Midwest.
- Defeat of the South and the passage of the Thirteenth, Fourteenth, and Fifteenth Amendments that established national citizenship over state citizenship.
- Development of Theodore Roosevelt's "new nationalism" that provided the intellectual foundations for an activist national government.
- Passage of the Immigration Restriction Act of 1924, which permitted a degree of homogenization of the population.
- Development of radio and television, which nationalized politics and popular culture.
- The automobile and interstate highway system made the country internally mobile.
- The Great Depression, World War II, and the onset of the Cold War, all of which increased the need for a strong centralized national government.

These forces contributed to an exceptional uniformity that characterized the U.S. society in the early post–World War II period (Clough, 1997). Another perspective is to recognize that the various groups comprising the United States have, to some extent, diverse cultural patterns. They may overlap, but they do differ. To talk about a dominant cultural pattern from this perspective is to talk about the cultural patterns of the group that controls the society.

International opinion polls continue to show that U.S. residents have values different from those of other cultures. It was Tocqueville who coined the phrase "American exceptionalism" to express the idea that the United States *is* different. Understanding these values and their development contributes to improved intercultural communication, for as you learn to understand and accept your own culture, your intercultural communication improves. As you go through this chapter, then, you must keep in mind that it is generalizing the values of an entire culture. You may find that you as an individual do not agree with all the values identified as typical in the United States, and you surely will know of others who would not agree. This chapter is about the dominant cultural values said to be characteristic of the majority of U.S. citizens.

FOCUS ON THEORY 8.1

Hofstede's original research identified four dimensions of cultural variation. The business-oriented *Global Leadership and Organizational Behavior Effectiveness* (GLOBE) research project (House, Hanges, Javidan, Dorfman, & Gupta, 2004) of 17,000 managers from 951 organizations in 62 societies used nine:

Institutional collectivism, related to Hofstede's individualism dimension, is the degree to which organizational and societal institutional practices encourage and reward collective distribution of resources and collective action. It is especially high in Confucian Asian cultures, which tend to be less segmented societies. *In-group collectivism,* also related to Hofstede's individualism dimension, reflects the degree to which individuals express pride, loyalty, and cohesiveness in their organizations and families. It's related to low divorce rates.

Gender equality is one of two concepts substituted for Hofstede's masculinity dimension. It represents the degree to which an organization or society minimizes gender role differences while promoting gender equality, women earning an income, and women having access to resources. *Assertiveness* is the second concept substituted for Hofstede's masculinity dimension. It represents the degree to which individuals in organizations and societies are assertive, confrontational, and aggressive in social relationships.

Power distance (Hofstede's power distance dimension) is the degree to which members of an organization or society expect and agree that power should be concentrated at higher levels of the organization or government. *Uncertainty avoidance* (Hofstede's uncertainty avoidance dimension) is the extent to which members of an organization or society strive to avoid uncertainty by relying on established social norms, rituals, and bureaucratic practices. *Future orientation* (more closely related to Kluckhohn and Strodtbeck's [1961] temporal dimension, described later in this chapter, than the long-term orientation discussed below) is the degree to which individuals in organizations or societies engage in future-oriented behaviors such as planning, investing in the future, and delaying individual and collective gratification.

Human orientation (related to Kluckhohn and Strodtbeck's [1961] human nature dimension, described later in this chapter) is the degree to which individuals in organizations and societies encourage and reward individuals for being fair, friendly, generous, caring, and kind to others. People in societies high on this attribute show empathy, are very high in satisfaction, and tend to use extended, warm greetings. *Performance orientation* (derived from McClelland's 1976 work on need for achievement, described later in this chapter) is the degree to which an organization encourages and rewards group members for performance improvement and excellence.

As you examine these values, remember too how everything that occurs in a culture is related to and consistent with other things in that culture. None of the values presented is discrete—all are related to and reinforce each other.

VALUE ORIENTATION THEORY

Kluckhohn and Strodtbeck (1961) argue that all human cultures are confronted with universally shared problems emerging from relationships with fellow beings, time, activities, and nature. These five basic problems are as follows:

- What is a human being's relation to nature? (human being–nature orientation)
- What is the modality of human activity? (activity orientation)
- What is the temporal focus of human life? (time orientation)
- What is the character of innate human nature? (human nature orientation)
- What is the relationship of the individual to others? (relational orientation)

Kluckhohn and Strodtbeck's value orientation theory suggests that cultures develop unique positions in these five value orientations: human being–nature, activity, time, human nature, and relational. Human being–nature is described here as worldview (after Samovar, Porter, & Jain, 1981) and considers how humans dominate, live with, or are subjugated to nature. Activity orientation deals with people in the culture "being" (passively accepting), "being-in-becoming" (transforming), or "doing" (initiating action). Time orientation deals with the emphasis the culture places on the past, the present, or the future. Human nature orientation considers whether humans are primarily evil, primarily good, or a mixture of both. And relational orientation considers the way the culture organizes interpersonal relationships: linear hierarchy, group identification, or individualism.

There have been many excellent descriptions of U.S. cultural patterns (Kohls, 1984; Samovar et al., 1981; Stewart, 1972). The one used in this chapter is based on Kluckhohn and Strodtbeck's (1961) value orientations and modifies and adds to their categories as necessary to describe the cultural patterns that are characteristic of the majority of U.S. citizens and have an influence on communication.

The Kluckhohn and Strodtbeck value orientations can be used to describe other cultures and provide, then, a systematic way of comparing cultural values.

WHAT IS A HUMAN BEING'S RELATION TO NATURE?

The term worldview deals with a culture's most fundamental beliefs about its place in the cosmos, beliefs about God, and beliefs about the nature of humanity and nature. Worldview refers to the philosophical ideas of being. Huntington (1993, 1996) has argued that the world can be divided into eight major "cultural zones" that have been shaped by religious tradition still powerful today. The zones are Western Christianity, the Orthodox world, the Islamic world, and the Confucian, Japanese, Hindu, African, and Latin American zones. Throughout the 19th century, religious discourse in the United States was dominated by White male Protestant conservatives of European heritage (Eck, 1993). In the 20th century, the United States became a meeting place for all the world's religions.

Sociologist Seymour Martin Lipset (1990) argues that because the United States separates church and state, thus making religion totally voluntary, people in the United States are more likely to believe that religion provides spiritual needs. In countries with a state religion, that religion is in many ways a person's only choice, whereas in the United States, the wide diversity of religious options provides more opportunities for an individual to identify with a religious denomination.

Among the world's industrialized nations, the United States is the most religious. U.S. citizens are more likely to believe in heaven, hell, the Devil, and life after death. In fact, some 92% of U.S. citizens believe there is a God or universal spirit (Pew Forum on Religion and Public Life, 2008). This compares dramatically with England's 31% and Sweden's 19%. Another study comparing the United States with European countries found that 87% of U.S. citizens report never having doubted the existence of God. A Pew Research Center survey showed that 59% of people in the United States say that religion is very important in their lives. This contrasts to 33% of Britons, 21% of Germans, and 11% of the French. Consistent with previous research, a recent analysis of the World Values Survey clearly shows again that the United States continues to have a much more traditional value system than any other advanced industrial society. In fact, the United States has levels of religiosity and national pride comparable to those found in developing societies (Inglehart & Baker, 2000). (See Table 8.1 for a survey on religion and environmental laws in the United States.)

Samovar et al. (1981) identified three parts to worldview: the individual-and-nature relationship, science and technology, and materialism.

The Individual-and-Nature Relationship

In the United States, people typically make a clear and separate distinction between human life and nature, valuing nature but clearly placing a higher value on human life. This belief that humans have "dominion over nature" has made it possible for the United States to change the course of rivers, harvest forests for wood and paper, breed cattle for increased meat production, and destroy disease-causing bacteria. There can be little doubt that this

Table 8.1   Religion and Environmental Laws

U.S. citizens were read two statements: "Stricter environmental laws and regulations cost too many jobs and hurt the economy" and "Stricter environmental laws and regulations are worth the cost." They were asked if the first statement or the second statement was closer to their own views.

	Hurt Economy (%)	Worth the Cost (%)
Jews	16	77
Buddhist	19	75
Muslim	26	69
Mainline churches	28	64
National average	30	61
Evangelical churches	35	54
Historically Black churches	38	52

Source: Pew Forum on Religion & Public Life (2008).

Note: Poll of 35,556 adults nationwide. Responses for "neither/both" and "don't know/refuse to answer" omitted.

Global Voices

There is no country in the world where the Christian religion retains a greater influence over the souls of men.

—Alexis de Tocqueville, *Democracy in America* (1835/1945)

The United States "now has a greater diversity of religious groups than any country in recorded history."

—J. Gordon Melton, *Encyclopedia of American Religions* (1991)

belief has contributed to the material wealth of the United States. The environmental movement and the animal rights movement are not contradictory to this belief. Both movements share the basic assumption that humans have a responsibility to protect nature. For the most part, these activists agree that humans should act to protect nature—that is, that humans are different from the rest of nature and in some ways superior to it. Having a responsibility to protect nature implies a dominant role.

Other views are that humans are a part of nature and should attempt to live in harmony with it—not exploit or protect it—and that humans are subjugated by nature.

FOCUS ON THE ENVIRONMENT 8.1

The Judeo-Christian tradition has multiple views. The traditional dualistic view emphasizes differences between humans and the rest of creation. While the Torah may give humanity a privileged place in the order of creation, it isn't the "domination of a tyrant." The unifying view is represented by the idea that humans were created from dust or nature. Finally, the transcendentalist view affirms that "nature is God and God is nature," and, indeed, many commandments concern the preservation of the natural environment.

Theologians from a wide range of Christian traditions have addressed environmental issues. A papal decree by Pope John Paul in 1990 stated that "environmental degradation damages not just creation, but our human neighbors." Pope Benedict XVI has a growing interest in the environment and has said, "Before it's too late, we need to make courageous choices that will re-create a strong alliance between man and Earth." In 2008 Vatican official Msgr. Gianfranco Girotti said that an offense against God is also destroying the environment. Church hierarchy had been divided with some believing that ecology is a concern of rich, developed nations, not the poor regions of the world. But scarcity of resources and natural disasters are hurting the poor, making care for the environment a moral responsibility for all the faithful.

Sources: United Nations Development Programme (2008, p. 61) and Hull (2006)

Science and Technology

People in the United States have a strong faith in the scientific method of solving problems. In the United States, it's a common belief that events have causes, that those causes can be discovered, and that humans can and should alter that relationship.

That events have causes rather than being random has a long tradition. The early colonists felt that nothing that occurred in the world was a random event but, rather, was the product of intent by some mover. A New England earthquake in 1727 "filled the houses of God" and contributed to the first Great Awakening. Pennsylvania's Johnstown Flood in 1889, the sinking of the *Titanic* in 1912, and the Great Depression of the 1930s were all attributed to the wrath of God.

Modern acceptance of the scientific method is reflected in much communication and logic. Objectivity, empirical evidence, and facts are valued. Consider the majority approach to the AIDS epidemic. Most people in the United States recognized that the disease had a viral cause and that the virus could be identified and eradicated as polio had been.

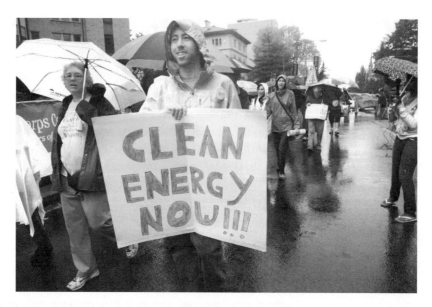

The relationship between science and technology and the environmental movement is multifaceted. Environmentalists point to environmental degradation and call for clean energy. Governments and companies point to new clean "green" jobs.

FOCUS ON THEORY 8.2

Carolyn Merchant's book *The Death of Nature: Women, Ecology, and the Scientific Revolution,* published in 1980, presented a view of the Scientific Revolution that challenged science as progress. It argued that the outcomes of science include the ecological crisis, the domination of nature, and the devaluation of women in the production of scientific knowledge.

"Yet the notion of a "Scientific Revolution" in the sixteenth and seventeenth centuries is part of a larger mainstream narrative of Western culture that has propelled science, technology, and capitalism's efforts to "master" nature—a narrative into which most Westerners have unconsciously been socialized and within which we ourselves have become actors in a storyline of upward progress. Demoting the "Scientific Revolution" to the mere nomer of "early modern science" obscures the power of the dominant narratives of colonialism and imperialism that have helped to shape Western culture since the seventeenth century at the expense of nature, women, minorities, and indigenous peoples. This move hides the political power of scientific narratives in remaking the earth and its natural resources as objects for human use" (Merchant, 2006, p. 517).

The United States has strong faith in science and technology. The 1939 World's Fair celebrated technology in the United States. Also in 1939, the U.S. Army numbered 175,000 officers and men, 16th largest in the world, right behind Romania. World War II changed that. In 1945, Germany built 40,593 aircraft and Japan 28,180. The United States built 96,318. By 1945, half of all ships afloat in the world had been built in the United States. U.S. industry made the military the best equipped in the world.

Adoption of media has been far reaching in the United States. The country has 141 million land line telephones (second in the world, one for every 2.2 people), 286 million cell phones (third in the world, one for every 1.1 person), and 245 million Internet users (second in the world, one for every 1.3 people). In the years before the 2008 financial crisis, the only major U.S. industry other than health care that consistently grew was consumer electronics. In 2009 people over the age of 15 devoted 58% of their leisure time watching television, playing games, and using the Internet.

Materialism

If there is one value that most of the rest of the world attributes to the United States, it is materialism, or the belief that possessions are important in life. In *Democracy in America,* Tocqueville (1835/1945) wrote about how materialistic people in the United States were even in 1831. In many ways, the miracle of the economic system of the United States is that most people have jobs that provide an income sufficient to buy things and services and, in turn, create jobs for others. The system is dynamic and depends on the constant circulation of money to ensure full employment. Consumer spending accounts for more than two thirds of total economic activity in the United States.

The U.S. system encourages people to buy things and then to buy the "new improved" versions as new things quickly become obsolete. It's said that a man is a boy with more expensive toys. Others are judged by their possessions: Where do they live? What kind of car does she drive? What did he wear to the party? You can even express positive feelings about yourself by acquiring and showing things. The difference between clothes and designer clothes is price and how you feel about yourself when you wear them. (See Table 8.2 for a list of what people in the United States buy daily and Table 8.3 on page 209 for pounds of garbage produced in 2004.)

A materialistic system encourages high turnover, disposability, and "supersizing." Last season's styles are not as desirable. Last year's toys are in the attic. The phonograph is in the garage to make space for the CD player. The landfill is the final resting point for yesterday's materialistic purchases still unpaid on today's credit card statement. Ford Excursions are 19 feet long, Double Gulp drinks are 64 ounces, McDonald's has SuperSize portions, and Starbucks has Venti cappuccino.

Table 8.2	What the United States Buys Daily
50,051,507	12-oz. cans of Pepsi
35,079,448	12-oz. servings of Bud Light
8,179,726	20-oz. bottles of Aquafina water
2,400,000	Burger King Whoppers
500,000	Hostess Twinkies
300,000	Packs of Pampers
153,424	Lbs. of Starbucks coffee
150,000	Hot Wheels Basic Cars (small size)
125,000	Barbie dolls
123,287	Trojan Ultra Thin condoms
87,431	Slim-Fast Optima multipack shakes
14,100	First Response pregnancy tests
3,160	Men's Rogaine 5% Solution
34	Porsche 911s

Source: "America by the Numbers," (2007, p. 54).

The annual survey conducted by the Higher Education Research Institute at the University of California, Los Angeles (Sax, Lindholm, Astin, Korn, & Mahoney, 2001). shows that the number of college freshmen who said it was essential or very important to be very well off financially grew from 41% in 1968 to 73% in 2001. During the same period, the number who said "developing a meaningful philosophy of life" was a top priority fell from 83% to 41%. The desire to have possessions is also related to the high level of consumer debt in the United States.

Borrowing money has a long history, but for the most part, money was loaned only to start businesses because those businesses would generate profits to repay the loans. Consumer loans, which make instant gratification possible by using borrowed money to buy things, are a much more recent innovation.

Gasoline and store charge cards were the standard until 1950, when Diners Club established the first credit card. In 1986, the average cardholder debt was $900. By 1996, the average cardholder debt was $2,900; it's now estimated to be more than $14,743 per household with credit card debt. The typical U.S. cardholder has 3.5 credit cards. About 76% of college students have at least one credit card. Debt on these cards averages more than $2,200. That people are evaluated by their possessions can be seen in reactions to occasional stories of individuals who die in poor surroundings yet whose mattresses are stuffed with cash. The popular reaction is that these people must have been crazy.

Yet the genius of the U.S. economic system is that materialism makes high employment and a comfortable standard of living possible for a vast number of people and the huge middle class.

Table 8.3	Pounds of Garbage Produced per Person Each Year
United States	1,637
Norway	1,184
Netherlands	1,100
Germany	823
Sweden	662
France	572
Italy	548
Portugal	367

Source: "Recycling Advocates." (2004, p. 41).

Global Voices

When do you have enough in America? Never! It's a culture of excess, a permanently nouveau riche mentality. We want the biggest, the most extreme of everything.

—G. Clotaire Rapaille, French anthropologist (quoted in *Los Angeles Times Magazine*, June 9, 2002, p. 12)

WHAT IS THE MODALITY OF HUMAN ACTIVITY?

The term **activity orientation** refers to the use of time for self-expression and play, self-improvement and development, and work. Most visitors to the United States find it a hectic, busy culture. You can see this in the following three aspects.

Table 8.4	Average Paid Vacation in Days per Year
Germany	30
Spain	30
Britain	25
Australia	25
Netherlands	25
Japan	18
China	15
United States	10

Source: From European Industrial Relations Observatory, World Tourism Organization, *Los Angeles Times,* Bureau of Labor Statistics ("Snapshot of America," 2004, p. 41).

Activity and Work

It would seem from the preceding section that people in the United States work only to earn money to buy more things. Yet people in the United States have a special feeling about jobs, defining self and others by occupation. Work becomes part of one's identity. About half of U.S. citizens agree that a "feeling of accomplishment" is the most important aspect of work. This is about twice the agreement rate in other countries, where work is a means to get money and where self-identity and self-accomplishment come more from what one does outside work.

Work is taken very seriously in the United States. It's separated from play, which is something done outside work. To support that, a complex recreation industry has been developed to provide play away from work. (See Table 8.4 for a comparative list of worker vacation time.)

Efficiency and Practicality

People in the United States are perceived as placing such a high value on time that "efficiency experts," whose emphasis is on getting things done on time, cause lives to be organized for *efficiency,* so that the most can be accomplished. How many people organize their lives according to lists? Or at least think about organizing the day to accomplish the most?

It's possible that the emphasis on efficiency results in losing sight of other values, such as contemplation and aesthetic values. For example, most people plan commutes for the shortest possible drive time. Rarely would a person think about going the scenic route—unless on vacation and with "time to kill."

Practicality refers here to a preference for short-term goals over long-term goals. This means planning for what works best for the short time—the most practical. As a culture, the United States is less likely to make short-term sacrifices for long-term gain because progress is judged so much by monthly and quarterly goals. Meaningful 10-year goals, much less 100-year goals, are very unlikely. It may appear that education is a long-term activity. However, a college education is divided into 40 or so courses. Education is viewed as a series of courses, each of which must be completed successfully. The focus on short-term practicality may appear shortsighted, but tomorrow is another day, with new problems and new opportunities.

Global Voices

Democratic nations will habitually prefer the useful to the beautiful, and they will require that the beautiful should be useful.

—Alexis de Tocqueville, *Democracy in America* (1835/1945)

Progress and Change

Related to practicality and to materialism is an unwavering fundamental faith in the future. The belief is that change is basically good, that the new is better than the old. For example, 4G is better than 3G. Not only is the new viewed as better, but the new is often adopted without critically examining its effect on other aspects of the culture. For example, the microwave oven does make food preparation faster, but it also may lessen even more the time that families spend together. Such consequences usually are not considered in the adoption of the new. Perhaps the willingness to accept change also explains why the United States has one of the highest moving rates in the world. Each year, nearly one in five U.S. households changes location.

The belief that progress and change are good is associated with technological developments. Some observers, however, contend that the faith in progress and change also is being applied to values.

U.S. values or standards of what is right and wrong do change, and most would agree that these changes are proper. Public school integration is not that old, but you would agree that that change was right. Because social beliefs are changed so easily and so frequently in the United States, some say there are no longer any beliefs that are permanent.

WHAT IS THE TEMPORAL FOCUS OF HUMAN LIFE?

Cultures differ widely in their conceptions of time, as was first mentioned in the chronemics section of Chapter 5.

First of all, in the United States, time is viewed as a commodity. Such phrases as "time is money," "how much time do you have?" "don't waste time," and "budget your time" are common. Think about the conception of time as a commodity and the consequences of that belief. When time is thought of as a commodity, one needs to be constantly aware of it. Time clocks are everywhere: in homes, cars, work sites, on wrists, at organized play sites. Many people report feeling uncomfortable not knowing the time. Perhaps only camping in the woods—without a radio and clocks—can one be free of time awareness in the United States. When time is considered a resource, it becomes something to be managed and used responsibly. It can become a master if one

> ### Global Voices
>
> [In the United States] they all consider society as a body in a state of improvement, humanity as a changing scene, in which nothing is, or ought to be, permanent; and they admit that what appears to them today to be good, may be superseded by something better tomorrow.
>
> —Alexis de Tocqueville, *Democracy in America* (1835/1945)

becomes a slave to it. How many people do you know who carry schedules of their day, week, or year?

Second, when time is viewed in a linear fashion, it obviously has a past, a present, and a future. Most will admit to being motivated by the future in how to act in the present: going to school to get a degree and a satisfying job, working to provide for oneself and one's family in the future, dieting so as to have a better figure and more friends in the future, training so as to be better at sports in the future, and living the future in the present. Some would say that, because of living the future in the present, one is less aware of the present, having less time and appreciation for what is happening in the moment. Some would even say that living the future in the present is an illusion because the future is not yet here—it is unreal. In living for something that isn't real, one misses much of the reality of the present.

WHAT IS THE CHARACTER OF INNATE HUMAN NATURE?

What does it mean to be human? What is human nature? What are human rights and responsibilities? These are the types of questions meant by human nature orientation.

Goodness

This area refers to the question of the innate nature of humans. Are we born good? Evil? With the potential for both? It has been argued that the Puritan ancestry of the United States suggests a view that people are born evil but have the potential to be good. To achieve good in this view, one must control and discipline the self. Others argue that contemporary beliefs in the United States are that people are born with a mixture of or a potential for both good and evil.

Rationality

Related to the concept of the innate nature of humans is rationality. To believe that humans are rational is to believe that humans act on the basis of reason. In other words, if you believe that humans have the potential for both good and evil, you also believe that humans have free choice and therefore responsibility for their actions. However, if you believe that humans are innately evil and lacking in rationality, you also believe that human evil is natural.

A belief in rationality, then, is consistent with a belief in the scientific method. Truth can be discovered through human reason. That being accepted, democracy, trial by jury, and a free enterprise system are all consistent beliefs because they assume that individuals can be trusted to make decisions for themselves.

It can be argued that the fundamental reason for the rise of the West was an extraordinary faith in reason. Christianity alone embraced reason and logic as the primary guide to religious truth. Christianity taught that reason was the supreme gift from God. Consequently, Christianity is oriented to the future while other religions assert the superiority of the past. Faith in the power of reason infused Western culture and stimulated the pursuit of science, democracy, and capitalism (Stark, 2005).

Mutability

The term **mutability** means subject to change. This, then, refers to the belief that human nature can be changed by society. This is reflected in the belief that education is a positive force in improving human nature. It's also fundamental to the belief that the prison system can rehabilitate wrongdoers, that although an individual chose to do evil, that individual can be changed by society to choose to do good.

Through science, this belief is now open to renewed public debate. In studies linking biology and human behavior, some scientists believe they are finding a sub-

> ## Global Voices
>
> Every adult, no matter how unfortunate a childhood he had or how habit-ridden he may be, is free to make choices about his life. To say of Hitler, to say of the criminal, that he did not choose to be bad but was a victim of his upbringing is to make all morality, all discussion of right and wrong, impossible. It leaves unanswered the question of why people in similar circumstances did not all become Hitlers.
>
> But worse, to say "It is not his fault; he was not free to choose" is to rob a person of his humanity, and reduce him to the level of an animal who is bound by instinct.
>
> —Harold S. Kushner, *When Bad Things Happen to Good People* (1982)

stantial genetic underpinning for human behavior, having now demonstrated a genetic role in intelligence and aggression, and the personality trait "novelty seeking." Genetic determinism diminishes the power of one's capacity to choose and accept responsibility for those choices. Is the alcoholic a helpless victim of biology or a willful agent with control over behavior?

Public debate also extends to whether unhealthy circumstances can lead individuals to do evil. Notice a contradiction here to the belief in rationality if you believe that a person who was abused as a child is more likely to abuse children and allow that fact in court to mitigate the individual's responsibility to have chosen rationally not to be abusive.

WHAT IS THE RELATIONSHIP OF THE INDIVIDUAL TO OTHERS?

This cultural pattern refers to perceptions of the self and the ways society is organized. Persons of diverse cultures tend to have differing perceptions of the self. In U.S. culture, people tend to define the self in terms of one's role and responsibilities in the society. Generally, people in the United States define self in terms of occupation rather than in terms of family or other relationships.

Individualism

Remember, as was discussed in the preceding chapter, the United States is characterized to a high degree by individualism as opposed to collectivism. In fact, surveys in the industrialized nations during the 1980s clearly show that the most distinctive and perhaps permanent characteristics of the U.S. character are independence and individuality. Yet the word *individualism* did not enter the English vocabulary until 1835, when Tocqueville used it to describe what he found in the United States. Those characteristics are echoes of constitutional guarantees of free speech and free press. Freedom for people in the United States is the freedom to be an individual. People in the United States have a passion for freedom. Patterson (1991) links this passion with the country's history of slavery. The concept of freedom that emerged from slave-holding Virginia was mass based and egalitarian.

This value is enforced early. According to a Chinese proverb, "You have to have the right name to do the right thing." In some cultures, names given to children have traditional or family meaning. Today, in the United States, names are more likely chosen by sound alone. Instead of tradition or family, children's names help reinforce individualism. Months-old infants are put in cribs in rooms separate from other people and crying is tolerated because of the importance placed on learning to be an individual. In contrast, in virtually all preindustrial societies, mothers sleep with babies for many months—and might well consider the U.S. practice cruel, or certainly not attentive to the child's needs. Children in the United States are encouraged to be autonomous, make independent decisions, solve problems independently, and generally view the world from the point of view of the self.

In the United States, adults maintain a separate self-concept when working in groups and organizations and are encouraged to accept responsibility as separate, independent individuals. Keep in mind, however, that independent individuals can cooperate—or compete—according to what maximizes benefits for the individual relative to costs.

A concern for individualism relates to views on love and marriage and life after death. In other cultures, marriage decisions are too important to be left to the individuals because, where families are most important, marriages present opportunities for alliances between families. Love develops after the marriage. Only in cultures that value individualism is romantic love the reason for marriage. Individualism also is reflected in beliefs in an existence beyond death. Most people in the United States believe in an afterlife as an individual (Segal, 2004).

In contrast to some cultures, the emphasis on individuality may make it somewhat difficult to experience the comfort and security of association that other cultures experience. It also may explain a weaker family structure than is found in other cultures. One fourth of U.S. households consist of a single person. And families in the United States are likely to be nontraditional: It is estimated that less than 10% of households now are made up of career fathers, homemaker mothers, and school-age children and that one third of all U.S. families are single-parent ones. Tocqueville predicted that the United States would succumb to the excesses of individualism, which he called egoism. Glendon (1991) calls this **hyperindividualism**, a withdrawing into individual private shells.

> **Global Voices**
>
> I swear by my life and my love of it that I will never live for the sake of another man, nor ask another man to live for mine.
>
> —Ayn Rand, *Atlas Shrugged*

Self-Motivation

The value of individualism in the United States is reflected in the belief that individuals should set their own goals and then pursue them independently. Motivation should originate in the individual; individuals have the power to determine their own destiny. Rather than favoring group decisions or having others decide for the person most affected, individual responsibility for decision making is favored.

A possible explanation for the emphasis on individualism and self-motivation can be seen in the history of Western religion and industrialization. What may appear to be an unlikely relationship has been clearly described by David McClelland (1976). In medieval Europe, society was rigidly structured. A person's place in society, or birthright, was defined by gender, social class, and lineage. The most holy life that one could aspire to on earth was to be a part of the church as a brother or nun and, in a sense, to be apart from the world. In medieval Catholicism, priests, nuns, saints, and rituals interceded with God for the masses. The Protestant Reformation changed this view. Protestant religious beliefs influenced attitudes toward work and relationships with God. Martin Luther taught that all forms of work are legitimate; that is, earthly work was not subordinate to spiritual work. Calvin and others taught that it was godly to be hardworking and that success was evidence of one's godliness. Within the Catholic Church, the Council of Trent (1545–1563) eliminated the abuses identified by the Protestant Reformers. These actions represented a significant shift in attitude. Whereas in the distant past, a talented person might find opportunity in the church apart from the world, after the Reformation, a talented person who worked hard might succeed in business. Success in the world became consistent with religious beliefs.

In addition, Protestantism of every kind argued for the private nature of religion. Protestantism sought to diminish the gap between people and God, thus supporting the growing individualism. Another influence was the Industrial Revolution. In the agricultural lifestyle, sons did what their fathers had done and daughters did what their mothers had done generation after generation. The Reformation and the Industrial Revolution made entrepreneurism, winning, personal ambition, and individualism a good thing.

McClelland (1976) labeled the consequences of this shift a "need for achievement." Individuals in cultures with a high need for achievement want to excel because of the feeling of accomplishment that it brings. McClelland showed that economic development in the West was largely built by individuals so motivated.

A particularly interesting part of McClelland's 1976 study was to use popular literature as an indicator of a culture's degree of need for achievement at any time. He studied the prevailing ideas and concerns in popular stories, songs, poems, plays, and speeches to index a culture's degree of need for achievement at any one time. He then correlated industrial activity in the culture to the presence of the achievement theme in popular literature. Not surprising was his finding that a peak in U.S. industrial activity was also a peak of this theme in popular literature, such as the Horatio Alger stories of the 1850s. Most of the 135 books that Horatio Alger wrote for boys in the 19th century stressed that a bright, self-reliant boy who works hard can go from "rags to riches."

The majority of the popular literature of the United States continues to stress the theme that an individual who works hard can succeed. The United States is called the land of opportunity, the country where people believe that if you work hard, you succeed. Many mistakenly believe that the saying "God helps those who help themselves" is from the Bible. Actually, the saying is attributed to Benjamin Franklin.

Table 8.5	Support for the Welfare State, by Country: Affirmative Responses	
Country	Percentage
Italy	81.0
Hungary	77.0
The Netherlands	64.0
Great Britain	62.9
All	58.6
West Germany	55.6
Australia	41.6
United States	27.9

Source: Adapted from a table in *U.S. News & World Report,* August 7, 1989, p. 25. Copyright © 1989, *U.S. News & World Report.*

The class structure of the United States places strong emphasis on status-defining boundaries of power, money, and involvement in influential social circles. This contrasts sharply with the French, who define class boundaries based more on intelligence, cosmopolitanism, and refinement.

Closely related to individualism and self-motivation is the presence of competition. Competition is a part of life from early childhood. Children play games in which only one person can win. Video games are competitive. Schools are competitive. And that competition is carried into the workplace. The overwhelming presence of competition in U.S. society can be seen in the ever-present sports metaphor. Many human endeavors are spoken of in sports language: a playing field, competitors, scores, winners, rankings. A good book or a good movie is ranked "No. 1" by the newspapers. Presidential candidates are given daily scores by the media—one candidate is so many points ahead of the competition.

Surveys suggest that because of individualistic values, U.S. citizens are less likely to vote on the basis of economic class. U.S. citizens are less likely to favor government redistributing income from rich to poor or providing jobs for all. In fact, surveys show that only 23% of U.S. citizens favor the state taking care of the poor. The next lowest in Europe is Germany at 50%. People in the United States, though, are far more likely to do volunteer work. More than half do. People in the United States prefer to help the needy independently. And, as an opportunity society, the United States ranks first among nations believing that people should have the chance to attend college. (See Table 8.5.)

Social Organization

This cultural pattern refers to ways society is organized. For example, the United States separates religion and state. Other cultures integrate church and state. Two major social organization patterns—equality and conformity—may explain many others characteristic of the United States.

Equality

Equality is an important cultural myth in the United States, although beliefs may appear contradictory to actions. The U.S. legal system promises equal treatment, yet evidence can be cited that questions this assertion. It is popularly said, though, that everyone should be treated equally.

The United States has "equal opportunity" laws. That choice of words is clearly important: Everyone should have the same opportunity to work hard and succeed. It's in the area of employment that the laws struggle to define equality. Employment decisions cannot be made on the basis of age, ancestry or ethnicity, disability, marital or parental status, race, religion, or sex. Again, though, evidence can be cited that demonstrates that people are different in achievements, successes, and rewards. (See Table 8.6 for a comparison of the importance of equality and freedom, by country.)

Table 8.6 Importance of Equality and Freedom, by Country: Affirmative Responses

Country	Importance of	
	Equality (%)	Freedom (%)
United States	20	72
Great Britain	23	69
France	32	54
Ireland	38	46
Italy	45	43
West Germany	39	37
Japan	32	37
Spain	39	36

Source: Adapted from *U.S. News & World Report,* August 7, 1989. Copyright © 1989, *U.S. News & World Report.*

The struggle for an Equal Rights Amendment highlights a very real struggle in the United States to define equality of the sexes. The sense of equality extends to freedom to decide with whom to associate and occasional disregard for hierarchical structures. Most people in the United States call each other by first names. Employees associate with bosses off the job, and all feel—perhaps mistakenly—that it's a "right" to go to the "top" to deal directly with the boss.

Conformity

Cultures differ in the content or type of conformity. Some emphasize conformity

Global Voices

Civil rights for all Americans—black, white, red, yellow, the rich, poor, young, old, gay, straight, et cetera—is not a liberal or a conservative value. It's an American value that I would think that we pretty much all agree on.

—Reverend Jerry Falwell speaking to commentator Tucker Carlson on MSNBC's *The Situation* (Wolff, 2005)

to traditional or past-oriented norms, whereas others exhibit conformity to modern or future-oriented norms. People in the United States tend to emphasize conformity to modern norms. U.S. citizens seem to conform to what is "in."

Though these fads may be short-lived, they involve much of the society in some way. Consider the following: name-brand athletic shoes, designer jeans, haircut styles, bottled water, exercise and food trends, television programs from *American Idol* to *Survivor,* and Super Bowl Sunday. Overall, people in the United States exhibit an unusual confidence in U.S. institutions, such as schools, the military, and the judiciary. U.S. citizens have an 80% rate of confidence compared to about 50% in major European nations.

U.S. citizens are also unusually patriotic. Fully 80% are proud to be a citizen—some polls have placed that figure at 97%. The average in Europe is 38%. In some polls, 71% of U.S. citizens would be willing to fight for the country. Other polls show a lower percentage but still a majority. The all-Europe average is 43%; Japan's is 22%. Some may interpret that pride as arrogance. In 2003, a poll conducted for the British Broadcasting Corporation (BBC) of 11,000 people in Australia, Brazil, Britain, Canada, France, Indonesia, Israel, Jordan, Russia, South Korea, and the United States revealed that 65%, a majority in every country—including the United States—said that the United States is arrogant ("Int'l poll finds," 2003).

As a populous and powerful nation, the United States has admirers and detractors. In a 2007 BBC poll, countries that were most admired included Canada, Japan, France, Britain, and China. The least admired countries included Russia, North Korea, the United States, Iran, and Israel. Table 8.7 identifies countries where more than half of the population believes that the United States has a positive or negative influence in the world.

> **Global Voices**
>
> While Tocqueville praised the United States, he also wrote that he knew of no other country with "less independence of mind and true freedom of discussion."

FORCES TOWARD THE DEVELOPMENT OF REGIONAL CULTURES

You've read about the various events that resulted in the development of a national culture during the early post–World War II period. Today, that national unity is fragmenting into new cultural regions. Let's look at the forces fragmenting the national culture.

- The old industrial heartland is being replaced with new regional economic centers in the South and West, while at the same time, the United States is becoming part of an integrated global economy.

Table 8.7   Perceptions of U.S. Influence in the World

Countries Where More Than Half the Population Believe:			
United States Has Positive Influence in the World	Percentage	United States Has Negative Influence in the World	Percentage
Philippines	72	Greece	78
Nigeria	72	Germany	74
Kenya	70	Indonesia	71
		France	69
		Turkey	69
		Argentina	64
		Australia	60
		Egypt	59
		Russia	59
		Lebanon	58
		Brazil	57
		Britain	57
		UAE	57
		Canada	56
		Portugal	55
		South Korea	54
		Mexico	53
		China	52
		Chile	51

Source: "Hearts and minds" (2007, pp. 16–17).

Note: Margin of error ranges from ±3.1 to ±4.9 percentage points.

- Integration and equal rights have resulted in recognition and acceptance of social and cultural differences.
- Immigration has eroded the homogeneity of the U.S. population and created ties between U.S. society and other societies around the world.
- As national media have grown into global media, new forms of local, special interest, and multilanguage media have appeared.
- International air transportation makes it easier and less expensive to travel abroad than to rural U.S. locations.
- The end of the Cold War lessened for a time the need for a large national security establishment.

These forces are still in their beginning stages, but the trend is becoming increasingly clear that the United States is returning to a country of distinct, relatively independent regions (Clough, 1997).

Global Voices

There is a fashionable intellectual perception that America is becoming more and more alike from one end to the other, that it's all covered with interstate highways and Howard Johnsons. Horsepucky. The most amazing thing about this country is its diversity, and the persistence of its regional and cultural differences.

—Molly Ivins, journalist (1991, p. 123)

Consistent with regionalism is the growing strength of regional dialects in the United States. Recent research (Labov, Ash, & Boberg, 1997) found that accents in Philadelphia, the cities of the Great Lakes region, and most of the South are getting stronger. The dialects of U.S. cities are more different from each other now than 50 or 100 years ago.

And regional words and sayings also are continuing in use, despite mass media homogenized English. If you know a "preacher's nose" is a part of a chicken's rump, you're probably from the South, and if you know that a "dropped egg" is an egg taken out of its shell and boiled in water, you're probably from New England (J. H. Hall, 2004).

The New Regions

About 25 years ago, Garreau (1981) described what he called the "nine nations" of North America. Today, it's possible to imagine even more. Some of the metropolitan areas that have taken on distinct cultures within the larger U.S. culture include the following.

- Atlanta, Georgia, site of leading global corporations Coca-Cola and Delta Air Lines, and CNN headquarters, has strong ties to developing countries from the presence of the Centers for Disease Control and Prevention and CARE, the world's largest relief organization, and interest in Africa by the city's African-American majority.
- Charlotte, North Carolina, the center of a new southern industrial belt dominated by manufacturing and banking, has close ties to Europe, especially Germany.
- Miami, Florida, is heavily linked to Cuba, Haiti, and Latin America and has diverse Hispanic and Caribbean immigrant populations.

- Houston, and the rest of Texas and the Southwest, is an oil producer with increasing ties to Mexico as its culture and economic interests become ever more distinct from those of other parts of the United States.
- Los Angeles and Southern California, with the nation's largest and most ethnically diverse immigrant community and global entertainment and tourist industries, is the leading entry port for trade with Asia.
- San Francisco's Bay Area is the capital of the world's high-tech industry.
- Seattle, Washington, home of Starbucks and Microsoft, has economic ties to Asia.

Evidence for the existence of distinct regions is the continuing existence of English dialects in the U.S. Figure 8.1 illustrates these regions.

Figure 8.1   From Sea to See

Contrary to common perceptions that regional dialects are slowly disappearing into a homogenized stew, the dialects of North America are actually a dynamic mosaic of still-evolving pronunciation patterns, separated by unusually sharp boundaries.

Regional Dialects
The map illustrates dialect boundaries and pronunciation changes over the last century in their most extreme form.

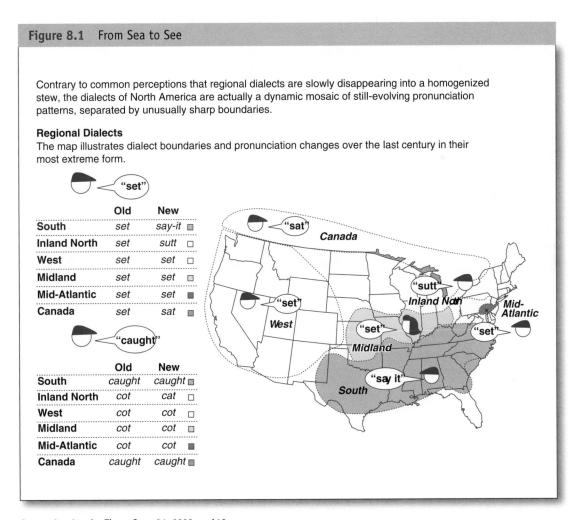

"set"

	Old	New
South	set	say-it ▣
Inland North	set	sutt ☐
West	set	set ☐
Midland	set	set ☐
Mid-Atlantic	set	set ■
Canada	set	sat ▣

"caught"

	Old	New
South	caught	caught ▣
Inland North	cot	cat ☐
West	cot	cot ☐
Midland	cot	cot ☐
Mid-Atlantic	cot	cot ■
Canada	caught	caught ▣

Source: Los Angeles Times, June 24, 2002, p. A12.

SUMMARY

Two thirds of U.S. residents see the past decade as a period of decline. The focus of this chapter is the fundamental values people in the United States share. Alexis de Tocqueville's 1831 tour resulted in long-lasting insights into U.S. values.

Kluckhohn and Strodtbeck's value orientation theory provides a way to describe U.S. culture:

- *Human being–nature orientation.* The United States is the most religious of the world's industrialized states. People in the United States make a clear distinction between human life and nature, placing a higher value on human life, and have a strong faith in the scientific method. Much of the rest of world attribute materialism, or the belief that possessions are important. to the United States
- *Activity orientation.* In the United States, work becomes part of one's identity. A positive value is placed on change.
- *Time orientation.* Time is viewed as a commodity and viewed in a linear fashion.
- *Human nature orientation.* People are viewed as having the potential for good and evil, as having free choice, and as being able to change.
- *Relational.* Perhaps the most defining value in the United States is the emphasis placed on individualism and self-motivation. The belief that everyone should have equal opportunity is an important cultural myth in the United States. And, finally, people in the United States to tend to emphasize conformity to modern norms.

The early United States may have been fragmented into many groups, but over the years many pressures contributed to a single culture. More recently, there may be renewed pressures for regional cultures.

DISCUSSION QUESTIONS

1. Discuss how unique cultural patterns developed in the United States, a country of immigrants from other nations.

2. Use the Kluckhohn and Strodtbeck (1961) value orientations to describe a culture other than the United States with which you have some knowledge.

3. What positive and negative consequences on the environment have resulted from the U.S. worldview?

4. What positive and negative consequences have resulted from each of the U.S. value orientations?

5. What do you believe is the most significant U.S. cultural pattern?

6. Consider the implications of the development of a dominant U.S. culture and of a fragmenting national culture.

KEY TERMS

activity orientation   209

change   210

conformity   217

emic   197

equality   216

etic   197

hyperindividualism   214

materialism   207

mutability   213

need for achievement   215

rationality   212

scientific method   205

worldview   202

READINGS

All readings are from *Intercultural Communication: A Global Reader* (Jandt, 2004).
M. Gene Aldridge, "What Is the Basis of American Culture?" (p. 84)
Ashis Nandy, "Consumerism: Its Hidden Beauties and Politics" (p. 400)
Mohan R. Limaye, "Five Ways to Reduce the Foreign Terrorist Threat to the United States" (p. 438)

STUDENT STUDY SITE

Visit the student study site at **www.sagepub.com/jandt7e** for these additional learning tools:

- Web Resources
- Audio and Video Links
- SAGE journal articles
- eFlashcards
- Web Quizzes
- Sample Essays

CHAPTER

9

FOCUS QUESTIONS

- What defines Arab culture?
- What are the major beliefs of the Islamic faith?
- How do Arab and U.S. cultural values compare?
- What are some of the difficulties in intercultural communication between Arab and Western cultures?

Comparative Cultural Patterns

Arab Culture

The Arab States
The Islamic Faith
> Muhammad, the Prophet
> The Koran
> Religious Practices
Saudi Arabia
> Geography
> Discovery of Oil
> Ruling Saud Family and Conservative Wahhabism
> Media
> Matawain
>> Contact With the United States
Dubai
Dominant Cultural Patterns
> Worldview
> Activity Orientation
> Time Orientation
> Human Nature Orientation
> Relational Orientation
>> Role of Women
Communication Barriers
> Political Unrest and Terrorism
> Political Unrest and Social Media
> Westernization Versus Cultural Norms
> Stereotypes
Summary
Discussion Questions
Key Terms
Student Study Site

Any two cultures could be compared as a way of learning more about both. Knowledge of other cultures is critical. You remember that cultural awareness is identified as a critical intercultural communication skill. In this chapter, the same categories used in the previous chapter to describe dominant U.S. cultural values are used here to learn more about Arab culture—a culture often misunderstood in the United States.

This chapter is devoted to how religion and language define Arab culture and then extends that with an examination of the conservative Arab state Saudi Arabia and the more tolerant emirate Dubai. The chapter concludes by identifying some of the communication barriers among the Arab states and the United States. Two key things to remember before you begin reading this chapter: While it is stated that religion, in part, defines Arab culture, it's important to remember that more Muslims live outside of the Arab states than in them. Second, the Arab states are very diverse. Every attempt has been made to be accurate, yet remember that generalized information is only that. It may not accurately reflect individuals or smaller groups.

As you study this chapter, make comparisons to the previous chapter on dominant U.S. cultural values. What intercultural communication problems could arise between individuals from these diverse cultures?

THE ARAB STATES

There is much diversity in the Arab world today, composed of 22 countries with a total population of 338 million. The population per country in 2007 ranges from 600,000 in Qatar to 80 million in Egypt. Iran is not considered an Arab country because its language is Persian (Farsi). Annual per capita gross domestic product (GDP) ranges from $1,176 in Comoros to more than $79,426 in Qatar. Literacy rates range from 56% in Mauritania and Morocco to 95% in Kuwait. (See Table 9.1.)

The Arab world's history spans more than 5,000 years. Yet from the time of Napoleon, who invaded Egypt in 1798, until the end of World War I, European countries conquered close to 90% of the Arab world by military force. After World War I, the European colonial powers began a slow retreat.

THE ISLAMIC FAITH

Traditionally, Arabs have had three main political and cultural trends: nationalism, pan-Arabism, and Islam. After the 1970 death of Egypt's pan-Arab leader, Gamal Abdel Nasser, secular Arab nationalism has not regained the influence it had. Later, Iraq's Saddam Hussein appealed to secular Arab nationalism. And in some countries such as Egypt and Lebanon, many people identify themselves as Egyptians or Lebanese. But in much of the Arab world, people identify themselves as Arab or Muslim.

Table 9.1 Overview of 22 Arab Countries

Country	2007 Population (Millions)	2008 Internet users/1000 people	2007 Adult Literacy (%)	GDP per Capita (US$)
Algeria	33.9	120	75.4	8,320
Bahrain	0.8	520	88.8	26,664
Comoros	0.6	40	75.1	1,176
Djibouti	0.8	20	N/A	2,471
Egypt	80.1	170	66.4	5,889
Iraq	29.5	10	74.1	N/A
Jordan	5.9	270	91.1	5,956
Kuwait	2.9	370	94.5	55,719
Lebanon	4.2	230	89.6	13,475
Libya	6.2	50	86.8	17,068
Mauritania	3.1	20	55.8	2,118
Morocco	31.2	330	55.6	4,628
Oman	2.7	200	84.4	25,653
Palestine*	4.0	90	93.8	N/A
Qatar	1.1	340	93.1	79,426
Saudi Arabia	24.7	310	85.0	24,726
Somalia	8.7	10	N/A	N/A
Sudan	40.4	100	60.9	2,051
Syria	20.5	170	83.1	4,760
Tunisia	10.1	270	77.7	7,979
United Arab Emirates	4.4	650	90.0	58,006
Yemen	22.3	20	58.9	2,387

Source: Data from United Nations Development Programme on Governance in the Arab Region website (http://www.arabstats.org/).

Note: The State of Palestine is recognized by many countries. Many of those that do not recognize the State of Palestine do recognize the PLO as the "representative of the Palestinian people."

FOCUS ON THEORY 9.1

Christianity's New Testament makes no claims for religious orthodoxy, but in the 4th century, once it had been embraced by Emperor Constantine, its leaders began to demand it, converting some by the sword and burning alleged heretics at the stake. Achieving religious freedom without abandoning religious belief was the difficult challenge. The struggle for religious freedom paved the way for discussions of freedom of speech and the press. Zagorin (2003) argues that a nation's progress depends on the creation and maintenance of human freedom, which in turn depends on religious freedom. Freedom in the modern sense of the term was introduced into the Arab culture through contact with Europe—particularly France. The scholar Ahmed bin Khalid al-Nasseri wrote that "the notion of freedom invented by the ferenja (foreigners or French) is, undoubtedly, the work of heretics. It requires disregard of the rights of God, the rights of parents and even the rights of humanity" (United Nations Development Programme, 2004, p. 54). On the other hand, the liberal Ahmed Lutfi al-Sayyid wrote, "Our freedom is our very being and our being is our freedom" (United Nations Development Programme, 2004, p. 55). Lewis (2002) recognizes the argument that Islam was once the pioneer of freedom, science, and economic development yet also raises the same point that in modern times, it's the separation of church and state and the creation of societies governed by secular laws that have fostered freedom of thought and expression, which have made progress possible.

The Arab culture transcends time and space, particularly through its language and its Islamic faith, the second largest in the world after Christianity, with some 1.2 billion followers, or about 20% of the world's population. **Arabs**, the ethnic group that originally spread Islam, are now a minority in the religion (see Tables 9.2 and 9.3). The **Muslim** religion extends far beyond the Arab world, from Africa to Europe to Asia, including republics of the former Soviet Union, which had experienced suppression of religion and language since the time of the Russian czars. Today, some 75 countries have large Muslim populations. Just as the Muslim religion includes more than Arabs, not all Arabs are Muslim. The Arab world, however, is connected largely by a shared culture that developed in the Islamic faith. Of course there is diversity within Islam, but it can be said that Islam is a "multidimensional system of beliefs that embraces the spiritual and the material, the divine and the earthly, the heavenly soul and mortal worldly deeds" (United Nations Development Programme, 2003, p. 118).

People who practice this religion are called Muslims (literally "submitters" to the will of God). Islam is a nonhierarchical religion; there is no priesthood. No one institution or individual speaks for all Muslims.

Table 9.2   Muslim Populations Outside of the Arab States

Although Islam is often associated with the Arab world and the Middle East, fewer than 15% of Muslims are Arab.

Country	Number of Muslims
Indonesia	204.8 million
Pakistan	178.1 million
India	177.3 million
Bangladesh	148.6 million
Nigeria	75.7 million
Iran	74.8 million
Turkey	74.7 million
China	22 million
Russia	16 million

Source: Population estimates are from Mapping the Global Muslim Population, Pew Research Center's Forum on Religion & Public Life, 2009.

Table 9.3   Muslims and Mosques in the West

	Total Population (in millions)	Muslim Population (in millions)	Mosques
United States	305.5	2.5	1,900
Germany	82	3.2 to 3.4	2,600
France	65	5.5	2,100
United Kingdom	62	2.4	1,500
Spain	46	.8 to 1.0	454
Canada	34	1.0	198

Source: Ghosh (2010, p. 23).

Muhammad, the Prophet

The prophet Muhammad (born circa 570, died 632) founded the religion in the early 7th century in Arabia. Orphaned at an early age, Muhammad ibn Abdullah was a businessman

FOCUS ON CULTURE 9.1

The first Muslims in the Americas were enslaved Africans brought over in the 17th century. African-Americans account for the majority of all converts to Islam in the United States. Among African-Americans, the Nation of Islam grew most rapidly in the 1960s. Most of its mosques underwent reforms after 1975 to join conventional Islam. Today, the Nation of Islam represents a small fraction of Muslims in the United States. Most South Asian and Arab Muslims' immigration dates to the 1960s and later. Today, Islam is one of the fastest growing religions in the United States. Islam's presence is being felt in the United States: Casio markets a watch that sounds an electronic call to prayer, some banks have set up "Islamic accounts" in response to the Muslim prohibition against paying or receiving interest, Warith Deen was the first Muslim to open the U.S. Senate with a prayer, and Keith Ellison was the first Muslim elected to Congress in 2006. Minnesotan Ellison took the oath of office on a copy of the Koran owned by President Thomas Jefferson.

Source: J. I. Smith (2000) and Dannin (2002).

when, in 610, it is said he received his first revelations through the angel Gabriel. These continued for another 20 years and form the Koran, the holy book of Islam.

By the 8th century, a system of political-religious leadership that originated with the first successor to Muhammad held authority over parts of three continents, from what is now Pakistan across the Middle East and North Africa to Spain. **Caliphates** is the name given to geographical areas ruled by a chief Muslim civil and religious leader. The leader, known as the caliph, governed as a successor to Muhammad. By the 10th century, the office had become more political. Then, in 1924, the office was abolished by Kamal Ataturk, the founder of modern Turkey. Today some Muslims are campaigning for the restoration of the caliphates in a form resembling the Roman Catholic papacy as a means of restoring order. Today, any imam, or religious leader claiming descent from Muhammad, can assert authority.

> **Global Voices**
>
> A British schoolteacher was arrested in Sudan in 2007, accused of insulting Islam's Prophet, after she allowed her pupils to name a teddy bear Muhammad. It was seen as an insult to Islam to attempt to create an image of the Prophet Muhammad.

The Koran

The Koran (often spelled Quran), it is said, was revealed by God to the prophet Muhammad in Arabic and generally is considered to contain the literal words of Allah, or God. The Koran contains stories, admonitions, verse and prophetic segments, and social, political, and economic laws. The Koran embraces all areas of human affairs, from the most personal to international relations. Not only is it unique in its completeness, but it also deals with human transactions in such a way as to make God's presence felt in every human interaction. There is no separation of church and state as in the United States. The Koran is a spiritual guide, a system of law, a code of ethics, and a way of life. Islam is the only world religion that offers rules by which to govern a state as well as a set of spiritual beliefs.

Dubai's ruler sponsors an annual competition for young men 21 and younger to recite the Koran from memory. This is to encourage young Muslims to better understand their faith. He provides nearly $700,000 in prize money. This competition is one of the most prestigious Koran recitation competitions in the world. The judges choose a section from the Koran at random, recite the beginning, and then the contestant is expected to pick up where the judges left off. The contestants must recite in Arabic in a melodic chant that follows rules known as *tajweed*. Tapes of the best reciters are sold across the Arabic world.

Religious Practices

Westerners once called Islam "Muhammadanism," but Muslims objected to the term because Muhammad is not regarded as divine. He is considered the last and most important prophet in a line that includes Abraham, Noah, Moses, and Jesus. The accounts of Muhammad's life and teachings are second only to the Koran as authoritative guidelines in Muslim faith and law. Many Muslims stress the similarities between Islam and the principal Abrahamic faiths in the United States. (The three Abrahamic faiths are Judaism, Christianity, and Islam.) For example, Jewish and Islamic dietary laws resemble one another very closely. According to Islamic law, Muslims may not drink alcoholic beverages, eat pork, or gamble. Muslims honor Jesus as one of the prophets of the Bible but not as the son of God. Most who practice the faith are religious conservatives with a literalist view of the holy book of Muslims.

The five religious obligations of Muslims begin with the public witness, or *shahadah*, "I testify that there is no God but God; I testify that Muhammad is the Messenger of God." Expressing this with conviction, it is said, is what makes one a Muslim. Short prayers, or *salah*, are recited by individuals five times daily at intervals from early morning to evening, each time after washing hands, arms, face, hair, and feet (although rubbing water lightly over socks is permissible). Facing toward Mecca, Muslims go through prescribed motions of standing, kneeling, and touching the floor with the forehead and palms. Congregational prayers at Friday noon are led by an imam, or spiritual leader. Alms giving, or *zakat*, is the duty of sharing with the poor a small percentage of the wealth beyond one's basic expenses.

Fasting, or *sawm*, is central during **Ramadan**, the ninth month on Islam's lunar calendar. Ramadan commemorates the prophet Muhammad receiving revelations from the angel Gabriel. Ramadan is a time to reflect on the meaning of Islam, to rejuvenate faith. Fasting Muslims abstain from food, drink, and sexual intercourse during the daylight hours. Nourishment is allowed only for the sick, the elderly, the pregnant, and the very young.

At least once in a Muslim's lifetime, a believer is expected to make a pilgrimage, or hajj, to Mecca. It's an elaborate series of rites requiring several days.

Muslims generally fall into either the Sunni or the Shiite branch. The **Sunni**, who account for about 90% of the world's Muslims, believe that Muslim leadership in the early years passed to a series of caliphs, whereas the **Shiite** Muslims believe that leadership should be passed down Muhammad's bloodline, starting with his martyred cousin and son-in-law Ali and his descendants. Shiites tend to be more ecstatic in religious practice and have messianic expectations of a future imam who will bring justice to the world. Shiites form the majority in Iraq, Iran, Bahrain, Azerbaijan, and eastern Saudi Arabia. Sufism is an ascetic movement throughout Islam directed toward mysticism and a direct personal experience with God.

The *sunnah* are the traditions relating to the deeds and utterances of Muhammad. Together with the Koran, they are the basis of the *sharia,* or canonic law. The legal system is different from Western models. The sharia system relies far less on physical evidence than on the accused's statements and answers to questions posed by judges. Cleric-scholars using the Koran and the acts of Muhammad as their guide get to the truth through patient questioning. If they err, they must answer to Allah. Anecdotal evidence indicates that the crime rate is low by Western standards. The Koran and *sunnah* dictate specific penalties for some crimes, such as amputating a thief's hand. Contrary to popular belief, these are rarely carried out because the crimes are narrowly defined and proof is strict. For example, a shoplifter would not suffer amputation because shoplifting is not considered a theft as the goods were not locked up. Executions occur only if all heirs of the victim demand it. Judges often encourage the family to accept "blood money," traditionally the price of 100 camels, instead. Punishment is often mild by Western standards. Some trials fall short of international standards—even "divine law must be carried out by mortals."

Most cultural differences come from the religion's conservatism. Muslims are known for preserving ethics and family values. Prohibitions against alcohol, smoking, and premarital sex are strict. To many Muslims, people in the United States don't care about families, abandon parents when they grow old, and have an epidemic of AIDS, pornography, pregnant teenagers, abortions, and illegitimate babies. These aspects of U.S. culture are not desired by Muslims as they bring shame on the family. To Muslims, God and family are most important. The dividing line between the Arab and Western worlds is religion. Islam is a religion, but also a way of life and the central force of Arab existence.

The prophet Muhammad achieved victory as a military commander and political ruler. The state has been the instrument of Islam, and God was considered to be head of both the state and the religion. This is in sharp contrast to Western Christian countries, which separated church and state. Perhaps as a consequence, only four (Comoros, Mauritania, Lebanon, and Kuwait) of the Arab states have developed even nominal democracies (Lewis, 2002).

Between the 9th and 13th centuries, Muslim scholars improved and named algebra, refined techniques for surgery, advanced the study of optics, produced astronomical tables, proposed that the Earth turns on an axis, and proposed a sun-centered universe. Then the scientific spirit died (Masood, 2008). Today there are an average of 8.5 scientists per 1,000 population in Islamic countries compared to 40.7 worldwide (Tolson, 2007). Nasr (2003) proposes that science in Islamic culture should not be seen as an extension of Western science but should be seen as an independent way of looking at nature. Rather than accepting that humans can only know the world through its quantifiable properties, Muslim scientists believe that full understanding requires seeing the world as signs of divine purpose.

Despite the economic slowdown, construction continues in Dubai as the cost of canceling projects can exceed the cost of completing them.

Global Voices

My Islam is a religion of tolerance and brotherhood.

—Sai'd Al-Ashmawy, former chief justice, Egypt's Supreme Court

Jews and Christians and whoever believes in God . . . and does what is right shall have nothing to fear or regret. Among his other signs are the creation of the heavens and the earth and the diversity of your tongues and colors. Surely there are signs in this for all mankind.

—Koran

SAUDI ARABIA

Geography

Because of the importance of Saudi Arabia in the Arab world, we need to pay particular attention to this country. Saudi Arabia occupies nearly 90 % of the Arabian peninsula and is the 12th largest country in the world—2,250,000 square kilometers (868,730 square miles), or one fourth the size of the United States. As 98 % of the land is desert, most cities are built on the coast and on oases. With an average of only 10 centimeters of rainfall a year, Saudi Arabia gets most of its water from underground aquifers filled with fossil water thousands of years old. This water—like oil—is a nonrenewable resource. Desalination provides only a small percentage of Saudi Arabia's water.

Discovery of Oil

In the 1940s, Saudi Arabia was mostly unknown to the rest of the world, and the rest of the world was unknown to most Saudis. Nomads outnumbered the settled. The economy was on a subsistence level. Illiteracy was high. In 1933, U.S. oil companies launched the California Arabian Standard Oil Company, which later became the Arabian-American Oil Co. (ARAMCO). With monies from the oil discovered in the late 1930s, Saudi Arabia developed at a pace unparalleled in history. With 25% to 30% of the world's proven oil reserves, Saudi Arabia became one of the strongest economies in the world, with oil as the source of its income. With a population of 9.5 million in the 1970s, oil raised its citizens to riches.

In the early 1980s, per capita income in Saudi Arabia was about $18,000, but by 2003, it had fallen to around $7,200, with many young Saudis no longer guaranteed good salaries and prestigious jobs. By 2007, the United States was importing 1.453 million barrels of oil a day from Saudi Arabia. By 2010, the country's population of 26 million citizens had a per capita income of $24,200. (Actually this was far from the wealthiest of the region. Qatar's per capita was $179,000.) The kingdom is wealthy but must import most of its essential goods.

Ruling Saud Family and Conservative Wahhabism

Saudi Arabia's ruling Saud family gained power in the 1920s by consolidating feudal tribes through an alliance with an ultraconservative brand of Islam, known as Wahhabism, that frowned on smoking, drinking, and virtually any contact between unmarried members of the opposite sex. In this sense, Wahhabism can be compared to the Puritans. Even today, as guardian of the two holy Muslim mosques in Mecca and Medina, Saudi Arabia is the most conservative Islamic country in the world. It is said that Islam, as practiced in Saudi Arabia today, remains much as it was in the time of Muhammad.

Media

The government licenses all bookshops, printing presses, and public relations agencies to ensure that standards of taste are maintained. At least 10 daily newspapers and nine weekly or monthly magazines are published in Saudi Arabia. All are privately owned but subsidized in varying degrees by the government. Editors patrol themselves, deferring to the government's Ministry of Information in questionable cases.

Some advertisers have attempted to adapt to Arab cultural values, such as in the portrayal of women. European ads for the men's cologne

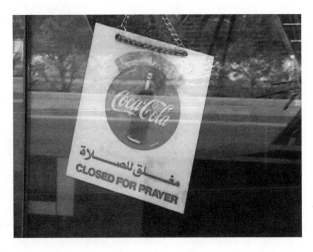

A shop closed during Muslim prayers is a typical sight in Saudi Arabia.

Drakkar Noir by Guy Laroche showed a man's hand clutching the cologne bottle and a woman's hand seizing his bare forearm. In the Saudi version, the man's arm is clothed in a dark jacket sleeve, and the woman is touching the man's hand only with her fingertips. Even so, some might find such ads objectionable in that they suggest sexual temptation (Nafeesi, 1986).

Broadcast media are state-controlled. State-run TV operates four networks; state-run radio operates several networks. Multiple international broadcasters are also available. Satellite television and the Internet bring in *Desperate Housewives,* David Letterman, and other U.S. shows. Saudi Arabia is saturated with symbols of U.S. culture but at the same time promotes hostility against U.S. foreign policy, values, and Judeo-Christian beliefs.

Matawain

Public morality committees, the **matawain** or the regional Societies for the Preservation of Virtue and the Prevention of Vice, ensure strict compliance with religious requirements. Salaried morals police patrol the public domain, making sure that businesses close at prayer times and that women are properly covered. The religious police have declared Barbie dolls with their revealing clothing as a threat to morality and offensive to Islam. There are no public worship services of any religion except Islam. There is no church, no temple of any kind, and no missionary work allowed. In fact, the Koran is part of Saudi Arabia's constitution. The country bases its legitimacy on its commitment to Islam and the implementation of sharia, or Islamic law. Anything that isn't allowed in Islam will not happen.

Saudi Arabia has parallel legal systems—one civil and the other, more prominent sharia system, based on the Koran. Criminal cases are presided over by religiously conservative judges not bound by civil law. For example, in late 2007, a married woman was meeting a man alone when the pair was accosted and she was gang raped. The assailants received 5-year prison terms. She was sentenced to 200 lashes and 6 months in prison. The sentence had been 90 lashes but was raised after she appealed. The religious judges hold power and are considered by some a check and balance on the monarchy.

Contact With the United States

Just weeks before his death, President Franklin Roosevelt hosted King Saud aboard a U.S. ship and gave the aging king his wheelchair. They formed a relationship that has continued between the two countries. President Harry S. Truman signed the first security agreement with Saudi Arabia in 1947. For years, American and Saudi peoples worked together, liked each other, but did not know much about each other. For example, the ARAMCO compound in Dhahran is like a 1950s midwestern U.S. small town isolated from the rest of the country with well-sprinkled lawns, neat houses, U.S.-brand groceries in stores, and even U.S. electrical current—not Saudi.

Today, the United States is the world's largest oil consumer, and Saudi Arabia is the largest market for U.S. consumer products in the Middle East. For years, Saudi Arabia has worked with the United States to keep oil markets stable and advance common political goals. In the 1980s, Saudi Arabia kept oil prices low, which helped weaken the Soviet Union. Again in the 1990s, Saudi Arabia kept the market stable after Iraq's invasion of Kuwait. Saudi Arabia has spent tens of billions of dollars on Western technology, including $270 billion on high-tech weapons since the 1991 Gulf War.

The 1991 war in the Persian Gulf (for which Saudi Arabia provided water, food, shelter, and fuel for coalition forces and made monetary payments to some coalition partners including

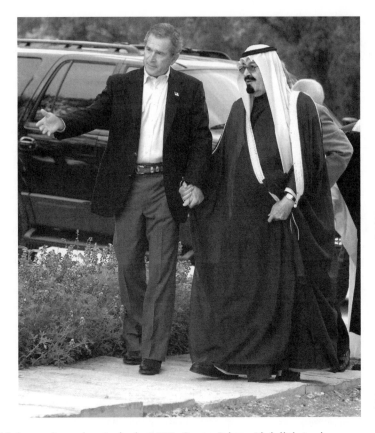

After King Fahd experienced a stroke in 1995, Crown Prince Abdullah took over governing the country. President George W. Bush is shown here with the Saudi Crown Prince. After Fahd's death in 2005, Abdullah became king. Saudi Arabia citizens like the idea that U.S. leaders come to Saudi Arabia as supplicants.

$15 billion to the United States) brought individuals from the two cultures into contact, and, as we have seen, neither will be the same in the future. A number of reform-minded Saudi businessmen, government officials, and academics used the 1991 war as an opportunity to advocate for expanded rights for women, a reliable court system, and an elected parliament. The Bush administration hoped that the 2003 war with Iraq would lead to more democratic changes in conservative regimes elsewhere in the Middle East. The conservatives have worked to make Islamic Saudi Arabia even more fundamentalist—particularly in the areas of economic policies (i.e., eliminating Western-oriented banks), the parts of the legal system not fully based on sharia law, censorship of foreign media with secular ideas, and a heavy dependence on the West in foreign and defense policies—particularly in light of the war with Iraq.

Saudi Arabia is a monarchy, but an age-old practice of majlis provides any citizen access to the king and local governors. Also in Bedouin tradition are diwaniyahs, political meetings where

Table 9.4	Year Women Received Right to Vote
1946	Djobouti
1949	Syria
1952	Lebanon
1956	Egypt, Somalia
1959	Tunisia
1961	Mauritania
1962	Algeria
1963	Morocco
1964	Libya, Sudan
1970	Yeman
1973	Bahrain
1974	Jordan
1980	Iraq
1994	Oman
2003	Qatar
2005	Kuwait

men discuss community issues and debate politics. Perhaps in response to calls for change from both religious conservatives who resented the influx of Western forces during the Gulf War and liberals who saw the war as an impetus for opening the kingdom more to the West, early in 1992, King Fahd announced on national television a new administrative structure for the country. The king created a national consultative council that would review government policies and advise the Cabinet of Ministers, thus providing citizens a voice in government, and he announced guarantees for personal liberties, such as freedom from unreasonable searches, for the first time in history. In 2005, municipal elections were held in Riyadh, Mecca, and Jidda. These elected officials have some latitude in overseeing development in their cities. A second round of municipal elections were schedule for 2009, but repeatedly delayed until the fall 2011. Only men were eligible to vote in these elections.

Before the second round of municipal elections, King Abdullah announced that women would be able to participate in future municipal elections. Those may occur in 2015. The king further said he would consider appointing women to the consultative council: "Muslim women in our Islamic history have demonstrated positions that expressed correct opinions" (Murphy, 2011).

King Abdullah is widely regarded as a modernizer in a royal family balanced between those favoring changes and those who insist on maintaining a strict Wahhabi interpretation of Islam. In early 2009, King Abdullah appointed the first woman to a ministerial post (a new post of deputy minister of women's education) and dismissed a leading fundamentalist cleric and the head of the nation's powerful religious police (The year women received the right to vote in selected Arab states is shown on Table 9.4). Some fear that hurried reforms will lead to religious revolt.

DUBAI

Dubai is the second largest of the seven emirates that make up the United Arab Emirates. The emirate has just about depleted its own oil supply and has transformed itself into a post-oil economy.

Dubai represents a significant change in the Persian Gulf region. In the past, oil profits were reinvested in the West. Today Gulf states like Saudi Arabia, Qatar, and the United Arab Emirates are investing those profits at home. More than $1 trillion of construction is under way in the Persian Gulf states. Dubai is the high-profile example of that transformation. Two generations ago, Dubai was a small merchant community. Its ruler, Sheik Mohammed bin Rashid al-Maktoum, is constructing a city on par with New York and Hong Kong. Dubai has become the business and financial center of the Persian Gulf region and, in doing so, has an unusually tolerant society open to foreigners. The city of Dubai claims the world's tallest building, the world's tallest all-suite hotel, the world's largest artificial island, the first indoor ski slope in the desert, one of the world's largest shopping malls, and an airport double the capacity of New York's JFK International Airport. The Burj Dubai, a hotel, business, and residential complex, topped at 828 m (2716 feet) and became the world's tallest freestanding structure. The list of international companies that have facilities in Dubai demonstrates the emirate's open society: Morgan Stanley, Goldman Sachs, Microsoft, CNN, MTV Arabia, Harvard Medical School. There is even a Tiger Woods–designed golf course. The worldwide economic turndown has had a major impact on Dubai's development, however. The government and government controlled companies had to manage over $100 billion in debt.

Building this new oasis are foreign workers from the Indian subcontinent and Southeast Asia. Estimates are the expatriates make up as much as 95% of Dubai's population. Many live in camps, work 12-hour shifts, and earn an average of $175 a month. Dissidents lose their visas and are deported (Davidson, 2008). By nationality, Indians make up 42% of the population; Pakistani, 13%.

Dubai has been called the Las Vegas of the Middle East and, in doing so, has become a tourist center. While it may appear to be an unusually tolerant society open to foreigners, its indigenous population has long demanded that the government preserve their religious values and traditions. Dubai attempts to balance Western interests and Muslim sensibilities. Alcohol is served in hotel restaurants but not in other restaurants. Western women may wear bikinis on the same beaches where Arab women wear abayas. Very little democracy exists as all important decisions are imposed by the royal family.

To the south, the emirate Abu Dhabi produces some 3 million barrels of oil daily. It is using its wealth more conservatively by developing infrastructure first and investing in renewal and clean energy.

FOCUS ON THE ENVIRONMENT 9.1

 Masdar City is a planned community being built in Abu Dhabi, United Arab Emirates, with the majority of capital provided by the government of Abu Dhabi. The city is being built to function entirely on solar energy and other renewable energy sources with a sustainable, zero-carbon, zero-waste ecology. The city's perimeter wall will provide a barrier to the desert heat while narrow, shaded streets make cool breezes possible. No automobiles will be permitted within the city. A solar-powered desalination plant will provide for the city's water. The city also will attempt to reduce waste to zero. Progress has been slowed by the recent global financial crisis.

Source: Masdar City website (http://www.masdarcity.ae/en/).

DOMINANT CULTURAL PATTERNS

Muslims represent a growing social and political force that questions some of the West's dominant cultural patterns, particularly the following:

- The Relationship Between God and Humankind
- The Role of Morality in Human Affairs
- The Role of Technology and Modernization
- The Nature of Progress

We will use the Kluckhohn and Strodtbeck (1961) universally shared problems, discussed in the previous chapter to describe U.S. cultural patterns, again here to describe Arab cultural patterns and to provide a useful comparison.

Worldview

As mentioned in Chapter 8, a worldview is the outlook that a culture has concerning the nature of the universe, the nature of humankind, the relationship between humanity and the universe, and other philosophical issues defining humans' place in the cosmos.

In virtually all aspects, the Arab worldview is derived from Islam and expressed in its language. Islam draws no distinction between religion and the temporal aspects of life. According to Islam, everything in the world except humans is administered by God-made laws. The physical world has no choice but obedience to God. Humans alone possess the qualities of intelligence and choice. Humans can choose to submit to the Law of God and, in so doing, will be in harmony with all other elements of nature.

Islam holds that the world is totally real. It is incumbent upon every Muslim to seek knowledge in the broadest sense from the created universe, as it reveals knowledge and truth. Though Islam demands faith in God as the basis of knowledge and research, it encourages all methods of gaining knowledge, whether rational or experimental. This overwhelming quest for knowledge gave birth to, among other things, the modern sciences of mathematics, physics, chemistry, and medicine and triggered the Renaissance in Europe (Haiek, 1992).

While Islam generally does not hinder private enterprise or condemn private possessions, it does not tolerate selfish and greedy capitalism. This is an expression of the general philosophy of Islam of a moderate and middle but positive and effective course between the individual and the state—yet among the most egregious violators of human rights are the authoritarian regimes in the Muslim world, such as Saddam Hussein's former Iraqi regime.

Activity Orientation

Earning a living through labor is not only a duty but also a virtue. Islam respects all kinds of work as long as there is no indecency or wrong involved. Whatever a person makes is one's private possession that no one else may claim. Islam encourages Muslims to work, to engage in free enterprise, and to earn and possess, but the "owner" is God and the human is the trustee. This means the Muslim has a responsibility to invest and spend wisely. Just as Islam

FOCUS ON THE ENVIRONMENT 9.2

The primary sources of Islamic teaching about the natural environment are the Koran and Islamic law. Because humans are seen as part of nature, a recurrent theme in these sources is opposition to wastefulness and environmental destruction. Islamic law has numerous injunctions to protect and guard common environmental resources on a shared basis. There is also an injunction that the Earth and its natural resources must be preserved for future generations, with human beings acting as custodians of the natural world.

Source: United Nations Development Programme (2008, p. 61).

provides the values for work, it also guides other aspects of human activity. Islam encourages practicality. It does not encourage wishful thinking but does encourage one to accept and deal with the reality within one's reach.

Adherence to Islam largely conflicts with uncritical acceptance of progress and change. Islam is conservative because of its adherence to the Koran.

Time Orientation

Saudi accounting of time shows a strong relationship to the cosmos. Saudi Arabia adheres to the traditional *Hijrah* (or *Hegirian*) calendar, which is based on the cycles of the moon. A lunar month is the time between two new moons. The Hijrah year contains 12 months and so is 11 days shorter than the solar year. As a result, the months shift gradually from one season to another. Months in the Hijrah calendar have no relation to the seasons. The first day of the first year of the Hijrah calendar corresponds to July 15, 622, the date on which Muhammad fled Mecca for Medina to escape persecution at the hands of the Quraish. The Western method of designating Islamic dates is AH (*anno Hegira*).

Global Voices

Muslims celebrate the Prophet Muhammad's birthday on the 12th Rabi' al-awwal month on the Islamic calendar with festivities and religious fervor.

The traditional system of accounting time during the day is tied to the rising and setting of the sun. International communications, however, has forced Saudi Arabia to adopt Greenwich mean time.

Arab markets and stores appear to be in a state of mass confusion as customers all try to get the attention of a single clerk. Arab government offices may have large reception areas where groups of people are all conducting affairs at the same time. As a polychronic culture, Arabs can interact with several people at once and still be immersed in each other's business. Polychronic managers can supervise a large number of people. By their actions, polychronic cultures demonstrate that they are oriented to people, human relationships, and family.

Human Nature Orientation

Muslims believe that every person is born free of sin. It is said that when a person reaches the age of maturity, the individual becomes accountable for deeds and intentions. Thus, human nature is more good than evil, and the probability of positive change is greater than the probability of failure. God endowed only humans with intelligence and choice. The purpose of human life is to worship God by knowing, loving, and obeying him.

Relational Orientation

As we have seen, Arab culture is more group oriented. Social lives are traditionally organized around the family and tribal line. Loyalties are to family, clan, tribe, and government in that order. Individuals subordinate personal needs to the family and the community.

Many Saudis live in large extended families, and devotion to the family is central. In contrast to Western culture, the concept of individuality is absent. There is a strong sense of identity with the family. Saudis see themselves in the context of family. Duty is not to oneself but to the group. Loyalty is first to the family. All family members suffer from the dishonorable act of any one of them. Honor is the collective property of the family. Islam unifies humanity on the basis of equality. There are no bounds of race, country, or wealth. All are born equal and should have equal civil, political, and spiritual rights. In this sense, Islam is an international religion. Central to the Arab culture's social organization is family and Islam. Generous hospitality is a manner of honor and a sacred duty.

A man is usually considered to be a descendant only of his father and his paternal grandfather. A man's honor resides in the number of sons he sires. A man belongs to his father's family. Decisions are made by the family patriarch—not by the individual.

Role of Women

Most Muslims would say that women in Arab cultures are equal to men. The prophet Muhammad revolutionized life for women in the 7th century by granting women access to the mosque, full participation in public affairs, and the right to inherit property. The rights and responsibilities of women are equal to those of men but not identical with them. In Arab cultures, equality and sameness are two quite different things. It is said that women are deprived in some ways but are compensated in other ways. Thus, Arab women are equal as independent human beings, equal in the pursuit of knowledge, and equal in the freedom of expression. An Arab woman who is a wife and mother is entitled to complete provision and total maintenance by her husband. She may work and own property herself.

A traditional Saudi woman does not go out alone. She speaks to no man other than her husband or blood kin. Public facilities are segregated by sex. Even the takeout counters at McDonald's and Häagen-Dazs have two sections split by plywood dividers. Women who work outside the home work in capacities with other women exclusively. Saudi society is structured to keep a woman within strictly defined limits to protect her chastity.

Wearing the abaya and the veil is an old tradition to safeguard women from the actions of strange men. A woman is not permitted to expose any part of her body before strangers. Thus, the abaya and the veil represent honor, dignity, chastity, purity, and integrity. The great majority of Saudi women are willing to accept this position in society in return for the guarantee of security that Arab traditions provide. Those who want change want it within the context of the Arab culture.

Saudi women order in the women's section of McDonald's in the Kingdom Mall. Most coffee shops and restaurants have a "family section" where women and children are allowed to frequent with or without their husbands. Women are not allowed in strictly male cafés due to the religious restrictions of separating men and women in Islam.

FOCUS ON THE ENVIRONMENT 9.3

 Arab countries score below average on 17 of the Environmental Sustainability Index's 20 indicators. The Arab states are, in general, far below average on measures of environmental systems (the quality of air and water, for example) and on measures of social and institutional capacity and global stewardship. Water shortages are serious in many Arab countries. With 10% of the world's land, the Arab region controls only 1.2% of the global water reserves and relies on imports from outside the region for 60% of its needs. Arab countries generally exhibit higher levels of air emissions than other countries, particularly of oxides of nitrogen and volatile organic compounds. The United Arab Emirates has almost double the per capita carbon dioxide emissions of the United States. Representative of a pattern of environmental disengagement is that not a single Arab League member contributes payments to the Global Environmental Facility.

By contrast, they score above average on preserving land from human influence and in reducing human vulnerability to environmental harms (low proportion of undernourished, low child death rate from respiratory diseases, low death rate from intestinal infectious diseases, and low age 5 and younger mortality rate). The above-average performance in reducing human vulnerability is especially notable. A number of Arab countries take wildlife stewardship seriously and have launched programs to protect species and habitat.

Source: Esty, Levy, and Winston (2002, 2003).

COMMUNICATION BARRIERS

In summer 1990, there were no Western journalists and only a few thousand U.S. military advisers in Saudi Arabia. The war in the Persian Gulf changed that. By February 1991, more than 700 journalists and half a million U.S. troops were stationed there. Many U.S. soldiers spent up to 20 classroom hours learning about Arabs and Arab culture before being sent to Saudi Arabia. U.S. soldiers and Saudis started to get to know each other as individuals.

Political Unrest and Terrorism

Several barriers unique to the United States and Arab countries impede effective intercultural communication. One is the continuing political unrest in the region.

Islam emphasizes community over individual rights, and because the Koran provides rules for governing society, the line between religion and politics is blurred. Eight of the world's most authoritarian monarchies are in Islamic countries. Three Arab states—Iraq, Libya, and Sudan—have at times been labeled "outlaw" states by the United States and other countries. And 15 of the 19 suspected hijackers in the September 11, 2001, attacks on the World Trade Center and the Pentagon were Saudis. Saudi King Abdullah, in a 2005 interview on ABC-TV, said that the kingdom will fight terrorists and characterized Al-Qaida as the "work of the devil."

The effect of the 2003 war with Iraq is yet to be fully known. Initially, the televised images of the rapid U.S. thrust into Baghdad were seen as occupation—not liberation. In 1917, the British took Baghdad from the Ottoman Turks. The British general Frederick Stanley Maude told the citizens the British came not as conquerors but as liberators. The British stayed as colonialists until 1932. Some saw the United States acting to protect oil reserves and to create governments that would not threaten Israel. And some view the war on terrorism as a war on Islam. A Pew Global Attitudes Project (www.pewglobal.org) survey in six Arab countries in 2005 found that support for violence against civilian targets had fallen, but that there remains substantial support for attacks in defense of Islam. Conversely, some in the United States view Islam as the source of the terrorist problem.

Before and after the 1991 war in the Persian Gulf and the 2003 war with Iraq, the major issue between the United States and the Arab world was Israel. The United States recognized Israel as a country within minutes of its creation in 1948 and has been its staunchest ally ever since.

Political Unrest and Social Media

Early 2011 saw political unrest in the Middle East and North Africa. Protests occurred throughout the region, including the Algeria, Bahrain, Djibouti, Egypt, Iran, Iraq, Jordan, Kuwait, Libya,

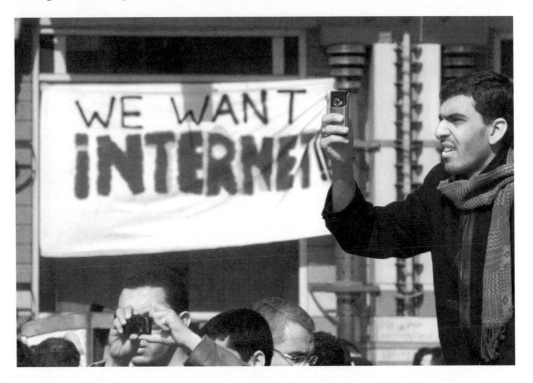

A man takes pictures with his cell phone on Tahrir, or Liberation Square, in Cairo, Egypt, Monday Jan. 31, 2011, the epicenter of the popular revolt that drove veteran strongman Hosni Mubarak from power, on February 12, 2011.

Global Voices

Micah Sifry:

The biggest factor in the unfolding events, to me, appears to be the emergent power of young people, compounded by how urbanized they are and how connected they are by mobile phones.

If you look at the available data on degree of internet penetration, number of mobile cellular subscriptions per 100 people, percentage of population under the age of 15 and degree of urbanization, what jumps out is how the last three factors seem to matter more.

Blogger Andrew Trench:

Social networks have also been given plenty of credit for the revolution unfolding in Egypt.

So I went and had a look at the numbers over on www.internetworldstats.com to see what they could tell us about these two scenarios. Well, fascinatingly, both Egypt and Tunisia have seen a massive growth in internet users and internet penetration over the last 10 years. Both have now got internet penetration of over 20% and in Tunisia's case it was as high as 34%.

While it is clearly simplistic to overstate this factor and there must be many more drivers contributing to such a rapid political uprising, it is obviously a factor as evidenced by the Egyptian regime pulling the plug on the country's internet access to try and block the rising tide of revolt.

My back-of-napkin theory is this: that a rapid increase in internet penetration in a repressive regime does play an important role as it provides an unfettered channel of communication allowing disaffected citizens to share views—and more importantly—to rapidly organise and mobilise.

If Egypt and Tunisia are valid case studies, it looks like internet penetration of around 20% is the mark.

Source: York (2011).

Mauritania, Morocco, Oman, Palestine, Saudi Arabia, Somalia, Sudan, Syria, Tunisia, Western Sahara, and Yemen. Local, regional, and global issues varied throughout the region. Some protests, such as in Oman, have been nonviolent, while others have been violent, such as in Libya. Following protests in Saudi Arabia, the government banned all protests, and at the same time announced a 15% pay raise for state employees and additional funds for various groups (NPR, 2011).

By the summer of 2011, in the Middle East and North Africa, 11.9 million people use Facebook in English; at the same time 10.1 million people use Facebook in Arabic. In the United Arab Emirates, more than half of the population is a Facebook user. Some of the protests were driven by well-educated, disaffected youth comfortable with social media. It is no surprise then that some described the protests, particularly the one in Egypt, as a Facebook revolution or Twitter revolution, referring to the social media websites that facilitate much easier information sharing. One Facebook page devoted to one day's planned protests had more than 80,000 followers the day before the planned protest. Social media did facilitate communication up to a point. The Egyptian government forced various companies to turn off their services at short notice, limiting the effectiveness of the social media. (Information compiled from various blogs posted in 2011.)

Westernization Versus Cultural Norms

The conflict that Westernization provides is a lingering problem. The West has technological and organizational superiority. Petrodollars brought a modern infrastructure to Saudi Arabia. To operate that infrastructure, Saudi Arabia relies on foreign workers. Up to one third of the residents and up to half of the workforce are foreigners with diverse religious and cultural backgrounds. Westernization and the presence of the foreign workforce have put a strain on family life, caused women to question women's roles, and put corrupting pressures on the devout. Negative aspects of family life in U.S. culture, such as divorce, are not desired by Arabs. In the face of Westernization, Saudi Arabia remains committed to traditional values. That also poses a barrier to intercultural communication.

In 2009, King Abdullah University of Science and Technology (known as KAUST) opened for coed classes with Western professors and a curriculum in English. This $20 billion university promises academic freedom and the mixing of cultures and religions. Interestingly, it isn't under the jurisdiction of the Education Ministry, which is controlled by fundamentalists. Rather, it is overseen by ARAMCO, the Saudi oil company. One of the objectives of the new university is that it will bring Western ingenuity to revive the Saudi economy.

Stereotypes

However, the major barrier to intercultural communication between U.S. and Arab peoples appears to be the stereotypes each holds of the other. Shaheen (2001) contends that U.S. media have vilified Arab Muslims in the aftermath of the September 11 attacks.

Arabs tend to stereotype Western women as loose or immoral. Men in other cultures are stereotyped as well: the British as obnoxious, the Germans like a mechanized tank division, the French as impossible, and the Americans as cowboys—not all that different from how some in the United States stereotype the Arabs as Bedouins who roam the desert.

To counter Arab-language radio and television in the Middle East that U.S. officials say feeds public stereotypes against Israel and the United States, the United States funds Radio Sawa, which targets Arab youths younger than age 30. *Sawa* means "together" in Arabic. Its message is that the West and the Arab world are not as estranged as it may appear. The United States also funds the satellite television station Alhurra, or the Free One.

The Islamic Center of Greater Toledo is the third mosque ever built in the United States. It has been around since the early 1950s and, since 1981, has been located off of I-75 in its current iteration. It is perhaps the grandest and most beautiful mosque in the United States. Its unique design and structure lend it immediate recognition as a place of worship.

SUMMARY

Twenty-two countries with a combined population of 338 million make up the Arab world. It is characterized by the Islamic faith and Arabic language use. While there is much diversity among the countries, this chapter focuses on values using the same Kluckhohn and Strodtbeck value orientation theory as used in Chapter 8 to describe U.S. dominant cultural values.

Islam is a monotheistic religion. A follower of Islam is a Muslim. The Koran is considered by believers be the verbatim word of God; Muhammad is believed to be the last prophet of God after Abraham, Moses, and Jesus. Some 80% to 90% of Muslims are Sunni and 10% to 20% are Shiite. Saudi Arabia, the guardian of the two holy sites Mecca and Medina, is the most conservative Islamic country. Dubai, one of the United Arab Emirates, is transforming itself into a post-oil economy and balancing Western interests with Muslim sensibilities.

Arab worldview is derived from Islam and expressed in its language. Islam respects all kinds of work as long as there is no indecency or wrong involved. Saudi accounting of time shows a strong relationship to the cosmos; Saudi Arabia adheres to the traditional *Hijrah* calendar, which is based on the cycles of the moon. Muslims believe God created only humans with intelligence and choice, and that the purpose of human life is to worship God. Arab culture is more group oriented, organized around the family and tribal line.

Communication barriers between Western and Arab states focus on the issues of political unrest and terrorism, Westernization, and stereotypes each holds of the other.

DISCUSSION QUESTIONS

1. Compare the relationship of Islam to Arab culture and Christianity to Western culture.

2. How can contemporary U.S. society be seen from the perspective of fundamentalist Islam?

3. Contrast Arab and U.S. cultural patterns.

4. Discuss the role of social media in bringing change to the Middle East.

5. Identify intercultural communication barriers between Arab culture and the United States.

KEY TERMS

Arabs 227	hajj 231	Muslim 227
caliph 229	imam 229	Ramadan 230
caliphate 229	majlis 235	Shiite 231
gross domestic product (GDP) 225	matawain 234	Sunni 231
	Muhammad 228	

READINGS

All readings are from *Intercultural Communication: A Global Reader* (Jandt, 2004).

Mark Warschauer, Ghada R. El Said, and Ayman Zohry, "Language Choice Online: Globalization and Identity in Egypt" (p. 160)
George E. Irani, "Islamic Mediation Techniques for Middle East Conflicts" (p. 360)

STUDENT STUDY SITE

Visit the student study site at **www.sagepub.com/jandt7e** for these additional learning tools:

- Web Resources
- Audio and Video Links
- SAGE journal articles
- eFlashcards
- Web Quizzes
- Sample Essays

CHAPTER 10

Culture and Gender

FOCUS QUESTIONS

- How does the status of women vary worldwide?
- How is the status of women related to cultural factors?
- How does family structure relate to cultural factors?

Gender and Communication
Status of Women
        United Nations Studies
World Economic Forum Study
            Health
            Education
            Economics
            Political Participation
Comparison of Individual Countries
        Nordic Countries
        Mexico
        China
        Japan
        South Korea
        India
        Sub-Saharan Africa
        Arab States
Family Units
        Marriage
Summary
Discussion Questions
Key Terms
Student Study Site

The purpose of this chapter is to examine the impact of culture on gender. When scholars and researchers use the words *sex* and *gender* today, they refer to different concepts. The word sex is most used to refer to the biological features based on chromosomal evidence that distinguish males from females (Brettell & Sargent, 1993). The word gender is most often used to refer to the learned behaviors and attitudes associated with the words *feminine* and *masculine*. Gender, then, can be said to be socially constructed (Condit, 2000; Wood, 2005).

From antiquity to the end of the 17th century, there was no concept of gender. The female body was a variation of the male body (Laqueur, 1990). The distinction between sex and gender and the understanding that sex is fixed before gender are products of the modern era. Gender is learned through language, the toys we play with, the occupations we are encouraged to hold, the behaviors that are rewarded. Since gender is socially constructed or learned, we can study how gender varies by culture. In the United States and a number of other cultures, traits that are considered feminine traits are attributes such as affection, compassion, nurturance, and emotionality. Traits that are considered masculine traits are typically attributes such as strength, assertiveness, competitiveness, and ambitiousness (Doyle, 1994; Wood, 2005). In the United States, children are aware of gender role differences by the age of 2 (Witt, 1997). By the age of 3, boys compete, wrestle, and play flight more than girls (Geary, 1998). In the United States and a number of other cultures, fathers reward gender-appropriate behavior more than mothers do. Boys experience more pressure to behavior in gender-appropriate ways than girls (Levy, Taylor, & Gelman, 1995).

FOCUS ON THEORY 10.1

Feminist theory is more of a variety of voices rather than a single theory. Feminist theorists contend that many aspects of life are experienced in terms of feminine and masculine. Furthermore, feminist theorists assume that gender is socially constructed and dominated by a male perspective that is oppressive to women in economic development, education, health care, family roles, and political participation (Foss & Foss, 1994). Feminist standpoint theories assume that women's experiences enable women to see privilege and power in ways that men cannot in not only such things as wages and exclusion from power and decision making but also in the very way society itself is constructed (Hallstein, 1999). The relationship between language and power has been a focus in feminist theory. Muted-group theory contends that men created the meanings for a group through its language, which suppresses women. One result is that women develop unique forms of expression.

GENDER AND COMMUNICATION

You know the importance of language in defining a culture. One important consideration, then, for saying there are separate groups—real or constructed—would be the use of a unique language code.

Anthropologists have shown that women share some common communication behaviors across cultures. Women in completely different cultures are known to engage in ritual laments, spontaneously producing rhyming couplets that express pain, such as over the loss of a loved one. Men are more likely to use language to compete with one another by trading playful insults and put-downs. Women are pressured to be submissive and dependent, regardless of individual personality traits, and men are pressured to be assertive, competitive, and in control, regardless of individual personality traits. That pressure is reflected in the language that parents use with children: Girls are more likely to hear twice as many diminutives—affectionate words like *kitty* or *dolly* in place of *cat* or *doll*—than are boys.

FOCUS ON CULTURE 10.1

Language use does have important consequences: How would you refer to a group of both sexes—"men and women" or "women and men"? Does the word order convey any message? Did you notice that this book uses "women and men"?

The ability of the culture to mold our conception of what is natural or normal behavior for females and males is immense. Female and male infants are born with similar potentials, but parents and other socializing agencies impose different standards of behavior on the offspring in accordance with cultural guidelines. You learn as children what actions and attitudes are associated with your biological self. Along with different communication patterns are different normative expectations. Women clearly exhibit characteristic patterns of behavior that are sufficient to distinguish women from men. In certain languages, great differences exist between the sexes—so much so that speakers of other languages might think that the women and men in that culture were speaking totally different languages. In Zulu, for example, women and men use different words to refer to the same thing. In Japanese, the words for "it's beautiful" are *kirei dawa* if the speaker is a woman and *kirei dana* if the speaker is a man; the words for "(I) want to eat" are *tabetai wa* if the speaker is a woman and *tabetai na* if the speaker is a man. For the most part, women and men use the same nouns, but, as in these examples, the final particle indicates female or male speech. In general, *wa* is used by females and *na* by males. The resulting difference is one of tone rather than of meaning. Japanese male language sounds "stronger, less refined, more direct." Some members of the U.S. military who were taught Japanese by Japanese women learned the female style. To Japanese men, the language sounded "feminine, weak, sensitive." Within U.S. culture, M. D. Miller, Reynolds, and Cambra (1987) have demonstrated that Japanese-American and Chinese-American males use more intense language than female counterparts. A thousand years ago in rural China, women devised a secret language called **Nushu,** or woman's writing, to communicate with other women in male-dominated China. The women in Hunan province took characters from **standard Chinese** and gave them a new value corresponding to phonetic sounds in the local dialect. At its height,

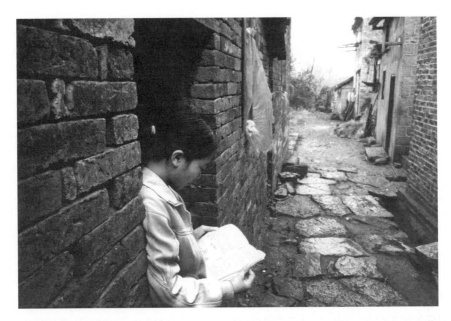

Nushu is a language in which women could communicate without men understanding them. Nushu when written is a series of strokes, dots, and horizontals and arcs similar to Chinese. The language is being documented and preserved by linguists in China.

women in central China corresponded in the language. Nushu poems were common wedding gifts, and women often took Nushu books to the grave. Thousands of poems, songs, letters, and historical anecdotes were written in Nushu over the centuries. The language fell out of use when women were allowed to attend schools and learn written Chinese.

STATUS OF WOMEN

More studies are now available on the status of women, and these serve as the basis for our study of cultural influences.

United Nations Studies

In 1990, the United Nations Development Programme (UNDP) first used the Human Development Index (HDI) as a measure of life expectancy at birth, educational attainment, and adjusted per capita income. These were selected as quantitative measures of leading a long life, being knowledgeable, and enjoying a decent standard of living. Table 10.1 shows the 20 countries with the highest scores on the HDI.

In its 1993 report, the UNDP calculated separate HDI scores for females for 33 countries from which comparable data were available. The report concluded that no country treated its

Table 10.1	Twenty Highest Scoring Countries on the Human Development Index
1.	Norway
2.	Australia
3.	Netherlands
4.	United States
5.	New Zealand
6.	Canada
7.	Ireland
8.	Liechtenstein
9.	Germany
10.	Sweden
11.	Switzerland
12.	Japan
13.	Hong Kong, China (SAR)
14.	Iceland
15.	Korea (Republic of)
16.	Denmark
17.	Israel
18.	Belgium
19.	Austria
20.	France

Source: United Nations Development Programme (2011).

women as well as it treated its men. In some cases, the gap was substantial. Japan had the world's highest HDI rating that year but fell to 17th on the female HDI scale. Sweden was 5th overall but 1st on the female version. Gender equality is not dependent on the income level of a country. Several developing countries outperform much richer countries in the opportunities afforded women.

The HDI masks the differences in human development for women and men. In its 1995 report, the UNDP focused even more sharply on the status of women by using two new measures: the Gender-Related Development Index (GDI), to reflect gender imbalances in basic health, education, and income for 130 countries from which comparable data were available, and the Gender Empowerment Measure (GEM), to evaluate a country's progress in political and economic advancement of women. The GEM ranked 116 countries with comparable data on women's representation in parliaments, share of positions classified as managerial or professional, participation in the active labor force, and share of national income. The GDI for every country remained lower than its HDI, implying that there continues to be gender inequality in every country.

Recently a new measure was introduced to better show the differences in the status of women and men across countries. The Gender Inequality Index (GII) is a composite measure of three dimensions: health (maternal mortality ratio and the adolescent fertility rate), empowerment (share of parliamentary seats held by each sex and secondary and higher education attainment levels), and labor (participation in the work force). Table 10.2 shows the countries with the lowest gender inequality from 2008 data. And Table 10.3 shows countries with the

Table 10.2	Countries With the Lowest Gender Inequality, 2008 Data
1.	Netherlands
2.	Denmark
3.	Sweden
4.	Switzerland
5.	Norway
6.	Belgium
7.	Germany
8.	Finland
9.	Italy
10.	Singapore
11.	France
12.	Japan
13.	Iceland
14.	Spain
15.	Cypress
16.	Canada
17.	Slovenia
18.	Australia
19.	Austria
20.	Republic of Korea

Source: United Nations Development Programme (2010).

Note: The United States ranks 37th.

highest gender inequality. Generally, gender inequality is highest in South Asia, Sub-Saharan Africa, and the Arab states.

WORLD ECONOMIC FORUM STUDY

Independent of the United Nations, the World Economic Forum released its fifth annual report on world gender inequality ranking 134 countries. This study is based on health, education, politics, and economic opportunity. Table 10.4 shows the countries with the greatest and least gender equality.

Table 10.3	Countries With the Highest Gender Inequality, 2008 Data
119	Haiti
120	Gambia
121	Congo
122	India
123	Iraq
124	Zambia
125	Sierra Leone
126	Malawi
127	Benin
128	Saudia Arabia
129	Cameroon
130	Côte d'Ivoire
131	Liberia
132	Central African Republic
133	Papua New Guinea
134	Afghanistan
135	Mali
136	Niger
137	Democratic Republic of the Congo
138	Yemen

Source: United Nations Development Programme (2010).

Table 10.4 The Global Gender Gap 2010 Rankings	
Country	*Score*
Top Ranking	
Iceland	85.0%
Norway	84.0%
Finland	82.6%
Sweden	80.2%
New Zealand	78.1%
Ireland	77.7%
Denmark	77.2%
Lowest Ranking	
Côte d'Ivoire	57%
Mali	57%
Pakistan	55%
Chad	53%
Yeman	46%

Source: Adapted from Hausmann, Tyson, and Zahidi. (2010, Table 3).

Consistent with the United Nations report, the World Economic Forum report shows the Nordic countries to have the least gender inequality.

Let's look in more detail into the bases of these rankings.

Health

In the area of health, the reports examined maternal mortality, sex ratio, adolescent fertility, and life expectancy. In industrial nations, maternal deaths are rare. Almost all births are attended by trained health personnel. But according to the World Health Organization, Bangladesh, India, and Pakistan account for 28 % of the world's births and 46 % of its maternal deaths. In developing countries, fewer than half the births, and in South Asia fewer than a third, are attended by any health personnel.

Sex ratio at birth has become a reliable indicator of sex discrimination. The most recent data in The World Factbook (CIA, 2011) shows the following countries with male births greater than 110 to 100 female births: China 113.3, India and Armenia 112, followed by Albania, Vietnam, Azerbaijan, Curacao, and Georgia. The high sex ratios at birth in some Asian countries can be attributed to sex-selective abortion and infanticide due to a strong preference for sons.

Women internationally are the victims of violence rooted in patriarchy and its underlying assumption of the subjugation of women. Many countries have no laws on violence against women. In much of Latin America, the law excuses the murder of a woman by her husband if she is caught in the act of adultery. In other countries, the laws offer limited protection. Domestic violence is treated as a private, family matter.

Female genital mutilation flourishes in many countries in the belief that it prevents promiscuity among women. It is performed on an estimated 2 million children each year in more than 30 countries, primarily throughout the central belt of Africa, from Senegal to Somalia, and by minority groups in the Middle East and Asia. No state or federal laws ban the practice in the United States.

Women are victims of neglect, trafficking into prostitution, rape, incest, wife battering, political torture, abuses of refugees, and the ravages of war. One-third of women in Barbados, Canada, the Netherlands, New Zealand, Norway, and the United States report sexual abuse during childhood or adolescence. As stated earlier, an estimated 1 million children, mostly girls in Asia, are forced into prostitution. Studies from Canada, New Zealand, the United Kingdom, and the United States show that one woman in six is raped in her lifetime. And studies from Chile, Mexico, Papua New Guinea, and the Republic of Korea indicate that two-thirds or more of married women have suffered domestic violence.

For example, during most of Korea's history, the wife stayed home and cared for the children and the husband's mother, who lived with them when she became a widow. The husband worked during the day and often spent evenings with his friends. At times, the husband came home after an evening of drinking, and the conflict with his wife over this often resulted in physical abuse that was so common it was not thought of as a problem, just an aspect of marriage. Only recently have Korean married couples recognized equality, shared responsibility, and mutual respect.

Education

Nearly two thirds of the world's 862 million illiterate people are women. South Asia reduced its female illiteracy rate from 81% to 67% between 1970 and 1990. The Arab states more than doubled the reduction in women's illiteracy rate from 45% to 19% during the same period. More than one in four women aged 15 to 24 are illiterate in at least 20 countries. More than 40% of African women (except in South Africa) and 29% in South Asia are illiterate (United Nations, 2000).

Women's access to education has increased dramatically. In developed regions of the world, enrollment in primary and secondary education is nearly universal. In South America, the Caribbean, and South Africa, more than 90 per 100 school-aged girls are enrolled. In Southeast Asia, western Asia, and northern Africa, the ratios are about 70 for girls and 80 for boys. In South Asia, the ratios are 64 for girls and 77 for boys. In sub-Saharan Africa (excluding South Africa), the ratios are 47 for girls and 59 for boys (United Nations, 2000).

In higher education, female enrollment was less than half the male rate in 1970. By 1990, it had reached 70%. More women than men are enrolled in higher education in 32 countries.

Economics

Women represent more than 40% of the global workforce. Outside agriculture, the average wage for women is about three fourths of men's, ranging from 92% in Tanzania to 42% in Bangladesh (see Table 10.5). Canada ranked first on the overall HDI in 1995 but ninth on the GDI due to the lower participation of women in the labor force and lower average wage rates

Table 10.5   Women's Wage as Percentage of Men's Wage, by Selected Countries

Country	Percentage
Mozambique	102
Burundi	99
Papua New Guinea	96
Norway	87
Sweden	87
Finland	86
Iceland	86
Canada	84
Denmark	84
China	83
New Zealand	82
United States	82
Australia	80
United Kingdom	80
Ireland	74
Japan	66
Spain	66
Italy	62
India	42
Turkey	36
Oman	28
Egypt	27
Saudi Arabia	22
Occupied Palestinian Territories	15

Source: United Nations Development Programme (2007).

Note: World average = 67%; high human development index states = 73%; medium human development index states = 64%; low human development index states = 72%; Arab states = 34%.

for women. In the United States in 2000, women earned 76.5% of what men earned—up from 59% in 1977. Women with 4 years of college earn roughly the same median salary as men with a high school education. These statistics need to be interpreted carefully. The 1963 federal Equal Pay Act outlawed gender-based wage discrimination and requires employers to pay women and men the same wages for the same work. The difference in earnings results from women being available to work fewer hours than men, on average, and from lower salaries paid in fields traditionally held by women.

The proportion of women in managerial and administrative positions worldwide is 14%, ranging from 28% in industrial countries to 3% in sub-Saharan Africa. In most of the Arab states and in South Asia, the proportion is less than 10%. In the United States and Canada, women make up 46% and 42% of management, respectively; however, women in management tend to be concentrated in functions such as labor relations and personnel.

The majority of women in the workforce perform manual labor that requires minimal skills. As economies move toward greater use of technology, women are often the first unemployed by the changes. Of the estimated 1.3 billion people living in poverty, more than 70% are women. In the United States in 1940, 40% of the poor were women; in 1980, it was 62%. Poverty has long been a women's issue. In the 1990s, two out of three poor adults were women, one in three female-headed families lived below the poverty line, and one in two poor families was headed by a woman.

Political Participation

In the ancient Roman era, women were not considered citizens. By the 1860s, middle-class women in Great Britain were organizing for voting rights. John Stuart Mill, who had recently elected to the British Parliament, presented a women's petition for suffrage in 1866, initiating the first parliamentary debate on the subject. Later, in 1869, Mill published *On the Subjection of Women,* in which he argued the feminist case in terms of liberal individualism. Particularly in Australia, New Zealand, and the United States, the women's suffrage movement gained strength from the temperance movement. New Zealand became the first country in the world to grant women the vote in 1893. A South Australia state followed the next year and Australia as a whole in 1902. Only in the 20th century did women gain the right to vote and to be elected to political office in almost all countries that have representative governments (see Table 10.6). Until 1918, the Texas Constitution excluded "idiots, imbeciles,

Table 10.6	Year in Selected Countries That Women First Won the Right to Vote
Country	*Year*
New Zealand	1893
Australia	1902
Finland	1906
Norway	1913
Denmark	1915
Iceland	1915
Canada	1917
Germany	1918
United Kingdom	1918
Sweden	1919
United States	1920
India	1935
Italy	1945
Japan	1945
Mexico	1947
China	1949
Egypt	1956
Switzerland	1971
Oman	1994
Kuwait	2005

Source: United Nations Development Programme (2007).

aliens, the insane, and women" from voting. Today, women cannot vote in Kuwait; only men older than age 21 who have held Kuwaiti nationality for at least 20 years can vote.

Worldwide, women's representation in national parliaments is about 13.1%, ranging from 3.6% in the Arab states to 38.9% in the Nordic countries. In 50 countries, women constitute 5% or less of the parliament. These countries range from very poor to reasonably affluent. This would seem to indicate that exclusion from politics is not as much a function of a country's level of development or the educational and income level of women as it is of social and cultural constraints.

Only six countries have more than one-third female representation: Sweden, Denmark, Finland, Norway, the Netherlands, and Iceland (see Table 10.7). The leaders in female representation among developing nations are South Africa (30%), Argentina (28%), Cuba (28%), and China (21.8%). Local representation surpasses national representation in about half of the countries. In 2005, 22.5% of all U.S. state legislators were women—a percentage that has remained constant over the past 5 years. The range of women legislators was one-third in Arizona, Colorado, Delaware, Kansas, Maryland, Nevada, Vermont, and Washington to 9% in South Carolina in 2005. In 2006, 84 women served in the U.S. Congress (14 in the Senate and 70 in the House). The number of women in statewide elective executive posts is 79.

Table 10.7 Percentage of Parliament Seats Held by Women as of 2007

Selected Countries	Lower or Single House	Upper House
Rwanda	48.8	34.6
Sweden	47.3	
Finland	42.0	
Costa Rica	38.6	
Norway	37.9	
Denmark	36.9	
Netherlands	36.7	34.7
Cuba	36.0	
Spain	36.0	23.2
Argentina	35.0	43.1
Australia	24.7	35.5
Mexico	22.6	17.2
Canada	20.8	35.0
China	20.3	
United Kingdom	19.7	18.9

(Continued)

Table 10.7 (Continued)		
Selected Countries	*Lower or Single House*	*Upper House*
United States	16.3	16.0
Republic of Korea	13.4	
Japan	9.4	14.5
India	8.3	10.7
Turkey	4.4	
Kuwait	3.1	
Egypt	2.0	6.8
Qatar	0.0	
Saudi Arabia	0.0	

Source: United Nations Development Programme (2007).

Representation will increase as more countries reserve seats for women. According to the United Nations Development Fund for Women (UNIFEM), 32 countries have some kind of female quota for local or national assemblies. Beginning in 1994, India reserved a third of all *panchayat* (local council) seats for women, and in Uganda, by law a third of local council seats must go to women. Other countries have a quota for candidates. Germany's Christian Democratic Union (former Chancellor Helmut Kohl's party) reserved a third of party posts and election candidates for women beginning in 1995. And in Belgium, one gender cannot make up more than two thirds of the candidates for the Chamber of Representatives and the Senate.

Worldwide, women's representation in cabinets was about 6.8% in 1996. Nearly 30% of governments worldwide had no women members, and many who did limited women's participation to areas such as social services and health. Leading countries include Finland (39%), Norway (35%), and the Netherlands and Seychelles (31% each). In 1995, Sweden formed the world's first gender-balanced cabinet: 50% of the ministers were women. In 1997, 4 countries had a woman head of state, 10 had women United Nations ambassadors, and 17 had women speakers of parliament.

With limited participation in political decision making, women worldwide are not treated as equal to men in laws governing travel, marriage and divorce, acquisition of nationality, property management, employment seeking, and property inheritance

In 1979, the United Nations adopted the Convention on the Elimination of All Forms of Discrimination Against Women. Forty-one countries have not signed it; 139 have. Of those 139, 6 have signed without ratification (including the United States), and 43 have ratified it with reservations.

FOCUS ON THE ENVIRONMENT 10.1

There has been a growing understanding that environmental degradation does not necessarily affect women and men in the same way. "Governments at the various United Nations conferences in the 1990s, such as the Fourth World Conference on Women and the Rio Summit on Development and Environment, have recognized that sustainable development can only be achieved when gender inequalities in natural resource management are addressed" ("Strengthen Women's Role," 1999).

For example, in many countries, "adult women are in charge of water collection in more than half of the households. Women's responsibility for water collection tends to coincide with poor access to water, thus suggesting a high time burden on women." (United Nations Development Fund for Women, 2011, para. 2). Others ask if women taking on greater responsibility for activities such as recycling is an extension of socialization in a patriarchal culture.

Source: MacGregor (2005).

COMPARISON OF INDIVIDUAL COUNTRIES

It is no surprise that gender equality is not explained by a country's income level. Hofstede (1980) identified masculinity as one value dimension across which cultures vary. The status of women is dependent on a culture's values.

Nordic Countries

Denmark, Finland, Iceland, Norway, and Sweden have a shared political, economic, and cultural development. Danish, Faroese, Icelandic, Norwegian, and Swedish are all North Germanic languages. A Dane, a Norwegian, and a Swede can understand each other with varying degrees of difficulty, but none will fully understand Faroese or Icelandic without studying the language. Finnish, however, is a Finno-Ugric language related to Estonian and Hungarian. The term *Nordic countries* is used to refer exclusively to these countries.

On Hofstede's dimension of masculinity versus femininity, the Nordic countries rank high in femininity and, as shown in Table 10.2, rank the lowest in gender inequality. Hofstede (1997) argues that the concentration of feminine cultures in northwestern Europe (Denmark, Finland, the Netherlands, Norway, and Sweden) derives from shared historical factors. During major portions of their history, values associated with femininity were functional. A culture based on sailing and trading would value maintaining good interpersonal relationships and caring for ships and merchandise. During the Viking period, women managed the villages while men were away on long trips. And later, the association of trading towns of the Hanseatic League required feminine values to maintain such an association.

The Nordic countries have a strong value for personal freedom. One of the expressions of this freedom is that in Finland, Norway, and Sweden, all residents have free access to the

Finnish Prime Minister Matti Vanhanen and the ministers of his new government in Helsinki, Finland, 19 April 2007.

forests, seas, and uncultivated land. The Nordic people were converted to Catholicism in the 10th to 12th centuries, but the Lutheran Reformation overcame most Catholic customs and memories in the 16th century. The Lutheran ideal of enabling everyone to read the Bible on his or her own encouraged strong education programs that, with a strong work ethic, contributed to decreasing social inequality.

A long tradition of egalitarianism and a strong women's movement contributed to the low degree of gender inequality in the Nordic countries. There has been a strong correlation between women's social movements and other forms of political participation. Women's movements since the beginning of the 20th century have had a politics-first strategy. As a result, women have had a prominent role in politics. In parliaments, there has been a marked equalization of the gender composition of political posts within the democratic institutions. Since the mid-1970s, political parties have instituted quotas for female representation. Women in political parties have used the slogan "women representing women." In 1999, Bergqvist and colleagues reported that women accounted for 11% in all parliaments across the world and 13% in Europe. In that year four Nordic parliaments were among the five national parliaments in the world with more than 30% women participation. In 1981 (and again in 1986–1989 and 1990–1996), the head of Norway's Labour Party, Gro Harlem Brundtland, was Norway's first woman prime minister. In 2003, Finland became the first country in Europe to have women serving as prime minister and president at the same time. Social and gender equality in the Nordic countries has developed with increasing proportion of women in politics. (See Figure 10.1 for a visual comparison of the status of women in selected areas in Sweden.)

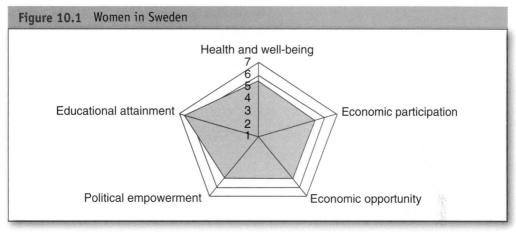

Source: World Economic Forum, Women's Emporwement: Measuring the Global Gender Gap. https://members.weforum
.org/pdf/Global_competitiveness_Reports/Reports/gender_gap.pdf

It is not surprising that these countries have adopted gender equality and women's empowerment as national policies. Consultative rather than confrontational politics focus political competition on issues. The Nordic countries have legislated equal rights, inexpensive child care, free contraception and abortions, and parental leave policies. The women's movement now addresses the issues of wage differences, job segregation, and violence against women, the environment, and peace (Borchorst, Christensen, & Raaum, 1999). Table 10.8 shows that the Nordic countries also rank high on foreign aid and peacefulness.

Table 10.8   Rankings of Countries by Development Assistance and Peacefulness

Per Capita Development Assistance for Selected Donor Countries	
Country	*2005 U.S.$ in millions (Percentage of Gross National Income)*
Norway	600 (0.94)
Luxembourg	570 (0.82)
Denmark	388 (0.81)
Sweden	371 (0.94)
Netherlands	313 (0.82)
Switzerland	237 (0.44)
Austria	191 (0.52)
Belgium	188 (0.53)

(Continued)

Table 10.8 (Continued)

Ireland	180 (0.42)
United Kingdom	179 (0.47)
Finland	171 (0.46)
France	165 (0.47)
Germany	122 (0.36)
Canada	116 (0.34)
Japan	103 (0.28)
United States	93 (0.22)
Italy	87 (0.29)
Australia	83 (0.25)
Spain	70 (0.27)
New Zealand	67 (0.27)

Ranking of Countries by Peacefulness, 2008	
1. Iceland	13. Sweden
2. Denmark	14. Germany
3. Norway	15. Belgium
4. New Zealand	49. United Kingdom
5. Japan	67. China
6. Ireland	97. United States
7. Portugal	131. Russia
8. Finland	136. Israel
9. Luxembourg	137. Afghanistan
10. Austria	138. Sudan
11. Canada	139. Somalia
12. Switzerland	140. Iraq

Sources: United Nations Development Programme (2007) and Vision of Humanity (2008).

Mexico

On the Hofstede ranking, Mexico ranks sixth highest in masculinity. It ranks fairly low on both the World Economic Forum gender inequality study and the Gender Inequality Index. Women and men both have a 14-year school life expectancy and 86% and 87% literacy rates. Life expectancy is 80 years for women and 74 for men. Some 84.6% of men participate in the labor market, compared to 46.3% of women. Women account for some 22.1% of the parliament.

For most of the 20th century, Mexican politics were dominated by what was called the "revolutionary family"—men who fought the Mexican Revolution and their offspring—and by groups of male politicians known as *camarillas*. Women have become more prominent in recent years. In the 1980s, enrollment of women in the universities skyrocketed. Economic crises forced more women into the workforce. And while the government's response to the 1985 Mexico City earthquake was ineffectual, grassroots women's groups formed to deal with the emergency.

In government, the left-wing Democratic Revolution Party (PRD) in 1998 announced that women would make up half of its candidates for high offices by 2000. The dominant Institutional Revolutionary Party (PRI) set a quota of 30% for congressional candidates on the nationwide slate. Women in the legislature from different parties are working together to promote women's issues, such as laws punishing violence within the family and sexual harassment. In 1998, Rosario Green was appointed Mexico's foreign minister, the highest ranking woman ever in the nation's government. Vicente Fox's inner cabinet included three women out of 19 appointees, and more than half of the cabinet of the Mexico City mayor were women.

Yet in 2007, Mexico's new President Felipe Calderon said that despite antidiscrimination laws, millions of women suffer from workplace discrimination and physical and psychological abuse due to Mexico's enduring "culture of machismo." In 2006, some 30 million Mexican women suffered some type of violence, and more than 80% of women who were murdered were killed in their own homes.

Almost 150 years ago, when Mexican liberals were stripping away the Roman Catholic Church's control over much of the country's life, Melchor Ocampo, a Mexican lawyer and liberal politician, wrote new marriage vows to replace the religious vows. Ocampo was later executed for promoting the separation of church and state, but his new vows were kept in the civil marriage law. His new vows portrayed women as delicate or weak. In 2006, Mexico's lower house of Congress adopted a resolution urging judges to skip Ocampo's wording. Today judges are using new vows that stress equality and mutual support.

China

China ranks 38th overall on the World Economic Forum gender inequality study, ranking high in economic participation and economic opportunity for women. China was not included in the original Hofstede studies.

In traditional Chinese culture, the family comes before the individual, and boys are valued more than girls. Before the communist revolution, girls were subjected to feet-binding, and peasant girls were at risk of being kidnapped and sold into marriage. In the family, the respect for age exists, as does pride in sons. Women have lived by the Confucian ethic of serving fathers in their youth, husbands in marriage, and sons in old age. Confucian cultures consider not having children the greatest sin a son or daughter can commit against his or her parents.

Even though the improved status of women in China was state initiated, barriers such as Confucian traditions still remain (Wang, 1996). The very first law passed by the Chinese Communist Party abolished the holding of concubines and gave women the right to own property, choose husbands, sue for divorce, and use their own names. China's constitution states, "Women enjoy equal rights as men in all aspects, including politics, economy, culture, society, and family life."

In 2009, the school life expectancy for women in China was 12 years (11 for men). China's literacy rate for women is 87.6% (95.7% for men). The average life expectancy of women in China climbed from 36 years in 1949 to 77 years in 2011, 4 years longer than the average life expectancy for men in China. Women make up 45% of the nation's workforce. More than a fifth (21.3%) of parliamentary deputies are women. That gives China the fourth highest female participation rate among developing countries and the 12th highest in the world. (See Figure 10.2 for a visual comparison of the status of women in selected areas in China.)

Since the 1980s, China's free market policies helped lift hundreds of millions of its people out of poverty and economic conditions improved for many women. Women gained equality in education, marriage, rights and freedoms, but in some villages and rural areas, the laws are ignored. Significant problems continue to exist as a result of the country's one-child policy and in human trafficking. Family planning has been well established in China since 1956. It was not until 1971, though, that a reduction in the **fertility rate** became a national priority. That year, the third family planning campaign, known as the *Wan, Xi, Shao* program, was initiated. These terms represent the three slogans of the campaign: late marriage, longer intervals between children, and fewer children. The fertility rate fell from 5.4% in 1971 to 2.7% in 1979.

Figure 10.2   Women in China

Source: World Economic Forum, Women's Emporwement: Measujring the Global Gender Gap. https://members.weforum .org/pdf/Global_competitiveness_Reports/Reports/gender_gap.pdf

In 1979, the **one-child campaign** was introduced. The goals of the program were to eliminate all births above or equal to three per family and to encourage most families, particularly in urban areas, to have no more than one child. This program was undertaken to hold China's population at 1.3 billion by the end of the 20th century.

The Chinese government went to great lengths to ensure the success of the one-child policy. Couples were supposed to get a birth permit before conceiving. The mother must be at least 20, and the father, 24. It was a familiar sight in China to see billboards advertising birth control and the one-child goals, yet enforcement became sporadic because of loopholes, corruption, and defiance. Families with unauthorized births paid a fee up to six times their annual income. Also, it was not unusual to hear of coercion, abortions, and sterilizations being used to enforce the one-child policy. Sonogram technology has contributed to abortions of female fetuses—a practice the government condemns. In 1999, China had a ratio at birth of 100 girls to 117 boys. As of 2011, the ratio at birth was 100 girls to 113 boys. In some provinces, the ratio may be as high as 130 boys to 100 girls. That the ratio was higher is shown in the statistic that the ratio of all children under 15 is 117 boys to 100 girls.

The people of China made a critical choice. As a family-oriented culture, it was not unusual for one couple to have as many as eight children. Now, with the one-child policy, large families are much less common. The children of today's children will have no brothers or sisters and no aunts, uncles, or cousins. The family will consist only of grandmothers, grandfathers, mother, father, and child. Implications for the society range from pampered overweight children dubbed "Little Emperors"—four grandparents to spoil one child—to the world's largest elderly population no longer being able to rely on a large family to provide care in old age. But the policy did stabilize the population at 1.3 billion and did lift the country's standard of living. By 2006, the policy was beginning to soften, and discussions of overhauling the policy became more common. Before the 2008 Olympics, China banned insensitive slogans promoting the one-child policy such as "Raise fewer babies, but more piggies." The policy continues to engender anger and resentment among farmers.

China is a source, transit, and destination country for women and children trafficked for the purposes of sexual exploitation. Chinese women are promised legitimate employment, but find themselves forced into commercial sexual exploitation, largely in Taiwan, Thailand, Malaysia, and Japan (CIA, 2011). Since the early 1990s, more than 80,000 Chinese children, mostly girls and many abandoned by their parents, have been adopted abroad (Demick, 2009).

In May, 2008, China's top population official affirmed that the one-child policy will not be eliminated for at least a decade (Fitzpatrick, 2009).

Japan

Japan has a similar rank to China on the World Economic Forum gender inequality study, but ranks 12th on Gender Inequality Index. Hofstede placed Japan highest in masculinity. But unlike China, Japan ranks extremely high on women's health (third worldwide) and lower on all other areas.

In pre–World War II Japan, education was completely segregated by gender. Women were effectively forbidden from voting or going to 4-year colleges. In 1925, Japan's fertility rate averaged 5.1 children per woman. The postwar constitution clearly stipulated equality under law and excluded discrimination on the basis of sex, but in the 1993 HDI report, Japan had the world's highest HDI rating but fell to 17th on the female HDI scale.

Japanese women and men have the same school life expectancy (15 years), the same literacy rate (99%), but women have significantly greater life expectancy (86 years compared with 79 years for men). With high levels of education, health care, and income, Japanese women have more choices than ever before. Japanese women are postponing marriage. Japanese women's average age at first marriage is 28.6, and for Japanese men, it is 30.4 (per 2009 data). (In the United States, the average age in 2008 was 26 for women and 28 for men.) The fertility rate has plummeted to a low 1.21 in 2011 (ranks 219th out of 223 world countries. During the 2005 to 2010 period, the population of Japan remained nearly stable. The decline in the marriage rate and the relatively older age at which couples now get married, on average, are considered to be two factors behind the downtrend in the birthrate. Unlike in Japan, women in the United States rank less well in health and well-being (see Figure 10.3).

The modern trend is away from traditional large multigenerational families and toward small families consisting of a husband and wife and one or two children. Some writers have described Japanese families today as like families in the United States in the 1950s—except the houses are much smaller. High-rise apartments are common. The average home in Tokyo is a four-room condo of less than 1,000 square feet. Within the home, women control the

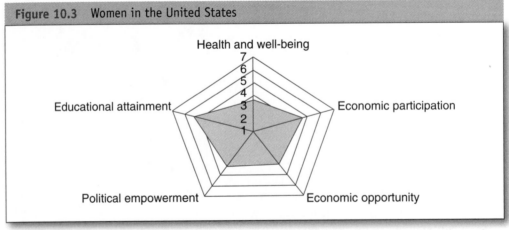

Figure 10.3 Women in the United States

Source: World Economic Forum, Women's Emporwement: Measuring the Global Gender Gap. https://members.weforum .org/pdf/Global_competitiveness_Reports/Reports/gender_gap.pdf household income and family life. It is the wife who handles the money and makes all of the family's financial decisions. In a country, where serving men had been the long-accepted female role, some continue to want the woman inside the house all the time to serve her husband's needs day and night.

Women are increasingly active outside the home. A higher proportion of women than of men have voted in elections since 1980, but women constitute only about 12.3% of the Japanese legislature. Even though the national legislature and cabinet remain male dominated, women are a significant force in local government.

> ## Global Voices
>
> Japanese men have a saying: "To have the best of all worlds is to have an American house, eat Chinese food, and have a Japanese wife. To have the worst of all worlds is to have a Japanese house, eat British food, and have an American wife."

A 1986 equal employment opportunity law prevents discrimination against women in hiring. Some companies are using a two-track hiring system, which puts most female employees on career tracks to lower paying positions. The traditional female role reappeared during Japan's economic slump in the mid-1990s, when there was a scarcity of jobs. Women job applicants and existing female employees began to experience increased sexual harassment. Some accepted the harassment as normal in Japan's male-centered workplace. Today, approximately 62% of Japanese women participate in the labor force compared with 85.2% of men (CIA, 2011; Japanese Ministry of Internal Affairs & Communications, 2011).

Nonetheless, the most dramatic change in modern Japan is the changing role of women. Prescribed gender roles are breaking down. Japanese women are defining a unique interpretation of equality in gender relations in the home and in society. Along with changes affecting family structure, views on the proper relationship between women and men, student and teacher, and employee and employer are all changing. Yet concerns over Japan's royal family demonstrate the culture's continuation of male dominance. The current emperor, Akihoto, has two sons. Between them they have three daughters. For a time, the lack of a male heir may have become a catalyst for legal, cultural, and social change to redefine women's roles. The crisis was forestalled when in 2006, Prince Akishino fathered a male heir, Hisahito.

South Korea

South Korea (Republic of Korea) is an extremely homogeneous country (like Japan). Other than Koreans, only about 20,000 Chinese live in the country. Korea ranks lower than China or Japan on the World Economic Forum global gender gap (54 compared to 33 and 38), with, like Japan, the highest ranking for health. Similar to Japan's high ranking of 12 on the Gender Inequality Index, Korea's rank is 20th. On Hofstede's masculinity scale, Korea ranks 41st. Korea's version of Confucianism is a "neo-Confucian" set of values devised as a formal state ideology in 1392 by Yi Seong-gye, the first king of the last Korean dynasty, imposed as a way to consolidate power. So deeply rooted and pervasive are these ethics that the average citizen does not think of them as Confucian.

South Korea's family law institutionalizes many elements of this traditional male-dominated family succession system. In many households, the eldest son is held in highest esteem to continue the lineage of an unbroken line of male-linked kin, perpetuate the family name, inherit the family property, and preside over ancestral rites. A bride is absorbed into her husband's household and is expected to adopt to its ways in everything from laundry methods to cooking styles.

A Korean wife who does not produce a healthy son under Korean custom could be driven from the home and deprived of her status as a wife. Under the law, women are denied the right to become heads of household—a condition with implications for divorce, child custody, and communal property ownership. Most of the Confucian-based discrimination against women in the nation's laws has been eliminated in recent years, although women's participation in parliament is only 13.7%.

India

Early census data released in 2011 reported that India's population is now more than 1.2 billion. India could become the world's most populated country by 2030. India today has a thriving economy, yet 300 million live in desperate conditions. India's rank on the World Economic Forum global gender gap is similar to South Korea's. India's literacy rate for women is 47.8% compared to 73.4% of men; 39.4% of Indian women participate in the labor force compared to 84.5% of men. The number of working women has doubled in 15 years. But violence against women has increased as well. Between 2003 and 2007, rape cases rose by more than 30%, kidnapping or abduction cases rose by more than 50%, and torture and molestation cases also increased.

Similar to China, India has a history of female infanticide, which explains why there are 37 million fewer females than males. Most Indian parents prefer to have boys because girls require a costly dowry at marriage. The advent of ultrasound and amniocentesis tests led to widespread abortions of unwanted females. India has passed a law preventing doctors from telling parents the sex of the fetus, but still, in 2011, there were 914 girls younger than 6 for every 1,000 boys, down from 927 girls to 1,000 boys a decade ago. The reasons are complex and deeply rooted. In India, wedding costs and dowries are required of the bride's parents, and sons are the only ones permitted by the Hindu religion to perform last rites when their fathers die. Some of the worst statistics come from the relatively wealthy northern states of Punjab and Haryana. Federal and state governments have programs to encourage parents to take care of their girls ranging from free meals to fee education. Yet, India's Home Secretary G. K. Pillai said at announcing new census numbers in 2011, "Whatever measures that have been put in over the last 40 years have not had any impact."

A few Indian women have obtained some of the highest positions in politics (such as Prime Minister Indira Gandhi) and business (such as PepsiCo CEO Indra Nooyi). India is one country with female quotas for a seat in parliament. India already had 50 years of a tradition of quotas for indigenous peoples, outcasts, and Indians of British descent in state and national parliaments. The idea of extending quotas to women was suggested by former Prime Minister Rajiv Gandhi, son of Indira Gandhi. At present, though, only 9.2% of parliament are women. India's parliament has not extended the female quota to higher offices (French, 2011).

Despite laws banning prenatal gender tests, the abortion of female fetuses is still common in some parts of India. Estimates are that some 12 million girls have been aborted over the past three decades.

Sub-Saharan Africa

African societies are largely patriarchal societies. Despite constitutional guarantees of female equality, Zimbabwe's Supreme Court issued a ruling in 1999 declaring that it is in "the nature of African society that women are not equal to men. Women should never be considered adults within the family, but only as a junior male or teenager." Women have fared better in countries where there was participation in campaigns against colonialism, White minority rule, or authoritarian regimes. South Africa's postapartheid constitution, for example, bars discrimination based on gender, marital status, sexual orientation, and pregnancy.

In Uganda, one-third of local council seats must, by law, go to women. Uganda's quotas grew out of the National Resistance Army's (NRA) guerrilla war in the 1980s when women fought side by side with men. In recognition, each of the rebel councils includes a secretary for women's affairs. After the NRA victory, the new president applied the same policy to national politics. The women in Uganda's parliament were successful in amending a land act to allow married women to share property ownership with husbands and in increasing women's access to education. In Kenya, women are taught that, other than that to conceive children, the purpose of sex is to give pleasure to men.

Every year 265,000 mothers and 4.4 million children—including 1.2 million newborns—die in sub-Saharan Africa. Sub-Saharan Africa has half of the world's maternal, newborn, and child deaths resulting from pregnancy and childbirth complications, newborn illness, childhood infections, malnutrition, and HIV/AIDS (Kinney et al., 2010). Many African governments are underutilizing medicines, immunizations, insecticide-treated bed nets, and equipment for emergency obstetric care to save women's and children's lives. On the other side of the world, anthropologist Nancy Scheper-Hughes studied the lives of women and children in a shantytown in northeast Brazil between 1982 and 1989, the same community she had visited as a 20-year-old Peace Corps volunteer years earlier. Her controversial study of the relationship between poverty, childrens' deaths, and mothers' maternal love is that with high fertility and high infant death rates, mothers withdraw care from vulnerable infants, do not grieve when a fragile child dies and, instead, focus on those infants likely to survive. Her study raised controversy because it countered the notion that a mother's love is a universal phenomenon (Scheper-Hughes, 1993).

Arab States

In 7th-century pre-Islamic Arabia, girls were seen as having little value. Female infants could be buried alive. The Koran, which was revealed to the prophet Muhammad, revolutionized life for women. In the Koran, all are equal in God's eyes—women and men, slave and master, subject and ruler. Against the status quo of the time, Islam gave women rights in marriage, divorce, property ownership, business, and inheritance. Muhammad welcomed women in the mosque as members of the community of believers.

Muslims would say that women in Arab cultures are equal to men. The rights and responsibilities of women are equal to, but not identical with, those of men. In Arab cultures, equality and sameness are two quite different things. It is said that in some ways, women are deprived but are compensated in other ways. Thus, the Arab woman is equal as an independent human being, equal in the pursuit of knowledge, and equal in the freedom of expression. She is the wife and mother and is entitled to complete provision and total maintenance by her husband. She may work and own property herself.

Actual practices have not met Islam's ideal. Many Muslims contend, then, that the repressive practices against women ascribed to Islam are based on patriarchal cultural traditions, social considerations, and contested interpretations of the Koran. Even though women's education has advanced in the Arab states, women face barriers in building and using their capabilities. Several Arab states rank markedly higher in terms of average levels of human development than in terms of gender equality.

In Arab cultures, a man is considered a descendant only of his father and his paternal grandfather. A man's honor resides in the number of sons he sires. A man belongs to his father's family. A divorced woman may keep her children until they are 7 years old, but then they go to the father's family. Decisions are made by the family patriarch—not by the individual. Marriages in Saudi Arabia today may still be alliances between families. Islamic law gives the Saudi woman the right to approve or reject her family's choice.

Legally, a Muslim man can have four wives at once—if he can give each wife equal material goods and equal time—but a woman can marry only one man. Monogamy is the common practice today. "Strict disciplining" of women is openly encouraged. Divorce is discouraged, but marriage can be terminated by mutual consent, judicial ruling on the wife's request, or repudiation by the husband. He needs only to say, "I divorce you" in front of a witness. He does not need to give a reason. If the woman does not want the divorce, she can claim her rights in court according to Islamic law.

While not true of all Islamic countries, Saudi Arabia does enforce strict codes of behavior for women. Women may not vote except for chamber of commerce elections in two cities. No woman can sit on the kingdom's cabinet. Women are not allowed to register in hotels or leave the country without a male relative's or husband's written permission. Saudi Arabia is the only country in the world where women—including foreigners—were not permitted to drive cars. Since 1999, Saudi Arabian women who are married and over 35 years old have been allowed to drive cars during daylight hours, provided they have the husband's written permission; however, it is not clear that this change was ever enacted. Even Saudi-trained scholars agree that the restriction on women driving is not grounded in the Koran but is a modern social consideration to prevent women and men from being together in unsafe or unexpected circumstances. Families that can't afford a driver must rely on male relatives to drive women to school, work, or shopping. The year 2011 brought challenges. On June 17 of that year, the first woman received a traffic ticket. Saudi religious authorities detained a Saudi woman who had posted a video of herself behind the wheel on Facebook and YouTube where she hoped to encourage other women to copy her. Later a campaign waged on Twitter as well as Facebook led to a "driving demonstration." Amnesty International issued a statement calling for Saudi Arabia to stop treating women as second-class citizens and allow them to drive. Driving became a symbol. For some it represented a change that could fundamentally alter Saudi society; for others, it represented the first step to other freedoms.

A traditional Saudi woman does not go out alone. She speaks to no man other than her husband or blood kin. All public facilities are segregated by sex. Women who work outside the home work in capacities in which the customers or clients are other women exclusively. Today's Saudi women may be teachers, computer technicians, social workers, laboratory technicians, physicists, engineers, bankers, or filmmakers, but most work in all-female facilities. Saudi society is structured to keep a woman within strictly defined limits to protect her chastity.

In Saudi Arabia, women must follow a rigid dress code. Observant Muslim women dress modestly and must be completely covered except for face and hands. Women walk the streets wearing a long black cloak called an **abaya** (also known by the Persian word *chador*). Most use veils to cover the face. Under the abaya, however, anything goes—from colorful cottons to blue jeans to haute couture.

The abaya and the veil represent an old tradition to safeguard women from advances by strange men. She is not permitted to expose her body before strangers—thus the abaya and the veil represent honor, dignity, chastity, purity, and integrity. The majority of Saudi women are willing to accept women's position in society in return for the guarantee of security that Islamic traditions provide. Those who want change want it within the context of the Arab culture.

FAMILY UNITS

The family unit—however defined—remains the organization in which the majority of human beings continue to exist. Women's role in the family unit has a relationship to cultural values. Family could mean any one of several groupings. The **nuclear family** is composed of one married pair and their unmarried offspring. Anthropologist George P. Murdock found that in 92 of the 192 societies he studied, the extended family was predominant. The **extended family** is composed of two or more nuclear families joined by an extension of the parent-child relationship (Murdock, 1949).

French social historian Emmanuel Todd (1985) developed a schema of family types in an attempt to link a country's prevailing family structure with its political ideology, arguing that why a country has a particular form of government is that it is consistent with the prevailing family structure. Todd based his schema on the earlier work of 19th-century French political philosopher Le Play (1884). Le Play identified two criteria: (a) whether sons continued to live with their parents after marriage (community family) or set up independent homes (nuclear family) and (b) whether inheritance was shared among all sons or whether one son only inherited.

Todd (1985) added the criteria of marriage partner choice. **Exogamy** refers to the practice of marrying outside a defined group. **Endogamy** refers to the practice of marrying within a defined group. Todd focused on whether marriage between first cousins was accepted or not. Using these criteria, Todd developed the following family types, which he related to the countries in which they were dominant:

- *Exogamous community family,* in which equality of brothers is defined by rules of inheritance, married sons cohabit with their parents, and cousins do not marry. Spouses are selected by custom. Typical in China, Vietnam, Russia, Hungary, and northern India.
- *Authoritarian family,* in which there is inequality of brothers as inheritance rules transfer patrimony to one of the sons, the married heir cohabits with his parents, and there is little or no marriage between the children of two brothers. Spouses are selected by parents. Typical in Japan, Korea, Germany, Austria, Sweden, Norway, Scotland, and Ireland.
- *Egalitarian nuclear family,* in which equality of brothers is laid down by inheritance rules, married children do not cohabit with their parents, and there is no marriage

between the children of brothers. Spouses are selected by the individual with a strong exogamous obligation. Typical in northern France, northern Italy, central and southern Spain, central Portugal, Greece, Poland, and Latin America.

- *Absolute nuclear family,* in which there are no precise inheritance rules so there is frequent use of wills, married children do not cohabit with their parents, and there is no marriage between children of brothers. Spouses are selected by the individual with a strong exogamous obligation. Typical in Holland, Denmark, and the Anglo-Saxon world.
- *Endogamous community family,* in which there is equality between brothers established by inheritance rules, married children cohabit with their parents, and there is frequent marriage between children of brothers. Spouses are selected by custom. Typical in the Arab world, Turkey, Iran, Afghanistan, and Pakistan.
- *Asymmetrical community family,* in which equality between brothers is established by inheritance rules, married sons cohabit with their parents, and marriages between the children of brothers is prohibited, but there is a preference for marriages between the children of brothers and sisters. Spouses are selected by custom. Typical in southern India.
- *Anomie family,* in which there is uncertainty about equality between brothers since inheritance rules are egalitarian in theory but flexible in practice, cohabitation of married children with parents is rejected in theory but accepted in practice, and consanguine marriage is possible and sometimes frequent. Spouses are selected by the individual with a weak exogamous obligation. Typical in Cambodia, Laos, Thailand, Indonesia, the Philippines, and South American Indian cultures.

Knighton (1999) demonstrated a correlation between Hofstede's (1980, 1983, 1984, 1991, 1994, 1996, 1997, 1998, 2001) individualism dimension and Todd's family types. Countries with predominantly absolute nuclear families and with authoritarian families tend to be individualistic; those with egalitarian nuclear families tend to be collectivist. Countries that have rules regarding equal partition of parental property among all offspring tend to be collectivist. Those countries that have rules prescribing unequal partition of inheritance and those that have historically allowed parents (usually fathers) to have full freedom in deciding who will inherit tend to be individualist.

Marriage

Cultures regulate how many spouses a person can have, which partner has more authority and dominance in the union, and from what group a person can choose. Buss (1989, 1994) reported a study of criteria for selecting marriage partners in 37 countries. Mutual love, kindness, emotional stability, intelligence, and health were universally desired, but others varied by cultural dimensions. Brides in collectivist countries want age differences at marriage to be larger, and they want their husbands to be wealthy. Industriousness is a minor factor and chastity not at all. Bridegrooms in collectivist countries want age differences at marriage to be larger and put more stress on the bride being industrious, wealthy, and chaste. Grooms in high uncertainty avoidance and in masculine countries more highly value chastity. And in masculine countries, industriousness is deemed more important for women than for men; in feminine countries, it is equally important or unimportant.

Hofstede (1996) studied boyfriend and husband preferences of women in eight Asian cities. In the more masculine cultures, boyfriends should have more personality and more affection, intelligence, and sense of humor. Husbands should be more healthy, wealthy, and understanding. In the more feminine cultures, there was little or no difference between the preferred characteristics of boyfriends and husbands. Hofstede concludes then that in masculine countries, love and family life may be seen as separated, whereas in feminine countries, they are the same.

In Western countries, marriage as an institution has waned (see Table 10.9). More than a quarter of all children born in the United States, a third of those in France, and half of those in Sweden and Denmark are born outside marriage. With economic reforms and increasing Western influence, divorce rates in China have soared, particularly in urban areas. In 2003, the divorce process was simplified in China from a months-long ordeal to a 15-minute civil affair. The Population Council research found that between the early 1970s and mid-1980s, the number of single-parent households rose worldwide. In the United States, the figure rose from 13% to 23.9%. In the United States, Australia, and Canada, more than half of all one-parent families are considered poor. In Great Britain and Germany, it is about one-third. In the industrialized world, only in the Nordic countries is the poverty rate below 10% for one-parent families.

Worldwide, with more women moving into the workforce, the parents' role in preparing children for adulthood is diminishing. A Population Council report (Bruce, Lloyd, & Leonard, 1995) found that in only 1 of 10 diverse nations—Indonesia—did both parents devote more than a combined average of 7.5 hours a week in direct child care. In parts of Africa where the extended family had an important role in children's socialization, the decline of the kinship system has left children without their traditional direction. The Nordic countries with the greatest gender equity and the United States with strong individualism values may demonstrate that individual freedom and self-fulfillment affect the form and duration of the family. The authoritarian father rule has given way to a democratization in these cultures, freeing women and children from domestic tyrannies. Of course, families held together by duty and social responsibility still exist, but the trends demonstrate that cultural values affect the composition, size, and role of families.

Table 10.9   Divorce Rates by Country in 2000

Country	Per 1,000 Population Aged 15–64
United States	6.2
Denmark	4.0
United Kingdom	4.0
Sweden	3.8
Germany	3.5
Canada	3.4
Netherlands	3.2
Japan	3.1
France	3.0
Spain	1.4
Ireland	1.0
Italy	1.0

Source: U.S. Census Bureau. (2010, Table 1335).

SUMMARY

Gender is learned through language since gender is socially constructed or learned, we can study how gender varies by culture. Anthropologists have shown that women share some common communication behaviors across cultures. A thousand years ago in rural China, women devised a secret language called Nushu, or woman's writing, for use in communicating with other women in male-dominated China.

The United Nations has developed a measure to assess the status of women in the world's countries. In 1990, the United Nations Development Programme first used the Human Development Index (HDI) as a measure of life expectancy at birth, educational attainment, and adjusted per capita income. In a 1993 report, separate HDI scores for females were calculated for 33 countries from which comparable data were available. The report concluded that no country treated its women as well as it treated its men. Recently a new measure was introduced to better show the differences in the status of women and men across countries. The Gender Inequality Index (GII) is a composite measure of three dimensions: health (maternal mortality ratio and the adolescent fertility rate), empowerment (share of parliamentary seats held by each sex and secondary and higher education attainment levels), and labor (participation in the work force). Consistent with the United Nations report, a World Economic Forum report shows the Nordic countries to have the least gender inequality.

Individual countries are then compared: Nordic countries, Mexico, China, Japan, South Korea, India, Sub-Saharan Africa, and Arab states. Finally, family types are linked to cultural factors.

DISCUSSION QUESTIONS

1. Is there such a thing as women's language?
2. Give explanations for the differing status of women in cultures worldwide.
3. What possible explanations can be given for why the Nordic countries have the least distinctions between women and men?
4. In what ways will China's one-child campaign change the culture?
5. Project the future status of women in the Arab states.
6. Discuss the relationships between marriage and family types and Hofstede's dimensions.

KEY TERMS

abaya   273
endogamy   274
exogamy   274
extended family   273

fertility rate   266
gender   249
nuclear family   273
Nushu   250

one-child campaign   267
sex   249
standard Chinese   250
sub-Saharan Africa   256

STUDENT STUDY SITE

Visit the student study site at www.sagepub.com/jandt7e for these additional learning tools:

- Web Resources
- Audio and Video Links
- SAGE journal articles
- eFlashcards
- Web Quizzes
- Sample Essays

CHAPTER 11

Contact Between Cultures

FOCUS QUESTIONS

- What characterized intercultural communication in the age of colonialism?
- Why do some fear the influence one culture can develop over another?
- What characterizes the marketing of U.S. cultural icons?
- What explains the spread of innovations from one culture to others?

Colonialism
    Hawai'i
    Australia
Cultural Imperialism
Cultural Icons
Cultural Hegemony
    Japanese Icon in Mexico
U.S. Cultural Icons
    Coca-Cola and Pepsi
    Euro Disney and Hong Kong Disneyland
    McDonald's
    Kentucky Fried Chicken
    Budweiser
    SPAM®
    Barbie
    Marlboro
Diffusion Model
Roles in the Diffusion Process
    Opinion Leadership and Change Agents
    Adopters
    Change Agent Ethics
    Case Study: Quality Circles
Convergence Model
Adapting The Message
    Case Study: Marketing Gerber Baby Foods Worldwide
    Case Study: Religious Missionary Work in New Guinea
Summary
Discussion Questions
Key Terms
Readings
Student Study Site

In this chapter, you will examine what happens when people from diverse cultures interact with one another. First, we focus on colonialism and cultural imperialism. Then you will look at cultural icons such as Japanese instant ramen and U.S. cultural icons such as Coca-Cola, Disney, McDonald's, and KFC. In contrast to other products, icons are minimally changed for the receiving culture. Next comes a look at cultural hegemony, or the fear of the influence one culture can develop over another. Finally, we focus on diffusion, or the spread of practices from one culture to another. You will identify the roles in the diffusion process and the characteristics of those most likely to adopt new practices first. And you will see, through examples, that key to successful diffusion is adapting the new practice to the receiving culture.

COLONIALISM

For tens of thousands of years, humans lived in isolated communities. Cultures developed largely independently and many were unaware of the others' existence. The initiation of contact among previously separate cultures has been the major world event of the past centuries. Mary Pratt coined the term **contact zone** to refer to "the space in which peoples geographically and historically separated come into contact with each other and establish ongoing relations, usually involving conditions of coercion, radical inequality, and intractable conflict" (1992, p. 6) During the 16th, 17th, 18th, and 19th centuries, new contacts dominated the EuroAmerican cultures. For a time, travel writings, explorer's lectures, exhibits of peoples from other cultures, and the proceedings of academic and scientific communities were major popular activities. Yet in the EuroAmerican cultures, the peoples and cultures from other lands were devalued and information from them ignored. The perception of difference lead to violence and extermination.

From the time of Columbus, Spain debated the rationality of the Indians—are the Indians rational humans with souls? The monarchy did issue laws intended to regulate Indian-Spaniard relations, including the Laws of Burgos, which mandated that Spaniards who benefited from forced Indian labor must instruct their subjects in Christianity. A 1537 papal bull proclaimed the Indians rational beings by confirming the Indians' capability to understand and receive the Christian faith. In 1539 Bartolomé de las Casas in his *The Devastation of the Indies* called attention to the actual treatment of the Indians, which was far from that of rational humans with souls. A disputation or debate resulted between Las Casas and Juan Ginés de Sepúlveda, a Dominican, in the city of Valladolid in 1550 and 1551, which, for a time, held the attention of Spain.

Sepúlveda made four arguments for enslaving the Indians: First, the state of their culture make them fit for slavery and it was the responsibility of the Spaniards to act as masters. Second, Spaniards were obligated to prevent Indians from engaging in cannibalism. Third, Spaniards were obligated to stop human sacrifices to their Gods. Finally, slavery was an effective method of converting Indians to Christianity (Losada, 1971). Las Casas argued that the Indians were rational, free humans in the natural order, deserved the same treatment as others, and could be brought to Christianity without force.

The Valladolid disputation was not so much about the treatment of the Indians nor about Christianity as it was an enactment of European Spaniards believing they had the right to decide if the Indians were rational humans. If the decision was that they were not, then Spanish treatment of the Indians as slaves and property was justified.

Hawai'i

In chants, legends, and *mele* ("vocal music"), Hawaiians trace the origins of the culture to daring seafarers who discovered and colonized the islands. Sometime around 1000 CE, isolated from further outside influence, a unique culture emerged. Hawai'i's society was hereditary and composed of the *ali'I* ("ruling class"), *kahuna* ("priests" or "experts"), *maka'ainana* ("commoners"), and *kauwā* ("slaves"). The society operated under a strict *kapu* ("restriction," "consequence," "separation," or "forbidden") system that dictated daily activity between the classes and between the people and nature and the Gods. A culture of about 1 million people had developed a harmony with its isolated island environment (Young, 1980).

British Captain James Cook departed on his third voyage in 1776 arriving in Hawai'i in 1778. Edward Said (1978, 1981) describes the contact and subsequent linguistic construction of non-Western cultures as "Orientalism," a process of labeling the peoples of "underdeveloped" cultures as insignificant "others." Captain Cook and his men, for example, wrote of the Hawaiians as "savage or animal-like or heathen." While the Hawaiians were labeled as savages, the Europeans interpreted the Hawaiians' actions as deifying Captain Cook. The ship's journals state that "they [the Hawaiians] venerated [Cook] almost to adoration," looked upon Cook as "a kind of superior being," honored him "like a god," and "as far as related to the person of Captain Cook, they seemed close to adoration" (Obeyesekere, 1992). The Europeans labeled the Hawaiians not by any uniqueness but on the basis of what the Hawaiians were not (i.e., not civilized by European standards). Shome (1996) calls this discursive imperialism (also see Tanno & Jandt, 1994).

The dehumanization of the Hawaiians into "others" contributed to near destruction of the Hawaiian culture. Native Hawaiians lost government, lands, and cultural identity with the U.S.-backed 1893 overthrow of the Hawaiian monarchy.

Today, Native Hawaiians number some 80,000 out of the state's population of 1.36 million. In 1993, a U.S. congressional resolution apologized to Hawaiians for the 1893 overthrow, noting that economic and social changes since then have been devastating to the population and to the health and well-being of the Hawaiian people. In 2005, Senator Daniel Akaka sponsored a bill in the U.S. Senate that would grant Native Hawaiians the same rights of self-government as American Indians and Native Alaskans and would lead to recognition of a native government entity. The bill was blocked by a Nevada senator out of fears that it would lead to legal gambling in Hawai'i.

Several native organizations claim sovereignty and are working for reparations and some form of self-government. The Native Hawaiian Government Reorganization Act, sponsored by Senator Daniel Akaka, would create a "Native Hawaiian Governing Entity" that would exempt the entity from the First, Fifth, and Fourteenth Amendments and permit negotiations over land, natural resources, criminal and civil jurisdiction, and historical grievances. The act defines Native Hawaiians as direct lineal descendants of indigenous people who lived on the islands before 1893. The legislation would, in effect, create a "tribe."

Australia

In a similar way, all that is known of the European contact with Australia's Aboriginals is from the written journals and history of the Europeans. Eighteen years after Captain Cook first arrived off the eastern coast of Australia, Captain Arthur Phillip arrived with 11 ships and their cargo of prisoners, who established the British settlement on the shores of Sydney Harbor in January 1788.

Captain Phillip's view of the colonists as "guests" of the indigenous inhabitants and his edict prohibiting molesting or killing Aboriginals was not long lasting. The Europeans occupied coastal hunting grounds and disturbed sacred sites of local Aboriginals, not having learned of their existence, much less importance. There were no large-scale wars like those with American Indians and New Zealand's M ori. The Aboriginals resisted with spears and stone weapons in encounters that would later be called "guerrilla warfare."

In the book *Ancient Society* published in 1877, the Australian Aboriginal was described as "the living representatives of that worldwide primeval culture from which all other cultures had evolved." The Aboriginal was labeled as not evolved, an oddity, or semihuman. As the Europeans moved further into the continent with farming and cattle raising, the Aboriginal population was decimated. Arsenic was mixed with the flour or inserted into the carcasses of sheep given to the Aboriginals for food. Numerous instances of large-scale slaughter have been documented, including the entire Aboriginal population of Tasmania (Isaacs, 1980).

In 2008, Labor Prime Minister Kevin Rudd issued a comprehensive apology for past wrongs and called for action to improve the lives of Australia's Aborigines and Torres Strait Islanders. He particularly addressed the "Stolen Generations," the tens of thousands of indigenous children who were removed from their families in a policy of forced assimilation that only ended in the 1970s.

FOCUS ON THEORY 11.1

Cultural studies focus on the ways culture is formed through struggles among ideologies (Agger, 1992). Cultural studies scholars have as an objective to change Western cultures, in part, through their scholarship, which helps people understand domination and pathways to reform. Media have been a focus for study as media are seen as tools of the powerful in disseminating information along with the social institutions of education, religion, and government. Cultural studies expose the ways the ideology of powerful groups is established. Postcolonial theory refers to the study of cultures affected by colonization (Shome & Hegde, 2002). At its core is Edward Said's (1978) notion of "othering"—the stereotypic images of non-White populations. Postcolonial scholars study many of the same issues as cultural studies scholars.

Global Voices

The Declaration on the Rights of Indigenous Peoples was adopted by the U.N. General Assembly on Thursday September 13, 2007 by a of 144 states in favor, four votes against (Australia, Canada, New Zealand and the United States) and 11 abstentions. Since its adoption, Australia, New Zealand, Canada, and the United States have all reversed their positions and now endorse the declaration.

Selected sections from the declaration:

Affirming that indigenous peoples are equal to all other peoples, while recognizing the right of all peoples to be different, to consider themselves different, and to be respected as such,

Affirming further that all doctrines, policies and practices based on or advocating superiority of peoples or individuals on the basis of national origin or racial, religious, ethnic or cultural differences are racist, scientifically false, legally invalid, morally condemnable and socially unjust,

Concerned that indigenous peoples have suffered from historic injustices as a result of, inter alia, their colonization and dispossession of their lands, territories and resources, thus preventing them from exercising, in particular, their right to development in accordance with their own needs and interests,

Recognizing that respect for indigenous knowledge, cultures and traditional practices contributes to sustainable and equitable development and proper management of the environment,

Article 1

Indigenous peoples have the right to the full enjoyment, as a collective or as individuals, of all human rights and fundamental freedoms as recognized in the Charter of the United Nations, the Universal Declaration of Human Rights(4) and international human rights law.

Article 8

1. Indigenous peoples and individuals have the right not to be subjected to forced assimilation or destruction of their culture.

CULTURAL IMPERIALISM

Is the age of colonialism past? Some argue that colonialism continues in many ways, including corporate colonialism. Nigeria is Africa's most populous country, and with proven oil reserves of 37.5 billion barrels, it has a petroleum-based economy. With 606 oilfields, the Niger delta supplies 40% of all the crude the United States imports. The Niger delta is also the world capital of oil pollution. More oil is spilled In the Niger delta every year than was spilled in the Gulf of Mexico at BP's Deepwater Horizon site in 2010. Media coverage of the Gulf of Mexico spill was worldwide; little is made available about the Niger delta.

A worker subcontracted by Shell Oil Company cleans up an oil spill from an abandoned Shell Petroleum wellhead in the Nigerian town of Oloibiri. Wellhead 14 was closed in 1977 and has been leaking since. By June of 2004, it had released over 20,000 barrels of crude oil.

Shell admits to spilling 14,000 tons of oil in 2009. In 2010 ExxonMobil spilled more than a million gallons into the delta over seven days. The Nigerian government's national oil spill detection and response agency reported that between 1976 and 1996 alone, more than 2.4 million barrels contaminated the environment. Oil spills have polluted drinking wells, forests, farming, and fishing areas. Nnimo Bassey, Nigerian head of Friends of the Earth International, was quoted as saying that the oil companies "have been living above the law. They are now clearly a danger to the planet. The dangers of this happening again and again are high. They must be taken to the international court of justice" (Vidal, 2010).

While international media may not report examples of corporate colonialism, others contend that media can itself contribute to colonialism. The cultural imperialist approach to communication recognizes that mass media is not value free—the media also carry important cultural values (Nordenstreng & Schiller, 1979; Schiller, 1976). In this theory, countries with media that can capture and dominate international markets serve the originating country's

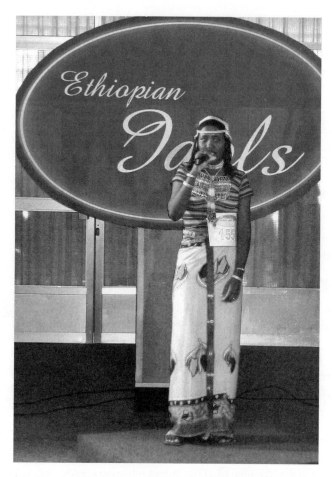

Even where most of people cannot afford a television set of their own, on some level Ethiopian Idol promises the glamor and fame of the British and U.S. versions.

intentions. The single largest export industry for the United States is not aircraft. It's entertainment. Hollywood films grossed more than $30 billion worldwide in 1997. Hollywood gets 50% of its revenues overseas (United Nations Development Programme, 1999). Schiller (1976) points to the unrestricted flow of media from the United States having the effect of surreptitiously affecting other people's goals and aspirations. It was just that concern that led Canada to require that radio stations devote at least 30% of their programming to Canadian music. And MTV, with its Western images of cars, clothes, and relationships, is now seen from Senegal to Russia and claims to be the largest television network in the world. Something as simple as *American Idol* carries a message: In Ethopian culture it's not common to be brutally frank or critical. Ethiopian contestants were not prepared for the British-American style "put downs."

In Taiwan, some are talking about a "new colonialism," and one newspaper carried the headline, "Be Careful! Your Kids Are Becoming Japanese." Japanese television reaches 75% of Taiwanese households on cable. Japanese comic books and trendy fashion magazines such as *Non-No* and *Check* are popular among teens, as are Japanese merchandise and pop singers. Teens say that Japanese popular culture is easy to relate to because the cultures are similar. Older people remember Japan's 50-year rule of Taiwan and have called for a boycott of Japanese products so as to preserve Chinese heritage.

> ### Global Voices
>
> I do not want my house to be walled in on all sides and my windows stuffed. I want the cultures of all the lands to be blown about my house as freely as possible. But I refuse to be blown off my feet by any.
>
> —Mahatma Gandhi, quoted in United Nations Development Programme (1999)

FOCUS ON CULTURE 11.1

The term *ecoimperialism* refers to global governance that protects the existing power structure at the expense of poor countries.

Fundamentally, ecoimperialism undermines the capacity of people to escape poverty. Ecoimperialists impose a set of beliefs on people in poor countries, through environmental regulations, restrictions on trade, and through their fundamental belief that they should make decisions for everyone else. People in poor countries need more development, more technology, more resource consumption, and more energy consumption—and they should reject ecoimperialism, just as they rejected imperialism. People everywhere should be empowered to make choices for their own lives—and not be prevented from so doing by people and governments in wealthy countries (Sustainable Development Network).

For example, should a worldwide ban on the use of DDT take priority over a poor country's attempt to deal with immediate problems of human suffering from malaria? (Elliott, 1998, p. 118)

CULTURAL ICONS

Products can carry cultural values as well, and many products that are seen to represent a culture have been both widely popular and resisted. In his book *Mediamerica*, Edward Jay Whetmore (1987) writes of icons and artifacts as aspects of popular culture. An icon is a special symbol that tends to be idolized in a culture. (U.S. baseball is an example, with successes in Japan, South Korea, and Taiwan. See Focus on Culture 7.2 in Chapter 7.) An artifact is an object

Table 11.1 Twenty Most Powerful Brand Names, 2010	
	Country of Origin
1. Coca-Cola	United States
2. IBM	United States
3. Microsoft	United States
4. Google	United States
5. General Electric	United States
6. McDonald's	United States
7. Intel	United States
8. Nokia	Finland
9. Disney	United States
10. Hewlett-Packard	United States
11. Toyota	Japan
12. Mercedes-Benz	Germany
13. Gillette	United States
14. Cisco	United States
15. BMW	Germany
16. Louis Vuitton	France
17. Apple	United States
18. Marlboro	United States
19. Samsung	South Korea
20. Honda	Japan

Source: Interbrand (2010).

less widely recognized. English gardens, golf, English tea, Winnie the Pooh, Burberry, Laura Ashley, and the Body Shop represent British culture to many. Kangaroos, koalas, and boomerangs represent Australia to many. Louis Vuitton bags, France, and Ferragamo shoes, Italy. A global brand carries the same brand name or logo worldwide. Table 11.1 shows which ones are readily known worldwide.

Other examples of global brands are Braun, Budweiser, Canon, Cartier, Club Med, KFC, Levi's, Mercedes, Mitsubishi, Philips, and Sony. Most global brands are of U.S. origin and to many they represent the U.S. lifestyle and culture (de Mooij, 1998). The positioning and values of global brands are identical in all countries, and they have brand loyalty in all countries in which they are marketed. Marlboro is an example. It is positioned worldwide as an urban premium brand appealing to the desire for freedom and open physical space symbolized by the "Marlboro man" and "Marlboro Country." The product itself may be modified to meet local consumer needs and competitive requirements. For example, both Coca-Cola and Pepsi are sweeter in the Middle East, where consumers prefer a sweeter drink.

CULTURAL HEGEMONY

Some nations, like the United States, are major exporters of their own cultures. Though some societies are excellent markets for U.S. icons, other societies may resist adopting these ideas because they fear the changes that may accompany the new ideas. Some societies may perceive the increasing popularity of those icons as a form of cultural **hegemony**, or the fear of the predominant influence that one culture can develop over another. It is believed that what is being transmitted are the values of the culture. The receiving culture can unconsciously, or perhaps uncritically, absorb the values. *Cultural dependency* is the belief that a receiving culture becomes accustomed to cars from Japan or movies and TV from Great Britain and the United States, and that it's natural that they come from there, thus discouraging local businesses.

Japanese Icon in Mexico

In Japan, instant ramen was a post–World War II invention. The product soon became a cultural icon. Thousands visit a museum each year to see a replica of the workshop where instant ramen was developed.

Japanese fast-food noodles were first imported into Mexico in the 1980s. Today, Mexico is Latin American's largest per capita consumer of instant ramen—1 billion servings in 2004, a threefold increase since 1999. Instant ramen noodles, such as those marketed under the brand name Maruchan, which has an 85% share of the market, are supplanting beans and rice for many in Mexico. Convenience stores sell ramen, or *preparada,* with packets of salsa, and the Mexican government distributes it to remote rural areas. A cup of Maruchan costs 4 pesos (about 35 U.S. cents); a serving of beans costs much less, but Maruchan is ready to eat in minutes. Defenders of the nation's cuisine point to the relationship between food and culture. Ancient ancestors believed that humankind descended from corn. Mexican food traditionally has fresh ingredients, slow-cooked sauces, and hand-worked doughs. Today's culture defenders see a threat to family and other traditional values.

U.S. CULTURAL ICONS

Coca-Cola and Pepsi

Without doubt, the most widely recognized U.S. icon worldwide is Coca-Cola. Coca-Cola products are sold in more countries than the United Nations has members, and it is claimed that *Coke* is the second most universally understood term in English after *okay.* The company has marketed internationally since 1900. Today, Coke sells 1.2 billion servings daily in nearly 200 countries. Although U.S. residents drink 524 million servings daily, 75% of the company's operating income comes from outside the United States.

Beginning in 1992, Coke began its first global marketing campaign—six commercials broadcast at the same time all over the world. So it's not all that surprising that Coca-Cola wanted Chinese characters that "sounded like" its name in English. That's what it was selling and why it has, on occasion, been met with opposition. China was one of Coca-Cola's first overseas markets when bottling plants were established in Shanghai and Tianjin in 1927. Forced to leave in 1949 by China's Communist Party as a symbol of U.S. imperialism, Coke returned in 1979. There have been new movements in China to limit the growing sales of U.S.-made Coke and Pepsi to protect local beverages. Coca-Cola was forced to leave India in 1977 after pressures from socialists, who labeled the soft drink a new form of colonialism pushing the American culture. Coke returned to India in 1993.

Coca-Cola markets an international T-shirt showing the various spellings of its name. Note that the trademark ribbon, part of Coke's logo, is always present.

The first U.S. factory to open in Vietnam since the United States restored diplomatic relations in 1995 was Coke's. Coke is seen as a status symbol. The Vietnamese pay 10% more for Coke than for a Vietnamese cola. Pepsi is second to Coke worldwide except in Pakistan, parts of the Middle East, and in Quebec, where Pepsi leads 2 to 1. Pepsi had been using U.S. ads translated into French in Quebec. Then its advertising agency started using a comedian with caricatures drawn from stereotypical *Quebecois* characters, such as a bizarre ice hockey player who could not pronounce *Pepsi* correctly. Sales soared.

Some Arabs and other Muslims boycott U.S. products over the U.S. backing of Israel. Sales of the Iranian soft drink Zam Zam Cola, with its name taken from a holy spring in Saudi Arabia, increased in 2002. Another, Mecca-Cola, now sold in more than 60 countries, is marketed as a protest to U.S. foreign policy.

Mecca-Cola, a new soft drink and part of anti-American sentiment around the world.

Euro Disney and Hong Kong Disneyland

The first Disneyland outside the United States opened in 1983 in Tokyo and was totally owned by Japanese companies. Disney's $4.4 billion Euro Disney opened near Paris in April 1992. Some European intellectuals labeled the park a "cultural Chernobyl." Some were concerned how the park would affect French culture.

Disney made an attempt to "Europeanize" its attractions and products and downplayed the U.S. culture. Souvenir shops carried sweatshirts with small, discreet Disney logos. Rather than only fast-food restaurants, Euro Disney offered table-service restaurants. Disney's objective was to attract people from all over Europe and thus hired multilingual workers from all over the continent.

FOCUS ON THE ENVIRONMENT 11.1

Why does Coca-Cola continue to sell bottled water despite environmental impacts?

Coca-Cola has received criticism in many countries for its environmental record. In India, it is alleged that the production of Coke requires so much water that aquifers are drying up. Elsewhere Coca-Cola receives criticism for its bottled water products. Criticism has revolved around ground water extraction, plastic packaging, transportation, and water quality. Does Coca-Cola's corporate policy statement adequately address these concerns?

Bottled water is a convenient, safe and refreshing beverage, and its portability makes it a popular choice. With our water brands, as with all our beverages, we are committed to using resources responsibly, reducing our environmental footprint and protecting natural resources.

We are making our packages lighter, using more recycled content and supporting comprehensive consumer recycling programs. Lighter packages require less fuel to transport and save energy during production. Increasing the use of recycled content in our water packaging reduces the need to generate new materials from non-recycled content.

All of our waters are packaged in either PET or refillable glass bottles—materials that are 100 percent recyclable. Our bottles are clear, green and light blue because these colors have the highest recycling value. Even our caps and labels are designed to be recycled along with the bottle and are compatible with local recycling systems.

To further reduce waste, we have launched recycling initiatives throughout the world on our own and with third-party partners. We have also invested more than $80 million to build six plastic bottle-to-bottle recycling plants throughout the world, including the world's largest PET recycling plant in Spartanburg, South Carolina.

Our operations and distribution are local, which means that for most of our water brands the water is collected, bottled and transported locally, with minimal transportation to consumer outlets. ("Addressing Your Questions," 2006)

The French have had little experience with theme parks. The French often dedicate Sunday—and only Sunday—to family outings. Most French do not snack and insist on eating at 12:30 p.m. This could create enormous and hostile bottlenecks at park restaurants. And French employees have an aversion to providing the smiles and friendly greetings so expected at any amusement park. Food, merchandise, and hotel business was weak: Europeans brought bag lunches and left early—not spending money at the park's gourmet restaurants and showcase hotels. Some European investors complained about a rigid, myopic U.S. management style.

At one point, the park was losing $1 million a day, forcing Disney to bring in a Saudi prince as a major investor and rename the park Disneyland Paris. Disney had discounted its own value as a U.S. icon, which is just what the French wanted to experience. Frontierland was just as popular as Discoveryland. French visitors to the park didn't want a leisurely, sit-down lunch; they wanted fast food. European visitors to the park didn't want discreet sweatshirts; they wanted sweatshirts with huge letters and big pictures of Mickey Mouse. After these changes, the park made its first small profit in the fiscal year ending in 1995. It became the most popular tourist attraction in France but was losing money again in 2002, attributed to a downturn in European travel and general economic conditions.

In Asia, Disney opened the $3.5 billion Disneyland Hong Kong in 2005. Disney owns 43% and the Hong Kong government owns the remainder. In contrast to Europe, China, Taiwan, Singapore, Malaysia, and other countries close to Hong Kong don't have extensive acquaintance with the Disney culture and stories. Disney cartoons first appeared on Chinese television only in 1986. To counter that, Disney launched a Chinese television program *The Magical World of Disneyland,* which had segments on the park; Disney merchandise appeared in more than 1,000 stores; and Disney used an alliance with an after-school program and the China Youth League to introduce Disney stories. Disney modeled this park closely after the original Disneyland, with only some features unique to Asian cultures. Guests meet the characters and take pictures with them in a large garden with five pavilions. Also, the vast majority of the food is Asian cuisine. The park missed its attendance targets for 2 years in a row. The park is small and lacks the high-profile rides of other Disney parks. Disney plans to expand the park with scores of new attractions.

Disney was criticized for not giving attention to the French culture when it built Disneyland Paris in the 1990s. When designing Hong Kong Disneyland, the company consulted feng shui experts to place elements in harmony to bring good luck. (Holson, 2005)

In 2011, Disney began construction of a $3.7 billion 963 acre (390 hectares) Shanghai Disneyland. To be built in partnership with the Shanghai Shendi Group, a government-controlled entity, Disney will own 43% of the park. The stated objective is to build a park that is "distinctly Disney, yet authentically Chinese." To prepare China for Disneyland (where Mickey Mouse is still known as Mi Lao Shu), Disney has partnered with China's two dominant online video sites to stream Disney's ABC primetime shows and is operating Disney English centers for children aged 2 to 12. The centers use learning materials filled with Disney images.

McDonald's

Restaurant chains have become cultural icons. As seen in Table 11.2, most are identified with the United States.

Most influential, by far, is McDonald's. The McDonald brothers operated a hamburger stand in San Bernardino, California, that offered a limited menu and used "assembly-line" procedures for cooking and serving food. Ray Kroc first visited it in 1954 and, in the following year, in partnership with the McDonald brothers, opened the first restaurant (Ritzer, 1993). By 1998, McDonald's had about 25,000 restaurants in more than 110 countries. In a 1986 survey, 96% of the schoolchildren surveyed could identify Ronald McDonald—second only to Santa Claus in name recognition. In each country, the company faces the challenge of adapting its menu to local tastes without weakening its appeal as a U.S. icon.

Table 11.2   Top U.S. International Franchise Restaurant Chains, Ranked by 2006 International Sales

International Chain	Total Units	Percentage of Units Outside the United States	International Sales ($1,000,000s)
McDonald's	31,046	56	56,800
KFC (Kentucky Fried Chicken)	14,258	62	14,200
Burger King	11,184	33	12,700
Subway	26,893	33	10,000
Pizza Hut	12,685	33	9,300
Wendy's	6,674	11	8,727
Taco Bell	5,846	4	6,500
Domino's Pizza	8,366	39	5,103
Dunkin' Donuts	7,293	26	5,000
Tim Horton's	3,047	89	4,750

Source: "Top 200 Franchise Systems" (2007, p. 4).

Note: Tim Horton's offers coffee and baked goods. It was founded in Canada and named after a Toronto Maple Leaf hockey player.

When McDonald's opened its first restaurant in Singapore in 1982, it quickly became the largest selling McDonald's in the world. In early 1990, McDonald's opened its first restaurant in Moscow. One journalist described it as the "ultimate icon of Americana." Russians were unaccustomed to eating finger food, and Russian workers were unaccustomed to smiling and looking customers directly in the eye. McDonald's knew it was selling U.S. popular culture and kept much of the product the same. In 1992, McDonald's opened its largest restaurant at that time in Beijing, with 700 seats, 29 cash registers, and nearly 1,000 employees. On its first day of business, it served about 40,000 customers (Ritzer, 1993). Today, McDonald's has some 1,000 restaurants in China and plans to double that number by 2013.

McDonald's now stresses its ties to local economies. The Kiwiburger packaging features New Zealand icons.

In 1996, McDonald's opened in New Delhi, India, but without all-beef patties because 80% of the population is Hindu, a religion whose followers don't eat beef. The menu features the Maharaja Mac—"two all-mutton patties, special sauce, lettuce, cheese, pickles, onions on a sesame-seed bun." The restaurant opened with a traditional Hindu ceremony. In Jerusalem, McDonald's has nonkosher and kosher restaurants. As Jewish law forbids the cooking, serving, or eating of meat and milk products together, the kosher restaurants don't have cheeseburgers, milkshakes, or ice cream. The restaurants also closed on Saturdays to observe the religious injunction against working on the Sabbath.

McDonald's in Great Britain, France, Germany, and Brazil serve beer and wine. McDonald's in Brazil has "happy hours" with salsa bands. But McDonald's has found that adaptations to local tastes can go too far: The McPloughman's sandwich, a version of the British pub staple featuring bread, cheese, and pickle, was not popular, nor was the forced "Thank you, please call again."

FOCUS ON CULTURE 11.2

Hamburger Colonialism

When European germs wiped out Indians, at least that aspect of conquest was unintentional. Burger King has no such excuse.

The modern colonizers currently have an ad campaign called "Whopper Virgins." Commercials are running during televised sports events, and the company has a nearly 8-minute video on its website. In a bizarre parody of an actual documentary, Burger King sent a crew out to remote Hmong parts of Thailand, Inuit parts of Greenland, and a village in Romania where people have both never seen a hamburger nor ever heard of one through advertising. The narration starts, "The hamburger is a culinary culture and it's actually an American phenomenon," (as if we didn't know this).

The first part of the video involved plucking some villagers to come to a modern office in local and native dress to compare Burger King's signature burger with a McDonald's Big Mac. Villagers are shown fumbling with the burger, with a patronizing narrator saying, "It's been very interesting to see their reaction to the hamburger because they've never seen such a foreign piece of food before and they didn't even quite know how to pick it up and they didn't know how to—from what end to eat. It was really interesting. We were able to see these people's first bite of a hamburger."

Remarking on the villagers' awkwardness in handling the burger, the narrator added: "It took them awhile to understand the dynamics of it and so that was fascinating to see because we take it for granted 'cause we live in America where hamburgers are consumed like a staple."

After the guinea pig villagers decided (of course!) that the Whopper tasted better than the Big Mac, Burger King sent a production crew out to the villages to cook burgers. Under the guise of "sharing things about both our cultures" (Gee, where have we heard that before in sanitized colonial history?), shots of a burger broiler being airlifted and sledded in by dog are shown. The villagers, of course, like the burger, with the narrator saying, "They told us yesterday, 'No, we want to experience other things in this world, too. We want to taste other foods. We want to see other people. We want to see other things.'"

Right out of the most banal of Thanksgiving scripts, the narrator says, as one of the crew receives a coat, "And they've been extraordinarily gracious to us." Burger King defends the ads, saying it worked hard to respect cultural sensitivities.

All this, to spread disease to developing peoples. And Burger King knows it. The Westernization of the global diet, led by America's fast-food giants, is helping spread obesity and diabetes as it has

(Continued)

never been seen before. It's not enough that those diseases are off the charts with Native Americans here at home. Now we want to seduce Inuits abroad. Even if levels of obesity stay what they are now, the number of people around the world with diabetes will explode from the 171 million people of 2000 to 366 million by 2030.

The numbers will more than triple in places ranging from the Democratic Republic of the Congo to Bangladesh to Guatemala. They will more than double or nearly triple in China, India, Brazil, and Mexico. According to WHO researchers, diabetes was already responsible in 2000 for nearly 3 million deaths around the world. "Given the increasing prevalence of obesity, it is likely that these figures provide an underestimate of future diabetes prevalence," those researchers said. Translated, even more people will die.

The WHO, not surprisingly, says, "Initiatives by the food industry to reduce the fat, sugar, and salt content of processed foods . . . could accelerate health gains worldwide."

But no, Burger King wants to colonize the farthest reaches with fat, sugar, and salt.

The irony was when the locals made the crew their native food in the video. The meal ladled out for them was smothered in vegetables. The crew yum-yummed "Nice," "Wonderful," "So good," and even, "Insane." That was the height of patronization given their mission. Burger King's violation of the "Whopper Virgins" is an insane reenactment of the worst of American colonial history.

Source: Jackson (2008) © Globe Newspaper Company.

By 1992, McDonald's had 882 outlets in Japan. These offer soup and fried rice to cater to Japanese eating habits, but the golden arches are there. McDonald's competitor in Japan is Japanese-owned MOS (Mountain, Ocean, Sea). Ironically, the MOS burger is based on the one made at Tommy's, a famous Los Angeles hamburger franchise.

What "message" representing the United States does McDonald's communicate to the world? Ritzer (1993) identified the principles of the fast-food restaurant that are coming to dominate more and more sectors worldwide. He calls this the "McDonaldization of society."

- *Efficiency.* The McDonald's fast-food model offers an efficient method of satisfying many needs.
- *Quantification.* Time is quantified in terms of how quickly one is served, and quantity ("bigger is better") becomes more important than quality.
- *Predictability.* The food McDonald's serves in Baltimore is essentially identical to the food it serves in Houston. It offers no surprises.
- *Control.* Employees are trained to do a very limited number of things, and customers as well are controlled through limited options.

Kentucky Fried Chicken

Kentucky Fried Chicken, now simply known as KFC, was a leader in the international market. Today, it has more than 14,000 restaurants in 100 countries, including some 1,100 outlets in Japan. Its Original Recipe offerings are sold in every KFC restaurant around the world. The KFCs in Japan adapt to the Japanese palate by making the coleslaw a little less sweet than the U.S. version of the popular side dish. The Colonel still smiles at every purchase.

In 1987, KFC opened the first Western fast-food restaurant in China in Beijing's Tiananmen Square. KFC meals became a political statement at the prodemocracy demonstrations there. Since then, some 3,700 restaurants have been built. In 2007, it was opening a new restaurant every day. The target is 20,000 restaurants within two decades. As a result, KFC is the most recognizable international icon of any kind in China. KFC remains popular in Muslim Indonesia despite less than favorable attitudes to the U.S. government. In the world's largest Muslim nation, KFC remains lucrative during Ramadan. Perhaps Muslims in Indonesia have divergent attitudes about the U.S. government and U.S. popular culture.

Chinese fast food courtesy of the KFC Colonel in Chaoyang shopping district in Nanning.

Budweiser

Anheuser-Busch, the world's largest brewer, entered China more than a decade ago and, in 2004, bought Harbin Brewery Group, China's fourth largest beer producer. More than 800 breweries compete for the Chinese market. Other international competitors coming into China are San Miguel of the Philippines, Fosters Brewing Group of Australia, and Denmark's Carlsberg and Heineken. Anheuser-Busch's successful international strategy has been to form partnerships with leading local brewers around the world through joint ventures or licensing agreements. The local partners know the local market and the local distribution system. Budweiser was a corporate sponsor of the 2008 Beijing Olympics, and it's known for having the same taste worldwide. In focus groups conducted in China, it became clear that the Chinese knew nothing about the name Budweiser. So Anheuser-Busch will market Budweiser with the U.S. value of personal independence, the freedom to do what you want to do, along with popular sports and the outdoors.

SPAM®

The "Miracle Meat in a Can" was launched in the United States in 1937. It traveled with the U.S. military during World War II and the Korean War. Spam® remains popular in the Philippines, Okinawa, Guam, and Saipan, all places with a history of U.S. military presence.

World War II brought thousands of U.S. military to Hawai'i and, with them, came mainland cultural influences that dominated and replaced existing traditions. One, which remains a staple to this day, is Spam®.

Today, Spam® is a luxury item in South Korea. *Chusok,* the Korean equivalent of U.S. Thanksgiving, is the biggest gift-giving occasion of the year. On this day alone, some 8 million cans of Spam® are given as gifts, some in boxed sets.

Barbie

Barbie dolls are considered anti-Islamic, and importing them into Iran is prohibited. Barbie's makeup and "indecent" clothes are considered Western cultural influences. An Iranian government-sponsored project designed Sara and Dara dolls. Sara wears long, flowing clothes and wraps. Her companion, Dara, is her brother, who comes with the long coat and turban of an Islamic cleric.

Marlboro

Another U.S. product being marketed internationally today as a cultural icon is cigarettes. According to the World Health Organization, 25 years ago, the industrialized West led the world in smoking; today, poor countries lead the list. Cigarette advertising in developing countries shows glamorous scenes of life in the United States. Smoking is advertised as sophisticated and cosmopolitan to match the way many of its audience see the United States.

Marlboro is among the most advertised foreign products in China. The "Marlboro man" can be seen on billboards in China even though the government has banned cigarette advertising. In Hong Kong, the Marlboro man is presented as a clean-cut man of property who lives in a big ranch house and rides a white horse—a symbol of good luck. U.S. cigarettes have associated themselves with a social and political message that says freedom, modernity, and luxury. The unofficial cigarette of protest at Tiananmen Square was Marlboro. In Russia, cigarettes are advertised with images of the U.S. good life: L&M cigarettes were superimposed on a photo of the Golden Gate Bridge with the slogan "Date with America."

The counterargument to cultural imperialism is that no surveys show that people are becoming more alike. While media flow globally, people receive and use the messages differently. Global marketing may symbolize the lifestyles that people aspire to, but evidence grows that local cultures have taken on a renewed significance as political movements promote local cultures and local identities. Finally, there is evidence that cultures do not flow in only one direction. Salsa music originated in the Caribbean but is now known worldwide, as are Ethiopian and Thai cuisines. German game shows and a Brazilian soap opera are popular on Cameroon television. And international students from Kenya are relieved to discover that KFC is available in the United States too.

Global Voices

The United Nationals Global Compact was officially launched in July 2000. The initiative encourages businesses to adopt sustainable and socially responsible policies and report their progress. Three of its 10 principles (United Nationals Global Compact, 2005) relate to the environment. Businesses should:

- Should support a precautionary approach to environmental challenges.
- Undertake initiatives to promote greater environmental responsibility.
- Encourage the development and diffusion of environmentally friendly technologies.

Here are some examples of corporate statements on environmental issues:

BP: "We expect that the world will require a more diverse energy mix as the basis for a secure supply of energy over time. . . . We will deliver on our commitments from the Gulf Coast incident and work hard to earn back the trust in our operations. We will rebuild value for our shareholders by re-establishing our competitive position within the sector by playing our part in meeting the world's growing demand for energy, as well as participating in the transition to a low-carbon economy." ("Our strategy," 2011)

Dow: "As a world leader in applied chemistry, Dow is uniquely positioned to drive change by delivering sustainable and innovative solutions that contribute to human progress and the growth of our business." ("Sustainability pillars," 2011)

Air France: "Beyond their CO_2 emissions, the main environmental impacts of airlines are noise, energy and water consumption, local emissions and waste production. . . . Despite the economic crisis, the Group continued to modernise its fleet in 2010, therefore cutting aircraft noise, its major impact for local communities close to airports. In order to limit its energy consumption on the ground, the Group is using various means, from electric vehicles to the construction of new buildings with the highest environmental standards" ("Environment and climate," 2010).

DIFFUSION MODEL

One result of contact between cultures is that through interaction, one culture may learn and adopt certain practices of the other culture. Perhaps the most significant example of adopting new practices resulted from Columbus's voyages linking two separate worlds into one. The Old World brought horses, cows, sheep, chickens, honeybees, coffee, wheat, cabbage, lettuce, bananas, olives, tulips, and daisies. The New World provided turkeys, sugarcane, corn, sweet potatoes, tomatoes, pumpkins, pineapples, petunias, poinsettias, and the practice of daily baths—a practice abhorred by Europeans.

This is the process of diffusion. Everett Rogers (Rogers & Shoemarker, 1971) has studied the communication process by which innovations are spread to members of a social system. Since the early 1960s, communication researchers have investigated the agricultural, health, educational, and family planning innovations in developing nations. The communication model presented in Chapter 2 has been particularly robust in analyzing and planning innovation diffusion.

FOCUS ON THEORY 11.2

Political scientist Daniel Lerner (1958) proposed that media helped transition from a traditional to a modernized country. Lerner argued that mass media expose people to events and ideas in other societies. That exposure would encourage them to reassess their current lifestyle and aspire to modern ways of life. Mass media at the societal level and interpersonal communication at the local level were seen as the paths to modernization. Studies from this perspective represent an area known as *development communication*. Development communication began as a Western political construct.

Non-Western scholars, particularly in Latin America, were critical of the imperialism of modernization in the dominant model (Beltran, 1976) and used cultural studies methods to focus more on the barriers that perpetuate inequalities. What is labeled as the *neomodernization* approach rejects the top-down perspective of the earlier modernization models and focuses on decentralized decision making and adopts a local bottom-up view of modernization (Melkote, 2003).

ROLES IN THE DIFFUSION PROCESS

Opinion Leadership and Change Agents

Important roles in the diffusion process are opinion leadership and change agents. Opinion leadership is accomplished by individuals who can influence informally other individuals' attitudes or overt behavior in a desired way with relative frequency. A change agent is a person who influences innovation decisions in a direction deemed desirable by a change agency.

Adopters

The rate of adoption is the relative speed with which an innovation is adopted by members of a social system. Important to understanding the diffusion process are adoption categories or classifications of the members of a social system on the basis of innovativeness. In order of their adoption of a change are innovators, early adopters, early majority, late majority, and laggards.

The diffusion process also can be observed within a culture as it adopts new technologies. Everett Rogers (1986), in his book *Communication Technology,* recounts the introduction and adoption of bank automated teller machines (ATMs). For banks, ATM technology has many advantages: The machines seldom make mistakes, and they save on labor costs. Each ATM transaction costs banks 21 cents, whereas each transaction completed face-to-face with a human teller costs banks more than twice as much. With these advantages, it isn't surprising that banks across the country installed some 70,000 ATMs in the late 1970s and early 1980s at a cost of some $1 billion.

By 1985, only about one in three customers used them. The innovators, early adopters, and some of the early majority were users. As this 33% use seemed to be fairly stable, bankers began to speak of "smashing the wall"; that is, bankers began to try incentives to increase the percentage of customers using the ATM—or converting the late majority and laggards.

Who are the innovators? Studies of adaptation potential, or an individual's possible success in adapting to a new culture, give us hints of likely innovators. Age and educational background are good predictors as innovators tend to be younger and better educated. Another characteristic of innovators is familiarity with the new technology or belief through previous contact, interpersonal contacts, and mass media. Personality factors, such as gregariousness, tolerance for ambiguity, risk taking, open-mindedness, and other related factors, are also good predictors of cultural adaptation and likely characteristics of innovators.

Change Agent Ethics

One final aspect of the diffusion process is change agent ethics. You might ask yourself the "pill question." If you had a pill that could cure cancer, would you give it to a society? It would cure cancer, but the result would be the loss of jobs in health care. It also might cause people to live longer, thus putting a strain on the resources of that society. In response to that strain, that society may move to mandatory deaths of its citizens at age 70. Would you want that to happen?

The introduction or rejection of an innovation has consequences for a society. It is important to recognize that the adoption—or rejection—of any innovation has consequences for the society. Introducing axes to the indigenous Australian tribes by missionaries (the change agents) resulted in an improved standard of living for the tribes but also contributed to the breakdown of the family structure, the rise of prostitution, and "misuse" of the axes themselves. Axes made hunting possible, which required men to live apart from their families, and axes could be used to kill humans as well as animals.

What are the consequences of providing birth control information and technology to a developing country? What might be the consequences on family size? The role of women? Support for the elderly? This fear of the consequences of culture contact is one reason why products are rejected.

Case Study: Quality Circles

In the following case study, you will see an example of the diffusion of management concepts from the United States to Japan and then from Japan back to the United States.

After World War II Japan had its industry destroyed. Japanese products of the time were popularly known as "junk"—they might last a day or two. "Made in Japan" meant the same thing as cheap and shoddy merchandise. General Douglas MacArthur asked Washington to send someone to help conduct a national census and assess Japan's ability to rebuild. Dr. W. Edward Deming, a relatively unknown statistician for the U.S. government, was sent.

Beginning in 1948, he gave lectures for the Union of Japanese Scientists and Engineers (JUSE), eventually lecturing to representatives of virtually every major Japanese corporation. Deming's message was that quality is the result of consistency, efficiency, and continual improvement. Deming believed that workers are intrinsically motivated to do well but that efforts are thwarted by incompetent, narrow-minded management. Deming stressed achieving uniform results during production rather than through inspection at the end of the production line. Deming's message was empowering workers with quality control decisions, monitoring the results statistically, and systematic cooperation with suppliers and buyers. In 1951, the JUSE honored his services by establishing the Deming Award for Quality. His portrait in Toyota headquarters is larger than that of the company's founder.

Later, Dr. Joseph Juran lectured in Japan on extending quality from just manufacturing to the entire process, from product design to product delivery to the customer. By 1956, there was a weekly radio series on quality, and in 1960, the government declared November "National Quality Month." From Deming's and Juran's work, Japan developed by 1962 the concept of the quality circle—a group of 3 to 10 employees who meet on the job to discuss and solve quality problems (Ingle, 1982). This and other efforts had, by the 1970s, resulted in top-quality cameras, electronics, motorcycles, television sets, and radios.

Why did the quality circle as a concept succeed so well in Japan? The most important reason, as you have seen, is that the concept of working together in groups to benefit organization matched with the Japanese cultural value placed on group affiliation or homogeneity. But the story isn't over. In the 1960s, the United States was beginning to lose its lead in manufacturing. In the late 1960s, Dr. Juran published stories describing Japanese quality circles. Companies such as Lockheed and Honeywell started similar pilot programs. By 1973, Lockheed's programs were receiving wide publicity and wide imitation. Although many Fortune 500 companies began using quality circles, the programs did not have the same impact they had in Japan. Quality circles did not fit in well with the dominant U.S. value of individualism.

In the first part of this example, General MacArthur provided the opinion leadership, and Dr. Deming was the change agent. In the second part of the example, Dr. Juran provided the opinion leadership for the United States. As for the quality circles coming to the United States, the innovator was a corporation: Lockheed was the innovator in using Japanese quality circles in the United States.

CONVERGENCE MODEL

There has been much criticism of the diffusion model, including its heavy identification with mass media channels. The model has been modified to treat communication as a process of convergence among members of interpersonal networks (Rogers & Kincaid, 1981). In the convergence model, communication is defined as a process in which information is shared by two or more individuals who converge over time toward a greater degree of mutual agreement. Whereas the diffusion model focuses on what one individual does to another, the convergence model focuses on the relationship between those who share information. Thus, the level of analysis shifts from the individual to the dyad or, on the macro level, to groups and cultures.

ADAPTING THE MESSAGE

As you have seen, key to the diffusion and convergence processes across cultures is adaptation of the message to the receiving culture. The key is to adapt to the local culture, localize thinking, localize the product, and localize the marketing strategy.

De Mooij (1998) has reviewed research and been able to relate advertising styles to Hofstede's dimensions: Japanese advertising reflects Confucian and collectivistic values. Concepts of face and harmony relate to an indirect communication style. It is said that the goal of Japanese advertising is to win the trust and respect of the consumer. Advertising is serene, mood creating, and subtle, with much symbolism. Dependency, nature, and respect for elders can be seen.

In commercials seen in the United States, AFLAC makes use of an abrasive quacking duck. About 70% of the company's income comes from the Japanese market. For commercials in Japan, the AFLAC duck has a more "smoothing" tone. And in Japan, the actors talk directly to the duck, while in the U.S. commercials, the actors never notice the duck.

Taiwan advertising generally links the product to the consumer's traditional Chinese values, such as family relations and respect for authority. The advertising is indirect and promises an ideal that may be reached through the use of the product. Spanish advertising is less direct than the advertising style of northern European countries because Spain's culture is more collectivistic. People are depicted in family and other groups. Feminine aspects of the culture are seen in the softer approaches and relatively low use of celebrity endorsements. The use of art, color, and beauty is related to a strong uncertainty avoidance.

U.S. advertising reflects assertiveness, the direct approach, and competitiveness, which de Mooij relates to a configuration of masculinity and individualism. Overstatement and hyperbole are typical, as are direct comparisons. Two examples of message adaptation are the marketing of baby food worldwide and missionary work in New Guinea.

Case Study: Marketing Gerber Baby Foods Worldwide

Gerber Products first entered Australia in 1959, Japan in 1960, and the Philippines in 1972 under the assumption that the world would like and buy what was popularly used in the

United States. The company discovered that each country not only likes different foods but also has different baby-feeding practices. Gerber then established advisory committees in those countries to determine what products would be acceptable. Out of that came "lamb stock stew" for Australia, "rice with young sardines" for Japan, and "strained mango" for the Philippines.

In Japan and South Korea, mothers are pressured to make meals for the family from scratch. Here Gerber positions itself by marketing its products as part of a "scientifically based" feeding plan. The food containers are labeled as "lessons" to demonstrate that Gerber provides something that the mothers cannot make for babies.

Case Study: Religious Missionary Work in New Guinea

Before reading how missionaries took Christianity to the peoples of New Guinea, understand that missionaries look for what is called a redemptive analogy, or something in the culture that can be compared to the gospel and hence makes the unknown knowable to the culture (Richardson, 1974). One missionary came upon the practice of peace making between two villages. A man from each village handed over to the other village one of each village's babies to live among the other people. The people in New Guinea called these children *tarop tim,* or "peace child." According to the tradition, everyone in the village must then touch the peace child as a symbol of accepting the peace. As long as the children were alive, no fighting was allowed to occur between the villages.

The missionary built his message around the concept of the peace child. He explained how God gave his "peace child" to the world. In the local culture, fighting could begin again if the children died, but God's peace child is eternal because he rose from the dead and is still alive.

SUMMARY

Mary Pratt coined the term *contact zone* to refer to "the space in which peoples geographically and historically separated come into contact with each other and establish ongoing relations, usually involving conditions of coercion, radical inequality, and intractable conflict" (1992, p. 6). Edward Said describes the contact and subsequent linguistic construction of non-Western cultures as "Orientalism," a process of labeling the peoples of "underdeveloped" cultures, particularly indigenous cultures, as insignificant "others." That cultural imperialism continues in the actions of multinational corporations. Products can carry cultural values, and many products that are seen to represent a culture have both been widely popular and resisted. A cultural icon is a special symbol that tends to be idolized in a culture. U.S. cultural icons include Coca-Cola, Disneyland, McDonald's, KFC, Budweiser, Spam®, Barbie, and Marlboro.

Diffusion is the communication process by which innovations are spread to members of a social system. Roles in the diffusion process include opinion leadership (individuals who can informally influence others), change agents (people who influence innovation decisions), and adopters (people who accept and use the innovation). Early adopters tend to be younger and more educated, to have had previous contact with the innovation, and to have personality characteristics such as gregariousness. The key to successful diffusion across cultures is adapting the message to the receiving culture.

DISCUSSION QUESTIONS

1. In what ways can it be said that colonialism is a continuing world theme today?

2. Can there be a balance between cultural imperialism and diffusion of cultural icons?

3. What are the arguments for and against anyone or any government introducing new ideas or technology into a culture?

4. Describe examples of advertising from countries that reflect those countries' cultural dimensions.

KEY TERMS

adaptation potential   299

artifact   285

change agent   298

change agent ethics   299

contact zone   279

convergence   301

diffusion   298

discursive imperialism   280

hegemony   286

icon   285

opinion leadership   298

quality circle   300

redemptive analogy   302

READINGS

All readings are from *Intercultural Communication: A Global Reader* (Jandt, 2004).

He-Soo Kim, Greg Hearn, Caroline Hatcher, and Ian Weber, "Online Communication Between Australians and Koreans: Learning to Manage Differences That Matter" (p. 143)

Akira Miyahara, "Toward Theorizing Japanese Interpersonal Communication Competence From a Non-Western Perspective" (p. 279)

Wole Soyinka, "Nobel Lecture, December 8, 1986" (p. 387)

Lalita Rajasingham, "The Impact of Universities on Globalisation" (p. 413)

STUDENT STUDY SITE

Visit the student study site at **www.sagepub.com/jandt7e** for these additional learning tools:

- Web Resources
- Audio and Video Links
- SAGE journal articles
- eFlashcards
- Web Quizzes
- Sample Essays

PART 4

Cultures Within Cultures

National boundaries do not necessarily overlap cultural boundaries. At some national boundaries, a unique blended culture can develop. In some ways, parts of the Mexico-Southwest U.S. border became a blended culture. For example, at the Tijuana and San Diego border, some people cross relatively freely, even working on one side and living on the other side of the border.

Within national boundaries, distinct co-cultures can exist in voluntary or fixed separation. Harlem in New York City has a long and varied history stretching from the Manhattan Indians through Dutch, British, and German immigrants. Early in the 20th century, the Afro-American Realty Company began renting properties to the city's Black middle class. The area's evolving culture became the home and inspiration to generations of writers and artists, as well as many of the past century's African-American politicians.

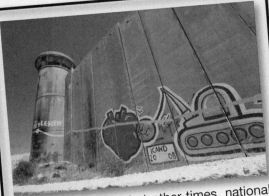

At other places and at other times, national boundaries can be used to define cultural boundaries, and political tensions may arise.

On the other side of the continent, by the 1850s, thousands of Chinese lived in a tent community in Victoria, Canada. A future premier of British Columbia referred to Victoria as Little Canton. And by 1880, Victoria's Chinatown became the largest community of Chinese in Canada. In the 20th century, urban renewal reduced its size until community planning by the city revitalized the area.

What is known as JapanTown in San Francisco was formed after the 1906 earthquake. Most Japanese immigrants entered the United States through San Francisco, and many stayed in the city. Like Chinatown in Victoria, JapanTown in San Francisco was negatively affected by urban renewal. Today, the Peace Plaza and five-story Pagoda remains as the dominant architectural structure in JapanTown.

CHAPTER

12

Immigration and Acculturation

FOCUS QUESTIONS

- What is meant by the term *culture shock?*

- How is China an example of the pressures of internal migration?

- How does one become a citizen of a country?

- What can be learned from examples of immigration experiences?

- What are the predictors of an immigrant's success in a new country?

Culture Shock
    Stages of Culture Shock
    Reverse Culture Shock
    Symptoms
Third-Culture Kids
Migration Within One Country
Citizenship Policies
    Germany
    Israel
    Japan
Immigration
    Migration From Japan to Brazil and Peru
    Migration From Korea to Brazil and Argentina
    Migration From Europe to Argentina
    Migration From the United States to Brazil
    Recent Immigration to Western Europe
    Immigration to the United States
        Colonial Policies on Immigration
        U.S. Policies on Immigration
        Contributing Countries Prior to 1800
        Contributing Countries Since 1800
Predictors of Acculturation
    Similarity of Culture
    Personal Characteristics and Experiences
    Effect of Media and Transportation Advances
Categories of Acculturation
Summary
Discussion Questions
Key Terms
Reading
Student Study Site

Perhaps there can be no greater test of one's intercultural communication skills than immigration. A tourist visits a country for a short time for such goals as relaxation and self-enlightenment. And a **sojourner** lives in a country for a limited time, from as little as 6 months to as long as 5 years, with a specific and goal-oriented purpose, such as education. Both tourists and sojourners fully expect to return home, and hence don't face the same challenges as immigrants.

The word **expatriate** is more often used to refer to a noncitizen worker who lives in a country for an indeterminate length of time. Many people labeled "immigrants" in the United States and Europe are in fact expatriates whose intent is to work but not to become full-fledged members of the culture. (Furnham, 1987). It is immigrants who face the greatest challenges. Immigrants include refugees and asylees. A **refugee** is a person in any location who is unable or unwilling to return to the country of nationality because of persecution or a well-founded fear of persecution. An **asylee** is a person in a country who is unable or unwilling to return to the country of nationality because of persecution or a well-founded fear of persecution.

While many immigrants may relocate with their immediate family, everything else in their worlds changes. Most face the challenge of learning a new language; all are challenged with a new culture—everything from living arrangements, food, landscapes, social customs, government, education, popular culture, and more.

This chapter first looks at the experience of culture shock, the feelings one can experience on introduction to a new culture. Then you will read about the largest example of migration within one culture. Then after a review of citizenship policies come examples of immigration throughout the world. Finally, you will read about the predictors of immigrants becoming fully functioning in a new culture. You will discover how modern media and transportation systems have significantly changed immigration and acculturation from what immigrants of a century ago experienced.

CULTURE SHOCK

Whether an individual enters a host culture as a sojourner or as an immigrant, **culture shock** is the first likely response (Furnham & Bochner, 1986). Using public transportation where the systems are different can present challenges. Unless you are prepared to function in the new culture, the situation can be highly stressful. Refer back to the intercultural barrier identified in Chapter 4 as anxiety. This form of stress and anxiety is called culture shock. Studies show that from 30% to 60% of expatriates suffer serious culture shock, whereas about 20% have no difficulty and enjoy the challenge.

The phrase was popularized by anthropologist Kalvero Oberg (1960) to describe the feelings of disorientation and anxiety that many people experience for a time while living in a foreign country. It results from an awareness that one's basic assumptions about life and one's familiar ways of behaving are no longer appropriate or functional.

Stages of Culture Shock

Adler (1975), Pedersen (1995), and others have described culture shock as a five-stage process.

The first stage of initial contact, sometimes called the "honeymoon stage" or initial euphoria, is where everything is new and exciting. The person is basically a tourist with her or his basic identity rooted in the home culture.

The second stage involves disintegration of familiar cues and irritation and hostility with the differences experienced in the new culture. For example, an international student in a U.S. grocery store may be asked, "Paper or plastic?" The student knows what paper is and what plastic is but doesn't understand the question. The student can experience feelings of inadequacy and can withdraw or become isolated.

The third stage involves a reintegration of new cues and an increased ability to function in the new culture. Perhaps surprisingly, though, the emotions experienced at this stage are typically anger and resentment toward the new culture for "being different."

In the fourth stage, gradual adjustment continues toward gradual autonomy and seeing "good" and "bad" elements in both the home and new cultures. The individual becomes more comfortable in the new culture as more things are predictable. Feelings of isolation are fewer, and people feel more in control and more comfortable.

Global Voices

Soon after arriving in the United States from Peru, I cried almost every day. I was so tense I heard without hearing, and this made me feel foolish. I also escaped into sleeping more than twelve hours at a time and dreamed of my life, family, and friends in Lima. After three months of isolating myself in the house and speaking to no one, I ventured out. I then began to criticize everything about this new culture: values, customs, climate, and its people. During this time I began to idealize my own homeland. I also began to have severe headaches. Finally I consulted a doctor, but she only gave me a lot of drugs to relieve the pain. Neither my doctor nor my teachers ever mentioned the two magic words that could have changed my life drastically during those times: culture shock! When I learned about this I began to see things from a new point of view and was better able to accept myself and my feelings.

I now realize most of the Americans I met in Lima before I came to the U.S. were also in one of the stages of culture shock. They demonstrated a somewhat hostile attitude toward Peru, making crude jokes and fun of the people and culture around them. Peruvians sensed this hostility and usually moved from an initially friendly attitude to a defensive, aggressive attitude or to avoidance as in my case. The Americans mostly stayed within the safe cultural familiarity of the embassy compound. Many seemed to feel that the difficulties they were experiencing in Peru were specially created by Peruvians to create discomfort for "gringos." In other words, they displaced their problem of adjustment and blamed everything on Peru for being an underdeveloped culture.

—R. Bimrose, July 1981, quoted in *Handbook of Intercultural Training* (Landis & Brislin, 1983, p. 30)

The final, fifth stage is described as reciprocal interdependence, where the person has achieved **biculturalism** by developing the ability to cope comfortably in both the home and new cultures. Full adjustment can take years.

Reverse Culture Shock

If a person has adjusted exceptionally well to the host culture, **reverse culture shock** may occur upon return to the home country. This type of culture shock may cause greater distress and confusion than the original had. In reverse culture shock, the home culture is compared adversely to the admired aspects of the new culture.

Symptoms

The symptoms of culture shock are pervasive and vary in intensity, duration, and severity among individuals. Individuals can experience both physical and psychological symptoms.

Physical symptoms are overconcern about cleanliness of food, bedding, and dishes; extreme stress on health and safety; fear of physical contact with anyone in the new country; great concern over minor pains and skin eruptions; craving "home cooking"; use of alcohol and drugs; and a decline in work quality.

Psychological symptoms are insomnia, fatigue, isolation and loneliness, disorientation, frustration, criticism of the new country, nervousness, self-doubt, irritability, depression, anger, and emotional and intellectual withdrawal. The effects of culture shock on intercultural communication are obvious: The immigrant's—or visitor's—intercultural communication becomes less effective. For example, frustrations with the new culture may be interpreted by intercultural receivers as hostility toward them. Intercultural communication receivers need to be sensitive to the difficulties of culture shock that an individual may experience.

THIRD-CULTURE KIDS

The term *third culture* has been used by some to refer to a lifestyle shared by individuals acting in missionary, diplomatic, and business roles as they attempt to relate their home and sojourn cultures. Ruth Hill Useem (Useem & Downie, 1976) first coined the term *third-culture kids* to refer to children in expatriate families who reside outside of their home culture for years at a time. Other terms that have been used are *global nomads, transnationals,* and *internationally mobile children* (Gerner, Perry, Moselle, & Archbold, 1992). Eakin (1998) and Useem (1999) (cited in Kidd & Lankenau, 2007) argue that these people integrate elements of their home culture and their various cultures of residence into a third, different and distinct culture and may experience cultural marginality because of no longer feeling comfortable in any specific culture. In some ways, President Obama is a third-culture kid. He was born in Honolulu. At age 2, his father returned to Kenya. His mother remarried and moved to her new husband's home-land, Indonesia. Obama attended public school in Indonesia until he was 10 and then returned to Honolulu to live with his grandparents. *New York Times* columnist David Brooks described Obama as a "sojourner who lives apart" (2008, p. A33).

While most research has been with children from the United States, studies have shown that third-culture kids have a high level of interest in travel and learning languages and feel accepting of cultures and diversity (Gerner et al., 1992). Iwama (1990) found third-culture kids to be more self-confident, flexible, active, and curious and to have greater bilingual ability.

Does biculturalism as represented by third-culture kids represent a way to transcend nationalism and ethnocentrism and a way to create diverse communities (Willis, 1994)? There are suggestions of difficulties: Third-culture kids may have difficulty in maintaining relationships and in direct problem solving (C. A. Smith, 1991).

MIGRATION WITHIN ONE COUNTRY

The world's largest human migration occurs annually within the borders of China. Each year millions of workers travel from urban cities to their rural home villages. In the 1950s, China established the Hukou system under which every person is registered with a specific location, usually their place of birth. Changes in residences must be approved by both the place of origin and the place of destination. Individuals with an urban Hukou are entitled to employment, health care, housing, pension, and food subsidies. None of these are available to people with a rural registration (Zhao, 2000).

Official estimates place the number of migrant workers at more than 98 million in 2003. Most of the migrants originate from the central and western inland regions and move to the cities in the eastern coastal provinces of Beijing, Shanghai, Guangdong, Zhejiang, and Fujian.

Chinese migrant workers carry heavy loads of bricks over a narrow wooden plank at a construction site in Shenzhen, Guangdong province. The migrant workers are the backbone of China's amazing construction boom.

Many factors contribute to this migration, including China's market economy, surplus labor in agriculture, and rural-urban income disparity (Wong, Li, & Song, 2007).

Each year millions leave the cities for annual visits to their villages to see their spouses, children, and parents for two weeks of holiday at Chinese New Year. Others alternate work in the cities with seasonal agriculture jobs. The migrants are usually young males, with a higher-than-average level of education than others from their place of emigration. They tend to gain employment in factories and service industries, and they work longer hours, yet have lower household incomes than the urban residents (Hu, Wang, & Zou, 2002).

China needs these migrants for economic growth, but they are not accorded the rights of urban residents. They work at jobs that China's urban residents are unwilling to do. They live in very poor housing conditions. In the media they have been portrayed as ignorant and a threat to social stability and are linked to the increase in crime rates in the cities. They are perceived also as competing with unemployed urban residents who have been laid off from the state-owned enterprises. Furthermore, the general public holds the view that migrant workers are stupid and ignorant, and should be blamed for their misfortunes (Davin, 2000). It's no surprise, then, that China's migrant workers display many of the symptoms of culture shock: sleep disturbance, anxiety, depression, inadequate coping, and social dysfunction (Wong et al., 2007).

> **Global Voices**
>
> "It may take longer than 100 years to even out the disparity between East and West (China)."
>
> —Li Zibin, the former vice chairman of the West Development Office of the State Council quoted in *News China*, May 5, 2010, p. 8.

CITIZENSHIP POLICIES

Citizenship in a country may be acquired in three ways: by birth, by blood, or by naturalization. By birth, or *jus soli,* is that one who is born within the borders of a country is automatically a citizen. By blood, or *jus sanguinis,* is that if one's parents are citizens of a country, no matter where one is born, one is a citizen of the parents' country. Naturalization requires a period of residency, an exam, an oath, or some combination of these. The following are some noteworthy examples of the ways citizenship is acquired.

Germany

Germany had the industrialized world's most liberal political asylum law (Marshall, 1992). After World War II, Germany wrote into its constitution a guarantee to shelter all persecuted people. In the first year after unification, about 250,000 foreigners sought asylum—most in the Eastern sector and most not political exiles but economic refugees hoping for a better life. That number doubled over the next year. The hearing process for refugees could take up to 3 years, and less than 5% were finally granted permanent asylum. During that waiting period, the refugees were given full access to Germany's generous welfare system that provided free housing, electricity, medical care, schooling for children, and stipends of up to approximately $10,000 a year. These benefits often far exceeded what refugees could make at home—and exceeded what many Germans, particularly Easterners, made.

Chancellor Helmut Kohl labeled the asylum issue second in importance only to monetary stability. In 1992, Germany announced plans to repatriate thousands of Romanians (most being denied asylum of this group are Roma), and in 1993, the German parliament voted to end the constitutional right of foreigners to seek asylum. Only those foreigners who arrive by air from dangerous homelands and who hold proper travel documents may now file for refugee status.

In addition, the German constitution gives automatic right of abode to ethnic Germans scattered throughout Eastern Europe and the former Soviet Union. As a result, more than 1.5 million immigrants from the former Soviet Union, most with little or no German-language proficiency, have received citizenship over the past decade based on their forebears having settled along the Volga River as much as 300 years ago.

Postwar immigration brought the percentage of nonethnic Germans to about 5% of Germany's population. Germany did not strive to be a melting pot. Hundreds of thousands of Turks, for example, fluent in German and whose families have lived in Germany for two or three generations, were referred to as guest workers and not eligible for citizenship. People of nonethnic German heritage who have lived in Germany for some time are called *ausländer,* which translates as outlander or foreigner. Immigrants came and were accepted as laborers in Germany's booming economy. Most expected to return home. By 1999, there were 7.3 million foreign nationals among Germany's 81 million residents. Approximately half had lived in Germany at least 10 years, 30% at least 20 years, and at least 1.5 million were born in Germany.

Social movements beginning in the late 1960s encouraged immigrants to become more involved in public life. But without voting rights or a voice in social affairs, immigrants experienced antiforeigner sentiments, particularly in regions with high unemployment. Attacks on these foreigners and on those seeking asylum led to renewed charges of German **xenophobia**, or fear of strangers or foreigners, and of extreme nationalism. The violence, however, has been concentrated almost exclusively among the small-fringe skinhead youth group, and thousands of Germans have protested the violence against foreigners.

There were three ways of becoming a citizen of Germany: by birth, by naturalization, and, for ethnic Germans from Eastern Europe and the Soviet successor states, by claim under the "right of return." Traditionally, Germany granted citizenship on the basis of descent, the principle of *jus sanguinis* or of defining citizenship by inheritance. Effective in 2000, a new nationality law came into effect that grants citizenship by place of birth, the principle of *jus soli,* in an attempt to ensure social and domestic peace.

The German government estimated that half of the foreigners living in Germany became eligible for citizenship under the new law. All children born in Germany now automatically receive citizenship if at least one of their parents lived in Germany for at least 8 years. Children of foreign parents born in Germany are now entitled to dual citizenship until age 23, when they must then choose one or the other. To receive German citizenship, they must be loyal to Germany and its people and have a good command of the German language. The new citizenship law also facilitates the naturalization of foreign nationals who have lived in Germany for many years. Germans are struggling with the consequence of the change in immigrant policy. There is a growing differentiation between an ethnic identity and a civil identity (e.g., a Turk who carries a German passport).

Israel

Proclaimed on May 14, 1948, Israel was a relatively poor, besieged nation in need of building the country's population. Citizenship may be acquired by birth, residence, naturalization, and the Law of Return. The Proclamation of the Establishment of the State of Israel stated, "The State of Israel will be open for Jewish immigration and the ingathering of the exiles; it will foster the development of the country for all its inhabitants; it will be based on freedom, justice, and peace as envisaged by the prophets of Israel; it will ensure complete equality of social and political rights to all its inhabitants irrespective of religion, race or sex." A fundamental aspiration of the State of Israel is *aliyah,* literally "ascending," the Hebrew word for immigration into Israel. The Law of Return, enacted in 1950, granted anyone with a Jewish mother or who had converted to Judaism the right to come to Israel as an **oleh** (a Jew immigrating to Israel) and become a citizen. By 1951, the number of immigrants more than doubled what the Jewish population of the country had been in 1948. The government devoted much effort to absorbing the immigrants through residence construction, job creation, Hebrew-language instruction, and educational expansion to meet the needs of children from diverse cultural backgrounds. (See Table 12.1 for immigration into Israel by year.)

Since 1970, the right to immigrate under the Law of Return has been extended to include the child and the grandchild of a Jew, the spouse of a child of a Jew, and the spouse of the grandchild of a Jew. The purpose of the change was to ensure the unity of families where intermarriage had occurred, even though the Halakhah, or Jewish religious law, specifies that only those born to a Jewish mother and those who have converted are Jews. Since the establishment of Israel, more than 2.5 million people have immigrated, with the largest numbers from "countries of distress," places where Jews are unwelcome, harassed, or persecuted.

Today, Israel is a prosperous nation but with a mosaic of ultra-Orthodox Jewish immigrants who fled from Europe and distinguish themselves from immigrants from North Africa and the Middle East. Israel's population today is about 7.5 million. About 24% of the population is non-Jewish and mostly Arab. Soviet Jews were permitted to leave the Soviet Union in large numbers in the late 1980s. The collapse of the Soviet Union in late 1991 brought more Soviet immigrants, many nonpracticing Jews. Some of these have a spouse, father, or grandparent

Table 12.1 Immigration Into Israel, by Year

1948–1951	(4-year total)	687,624
1952–1959	(8-year total)	272,446
1960–1969	(10-year total)	373,840
1970–1979	(10-year total)	346,260
1980–1989	(10-year total)	153,833
1990–1991	(2-year total; Soviet immigration)	375,616
1992–1999	(8-year total)	580,703
2000–2010	(10-year total)	285,697

Source: The State of Israel, Central Bureau of Statistics (2012, p. 5). Adapted with permission.

who is Jewish but are not Jews themselves under Jewish religious law. Some Israelis fear that the country has become a preferred destination for non-Jews from the former Soviet Union and other economically depressed areas who immigrated only for economic reasons and who have no desire to become Jewish. Some have proposed limiting immigration. The issue is no less than the character of Israel as a Jewish state.

In addition, the Palestinians demand a partnership in governing the country to ensure that Arab citizens get equal treatment. The Palestinians object to the Star of David on Israel's flag and the national anthem that expresses the Jewish yearning for a return to Zion.

Japan

Unlike the in United States, immigration was not a concern in Japan until recently. Between 1976 and 1983, the total inflow of documented immigrant workers into Japan was between 20,000 and 30,000 a year. The numbers began to increase in 1984 and reached 95,000 in 1990. From violations of the Immigration Act, it is estimated that undocumented immigrant workers numbered only 1,889 in 1982 but grew to 36,264 in 1990. Estimates of the number of undocumented workers in 1991 ranged from 200,000 to 500,000.

In 2000, a new immigration law went into effect, under which illegal immigrants can no longer avoid the possibility of being fined or imprisoned after being in Japan for 3 years. And once deported, illegal immigrants are banned from returning for 5 years. However, as in the United States and Germany, the number of undocumented workers is increasing.

IMMIGRATION

The number of people counted as living outside their country of birth has almost doubled during the past 50 years, increasing to 191 million in 2005, up from 84 million in 1975 and 104 million in 1985 (United Nations, 2006a, 2006b). People migrate for a variety of reasons—from fleeing from war or persecution to seeking better economic opportunity, from political conflict to labor surpluses.

FOCUS ON THEORY 12.1

The terms *adaptation, acculturation, assimilation, adjustment,* and *integration* have all been used to refer to the process in which individual sojourners and immigrants develop functional and psychological fitness in a new culture. Young Yun Kim (2005) has developed a communication theory of adaptation that conceives of adaptation as a process of "stress-adaptation-growth" that leads to greater functional and psychological fitness. Kim also identifies the key factors that facilitate the adaptation process—intrapersonal communication, interpersonal communication, mass communication, the new environment, and the individual's own background.

Migration From Japan to Brazil and Peru

Brazil is home to the largest Japanese community outside Japan. Some 1.6 million people of Japanese origin now live in Brazil. Most arrived in Brazil to work on coffee plantations. Some have built up large agricultural concerns. Similarly, the Japanese who migrated to Peru went as contract laborers. The Japanese in Peru have gone through periods of prejudice to assimilation as an immigrant's son became a popular president of the country. Japanese migration to Peru began in 1899, when contract workers began to arrive to work on large haciendas. By 1923, when contract labor was stopped, some 18,000 Japanese lived in Peru. Relatives of previous immigrants continued to arrive.

Many of the Japanese settled in Lima and other cities and opened small businesses. Before World War II, two incidents greatly affected the Japanese immigrants: A popular book by a Peruvian journalist contended that the Inca Empire founder had been a Japanese fisherman. This led to speculation that Japan would try to lead Peru's Indian majority in an uprising against the White government. Then, rumors spread that caches of weapons had been found on property owned by Japanese immigrants. So after the attack on Pearl Harbor, the government closed Japanese schools and social organizations, seized business properties, and deported more than 1,700 *nikkei,* or people of Japanese descent, to relocation camps in the United States. Some were deported to Japan in exchange for U.S. civilian prisoners held in Japanese-controlled territories.

Today, the nikkei population is estimated at some 40,000, a small percentage of Peru's 30 million residents. Like Indians and Blacks, the nikkei experience racial prejudice from Peru's White upper class, but the nikkei are assimilating. Half of the Japanese-Peruvians are of mixed origin, and most do not speak Japanese. A 1989 census found that more than 90% of Japanese-Peruvians are Roman Catholic, with fewer than 3% Buddhist. At least 40% maintain no contact with nikkei social organizations.

Migration From Korea to Brazil and Argentina

In 1962, Korea and Brazil reached an agreement to ease unemployment in South Korea and to develop farmlands in Brazil. Tens of thousands of middle-class Koreans from South Korea and North Korea with little Portuguese or Spanish language ability sailed for Brazil and Argentina. Some did become farmers. Many others, however, sold their clothes from their trunks on arrival and became garment peddlers, replacing the Jewish and Armenian immigrants who had dominated the apparel trade in São Paulo and Buenos Aires. Thirty years later, some 50,000 Korean immigrants worked as entrepreneurs in the garment trade.

In the early 21st century, many migrated again but this time to New York and Los Angeles. They demonstrate a unique mix of Confucian and Latin American culture, prize business ownership (traditional Koreans look down on merchants), are apt to peck each other on the cheek and interact easily with others, and speak the language of their Latino production workers and buyers.

Migration From Europe to Argentina

Like the United States, Argentina, with a population of about 42 million, is a nation of immigrants. One group arrived in 1865 from mining towns in Wales seeking to escape English rule and establish a Welsh state. They were welcomed by an Argentine government eager for growth. The Welsh built self-contained farming and sheep ranching communities in Patagonia on the eastern slopes of the Andes. Their town councils were notably democratic, allowing women to vote.

The immigrants remained nationalistic. The great-grandchildren of the original immigrants are Argentine, yet their language and customs are in some ways more traditional than modern-day Wales. Exchange students study in Wales, and the regional government invites teachers from Wales to keep the language and culture alive.

Late into the 19th century, Argentina was still only sparsely populated, largely with descendants of Spanish settlers and only the remnants of indigenous groups. A strong agricultural economy brought immigrants from southern and eastern Europe—primarily Italy and Spain. Argentina became a blend of Italian and Spanish. Writer Abel Posse, in *Dogs of Paradise* (1989), for example, describes Christopher Columbus as a typical Argentine—"an Italian who learned Spanish." By 1914, more than a third of Argentina's population was foreign born.

Argentina has been described as the "most European" of the Americas. The third largest ethnic group is made up of Jews from Russia, followed by Arabs. Argentina continues to be a magnet for immigrants, a land of promise. However, the "Latinamericanization" of new immigrants has raised concerns. The new immigrants are more likely to be racially mixed and darker skinned. And competition for jobs has become an issue. To deal with the increasing illegal immigration, Argentina is attempting to control its borders.

Migration From the United States to Brazil

Following the Civil War in the latter half of the 19th century, thousands of people from all over the South migrated to Mexico, Cuba, and Brazil. Ellsworths, Lees, McKnights, Stegalls, and Yancys were part of an estimated 10,000 to 40,000 Confederates who emmigrated, many to Brazil, where the government promised cheap land in the hope that the immigrants would establish Brazil as a cotton-producing country where slavery was still legal.

The immigrants settled in several parts of Brazil: in an area located 500 miles from the mouth of the Amazon River, which became the city of Santarem; in Rio Doce near the coast; and in settlements called Juquia, New Texas, Villa Americana, and Xiririca in southern Brazil near São Paulo. Only Villa Americana prospered.

Some failed and moved to the cities or returned to the United States. Others were successful and made fortunes in cotton and watermelons. The immigrants brought baseball, peaches, pecans, and various strains of rice to Brazil. The immigrants remained in cloistered communities and established schools, churches, and cemeteries because the Roman Catholic Church in Brazil would not allow the Protestant Confederates to be buried with Catholics. Even 80 years later, many spoke English exclusively in homes. But with time, more and more of the descendants moved to the cities and assimilated into the Brazilian culture.

Today, the descendants of the Confederates are attempting to recover this heritage by having picnics and celebrations where they wear antebellum gowns and Civil War uniforms, by flying the Confederate flag and sharing old photographs and stories, as well as speaking Portuguese in a Southern drawl. The experience of the Confederates in Brazil is not unlike the experiences of immigrants in the United States.

Recent Immigration to Western Europe

Western Europe is beginning to deal with increasing immigration, particularly from Muslim countries (see Table 12.2). Overall, the Islamic population in the European Union grew to as much as 16 million by 2007. Italy, for example, has one of the world's lowest birthrates and oldest populations. It had been a largely homogeneous society with little immigration. Since 2000, the number of legal immigrants has risen by 66%, stabilizing what had been a decline in the population. In Lazio, the province that includes Rome, immigrant labor now accounts for 10% of the economy. Yet immigration remains a source of constant debate as the profile of Italy's immigrant community is becoming more Muslim with Moroccans, Tunisians, and Bangladeshis.

Table 12.2 Muslims in the European Union, 2006

Country	Number	Percentage of Total Population
France	3,516,824	5.4
Germany	3,400,000	4.2
United Kingdom	1,588,890	2.5
Spain	1,064,904	2.3
Netherlands	945,000	5.6
Italy	723,188	1.2
Sweden	400,000	4.4
Belgium	360,000	3.5
Greece	360,000	3.3
Austria	338,988	4.1

Source: Adapted from European Monitoring Centre on Racism and Xenophobia, Muslims in the European Union, (2006, pp. 27–29).

A similar debate grows in the Netherlands, where a half century ago, there were few foreigners. Today, about 4.4% of the population is immigrant. The Dutch did welcome guest workers in the 1960s and 1970s and did accept many seeking asylum from wars in Iraq, Kosovo, Africa, and Afghanistan. But that was before the September 11, 2001, attacks on the World Trade Center and Madrid bombings in 2004. Long considered one of Europe's most tolerant societies, the Netherlands' parliament voted in 2002 to deport 26,000 foreigners who had requested political asylum.

FOCUS ON CULTURE 12.1

Would-be immigrants to the Netherlands must purchase and view a film that includes scenes of two gay men kissing in a park and a topless woman emerging from the sea walking onto a crowded beach. The film is a test of the immigrant's readiness to participate in the liberal Dutch culture.

The same pressure is developing in the Nordic states. Norway is struggling to integrate 70,000 Muslims into its 4.5 million population. Six of Norway's 10 most populous immigrant groups come from Muslim countries. Denmark, a Christian country for 1,000 years and a culture that prides itself on racial parity, has experienced growing Muslim immigration—currently at 150,000 in a country of 5.5 million people. Muslims in Denmark feel that, because of the country's fear of terrorism, pressure to assimilate is increasing. The summer of 2011 saw a lone terrorist kill some 93 people in Norway by bombing in Oslo followed by a shooting spree at a youth camp. The accused terrorist had posed a manifesto advocating an armed campaign against Muslims it says are overrunning Europe. Sweden has given shelter to 100,000 Iraquis, 40,000 since the U.S. invasion in 2003. Sweden has gradually tightened its asylum rules, responding to fears that its generous welfare system cannot cope with the immigrant numbers.

European countries have adopted various policies to the growing Muslim immigration. Britain's approach allowed immigrants to keep distinctive cultural backgrounds and identities. Now there is fear that radical elements flourish in ethnic neighborhoods. France has encouraged immigrants to adopt all things French, a policy that has angered Muslims living in the slums outside of Paris. In fact, France does not compile statistics on foreign-born residents. Critics argue that this policy limits France's ability to recognize and treat the difficulties minorities face. The fall of 2005 and again in 2007 saw the worst civil unrest in France in nearly 40 years break out in the poor neighborhoods populated by immigrants, largely Black and Arab.

France's Muslim population is expected to climb from 4.7 million in 2010 to 6.9 million in 2030, according to the Pew Forum on Religion & Public Life (2011).

Immigration to the United States

Perhaps the least understood immigration into the Americas was the first one. The migration experiences of the groups now known as American Indians are lost in history, so this section begins with immigration to colonial America.

Colonial Policies on Immigration

In colonial America, three principal responses to immigration developed. Massachusetts wanted settlers who were "religiously pure." Virginia and Maryland recruited immigrants for cheap labor but did not allow full participation in government. Pennsylvania welcomed all European settlers on equal terms and as equal participants in the colony. Later, the Pennsylvania model largely prevailed in the new nation, which in its first 100 years encouraged immigration.

U.S. Policies on Immigration

Congress has total and complete authority over immigration. The president is limited to policies on refugees.

In 1798, Congress passed the Act Concerning Aliens, which gave the president power to deport all immigrants deemed dangerous to national security. But it was the Fourteenth Amendment, ratified in 1868, that established an important foundation for U.S. immigration and citizenship laws. The Fourteenth Amendment was not drafted in response to immigration; by establishing that anyone born in the country was a citizen, it was drafted to establish that former slaves were citizens with all rights of citizens. The Supreme Court held in 1898 that a man born in California to noncitizen Chinese immigrants was U.S. citizen under the Fourteenth Amendment. One result of the amendment is that the United States is one of the last countries in the world to follow the principle of birthright citizenship.

Beginning in 1875, the first federal laws limiting immigration were enacted to bar convicts and prostitutes. Over the years, other laws excluded those having "physical, mental, and moral defects"; those who advocated "subversive doctrines"; and those who had "economic disqualifications" or were illiterate (Carliner, 1977; Carliner, Guttentag, Helton, & Henderson, 1990).

Beginning in 1921, the U.S. Congress established country quotas based on the origins of the U.S. population using 1910 census data to prevent major changes in the country's racial and ethnic makeup. During the Prohibition era three years later, Congress chose to use the 1890 census data, which had the effect of favoring immigration from northern and western Europe. In 1965, country quotas were replaced with hemisphere quotas.

The Immigration Act of 1990 raised the annual immigration level from 540,000 to 700,000 in 1992 through 1994, thereafter dropping it to an annual minimum of 675,000. The new law also cuts back on provisions under which potential immigrants have been denied entry in the past on grounds of ideology or sexual orientation and allows more immigrants to qualify for permanent residency by virtue of investment capital and professional skills rather than family ties. Current immigration policy favors foreigners with immediate relatives in the United States. This benefits the relatives of the more recent immigrants—Asians and Latin Americans. To diversify the flow of immigrants, Congress created a permanent immigration "lottery" that will provide from 40,000 to 55,000 visas to residents of mostly European countries.

One consequence of the September 11, 2001, attacks on the United States is that immigration law has achieved new visibility and a much greater sense of national importance in the minds of legislators, the Obama administration, the media, and the public. This attention has already resulted in changes in immigration law and practice in the post–September 11 era. Many more changes are likely in the future. Illegal immigrants who enter the United States come from all over the world. In 1997, the U.S. Immigration and Naturalization Service (now the Bureau of Citizenship

Global Voices

Uncontrolled immigration threatens to deconstruct the nation we grew up in. . . . Balkanization beckons.

—Patrick J. Buchanan, *The Death of the West* (2002, p. 3)

Once I thought to write a history of the immigrants in America. Then, I discovered that the immigrants were American history.

—Oscar Handlin, Pulitzer Prize–winning historian, in *The Uprooted* (1952, p. 3)

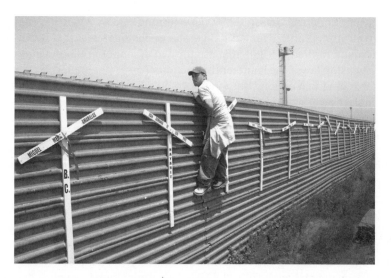

A man on the Mexican side of the U.S.-Mexico border looks over the fence. The crosses on the fence represent those who have died attempting to cross the border.

and Immigration Services [BCIS], a part of the U.S. Department of Homeland Security) put the number of illegal immigrants at 5 million—half being in California. Half of these arrive with temporary visas, typically at airports. The remainder enter without valid documents, usually across the U.S.-Mexico border. About half of the total originate from Mexico. Today, the children of illegal immigrants have the same right to attend school as do U.S. citizens and permanent residents based on the 1982 Supreme Court ruling on *Plyler v. Doe.*

Voters in Texas and California have challenged this practice in the belief that recent immigration unfairly burdens the states' economies. That immigration remains a major issue in the United States is reflected in new state laws passed in response to what was seen as a lack federal government action. Arizona, Georgia, Utah, Indiana, Alabama, and South Carolina passed laws designed to decrease illegal immigration by, among other provisions, making it a crime not to carry documents and by granting law enforcement powers to detain any suspected to be in the country illegally not in possession of appropriate documents. Federal courts have suspended portions of these laws largely based on the issue that immigration policy is a federal prerogative.

Contributing Countries Prior to 1800

Prior to 1800, the number of immigrants from Europe to the New World was between 4 and 5 million. In comparison, the largest migration was the involuntary movement of slaves from Africa mainly to the New World. It is estimated that 12 million people were transported as slaves, with 10 million actually surviving the trip. Table 12.3 shows where slaves were taken. This group was largely held in a state of separation and segregation.

Contributing Countries Since 1800

Since the beginning of the 19th century, as many as 70 million people have immigrated to the Western Hemisphere. Between 1846 and 1932, 53 million people migrated, all but 2 million from Europe and more than three-quarters of that number from five areas: the British Isles, Italy, Austria-Hungary, Germany, and Spain. The United States received 60% of those.

Ellis Island processed its first immigrant in 1892 and its last in 1954. More than half of the immigrants entering the United States between 1892 and 1924 passed through its gates. In its peak year, 1907, 1 million immigrants were processed. The center handled 17 million newcomers from more than 90 countries. Of the total, 2.5 million were from Italy, 2.2 million from Austria-Hungary, 1.9 million from Russia, and 633,000 from Germany

Table 12.3 Slave Trade, 1450–1870	
Location	*Number*
1. Brazil	4,000,000
2. Spanish Empire	2,500,000
3. British West Indies	2,000,000
4. French West Indies	1,600,000
5. British North America and United States	500,000
6. Dutch West Indies	500,000
7. Europe	200,000
8. Danish West Indies	28,000

Source: Stauffer (2005, p. 61).

Note: The United States banned the importation of slaves in 1808.

Today, 35% to 40% of the country's population can trace a heritage to a family member who passed through the immigration processing station on Ellis Island, a half mile from the Statue of Liberty. In 1990, the facility was restored as a museum.

1907 was the peak year for immigration at Ellis Island. More than 1 million immigrants were processed.

FOCUS ON CULTURE 12.2

You probably have heard some of these lines from this poem mounted on the pedestal of the Statue of Liberty. Are there any that change the meaning of the commonly known ones?

The New Colossus

Not like the brazen giant of Greek fame,
With conquering limbs astride from land to land;
Here at our sea-washed, sunset gates shall stand
A mighty woman with a torch, whose flame
Is the imprisoned lightning, and her name Mother of Exiles.
From her beacon hand
Glows world-wide welcome;
her mild eyes command
The air-bridged harbor that twin cities frame.
"Keep, ancient lands, your storied pomp!" cries she
With silent lips. "Give me your tired, your poor,
Your huddled masses yearning to breathe free,
The wretched refuse of your teeming shore,
Send these, the homeless, tempest-tost to me,
I lift my lamp beside the golden door!"

Source: Poem written in 1883 by Emma Lazarus, a Sephardic Jew.

As you study the history of immigration presented in Table 12.4, identify the years of the least and most number of immigrants. What happened in those years that affected immigration? Identify the decades of significant shifts in the major contributing countries. What impacts did those shifts have on the United States?

Each major wave of immigrants experienced discrimination. In the 1850s, the Germans and Irish who were fleeing economic destitution were largely viewed as a "lower class of people." In the 1880s and 1890s, eastern and southern European immigrants were viewed with suspicion because of darker skin and the religion of Catholicism. The Irish were blamed for bringing cholera, the Italians for bringing polio, the Chinese for carrying bubonic plague, the Jews for spreading tuberculosis, and the Haitians for bringing AIDS (Kraut, 1994). Between 1870 and 1920, approximately 15% of the U.S. population was foreign born (see Table 12.5). President Theodore Roosevelt (1901–1909) urged "native Americans" (he didn't mean indigenous peoples) to have more children to combat the disintegration of racial

Table 12.4 Immigration to the United States

Decade	Number	Immigrated Major Contributing Countries
1820s	152,000	Ireland, Great Britain, France
1830s	599,000	Ireland, Germany, Great Britain
1840s	1,713,000	Ireland, Germany, Great Britain
1850s	2,598,000	Germany, Ireland, Great Britain
1860s	2,315,000	Germany, Great Britain, Ireland
1870s	2,812,000	Germany, Great Britain, Ireland
1880s	5,247,000	Germany, Great Britain, Ireland
1890s	3,688,000	Italy, Austria-Hungary, Russia, Germany
1900s	8,795,000	Austria-Hungary, Italy, Russia
1910s	5,736,000	Italy, Russia, Austria-Hungary
1920s	4,107,000	Italy, Germany, Great Britain
1930s	528,000	Germany, Italy, Great Britain
1940s	1,035,000	Germany, Great Britain, Italy
1950s	2,515,000	Germany, Canada, Mexico, Italy
1960s	3,321,700	Mexico, Canada, Cuba
1970s	4,493,300	Mexico, Philippines, Cuba, Korea
1980s	8,500,000[a]	Mexico, Philippines, Vietnam, China
1990s	9,095,400	Mexico, Caribbean, Soviet Union, China
2000s	10,000,000[b]	Not yet known

Source: U.S. Bureau of the Census, *Statistical Abstract of the United States,* various editions.

Note: a. Not including 2.3 million under the 1986 amnesty law. b. Estimate by Center for Immigration Studies, Washington, DC.

purity that he said was threatening the American way of life. Charles Davenport, a leader of the eugenics movement, argued for protecting racial purity from eastern and southern European immigration. His lobby helped pass the Immigration Act of 1924, which is one of the most restrictive and discriminatory immigration statutes ever enacted in the United States.

Studies of immigration in the 1990s have shown that the educational level of immigrants has increased. In 1960, about one third of all new immigrants had less than 8 years of

Global Voices

In 1880, encouraged by the success of the Swiss settlers in Texas, a group of capitalists in Basel, Switzerland, organized a land company called the Basle Land Gesellschaft. The company provided the finances for the founding of a Swiss colony on the Guadalupe River approximately three miles south from Seguin. Around 1880, ten families left Switzerland and settled on the company's land. Each one was provided with sixty acres of land, a log cabin, a horse, a cow, chickens, hogs, and two hundred dollars per year to take care of the family needs.

Samuel Prabst was the first administrator of the colony. He was succeeded by Fredrick Wilhelm Naumann, who was given four hundred acres of land for his service. After a few years the colony failed and many of the original settlers moved to other parts of the state leaving only a few of the first settlers.

—Texas Institute of Cultures, San Antonio

Immigrant recollections:

Bismarck united Germany and in 1871 our father was on Germany's side against Napoleon III of France. He was in the reserves, and saw no fighting. He disliked militarism and the ungodly life of most soldiers. Therefore he moved to America before his oldest son, John, would be registered for service.

I am quite sure the ship's name was "Werra." We sailed on the Rhine River to the City of Köln (Cologne), then by rail to Bremen; on the "Werra" to New York; and by rail to New Braunfels, Comal County, Texas, March 9, 1885. I remember red hot pipes (too hot to sit on) on board ship; also the immigrants standing on deck singing:

"Noah's Arche schwankte / Lang of grauser Fluth,
Wie das Schiff auch wankte / Ihm sank nicht der Muth."

—Phillip Herbold, German immigrant

Sources: Personal archives of the author.

education. In the 1990s, that dropped to one-quarter. The immigrants of the 1990s did not draw on welfare any more than others. The percentage of foreign born on welfare is presently 6.6%. Refugees are guaranteed welfare by federal law. Taking out that group, 5.1% of nonrefugee working-age immigrants receive welfare, compared to 5.3% of working-age native born. A study (Hanson, 2009) showed that, overall, immigrants were a net economic gain for the country but that the six states with the highest concentration of immigrants were experiencing pressures as taxes go mostly to the federal government. Table 12.6 on page 328 shows the states with the largest immigrant populations.

Table 12.5   Profile of the U.S. Foreign-Born Population

Period	Number (in Millions)	Percentage of Population
1850	2.2	9.7
1860	4.1	13.2
1870	5.6	14.4
1880	6.7	13.3
1890	9.2	14.8
1900	10.3	13.6
1910	13.5	14.7
1920	13.9	13.2
1930	14.2	11.6
1940	11.6	8.8
1950	10.3	6.9
1960	9.7	5.4
1970	9.6	4.7
1980	14.1	6.2
1990	19.8	7.9
2000	28.4	10.4
2006	37.5	12.5

Countries of Birth of the U.S. Foreign-Born Population, 2007	Number (in Thousands)
Mexico	11,700
China	1,900
Philippines	1,700
India	1,500
Vietnam	1,100
El Salvador	1,100
Korea	1,000

Source: U.S. Census Bureau (2009b).

Table 12.6   U.S. Foreign-Born Population, by State, 2004

State	Immigrant Population	Percentage of Population
California	9,902,000	27.2
New York	4,179,000	21.6
Texas	3,741,000	15.9
Florida	3,426,000	18.9
Illinois	1,774,000	13.8
New Jersey	1,754,000	20.1
Arizona	929,000	15.1
Massachusetts	908,000	14.1
U.S. total	37,548,000	12.5

Source: U.S. Census Bureau (2009b).

The recent U.S. economic recession seemed to cause a dramatic slowdown in immigration beginning in 2007. In 2006, the United States recorded adding 1.8 million immigrants; in 2007, the number had dropped to about a half million.

FOCUS ON THE ENVIRONMENT 12.1

Some have used concerns for the environment as an argument against immigration. Their arguments are below:

The rate of environmental degradation is the speed at which a person does damage to the environment through consumption of its resources. Most immigrants to the United States come from less technologically advanced countries. Because of the lifestyles of those countries, their people tend to consume and damage the earth's resources more slowly; that is, they have a low rate of environment degradation.

When immigrants come to the United States, they do not maintain the old lifestyle of their home country. They begin to adapt to the American lifestyle. As they do, they become greater consumers and damagers of natural resources; their individual rate of environment degradation increases.

But it is not just that immigrants' individual rates of environment degradation goes up after they get here (although that is obviously a serious problem in itself). The worst thing about immigration for the environment is that it is causing overpopulation. Environment degradation is not simply about the rate at which individuals degrade the environment; it is also a result of how many people there are.

The more people there are in the United States, the more we as a whole degrade the environment. This is the problem of population growth, and immigration worsens it severely.

Immigration is responsible for over forty percent of the population growth since 1970. The United States will never be able to level off or reduce the amount of overall damage we do to the environment unless we can get the size of our population to level off. But the size of our population can never level off as long as we continue to have the heavy immigration we have now. For the sake of our environment, we need a moratorium on immigration.

Source: Federation for American Immigration Reform (2002).

PREDICTORS OF ACCULTURATION

No immigrant, as long as livelihood needs are to be met in a new country, can escape acculturation. Individuals do differ, however, as to what degree they become acculturated. Young Yun Kim (1986, 1988) has identified background characteristics that are accurate predictors of an immigrant's success in acculturation.

Global Voices

We find ourselves threatened by hordes of Yankee emigrants. What are we to do?

—Manuel Micheltorena,
Mexican governor of
California, 1846

Similarity of Culture

The similarity of the original culture to the new host culture is one of the most important factors in successful acculturation. For example, an immigrant from Canada to the United States finds acculturation easier than a Vietnamese immigrant from Southeast Asia will. There can be differences among immigrants from the same country—depending on, for example, whether they grew up in a cosmopolitan urban center or in a rural area where there existed relatively less outside influence.

Personal Characteristics and Experiences

Younger immigrants adapt more easily than older ones. Educational background also plays a part, and a person's personality (risk taking or being gregarious and curious or not, for example) can determine how readily she or he will desire to blend in with a new culture. Finally, previous travel, contact with overseas friends or family, and mass media influence also come into play.

Effect of Media and Transportation Advances

It's useful to compare the immigration peaks of the early 1900s with today's. The European immigration of the early 1900s brought millions of people who at the time seemed just as alien to many native-born U.S. citizens as Salvadorans or Koreans do today. However, there are some important—and critical—differences in the intercultural communication context: Media and transportation advances contribute to the difference.

The immigrants of the 1900s left homes permanently, with little hope of returning even for a visit, and thus lost much of the original culture in assimilation. The immigrants of the 1900s had little contact with friends and families left behind. Letters and messages brought by friends were slow. Immigrants in the United States did find newspapers and periodicals printed entirely or in part in languages other than English. These helped immigrants not only maintain contacts with other immigrants but also adjust to life in the United States. The non-English press was weakened by restrictive legislation in the 1920s and by a drop in the number of new immigrants. At the same time, members of the second generation were not interested in newspapers in the languages of their parents (Govorchin, 1961). According to the 1940 U.S. census, there were 8,354,700 people in the United States whose native language was one other than English. At that time, about 1,000 newspapers and periodicals were printed entirely or in part in languages other than English (Chyz, 1945). In 1942, there were nearly 1,000 radio stations in the United States, 200 of which broadcast in some 26 languages. In fact, though, the media contributed to assimilation. Today, some 200 ethnic newspapers and magazines can be found in New York. San Jose, California, has dozens of Vietnamese publications.

Czech immigrants founded dozens of communities in Texas, making the language the third most spoken in the state. Annual fests renew ties to the culture with music and kolaches.

The U.S. Bureau of Citizenship and Immigration Services uses various social media including a blog, YouTube, and Twitter sites to disseminate information to immigrants. Social media platforms also provide a way for those seeking citizenship to form online communities. A youth-oriented informal group, who call themselves *Dreamers,* use social media to find each other without travelling or exposing their status. They use social media to appeal to supporters nationwide and petition en masse for extensions on deportation dates.

A Canadian platform LoonLounge, developed by a Canadian immigration attorney, is a social networking site where Canadian citizens and prospective Canadians can connect. The site eases the process of Canadian immigration and settlement in Canada through the creation of personal and professional networks prior to and following their arrival in Canada. For today's immigrants, social media is taking the place of other forms of media immigrants from the past relied on for information and support.

FOCUS ON CULTURE 12.3

Western Union was a telegraph company. Air travel, fax, and the Internet made telegraphs a thing of the past and the company went bankrupt in 1992. The company emerged 2 years later as a money transfer company. Today the company has five times as many locations as McDonald's, Starbucks, Burger King, and Walmart combined and transfers some $300 billion annually for immigrants across the globe to their home countries.

Today's immigrants can easily return for visits. They can watch television programs from their home countries and be in easy telephone contact. The pressure to assimilate is not as great. It's quite possible to maintain their original cultural identity and participate in a meaningful way in the larger society (see Focus on Culture 12.4).

CATEGORIES OF ACCULTURATION

Acculturation, or **cultural adaptation**, refers to an immigrant's learning and adopting the norms and values of the new host culture. Unlike a temporary visitor, the immigrant must find a new source of livelihood and build a new life. This adapting to a new host culture is called acculturation. Berry, Kim, and Boski (1987) have described acculturation in relation to two dimensions: the value placed on maintaining one's original cultural identity and the value given to maintaining relationships with other groups in one's new culture.

FOCUS ON CULTURE 12.4

Germans' Reminder of Home Lives On

 Germans first arrived in large numbers in the 1720s, settling in Pennsylvania. A second and larger wave arrived between the 1830s and 1930s, with most going to the Midwest and the Upper Plains states. Today, about 23% of the U.S. population list German ancestry first on census forms. The German-born population was a record high 30% in 1890.

Immigrant farmers from the fertile lowlands of northern Germany—conquerors of Ohio's Great Black Swamp—turned Henry County into what some believe is a mirror image of their "fatherland."

Walter Delventhal, who recently shepherded the organization of the Low German Club through Napoleon and Henry County officials, said the majority of the German people in Henry County came from the Visselhovede area, a small community in the northern German lowlands generally between Bremen and Hamburg. And the majority of people in Henry County are of German descent. A sampling of ancestry of Henry County residents, taken from 1990 Census reports, showed that 18,832 residents claimed to be of German ancestry. The second-largest group, by ancestry, were the English, with a total of 1,518. . . .

Earlier this month, the county commissioners and Napoleon Mayor Don Strange signed an agreement establishing a sister city-county relationship with Visselhovede. They hope the relationship will encourage Henry County residents to seek their roots in Germany.

Mr. Delventhal and his wife, Lucia, have returned to their hometown of Visselhovede three times, in 1972, 1983, and 1984.

"It's just like going home," he said with a smile. "They talk just like we do." The Delventhals still speak "Low German" at home as their first language. Their children can understand it but do not speak it. The phrase "Low German" refers to the flat lowlands of northern Germany. The language is different from "High German," which is spoken in the southern highlands, including the Black Forest.

The Delventhals attend St. John Lutheran Church in Freedom Township, which until the 1960s had both German and English services. Germans traditionally had strong ties with their churches, and that continued when they came to the United States.

"What happened was that one family moved from Visselhovede or Walsrode, a village to the south, then wrote back to their relatives talking about how good things are in their new home," he explained. Soon, their relatives wanted to come too. Speeding the exodus was the German tradition that the oldest son always inherits the family farm. That left a lot of other family members disgruntled and anxious to move to the new world, he said.

Russell Patterson, a Napoleon druggist and grandson of a German immigrant, said his grandfather, Wilhelm Frederick Franz Bernicke, paid $30 for steerage passage to the United States. Like others, he arrived on the East Coast in 1893 to find that all of the farmland already was owned, so he used his money for a train ride west. He ultimately landed in Henry County. Hamler, once the hunting grounds of the Ottawa, Shawnee, Seneca, and Miami Indians, today is best known for its summer festival, when upwards of 25,000 or more polka lovers descend on the town.

Source: W. Ferguson (1997, pp. A11–A12). Reprinted with permission.

Global Voices

"Being able to meet other undocumented students online, join a Facebook group, and be able to share the experiences, the fears, the hopes and the aspirations of other undocumented people—online tools are great for doing that."

—Nathan Ryan, Illinois Coalition for Immigrant and Refugee Rights advocacy, web and technology manager

"You're free to reveal as much of your identity as you wish to. . . . You kind of grow up with that fear and that whole perspective that nobody is ever supposed to know about your immigration status. Once you eventually get over that hurdle, naturally the next thing that is going to go is that you're going to write up something and post it anonymously online. . . . The more we hide, the harder it becomes to connect."

—Juan, communications director for Dream Activist, a website that provides information and resources for undocumented students. Juan won't reveal his last name out of fear that the university where he is attending will find out about his immigration status.

Source: Hing (2010).

As shown in Figure 12.1, **marginalization** refers to losing one's cultural identity and not having any psychological contact with the larger society. The person has feelings of "not

Figure 12.1 Dimensions of Acculturation Include Original Cultural Identity and Relationships With Other Groups

		Value to Maintain Original Cultural Identity	
		Yes	No
Value to Build and Maintain Relationship With New Culture	Yes	Integration	Assimilation
	No	Separation(or Segregation)	Marginalization

belonging anywhere." **Separation** and **segregation** refer to maintaining one's original culture and not participating in the new culture. To some, segregation connotes a judgment of superiority and inferiority, as well as prejudice and hatred between groups. Others use the term *insularity* to connote separation only. The person has a strong sense of ethnic identity.

Assimilation results from giving up one's original cultural identity and moving into full participation in the new culture. The person identifies with the country and not the ethnic group. Assimilation is a long-term and sometimes multigenerational process. True **integration** is maintaining important parts of one's original culture as well as becoming an integral part of the new culture. Integration ensures a continuity of culture. One contrast between assimilation and integration is that under assimilation policies, groups disappear through intermarriage but that in integration, groups continue to exist. The words *biculturalism* and *pluralism* also have been used to describe integration. The person feels as loyal to the country as to any ethnic group. Integration is supported by the dual-nationality trend, which allows expatriates from immigrant-sending nations to retain rights as nationals while taking on citizenship status in the United States or elsewhere. In a seeming paradox, new U.S. citizens must formally renounce allegiances to foreign governments as part of the naturalization process, but U.S. law still permits citizens to possess other nationalities. Keep these terms in mind as you read the following chapter, which describe various cultures within U.S. culture.

SUMMARY

The phrase *culture shock* describes the feelings of disorientation and anxiety that many people experience for a time while living in a foreign country. It results from an awareness that one's basic assumptions about life and one's familiar ways of behaving are no longer appropriate or functional. Reverse culture shock also can occur upon returning home after a long stay outside one's home country. *Third-culture kids* refers to children in expatriate families who reside outside of their home culture for years at a time.

The world's largest human migration occurs annually within the borders of China. Each year millions of workers travel from rural home villages to work in urban cities and return for visits.

Citizenship in a country may be acquired by birth, by blood, or by naturalization. By birth, or *jus soli,* is that if one is born within the borders of a country, you are automatically a citizen. By blood, or *jus sanguinis,* is that if one's parents are citizens of a country, no matter where you are born, you are a citizen of your parents' country. Naturalization requires a period of residency, an exam, an oath, or some combination of these.

Today, Western Europe is dealing with increasing immigration, particularly from Muslim countries. U.S. immigration has come in distinct waves. In the 1850s, the Germans and Irish who were fleeing economic destitution were largely viewed as a "lower class of people." In the 1880s and 1890s, eastern and southern European immigrants were viewed with suspicion because of darker skin and the religion of Catholicism. The Irish were blamed for bringing cholera, the Italians for bringing polio, the Chinese for carrying bubonic plague, the Jews for spreading tuberculosis, and the Haitians for bringing AIDS. Recent immigration from Spanish-speaking countries has brought calls for official English language laws.

Predictors of an immigrant's success are the similarity of home and new cultures, age, educational background, and personality (risk-taking and being gregarious). Other factors are previous travel, contact with overseas friends and family, and mass media influence. Categories of acculturation can be based on the value to maintain original cultural identity and value to maintain relationship with new culture.

DISCUSSION QUESTIONS

1. What are advantages and disadvantages of having been reared as a third-culture kid?

2. What challenges and opportunities does immigration present to a country?

3. How could countries use predictors of an immigrant's success in acculturation in immigration policies or in facilitating acculturation?

4. What factors today make the melting pot concept a less accurate description of immigration into the United States?

5. What factors contribute to a country's immigration and citizenship laws?

KEY TERMS

acculturation   331

assimilation   334

asylee   309

biculturalism   311

cultural adaptation   331

culture shock   309

expatriate   309

integration   334

marginalization   333

oleh   315

refugee   309

reverse culture shock   311

segregation   334

separation   334

sojourner   309

xenophobia   314

READING

This reading is from *Intercultural Communication: A Global Reader* (Jandt, 2004).

Flora Keshishian, "Acculturation, Communication, and the U.S. Mass Media: The Experience of an Iranian Immigrant" (p. 230)

STUDENT STUDY SITE

Visit the student study site at **www.sagepub.com/jandt7e** for these additional learning tools:

- Web Resources
- Audio and Video Links
- SAGE journal articles
- Flashcards
- Web Quizzes
- Sample Essays

CHAPTER 13

Cultures Within Cultures

FOCUS QUESTIONS

- What has been the effect of marginalization on the Hmong?

- How does the voluntary separation of the Amish support cultural values that contrast to dominant U.S. cultural values?

- What is the status of indigenous languages and cultures?

- What have been U.S. immigration and acculturation policies?

- What communication factors are acting to maintain Hispanic groups' cultural identity?

Marginalization: The Hmong
    History
    Cultural Patterns
Separation: Koreans In Russia
Separation: The Amish
    History
Values
    Religion
    Controlled Use of Technology
    Accepting Amish Identity
    Education
    Work
    Change
    Diversity Among the Amish
Indigenous Cultures
Assimilation: United States
    Melting Pot Concept
Integration: United States
    From Melting Pot to Symphony and Stew
Hispanic Cultures
    Terminology
    Spanish-Language Use
    Values
    Cultural Identity and Media
    Print
    Radio
    Television
            Spanish-Language Internet and
                Social Media
    Cultural Identity and Marketing
Postethnic Cultures
Summary
Discussion Questions
Key Terms
Readings
Student Study Site

You read in Chapter 1 about the controversy over the use of the words *subculture* and *co-culture* and the reasons why this text uses the phrase "cultures within cultures." Cultures within cultures are most often based on economic or social class, ethnicity, race, or geographic region. Cultures within cultures usually encompass a relatively large number of people and represent the accumulation of generations of human striving. Awareness of cultures within cultures is a critical intercultural communication skill.

If you haven't read the previous chapter, you should review the section "Categories of Acculturation" before reading this chapter. The previous chapter identified the four categories of acculturation. Remember that *marginalization* refers to losing one's cultural identity and not having any psychological contact with the larger society. As an example of marginalization, this chapter discusses the Hmong, who were forced to leave Laos.

Remember that *separation and segregation* refer to maintaining one's cultural identity while not participating in the larger culture. Separation may be voluntary and reflect a strong cultural identity. As an example of separation, you will read about the Koryo-saram in Russian and the Amish in the United States. As a culture with strongly defined and communicated values, the Amish have long resisted acculturation through voluntary separation. On the other hand, segregation connotes a forced condition involving power, prejudice, and hatred. As an example of segregation, you will read about the special case of indigenous cultures that continued to experience cultural domination.

Remember that *assimilation* refers to giving up one's original cultural identity and moving into full participation in the new culture, while *integration* refers to maintaining important parts of one's original culture as well as becoming an integral part of the new culture. This chapter briefly discusses the assimilation policies in Australia and then looks in depth at when assimilation was more characteristic of the United States than today. You will see how Hispanic cultures are maintaining multiple cultural identities. What is called the Hispanic culture in the United States is a vast, dispersed, heterogeneous, multilingual, multiclass with Mexican, Puerto Rican, Cuban, and Central American origins yet bound by the shared Spanish language and culture. You will read about specialized communication media and segmented marketing as forces against assimilation. As you have seen in the previous two chapters, modern transportation and communication technology have modified immigrants' pressures to acculturate. In contrast to a century ago, specialized communication media and segmented marketing can have the effect of strengthening a culture's identity and lessening the pressures it feels to acculturate.

Finally, you will read about postethnicity, or the idea that today we can all identify ourselves with various groups, and about communication barriers that can arise when multiple identities are stronger than one assimilated identity.

MARGINALIZATION: THE HMONG

When you think of cultures within cultures, you probably think of immigrant groups. Scholars first used the word **diaspora** to refer to the experiences of Jews and, later, Armenians who were both forcibly exiled from their homelands. More recently, scholars have expanded that definition to include all groups that move from one part of the world to another, even if that migration was of free choice. Diaspora, of course, can have the effect of creating cultures within cultures in the country into which peoples move, as is the case with the Iu Mien and the **Hmong**, who left the villages of Laos for life in the United States. Particularly, many of the older Hmong immigrants lost their identity provided by their homeland and were unable to establish a new identity in the United States, and thus are an example of marginalization.

The Hmong (pronounced MONG and literally meaning "free men") are among recent immigrants who have been called the most ill-prepared people ever to immigrate to the United States. The extent of differences to dominant U.S. cultural patterns places these immigrants in a state of marginalization and raises the question of whether this group will maintain a separate identity in the United States or someday will assimilate into the dominant culture.

Tran Minh Tung (1990) described the groups within the Cambodian, Laotian, Hmong, and Vietnamese refugee cultures most at risk for marginalization:

- *Newcomers.* Those who went through relocation camps experienced fear and humiliation in dehumanizing conditions, resulting in passivity, dependency, and learned helplessness. The first year of relocation to the United States can be a disappointment compared to what dreams had been. Newcomers see opportunities but also experience fear, uncertainty, and unhappiness.
- *Refugee teenagers.* While the majority of refugee teenagers are well adjusted and do well in school, a significant number become involved in gang criminal behavior. Loss of traditional values and lack of support and guidance from parents themselves experiencing stress may be contributing factors.
- *Elderly refugees.* Minimal or nonexistent English-language skills result in social isolation. Family structure changes as children and grandchildren begin to take places in the new culture and become strangers. The U.S. urban environment and value placed on individualism reduce the need for interdependence traditionally provided by the family.
- *Rural refugees.* Often less sophisticated than urban counterparts, rural refugees do not fare well in a capitalistic society, although the children progress economically and socially. The majority of young refugee adults have jobs, homes, and cordial, even if brief and infrequent, relations with U.S. colleagues and neighbors. Most of the refugees' social interactions occur within a small circle of relatives and friends in the numerous Little Saigons that have sprung up in several urban areas and re-create some feeling of home.

History

The Hmong, also known as Montagnards (Geddes, 1976), are an ancient Asian hill tribe that has resisted assimilation for millennia. A people long persecuted, the Hmong written language was destroyed centuries ago. The Hmong are thought to have originated in the Russian steppes and to have been pushed out of China in the early 1800s for refusing to discard unique ways. The Hmong kept migrating south to the highlands of northern Laos. The term *Hmong* actually refers to a diverse group, including the Hmong Der or White Hmong, the Mong Leng or Blue or Green Mong, Striped Hmong, Black Hmong, and Red Hmong—classifications based on costume and custom.

As mercenaries for the Central Intelligence Agency (CIA) in the 1960s and 1970s, the Hmong fought the communists in Laos. More than 40,000 died in that war. After the U.S. withdrawal from Vietnam, Hmong villages in Laos were attacked by the Laotians and Vietnamese. Many Hmong fled to refugee camps in Thailand.

Hmong refugees migrated to Australia, Canada, France, the United States, and other parts of the world. Hmong immigration to the United States started in the late 1970s. Today, more than 200,000 Hmong reside in the United States, primarily in California, Minnesota, and Wisconsin. The San Joaquin Valley in central California has become home to some 88,000 Hmong; some 32,000 reside in St. Paul, Minnesota; and 15% of the population of the small town of Wausau in Wisconsin is now Hmong.

Cultural Patterns

Hmong culture is evident in the United States: grocery stores with familiar food, radio programs with familiar music and community news, Lao family centers and festivals, and traditional farming and funeral practices.

The Hmong continue religious practices that blend ancestor worship, animal sacrifice, and shaman healing. The killing of chickens, pigs, and an occasional dog inside the home of the ill is practiced by shamans to placate evil spirits. Rites for the dead stretch some 72 hours and mix mourning, feasting, and woodwind music. The Hmong believe that any metal in and around the body prevents passage to the other life. Hence, gold and silver tooth fillings are removed. Instead of metal coffins, the Hmong use handmade oak Orthodox Jewish caskets. Red twine is strung from the casket to a cow outside the funeral chapel. The cow is sacrificed, and the meat is then cooked and brought back to the chapel where it's eaten in honor of the deceased. Hmong religious practices are misunderstood and a source of prejudice in the United States.

Hmong practices of early marriage age for females and fertility rates of 9.5 children per mother are continued by many. Between 50% and 70% of Hmong females are married before the age of 17—many at the age of 12, even though these marriages are not recognized by the state. The Hmong tribal tradition of "marriage by capture" is considered an acceptable form of elopement.

Traditionally, the girl feigns resistance as the male takes his intended to his family's home. There the father performs a 30-second ceremony using a live chicken. The bride's parents are then notified, and the payment due from the bride's family is negotiated. In Fresno, California, a Hmong immigrant kidnapped and raped a Hmong woman. His defense for abuse was to claim that marriage by capture is a form of courtship in his native Laos. His cultural defense served to reduce the criminal charges against him to false imprisonment.

Ill prepared for life in the United States and with few marketable skills, the Hmong have the highest welfare dependency rate of any refugee group in the United States. Some Hmong youths are acculturating. Teenagers wear popular California sweatpants and sneakers. Many Hmong children are achievers in the school system and have been high school valedictorians. Some adults are adapting to the U.S. culture, but most older adults continue to exist in a state of marginalization—the homeland lost and the U.S. culture hostile and strange.

SEPARATION: KOREANS IN RUSSIA

The term *Koryo-saram* refers to ethnic Koreans in the post-Soviet states. Totaling some 470,000 people, the largest number are in Uzbekistan (198,000), Russia (125,000), and Kazakhstan (105,000). Koreans began migrating to Russia in the second half of the 19th century to escape famine, economic hardship, and Japanese imperialism in Korea. Prior to the construction of the Trans-Siberian Railway, Koreans actually outnumbered Russians in the Russian Far East. In the 1930s, Stalin's government relocated about 200,000 ethnic Koreans to central Russia under the pretense that the Koreans would act as spies for the Japanese.

The Koryo-saram actually lived in a state of separation from the Russian culture, interacting little with the nomadic peoples around them. They established rice farms. The Koryo-saram did maintain some Korean traditions: They maintained Korean food, adding only local ingredients, and maintained Korean birthday rituals. Rather than adopting the clothing of the peoples around them, they adopted Western-style clothing. The Koryo-saram maintained their own schools and colleges, as well as print media, with one large circulation newspaper. And as would be predicted from the years of separation, language use did change. Those who continued to speak Korean had some difficulties conversing with today's South Koreans. About half of the Korean-Russians spoke Russian as a first language (Back, 2004).

With the collapse of the Soviet state, the Koryo-saram are now facing marginalization, as in Uzbekistan, where there is a clash of ethnicity, religion, and language. Uzbekistan is Islamic and has adopted Uzbek as the official language of the country. The Koryo-saram are Russian-speaking ethnic Koreans and are either Russian Orthodox, Christian, or atheist.

Some Russian-speaking Koryo-saram have immigrated to the United States as refugees. In the United States, the Russian Koreans have found dealings with Korean-Americans to be difficult. The Koro-saram lack fluency in Korean and tend to have become more expressive, emotional, and Western in their mannerisms and behavior. They experience older Korean Americans as distant and reserved (Simmons, 2003).

SEPARATION: THE AMISH

While the Hmong had little choice but to leave their homeland, the Amish left voluntarily and have voluntarily chosen to remain apart from the dominant U.S. culture. The Amish immigrated to the United States as a religious community. Religion provides a complete defining cultural identity for the Amish, who have chosen to live apart from the dominant culture and resist acculturation. The Amish are an example of a subculture that has attempted to maintain its original culture and to participate as little as possible in the U.S. dominant culture. That voluntary separation extends to not voting.

History

The Amish and Mennonites grew out of the Anabaptist movement that developed in Switzerland during the 1500s. The Mennonites took their name from the Dutch reformer Menno Simons and adhered to pacifism and a strict separation of church and state. The Amish were named after the leader Jacob Ammann, a Swiss Mennonite bishop. In the late 17th century, the Amish broke away from the Mennonites, who had begun taking a more liberal view over the policy of shunning the excommunicated. As Anabaptists, the Amish believe in adult baptism and living apart from the world, preferring a simple, agrarian lifestyle. The Amish migrated from Switzerland in the 1720s to Pennsylvania, where they were welcomed by William Penn and found an abundance of land for farms and freedom to worship. About 5,000 Amish lived in the United States in 1900. Today, the Amish number about 250,000 in North America and are concentrated in Lancaster County and other parts of Pennsylvania, as well as living in parts of Ohio, Indiana, Wisconsin, New York, and Michigan. Two and a half centuries later, the Amish remain basically the same ("Amish Population," 2010; Aurand, 1938; Hostetler, 1980; Kraybill, 1989).

VALUES

Religion

Gelassenheit is a common German word in Amish life. Translated, it means submission. The Amish believe in complete submission to God and do not separate religion and life. The Amish home serves as the church. Every moment in Amish life is a religious one. The **Ordnung** contains the church rules and outlines the values of the community. Humility, obedience, simplicity, sharing, and community cooperation are valued. The Amish don't pay or accept Social Security; elderly Amish remain in the family's home.

Pride is a sin in the Amish community. Pride is the evil face of individualism that is believed to be the death of the community and of the family. This value is even reflected in clothing. Hooks and eyes replace buttons. Shirt pockets are prohibited as they can become a place to display fancy things and hence are prideful. Indeed, the Amish are often referred to as "plain people" because of dress and lifestyle.

Controlled Use of Technology

The Amish do not condone technology unless it's clearly beneficial to the community by making it possible to continue as a community (Kraybill, 1989). The most conservative and strict, the **Old Order Amish**, avoid any use of electricity and automobiles. **New Order Amish** use telephones and powered farm equipment but use batteries and generators rather than public electricity. The **Beachy Amish**, named after the leader Moses Beachy, separated from the more conservative Amish in 1927 and use both automobiles and electricity. The primary communication link among Amish communities across the country is the small newspaper *The Budget,* published since 1890. Its reporters are hundreds of volunteers who send in handwritten dispatches. About 80% of its 19,000 subscribers do not have electricity nor telephones (Huffstutter, 2009).

Automobiles threaten the family, so horses and carriages are used. They symbolize as well the tradition of a slower pace and a closeness to nature. Some Amish have adopted automatic milking machines and refrigeration because that continues to make the family farm possible. Telephones and answering machines are not permitted in homes based on a prohibition of wires from the outside world into homes, but Amish may be found phoning inside wooden shanties (an outhouse-type version of the phone booth) across the road from an Amish home. Telephones in the home could lead to a change in values. The Amish are, however, currently debating cell phone use. Internet pioneer Howard Rheingold (1999) visited the Amish to observe telephone use. He found that the Amish don't fear technology as such. Rather, they fear the ideas that technology is always beneficial, that individuality is a precious value, and that the goal of life is to get ahead. Rheingold asked, "If we decided that community came first, how would we use our tools differently?" (p. 131).

Accepting Amish Identity

Amish youth must chose to accept an Amish identity. During what is called "time out" or **rum-springa**, teenage Amish, beginning at the age of 16, are given quite a bit of freedom to investigate the outside world before deciding whether to rejoin the church for the rest of their lives. Young men may obtain driver's licenses, travel to large cities, and adopt contemporary clothing. Young Amish reportedly are using smart phones to connect with other Amish through social media. Occasional instances of drug possession have even been reported. To marry an Amish woman, though, a man must agree to be baptized and take up the responsibilities of being an adult member of the Amish community. Some 80% to 90% make the decision to join the church and choose the Amish way of life (Shachtman, 2006). Amish society is male dominated. Women are respected and run the household, but the men have the final say. The Amish have large families; seven children is about average.

Education

The Amish have received a unique status in the educational system of the United States. The practical skills of everyday life—spelling, English, German, mathematics, geography, and health—are taught in small private schools.

Parents are involved in the curriculum, instruction, and administration of the schools. Religion is not taught in the schools as it is believed to be too important to be taught there instead of in the family and church. After the eighth grade, Amish children may continue education at home on the farm to learn the practical skills of providing for family and community. Further education is discouraged as it instills feelings of superiority that would lead to placing the needs of the self over those of the community.

Work

Work is important to Amish life. Work is preferred over idleness, which is believed to breed laziness, a trait of the outside world. Work also becomes a way to bring generations together on the farm; grandparents, parents, and children all work together. Also, work can bring the community together in projects such as barn raisings. Now, a major source of income for the Amish is handicrafts, such as quilts, rugs, furniture, and other household products. Amish handicrafts, prized for their design and workmanship, are sold to the "English" world. (The Amish refer to anyone not Amish as English.)

Change

The most important characteristic of the Amish, in contrast to the dominant culture, is the way change is handled. Change does not come easily to the Amish. Many considerations must be examined before a change is adopted in the community. Tobacco-growing Amish participated in growing genetically engineered tobacco. This change permits the farming culture to continue.

Any change that decreases the amount of family or community solidarity, increases visibility, promotes individualism, or threatens the values of the Amish in any way is rejected. If a change will better the life of the community without threatening the Amish society as a whole, it may be gradually adopted into Amish life. The Amish try to control the use of technology.

The tradition of the Amish is farming—and the farms are profitable. Cultivating and nurturing the land is an important Amish value. But increasing population and land prices force change. Some Amish have emigrated to other areas to continue farming. Others have taken nonfarm employment to make it possible to remain near family and community.

In comparing Amish cultural patterns to dominant U.S. cultural patterns, major attention must be given to how the Amish control change. Each change is evaluated in terms of how it will affect the culture. A major factor in maintaining control of change was the dominant culture's allowing the Amish an educational system.

In the 1972 landmark Supreme Court ruling in *State of Wisconsin v. Jonas Yoder et al.,* Justice Burger wrote, "There can be no assumption that today's majority is right and the Amish and

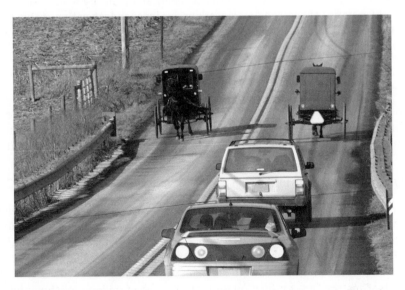

What makes it possible for the Amish to remain a distinct culture separate from the culture around them?

Another example of separation: The Basque region of northern Spain is the most autonomous and prosperous of Spain's 17 provinces and is home to 2.2 million people. The Basque region of Spain was granted autonomy after the death of Gen. Francisco Franco in 1975. Since then, the Basque have revived the language and taken charge of the local government and police force while the economy and judiciary remain answerable to Spain. A slight majority of the people are working for independent nation status to be known as Euskadia, which also would include parts of the neighboring Spanish province of Navarra and a couple of provinces in southern France.

others like them are wrong. A way of life that is odd or even erratic but interferes with no rights or interests of others is not to be condemned because it is different." No matter how much the world changes, the Amish will strive to preserve the serenity of Amish culture.

Diversity Among the Amish

An Amish settlement refers to a geographic area. Within each settlement, one or more affiliations of people share a set of theological rules and practices. Each affiliation makes its own decisions in meetings of members who, by consensus, develop their own set of rules. Each affiliation is made up of church districts or groups of 25 to 35 families. Each affiliation reacts to change from the same Amish religious value context but with seemingly contradictory results. Thus, the Dover affiliation prohibits the use of milking machines while others do not. The Lancaster affiliation permits the use of plows with two blades, while the Dover affiliation permits only the single-blade walking plow.

FOCUS ON THEORY 13.1

Critical researchers focus on the politics of identity and the struggles of nondominant groups (Y. Y. Kim, 2005). Orbe's (1998) theory of co-cultural communication explains the communication strategies of traditionally "muted" groups as avoiding, censoring self, bargaining, and attacking and the preferred communication outcome (e.g., accommodation and separation).

INDIGENOUS CULTURES

A state's immigration and acculturation policies can change over time. One example is policies toward indigenous cultures in countries worldwide. At different times in different countries, policies have ranged from forced assimilation to forced separation. The status of indigenous cultures after contact with colonizers can be traced as well through a historical study of the state of indigenous languages.

In Canada, after the 1812 war, British colonists no longer required indigenous peoples as allies, explorers, or traders. Instead, they came to be seen as obstacles to Canadian settlement. From the early 19th century on, Canada rejected extermination for its "Indian problem" but pursued a policy of absorbing the peoples by undermining the cultural distinctiveness of aboriginal society and subjecting the indigenous peoples to the rules and values of Euro-Canadian culture.

Mexico's indigenous peoples have been denied rights for centuries. It is estimated that by the 15th century, 40 million or more peoples lived in the Americas. These peoples varied greatly in physical appearance and culture. Different civilizations dominated at different times. Perhaps the most complex of these were the Mayas, with a reliable agricultural base, a polytheistic religion, and a developing mathematics, astronomy, and other sciences. As the Mayan culture declined, others arose, including the Aztecs, who, through military organization and trade, administered a large territory of some 10 million peoples. The Aztecs' special strength was synthesizing and using cultural elements from many conquered peoples. Its great city Tenochtitlán (Mexico City today) had a population of 100,000—four or five times that of contemporary London, Madrid, or Paris (Meier & Ribera, 1993).

The Aztecs were soon to meet the Spaniards, a people with a similar history of cultural synthesis. Spanish influence in the Americas was largely one of cultural blending rather than of cultural extinction, as occurred on the North American East Coast. Though the Spanish imposed government, religion, and technology, the basic Mesoamerican culture remained. While the heroes of Mexico's Aztec past are honored in monuments, the living descendants of the Aztec are not allowed to eat in some of the country's finest restaurants. From the Spanish founding of Mexico, social class has been determined by racial purity (i.e., those born in Spain at the top and full-blooded Indians on the bottom). In the United States, Congress passed the Indian Removal Act in 1820 to force American Indians west of the Mississippi River. Later, as colonists moved westward, the U.S. government sent many tribes to reservations and passed legislation intended to integrate American Indians into the rest of U.S. society. Only English-speaking teachers were employed to assimilate indigenous children into the dominant culture (Baron, 1990; Piatt, 1990).

Similar methods were widely used all over the world in an effort to assimilate indigenous peoples. In Taiwan, aboriginal tribes were dispossessed, forced to adopt Chinese names, and punished for speaking their languages. In Paraguay, the government banned Guaran from schools and required teachers to use only Spanish. The Sami people in Norway were prevented from renting or buying state-owned land by a 1902 law that required use of the Norwegian language in everyday life. In Australia, under a government policy that ran from 1910 until 1971, as many as 10% of all Aboriginal children were taken from their families to speed the process of assimilation. In countries all over the world, it was expected that the indigenous cultures and languages would eventually disappear naturally or by absorption into the population of an emerging national culture (Cobo, 1987).

Beginning in the second half of the 20th century, the situation began to shift. In the 1950s, Mexico was the scene of serious discussions, and by the middle of the 1960s, the policy had changed to early literacy in one's native language and teaching Spanish as a second language (Stavenhagen, 1990). The Zapatista rose up in the southern Mexican state of Chiapas in 1994 to protest the repression of Indians across the country. Mexico's army fought to contain the guerrilla movement. In 1996, the government of Mexico signed an agreement to amend the state's and nation's constitutions to guarantee respect for Indian languages and culture. This agreement marks the first time that the original peoples of Mexico have been recognized as equals.

The situation is different in Brazil: Brazil's indigenous population was approaching near-extinction in the mid-20th century (100,000 people in the 1950s). Today, the population has grown to 350,000. Eleven percent of the landmass of the country (260 million acres) is now reserved for the Indians. On the other hand, under Brazil's constitution, the Indians are not full citizens. Instead, they are legal minors with the status of a protected species.

In Norway, Sami was allowed back as a language of instruction in schools in 1959. In 1969 and 1990, the right of indigenous children to be instructed in the indigenous language was legally formalized. Now, Norway, Finland, and Sweden have elected Sami consultative "parliaments." Finally, in New Zealand, numerous court decisions confirmed that the Māori language is protected under the Treaty of Waitangi as a *te reo Māori,* a valued Māori treasure. Thus, in 1987, Māori was made an official language.

Without question, early laws had as an objective the assimilation of indigenous peoples into national cultures as quickly as possible and at any human cost. The trend today is decidedly different. Indigenous peoples are encouraged or forced to learn a national official language but also are allowed to, and in some cases assisted in, developing and promoting indigenous languages and cultures.

The United Nations Declaration on the Rights of Indigenous Peoples unequivocally suggests that indigenous peoples should occupy a privileged political and legal position. Indigenous peoples should have the right to autonomous governing and legal structures and institutions, including some power of taxation and control over resources and the right to use indigenous languages. In the cases where assimilation policies approached cultural genocide, such as in Australia and North America, the language of the declaration suggests that the governments could be obligated to assist in correcting past injustices and practices (Mikkelsen, 2010).

An extreme example of segregation occurred during World War II. After Japan attacked Pearl Harbor, President Franklin D. Roosevelt signed Executive Order 9066, which led to the forced evacuation of about 120,000 people of Japanese descent from the West Coast and their relocation to 10 internment centers. Approximately two thirds of those relocated were U.S. citizens. Internees lost their houses and farms, their livelihoods, and their freedom. Japanese-Americans remained loyal to the United States. In fact, the 422nd Regimental Combat Team, which included Japanese-American volunteers from these camps, is the most highly decorated unit in U.S. military history. This picture is of a Sunday school class at the Manzanar Relocation Center in California. In 1988, the U.S. government apologized for the internment and paid each camp survivor $20,000 as reparations. In 1998, President Bill Clinton apologized for the internment of more than 2,200 people of Japanese ancestry from 13 Latin American countries and pledged payments of $5,000 each. The Manzanar site is now a National Historic Site. One former internee said at its opening, "The worst part of camp was the psychological effect of being rejected by the public as an American citizen, as an equal."

ASSIMILATION: UNITED STATES

Immigration and acculturation policies in the United States have included forced separation, most notably slaves and their descendants, to assimilation for groups such as German immigrants, and now to acceptance of integration of subcultures such as Hispanics, in which maintaining important aspects of one's original culture is accepted. The United States proclaims the Latin phrase *E Pluribus Unum* ("from many, one") on its coins to symbolize the desire that the many will see themselves as one. This idea of the United States as a nation of people of many backgrounds has been a popular cultural myth. Many wrote of the diversity of the country's creation. Ralph Waldo Emerson (1909–1914) wrote of a "new race" drawing "the energy of Irish, Germans, Swedes, Poles, and Cossacks, and all the European tribes—of the Africans, and the Polynesians" (p. 116). Herman Melville (1849/1976) wrote, "On this Western Hemisphere all tribes and peoples are forming into one federated whole" (p. 239). More recently, former British Prime Minister Margaret Thatcher said of the United States that "no other nation has so successfully combined people of different races and nations within a single culture."

Melting Pot Concept

The phrase most often used to describe the assimilation of the early immigrants into the United States is "melting pot," which comes from Israel Zangwill's popular 1908 play *The Melting Pot*. The melting pot of old included English, German, Irish, French, and Italian immigrants and encouraged ethnic uniformity. Patriotic significance was placed on learning English and becoming "American." You seldom think of those of English, German, Irish, French, and Italian descent as "ethnic groups" because throughout the generations, these groups have become assimilated into a somewhat "homogenized" society. For example, more than 50 million people of German heritage live in the United States, yet that culture isn't particularly evident today. Automaker Henry Ford established for his company the "English Melting Pot School." The graduation ceremony featured the automaker's foreign-born employees, dressed in Old World costumes and carrying signs noting their birthplace, marching into a large, kettle-shaped prop labeled "Melting Pot." Moments later, the same people would emerge dressed in neat business suits and waving small U.S. flags.

Immigration has made the United States home to many ethnic groups. U.S. citizenship is easy to acquire, is hard to lose, and imposes few duties.

FOCUS ON THEORY 13.2

Generally, self-identity theories share the concept of self-consciousness in a network of relations with others or a socially constructed "object." Cultural identity can provide a sense of historical connection and a sense of connection to others. Such an understanding tends to a somewhat stable concept of the group that gives little recognition to individual variations within the group and the evolving nature of cultural identity throughout a person's life. Most researchers have conceived of cultural identity as an ascription-based, monolithic entity exclusive to a particular group of people (Y. Y. Kim, 2005). Collier and Thomas (1988) focused on identity negotiation as a key to intercultural communication competence. Similarly, Ting-Toomey and Kurogi (1998) focused on face negotiation.

INTEGRATION: UNITED STATES

From Melting Pot to Symphony and Stew

A century ago, there may have been a greater consensus as to cultural norms, religion, and what it meant to be a "true American." The traditional melting pot assimilation theory held that ethnic identity largely disappeared in one or two generations after arriving in the United States.

The melting pot metaphor was rejected as early as 1915 by philosopher Horace Kallen (1915, 1924/1970), who set forth the idea of cultural pluralism to describe the United States. He employed the metaphor of a symphony orchestra. Each instrument was an immigrant group that, together with other immigrant groups, created harmonious music. Kallen's opponents included John Dewey (Westbrook, 1991), who warned that cultural pluralism supported rigid segregation lines between groups.

Kallen's cultural pluralism predates today's debate over **multiculturalism**. Hollinger (1995) has described the issue as a two-sided confrontation between those who advocate a uniform culture grounded in Western civilization and those who promote diversity. Some use the word to refer to ethnic preservation, the drive to recover and preserve cultural and subgroup identification. This view raises the issue whether all cultures should receive equal attention in the schools. Others use the word to refer to globalism, the awareness of the interdependence of the world's peoples. Opponents to this view argue that an emphasis on differences between people actually impedes the goal of human equality.

Today, there may no longer be a consensus as to the cultural norms, religion, and behavior that define a U.S. culture. More recent immigrants experience less pressure to immediately learn fluent English and otherwise become Americanized than did earlier immigrants.

U.S. residents today increasingly recognize their own immigrant roots. Acculturation is defined more in terms of integration than assimilation. Today's immigrants find a much more ethnically diversified country. In some areas, people of similar ethnic origin reside together in large communities. People in the United States today can maintain some original cultural identity and values and participate meaningfully in the larger society. Some argue that the melting pot myth was never true. Today, you are more likely to hear the **salad analogy** or **stew analogy** to suggest that the elements maintain their own taste or identity but exist together to create the whole.

FOCUS ON THEORY 13.3

Gerbner, Morgan, and Signorielli (1986) identified television as having a homogenizing effect in a culture called *cultivation*. Television, it is believed, is a common experience of many and, therefore, provides a shared way of viewing the world. Cultivation analysis focuses on a totality communicated by television over a long period. Cultivation analysis contends that subcultures may retain their separate values, but the overriding images on television affect all social groups and subcultures. The contention is that culture becomes homogenized or mainstreamed through television. In other words, television is a stabilizing force for a culture.

HISPANIC CULTURES

The major example of integration in the United States today is the Hispanic subculture. Remember that Berry, Kim, and Baski (1987) defined integration as maintaining aspects of one's original culture as well as becoming an integral part of the new culture.

Terminology

Labeling has a long history in the Americas: For centuries in Mexico, Spain attempted to maintain a hierarchical racial order. Over time, intermarriage began to erode that order. By the time the settlement of the north began, the categories were more economic and culturally based. For example, Jose Vanegas, one of the original 46 settlers of Los Angeles, was first classified as an Indian in the Spanish census. Later, he was classified as mestizo. Similarly, Jose Navarro was first classified as mestizo in 1790 but later reclassified as Spanish. That fluidity continues today. Tanno (1994) and Mirandé and Tanno (1993) have called attention to the meaning and importance of ethnic labels. Remember from the discussion of othering the importance of labels imposed by an external, more powerful group or self-identified labels. For example, *Spanish speaking, Spanish surnamed, Spanish origin, Hispanic, Chicano, Latino,* and *Mexican-American* have all been used interchangeably to refer to that culture in the United States whose members originally came from a Spanish-speaking country. Antonio Guernica (1982) offers these distinctions:

- **Spanish speaking** refers to the population with the ability to speak and comprehend the Spanish language—whether as a primary or secondary language. This term encompasses non-Hispanics as well as Hispanics.
- **Spanish surnamed** refers to the population segment with last names that have been identified as Spanish by the U.S. Census Bureau.
- **Spanish origin** refers to that segment of the population that came from a Spanish-speaking country or that has ancestors came from a Spanish-speaking country. This term does not indicate that the person is Spanish speaking or personally identifies with Hispanic cultures.
- **Hispanic** came into common use as a result of the 1980 census to identify various U.S. Spanish speakers' shared roots to Spain. It refers to that population segment with the capability of speaking and comprehending the Spanish language, with ancestry based in a Spanish-speaking country, and that identify with Hispanic cultures. The Census Bureau considers it an ethnicity rather than a race, so in the U.S. census, someone of any race can be Hispanic. The term has been rejected by some because its use was imposed by the government.
- **Chicano** most often refers to that segment of the population born in the United States but with ancestors who came from Mexico. The label *Chicano* has a political meaning and is often used to represent a nationalist or separatist identity and a commitment to disassimilation (Sedano, 1980).
- **Latino** most often refers to Spanish-speaking individuals who came from, or whose ancestors came from, anywhere in Latin America. The term is more commonly used in the U.S. Southwest.

- **Mexican-American**, a term similar to Irish-American, indicates a person from a specific country of origin who is in the assimilation process (Hurstfield, 1978).
- **Tejano** is a term in widespread use in Texas to refer to people born in Texas of Mexican ancestry.

As Tanno (1994) argues, none of these terms is accurate and yet all are. An individual could identify with one or more of these at different times in her or his life and be enriched by the opportunities each provides.

Is there one label by which to identify a distinct culture? Any single label that includes Spaniards, Cubans, Mexican-Americans, Latinos, and Puerto Ricans groups together peoples with very diverse histories and cultures. A Black Cuban, a Uruguayan Jew, a multiracial Peruvian, and a multiracial Puerto Rican all living in New York City share a heritage of language and culture that originated in Spain; hence, it is accurate to say they are all Hispanic. Important differences, however, can be lost; for example, Cinco de Mayo is a Mexican holiday—not a Hispanic holiday. This text uses the terms *Hispanic* and *Hispanic cultures* to identify groups of diverse peoples as a survey has shown that that term, at least at this time, is preferred by the diverse group of peoples to whom it has been applied (see Table 13.1). The forces of media and marketing, among others, support a single identifying label even though some studies continue to show rejection of the term. It isn't clear, however, if the term or the forced labeling is being rejected (de la Garza, 1992).

The major consequence of labeling is categorization, the act of setting those labeled peoples as separate and apart. Gonzalez (1990) has identified in labeling the themes of inclusion and separation. Inclusion is desire for belonging on the basis of one's worth; separation is the fragmentation of not belonging, of being, for example, Mexican-American, not Mexican, not American, but somehow both. These themes can be seen in the complex feelings about language use and media and in feelings about ethnic identity and assimilation.

> ## Global Voices
>
> The interesting thing about Hispanics is that you will never meet us in Latin America. You may meet Chileans and Peruvians and Mexicans. You will not meet Hispanics. If you inquire in Lima or Bogotá about Hispanics, you will be referred to Dallas. For "Hispanic" is a gringo contrivance, a definition of the world according to European patterns of colonization.
>
> —Richard Rodriguez, (2003, p. 65) Editor at Pacific News Service and an essayist for PBS's News Hour, *The Chronicle of Higher Education*

Table 13.1 Hispanic Self-Identification Preferences, 2008

	Percentage
Hispanic	36
Latino	21
No preference	43

Source: Passel and Taylor (2009).

Global Voices

Mexicans have been the target of prejudice and racism. Arguing against the 1848 Peace Treaty of Guadalupe-Hidalgo, Senator John C. Calhoun of South Carolina said on the Senate floor:

> We have never dreamt of incorporating into our Union any but the Caucasian race—the free white race. To incorporate Mexico, would be the very first instance of the kind of incorporating an Indian race; for more than half of the Mexicans are Indians, and the other is composed chiefly of mixed tribes. I protest against such a union as that! Ours, sir, is the Government of a white race. The greatest misfortunes of Spanish America are to be traced to the fatal error of placing these colored races on an equality with the white race. That error destroyed the social arrangement which formed the basis of society. . . . Are we to overlook this fact? Are we to associate with ourselves as equals, companions, and fellow-citizens, the Indians and mixed race of Mexico? Sir, I should consider such a thing as fatal to our institutions.

Current U.S. Census Bureau policy is simple: Who's Hispanic? Those who says they are and nobody who says she or he isn't. Today, the Census Bureau relies totally on self-reporting. Self-identification is the official policy.

Immigration from Mexico has largely been tied to labor needs in Mexico and the United States. Late-19th-century immigrants worked in Southwest agriculture, in building railroads, and in mining. Immigration accelerated in the 1920s following the economic tumult of the Mexican Revolution.

The Depression era brought public outcry against illegal immigrants. Many illegal as well as legal immigrants and U.S. citizens were picked up for deportation. The changing labor market brought on by World War II saw the birth of the *bracero* program, a guest worker initiative for agriculture that lasted until the 1960s.

In 1960, fewer than 600,000 Mexican-born people resided in the United States. By 1980, that number had grown to more than 2 million and increased 50% from 1990 to 1996. This migration is the largest sustained mass migration of one group to the United States, far eclipsing earlier migrations of Irish and Italians. By 2007, for the first time, two Hispanic surnames, Garcia and Rodriguez, were among the top 10 most common names in the United States.

The total U.S. Hispanic population of some 50 million (one in six U.S. residents, according to the 2010 census) is regionally concentrated according to national origin and exhibits differences

(Szalay & Inn, 1987). Over 75% of the U.S. Mexican-origin population resides in the Southwest and the Pacific region and, over time, is dispersing beyond the border states to virtually every region of the country. More than 60% of the U.S. Puerto Rican population is found in New York, with another sizable population living in Chicago. The Cuban population is primarily concentrated in Florida, but a large Cuban population can be found in New York as well. The Central and South American population in the United States is dispersed geographically, with most centered in large urban centers such as New York, San Francisco, Los Angeles, Chicago, and Miami.

The Hispanic population in the United States has often been the subject of general-circulation media. The October 16, 1978, *Time* magazine had "Hispanic Americans: Soon the Biggest Majority" emblazoned on the cover ("It's your turn," 1978). *Newsweek* and *U.S. News & World Report* carried similar stories. In 1980, CBS-TV newscaster Walter Cronkite anchored a series of reports on the U.S. Hispanic population. Generally, these reports have taken the same approach as one would in writing about a foreign country and often present a stereotype of poverty.

Global Voices

I'm for making a cantonal system. The massive waves of Latinos sweeping across the border are quite correctly taking what they call "the occupied lands"—Southern California, Arizona, New Mexico, Texas. They're reoccupying it, and have no particular interest in the Anglo culture. My theory is that, essentially, the thing is never going to integrate anymore. . . . We're going to end up with, if we're lucky, something like Switzerland with sort of Spanish cantons. . . . I like the diversity of it.

—Gore Vidal, novelist and grandson of Senator Thomas Gore, quoted in Scheer, (1991, p. M3).

[Samuel P. Huntington argues that] the continuing Latin American immigration could create a cultural clash between Hispanics and Anglos that would "replace the racial division between blacks and whites as the most serious cleavage in U.S. society." He warns that Mexicans, in particular, will increasingly refuse to assimilate into the mainstream and will create "an autonomous, culturally and linguistically distinct and economically self-reliant bloc." The U.S. would be divided into two peoples, two cultures, and two languages.

—Samuel P. Huntington, author of *Who Are We? The Challenges to America's National Identity* (2004), quoted in G. Rodriguez (2004, p. M1).

Source: Los Angeles Times, December 15, 1991, p. M3. Copyright © 1991, Los Angeles Times.

Spanish-Language Use

The 1996 report "Toward a Latino Urban Policy Agenda," released by Latino Urban Policy Agenda (Puenta, 1996), shows that 93% of Hispanics born in the United States speak English well and that 66.1% of Colombian immigrants, 61.1% of Cuban immigrants, and 51.3% of Mexican immigrants speak English well. Those for whom Spanish is the usual or first language rose from 10.6 million in 1976 to 28.1 million by 2000 (Shin & Bruno, 2003). In 2007 the number 5 years of age and older using Spanish at home was 34.5 million (12% of the U.S. population; Shin & Kominski, 2010).

The Hispanic culture has two distinct characteristics: Spanish language and identification with all Hispanic cultures. Spanish has spread across the world for 500 years but has maintained an amazing coherence of grammar and vocabulary.

Nonetheless, the presence of Spanish and the interface of Spanish and English languages is producing **Spanglish** (or Tex-Mex or Cubonics)—a practice called **code switching** by linguists to refer to changing from one language to another for a single word, phrase, clause, or entire sentence (Eastman, 1992; Lipski, 1985). Spanglish used by Hispanics reflects both a knowledge of Spanish and an awareness of the U.S. culture. A teenage girl, for example, may admonish her mother by saying, "No seas tan old-fashioned!" Usually, the simpler word from either language is used. For example, "income tax" is used for *impuesto sobre la renta* and "*ir al* supermarket" replaces a longer explanation for leaving.

Code switching goes both ways. In areas with a high concentration of Hispanics, Spanish words are used by those with no knowledge of Spanish. Examples are *gracias, bueno, amigo,* and *por favor.* Other words move into more general mainstream use through popular literature and music. Immigrants of the 1960s and 1970s who experienced discrimination believed that the children would do better speaking unaccented English. These immigrants, like immigrants from other eras, did not speak Spanish with their children. One indicator of an increasing cultural identity is a growing number of people learning the Spanish of immigrant parents and grandparents. Yet, over all, as a 2009 study showed, among foreign-born 16- to 25-year-olds, 48% can carry on a conversation in English, but among their native-born counterparts the likelihood of speaking proficiently in English more than doubles, to 98% for the second generation. While proficiency with English does grow, young Hispanics do not abandon Spanish.

> About nine-in-ten immigrant youths and eight-in-ten second-generation youths are fluent in Spanish. Even among third-generation youths, nearly four-in-ten (38%) retain the ability to speak and understand Spanish, despite the fact that they were born in the United States to native-born parents who are mostly English dominant. And when it comes to music, some 30% of third-generation Latino youths report that at least half of the songs they listen to are in Spanish. (Pew Hispanic Center, 2009, p. 31)

Values

In 1996, the Tómas Rivera Center released "Hispanic Perspectives," a survey of Hispanic public attitudes in Texas, California, New York, and Florida. The majority supported affirmative action programs and thought Hispanic communities had benefited from these programs. Almost 70% of Hispanics in Texas believed that they had as much chance as an Anglo in getting a job for which both were qualified. In the other states, there was a simple majority agreement. The majority in all four states believed that most people receiving public aid do so because of not wanting to work. The majority, except for those in California, supported the issuance of government ID cards to all legal residents and citizens. And the majority agreed that illegal immigrants who pay taxes should receive government services.

Just from these few results, you could not say that Hispanics were conservative or liberal or that Hispanics in Texas held the same views as Hispanics in California.

What does exist behind this diversity are many shared values. Studies using 50 years of census data (Hayes-Bautista, 1992) show that, compared to non-Hispanic Whites, African-Americans, and Asians, Hispanics have consistently had the highest labor force participation, the least use of welfare programs, and the highest rate of family formation. Compared to non-Hispanic Whites and African-Americans, Hispanics have a longer life expectancy; less cancer, heart disease, and respiratory disease; the fewest low-birth-weight babies; the lowest infant mortality; and the fewest babies damaged by drugs. Such behaviors are related to strong shared cultural values—an explicit moral structure, a Roman Catholic tradition, and social integration that binds individuals and families together into a larger community.

Often referred to as family oriented (Sabogal, Marín, Otero-Sabogal, Marín, & Perez-Stable, 1987) compared to Anglo-Americans, Hispanics rely on extended families for emotional support and feel more anxiety when separated from families (Griffith & Villavicencio, 1985; Levine & Padilla, 1979).

A commemorative stamp was issued in 1984 to honor Hispanic Americans. In his remarks at a White House ceremony unveiling the stamp on October 31, President Reagan called attention to Hispanic values: "Devotion to family and respect for God, love of country and respect for honest work—these are the ingredients that have molded the character of Americans of Hispanic descent."

Global Voices

In 1800, if a reasonable person had asked which would be the dominant power in North America in two hundred years, the logical answer would have been Mexico. It was far more developed and sophisticated (Friedman, 2011, p. 203).

[T]here is a fundamentally geopolitical reason not to compare Mexican immigration with "immigration from distant countries." . . . Not only is Mexico adjacent to the United States, but in many cases the land the migrants are moving into is land that once belonged Mexico. When Mexicans move northward, they are not necessarily breaking ties with their homeland. Indeed, within the borderland, which can extend hundreds of miles into both countries, the movement north can require minimal cultural adjustment. . . . Within the borderland, they have the option of retaining their language and their national identity, distinct from whatever legal identity they adopt. This state of affairs creates serious tension between the legal border and the cultural border (p. 205).

—George Friedman, in *The Next Decade* (2011)

There also exists a growing shared appreciation for the art, music, dance, cuisine, literature, and other elements of an international Hispanic culture. Traditions that had been put aside are now gaining new followers. The Mexican tradition of *Dia de los Muertos,* the Day of the Dead, which combines Aztec and Catholic beliefs, has become a popular day to remember departed family members and reclaim a cultural tradition.

Cultural Identity and Media

Though many Spanish-origin individuals can neither read Spanish nor understand it when spoken, Hispanic cultures in the United States have a rich media—Spanish-language magazines, newspapers, radio, television, and social media. Hispanic media, like other forms of minority media, provide a forum where minority issues can be freely discussed (Downing, 1990). It is these media that help continue the culture and support an integrated status.

Print

In Mexico, well-read people patronize "libraries," which are bookstores, or pay a fee to take books from a lending library. It's frequently hypothesized that Hispanics in the United States have a reading tradition. Hispanic print media often appear in both Spanish and English to serve that portion of the culture who cannot read Spanish.

FOCUS ON THE ENVIRONMENT 13.1

Nueva Encuesta del Sierra Club Muestra a los Latinos Preocupados por el Calentamiento Global y la Energía, y Que Están Dispuestos a Actuar en Consecuencia

(New Sierra Club Poll Shows Hispanic Voters Concerned about Global Warming and Energy, Willing to Take Action)

In March 2008, the Sierra Club conducted the first-ever national survey of Hispanic voters on energy and environmental issues. Some 91% of Hispanics in the United States live in metropolitan areas, where polluted air may increase the risk of illnesses including asthma and cancer.

Some 80% of Hispanic voters view "energy and global warming" to be one of the two most important environmental problems for their families (the other was clean air and water).

Additionally 83% said that energy and environmental issues have "a lot" or "some" impact on the quality of life and health of their families. Two-thirds of respondents nationwide said they were aware of toxic sites close to their home or place of work, such as a refinery, chemical plant, factory, or incinerator. Forty-two percent of respondents said they had personally suffered health concerns due to environmental problems where they lived, the most common of which was air pollution.

Source: Sierra Club (2008).

Only four other countries in the world buy more Spanish-language books than the United States. More than half of the books that Mexico exports are sent to the United States.

The number of national Hispanic-oriented publications has grown from more than 700 in 1990 to more than 1,200 in 2000. More than 80% of these are in Spanish. Combined circulation was approximately 33 million. Traditionally, the most successful Spanish-language magazines in national distribution have been geared toward the Hispanic woman. *Vanidades* entered the U.S. market in 1961, making it the first Spanish-language women's magazine available nationally. Since then, the number of magazines has grown and diversified, although those for women retain prominence. The New York–based *Latina,* a bilingual quarterly for women, started publication in 1996, as did *People en Español* (the most widely read Spanish language newspaper) and *Newsweek en Español.* Other new magazines include *Moderna* and *Latina Style* (fashion, fitness, finances, and travel), *Frontera* (music and entertainment), *Generation Ñ* (Cuban culture), *POZ en Español* (HIV community), *Podor* (business), and *Urban Latino* (men's magazine).

Approximately 28 major Spanish-language newspapers can be found in the United States. *La Opinión,* published in Los Angeles, is the largest Spanish-language daily in the United States. It emphasizes coverage of Mexican-American personalities and events, features on specifically Mexican-interest topics, and news of Mexico itself—particularly U.S.-Mexico relations.

Popular English language magazines, such as *People,* have started Spanish-language editions.

Besides the dailies, hundreds of Spanish-language weeklies and biweeklies tend to emphasize news of local interest, such as community affairs and upcoming events in the local Hispanic community.

Radio

While Spanish-language newspapers have been largely owned by members of the immigrant community, radio stations that broadcast in Spanish were at first owned by majority-culture entrepreneurs (A. Rodriguez, 1999). In 2007, the number of Spanish-language radio stations was 872, more than double what it had been 10 years earlier (Arbitron, 2008). The growth of Spanish-language radio can be seen in Los Angeles, the largest and fastest growing Spanish radio market in the United States. Forty years ago, there was one full-time Spanish-language station. In 1997, 17 of the market's 82 radio stations were full-time Spanish-language stations. Two of the 17 are consistently in the top 10 highest rated stations. Both San Antonio and Los Angeles have had Spanish-language stations rated first in Arbitron's ratings.

Local independent radio stations are being replaced with national network affiliates. The top Spanish-language radio broadcaster in the United States, the Hispanic Broadcasting Corporation, which owned 65 Spanish-language stations in 11 of the top 15 Hispanic markets, was acquired by Univision in 2003. Rather than national programming, it provides regionally based programming.

Historically, radio has been an important medium in Spanish-speaking communities as more people can speak Spanish than can read it. Spanish-language stations serve as a primary source of news and information for much of the audience. Music, however, constitutes the bulk of the programming day, although a few stations in New York, Miami, and Los Angeles–Orange County have all-talk formats.

Spanish-language radio programming has been said to create a strong emotional tie to the Hispanic culture as Hispanics have higher-than-average station loyalty. Spanish-language radio stations frequently have close community involvement, providing information on voter registration, breast cancer screening, and the Better Business Bureau. A broadcast announcement of a family without housing or food because of fire or flood brings quick and generous responses.

Some stations have experimented with a bilingual format that attempts to bridge the two cultures by speaking both languages. These stations mix diverse musical styles with news and public affairs segments that focus on such issues as immigration, economic opportunities, and the problems in growing up in two cultures. The bilingual announcers switch often and effort-lessly from Spanish to English and back again—sometimes in midsentence. This is code switching in action. The changes are brief enough that a speaker of one language only never feels lost, and the context provided by the language one knows encourages learning the other language (Downing, 1990, Albarran & Hutton, 2009).

Television

In 1961, Mexican mogul Emilio Azcárraga Vidaurreta bought KCOR-TV in San Antonio, the nation's first Spanish-language TV station. SIN—Spanish International Network—grew in one decade to nine stations and experimented with cable outlets, microwave and satellite intercon-nections, and repeater television stations (A. Rodriguez, 1999).

By early 1982, there were 12 Spanish-language television stations in the United States. Ten of them were SIN affiliates. SIN's programming was carried also by more than 100 cable sys-tems and translators (low-power repeater stations). Hallmark Cards bought SIN in 1987, renaming it Univision and then in 1992 announced its sale to an investment group linked with the huge Mexican media conglomerate Grupo Televisa, making it the dominant force in Spanish-language broadcasting in the United States and the fifth largest U.S. prime-time net-work. Univision grew to command 80% of the U.S. Spanish-language market and some 92% share of the prime-time audience that watches TV in Spanish.

The second place Spanish-language network, Telemundo, was created by Saul Steinberg and based in Miami. In 2001, NBC purchased Telemundo for $2.7 billion. In addition to Univi-sion and Telemundo, there are now several major Spanish-language broadcasters, including TeleFutura, V-me, Azteca América, Estrella TV, and LATV, all founded between 2001 and 2009. To demonstrate to advertisers that people were watching Spanish-language television, Nielsen Media Research, with financing by Univision and Telemundo, began to develop a national Hispanic television rating service to help Spanish-language television compete for advertising revenue. One consequence of these efforts is the reinforcement of the label *Hispanic* to refer to a single co-culture (A. Rodriguez, 1999). By 2007, Nielsen ended separate rating services as Hispanic viewers were fully integrated into its sampling methodology.

In Los Angeles, Univision's Spanish-language 34 KMEX regularly wins news ratings over English-language stations. In New York, WXTV has more viewers younger than age 49 for news than its English-language competitors. In Miami, Univision's WLTV in 1998 was the first Spanish-language station to get top ratings in both news and prime time. Spanish-language programming produced in the United States is, however, basically limited to local news pro-grams, talk shows, and public affairs presentations. Imported programming offers *novelas* (which, unlike U.S. "soaps," usually come to a conclusion within a few months), news shows, movies, magazine-style shows, children's shows, talk shows, and variety. The Nielsen study of Hispanic television viewing (A. Rodriguez, 1999) showed that Hispanics watch very different TV shows than the general public does. Adults prefer Univision and Telemundo to the English-language network shows three to one. Of English-language shows, only one in four of the top 10 shows preferred by the general public rated in the top 10 for Hispanics. The study showed that Spanish language was the most important factor in reaching the Hispanic audience. It's no surprise, then, that the major English-language networks began to program for Hispanics.

Spanish-Language Internet and Social Media

In the 7 years 2004 to 2010, the number of Hispanics online doubled to 28.4 million. English was the language of preference for 52% of users; 26% preferred both languages, and 22% preferred Spanish online (Fackler, 2010). The Pew Hispanic Center reported in 2007 that educational level and English language ability explained the lower Internet use among Hispanics. The report showed that 89% of Hispanics who have a college degree, 70% who completed high school, and 31% of who did not complete high school go online. And that 78% of Hispanics who are English-dominant and 76% of bilingual Latinos use the Internet, compared with 32% of Spanish-dominant Hispanic adults (Fox & Livingston, 2007).

The data reported in 2007 reported the same educational and language factors, but also showed that Hispanics who don't use the Internet are connecting via cell phone. Fully 59% of Hispanic adults have a cell phone and 49% of Hispanic cell phone users send and receive text messages on their phone (Fox & Livingston, 2007). A Pew report in 2011 reported the same trend: Hispanic cell phone owners are more likely than non-Hispanic White cell phone owners to access the Internet (40% versus 34%), e-mail (36% vs. 31%), or instant messages (45% vs. 24%) from their cell phone (Livingston, 2011). Another Pew study found that, compared to the general population, Hispanics use their cell phones more often, and they use more features on their phones.

These demographic differences don't represent a cultural difference. We need to look at the messages in the media to see how an integrated subcultural status is being supported.

Cultural Identity and Marketing

Attempts made to sell services and products to individuals in a culture by appealing to the values of that culture are undisputable evidence of the culture's existence. Such advertising also serves to continue and strengthen the culture.

Many attempts at marketing in Spanish revealed translation errors. The story goes that one cigarette company advertising "low-tar" cigarettes used a phrase that translated to "low asphalt." A Miller Lite slogan told readers that the beer was "Filling, and less delicious." And a Coors beer slogan "Get loose with Coors" became "Get the runs with Coors." As one restaurant chain learned, *nieve* means "ice cream" to some Mexican-Americans but "cocaine" to many Cuban-Americans. And in another ad, the word *point* was translated as *puta* (prostitute) instead of *punta*.

Advertisers discovered that marketing to the Hispanic community involves not only language and images that mean something to the buyer but also cultural traditions and values. And the larger advertisers have learned that the Hispanic culture is not one culture but many, with diverse experiences, all of which are changing and evolving. For example, advertisers now recognize a "boomerang effect" or "retro-acculturation" wherein Hispanic teens are attracted to general market media but then return to their roots when they marry to ensure that their children retain a sense of heritage.

Budweiser was early to advertise in Spanish. In a 1979 print and television campaign, Budweiser advertised to three regional subgroups. In California, Texas, and the Southwest, advertisements aimed at Spanish speakers of Mexican heritage featured cowboys and cactus. In the Northeast, advertisements aimed at Puerto Ricans featured cityscapes and salsa music. And in Florida, advertisements aimed at Cubans featured palm trees, cigars, and bananas. Each advertisement featured differently accented Spanish and national-origin-appropriate music. Other early advertisers, such as Procter & Gamble, Colgate-Palmolive, and Coca-Cola, used a similar strategy (A. Rodriguez, 1999). Miller Brewing, Chevron, Nike, and Ford have all had Spanish-language ads with English subtitles on English-language television stations.

A truly national advertising campaign would need to be based on some shared culture. Coca-Cola was the first major corporation to systematize segmenting Hispanics in advertising. Coke directs its ads not to the consumer but to the Hispanic *community,* showing sensitivity toward such issues as job training and education. For the 1992 quincentenary celebration of Columbus's landing in America, Coke planned advertising recognizing Hispanic contributions to U.S. culture and featuring prominent Hispanic-Americans, such as actress Rita Moreno. To communicate an interest in the community, both Coca-Cola and PepsiCo sponsor ethnic festivals and concert tours and place special promotional displays in neighborhood stores. Pepsi sponsored the U.S. tour of Santo Domingo native Guerra and his group 4.40. Pepsi also designed a Hispanic version of its "Gotta Have It" ad campaign, featuring Guerra, tennis star Gabriela Sabatini, and comedian Paul Rodriguez.

Budweiser and Bud Light beers sponsor Cinco de Mayo celebrations—U.S.-Mexican fiestas in honor of the 1862 Mexican victory over the French. In 1988, Budweiser began awarding about $1.5 million annually in college scholarships to Hispanic students. Because of these efforts, Anheuser-Busch has more than doubled the Hispanic market share of its nearest competitor. Appealing to similar values, Bank of America offers bilingual automated teller machines, envelopes, and checks. The check series, called *Im genes Familiares* ("Family Images"), portrays five Hispanic family scenes. The checks have "pay to the order of" and "dollars" in both English and Spanish. The message the bank wants to make is that it respects the Hispanic culture and wants to do business with Hispanics.

Burger chain Carl's Jr. simply wanted to translate its popular television ads into Spanish, but when it took its account to one of a growing number of Hispanic advertising agencies, the agency explained that the humor in the English-language ads directed at young males would confuse mothers in Hispanic households, who typically decide where families eat. The agency produced a series of highly successful ads for Carl's Jr. featuring Hispanic actors performing traditional dances. In 2001, Mattel introduced its first Hispanic-targeted brunette Barbie in the gown of the *quinceanera,* the traditional Mexican celebration marking a young girl's 15th birthday.

One in the five-check series painted by San Francisco artist Carmen Lomas Garza for Bank of America.

La harías *reina* del mundo si pudieras.

Le sirves pollo de *calidad* **totalmente natural** porque puedes.

*Todos los productos de pollo Tyson comienzan con pollo totalmente natural.
Esto quiere decir que no contienen aditivos y su procesamiento es mínimo.*

Lo que tu *familia* se merece.™

www.tyson.com

Since 2000, Tyson has spent more than $1 million per year on placing ads in Hispanic magazines, averaging 57 insertions a year in seven publications.

In 1989, Ford Motor Company introduced a Spanish-language version of its buying guide *Car and Truck Buying Made Easier*. Ford advertised its availability in cities with large Hispanic populations. Multilingual advertising is not new, of course. However, now it seems that all types of businesses have discovered that "money talks, but it speaks many languages." Not everyone approves of the growing trend. One English-as-the-official-language organization is campaigning against multilingual customer service, arguing that it perpetuates linguistic divisiveness and separation rather than promoting assimilation.

POSTETHNIC CULTURES

You read earlier in this chapter that John Dewey criticized cultural pluralism as encouraging people to identify themselves as a member of one group, and experience in the United States shows that that group is most often an ethnic group. If a person is born a woman in Texas of immigrant parents from Mexico who becomes an attorney, a Republican, and a Baptist who currently lives in Minneapolis, who is she? In the United States, can she identify herself as any one of these? As all of these? Will others most likely identify her first as Hispanic?

A postethnic perspective recognizes that each of us, like the Minneapolis attorney, lives in many diverse groups and so we aren't confined to only one group. Angela Davis (1992) used the image of "a rope attached to an anchor": While we may be anchored in one community, our "ropes" should be long enough to permit us to move into other communities.

A postethnic perspective does not assume that "everyone is the same." Rather, it recognizes our interdependent future and stretches the boundaries of "we."

Hollinger (1995) describes a postethnic perspective as a challenge to the "right" of our grandparents to establish our primary identity. **Postethnicity** "prefers voluntary to prescribed affiliations, appreciates multiple identities, pushes for communities of wide scope, recognizes the constructed character of ethno-racial groups, and accepts the formation of new groups as a part of the normal life of a democratic society" (p. 116). Postethnicity recognizes that groups based on affiliations are as substantive and authentic as groups based on blood and history.

In one sense, postethnicity is an idealistic attempt to redefine groups rigidly based on ethnicity into groups based on voluntary interests. However, if viewed from the perspective of dominant U.S. cultural values—particularly individualism—postethnicity is a reaffirmation of the individual's right to define herself or himself by individual interest and not by heritage. Postethnicity in the United States may be an extension of extreme individualism.

It's important to recognize the criticism of postethnicity: that it is idealistic to assume that others will not continue to label some people as members of a group and communicate with them as members of that group and not as individuals.

SUMMARY

The Hmong have been called the most ill-prepared people ever to immigrate to the United States. The Hmong left the villages of Laos to resettle in California, Minnesota, and Wisconsin. Many of the older Hmong immigrants lost their identity provided by their homeland and were unable to establish a new identity in the United States, and thus they are an example of marginalization. Another example of marginalization are the Koryo-saram, the ethnic Koreans in the post-Soviet states. The Koryo-saram actually lived in a state of separation from the Russian culture, interacting little with the nomadic peoples around them.

Indigeneous peoples across the world have faced separation and at other times faced forced assimilation. Over the years, immigration policy in the United States has changed. The melting pot of old included English, German, Irish, French, and Italian immigrants and encouraged ethnic uniformity. Patriotic significance was placed on learning English and becoming "American." The major example today in the United States of integration is the Hispanic subculture. Integration as an immigration status means maintaining aspects of one's original culture as well as becoming an integral part of the new culture.

Postethnicity recognizes that groups based on affiliations are as substantive and authentic as groups based on blood and history. In one sense, postethnicity is an idealistic attempt to redefine groups rigidly based on ethnicity into groups based on voluntary interests. However, if viewed from the perspective of dominant U.S. cultural values—particularly individualism—postethnicity is a reaffirmation of the individual's right to define herself or himself by individual interest and not by heritage. Postethnicity in the United States may be an extension of extreme individualism.

DISCUSSION QUESTIONS

1. What reasons can you give for the Hmong integrating, assimilating, or remaining a separate culture?

2. Contrast Amish cultural patterns to dominant U.S. cultural patterns.

3. Discuss the consequences of labeling diverse peoples with terms such as *Latino* or *Hispanic*.

4. Describe factors acting to maintain cultural identity.

5. In light of the official English movement, what are possible consequences of major political parties' candidates having Spanish-language websites?

6. Compare the experiences of Asian-Americans to Hispanic cultures in the United States.

7. Critique the concept of postethnicity.

KEY TERMS

Anabaptist 340	melting pot 348	Spanglish 354
Beachy Amish 341	Mexican-American 351	Spanish origin 350
Chicano 350	multiculturalism 349	Spanish speaking 350
code switching 354	New Order Amish 341	Spanish surnamed 350
diaspora 337	Old Order Amish 341	stew analogy 349
Gelassenheit 341	Ordnung 341	Tejano 351
Hispanic 350	postethnicity 362	Telemundo 359
Hmong 338	rumspringa 342	Univision 359
Latino 350	salad analogy 349	

READINGS

All readings are from *Intercultural Communication: A Global Reader* (Jandt, 2004).

Rujira Rojjanaprapayon, Porntipha Chiemprapha, and Achaya Kanchanakul, "Conflict Management in Thai Organizations" (p. 28)

Rueyling Chuang, "An Examination of Taoist and Buddhist Perspectives on Interpersonal Conflicts, Emotions, and Adversities" (p. 38)

Jung-huel Becky Yeh and Ling Chen, "Cultural Values and Argumentative Orientations for Chinese People in Taiwan, Hong Kong, and Mainland China" (p. 51)

Jonathan J. H. Zhu and Zhou He, "Information Accessibility, User Sophistication, and Source Credibility: The Impact of the Internet on Value Orientations in Mainland China" (p. 65)

Amadou Hampaté Bâ, "Africa: The Power of Speech" (p. 108)

Eric Aoki, "Mexican American Ethnicity in Biola, CA: An Ethnographic Account of Hard Work, Family, and Religion" (p. 112)

Wally Penetito, "Research and Context for a Theory of Māori Schooling" (p. 173)

Flora Keshishian, "Acculturation, Communication, and the U.S. Mass Media: The Experience of an Iranian Immigrant" (p. 230)

Tarla Rai Peterson, Susan J. Gilbertz, Kathi Groenendyk, Jay Todd, and Gary E. Varner, "Reconfiguring Borders: Health-Care Providers and Practical Environmentalism in Cameron County, Texas" (p. 243)

Richard D. Pineda, "Nuestro Espacio Cyber: The Internet as Expressive Space for Latina/os in the United States" (p. 252)

Ketra L. Armstrong, "Nike's Communication With Black Audiences" (p. 264)

Paul Wehr and John Paul Lederach, "Mediating Conflict in Central America" (p. 345)

Wole Soyinka, "Nobel Lecture, December 8, 1986" (p. 387)

STUDENT STUDY SITE

Visit the student study site at **www.sagepub.com/jandt7e** for these additional learning tools:

- Web Resources
- Audio and Video Links
- SAGE journal articles
- Flashcards
- Web Quizzes
- Sample Essays

CHAPTER

14

Identity and Subgroups

FOCUS QUESTIONS

- What purposes does argot service for subgroups?

- How can corporations present the same communication challenges as cultures?

- How does the subgroup of lesbians and gay men illustrate how subgroups can change over time and location?

- How do the observations of today's astronauts suggest the importance of studying intercultural communication?

Argot
  Specialized Vocabulary
  Argot and Subgroup Identity
  Argot and Subgroup Boundaries
  Argot and Meaning
Subgroup Media and Values
Examples of Subgroups
  The Working Class
  British Punk
  Corporate Cultures
  Case Study: Southwest Airlines
      Southwest Airlines Former
          CEO Herb Kelleher
  Case Study: Google
Sexual Orientation as a Basis for Subgroups
  Sexual Orientation and Othering
  Rejecting All Labels
  Attitudes Toward Sexual Orientation
  Cultural Bases for Attitudes
  Consequences of Othering
  Homophobia
  Traditional and Social Media
  From Separation to Assimilation
  Evidence of Separate Status
Integration or Assimilation of Subgroups
A Final Word
Summary
Discussion Questions
Key Terms
Readings
Student Study Site

In Chapter 1, you read that subgroups have similar communication dynamics as cultures and also are characterized by an identifiable distinction and shared interests and values. Subgroups usually do not involve the same large numbers of people as cultures, and they are not necessarily thought of as transmitting values and patterns of behavior over generations in the same way as cultures. Existing within cultures, subgroups do provide members with patterns of behavior.

This chapter explains the importance of language in communicating a subgroup identity and offers the examples of the working class, British punk, corporations, and lesbians and gay men. These were chosen because they illustrate the unique intercultural communication challenges presented by all types of subgroups. Remember that each of us is a member of various subgroups throughout our lives. As you read this chapter, examine the ways your subgroups support an identity.

ARGOT

In previous chapters you have seen the importance of the study of a culture's language as a way to know that culture. The equivalent to learning about a subgroup is studying its specialized language, its vocabulary.

Specialized Vocabulary

According to the Sapir-Whorf hypothesis (discussed in Chapter 6), language provides the conceptual categories that influence how its speakers' perceptions are encoded and stored. That same concept is true for subgroups but on the level of vocabulary. The specialized vocabulary identifies the subgroup and establishes the group's boundaries. The specialized vocabulary of subgroups, argot (pronounced AR-go), has been variously called *jargon, cant,* and *slang.*

Jargon has been used to refer to the technical language of a professional subgroup, such as doctors and lawyers. Jargon is the vocabulary that communicates the distinctions and specific meanings these professionals need to reference. Cant has been used to refer to the specialized vocabulary of any nonprofessional subgroup, such as truck drivers. Slang has been used to refer to the specialized vocabulary of "stigmatized" subgroups, such as gangs, drug dealers, and prostitutes, as well as to the specialized vocabulary of teenagers. As *argot* is becoming the more commonly recognized term, it is used in this chapter to refer to the specialized vocabulary of subgroups regardless of how these subgroups are thought of by the dominant culture.

Argot and Subgroup Identity

The study of argot originated with the work of David Maurer (1981) in the 1930s. Before his work, observations of nonstandard language were limited to the study of regional dialects. Maurer, who had studied Sapir's work, was the first to gather, analyze, and present the speech of subgroups. He was also the first to observe that argots were not primarily secret communications used to deceive outsiders but, rather, were an important aspect of group identity.

In Maurer's (1981) studies of professional crime, he showed that individual criminals were not abnormalities but fully integrated and well-adjusted members of a subgroup. Professional crime is much more than individual identity and subgroups' lawbreaking; it's actually a way of life within certain subgroups. Crime is not a mere facet of the life of some groups but is an entire way of life. Maurer's studies demonstrate that membership in the subgroup provides an identity and that the key to developing and understanding that identity is its language.

Argot and Subgroup Boundaries

Besides developing an identity, a subgroup's argot defines the boundaries of the subgroup. Because its argot can change rapidly, to be a member of the subgroup, you have to know the vocabulary. If you don't know the vocabulary, you're obviously not a member. Correct use of the argot, then, establishes the subgroup's boundary.

Gang slang, for example, serves several important functions. A special language can contribute to feeling special, to developing a group identity. Besides argot, there may be unique nonverbal symbols such as handshakes or clothing styles. The language and clothes say, "I'm somebody." Use of the argot and nonverbal codes establishes the boundaries of the gang.

A particular gang slang may appear in another part of the country when gang members move. It may die unnoticed when a gang dies out. Some argot may be absorbed into more mainstream language. For example, *four-twenty* was once an obscure San Francisco Bay Area term for marijuana. Later it began to show up nationally in advertising—420 Pale Ale, 420 Tours, and Highway 420 Radio.

Argot and Meaning

Argot also has specific, unambiguous meaning for a subgroup. Air traffic controllers and seafaring radio operators have an argot that has specific, unambiguous meaning. Various scientific disciplines have developed specialized argot to express nuances of meaning precisely. That preciseness of meaning is clear only to the subgroup's members.

The medical professions have developed an argot for preciseness of meaning to avoid misunderstandings that can hurt a patient's health. A limited vocabulary has been devised to ensure that each word has a precise, unambiguous meaning.

SUBGROUP MEDIA AND VALUES

Besides argot, media use and values contribute to defining subgroup identity and boundaries. Media distributed only to members can vary widely from graffiti to newsletters, but the subgroup's argot and pictorial images will be used. To get an idea of the media of subgroups, simply visit a large newsstand. You'll find specialty magazines that appeal to a wide variety of subgroup interests. Social media have also become particularly important for most subgroups in helping maintain interaction and, hence, shared identity.

Most important, however, are common values or worldviews shared by members of the subgroup. For many subgroups, that common value may be a reaction to society's disapproval—that is, "because we're outcasts, we're together"—but for other subgroups, the shared values may grow to provide a member with a relatively complete set of guiding values and patterns of behavior.

FOCUS ON THEORY 14.1

Each of us can have multiple group identities. Standpoint theory (Collins, 1990; Harding, 1991) focuses on how individuals understand and construct a social world. Rather than the belief that each of us must choose a single identity, standpoint theory contends that each of us can construct multiple identities. Standpoint theorists also incorporate the construct of power. Individuals whose identities include less powerful groups can see the world from that perspective as well as from the standpoint of those in power. However, those from more powerful groups never develop the need to see the world from the standpoint of the oppressed classes.

EXAMPLES OF SUBGROUPS

Just like cultures, ethnographic and cultural approaches can be applied to subgroups. There are many reports of observations of subgroups that range in method from "insider" to participant observer. Insider reports can be most interesting and valuable; some have been written for self-justification or profit. **Participant observer** reports are based on the researcher's orderly and scientific study of a subgroup by actually becoming accepted as a member. In one sense, these reports can be viewed as self-reports of the acculturation process of learning the culture of the subgroup. Several fascinating reports of this kind are available that provide insight into the argot, nonverbal symbols, media, and values.

The Working Class

In Chapter 1, social class was given as one basis for a subculture. Most scholars agree that working-class values include a high value placed on loyalty to one's community even at the cost of self-advancement, a lack of a sense of entitlement of privilege, and a shared resentment of perceived arrogance in wealthier classes (Denning, 1997; Roediger, 1999). And as you read in Chapter 1, working-class parents emphasize different values in child rearing than do middle-class parents.

While social class is more properly considered a subculture, studies by Gerry Philipsen (1975, 1976, 1989, 1992) of blue-collar, low-income Whites on the near south side of Chicago in the early 1970s are the best example of a study that focuses on the communication behavior of the group. Philipsen showed that to know how to present oneself as a man in this community, one needed to know the community's culture. In some situations, speech was appropriate in male role enactment, but in others it was not. To use speech where it wasn't appropriate casts doubts on the speaker's manliness. If the relationship was symmetrical—that is, matched on age, sex, ethnicity, occupation, and location of residence—then speech was appropriate. However, if the relationship was asymmetrical—that is, if a man was with his wife, child, or boss; was an outsider; or was of different ethnicity—then speech was not appropriate.

Studies seem to suggest that working class participation in social media is significantly less than others. Data was collected from more than 41,000 American adults surveyed between 2000 and 2008 in the Pew Internet and American Life Project (Schradie, 2011). Users' education level, income, gender, race and ethnicity, as well as use of Facebook, website building and design, blogging, photo- and video-sharing, and chat room and newsgroup participation, were tracked. In all online activities, a socioeconomic class divide existed. The study concluded that the working class is underrepresented on the Internet.

FOCUS ON THE ENVIRONMENT 14.1

In the 1960s, India's push for national economic development included clearing trees for export. In the Himalayan foothills, as food, fuel, and water gatherers, women have strong interests in reversing deforestation, desertification, and water pollution. In the 1970s a subgroup of mostly rural women in India developed, called Chipko, to save their environment. *Chipko* in Hindi means to cling, as in a protest throwing their arms around the tree trunks designated to be cut and refusing to move.

In the 1980s, the ideas of the Chipko movement spread by women talking about them at water places and in markets. Women decided they were not powerless; there were actions they could take and a movement that would support them. Songs and slogans were created.

"In one the contractor says:

'You foolish village women, do you know what these forest bear? Resin, timber, and therefore foreign exchange!'

The women answer:

'Yes, we know. What do the forests bear? Soil, water, and pure air, Soil, water, and pure air.'" Reese (2005, para. 5)

In 1987, Chipko was chosen for a Right to Livelihood Award, known as the "alternate Nobel" prize honor.

British Punk

A now-classic cultural studies analysis of a subgroup is Dick Hebdige's 1979 study of British punk youth culture. He described the use of random, mass-produced objects such as dog collars, safety pins, and school uniforms as a parody of consumerism.

Hebdige dates the origin of punk in the music press to the summer of 1976 as an alliance of diverse and superficial incompatible music traditions reproduced on the visual level in a clothing style. He interprets punk culture, in part, as a British White working-class "translation" of Black ethnicity and, in part, as the intentional self-construction of "otherness," which challenged, on a symbolic level, class and gender stereotypes.

Hebdige shows how subgroups develop a style through the intentional use of clothing, dance, argot, and music. Punks repositioned and recontextualized commodities by subverting the conventional uses and inventing new ones. It's how commodities are used in the subgroup that marks the subgroup off from the dominant culture. Lavatory chains became jewelry; school uniforms were covered with graffiti; sexual fetish clothing became street clothes; dance became robotic. What appeared as chaos was actually orderly.

Hebdige acknowledges that not all punks were aware of the signification on which the subgroup was based. The original or first wave of self-conscious innovators were aware and committed. The later "plastic punks" participated in the subgroup as a distraction from home, school, and work. Hebdige shows that the subgroup declined when punk's visual and verbal vocabulary became reassigned by the dominant culture as mass-produced commodities (clothing and music) and relabeled (boys wearing lipstick became "just kids dressing up" and girls in rubber dresses became "daughters just like ours").

Punk provides an interesting example of cultural diffusion. When record labels and music stores have surplus CDs, they often cut a little square notch out of the plastic case that then marks them as "remainder" products to be sold very cheaply. In China, punk was a rarity until Asian record labels and retailers trashed thousands of these surplus CDs, known in China as *dakou*. Through a network of scavengers and middlemen, these dakou CDs appeared in Chinese alternative record stores. The dakou CDs served as inspiration for launching a whole new generation of Chinese punk and Chinese punk rock bands who often sing in English to avoid Chinese censorship. And—just as in Britain—plastic punks now buy expensive punk clothing in Beijing.

Punk originated in London in the mid-1970s, recognizable by visual appearance and anarchic behavior. Scores of benefit punk concerts are held for social causes and medical research. Some punk bands run homeless shelters, mobilize youth to vote, and try to break down racial barriers.

Some bloggers suggest that social media is the punk of today. The mass market music industry of the 1970s was controlled and conservative. Punk of the 1970s was raw, confrontational, and passionate. It was about getting noticed and getting represented. Punk found niche audiences who listened and supported the artists. Their thesis is that today's social media have become the media for independent voices (Foster, 2011).

Corporate Cultures

One popular business buzzword of the 1980s was corporate culture. It has been defined as "the way we do things around here," or the set of values, goals, and priorities encouraged through the policies and procedures of the organization. Companies can act like cultures and present the same communication challenges (Deal & Kennedy, 1982; Pacanowsky & O'Donnell-Trujillo, 1982; L. Putnam & Pacanowsky, 1983; Sypher, 1985).

In Chapter 1, you read that Hofstede (1994) classified the elements of culture as symbols, heroes, rituals, and values. Organizations can have their own symbols: their own argot, their own dress codes, and status symbols recognized by insiders only. Organizational heroes are those people, dead or alive, who serve as models of the "ideal employee" or the "ideal manager" for behavior within the organization. Founders of organizations sometimes become mythical heroes later on, and incredible deeds are ascribed to them: Thomas Watson, Jr., at IBM, Ray Kroc at McDonald's, Walt Disney at Disney Productions, and so on. Rituals in organizations include celebrations and also the many activities common to the organization; for example, meetings, memos, who may speak to whom, who can be late for meetings.

Chapter 1 also described cultures as having myths. Corporate rituals can take the form of myths within organizations. Ruth Smith and Eric Eisenberg (1987) have shown, for example, how "drama" and "family" are important myths at Disneyland.

Finally, organizations can have their own values. Hofstede (1994) makes it clear that we enter work organizations as adults with most of our values firmly entrenched, but we do become socialized to the practices of the work environment. For many organizations, the value systems were established by the personality of the leader: These were value-shaping leaders with visions to excite thousands of employees.

IBM's Thomas J. Watson, Jr., (1963) wrote an entire book about values. He observed:

> Consider any great organization—one that has lasted over the years—I think you will find that it owes its resiliency not to its form of organization or administrative skills, but to the power of what we call beliefs and the appeal these beliefs have for its people. This then is my thesis: I firmly believe that any organization, in order to survive and achieve success, must have a sound set of beliefs on which it premises all its policies and actions. (p. 5)

But does having clearly defined and communicated values affect the profitability of a business? The book *In Search of Excellence* (Peters, 1982) argues that the better performing companies all have a well-defined set of values. The poorly performing companies either have no explicit values or only quantified ones, such as a "percentage increase over last year." The book makes it clear that a well-defined set of values motivates and serves to direct the behavior of thousands of employees.

Corporate culture became a major factor in recent corporate mergers. Exxon, an otherwise low-profile company known for the Valdez oil spill, merged with Mobil, known for sponsoring *Masterpiece Theatre* and for full-page ads expressing views on various issues. Daimler-Benz and Chrysler formed a postmerger integration team to deal with issues as far-ranging as language, clothing, clashing values (quality

> ## Global Voices
>
> When several workers at Disneyland's Jungle Cruise lost their jobs for telling their own jokes with contemporary references instead of following the company's official script, Disneyland issued a brief statement:
>
> Our philosophy is that Disneyland is very much a theatrical house or stage, which means we view our park as having both onstage and backstage presence. We entertain our guests with quality family entertainment and put on performances every day. Our goal is to deliver a consistent quality show daily.

vs. efficiency), labor-management relations, spending priorities, and even the German *vesper,* or employee beer break. And Time-Warner's suited executives met AOL's more casual dress style in what would prove to be an ill-fated merger that was to have brought Internet technology to Time-Warner.

Case Study: Southwest Airlines

Herb Kelleher, an attorney in a San Antonio, Texas, law firm, along with Rollin King, developed the idea for Southwest Airlines in 1966. The meeting at which the idea was born is now part of the company's mythology, as the story is told and retold like a legend. The plan, penciled on a cocktail napkin, was to establish the airline as an intrastate carrier between the cities of Dallas, Houston, and San Antonio. It overcame overwhelming resistance from the major interstate carriers, but it was probably that resistance itself that helped shape the character of the company as reflecting efficiency, sound business decisions, and fun.

The Southwest corporate culture has evolved through the years—undoubtedly influenced by the gregarious, self-deprecating, chain-smoking, whiskey-drinking Kelleher, who was known to dress as Elvis and arrive at Southwest parties on a Harley. Although no longer in a management role, Chairman Emeritus Kelleher still has the adulation of the Southwest workforce. Now, Employees eagerly await the unveiling of current CEO Gary Kelly's Halloween costume every year. The strong Southwest corporate culture is carefully reinforced in its hiring policy. Recruiters look for a certain "Southwest Spirit" in every job candidate. Southwest rejects most job applicants to find those who will not only fit, but who will thrive, within the Southwest culture.

Southwest Airlines Former CEO Herb Kelleher

Former Southwest Airlines CEO Herb Kelleher laughs as he recalls many of the good times he has had at Southwest Airlines, one of the biggest success stories the commercial airline industry has ever known.

The Southwest story was turned into a children's book, *Gumwrappers and Goggles* by Winifred Barnum. In the story, a small jet, TJ Love, is sued by two larger jets to stop him from flying. It just happens that TJ Love's colors are those of Southwest and the two larger jets are colored in Braniff and Continental's colors. The attorney who helps TJ Love resembles Herb Kelleher. The book was adapted into a stage musical, *Show Your Spirit,* that played only in cities serviced by Southwest (http://www.poohbooli.com/bio.html)

Photos of most of its 35,000-plus employees cover the walls of its corporate headquarters building in Dallas. A 100-member employee "Culture Committee" devises all sorts of celebrations and incentives to keep the Southwest Spirit alive. Southwest has grown to carry more passengers than any other carrier in the United States. It has one of the youngest fleets, the best safety record, and too numerous to count awards for customer service. In fact, the company capitalizes the "E" in Employee, and the "C" in Customer, to emphasize the importance of both. Continually profitable, Southwest was cited by a 1993 government study as the principal force behind fundamental changes in the airline transport business.

FOCUS ON CULTURE 14.1

On Southwest's Culture

Others can copy our business and operating models, but they can't copy our Employees, and for over 34 years, the People of Southwest Airlines have been proving that statement true on a 24/7/365 basis. Our Corporate Culture is a big reason for that difference.

Admittedly, as we have grown to 31,000+ Employees, it has been much harder to keep everyone on the same Culture "page." Although the most effective method of sharing our Culture is from one Employee to another, our Corporate Culture Committee and the Local Culture Committees in each location help this process. In turn, a group in my office, Culture Activities, coordinates our celebration of the traits that make our Culture unique, and some of those traits are Golden Rule behavior; the Warrior Spirit; Servant Leadership; and FUN. Culture Committee Members hold events like "Lounge LUV" for Crew Bases; "Maintenance Visits" for Mechanics; "Reservations Appreciation" at Reservations Centers; and airport "E-Team Visits." These events celebrate a job done well and provide encouragement, fun, and food. Local Culture Committees do much the same thing in their locations to recognize and assist Coworkers.

In addition to supporting all of the various Culture Committees, the Headquarters Culture Activities Team coordinates large Companywide events like our annual Awards Banquet, Spirit Parties, and yearly Messages to the Field.

Besides all of the fun "stuff" listed above, our formal Culture programs strive to instill in each Employee a sense of our proud history and tradition of excellence. By embracing our past and knowing "who we were," we can meet the challenges of the future and make the "who we are" that much stronger. It is vital that we treat each Customer and Coworker in the same manner in which we want to be treated. When we see how our Southwest predecessors banded together as a Team to ensure our survival, their Warrior Spirit becomes ours. Embracing our tradition of Leaders Serving others from the Heart, if you will, helps our future Leaders to enlarge upon this tradition. Our Culture, as exemplified in our Employees, really is that intangible, "uncloneable" Southwest difference.

The concept of Family is also critically important to our Culture, and this is the time of year for Family. We work very hard to enable you to be with your Family during the Holidays. As you sit with your Family around the Thanksgiving table, we hope that you will reflect upon your blessings, and we want you to know that we will be counting you, our Valued Customers, among our blessings around our Thanksgiving tables.

—Colleen Barrett, President, 2001–2008

Source: From *Southwest Airlines Spirit*, (Barrett, 2005).

Case Study: Google

Google was founded in 1998 by two Stanford graduate students Larry Page and Sergey Brin. Just as it was Herb Kelleher at Southwest who established Southwest's corporate culture, it was Page and Brin's outlook that dominates "how things are done at Google." Google is organized as a "flat" company with a small middle management and a hands-on upper management. The result is that Google's core employees have autonomy, but work with a single unifying philosophy.

On corporate teams everyone has equal authority. In its early years, new product ideas moved forward without any formal process. Now that it's a giant with 20,000 employees, Google has begun to hold regular meetings at which employees are encouraged to present new ideas directly to Larry Page and Sergey Brin.

FOCUS ON CULTURE 14.2

The Google Culture

Though Google has grown a lot since it opened in 1998, we still maintain a small company feel.

At lunchtime, almost everyone eats in the office café, sitting at whatever table has an opening and enjoying conversations with Googlers from different teams. Our commitment to innovation depends on everyone being comfortable sharing ideas and opinions. Every employee is a hands-on contributor, and everyone wears several hats. Because we believe that each Googler is an equally important part of our success, no one hesitates to pose questions directly to Larry or Sergey in our weekly all-hands ("TGIF") meetings—or spike a volleyball across the net at a corporate officer.

We are aggressively inclusive in our hiring, and we favor ability over experience. We have offices around the world and dozens of languages are spoken by Google staffers, from Turkish to Telugu. The result is a team that reflects the global audience Google serves. When not at work, Googlers pursue interests from cross-country cycling to wine tasting, from flying to frisbee.

As we continue to grow, we are always looking for those who share a commitment to creating search perfection and having a great time doing it.

Source: http://www.google.com/about/corporate/company/culture.html.

SEXUAL ORIENTATION AS A BASIS FOR SUBGROUPS

In this section we first revisit the concept of othering and then explore current attitudes about sexual orientation worldwide. As attitudes vary widely, you will look at some of the cultural bases for that variance and some of the consequences of othering.

Sexual Orientation and Othering

Othering applies to subgroups just as it does to subcultures. This is particularly true in the case of sexual orientation.

The language people use to describe their and others' gender identity and sexual orientation varies widely by location and over time. It is easier to trace such a change over time in the United States. Words and symbols used pejoratively by the dominating culture were claimed and embraced by the subgroup as an important part in the development of positive self-esteem. The turning point in gay male and lesbian identity was the June 28, 1969, riot at Stonewall, a gay bar located in New York's Greenwich Village, in which patrons fought back against the police raiding the bar. Previous to that event, people at a gay bar might have tried to hide or otherwise escape police recognition. After that event with the birth of the gay liberation movement as an active political force, it became "OK to be gay" (Katz, 1976).

The words *dyke* and *faggot* now became symbols of gay pride. In a like manner, the word lesbian changed from a medical word to a label of pride. Queer Nation, a spin-off of ACT-UP (AIDS Coalition to Unleash Power), used the chant "We're here, we're queer, we're fabulous—get used to it." This self-labeling had a clear political utility (Epstein, 1990) in efforts to gain legal protections (D. H. Miller, 1998; R. R. Smith & Windes, 1997).

In the same way that word symbols are given positive meanings, nonverbal symbols facilitate group identification. For example, the pink triangle had its origin in Hitler's concentration camps to label homosexuals. (Lesbians—and other women—were not judged to have any decision-making power or sovereignty and so were forced to wear black triangles, which labeled them "antisocials.") The rainbow flag, which had its first use in gay parades in San Francisco, is often seen now to identify the gay community.

Some individuals may not accept the identity their behavior would lead others to assume. For example, individuals may be "same-sex practicing" without accepting an identity associated by others with that behavior. The label gay came to refer in a positive way to individuals who form primary emotional attachments to members of the same sex and who value one another. One can be gay and not be sexual. Being gay means sharing certain beliefs and values with others. The same things later happened in other cultures, such as in Germany, with the word *schwul* and in Sweden with the word *boeg*. However, it's impossible to fully reflect the worldwide diversity of labels and behaviors associated with gender identity and sexual orientation.

Rejecting All Labels

Non-White, non-middle-class lesbians and gay men and people of sexualities of all kinds began to challenge the idea of a single gay/lesbian identity (Lorde, 1984). The label—both externally applied and later redefined—categorized a group only on the basis of one dimension of sexual orientation. Identity politics imposed "a unitary identity upon gay men, lesbians, and bisexuals [that] Identity and Subgroups is alienating to those who do not fit into the mold constructed by the leaders of the movement" (Slagle, 1995, p. 86).

Queer theory challenges the idea of a single identity and rejects the categorization of heterosexuality and homosexuality. Queer theory argues that identities are multiple (sexual orientation and race and class and gender and so forth). Accepting such a label, even as an indicator of pride, can be restrictive in defining self (Fuss, 1991; Warner, 1993).

FOCUS ON THEORY 14.2

Queer theorists (Yep, Lovaas, & Elia, 2003) challenge the concepts of binary categories such as female or male or homosexual or heterosexual, arguing that identities are not as restricted as suggested by binary categories. The focus in queer theory, then, is on identity as voluntary or as choice. Queer theorists advocate for social change by incorporating race, ethnicity, social class, and personal experience into theory and discussion. Queer theory suggests that every part of our identity is fluid and mixed. The use of the term *queer* itself is an example of queer theory. The meaning of the term has evolved from shame, to bonding, to sanction.

Robert Reid-Pharr (2002) raised a question for queer scholars: "Specifically, I wonder what we might encounter if we shifted our inquiry away from the question of how we 'subalterns" can make ourselves heard within 'dominant society' to how all of us—all Americans, all members of the human family—can take up the task of fashioning that society; indeed, how we can talk to one another. That is the next step for queer studies to take" (p. B9).

Attitudes Toward Sexual Orientation

The Pew Global Attitudes Project is a series of worldwide public opinion surveys encompassing a broad array of subjects ranging from people's assessments of their own lives to their views about the current state of the world and important issues of the day. Table 14.1 reports responses to the question if homosexuality should be accepted or rejected.

Table 14.1 Acceptance/Rejection of Homosexuality Worldwide

County	Percentage accepting	Percentage rejecting
Sweden	86	9
France	83	17
Czech Republic	83	16
Spain	82	9
Germany	81	17
Argentina	72	21
Britain	71	21
Canada	70	21
Slovakia	66	29
Italy	65	23
Brazil	65	30
Chile	64	31
Mexico	60	31

County	Percentage accepting	Percentage rejecting
Peru	51	43
United States	49	41
Japan	49	28
Venezuela	47	50
Poland	45	41
Bolivia	44	49
Bulgaria	39	38
Israel	38	50
South Africa	28	64
Russia	20	64
Ukraine	19	69
South Korea	18	77
Lebanon	18	79
China	17	69
Turkey	14	57
Côte d'Ivoire	11	89
India	10	81
Palestinian Ter.	9	58
Malaysia	8	83
Kuwait	6	85
Jordan	6	89
Bangladesh	4	84
Ghana	4	94
Indonesia	3	95
Tanzania	3	95
Kenya	3	96
Uganda	3	96
Senegal	3	97
Ethiopia	2	97
Nigeria	2	97
Mali	1	98
Egypt	1	95

Source: Pew Research Center (2007).

A clear majority believe that homosexuality should be accepted in Western Europe. Opinions are divided in North America. Seven in 10 Canadians believe society should accept homosexuality, compared to roughly half of U.S. residents. In Africa, Asia and the Middle East, attitudes toward homosexuals are negative. In 8 of 10 African countries, less than 5% feel society should accept homosexuality. Japan is the only country in Asia in which a plurality (49%) believe it should be accepted (Pew Research Center, 2007).

Hofstede (1998) reports that the masculinity cultural dimension is negatively related to the acceptance of homosexuality. Those cultures with a high acceptance of masculinity tend to be less accepting of homosexuality. Ross (1989) surveyed 600 gay men in Australia, Finland, Ireland, and Sweden. Ross reported that young gay men had more problems accepting a gay sexual orientation in Ireland and Australia, less in Finland, and least in Sweden. Ross ranks these societies in homophobia in the same order. Ross's study does tend to support Hofstede's hypothesis in that Ross's ranking on homophobia is also the order of these countries on Hofstede's masculinity dimension. Homosexuality tends to be perceived as a threat in masculine cultures (Bolton, 1994) and considered a fact of life in feminine cultures.

In 2008, France introduced the first declaration on gay rights read in the United Nations General Assembly. France used the format of a declaration because it did not have the support for an official resolution. The nonbinding measure sought to decriminalize homosexuality and won the support of 66 countries in the United Nations General Assembly. The declaration had support from European and Latin America countries. Those opposing the declaration included the United States, Russia, China, the Roman Catholic Church and members of the Organization of the Islamic Conference (Macfarquhar, 2008).

In June 2011, the United Nations endorsed rights of gay, lesbian, and transgender people for the first time when the Human Rights Council adopted a resolution expressing "grave concern at acts of violence and discrimination, in all regions of the world, committed against individuals because of their sexual orientation and gender identity." The resolution established a formal U.N. process to document human rights abuses against gays, including discriminatory laws and acts of violence.

The resolution was put forward by South Africa. The 23 states voting in favor included the United States, the European Union countries, Japan, Korea, Brazil, and other Latin American countries. The 19 states voting against included Russia, Saudi Arabia, Nigeria, and Pakistan. China, Burkina Faso, and Zambia abstained. Consistent with the Pew attitude survey in Table 14.1, some African and Muslim countries strongly opposed the resolution.

The same division of countries can be seen as to where same-sex marriage is legal. Canada and a growing number of European countries have legalized same-sex marriage: Sweden, Norway, Netherlands, Belgium, Spain, Portugal, and Iceland. Same-sex marriage is also legal in Mexico, South Africa, and some U.S. states. Civil unions are legal in Argentina, Finland; France, Germany, the United Kingdom, Switzerland, Australia, New Zealand, Israel, and some U.S. states.

Let's look at the cultural basis for opposition in African and Muslim countries.

Cultural Bases for Attitudes

According to the BBC homosexuality is outlawed in 38 African countries. In Mauritania, northern Nigeria, and Sudan, homosexuality can be punishable by death. In Uganda, homosexuals can be imprisoned for life. The one exception on the continent is South Africa. Not only did South Africa introduce the United Nations 2011 resolution, its constitution guarantees gay and lesbian rights and legalizes same-sex marriage.

Some Muslim scholars refer to the story in the Koran of the people of Lut (Sodom and Gomorrah) who were destroyed by Allah because they engaged in carnal acts between men. The Arabic words for homosexual behavior (*liwat*) and for a homosexual (*luti*) are both derived from the name Lut (Dynes, 1990). These scholars content that Islam disallows homosexuality and ordains capital punishment for homosexuals. And, in fact, homosexual activity is a crime in most Muslim-majority countries. In Iran, Mauritania, Saudi Arabia, Somalia, Sudan, Yemen, and parts of Nigeria, homosexual activity can be punished by death (ILGA, 2009). Islamic jurists have referenced *hadith* (sayings of Muhammad) and *akhbar* (accounts of his life), which are clear in their condemning of homosexual behavior (Dynes, 1990).

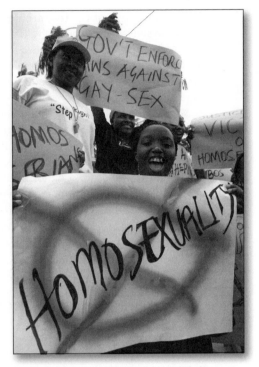

Campaigning against homosexuality at a rally in Kampala, Uganda in 2007.

Consequences of Othering

Among the consequences of othering are the potential for emotional and physical harm to those being labeled. The emotional and physical harm to those labeled by sexual orientation has been studied in the United States as homophobia. Another consequence, though, is the potential for alliances and a strengthening of a community identity among those being so labeled through traditional and social media.

Homophobia

The irrational fear of gay men and lesbians is called homophobia (Pharr, 1988). It is related to heterosexism, the assumption that the world is and must be heterosexual, and patriarchy, the enforced belief in heterosexual male dominance and control.

Homophobia is a learned attitude. Many historical studies have shown that homosexuals were not feared or despised in the past. Some point to the 20th-century psychiatrists, who created the paradigm of thinking of various forms of sexualities as diseases as resulting in negative stereotypes. Historian George Chauncey (1985) argues that the Cold War era of fear created the unfounded negative stereotype of homosexuals as subversive security risks.

In 1969, the year of the Stonewall riot, there were no policies, laws, or ordinances prohibiting discrimination against lesbians and gay men. In fact, in 1967, the New York State Liquor Authority forbade bars to serve homosexuals, 49 states had laws banning sodomy, and there were no hate crime laws.

Media portrayal of gay men and lesbians contributed to stereotyping. The Motion Picture Production Code of 1930 banned all mention of homosexuality in U.S. films for more than 30 years. Russo (1987) has shown how the portrayal of lesbians and gay men in film has, until recently, been derisive and as victims.

The early 1990s saw a nationwide rise in hate crimes against gay individuals, which has been attributed in part to increased visibility and activism in the gay community. These hate crimes include harassment, vandalism, assault, and police abuse: Lesbian and gay high school students are the targets of bullying, teasing, and violence.

Discrimination continues in employment. Only 11 states have laws that prohibit job discrimination against lesbians and gay men. Many major U.S. corporations, such as Harley-Davidson, IBM, Kodak, Time-Warner, and 3M, have policies banning discrimination based on sexual orientation. Gay activists argue that discrimination based on sexual orientation is still widespread. In 1991, Cracker Barrel Old Country Stores, a firm based in Lebanon, Tennessee, that runs restaurants along many Southeast interstates, fired several employees for being gay. The restaurant chain defended its actions by citing "traditional American values" and declared in a memo that it "is perceived to be inconsistent with those of our customer base to continue to employ individuals in our operating units whose sexual preferences fail to demonstrate normal heterosexual values which have been the foundation of families in our society" ("Decision to fire," 1991, para. 2). The restaurant chain later discontinued its practice, though gay activists say the rule still exists.

Problems that gay men and lesbians have faced in the workplace include being refused positions based on the perception of being gay, receiving anonymous harassing phone calls and letters, and not being promoted or retained when sexual orientation becomes known. Most discrimination against gays in employment in the 1990s was disguised. Employers who wanted to terminate a gay employee first found other reasons to disguise the termination. In early 2000, the Pentagon released a study of 72,000 troops. The results showed that 37% have witnessed or been targets of gay harassment. More than 80% reported hearing offensive speech, derogatory names, or jokes at least once over the past year, and more than 85% believed that antigay comments are tolerated at military installations or aboard ships (Richter, 2000). Just because homophobia is not public doesn't mean it isn't there. In 2011 a Southwest Airlines pilot had accidently turned on his microphone and his true beliefs were broadcast over an air traffic control frequency. Referring to flight attendants he said: *"Eleven f*****g over the top f*****g homosexuals and a granny. Eleven. I mean, think of the odds of that. I thought I was in Chicago, which was party-land. . . . After that, it was just a continuous stream of gays and granny"* (Johnson, 2011, para. 7).

Gay persons have experienced discrimination even in churches. In 1990, three Lutheran ministers were suspended for being "practicing homosexuals," a phrase that has developed a unique meaning. Most lesbians and gay men understand it to mean that one can be accepted if one doesn't "act gay"—that is, if without acknowledging an important part of one's identity. Their congregations refused to rescind the ordinations, and the ministers were later expelled from the church.

Traditional and Social Media

In countries with no acceptance of homosexuality, even private media use can lead to prosecution. In Egypt in 2002 and 2003, gay men were arrested and tried after having agreed to meet other men who they contacted through the Internet. The other men were security officers or police informants. The private Internet conversations were used as evidence against the gay men and their names were published in the media. In India in 2006, four men were arrested after the police traced the phone number of a gay man they got from a gay website. The police then forced him to call several of his friends who were arrested on charges of operating a "gay racket" on the Internet, as well as of belonging to and an "international gay club" and of engaging in "unnatural" sex (Amnesty International, 2008).

In countries with a greater acceptance of homosexuality, traditional media and social media can reinforce subgroup identity. This can more easily be seen in the United States. Specialized print media have long existed for the U.S. gay community and serve to reinforce its existence, just as they do with other cultures and subgroups. Lesbian literature has been more prominent than other forms of lesbian media and has reflected a feminist perspective. Gay male literature of the 1960s and 1970s by such authors as James Baldwin, Truman Capote, Gore Vidal, and Tennessee Williams generally depicted gay men as social outsiders. Later writers, such as Andrew Holleran, Armistead Maupin, and Edmund White, created positive characters functioning within a gay community.

Local newspapers across the United States focused on community events and contributed to a shared identity, as did national magazines. More recently, gay male magazines focused on human rights issues. They support responsibility, caring for and supporting one another, and maintaining identity in the face of AIDS in a largely indifferent society. It was the gay press—not the popular press or the medical community—that brought AIDS to the attention of gay men, and as a consequence, the spread of AIDS declined in the gay community while growing dramatically in other segments of society (Fejes & Petrich, 1993).

Market research has told advertisers that 6% to 10% of the U.S. market is gay. Surveys showed gays to be better educated, with 60% of those in the gay market holding a college degree, but less affluent than the general population. Seagrams's research of the psychographics of gay publication readers identified gay men as "fashion conscious and trend setting." Market research also has shown that gay men and lesbians are very brand loyal to companies that advertise first in the gay press.

Gay magazines have drawn advertising from car companies such as Saab and Saturn, from the travel industry such as Virgin Atlantic and American Express, from liquor companies such as Absolut vodka and Tanqueray gin, and from mainstream companies such as AT&T and MCI; Chase Bank, Chemical Bank, and Citibank; Evian and Perrier; Flowers Direct and Geffen records; and Quality Paperback Books and Viking/Penguin Press.

General-circulation magazines run "gay-vague" advertising as well as advertising using homosexuality as a means to draw attention. Seagrams once marketed Boodles gin with a bar mirror that featured "Six Famous Men of History" etched on it: Oscar Wilde, Lawrence of Arabia, Walt Whitman, Edgar Allan Poe, Ludwig van Beethoven, and Edgar Degas. Probably, most nonlesbians and nongay men did not recognize the six as homosexual, but the gay community did.

A 2010 survey of social media use in the United States by Harris Interactive revealed that the lesbian, gay, bisexual, and transgender community is more active on social networks than nongays and nonlesbians. Some of the specific findings were:

- 54% of the gay men and lesbians surveyed read some type of blog, compared to only 40% of heterosexuals;
- 73% of gay and lesbian adults are members of Facebook, compared to 65% of heterosexuals;
- 29% gay men and lesbians reported they were members of Twitter, while only 15% of heterosexual adults said they were; and
- 55% of gay men and lesbians say they visit social network sites at least once a day, while only 41% of heterosexual adults shared this frequency (Harris Interactive, 2010).

From Separation to Assimilation

We have seen that the language people use to describe their and others' gender identity and sexual orientation varies widely by location and over time. You have read about the effect of location on culture. We turn now to a consideration of how a subgroup's status within the dominant culture can change over time.

Some argue that some subgroups—particularly lesbians and gay men—can be studied as one would study an immigrant group in terms of acculturation. To apply this perspective, first we will look at the evidence of gay men and lesbians being treated as a separate or segregated group in the United States and now becoming either an integrated or assimilated group.

Evidence of Separate Status

You read earlier in this chapter that argot is an indicator of a subgroup. A strong, secret argot is evidence of separate status. In 1976, Joseph J. Hayes described "gayspeak" as the language one acquires when entering the gay community. He identified three settings in which gayspeak is important: secret or threatening situations (that is, in the presence of people who are not gay), social settings (that is, in the presence of other gays), and radical gay activist settings.

Although not all lesbians and gay men recognize gayspeak, its acceptance by some suggests a dual persona; that is, using one language in the gay community and another language in the gay subgroup community.

A second indicator of separate status would be that subgroup members could hide their identity until they felt comfortable revealing their identity. Accepting the label *gay* for oneself is part of the communication process of coming out. Communication scholar Larry Gross (1993) wrote, "The preponderance of lesbian and gay political rhetoric, both within the community and externally, reflects an essentialist position, insisting that one doesn't 'choose' to be gay, but recognizes and 'accepts' that one is so" (p. 113). Before Stonewall, coming out was a great risk that you took as it could affect your career and family relationships. Today, coming out is a positive act of self-expression and identity. You might feel different from others, but with publicly disclosing the reason comes an acceptance of the label *homosexual* or *gay*. Now everyone knows, and some will treat you differently. That different treatment confirms your personal identification as a gay person.

INTEGRATION OR ASSIMILATION OF SUBGROUPS

The change from separate or segregated status to integrated or assimilated status can be seen in today's discussions within the subgroup.

In a 1998 essay, Gabriel Rotello first framed the issue similar to one of immigration, as one of assimilationists versus the radicals. Assimilationists argue that lesbians and gay men should be "just like everybody else," whereas radicals argue that gay men and lesbians should maintain a separate culture. Rotello contends that cultural separation occurs only when society stigmatizes a group. As long as society in some way stigmatizes gay men and lesbians, a separate culture will exist. Or, as Harris (1997) wrote, if gay men and lesbians become too mainstream, what it means to be gay will be lost. Martin Duberman, distinguished professor of history at City University of New York and a pioneer in gay studies, also raises concerns about assimilation: "National organizations within the gay world are presenting themselves as just plain folks—'We're ordinary citizens. We're just like everybody else. So let us in. We're going to behave just the way you want us to behave.' As a people we've had a different historical experience, just as Black people have. The mainstream needs to know what we know" (Ricci & Biederman, 2004, p. B1).

FOCUS ON CULTURE 14.3

Most gays and lesbians, it seems, want to live, healthy, prosperous, fulfilled lives, pretty much the way their friends, relatives, and neighbors do. This perfectly reasonable desire is what is denounced as "assimilation."

But the word *assimilation* is somewhat disingenuous if it's meant to imply that gays are thereby sacrificing something that is part of their natural character or essential nature....

Much the opposite, in fact. More and more gays are insisting that they be accepted for who they are wherever they happen to be and however they want to live.

Better words for this process might be *inclusion* or *integration*—words that suggest that a person is regarded and treated equally at the same time he remains fully himself.

Source: Based on Varnell (2000).

Gay novelist Edmund White also has commented on the shift from separate to integrated or assimilated: "You go to a pride march and it's just like every other civic parade with its crass commercialism" (Hallett, 2003, p. 38). Suzanna Danuta Walters had the final word: "The real change will be when we don't talk about acceptance" (p. 38).

A FINAL WORD

If you read this book from the beginning, you have come to the end. You have studied how culture affects perception, how language and nonverbal communication are part of culture, and how language and nonverbal communication along with other factors can be barriers in effective intercultural communication. You have studied cultural values, including how they affect the role of women in societies. You have studied what happens when cultures come in contact and when people emigrate from one country to another. And you have studied how subcultures and, in this chapter, subgroups are like cultures.

The world has changed dramatically from when in 1405 the Chinese eunuch admiral Cheng Ho commanded 62 ships and explored Vietnam, Java, and Malacca, and then headed west across the Indian Ocean to cities on the southwest coast of India. And the world has changed dramatically from when in 1768 the British James Cook sailed in the *Endeavour* to Tahiti, New Zealand, Australia, and the Dutch East Indies. Both explorers encountered cultures with languages and behaviors that may have seemed new and strange to them.

Have the centuries of contact among cultures reduced the challenges presented to Cheng Ho and James Cook? Has our understanding of the planet changed over the centuries?

In the capsule on humanity's first voyage to the moon, looking back at the earth Neil Armstrong realized he could extend his arm and block his vision of the earth with his thumb. He was later asked if that made him feel like a giant. Armstrong responded: "No, it made me feel really, really small." Other astronauts who followed Armstrong made similar observations. Bill Anders described the earth as "very delicate." Stu Roosa said, "It's the abject smallness of the Earth that gets you." Another said, "Everything that I know, my family, my possessions, my friends, and my country, it's all down there on that little thing. And it's so insignificant in this great big vastness of space" (all quoted in Nelson, 2009, p. 274).

Later Neil Armstrong observed:

> From our position on the Earth it is difficult to observe where the Earth is and where it's going, or what its future course might be. Hopefully, we'll be able to make some people step back and reconsider their mission in the Universe, to think of themselves as a group of people who constitute the crew of a spaceship going through the universe. If you're going to run a spaceship, you've got to be pretty cautious about how you use your resources, how you use your crew, and how you treat your spacecraft. (Nelson, p. 327)

Perhaps our modern day explorers have helped set the objective for intercultural communication studies.

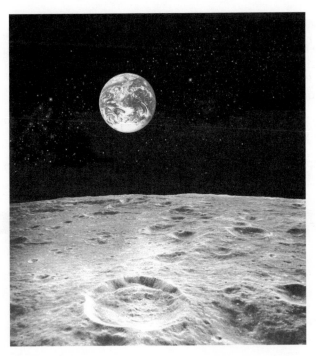

SUMMARY

While the Sapir-Whorf hypothesis establishes the relationship between cultures and languages, the same can be true for subgroups but on the level of vocabulary. The specialized vocabulary identifies the subgroup and establishes the group's boundaries. The specialized vocabulary of subgroups is known as *argot*. While social class is more properly considered a subculture, studies of blue-collar, low-income Whites on the near south side of Chicago in the early 1970s are the best example of a study that focuses on the communication behavior of the group. The British punk subgroup was about getting represented. Punk found niche audiences who listened and supported the artists.

Organizations can have their own symbols: their own argot, their own dress codes, and status symbols recognized by insiders only. And because of this, we can speak of organizations as corporate cultures. Herb Kelleher developed Southwest Airline's corporate culture, which has been cited as one of the reasons for its success. Larry Page and Sergey Brin developed Google's corporate culture.

Subgroups based on sexual orientation have been examples of othering in many cultures. The Pew Global Attitudes Project reported responses to the question if homosexuality should be accepted or rejected. A clear majority in Western Europe believe that homosexuality should be accepted. In Africa, Asia, and the Middle East, attitudes toward homosexuals are negative. In eight of 10 African countries, less than 5% feel society should accept homosexuality. Hofstede (1998) reports that the masculinity cultural dimension is negatively related to the acceptance of homosexuality. Homosexuality tends to be perceived as a threat in masculine cultures and considered a fact of life in feminine cultures. In the United States and some other cultures, lesbian and gay men have moved over time from separation to assimilation.

DISCUSSION QUESTIONS

1. Describe a subgroup you have identified with in terms of its argot, media use, and values.
2. How can corporations present the same communication challenges as cultures?
3. Give examples of the importance of labeling and identity with a subgroup.
4. Give examples of specialized media use by a subgroup.
5. Can a subgroup continue to exist as a subgroup under assimilation pressures?

KEY TERMS

argot 367	gay 377	lesbian 377
cant 367	homophobia 381	participant observer 369
coming out 385	homosexuals 377	slang 367
corporate culture 385	jargon 367	

READINGS

All readings are from *Intercultural Communication: A Global Reader* (Jandt, 2004).

Geert Hofstede, "Business Cultures" (p. 8)

Ashleigh C. Merritt and Robert L. Helmreich, "Human Factors on the Flight Deck: The Influence of National Culture" (p. 13)

Crispin Thurlow, "Naming the 'Outsider Within': Homophobic Pejoratives and the Verbal Abuse of Lesbian, Gay and Bisexual High-School Pupils" (p. 189)

STUDENT STUDY SITE

Visit the student study site at www.sagepub.com/jandt7e for these additional learning tools:

- Web Resources
- Audio and Video Links
- SAGE journal articles
- eFlashcards
- Web Quizzes
- Sample Essays

GLOSSARY

Abaya: A long black cloak worn in public by Muslim women

Aboriginal: The indigenous peoples of Australia (often applied to indigenous peoples in other countries)

Acculturation: An immigrant's learning and adopting the norms and values of the new host culture (*see also* Cultural adaptation)

Activity orientation: Use of time for self-expression and play, self-improvement and development, and work

Adaptation potential: An individual's possible success in adapting to a new culture

Amae: Japanese for a nurturing concern for and dependence on another

Anabaptist: A 16th-century Reformation movement that insisted that only adult baptism was valid and held that true Christians should not bear arms, use force, or hold government office

Anxiety: A diffuse state of being uneasy or worried about what may happen

Arabic The literary language of the Koran; the language and culture of the Arabs

Arabs: Ethnic group that originally spread Islam; the Semitic peoples originally from Arabia and now living throughout the Near East, North Africa, and the Arabian peninsula

Argot: The specialized vocabulary of subgroups

Artifact: An object from a culture

Assimilation: An immigrant's giving up the original culture identity and moving into full participation in the new culture

Asylee: A person living outside the country of nationality who is unable or unwilling to return because of persecution or a well-founded fear of persecution (*see also* Refugee)

Authoritarian personality: An individual who tends to overgeneralize and think in bipolar terms and who is highly conventional, moralistic, and uncritical of higher authority

Back translation: Translating from one language into another and then translating back into the original to compare the result to avoid errors in translation

Beachy Amish: A group that separated from the more conservative Amish over the use of automobiles and modern farm equipment

Biculturalism: The ability to function in two cultures

Burka: A loose garment worn by some Muslim women covering the entire body with a veiled opening for the eyes

Caliph: The secular and religious head of a Muslim state

Caliphate: The office, jurisdiction, or reign of a caliph

Cant: Specialized vocabulary of any nonprofessional subgroup

Change: Substitution of the new for existing

Change agent: A person who influences innovation decisions

Change agent ethics: Concern for the unanticipated consequences of introducing a new idea or product into a culture

Channel: The means by which a message is transmitted

Chicano: Refers to people born in the United States whose ancestors came from Mexico; often used to represent a nationalist identity and a commitment to disassimilation

Chronemics: The study of our use of time

Clothing: Can be a nonverbal communication message

Co-culture: An interdependent and equal subculture within a society

Code switching: Going from one language to another in the same sentence, as from Spanish to English and then back to Spanish

Collectivism: A dimension of culture; refers to interdependence, groupness, and social cohesion

Coming out: One's public disclosure of being gay

Communication: Intentionally stimulating meaning in other humans through the use of symbols

Communication apprehension: Fear or anxiety associated with either real or anticipated communication with another person or persons

Compound bilingual: People who learn a second language relatively late in life and who use it in a limited number of settings

Conformity: Compliance or acquiescence

Confucianism: An ethical system based on the teaching of Confucius, emphasizing personal virtue and devotion to family and society

Confucian work dynamism: A dimension of culture; persistence, commitment, and organizational identity and loyalty; relabeled by Hofstede as *long-term* versus *short-term orientation* (*see also* Long-term orientation, Short-term orientation)

Contact zone: The space in which geographically and historically separately peoples come into contact, usually establishing relations involving coercion, radical inequality, and intractable conflict

Context: The physical and social environment in which communication takes place

Convergence: A process in which information is shared by individuals who come together over time to a greater degree of agreement

Coordinate bilingual: People who learn a second language relatively early in life and who use it in a variety of settings

Corporate culture: Thinking of an organization as a culture; the values, goals, and priorities that guide policies and procedures of an organization

Creole: Language that develops from prolonged contact of two or more languages and acquired by children as their first language

Cultural adaptation: An immigrant's learning and adopting the norms and values of the new host culture (*see also* Acculturation)

Cultural identity: Identification with and perceived acceptance into a culture

Cultural invasion: One group penetrating the culture of another group to impose its own view of the world

Cultural relativism: A theory from anthropology that the differences in peoples are the results of historical, social, and geographic conditions and that all populations have complete and equally developed cultures

Cultural Revolution: Mao Zedong's attempt to purify China of outside influences and build a Marxist-Chinese culture

Cultural sensitivity: Making no value judgments based on one's own cultural values about other cultures' practices or artifacts (i.e., better or worse, right or wrong)

Cultural studies: An approach that attempts to develop an ideal personification of the culture, which is then used to explain the actions of individuals in the culture

Culture: Sum total of ways of living, including behavioral norms, linguistic expression, styles of communication, patterns of thinking, and beliefs and values of a group large enough to be self-sustaining and transmitted over the course of generations

Culture shock: Anxiety, disorientation, and stress that one experiences when in a new culture

Decoding: The process of assigning meaning to symbols

Dialect: A variety of speech differing from the standard

Diaspora: Dispersion of an originally homogeneous people

Diffusion: The spread of innovations into a culture

Discursive imperialism: Labeling of a group as a dehumanized "other," which facilitates actions taken against it

Emic: Knowledge learned from the inside; that is, the norms of culture known by its members (see also Etic)

Encoding: Process of putting the communication source's ideas into symbols

Endogamy: Marriage in which the partners must be members of the same group (e.g., a religious community)

Equality: Being alike or the same in some rank, ability, quantity, and so forth

Esperanto: A widely used universal language devised in 1887, based on European vocabularies and Latin grammar

Ethnic identity: Identification with and perceived acceptance into an ethnic group

Ethnicity: Subculture or subgroup identified by shared descent and heritage

Ethnocentrism: Negatively judging aspects of another culture by the standards of one's own culture

Ethnography: The direct observation and reporting of customary behavior of a culture

Etic: Knowledge learned by an outsider; that is, theoretical information about a culture developed by a researcher who is not a member of the culture (see also Emic)

Exogamy: Marriage in which the partner must be chosen from outside a defined group (e.g., members of the same extended family lineage may not marry)

Expatriate: A noncitizen worker in a foreign country

Extended family: A family group that includes parents and their married children

Face: In collectivist cultures, public image or reputation that one has achieved (mien in Chinese culture); also, the community's confidence in the integrity of one's moral character (lien in Chinese culture)

Feedback: That portion of receiver response that a source attends to

Femininity: A dimension of culture; both women and men being concerned with quality of life, interpersonal relationships, and concern for the weak

Feng shui: The Chinese art of manipulating the physical environment, such as homes and offices, to establish harmony with nature and achieve happiness, prosperity, and health

Fertility rate: The average number of children born alive to a woman in her lifetime; a fertility rate of 2.1 children per woman would eventually result in zero population growth

Field dependence: The degree to which perception is affected by the surrounding perceptual or contextual field

Four modernizations: Deng Xiaoping's economic programs in China in agriculture, industry, science, and technology

Gaijin: Japanese for foreigner or "outside person"

Gay: Refers in a positive way to individuals who form primary emotional attachments to members of the same sex and who value one another and similar others

GDP: *See* Gross domestic product

Gelassenheit: A German word used by the Amish to mean submission to God

Gender: Learned behaviors and attitudes associated with the words feminine and masculine

Ghutrah: A cloth worn by men in Saudi Arabia and some other Arabian countries to cover the head

Grammar: Linguistic rules governing sounds (or gestures in sign languages), meanings, and syntax of a language

Gregorian: A calendar based on the cycles of the sun

Gross domestic product (GDP): The total output of goods and services for final use produced by an economy

Hajj: The pilgrimage to Mecca that every Muslim is expected to undertake at least once

Haptics: Study of the use of touch to communicate

Hate speech: Threats or verbal slurs directed against specific groups or physical acts such as burning crosses or placing swastikas on public or private property

Hegemony: Predominant influence by one culture over another

Heroes: Real or imaginary persons who serve as a behavior model within a culture

High context: A dimension of culture; holds that much of the meaning of messages is determined by the context or environment

Hijrah: A calendar based on the cycles of the moon

Hispanic: Refers to people with the capability of speaking and comprehending the Spanish language whose ancestry is based on a Spanish-speaking country and who identify with the subculture

Hmong: A people living in Laos who sided with the United States in the Vietnam War and now have resettled in the United States

Homophobia: Irrational fear of lesbians and gay men

Homosexual: Refers to sexual activity with members of one's own sex

Hong Kong: A British Crown Colony returned to China in 1997

Honorific: Form of direct address used in some languages to show respect

Hyperindividualism: Excesses of individualism, disregard for others, and withdrawing into individual private shells

Icon: A popular symbol that represents a culture

Idiom: An expression whose meaning is not predictable from the usual meanings of its words

Imam: One of the leaders regarded by the Shiites as successors of Muhammad; any religious leader claiming descent from Muhammad

Individualism: A dimension of culture; refers to the rights and independent action of the individual

In-group: A cohesive group that offers protection in exchange for loyalty and provides its members with a sense of identity

Integration: Maintaining important parts of one's original culture as well as participating fully in a new culture

Intercultural communication: Communication between people and groups of diverse culture, subculture, or subgroup identifications

Interpretation: The step in the perception process referring to attaching meaning to sense data

Iqal: Also known as *agal,* the double ring of black rope or cord used to hold the *ghutrah* worn by men in Saudi Arabia and some other Arabian countries

Islam: The world's second largest religion, with nearly 1 billion followers, based on the teachings of the prophet Muhammad, believing in one God, and having a body of law put forth in the Koran and the *sunnah*

Jargon: Technical language of a professional subgroup

Kinesics: Gestures, body movements, facial expressions, and eye contact

Koran: The holy book of Islam, considered to contain the literal words of Allah or God; the Arabic text includes stories, admonitions, verse, and prophetic segments (also spelled *Quran*)

Language: A set of symbols shared by a community to communicate meaning and experience

Latino: Refers to Spanish-speaking individuals who themselves or whose ancestors came from anywhere in Latin America

Lesbian: Refers in a positive way to women who form primary emotional attachments to other women

Literacy rate: Percentage of people, age 15 and older, who can, with understanding, both read and write a short, simple statement on their everyday life

Long-term orientation: Fostering of virtues, particularly perseverance and thrift, oriented toward future rewards

Low context: A dimension of culture; holds that little of the meaning of messages is determined by the context or environment

Macau: A Portuguese colony returned to China in 1999

Majlis: The practice in Saudi Arabia allowing any citizen access to the king and local governors

Marginalization: Losing one's cultural identity and not having any psychological contact with society

Masculinity: A dimension of culture; refers to distinct traits of being assertive, tough, and focused on material success

Matawain: Public morality committees in Saudi Arabia that ensure compliance with religious requirements

Materialism: Emphasis on material objects, needs, and considerations over spiritual values

Melting pot: describe metaphor for the assimilation of early immigrants into a homogenized United States

Message: Encoded ideas of the communication source

Mexican-American: Someone from Mexico undergoing the assimilation process

Mitigated speech: Deferential or indirect speech between individuals of perceived high power distance

Monochronic time: In the use of time, doing one thing at a time in an orderly fashion

Mother tongue: The parent language of other languages or a person's first learned language

Muhammad: The founder of Islam; born circa 570, died 632

Multiculturalism: Understanding, acceptance, and constructive relations among people of many different cultures and subcultures

Muslim: Literally, one who submits to the will of God; one who practices the religion of Islam

Mutability: A state of changeability or variability

Myths: Stories and images representing a culture's values, handed down from generation to generation as a guide for living

Need for achievement: The desire to excel because of the feeling of accomplishment it brings

New Order Amish: A moderate group of the Amish, accepting some modern conveniences

Niqab: A veil worn by some Muslim women that covers all of the face except for the eyes

Noise: External, internal, or semantic limitations on the effectiveness of communication

Nonverbal communication: Actions and attributes with a socially shared meaning intentionally sent and received

Nuclear family: A family group including only parents and children

Nushu: Women's writing developed in rural China as a secret language to communicate with other women

Old Order Amish: The most conservative and strict of the Amish

Oleh: A Jew immigrating into Israel under the Law of Return; plural is *olim*

Olfactics: Communication by smells

One-child campaign: China's birth control program introduced in 1979 to encourage most families to have no more than one child

Opinion leadership: Individuals who can influence others' attitudes and behaviors

Ordnung: Church rules and values of the Amish

Organization: The step in the perception process referring to organizing sense data in some meaningful way

Othering: The degrading of cultures and groups outside of one's own and creating artificial divisions between cultures and groups by labeling language that emphasizes power relations and domination

Paralanguage: Nonverbal elements of the voice, including intensity, pitch, laughter, and so forth

Participant observer: A researcher's orderly and scientific study of a subgroup by actually participating in the group

Peace Corps: U.S. government organization established in 1961 to train and send volunteers abroad to work with people of developing countries in agricultural, educational, and technological projects

Perception: Becoming aware of, knowing, or identifying by means of the senses

Physical appearance: Personal appearance, clothing, grooming, and other factors that can be a nonverbal communication message

Pidgin: A mixture of two or more languages to form a new language

Polychronic time: In the use of time, placing a stress on the involvement of people and completion of transactions rather than on adherence to schedules

Postethnicity: Belief that associations or group memberships can be voluntary rather than determined by birth

Power distance: A dimension of culture; the extent to which the less powerful members of a culture expect and accept that power, prestige, and wealth are distributed unequally

Prejudice: Irrational suspicion or hatred of a particular group, race, religion, or sexual orientation

Profiling: A law enforcement practice of scrutinizing certain individuals based on characteristics thought to indicate the likelihood of criminal behavior

Proxemics: Use of fixed space, territoriality, and personal space

Quality circle: An employee group working to improve quality during the production process

Race: Biologically defined as groups who share some hereditary physical characteristics; sociohistorically defined by unstable social meanings constantly being transformed by debate

Racial profiling: *See* Profiling

Ramadan: The month of lunar Islamic calendar during which Muslims abstain from food and drink from sunrise to sunset in commemoration of God's revealing the Koran to Muhammad

Rationality: Mental powers to form conclusions and sound judgments; intelligent and dispassionate thought

Receiver: Someone who attends to a communication message

Receiver response: Anything the receiver of a communication message does after having decoded the message

Redemptive analogy: Something in a culture that can be compared to the Christian gospel

Reference group: A group to which one aspires to attain membership

Refugee: A person living outside the country of nationality who is unable or unwilling to return because of persecution or a well-founded fear of persecution (*see also* Asylee)

Reverse culture shock: Anxiety, disorientation, and stress that one can experience upon return to one's home country

Ritual: A socially essential collective activity within a culture

Rumspringa: Pennsylvania Dutch term usually translated as "running around"; late teenage years not subject to the church's rules and ending with the decision to be baptized into the church and become an adult member of the community

Salad analogy: In contrast to the melting pot analogy, a description of a culture in which individuals may retain elements of their original culture and still exist together without assimilating

Sapir-Whorf hypothesis: A useful way of thinking about the relationship between language and culture (also known as *Whorfian thesis* and *linguistic relativity*)

Scientific method: Identifying a problem, gathering data, and formulating and testing a hypothesis

Segregation: Maintaining one's original culture and not participating in the new culture

Selection: The step in the perception process referring to limiting attention only to part of the available sense data

Sensation: Neurological process of becoming aware through the senses of stimuli in the environment

Separation: Maintaining one's original culture and not participating in the new culture (*see also* Segregation)

Sex: Biological features that distinguish women from men

Shiite: The smaller branch of Islam that has messianic expectations of world justice

Shinto: The former state religion of Japan linking the people to ancestors and gods

Short-term orientation: A dimension of culture; the fostering of virtues related to the past and present, in particular respect for tradition, preservation of face, and fulfilling social obligations

Silence: Absence of verbal communication that can communicate messages nonverbally

Slang: The specialized vocabulary of subgroups

Sojourner: One who lives in a country for a specific time for a specific purpose, such as employment, and expects to return home

Source: Someone with an idea he or she desires to communicate

Spanglish: Spanish and English words mixed in one sentence

Spanish origin: Coming from or having ancestors from a Spanish-speaking country

Spanish speaking: Speaking and comprehending the Spanish language as a primary or secondary language

Spanish surnamed: Having a last name identified as Spanish by the U.S. Census Bureau

Standard Chinese: Mandarin dialect spoken by the majority of people in China

Stereotype: Judgment made about another solely on the basis of ethnic or other group membership

Stew analogy: *See* Salad analogy

Subculture: A group within a larger society that shares distinctive cultural characteristics to distinguish it from others

Subgroup: A group based on vocation, avocation, or special skills that, like cultures, provide patterns of behavior and values

Sub-Saharan Africa: Countries on the African continent south of the Sahara desert

Sunni: The largest branch of Islam

Symbol: Verbal and nonverbal language that is used to communicate the idea of a communication source

Syntax: Grammatical rules governing the way that words combine to form sentences

Taiwan: Republic of China, located on the island of Formosa off the southeastern coast of China

Taoism: A philosophical system originated by Lao-Tzu that advocated a simple life close to nature in order to be in harmony with the Tao, the underlying pattern of the universe

Tejano: A person born in Texas of Mexican ancestry

Telemundo: A Spanish-language television network

Territoriality: How space can be used to communicate messages

Thawb: Loose-fitting, ankle-length, usually white shirt worn by men in Saudi Arabia and some other Arab countries

Tibet: A country in South Asia north of the Himalayas under the suzerainty, or overlordship, of China

Uncertainty avoidance: A dimension of culture; the extent to which people are made nervous by unstructured or unpredictable situations

Univision: A Spanish-language television network

Value: A central organizing belief or belief system that shapes a person's goals and motivations

Wai: A nonverbal gesture used in Thailand to communicate greeting, farewell, respect, and appreciation

White privilege: Advantages that Whites have living in a White culture

Worldview: Philosophical ideas of being, a culture's beliefs about its place in the cosmos, and beliefs about the nature of humanity

Xenophobia: Unreasonable fear or hatred of foreigners

Yang: The bright, dry, warm aspect or principle in Chinese philosophy

Yin: The dark, moist, cool aspect or principle in Chinese philosophy

REFERENCES

Abeele, M. V., & Roe, K. (2011). New life, old friends: A cross-cultural comparison of the use of communication technologies in the social life of college freshmen. *Young: Nordic Journal of Youth Research, 19*(2), 219–240.

Adler, P. S. (1975). The transitional experience: An alternative view of culture shock. *Journal of Humanistic Psychology, 15*(4), 13–23.

Addressing your questions. (2006). *The Coca-Cola Company* [Website]. Retrieved from http://www .thecoca-colacompany.com/citizenship/challenges_ opportunities.html#environment

Adorno, T. W., Frenkel-Brunswick, E., Levinson, D. J., & Sanford, R. N. (1950). *The authoritarian personality.* New York: Harper.

Agger, B. (1992). *Cultural studies as critical theory.* London: Falmer.

Albarran, A. B., & Hutton, B. (2009). *A history of Spanish language radio in the United States.* Denton: University of North Texas, Center for Spanish Language Media.

Allen, H. G. (1982). *The betrayal of Liliuokalani: Last queen of Hawaii, 1838–1917.* Honolulu, HI: Mutual Publishing.

Allport, G. W. (1954). *The nature of prejudice.* Reading, MA: Addison-Wesley.

America by the numbers. (2007). *Time, 170*(21), 54.

Amish population by state: 2010. (2010). Elizabethtown PA: Elizabethtown College, Young Center for Anabaptist and Pietist Studies. Retrieved from http:// www2.etown.edu/amishstudies/Population_ by_State_2010.asp

Amnesty International. (2008). *Love, hate and the law: decriminalizing homosexuality.* London: Author.

Andersen, K. E. (1991). A history of communication ethics. In K. J. Greenberg (Ed.), *Conversations on communication ethics* (pp. 3–19). Norwood, NJ: Ablex.

Andersen, P. A., Lustig, M. W., & Andersen, J. F. (1987). Regional patterns of communication in the United States: A theoretical perspective. *Communication Monographs, 54*(2), 128–144.

Arbitron. (2008). *Hispanic radio today: 2008 edition.* Retrieved from http://www.arbitron.com/downloads/ hispanicradiotoday08.pdf

Argyle, M. (1988). *Bodily communication* (2nd ed.). New York: Methuen.

Argyle, M., & Ingham, R. (1972). Gaze, mutual gaze, and distance. *Semiotica, 6*(1), 32–49.

Arizonans for Official English v. Arizona, 520 U.S. 43 (1997).

Armstrong, N., & Wagner, M. (2003). *Field guide to gestures: How to identify and interpret virtually every gesture known to man.* Philadelphia: Quirk.

Asuncion-Lande, N. (1983). Language theory and linguistic principles. In W. B. Gudykunst (Ed.), *International and Intercultural Communication Annual* (Vol. 7, pp. 253–257). Beverly Hills, CA: Sage.

Aurand, A. M., Jr. (1938). *Little known facts about the Amish and the Mennonites.* Harrisburg, VA: Aurand Press.

Axtell, R. E. (1991). *Gestures: The do's and taboos of body language around the world.* New York: John Wiley.

Axtell, R. E. (1994). *The do's and taboos of international trade.* New York: John Wiley.

Back, T.-H. (2004). The social reality faced by ethnic Koreans in Central Asia. *Korean and Korean American Studies Bulletin 12*(2–3), 45–88.

Baker, I. (2004). *The heart of the world: A journey to the last secret place.* New York: Penguin.

Barber, W., & Badre, A. (1998, June). *Culturability: The merging of culture and usability.* Proceedings of the Fourth Conference on Human Factors and the Web, Basking Ridge, NJ. Retrieved from http://zing.ncsl. nist.gov/hfweb/att4/proceedings/barber/

Barer-Stein, T. (1999). *You eat what you are: People, culture, and food traditions* (2nd ed.). Willowdale, Ontario, Canada: Firefly.

Barna, L. M. (1997). Stumbling blocks in intercultural communication. In L. A. Samovar & R. E. Porter (Eds.), *Intercultural communication: A reader* (8th ed., pp. 337–346). Belmont, CA: Wadsworth.

Barnum, W. (1982). *Gumwrappers and goggles: The tale of a jet.* San Antonio, TX: Summit.

Baron, D. (1990). *The English-only question: An official language for Americans?* New Haven, CT: Yale University Press.

Barrett, C. (2005). On Southwest's culture. *Southwest Airlines Spirit.*

Baum, G. (2008, March 9). Paris politician introduces ethnicity into municipal race. *Los Angles Times,* p. A3.

Belay, G. (1993). Toward a paradigm shift for intercultural and international communication: New research directions. In S. A. Deetz (Ed.), *Communication yearbook 16* (pp. 437–457). Newbury Park, CA: Sage.

Beltran, L. R. S. (1976). Alien premises, objects, and methods in Latin American communication research. *Communication Research, 3*(2), 107–134.

Bennhold, K., & Castle, S. (2010, September 14). E.U. calls France's Roma expulsions a "disgrace." *New York Times,* p. A6. Retrieved from http://www.nytimes .com/2010/09/15/world/europe/15roma.html

Berger, C. R., & Calabrese, R. J. (1975). Some explorations in initial interaction and beyond: Toward a developmental theory of interpersonal communication. *Human Communication Research, 1*(2), 99–112.

Bergqvist, C., Borchorst, A., Christensen, A.-D., Ramstedt-Silén, V., Raaum, N. C., & Styrkársdottir, A. (Eds.). (1999). *Equal democracies? Gender and politics in the Nordic countries.* Oslo: Scandinavian University Press.

Berlo, D. K. (1960). *The process of communication.* New York: Holt, Rinehart & Winston.

Berry, J. W., Kim, U., & Boski, P. (1987). Psychological acculturation of immigrants. In Y. Y. Kim & W. B. Gundykunst (Eds.), *International and Intercultural Communication Annual* (Vol. 11, pp. 62–89). Newbury Park, CA: Sage.

Bickerton, D. (1981). *Roots of language.* Ann Arbor, MI: Karoma.

Bigelow, B. (1980). Roots and regions: A summary definition of the cultural geography of America. *Journal of Geography, 79*(6), 218–229.

Birke-Smith, K. (1959). *The Eskimos.* London: Methuen.

Black, G., & Munro, R. (1993). *Black hands of Beijing: Lives in defiance in China's democracy movement.* New York: John Wiley.

Blakeslee, M. (2002, June 24). Speech's utter dynamics. *Los Angeles Times,* p. A12.

Blanchard, F. A., Lilly, T., & Vaughn, L. A. (1991). Reducing the expression of racial prejudice. *Psychological Science, 2*(2), 101–105.

Bolton, R. (1994). Sex, science, and social responsibility: Cross-cultural research on same-sex eroticism and sexual intolerance. *Cross-Cultural Research, 28*(2), 134–190.

Borchorst A., Christensen A., & Raaum N. (1999), Equal democracies? Conclusions and perspectives. In C. Berqvist, A. Borchorst, A.-D. Christensen, V. Ramstedt-Silén, N. C.Raaum, & A. Styrkársdottir (Eds.), *Equal democracies? Gender and politics in the Nordic Countries* (pp. 227–289).Oslo: Scandinavian University Press.

Bosmajian, H. A. (1983). *The language of oppression.* Lanham, MD: University Press of America.

Boucher, J. D. (1974). Culture and the expression of emotion. In F. R. Casmir (Ed.), *International and Intercultural Communication Annual* (Vol. 1, pp. 82–86). New York: Speech Communication Association.

Brettell, C. B., & Sargent, C. F. (Eds.). (1993). *Gender in cross-cultural perspective.* Englewood Cliffs, NJ: Prentice Hall.

Brislin, R. W. (1988). Increasing awareness of class, ethnicity, culture, and race by expanding on students' own experiences. In I. Cohen (Ed.), *The G. Stanley Hall lecture series* (Vol. 8, pp. 137–180). Washington, DC: American Psychological Association.

Brooks, D. (2008, October 17). "Thinking About Obama." *New York Times,* p. A33.

Brown, M. (2008). *Managing nature—business as usual: Patterns of wording and patterns of meaning in corporate environmental discourse* (Unpublished doctoral thesis).University of Oslo.

Bruce, J., Lloyd, C. B., & Leonard A. (with Engle, P. L., & Duffy, N.) (1995). *Families in focus: New perspectives on mothers, fathers, and children.* New York: Population Council.

Buchanan, P. J. (2002). *The death of the west: How dying populations and immigrant invasions imperil our country and civilization.* New York: Thomas Dunne/ St. Martin's.

Buck, R. (1984). *The communication of emotion.* New York: Guilford Press.

Burgoon, J. K. (1986). Communication effects of gaze behavior: A test of two contrasting explanations. *Human Communication Research, 12,* 495–524.

Burgoon, J. K., Boller, D. B., & Woodall, W. G. (1988). *Nonverbal communication: The unspoken dialog.* New York: Harper & Row.

Burgoon, J. K., & Saine, T. J. (1978). *The unspoken dialogue: An introduction to nonverbal communication.* Boston: Houghton Mifflin.

Busari, S. (2008). *Tweeting the terror: How social media reacted to Mumbai.* CNN International. Retrieved from http://edition.cnn.com/2008/WORLD/ asiapcf/11/27/mumbai.twitter/index.html

Buss, D. M. (1989). Sex differences in human mate preferences: Evolutionary hypotheses tested in 37 cultures. *Behavioral and Brain Sciences, 12,* 1–14.

Buss, D. M. (1994). Mate preferences in 37 cultures. In W. Lonner & R. Malpass (Eds.), *Psychology and culture* (pp. 197–201). Needham Heights, MA: Allyn & Bacon.

Calhoun, J. C. (1848). *Conquest of Mexico.* Retrieved from http://teachingamericanhistory.org/library/index.asp?document = 478

Campbell, B. G. (1976). *Human-kind emerging.* Boston: Little, Brown.

Cann, R. L., Stoneking, M., & Wilson, A. C. (1987, January 1). Mitochondrial DNA and human evolution. *Nature, 325,* pp. 31–36.

Carey, J. W. (1989). *Communication as culture: Essays on media and society.* Boston: Unwin Hyman.

Carliner, D. (1977). *The rights of aliens: The basic ACLU guide to an alien's rights.* New York: Avon.

Carliner, D., Guttentag, L., Helton, A. C., & Henderson, W. J. (1990). *The rights of aliens and refugees: The basic ACLU guide to alien and refugee rights* (2nd ed.). Carbondale: Southern Illinois University Press.

Carroll, J. B. (Ed.). (1956). *Language, thought, and reality: Selected writings of Benjamin Lee Whorf.* New York: John Wiley.

Carson, R. (1962). *Silent spring.* New York: Houghton Mifflin.

Cavalli-Sforza, L., Menozzi, P., & Piazza, A. (1994). *The history and geography of human genes.* Princeton, NJ: Princeton University Press.

Cavalli-Sforza, L. L., Piazza, A., Menozzi, P., & Mountain, J. L. (1988). Reconstruction of human evolution: Bringing together genetic, archaeological and linguistic data. *Proceedings of the National Academy of Science USA, 85*(16), 6002–6006.

Chance, N. A. (1966). *The Eskimo of north Alaska.* New York: Holt, Rinehart & Winston.

Chang, H.-C., & Holt, G. R. (1991). More than relationship: Chinese interaction and the principle of Kuan-Hsi. *Communication Quarterly, 39*(3), 251–271.

Chapman, M. (1997). Preface: Social anthropology, business studies, and cultural issues. *International Studies of Management & Organization, 26*(4), 3–29.

Chauncey, G., Jr. (1985). Christian brotherhood or sexual perversion? Homosexual identities and the construction of sexual boundaries in the World War One era. *Journal of Social History, 19*(2), 189–211.

Chen, G.-M. (1989). Relationships of the dimensions of intercultural communication competence. *Communication Quarterly, 37*(2), 118–133.

Chen, G.-M. (1990). Intercultural communication competence: Some perspectives of research. *Howard Journal of Communications, 2*(3), 243–261.

Chen, G.-M., & Starosta, W. J. (1996). Intercultural communication competence: A synthesis. In B. R. Burleson (Ed.), *Communication yearbook 19* (pp. 353–383). Thousand Oaks, CA: Sage.

Cherry, C. (1957). *On human communication.* Cambridge: Technology Press of MIT.

Chinese Culture Connection. (1987). Chinese values and the search for culture-free dimensions of culture. *Journal of Cross-Cultural Psychology, 18*(2), 143–164.

Chiu, L.-H. (1972). A cross-cultural comparison of cognitive styles in Chinese and American children. *International Journal of Psychology, 7*(4), 235–242.

Chomsky, N. (1980). *Rules and representations.* New York: Columbia University Press.

Chu, G. C. (1977). *Radical change through communication in Mao's China.* Honolulu: University Press of Hawai'i.

Chyz, Y. J. (1945, October 13). Number, distribution, and circulation of the foreign language press in the United States. *Interpreter Releases, 20,* p. 290.

CIA (Central Intelligence Agency). (2011). *The world factbook.* Washington, DC: Central Intelligence Agency. Retrieved from https://www.cia.gov/library/publications/the-world-factbook/

Clinton, H. R. (2010, March). *Remarks on internet freedom.* Speech by U.S. Secretary of State Hillary Rodham Clinton, at Newseum, Washington DC.

Clough, M. (1997, July 27). Birth of nations. *Los Angeles Times,* pp. M1, M6.

Cobo, J. R. M. (1987). *Study of the problem of discrimination against indigenous populations.* New York: United Nations.

Cochrane, A. (2007). Environmental ethics. In *Internet Encyclopedia of Philosophy.* Retrieved from ttp://www.iep.utm.edu/e/envi-eth.htm

Cohen, M. N. (1998). *Culture of intolerance: Chauvinism, class, and racism in the United States.* New Haven, CT: Yale University Press.

Cole, M. (1996). *Cultural psychology.* Cambridge, MA: Belknap Press of Harvard University Press.

Collier, M. J. (1988). A comparison of conversations among and between domestic culture groups: How intra- and intercultural competencies vary. *Communication Quarterly, 36*(2), 122–144.

Collier, M. J., & Thomas, M. (1988). Cultural identity: An interpretive perspective. In *International and Intercultural Communication Annual* (Vol. 12, pp. 99–120).

Collins, P. H. (1990). *Black feminist thought: Knowledge, consciousness and the politics of empowerment.* Boston: Unwin Hyman.

Condit, C. M. (2000). Culture and biology in human communication: Toward a multi-causal model. *Communication Education, 49*(1), 7–24.

Costello, E. (1995). *Signing: How to speak with your hands.* New York: Bantam.

Coulton, T. M., & Glionna, J. M. (2011, September 23). In Japan, finders not keepers. *Los Angeles Times,* p. A1, A7.

Cowan, M. (Ed. & Trans.). (1963). *Humanist without portfolio: An anthology of the writing of Wilhelm von Humboldt.* Detroit, MI: Wayne State University Press.

Cowen, T. (2002). *Creative destruction: How globalization is changing the world's cultures.* Princeton, NJ: Princeton University Press.

Craig, R. T. (1999). Communication theory as a field. *Communication Theory, 9*(2), 119–161.

Crawford, J. (1992). *Hold your tongue: Bilingualism and the politics of English-only.* Reading, MA: Addison-Wesley.

Crosby, F., Bromley, S., & Saxe, L. (1980). Recent unobtrusive studies of black and white discrimination and prejudice: A literature review. *Psychological Bulletin, 87*(3), 546–563.

Damasio, A. R. (2010). *Self comes to mind: Constructing the conscious mind.* New York: Pantheon.

Dannin, R. (2002). *Black pilgrimage to Islam.* Oxford, UK: Oxford University Press.

Darwin, C. (1969). *The expression of the emotions in man and animals.* Westport, CT: Greenwood. (Original work published 1872)

Davidson, C. M. (2008). *Dubai: The vulnerability of success.* New York: Columbia University Press.

Davin, D. (2000). Migrants and the media: Concerns about rural migration in the Chinese press. In L. S. West & Y. H. Zhao (Eds.), *Rural labor flows in China* (pp. 278–291). Berkeley: University of California at Berkeley, USA, Institute of East Asian Studies.

Davis, A. (1992, May 24). Rope. *New York Times,* Sec. 4, p. 11.

Davis, E. W. (2007). *Light at the edge of the world: A journey through the realm of vanishing cultures.* Vancouver, Canada: Douglas & McIntyre.

Deal, T. E., & Kennedy, A. A. (1982). *Corporate cultures: The rites and rituals of corporate life.* Reading, MA: Addison-Wesley.

Decision to fire gays stirs anger. (1991, February 28). *Los Angeles Times.* Retrieved from http://articles.latimes.com/1991-02-28/news/mn-2871_1_gay-rights-activists

Deetz, S. (1973). An understanding of science and a hermeneutic science of understanding. *Journal of Communication, 23*(2), 139–159.

de la Garza, R. (1992). *Latino voices: Mexican, Puerto Rican and Cuban perspectives on American politics.* Hartford, CT: Westview.

de la Zerda, N., & Hopper, R. (1979). Employment interviewers' reactions to Mexican American speech. *Communication Monographs, 46*(2), 126–134.

Demick, B. (2009, September 20). Chinese babies stolen by officials for adoption fees. *Los Angeles Times,* p. A1ff.

Demick, B. (2011, April 2). Wary of unrest, China cracks down on dissent. *Los Angeles Times,* p. A9.

de Mooij, M. (1998). *Global marketing and advertising: Understanding cultural paradoxes.* Thousand Oaks, CA: Sage.

Denning, M. (1997). *The cultural front: The laboring of American culture in the twentieth century.* London: Verso Books.

DeVito, J. A. (1986). *The communication handbook: A dictionary.* New York: Harper & Row.

Diamond, J. (2005). *Collapse: How societies choose to fail or succeed.* New York: Viking Press.

Doi, L. T. (1956). Japanese language as an expression of Japanese psychology. *Western Speech, 20*(2), 90–96.

Doi, L. T. (1973). The Japanese patterns of communication and the concept of amae. *Quarterly Journal of Speech, 59*(2), 180–185.

Domhoff, G. W. (2011). Wealth, income and power. *Who Rules America?* Retrieved from http://sociology.ucsc.edu/whorulesamerica/power/wealth.html

Doty, R. L., Shaman, P., Applebaum, S. L., Giberson, R., Siksorski, L., & Rosenberg, L. (1984). Smell identification ability: Changes with age. *Science, 226,* 1441–1443.

Downing, J. D. H. (1990). Ethnic minority radio in the United States. *Howard Journal of Communications, 2*(2), 135–148.

Doyle, J. A. (1994). *The male experience* (3rd ed.). Dubuque, IA: William C. Brown.

Dresser, N. (1996). *Multicultural manners.* New York: John Wiley.

D'Souza, D. (2002, May 10). Two cheers for colonialism. *Chronicle of Higher Education.* pp. 7–10. Retrieved from http://chronicle.com/free/v48/i35/35b00701.htm

Dudley, M. K., & Agard, K. K. (1993). *A call for Hawaiian sovereignty.* Honolulu, HI: Na Kane O Ka Malo Press.

Duff-Brown, B. (2007, April 15). Those at home on the ice watch it slowly vanish. *Los Angeles Times.* Retrieved from http://articles.latimes.com/2007/apr/15/news/adfg-ice15

Duncan, D. E. (1998). *Calendar: Humanity's epic struggle to determine a true and accurate year.* New York: Avon.

Dunn, M., Greenhill, S. J., Levinson, S. C., & Gray, R. D. (2011). Evolved structure of language shows lineage-specific trends in word-order "universals." *Nature, 473,* 79–82. doi: 10.1038/nature09923

Dyer, R. (1997). *White.* New York: Routledge.

Dynes, W. (1990). *Encyclopaedia of homosexuality.* New York: Garland.

Eastman, C. (Ed.). (1992). *Code switching.* Avon, UK: Clevedon.

Eck, D. L. (1993). *Encountering God: A spiritual journey from Bozeman to Banaras.* Boston: Beacon.

Ehrlich, P. (1968). *The population bomb.* New York: Ballantine.

Ekman, P., Friesen, W. V., & Ellsworth, P. (1972). *Emotion in the human face: Guidelines for research and an integration of findings.* New York: Pergamon Press.

Ekman, P., Friesen, W. V., O'Sullivan, M., Chan, A., Diacoyanni-Tarlatzis, I., Heider, K., . . . Tzavaras, A. (1987). Universals and cultural differences in the judgments of facial expression of emotion. *Journal of Personality and Social Psychology, 53*(4), 712–717.

Ekman, P., & Heider, K. G. (1988). The universality of a contempt expression: A replication. *Motivation and Emotion, 12*(4), 303–308.

Elliott, L. (1998). *The global politics of the environment.* New York: New York University Press.

Emerson, R. W. (1909–1914). *Journals of Ralph Waldo Emerson* (Vol. 7). Boston: Houghton Mifflin.

Employment Division of Oregon v. Smith, 494 U.S. 872 (1990).

Environment and climate. (2010). Sustainable development. Air France [Website]. Retrieved from http://corporate.airfrance.com/en/sustainable-development/environment-and-climate/

Epstein, S. (1990). Gay politics, ethnic identity: The limits of social construction. In E. Stein (Ed.), *Forms of desire: Sexual orientation and the social constructionist controversy* (pp. 239–293). New York: Garland.

Essoungou, A.-M. (2010). A social media boom begins in Africa: Using mobile phones, Africans join the global conversation. *Africa Renewal, 24*(4), p. 3. Retrieved from http://www.un.org/ecosocdev/geninfo/afrec/vo124no4/social-media-boom.html

Esty, D. C., Levy, M. A., & Winston, A. (2002). *Environmental Sustainabilty Index (ESI).* New Haven, CT: Yale Center for Environmental Law & Policy.

Esty, D. C., Levy, M. A., & Winston, A. (2003). *Environmental sustainability in the Arab world.* In K. Schwab (Ed.), *Arab world competitiveness report 2002–2003* (pp. 236–248). Oxford, UK: Oxford University Press.

European Monitoring Centre on Racism and Xenophobia. (2006). *Muslims in the European Union: Discrimination and Islamophobia.* Vienna: Author. Retrieved from http://www.fra.europa.eu/fraWebsite/attachments/Manifestations_EN.pdf

Fackler, G. D. (2010, December 16). The new face of social media. *Hispanic Business.* Retrieved from http://www.hispanicbusiness.com/news/2010/12/16/the_new_face_of_social_media.htm

Federation for American Immigration Reform. (2002). *How immigration hastens destruction of the environment.* Retrieved from http://www.fairus.org/site/PageServer?pagename=iic_immigrationissuecentersa45e

Fejes, F., & Petrich, K. (1993). Invisibility, homophobia and heterosexism: Lesbians, gays and the media. *Critical Studies in Mass Communication, 10*(4), 395–422.

Ferguson, N. (2011). *Civilization: The West and the rest.* London: Penguin Press.

Ferguson, W. (1997, May 25). Germans' reminder of home lives on. *The Blade,* pp. A11–A12.

Finding the golden mean. (1987, January 9). *The Straits Times,* p. 24.

Fischer, D. H. (1989). *Albion's seed: Four British folkways in America.* New York: Oxford University Press.

Fishman, J. A. (1972). *The sociology of language.* Rowley, MA: Newbury House.

Fitzpatrick, L. (2009). A brief history of China's one-child policy. *Time.* Retrieved from http://www.time.com/time/world/article/0,8599,1912861,00.html#ixzz1TYhwWw00

Fong, M. (2000). "Luck talk" in celebrating the Chinese New Year. *Journal of Pragmatics, 32*(2), 219–237.

Foss, K. A., & Foss, S. K. (1994). Personal experience as evidence in feminist scholarship. *Western Journal of Communication, 58*(1), 39–43.

Foster, R. (2011, March 9). Social media = punk rock? *Is this binding* [Web log]. Retrieved from http://www.musicalfoster.com/blog/?p=675

Fox, S. & Livingston, G. (2007). *Latinos online.* Washington DC: Pew Hispanic Center. Retrieved from http://pewhispanic.org/reports/report.php?ReportID=73

Fragante v. City and County of Honolulu, 888 F.2d 591 (9th Cir. 1989).

Frank, T. (2000). *One market under God: Extreme capitalism, market populism, and the end of economic democracy.* Garden City, NY: Doubleday.

Freire, P. (1992). *Pedagogy of the oppressed* (M. B. Ramos, Trans.). New York: Continuum.

French, P. (2011). *India: A portrait*. New York: Knopf.

Friedman, G. (2011). *The next decade: Where we've been . . . and where we're going*. New York: Doubleday.

Fukuoka, Y. (1996). Koreans in Japan: Past and present. *Saitama University Review, 31*(1), 1–15.

Furnham, A. (1987). The adjustment of sojourners. In Y. . Y. Kim & W. B. Gundykunst (Eds.), *International and Intercultural Communication Annual* (Vol. 11, pp. 42–61). Newbury Park, CA: Sage.

Furnham, A., & Bochner, S. (1986). *Culture shock: Psychological reactions to unfamiliar environments*. New York: Methuen.

Fuss, D. (Ed.). (1991). *Inside/out*. New York: Routledge.

Gao, G., & Ting-Toomey, S. (1998). *Communicating effectively with the Chinese*. Thousand Oaks, CA: Sage.

Garreau, J. (1981). *The nine nations of North America*. Boston: Houghton Mifflin.

Geary, D. C. (1998). Male, female: The evolution of human sex differences. *Current Directions in Psychological Science, 8,* 115–120.

Geddes, R. W. (1976). *Migrants of the mountains: The cultural ecology of the Blue Miau (Hmong) of Thailand*. Oxford, UK: Clarendon.

Gerbner, G., Morgan, M., & Signorielli, N. (1986). Living with television: The dynamics of the cultivation process. In J. Bryant & D. Zillmann (Eds.), *Perspectives on media effects* (pp. 17–40). Hillsdale, NJ: Lawrence Erlbaum.

Gerner, M., Perry, F., Moselle, M. A., & Archbold, M. (1992). Moving between cultures: Recent research on the characteristics of internationally mobile adolescents. *Global Nomad Quarterly, 1*(2), 2–3, 8.

Ghosh, B. (2010). Muslims and mosques in the west. *Time, 176*(9), 23.

Gibson, C., & Jung, K. (2002), *Historical census statistics on population totals by race, 1790 to 1990, and by Hispanic origin, 1970 to 1990, for the United States, regions, divisions, and states*. Working Paper Series No. 56. Retrieved from http://www.census.gov/population/www/documentation/twps0056/twps0056.html

Gilbert, D., & Kahl, J. A. (1982). *The American class structure: A new synthesis*. Homewood, IL: Dorsey.

Gillette, J. (1991). Sporty Japanese import. *Westways*.

Gladwell, M. (2008). *Outliers: The story of success*. New York: Little, Brown.

Glendon, M. A. (1991). *Rights talk: The impoverishment of political discourse*. New York: Free Press.

Global Leaders. (2001). *Pilot environmental sustainability index*. Davos, Switzerland: World Economic Forum.

Goh, B. (2009, September 8). Asian social networking sites profit from virtual money. *Reuters*. Retrieved from http://www.reuters.com/article/idUSTRE5880 0D20090909

Gonzalez, A. (1990). Mexican "otherness" in the rhetoric of Mexican Americans. *Southern Communication Journal, 55*(3), 276–291.

Gordon, D. R. (1971). *The new literacy*. Toronto: University of Toronto Press.

Govorchin, G. G. (1961). *Americans from Yugoslavia*. Gainesville: University of Florida Press.

Greenberg, J., & Pyszczynski, T. (1985). The effect of an overheard ethnic slur on evaluations of the target: How to spread a social disease. *Journal of Experimental Social Psychology, 21,* 61–72.

Griffith, J. E., & Villavicencio, S. (1985). Relationships among acculturation, sociodemographic characteristics and social supports in Mexican American adults. *Hispanic Journal of Behavioral Sciences, 7*(1), 75–92.

Grosjean, F. (1982). *Life with two languages: An introduction to bilingualism*. Cambridge, MA: Harvard University Press.

Gross, L. (1993). *Contested closets: The politics and ethics of outing*. Minneapolis: University of Minnesota Press.

Gudykunst, W. B. (1983). Toward a typology of stranger-host relationships. *International Journal of Intercultural Relations, 7*(4), 401–413.

Gudykunst, W. B. (1985). The influence of cultural similarity, type of relationship, and self-monitoring on uncertainty reduction processes. *Communication Monographs, 52*(3), 203–217.

Guernica, A. (1982). *Reaching the Hispanic market effectively: The media, the market, the methods*. New York: McGraw-Hill.

Haiek, J. R. (1992). *Arab-American almanac*. (4th ed.). Glendale, CA: News Circle.

Haiman, F. S. (1994). *"Speech acts" and the First Amendment*. Carbondale: Southern Illinois University Press.

Hall, E. T. (1959). *The silent language*. Greenwich, CT: Fawcett.

Hall, E. T. (1976). *Beyond culture*. New York: Anchor.

Hall, E. T. (1983). *The dance of life: The other dimension of time*. New York: Doubleday.

Hall, E. T., & Hall, M. (1990). *Understanding cultural differences*. Yarmouth, ME: Intercultural Press.

Hall, J. H. (Ed.). (2004). *Dictionary of American regional English* (Vol. 4). Cambridge, MA: Harvard University Press.

Hallett, V. (2003, July 14, 2003). Who do you love? *U.S. News & World Report*, p. 38.

Hallstein, L. O. (1999). A postmodern caring: Feminist standpoint theories, revisioning caring, and communication ethics. *Western Journal of Communication, 63*(1), 32–56.

Hamilton, S., & Harwood, J. (1997). Cultural and structural differences in communication- related work values: The potential for conflict. In C. D. Brown, C. C. Snedecker, & B. Sykes (Eds.), *Conflict and diversity* (pp. 139–156). Cresskill, NJ: Hampton Press.

Hampden-Turner, C., & Trompenaars, F. (1997). *Riding the waves of culture: Understanding diversity in global business.* New York: McGraw-Hill.

Handlin, O. (1973). *The uprooted* (2nd ed.). Boston: Little, Brown.

Hanson, G. (2009). *The economics and policy of illegal immigration in the United States.* Washington, DC: Migration Policy Institute.

Harding, S. (1991). *Whose science? Whose knowledge? Thinking from women's lives.* Ithaca, NY: Cornell University Press.

Harper, R. G., Wiens, A. N., & Matarazzo, J. D. (1978). *Nonverbal communication: The state of the art.* New York: John Wiley.

Harris, D. (1997). *The rise and fall of gay culture.* New York: Hyperion.

Haris Interactive. (2010, July 13). Gay and lesbian adults are more likely and more frequent blog readers [Press release]. Retrieved from http://www.harrisinteractive.com/NewsRoom/PressReleases/tabid/446/mid/1506/articleId/435/ctl/ReadCustom%20Default/Default.aspx

Hausmann, R., Tyson, L. D., & Zahidi, S. (2010). *The global gender gap report 2010.* Geneva: World Economic Forum.

Hayakawa, S. I. (1978). *Through the communication barrier.* New York: Harper & Row.

Hayden, T. (2003, May 18). Losing our voices: Too many languages are speaking last words. *U.S. News & World Report.* Retrieved from http://www.usnews.com/usnews/culture/articles/030526/26tongue.htm

Hayes, J. J. (1976). Gayspeak. *Quarterly Journal of Speech, 62*(3), 256–266.

Hayes-Bautista, D. E. (1992). *No longer a minority: Latinos and social policy in California and redefining California. Latino social engagement in a multicultural society.* Los Angeles: UCLA Chicano Studies Research Center.

Hayman, R. L., Jr., & Levit, N. (1997). The constitutional ghetto. In R. Delgado & J. Stefancie (Eds.), *Critical white studies: Looking behind the mirror* (pp. 239–247). Philadelphia: Temple University Press.

Hearts and minds. (2007). *Time, 169*(13), 16–17.

Hebdige, D. (1979). *Subculture: The meaning of style.* London: Methuen.

Heidegger, M. (1972). Der weg zur sprache [The way to language]. In *Unterwegs zur sprache* [On the way to language] (P. D. Hertz, Trans.). New York: Harper & Row. (Original work published 1959)

Heider, F. (1958). *The psychology of interpersonal relations.* New York: John Wiley.

Hickson, M. L., III, & Stacks, D. W. (1989). *NVC, nonverbal communication: Studies and applications* (2nd ed.). Dubuque, IA: William C. Brown.

Hing, G. (2010, June 3). Social media connects immigrant activists. *Medill Reports.* Retrieved from http://news.medill.northwestern.edu/chicago/news.aspx?id=166332

Hofstede, G. (1980). *Culture's consequences.* Beverly Hills, CA: Sage.

Hofstede, G. (1983). Dimensions of national cultures in fifty countries and three regions. In J. B. Deregowski, S. Dziurawiec, & R. C. Annis (Eds.), *Expectations in cross-cultural psychology* (pp. 335–355). Lisse, Netherlands: Swets & Zeitlinger.

Hofstede, G. (1984). The cultural relativity of the quality of life concept. *Academy of Management Review, 9*(3), 389–398.

Hofstede, G. (1991). *Cultures and organizations: Software of the mind.* New York: McGraw-Hill.

Hofstede, G. (1994). Business cultures. *UNESCO Courier, 47*(4), 12–16.

Hofstede, G. (1996). Gender stereotypes and partner preferences of Asian women in masculine and feminine cultures. *Journal of Cross-Cultural Psychology, 27*(5), 533–546.

Hofstede, G. (1997). *Cultures and organizations: Software of the mind* (Rev. ed.). New York: McGraw-Hill.

Hofstede, G. (1998). Comparative studies of sexual behavior: Sex as achievement or as relationship? In G. Hofstede (Ed.), *Masculinity and femininity: The taboo dimension of national cultures* (pp. 153–178). Thousand Oaks, CA: Sage.

Hofstede, G. (2001). *Culture's consequences: Comparing values, behaviors, institutions, and organizations across nations* (2nd ed.). Thousand Oaks, CA: Sage.

Hofstede, G. (2002). Dimensions do not exist: A reply to Brendan McSweeney, *Human Relations, 55*(11), 1355–1361.

Hofstede, G., & Bond, M. H. (1984). Hofstede's culture dimensions: An independent validation using Rokeach's value survey. *Journal of Cross-Cultural Psychology, 15*(4), 417–433.

Hoijer, H. (Ed.). (1954). *Language in culture.* Chicago: University of Chicago Press.

Hollinger, D. A. (1995). *Post-ethnic America: Beyond multi-culturalism.* New York: Basic Books.

Holm, J. A. (1989). *Pidgins and creoles* (2 vols.). Cambridge, UK: Cambridge University Press.

Holson. L. M. (2005, April 25). Disney bows to feng shui. *New York Times.* Retrieved from http://www.nytimes.com/2005/04/24/business/worldbusiness/24iht-disney.html

Hostetler, J. A. (1980). *Amish society* (3rd ed.). Baltimore: Johns Hopkins University Press.

Hotz, R. L. (1995, April 15). Official racial definitions have shifted sharply and often. *Los Angeles Times,* p. A14.

House, R. J., Hanges, P. J., Javidan, M., Dorfman, P. W., & Gupta, V. (Eds.). (2004). *Culture, leadership, and organizations: The GLOBE study of 62 societies.* Thousand Oaks, CA: Sage.

Hu, H. C. (1944). The Chinese concepts of "face." *American Anthropologist, 46*(1), 45–64.

Hu, X. B., Wang, G. T., & Zou, Y. M. (2002). Political economy of the floating Chinese population. *Journal of Contemporary Asia 32*(4), 536–552.

Huffstutter, P. J. (2009, September 20). The news from Amish country. *Los Angeles Times,* p. A3.

Hull, R. B. (2006). *Infinite nature.* Chicago: University of Chicago Press.

Human Rights Council Res. A/HRC/17/L.9/Rev. 1, Res. on Human Rights, Sexual Orientation and Gender Identity, HRC 17th Sess. May 30-June 17, 2011

Huntington, S. P. (1993). The clash of civilizations? *Foreign Affairs, 72*(3), 22–49.

Huntington, S. P. (1996). *The clash of civilizations and the remaking of world order.* New York: Simon & Schuster.

Huntington, S. P. (2004). *Who are we? The challenges to America's national identity.* New York: Simon & Schuster.

Hurstfield, J. (1978). Internal colonialism: White, Black and Chicano self-conceptions. *Ethnic and Racial Studies, 1*(1), 60–79.

Husted, B. W. (2005). Culture and ecology: A cross-national study of the determinants of environmental sustainability. *Management International Review, 45*(3), 349–371.

ILGA. (2009). *Lesbian and gay rights in the world.* Retrieved from http://ilga.org/historic/Statehomophobia/ILGA_map_2009_A4.pdf

Imai, M., & Gentner, D. (1994). A cross-linguistic study of early word meaning: Universal ontology and linguistic influence. *Cognition, 62*(2), 169–200.

Infante, D. A., Rancer, A. S., & Womack, D. F. (1993). *Building communication theory* (2nd ed.). Prospect Heights, IL: Waveland.

Infomancie. (2008a, January 30). Nordic Ecolabel swan: Scandanavian co-operation. *Infomancy: The dark art of knowing clearly.* Retrieved from http://infomancie.wordpress.com/2008/01/30/nordic-ecolabel-swan-scandinavian-co-operation/

Infomancie. (2008b, March 10). The original recycling symbol. *Infomancy: The dark art of knowing clearly.* Retrieved from http://infomancie.wordpress.com/2008/03/10/the-original-recycling-symbol/

Ingle, S. (1982). *Quality circles master guide: Increasing productivity with people power.* Englewood Cliffs, NJ: Prentice Hall.

Inglehart, R., & Baker, W. E. (2000). Modernization, cultural change, and the persistence of traditional values. *American Sociological Review, 65*(1), 19–51.

In historic move, UN creates single entity to promote women's empowerment. (2010, July 2). UN News Centre. Retrieved from http://www.un.org/apps/news/story.asp?NewsID=35224

Interbrand. (2010). *Best global brands 2010.* New York: Author. Retrieved from http://issuu.com/interbrand/docs/bgb_report_us_version?mode=a_p

International covenant on civil and political rights. (1976). United Nations treaty series 171 (1977). Retrieved from http://www2.ohchr.org/english/law/ccpr.htm

Int'l poll finds US arrogant, threatening. (2003, June 19). *Shanghai Star.* Retrieved from http://app1.chinadaily.com.cn/star/2003/0619/cn9-2.html

Internet World Stats. (2011a). Facebook users in the world. Retrieved from http://www.internetworldstats.com/facebook.htm

Internet World Stats. (2011b). Internet world users by language. Retrieved from http://www.internetworldstats.com/stats7.htm

Isaacs, J. (1980). *Australian dreaming: 40,000 years of aboriginal history.* Sydney, Australia: Lansdowne.

Ishii, K., & Kitayama, S. (2003, July/August). *Selective attention to contextual information in Japan.* Poster presented at 25th annual meeting of Cognitive Science Society, Boston.

It's your turn in the sun. (1978). *Time, 112*(16). Retrieved from http://www.time.com/time/magazine/article/0,9171,916422,00.html

Ivins, M. (1991). *She can't say that, can she?* New York: Random House.

Iwama, H. F. (1990). *Factors influencing transculturation of Japanese overseas teenagers* (Unpublished doctoral dissertation). Pennsylvania State University, University Park, PA.

Jablonski, N., & Chaplin, G. (2000). The evolution of human skin color. *Journal of Human Evolution, 39*(1), 57–106.

Jackson, D. Z. (2008, December 9). Burger King's greasy campaign. Boston Globe. Retrieved from http://www.boston.com/bostonglobe/editorial_opinion/oped/articles/2008/12/09/burger_kings_greasy_campaign/

Jackson, R. L., II, Shin, C. I., & Wilson, K. B. (2000). The meaning of whiteness: Critical implications of communicating and negotiating race. *World Communication, 29*(1), 69–86.

Jain, N. C., & Matukumalli, A. (1993, April). *The functions of silence in India: Implications for intercultural communication research.* Paper presented at the Second International East Meets West Conference in Cross-Cultural Communication, Comparative Philosophy, and Comparative Religion, Long Beach, CA.

Jandt, F. (2004). *Intercultural communication: A global reader.* Thousand Oaks, CA: Sage.

Jandt, F. E., & Tanno, D. V. (2001). Decoding domination, encoding self-determination: Intercultural communication research process. *Howard Journal of Communications, 12*(3), 119–135.

Japanese Ministry of Internal Affairs & Communications. (2011). *Labour Force Survey.* Retrieved from http://www.stat.go.jp/english/index.htm

Johnson, R. (2011). Listen: Southwest pilot goes on homophobic sexist rant on an open frequency. *Business Insider.* Retrieved from http://www.businessinsider.com/listen-to-the-on-air-rant-of-this-suspended-southwest-airlines-pilot-2011-6

Jones, S. (1993). *The right touch: Understanding and using the language of physical contact.* Cresskill, NJ: Hampton Press.

Jones, S. E., & Yarbrough, A. E. (1985). A naturalistic study of the meanings of touch. *Communication Monographs, 52*(1), 19–56.

Jung, S. (2011). *Korean masculinities and transcultural consumption: Yonsama, Rain, Oldboy, K-Pop Idols* (Trans-Asia Screen Cultures Series). Hong Kong: Hong Kong University Press.

Kale, D. W. (1997). Peace as an ethic for intercultural communication. In L. A. Samovar & R. E. Porter (Eds.), *Intercultural communication: A reader* (8th ed., pp. 448–452). Belmont, CA: Wadsworth.

Kallen, H. (1915, February 18–25). Democracy versus the melting pot. *Nation,* pp. 190–194, 217–220.

Kallen, H. M. (1970). *Culture and democracy in the United States.* New York: Arno Press. (Original work published 1924)

Katz, J. (Ed.). (1976). *Gay American history: Lesbians and gay men in the U.S.A.* New York: Thomas Y. Crowell.

Katz, J. H., & Ivey, A. (1977). White awareness: The frontier of racism awareness training. *Personnel and Guidance Journal, 55*(8), 484–489.

Keesing, R. M. (1988). *Melanesian pidgin and the oceanic substrate.* Stanford, CA: Stanford University Press.

Kidd, J. K., & Lankenau, L. L. (2007). Third culture kids: Returning to their passport country. Retrieved from http://www.state.gov/m/dghr/flo/c22473.htm

Kim, M.-S. (1992). A comparative analysis of nonverbal expressions as portrayed by Korean and American print-media advertising. *Howard Journal of Communications, 3,* 317–339.

Kim, Y., Sohn, D., & Choi, S. (2011). Cultural difference in motivations for using social network sites: A comparative study of American and Korean college students. *Computers in Human Behavior, 27*(1), 365–372.

Kim, Y. Y. (1986). *Interethnic communication: Current research.* Beverly Hills, CA: Sage.

Kim, Y. Y. (1988). *Cross-cultural adaptation: Current approaches.* Newbury Park, CA: Sage.

Kim, Y. Y. (2005). Inquiry in intercultural and development communication. *Journal of Communication, 55*(3), 554–577.

King, R. D. (1997). Should English be the law? *Atlantic Monthly, 279*(4), 55–64.

Kinney, M. V., Kerber, K. J., Black, R. E., Cohen, B., Nkrumah, F., . . . Lawn, J. E. (2010) Sub-Saharan Africa's mothers, newborns, and children: Where and why do they die? *PLoS Medicine, 7*(6). doi:10.1371/journal.pmed.1000294

Kinver, M. (2006, December 1). Do mobile phones cost the earth? *BBC News.* Retrieved from http://news.bbc.co.uk/2/hi/science/nature/6174422.stm

Kirkland, S. L., Greenberg, J., & Pyszczynski, T. (1987). Further evidence of the deleterious effects of overheard derogatory ethnic labels: Derogation beyond the target. *Personality and Social Psychology Bulletin, 13,* 216–227.

Kissinger, H. (2011). *On China.* New York: Penguin Press.

Kitayama, S., Duffy, S., Kawamura, T., & Larsen, J. T. (2003). Perceiving an object and its context in different cultures: A cultural look at new look. *Psychological Science, 14*(3), 201–206.

Kluckhohn, F. R., & Strodtbeck, F. L. (1961). *Variations in value orientations.* Evanston, IL: Row, Peterson.

Knapp, M. L. (1990). Nonverbal communication. In G. L. Dahnke & G. W. Clatterbuck (Eds.), *Human communication: Theory and research* (pp. 50–69). Belmont, CA: Wadsworth.

Knighton, J. (1999). *Intergenerational transfer and the rise of individualism* (Unpublished paper). Victoria University of Wellington, New Zealand.

Kohls, L. R. (1984). *The values Americans live by*. New York: Meridian House International.

Kohn, G. C. (1986). *Dictionary of wars*. New York: Facts On File.

Kohn, M. L. (1977). *Class and conformity* (2nd ed.). Chicago: University of Chicago Press.

Kraut, A. H. (1994). *Silent travelers: Germs, genes, and the immigrant menace*. New York: Basic Books.

Kraybill, D. B. (1989). *The riddle of Amish culture*. Baltimore: Johns Hopkins University Press.

Krippendorff, K. (1993). Conversation or intellectual imperialism in comparing communication (theories). *Communication Theory, 3*(3), 252–266.

Kuhn, A. (2001, April 12). "Very sorry" proves to be the key phrase. *Los Angeles Times*, p. A14.

Kushner, H. S. (1982). *When bad things happen to good people*. Boston: G. K. Hall.

Labov, W., Ash, S., & Boberg, C. (1997). *A national map of the regional dialects of American English*. Retrieved from http://www.ling.upenn.edu/phono_atlas/NationalMap/NationalMap.html

Landis, D., & Brislin, R. (Eds.). (1983). *Handbook of intercultural training* (Vol. 2). Elmsford, NY: Pergamon Press.

Laqueur, T. (1990). *Making sex: Body and gender from the Greeks to Freud*. Cambridge: Harvard University Press.

Lau v. Nichols, 414 U.S. 563, 39 L. Ed. 2d 1, 94 S. Ct. 786 (1974).

Lee, W. S. (1994). On not missing the boat: A processual method for intercultural understanding of idioms and lifeworld. *Journal of Applied Communication Research, 22*(2), 141–161.

Leeds-Hurwitz, W. (1990). Notes in the history of intercultural communication: The Foreign Service Institute and the mandate for intercultural training. *Quarterly Journal of Speech, 76*(3), 262–281.

Le Play, F. (1884). *L'Organization de la famille* [The organization of the family]. Paris: Dentu Libre.

Lerner, D. (1958). *The passing of traditional society: Modernizing the Middle East*. New York: Free Press.

Lewis, B. (2002). *What went wrong? The clash between Islam and modernity in the Middle East*. New York: Oxford University Press.

Levine, E. S., & Padilla, A. M. (1979). *Crossing cultures in therapy: Pluralistic counseling for the Hispanic*. Monterey, CA: Brooks/Cole.

Levy, G. D., Taylor, M. G., & Gelman, S. A. (1995). Traditional and evaluative aspects of flexibility in gender roles, social conventions, moral rules, and physical laws. *Child Development, 66*(2), 515–531.

Liberman, K. (1981). Understanding Aborigines in Australian courts of law. *Human Organization, 40*(3), 247–255.

Liberman, K. (1990a). An ethnomethodological agenda in the study of intercultural communication. In D. Carbaugh (Ed.), *Cultural communication and intercultural contact* (pp. 185–192). Hillsdale, NJ: Lawrence Erlbaum.

Liberman, K. (1990b). Intercultural communication in central Australia. In D. Carbaugh (Ed.), *Cultural communication and intercultural contact* (pp. 177–183). Hillsdale, NJ: Lawrence Erlbaum.

Ling, R. (2005). The socio-linguistics of SMS: An analysis of SMS use by a random sample of Norwegians. In R. Ling & P. Pedersen (Eds.), *Mobile communications: Re-negotiation of the social sphere* (pp. 335–349). London: Springer.

Ling, R., & Baron, N. S. (2007). Text messaging and IM linguistic comparison of American college data. *Journal of Language & Social Psychology, 26*(3), 291–298.

Lipset, S. M. (1990). *Continental divide: The values and institutions of the United States and Canada*. New York: Routledge.

Lipski, J. (1985). *Linguistic aspects of Spanish-English language switching*. Tempe: Arizona State University Center for Latin American Studies.

Livingston, G. (2011). *Latinos and digital technology*. Washington DC: Pew Hispanic Center. Retrieved from http://pewresearch.org/pubs/1887/latinos-digital-technology-internet-broadband-cell-phone-use

Lopez-Claros, A., & Zahidi, S. (2005). *Women's empowerment: Measuring the global gender gap*. Geneva: World Economic Forum. Retrieved from https://members.weforum.org/pdf/Global_competitiveness_Reports/Reports/gender_gap.pdf

Lorde, A. (1984). *Sister outsider*. Freedom, CA: Crossing Press.

Losada, A. (1971). *Bartolome de las Casas in history: Toward an understanding of the man and his work*. DeKalb: Northern Illinois University Press.

Lyng v. Northwest Indian Cemetery Protection Association, 485 U.S. 439 (1988).

Ma, R. (1992). The role of unofficial intermediaries in interpersonal conflicts in the Chinese culture. *Communication Quarterly, 40*(3), 269–278.

Macfarquhar, N. (2008, December 18). In a first, gay rights are pressed at the U.N., *New York Times*. Retrieved from http://www.nytimes.com/2008/12/19/world/19nations.html

MacGregor, S. (2005). No sustainability without justice: A feminist critique of environmental citizenship. In A. Dobson & D. Bell (Eds.). *Environmental citizenship* (pp. 101–126). Cambridge: MIT Press.

Mack, A., & Rock, I. (1998). *Inattentional blindness: An overview.* Cambridge: MIT Press.

Maddox, K. B., & Gray, S. A. (2002). Cognitive representations of Black Americans: Reexploring the role of skin tone. *Personality & Social Psychology Bulletin, 28*(2), 250–259.

Magnier, M. (2011, March 18). In Japan, it's about the group. *Los Angeles Times,* p. A1ff.

Mäkinen, M., & Wangu Kuira, M. (2008). Social media and postelection crisis in Kenya, *International Journal of Press/Politics, 13*(3). 328–325.

Malotki, E. (1983). *Hopi time: A linguistic analysis of the temporal concepts in the Hopi language.* Berlin: Mouton.

Marcus, A., & Gould, E. W. (2000). Crosscurrents: Cultural dimensions and global web user-interface design. *Interactions, 7*(4), 32–46.

Marshall, T. (1992, November 13). Refugees: Germany may act to reduce asylum-seekers. *Los Angeles Times.* Retrieved from http://articles.latimes.com/1992-11-13/news/mn-293_1_asylum-law

Martin, J. (2000). World telephone cultures. Retrieved from http://www.netjeff.com/humor/item.cgi?file = HelloOnTelephoneWorldwide

Masakazu, Y. (1994). *Individualism and the Japanese: An alternative approach to cultural comparison* (B. Sugihara, Trans.). Tokyo: Japan Echo.

Masood, E. (2008). *Science and Islam: A history.* London: Icon Books.

Matthews, S., Polinsky, M., & Comrie, B. (Eds.). (1996). *The atlas of languages.* London: Quarto.

Maurer, D. W. (1981). *Language of the underworld.* Lexington: University Press of Kentucky.

Mayer, J. P. (with A. P. Kerr). (1981). *Journey to America by Alexis de Tocqueville* (G. Lawrence, Trans.). Westport, CT: Greenwood.

McClelland, D. C. (1976). *The achieving society.* New York: Irvington.

McCroskey, J. C., Burroughs, N. F., Daun, A., & Richmond, V. P. (1990). Correlates of quietness: Swedish and American perspectives. *Communication Quarterly, 38*(2), 127–137.

McIntosh, P. (1994). White privilege: Unpacking the invisible knapsack. *Hungry Mind Review* (Fall), 12–13.

McPhail, M. L. (2002). *Rhetoric of race revisited: Reparation or separation?* Lanham, MD: Rowman & Littlefield.

McSweeney, B. (2002a). The essentials of scholarship: A reply to Geert Hofstede. *Human Relations, 55*(11), 1363–1372.

McSweeney, B. (2002b). Hofstede's model of national cultural differences and their consequences: A triumph of faith—a failure of analysis. *Human Relations, 55*(1), 89–118.

Mehrabian, A. (1981). *Silent messages: Implicit communication of emotions and attitudes* (2nd ed.). Belmont, CA: Wadsworth.

Meier, M. S., & Ribera, F. (1993). *Mexican Americans/American Mexicans: From conquistadors to Chicanos* (Rev. ed.). New York: Hill & Wang.

Melkote, S. (2003). Theories of development communication. In B. Mody (Ed.), *International and development communication: A 21st- century perspective* (pp. 129–146). Thousand Oaks, CA: Sage.

Melton, J. G. (Ed.). (1991). *Encyclopedia of American religions: A comprehensive study of the major religious groups in the United States.* New York: Triumph.

Melville, H. (1976). *Redburn.* London: Harmondsworth. (Original work published 1849)

Mencken, H. L. (1935). The future of English. *Harper's Magazine,* (April), 541–548. Retrieved from http://www.harpers.org/archive/1935/04/0018932

Merchant, C. (1980). *The death of nature: Women, ecology, and the scientific revolution.* San Francisco: Harper & Row.

Merchant, C. (2006). The scientific revolution and the death of nature. *Isis, 97,* 513–533.

Merriam, A. H. (1974). Rhetoric and the Islamic tradition. *Today's Speech, 22*(1), 43–49.

Miike, Y. (2003). Toward an alternative metatheory of human communication: An Asiacentric vision. *Intercultural Communication Studies, 12*(4), 39–63.

Miike, Y. (2004). Rethinking humanity, culture, and communication: Asiacentric critiques and contributions. *Human Communication, 7*(1), 69–82.

Mikkelsen, C. (Ed.). (2010). *The indigenous world 2010.* Copenhagen, Denmark: International Work Group for Indigenous Affairs.

Miller, D. H. (1998). *Freedom to differ: The shaping of the gay and lesbian struggle for civil rights.* New York: New York University Press.

Miller, M. D., Reynolds, R. A., & Cambra, R. E. (1987). The influence of gender and culture on language intensity. *Communication Monographs, 54*(1), 101–105.

Milne, J. (1999, August 6). What makes a Māori? *The Dominion*, p. 9.

Mirandé, A., & Tanno, D. V. (1993). Labels, researcher perspective, and contextual validation: A commentary. *International Journal of Intercultural Relations, 17*(1), 149–155.

Miyamoto, Y., Nisbett, R. E., & Masuda, T. (2006). Culture and the physical environment: Holistic versus analytic perceptual affordances. *Psychological Science, 17*(2), 113–119.

Modley, R. (1976). *Handbook of pictorial symbols.* New York: Dover.

Montepare, J. M., & Opeyo, A. (2002). The relative salience of physiognomic cues in differentiating faces: A methodological tool. *Journal of Nonverbal Behavior, 26*(1), 43–59.

Moore, M. M. (1995). Courtship signaling and adolescents: "Girls just wanna have fun." *Journal of Sex Research, 32*(4), 319–328.

Morris, D. (1979). *Gestures.* Briarcliff Manor, NY: Stein & Day.

Morris, D. (1995). *Bodytalk: The meaning of human gestures.* New York: Crown Trade Paperbacks.

Mott, F. L., & Jorgenson, C. E. (Eds.). (1939). *Benjamin Franklin: Representative selections, with introduction, bibliography, and notes.* New York: American Book.

Murdock, G. P. (1949). *Social structures.* New York: Macmillan.

Murphy, D. (2011, September 25). Saudi women to vote . . . *Christian Science Monitor.* Retrieved from http://www.csmonitor.com/World/Backchannels/2011/0925/Saudi-women-to-vote

Nafeesi, S. (1986). *Advertising in Saudi Arabia* (Unpublished master's thesis). California State University, San Bernardino.

Nakamura, H. (1964). *Ways of thinking of Eastern peoples: India-China-Tibet-Japan.* Honolulu, HI: East-West Center.

Nasr, S. H. (2003). *Science and civilization in Islam.* Cambridge, UK: Islamic Texts Society.

Nelson, C. (2009). *Rocket men: The epic story of the first men on the moon.* New York: Viking Press.

Ng, S. H., & Bradac, J. J. (1993). *Power in language: Verbal communication and social influence* (Language and Language Behavior) Newbury Park, CA: Sage.

Nisbett, R. E. (1980). *Human inference: Strategies and shortcomings of social judgment.* Englewood Cliffs, NJ: Prentice Hall.

Nisbett, R. E. (2003). *The geography of thought: How Asians and Westerners think differently.* New York: Free Press.

Nordenstreng, K., & Schiller, H. I. (Eds.). (1979). *National sovereignty and international communication.* Honolulu, HI: East-West Center.

NPR. (2011). *A guide to protests in Middle East, North Africa.* Retrieved from http://www.npr.org/2011/04/14/133992421/a-guide-to-protests-in-middle-east-north-africa

Oberg, K. (1960). Cultural shock: Adjustment to new cultural environments. *Practical Anthropology, 7,* 177–182.

Obeyesekere, G. (1992). *The apotheosis of Captain Cook.* Princeton, NJ: Princeton University Press.

Olesen, A. (2011, August 6). China blasts U.S. over credit rating downgrade. Associated Press.

Oliver, R. T. (1971). *Communication and culture in ancient India and China.* Syracuse, NY: Syracuse University Press.

Omi, M., & Winant, H. (1986). *Racial formations in the United States from the 1960s to the 1980s.* New York: Routledge & Kegan Paul.

Onishi, N. (2004, December 23). What's Korean for "real man"? Ask Japanese women. *New York Times.* Retrieved from http://www.nytimes.com/2004/12/23/international/asia/23JAPAN.html

Orbe, M. P. (1998). *Constructing co-cultural theory: An explication of culture, power, and communication.* Thousand Oaks, CA: Sage.

Oregon Department of Transportation. (2007, February 4). *What is sustainability?* Retrieved from http://www.oregon.gov/ODOT/SUS/what_is_sustainability.shtml

Ostler, N. (2005). *Empires of the word: A language history of the world.* New York: HarperCollins.

Our strategy. (2011). *Sustainability.* BP [Website]. Retrieved from http://www.bp.com/sectiongenericarticle800.do?categoryId=9036153&contentId=7066889

Owens, K., & King, M. C. (1999). Genomic views of human history. *Science, 286,* 451–453.

Paabo, S. (2001). Genomics and society: The human genome and our view of ourselves. *Science, 291,* 1219–1220.

Pacanowsky, M. E., & O'Donnell-Trujillo, N. (1982). Communication and organizational cultures. *Western Journal of Speech Communication, 46,* 115–130.

Park, H., Russell, C., & Lee, J. (2007). National culture and environmental sustainability: A cross-national analysis. *Journal of Economics and Finance, 31*(1), 104–121.

Passel, J., & Taylor, P. (2009). *Who's Hispanic?* Washington DC: Pew Hispanic Center. Retrieved from http://pewhispanic.org/reports/report.php?ReportID=111

Patterson, O. (1991). *Freedom: Freedom in the making of Western culture* (Vol. 1). New York: Basic Books.

Pavlidou, T. S. (2006). Telephone talk. In J. L. Mey (Ed.), *Concise encyclopedia of pragmatics* (2nd ed., pp. 1072–1075). Oxford: Elsevier.

Pedersen, P. (1995). *The five stages of culture shock: Critical incidents around the world.* Westport, CT: Greenwood.

Peng, Y.-S., & Lin, S. (2009). National culture, economic development, population growth and environmental performance: The mediating role of education. *Journal of Business Ethics, 90*(2), 203–219.

Penn, M. J. (2011). The pessimism index. *Time, 178*(2), 36–37.

People labels. (1995, November 20). *U.S. News & World Report*, p, 28.

Peters, T. J. (1982). *In search of excellence: Lessons from America's best-run companies.* New York: Harper & Row.

Pew Forum on Religion & Public Life. (2008). *U.S. religious landscape survey.* Washington, DC: Author.

Pew Forum on Religion & Public Life. (2009). *Mapping the global Muslim population.* Washington, DC: Author.

Pew Forum on Religion & Public Life. (2011). *The future of the global Muslim population.* Washington, DC: Author.

Pew Hispanic Center. (2009). *Between two worlds: How young Latinos come of age in America.* Washington DC: Author. Retrieved from http://pewhispanic.org/reports/report.php?ReportID = 117

Pew Research Center. (2002). *What the world thinks in 2002.* Retrieved from http://people-press.org/2002/12/04/what-the-world-thinks-in-2002/

Pew Research Center. (2007). *The Pew global attitudes project: World publics welcome global trade—but not immigration.* Washington, DC: Author.

Pfeil, U., Zaphiris, P., & Ang, C. S. (2006). Cultural differences in collaborative authoring of Wikipedia. *Journal of Computer-Mediated Communication, 12*(1). Retrieved from http://jcmc.indiana.edu/vo112/issue1/pfeil.html

Pharr, S. (1988). *Homophobia: A weapon of sexism.* Inverness, CA: Chardon.

Philipsen, G. (1975). Speaking "like a man" in Teamsterville: Culture patterns of role enactment in an urban neighborhood. *Quarterly Journal of Speech, 61*(1), 13–22.

Philipsen, G. (1976). Places for speaking in Teamsterville. *Quarterly Journal of Speech, 62*(1), 15–25.

Philipsen, G. (1989). Speech and the communal function in four cultures. In S. Ting-Toomey & F. Korzenny (Eds.), *International and Intercultural Communication Annual* (Vol. 13, pp. 79–92). Newbury Park, CA: Sage.

Philipsen, G. (1992). *Speaking culturally: Explorations in social communication.* Albany: State University of New York Press.

Piatt, B. (1990). *Only English? Law and language policy in the United States.* Albuquerque: University of New Mexico Press.

Plyler v. Doe , 457 U.S. 202 (1982).

Posse, A. (1989). *Perros del paraiso* [Dogs of paradise] (M. S. Peden, Trans.). New York: Atheneum Books.

Pratt, M. L. (1992). *Imperial eyes: Travel writing and transculturation.* London: Routledge.

Profiling the Facebooks of the world. (2010, June 14). *Advertising Age*, p. 6. Retrieved from http://adage.coverleaf.com/advertisingage/20100614?pg = 10#pg10

Puenta, S. (1996, May). *Toward a Latino urban policy agenda.* Presented to Latino Urban Policy Agenda Project Conference in Washington, DC.

Putnam, L., & Pacanowsky, M. (Eds.). (1983). *Communication and organizations: An interpretive approach.* Beverly Hills, CA: Sage.

Putnam, R. E. (2007). E pluribus unum: Diversity and community in the twenty-first century—the 2006 Johan Skytte prize lecture. *Scandinavian Political Studies, 30*(2), 137–174.

Recycling Advocates. (2004, June 28). *U.S. News & World Report*, p. 41.

Reese, L. (2005). *The Chipko movement: India's call to save their forests.* Berkley, CA: Women in World History Curriculum. Retrieved from http://www.womeninworldhistory.com/contemporary-04.html

Reid-Pharr, R. (2002, August 16). Extending queer theory to race and ethnicity. Chronicle of Higher Education pp. B7–B9.

Rheingold, H. (1999). Look who's talking. *Wired, 7*(1), 128–131.

Ricci, J., & Biederman, P. W. (2004, March 30). Acceptance of gays on rise, polls show. *Los Angeles Times*, p. B1.

Richardson, D. (1974). *Peace child.* Marina del Rey, CA: GL Publications.

Richter, P. (2000, March 25). Armed forces find "disturbing" level of gay harassment. *Los Angeles Times.* Retrieved from http://articles.latimes.com/2000/mar/25/news/mn-12608

Riggins, S. H. (Ed.). (1997). *The language and politics of exclusion.* Thousand Oaks, CA: Sage.

Ritzer, G. (1993). *The McDonaldization of society.* Newbury Park, CA: Pine Forge.

Robbins, S. S., & Stylianou, A. C. (2002). A study of cultural differences in global corporate websites. *Journal of Computer Information Systems, 42*(2), 3–9.

Robertson, I. (1987). *Sociology.* New York: Worth.

Robinson, E. (1999). *Cool to cream: A Blackman's journey beyond color to an affirmation of race.* New York: Free Press.

Rodriguez, A. (1999). *Making Latino news: Race, language, class.* Thousand Oaks, CA: Sage.

Rodriguez, G. (2004, February 20). Mexican Americans are building no walls. *Los Angeles Times.* Retrieved from http://articles.latimes.com/2004/feb/29/opinion/op-rodriguez29

Rodriguez, R. (2003). The North American. In J. Roden & S. P. Steinberg (Eds.), *Public discourse in America* (pp. 60–70). Philadelphia: University of Pennsylvania Press.

Roediger, D. R. (1999). *The wages of whiteness: Race and the making of the American working class.* London: Verso Books.

Rogers, E. M. (1986). *Communication technology.* New York: Free Press.

Rogers, E. M. (1999). Georg Simmel's concept of the stranger and intercultural communication research. *Communication Theory, 9*(1), 58–74.

Rogers, E. M., & Kincaid, D. L. (1981). *Communication networks: A new paradigm for research.* New York: Free Press.

Rogers, E. M., & Shoemarker, F. F. (1971). *Communication of innovations: A crosscultural approach* (2nd ed.). New York: Free Press.

Rojas, R. (2011, March 27). When students' words go viral, schools react. *Los Angeles Times,* pp. A29, A33.

Rojjanaprapayon, W. (1997). *Communication patterns of Thai people in a non-Thai context* (Unpublished doctoral dissertation). Purdue University, West Lafayette, IN.

Romaine, S. (1988). *Pidgin and creole languages.* London: Longman.

Romaine, S. (1992). *Language, education and development: Urban and rural Tok Pisin in Papua New Guinea.* Oxford, UK: Oxford University Press.

Romero, D. (1996, March 3). Most signposts are in English along the info superhighway. *Los Angeles Times.* Retrieved from http://articles.latimes.com/1996-03-03/news/ls-42728_1_english-alphabet

Ross, M. W. (1989). Gay youth in four cultures: A comparative study. *Journal of Homosexuality, 17*(3–4), 299–314.

Rotello, G. (1998, January 20). Last word: Inside the circle. *The Advocate,* p. 112.

Rothenberg, P. S. (Ed.). (1992). *Race, class, and gender in the United States: An integrated study* (2nd ed.). New York: St. Martin's.

Roy, A. (2001). *Power politics.* Cambridge, MA: South End.

Rushing, J. H. (1983). The rhetoric of the American western myth. *Communication Monographs, 50,* 15–32.

Rushing, J. H., & Frentz, T. S. (1978). The rhetoric of "Rocky": A social value model of criticism. *Western Journal of Speech Communication, 42*(2), 63–72.

Russo, V. (1987). *The celluloid closet: Homosexuality in the movies* (Rev. ed.). New York: Harper & Row.

Ryan, M. G. (1974). The influence of speaker dialect and sex on stereotypic attribution. In F. L. Casmir (Ed.), *International and Intercultural Communication Annual* (Vol. 1, pp. 87–101). New York: Speech Communication Association.

Sabogal, F., Marín, G., Otero-Sabogal, R., Marín, B. V., & Perez-Stable, P. (1987). Hispanic familism and acculturation: What changes and what doesn't. *Hispanic Journal of Behavioral Sciences, 9*(4), 397–412.

Said, E. (1978). *Orientalism.* New York: Pantheon.

Said, E. (1981). *Covering Islam: How the media and the experts determine how we see the rest of the world.* New York: Pantheon.

Sakamoto, N., & Naotsuka, R. (1982). *Polite fictions: Why Japanese and Americans seem rude to each other.* Tokyo: Kinseido.

Samovar, L. A., Porter, R. E., & Jain, N. C. (1981). *Understanding intercultural communication.* Belmont, CA: Wadsworth.

Sapir, E. (1921). *Language: An introduction to the study of speech.* New York: Harcourt Brace Jovanovich.

Sapir, E. (1949). *Selected writings in language, culture, and personality.* Berkeley: University of California Press.

Sax, L. J., Lindholm, J. A., Astin, A. W., Korn, W. S., & Mahoney, K. M. (2001). *The American freshman: National norms for fall 2001.* Los Angeles: Higher Education Research Institute of UCLA.

Scheer, R. (1991, December 15). Gore Vidal: Novelist of U.S. past sees an empire replacing republic he so admired. *Los Angeles Times,* p. M3. Retrieved from http://articles.latimes.com/1991-12-15/opinion/op-725_1_gore-vidal

Scheper-Hughes, N. (1993). *Death without weeping: The violence of everyday life in Brazil.* Berkley: University of California Press.

Schiller, H. I. (1976). *Communication and cultural domination.* White Plains, NY: International Arts and Science Press.

Schmid-Isler, S. (2000, January). *The language of digital genres—A semiotic investigation of style and iconology on the world wide web.* Proceedings of the 33rd Hawaii International Conference on System Sciences

(HICSS 2000). http://csd12.computer.org/comp/proceedings/hicss/2000/0493/03/04933012.pdf

Schradie, J. (2011). The digital production gap: The digital divide and web 2.0 collide. *Poetics, 39*(2), 145–168.

Schroeder, H. W. (1991, April). *The spiritual aspect of nature: A perspective from depth psychology.* Paper presented at the Northeastern Recreation Research Symposium, Saratoga Springs, NY.

Scollon, R., & Scollon, S. W. (1991). Mass and count nouns in Chinese and English: A few further Whorfian considerations. In R. Blust (Ed.), *Currents in Pacific linguistics: Papers on Austronesian languages and ethnolinguistics in honor of George W. Grace* (pp. 465–475). Canberra, Australia: Pacific Linguistics.

Sechrest, L., Fay, T. L., & Zaidi, S. M. (1972). Problems of translation in cross-cultural communication. *Journal of Cross-Cultural Psychology, 3*(1), 41–56.

Sedano, M. V. (1980). Chicanismo: A rhetorical analysis of themes and images of selected poetry from the Chicano movement. *Western Journal of Speech Communication, 44*(3), 177–190.

Segal, A. F. (2004). *Life after death: A history of the afterlife in Western religion.* Garden City, NY: Doubleday.

Segall, M. H., Campbell, D. T., & Herskovits, M. J. (1966). *The influence of culture on visual perception.* Indianapolis, IN: Bobbs-Merrill.

S. Res. 76, 100th Cong, 134 Cong. Rec. S 29528 (1988).

Sennett, R. (1999).The spaces of democracy. *Harvard Design Magazine* (Summer), 68–72.

Shachtman, T. (2006). *Rumspringa: To be or not to be Amish.* New York: North Point Press.

Shaheen, J. G. (1984). *The TV Arab.* Bowling Green, OH: Bowling Green State University Popular Press.

Shaheen, J. G. (2001). *Reel bad Arabs: How Hollywood vilifies a people.* New York: Olive Branch.

Sherif, M., & Sherif, C. W. (1953). *Groups in harmony and tension.* New York: Harper.

Shin, H. B. & Bruno, R. A. (2003). *Language use and English-speaking ability: 2000.* Washington, DC: U.S. Census Bureau.

Shin, H. B. & Kominski, R. A. (2010). *Language use in the United States: 2007* (American Community Survey Reports, ACS-12). Washington, DC: U.S. Census Bureau.

Shioiri, T., Someya, T., Helmeste, D., & Tang, S. W. (1999). Misinterpretation of facial expression: A cross-cultural study. *Psychiatry and Clinical Neurosciences, 53*(1), 45–50.

Shome, R. (1996). Postcolonial interventions in the rhetorical canon: An "other" view. *Communication Theory, 6*(1), 40–59.

Shome, R., & Hegde, R. S. (2002). Postcolonial approaches to communication: Charting the terrain, engaging the intersections. *Communication Theory, 12*(3), 249–270.

Shuter, R. (1979). Gaze behavior in interracial and intraracial interactions. In Nemi C. Jain (Ed.), *International and Intercultural Communication Annual* (Vol, 5, pp. 48–54). Falls Church, VA: Speech Communication Association.

Shuter, R. & Chattopadhyay, S. (2010). Emerging interpersonal norms of text messaging in India and the United States. *Journal of Intercultural Communication Research, 39*(2), 123–147.

Sierra Club. (2008, April 23). New Sierra Club poll shows Hispanic voters concerned about global warming and energy [Press release]. Retrieved from http://action.sierraclub.org/site/MessageViewer?em_id = 50401.0

Simmons, A. M. (2003, December 21). Minority within a minority. *Los Angeles Times,* p. B1, B12.

Simons, D. J., & Chabris, C. F. (1999). Gorillas in our midst: Sustained inattentional blindness for dynamic events. *Perception, 28*(9), 1059–1074.

Singh, N., & Baak, D. W. (2004). Web site adaptation: A cross-cultural comparison of U.S. and Mexican web sites. *Journal of Computer-Mediated Communication, 9*(4). Retrieved from http://jcmc.indiana.edu/vol9/issue4/singh_baack.html

Singh, N., Zhao, H., & Hu, X. (2003). Cultural adaptation on the web: A study of American companies' domestic and Chinese websites. *International Journal of Global Information Management, 11*(3), 63–80.

Slagle, A. (1995). In defense of Queer Nation: From identity politics to a politics of difference. *Western Journal of Communication, 59*(2), 85–102.

Smith, A. G. (1966). *Communication and culture: Readings in the codes of human interaction.* New York: Holt, Rinehart & Winston.

Smith, C. A. (1991). *The absentee American.* New York: Praeger.

Smith, J. I. (2000). *Islam in America.* New York: Columbia University Press.

Smith, R. C., & Eisenberg, E. (1987). Conflict at Disneyland: A root-metaphor analysis. *Communication Monographs, 54*(4), 367–380.

Smith, R. R., & Windes, R. R. (1997). The progay and antigay issue culture: Interpretation, influence, and dissent. *Quarterly Journal of Speech, 83*(1), 28–48.

Smutkupt, S., & Barna, L. M. (1976). Impact of nonverbal communication in an intercultural setting: Thailand. In F. Casmir (Ed.), *International and Intercultural Communication Annual* (Vol. 3, pp. 130–138). Falls Church, VA: Speech Communication Association.

Snapshot of America. (2004). *U.S. News & World Report, 136*(23), 40–41.

Snyder, M., & Uranowitz, S. W. (1978). Reconstructing the past: Some cognitive consequences of person perception. *Journal of Personality & Social Psychology, 36*(9), 941–950.

Stark, R. (2005). *The victory of reason: How Christianity led to freedom, capitalism, and Western success*. New York: Random House.

State of Israel, Central Bureau of Statistics. (2011, February 24). *Immigration to Israel: 2010* [Press release]. Retrieved from http://www1.cbs.gov.il/www/hodaot2011n/21_11_045e.pdf

State of Wisconsin v. Jonas Yoder et al., 406 U.S. 205 (1972).

Stauffer, J. (2005). Across the great divide. *Time, 166*(1), 58–65.

Stavenhagen, R. (1986). *Problems and prospects of multiethnic states*. Tokyo: United Nations University Press.

Stavenhagen, R. (1990). Linguistic minorities and language policy in Latin America: The case of Mexico. In F. Coulmas (Ed.), *Linguistic minorities and literacy: Language policy issues in developing countries* (pp. 56–62). Berlin: Mouton.

Steele, C. M., & Aronson, J. (1995). Stereotype threat and the intellectual test performance of African Americans. *Journal of Personality & Social Psychology, 69*(5), 797–811.

Steinfatt, T. M. (1989). Linguistic relativity: Toward a broader view. In S. Ting-Toomey & F. Korzenny (Eds.), *International and Intercultural Communication Annual* (Vol. 13, pp. 35–75). Newbury Park, CA: Sage.

Stevenson, V. (1999). *The world of words: An illustrated history of Western languages* (Rev. ed.). New York: Sterling.

Stewart, E. C. (1972). *American cultural patterns: A cross-cultural perspective*. Chicago: Intercultural Press.

Stewart, E. C. (1982). Applications of intercultural communication in Japan. *Speech Education, 9*, 4–7.

Strengthen women's role in environmental sustainability. (1999). Retrieved from http://www.un.org/womenwatch/forums/beijing5/enviro/enviro.htm

Sugawara, Y. (1993). *Silence and avoidance: Japanese expatriate adjustment* (Unpublished master's thesis). California State University, San Bernardino.

Sustainability. (2008). *Portland: Oregon Department of Environmental Quality* [Website]. Retrieved from http://www.deq.state.or.us/programs/sustainability/

Sustainability pillars. (2011). *Sustainability*. Dow [Website]. Retrieved from http://www.dow.com/sustainability/pillars/

Sustainable Development Network (n.d.). *Ecological imperialism: A sustainable development network briefing paper*. Retrieved from http://sdnetwork.net

Sutherland, W. J. (2003). Parallel extinction risk and global distribution of languages and species. *Nature, 423*, 276–279.

Sypher, B. D. (1985). Culture and communication in organizations. In W. Gudykunst (Ed.), *International and Intercultural Communication Annual* (Vol. 9, pp. 13–29). Newbury Park, CA: Sage.

Szalay, L. B., & Inn, A. (1987). Cross-cultural adaptation and diversity: Hispanic Americans. In Y. . Y. Kim & W. B. Gundykunst (Eds.), *International and Intercultural Communication Annual* (Vol. 11, pp. 212–232). Newbury Park, CA: Sage.

Szalay, L. B., Moon, W. T., & Bryson, J. A. (1971). *Communication lexicon on three South Korean audiences: Social, national, and motivational domains; Communication lexicon on three South Korean audiences: Domains of family, education, and international relations*. Kensington, MD: American Institutes for Research.

Tajfel, H. (1969). Social and cultural factors in perception. In G. Lindzey & E. Aronson (Eds.), *The handbook of social psychology* (Vol. 3, 2nd ed., pp. 315–394). Reading, MA: Addison-Wesley.

Tanno, D. V. (1994). Names, narratives, and the evolution of ethnic identity. In A. Gonzalez, M. Houston, & V. Chen (Eds.), *Our voices: Essays in culture, ethnicity, and communication* (pp. 28–32). Los Angeles: Roxbury.

Tanno, D. V., & Jandt, F. E. (1994). Redefining the "other" in multicultural research. *Howard Journal of Communications, 5*(1–2), 36–45.

Taylor, D., Dubé, L., & Bellerose, J. (1986). Intergroup contact in Quebec. In M. Hewstone & R. Brown (Eds.), *Contact and conflict in intergroup encounters* (pp. 107–118). Oxford, UK: Basil Blackwell.

Tharoor, S. (2006). *India: From midnight to the millennium and beyond*. New York: Arcade.

Tharoor, S. (Ed.). (2007). *The elephant, the tiger and the cell phone: Reflections on India, the emerging 21st century power*. New York: Arcade.

Ting-Toomey, S. (1985). Toward a theory of conflict and culture. In W. Gudykunst (Ed.), *International and Intercultural Communication Annual* (Vol. 9, pp. 71–86). Newbury Park, CA: Sage.

Ting-Toomey, S., & Kurogi, A. (1998). Facework competence in intercultural conflict: An updated face-negotiation theory. *International Journal of Intercultural Relations, 22*(2), 187–225.

Tobin, J., & Dobard, R. G. (1999). *Hidden in plain view: The secret story of quilts and the underground.* Garden City, NY: Doubleday.

Tocqueville, A. de (1945). *Democracy in America.* New York: Vintage. (Original work published 1835)

Todd, E. (1985). *The explanation of ideology: Family structures and social systems* (D. Garrioch, Trans.). Oxford, UK: Basil Blackwell.

Tolson, J. (2007). Islam vs. science. *U.S. News & World Report, 143*(8), 48–49.

Tómas Rivera Center. (1996). *Hispanic perspectives.* Claremont, CA: Author.

Top 200 franchise systems. (2007). *Franchise Times,* Retrieved from http://www.scribd.com/doc/4965166/2007FranchiseTimesTop200

Triandis, H. C. (1964). Cultural influences upon cognitive processes. In L. Berkowitz (Ed.), *Advances in experimental psychology* (Vol. 2, pp. 1–48). New York: Academic Press.

Tsujimura, A. (1968). *Japanese culture and communication.* Tokyo: NHK Books.

Tsujimura, A. (1987). Some characteristics of the Japanese way of communication. In D. L. Kincaid (Ed.), *Communication theory: Eastern and Western perspectives* (pp. 115–126). San Diego: Academic Press.

Tung, T. M. (1990). Southeast Asia refugee mental health: Fourteen years later. *Journal of Vietnamese Studies, 1*(3), 56–64.

Tylor, E. B. (1871). *Primitive culture: Researches into the development of mythology, philosophy, religion, art, and custom.* London: J. Murray.

United Nations. (2000). *The world's women 2000: Trends and statistics.* New York: Author.

United Nations. (2006a). *Trends in total migrant stock: The 2005 revision: CD-ROM Documentation.* New York: United Nations, Department of Economic and Social Affairs, Population Division.

United Nations. (2006b). *World population monitoring, focusing on international migration and development: Report of the Secretary-General* (E/CN.9/2006/3). New York: Author.

United Nations Development Fund for Women. (2011). *MDGs and Gender: Goal 7: Ensure environmental sustainability.* Retrieved from http://www.unifem.org/progress/2008/mdgsGender7.html

United Nations Development Programme. (1990). *Human development report.* New York: Oxford University Press.

United Nations Development Programme. (1993). *Human development report.* New York: Oxford University Press.

United Nations Development Programme. (1995). *Human development report.* New York: Oxford University Press.

United Nations Development Programme. (1999). *Human development report.* New York: Oxford University Press.

United Nations Development Programme. (2003). *Arab human development report 2003: Building a knowledge society.* New York: Author.

United Nations Development Programme. (2004). *Arab human development report 2004: Towards freedom in the Arab world.* New York: Author.

United Nations Development Programme. (2007). *Human development report.* New York: Oxford University Press.

United Nations Development Programme. (2008). *Human development report 2007/2008.* New York: Oxford University Press.

United Nations Development Programme. (2010). *Human development report.* New York: Palgrave Macmillan.

United Nations Global Compact. (2005). *The ten principles.* Retrieved from http://www.unglobalcompact.org/AboutTheGC/TheTenPrinciples/index.html

United States v. Sandoval, 231 U.S. 28 (1913).

U.S. Census Bureau. (2009). *2005–2009 population and housing narrative profile for Puerto Rico.* Washington, DC: Author.

U.S. Census Bureau. (2010). *Statistical abstract of the United States: 2011.* Washington, DC: Author.

U.S. Supreme Court Reports, 29 L. Ed. 2d (1972).

Useem, R. H., & Downie, R. D. (1976). Third-culture kids. *Today's Education, 65*(3), 103–105.

Varnell, P. (2000, June 20). The threat of assimilation. *Chicago Free Press.* Retrieved from http://igfculturewatch.com/2000/06/28/the-threat-of-assimilation/

Vidal, J. (2010, May 29). Nigeria's agony dwarfs the Gulf oil spill: The US and Europe ignore it. *The Oberver.* Retrieved from http://www.guardian.co.uk/world/2010/may/30/oil-spills-nigeria-niger-delta-shell

Vision of Humanity (2008). *Global peace index 2008.* Retrieved from http://www.visonofhumanity.org

Walker, S. (1994). *Hate speech: The history of an American controversy.* Lincoln: University of Nebraska Press.

Wang, X. (1996). Conflict over the role of women in contemporary China: Prospects for liberation and resolution. In F. E. Jandt & P. B. Pedersen (Eds.), *Constructive conflict management: Asia-Pacific cases* (pp. 97–111). Thousand Oaks, CA: Sage.

Warner, M. (Ed.). (1993). *Fear of a queer planet.* Minneapolis: University of Minnesota Press.

Warschauer, M., El Said, G. R., & Zohry, A. (2002). Language choice online: Globalization and identity in

Egypt. *Journal of Computer Mediated Communication, 7*(4). Retrieved from http://jcmc.indiana.edu/vo17/issue4/warschauer.html

Wasserstrom, J. N. (1991). *Student protests in twentieth-century China: The view from Shanghai.* Stanford, CA: Stanford University Press.

Watson, T. J., Jr. (1963). *A business and its beliefs.* New York: McGraw-Hill.

Weiner, M. (1994). *Race and migration in imperial Japan.* London: Routledge.

Weinstein, N., Przybylski, A. K., & Ryan, R. M. (2009). Can nature make us more caring? Effects of immersion in nature on intrinsic aspirations and generosity. *Personality and Social Psychology Bulletin, 35*(10), 1315–1329.

Weller, A. (1998). Human pheromones: Communication through body odour. *Nature 392,* 126–127.

Wells, S. (2002). *The journey of man: A genetic odyssey.* Princeton, NJ: Princeton University Press.

Westbrook, R. B. (1991). *John Dewey and American democracy.* Ithaca, NY: Cornell University Press.

Wexler, B. E. (2008). *Brain and culture.* Cambridge: MIT Press.

Whetmore, E. J. (1987). *Mediamerica: Form, content, and consequence of mass communication* (3rd ed.). Belmont, CA: Wadsworth.

Willis, D. B. (1994). Transculturals, transnationals: The new diaspora. *International Schools Journal, 14*(1), 29–42.

Witt, S. D. (1997). Parental influences on children's socialization to gender roles. *Adolescence, 32*(126), 253–259.

Wolff, B. (Producer). (2005, August 5). *The situation* [Television broadcast]. New York: MSNBC.

Wong, D. F. K., Li, C. Y., & Song, H. X. (2007). Rural migrant workers in urban China: Living a marginalised life. *International Journal of Social Welfare, 16*(1), 32–40.

Wood, J. (2005). *Gendered lives: Communication, gender, and culture.* Belmont, CA: Wadsworth.

Woodring, A. A. (1995). Power distance and individualism among Japanese university students. *Hiroshima Shudo University Research Review, 11,* 61–75.

World Commission on Environment and Development. (1987). *Our common future.* Oxford, UK: Oxford University Press.

Yale Center for Environmental Law & Policy. (2010). *Country Scores.* Retrieved from http://epi.yale.edu/Countries

Yep, G. A., Lovaas, K. E., & Elia, J. P. (2003). *Queer theory and communication: From disciplining queers to queering the discipline(s).* Binghamton, NY: Harrington Park Press.

York, J. (2011). How much does internet access matter? *Global Voices Advocacy.* Retrieved from http://advocacy.globalvoicesonline.org/2011/03/10/how-much-does-internet-access-matter/

Young, B. B. C. (1980). The Hawaiians. In J. F. McDermott, Jr., W.-S. Tseng, & T. W. Maretzki (Eds.), *People and cultures of Hawaii: A psycho-cultural profile* (pp. 5–24). Honolulu: University Press of Hawai'i.

Yum, J. O. (1987). Korean philosophy and communication. In D. L. Kincaid (Ed.), *Communication theory: Eastern and Western perspectives* (pp. 71–86). San Diego: Academic Press.

Yum, J. O. (1988). The impact of Confucianism on interpersonal relationships and communications patterns in East Asia. *Communication Monographs, 55*(4), 374–388.

Yum, J. O., & Park, H. W. (1990). The effects of disconfirming information on stereotype change. *Howard Journal of Communication, 2*(4), 357–367.

Zagorin, P. (2003). *How the idea of religious toleration came to the West.* Princeton, NJ: Princeton University Press.

Zakaria, F. (2011, March 3). Are America's best days behind us? *Time.* 177(). Retrieved from http://www.time.com/time/magazine/article/0,9171,2056723,00.html

Zelinsky, W. (1973). *The cultural geography of the United States.* Englewood Cliffs, NJ: Prentice Hall.

Zenner, W. (1996). Ethnicity. In D. Levinson & M. Ember (Eds.), *Encyclopedia of cultural anthropology* (pp. 393–395). New York: Holt.

Zhao Y. H. (2000). Rural-to-urban labor migration in China: The past and the present. In: L. A. West, Y. H. Zhao (Eds.), *Rural labor flows in China* (pp. 231–250). Berkeley: University of California at Berkeley, Institute of East Asian Studies.

Zuckerman, M. B. (2008). China's gold-medal moment. *U.S. News & World Report, 145*(5), 94–96.

CREDITS

Photo Essay Background Image. Comstock Images/ Comstock/Thinkstock.

Part 1 Photo Essays

Photo Essay 1.1, page 2 (top). Digital Vision/ Digital Vision/Thinkstock.

Photo Essay 1.2, page 2 (bottom left). ©iStockphoto.com/ LL28.

Photo Essay 1.3, page 2 (bottom right). ©iStockphoto .com/ ElenaVizerskaya.

Photo Essay 1.4, page 3 (top). ©iStockphoto.com/ Soubrette.

Photo Essay 1.5, page 3 (bottom left). ©iStockphoto.com/ kycstudio.

Photo Essay 1.6, page 3 (bottom right). ©iStockphoto .com/tovfla.

Chapter 1

Photo 1.1, page 9. Photo courtesy of Mark Schumacher/ www.onmarkproductions.com.

Photo 1.2, page 15. Henryhbk/wikimedia.org.

Photo 1.3, page 24. ©iStockphoto.com/RollingEarth.

Photo 1.4, page 27. Image of euro provided by the author.

Chapter 2

Photo 2.1, page 37. Rasheed Irani.

Photo 2.2, page 45. ©Can Stock Photo Inc./Lvnel.

Photo 2.3, page 47. ©iStockphoto.com/peeterv.

Photo 2.4, page 51. CNTV http://www.cntv.cn.

Photo 2.5, page 53. Asian American Resource Workshop.

Chapter 3

Photo 3.1, page 66. Fred Jandt.

Photo 3.2, page 67. © Earl & Nazima Kowall/CORBIS.

Photo 3.3, page 68. Copyright © Johnston Pump Company. Reprinted with permission.

Photo 3.4, page 71. Digital Vision/ Digital Vision/ Thinkstock.

Photo 3.5, page 74. ©iStockphoto.com/fotoVoyager.

Part 2 Photo Essays

Photo Essay 2.1, page 78 (left). Digital Vision/ Digital Vision/Thinkstock.

Photo Essay 2.2, page 78 (right). BananaStock/ BananaStock/Thinkstock.

Photo Essay 2.3, page 79 (top). Christopher Robbins/ Photodisc/Thinkstock.

Photo Essay 2.4, page 79 (right). BananaStock/ BananaStock/Thinkstock.

Photo Essay 2.5, page 79 (bottom left). Jupiterimages/ Comstock/Thinkstock.

Chapter 4

Photo 4.1, page 88. ©Can Stock Photo Inc./monkey business.

Photo 4.2, page 91. Hedman/Wikimedia.

Photo 4.3, page 99. ©iStockphoto.com/grcorbin.

Photo 4.4, page 101. ©Can Stock Photo Inc./bbbar.

Photo 4.5, page 103. N/A.

Chapter 5

Photo 5.1, page 108. Stockbyte/Stockbyte/Thinkstock.

Photo 5.2, page 108. ©iStockphoto.com/brittak.

Photo 5.3, page 108. Thinkstock Images/Comstock/ Thinkstock.

Photo 5.4, page 110. ©Can Stock Photo Inc./kevers.

Photo 5.5, page 115. Jack Hollingsworth/Photodisc/ Thinkstock.

Photo 5.6, page 117. ©Can Stock Photo Inc./nito.
Photo 5.7, page 118. Jupiterimages/Goodshoot/Thinkstock.
Photo 5.8, page 118. ©Can Stock Photo Inc./Paha_L.
Photo 5.9, page 120. Brand X Pictures/Brand X Pictures/Thinkstock.
Photo 5.10, page 124. Comstock Images/Comstock/Thinkstock.
Photo 5.11, page 125. Photo courtesy of James Heremaia.
Photo 5.12, page 127. Chad Baker/ Photodisc/Thinkstock.
Photo 5.13, page 128. ©iStockphoto.com/Bearstudio.

Chapter 6

Photo 6.1, page 133. Drork/Wikimedia.
Photo 6.2, page 134. ©CreativeFire/istockphoto.com.
Photo 6.3, page 144. ©iStockphoto.com/petebax.
Photo 6.4, page 151. ©AFP/Getty Images.
Photo 6.5, page 154. Natalie Moxam/Wikimedia.
Photo 6.6, page 155. Editorial cartoon by Mike Thompson from La Opinion, November 20, 1995.
Photo 6.7, page 157. ©Can Stock Photo Inc./dgphotography.
Photo 6.8, page 160. ©iStockphoto.com.

Part 3 Photo Essays

Photo Essay 3.1, page 166 (left). Brand X Pictures/ Brand X Pictures/Thinkstock.
Photo Essay 3.2, page 166 (right). ©iStockphoto.com.
Photo Essay 3.3, page 167 (top). ©iStockphoto.com.
Photo Essay 3.4, page 167 (right). ©iStockphoto.com.
Photo Essay 3.5, page 167 (bottom left). ©iStockphoto.com.

Chapter 7

Photo 7.1, page 174. ©Can Stock Photo Inc./rssfhs.
Photo 7.2, page 175. ©meldayus / istockphoto.com.
Photo 7.3, page 178. ©Getty Images.
Photo 7.4, page 179. ©AFP/Getty Images.
Photo 7.5, page 180. ©Bloomberg/Getty Images.

Chapter 8

Photo 8.1, page 199. Beinecke Rare Book & Manuscript Library, Yale University.
Photo 8.2, page 203. ©iStockphoto.com.
Photo 8.3, page 206. ©iStockphoto.com.
Photo 8.4, page 211. ©iStockphoto.com.

Chapter 9

Photo 9.1, page 232. Tom Loos.
Photo 9.2, page 233. ©Pool/Getty Images.
Photo 9.3, page 235. ©Can Stock Photo Inc./philipus.
Photo 9.4, page 241. ©AFP/Getty Images.
Photo 9.5, page 242. ©Can Stock Photo Inc.
Photo 9.6, page 246. AP Photo/Ben Curtis.

Chapter 10

Photo 10.1, page 251. ©Fritz Hoffmann/Corbis.
Photo 10.2, page 262. ©LEHTIKUVA/X00718/Reuters/Corbis.
Photo 10.3, page 267. ©iStockphoto.com.
Photo 10.4, page 271. © AFP/Getty Images.
Photo 10.5, page 273. ©iStockphoto.com.

Chapter 11

Photo 11.1, page 283. ©Ed Kashi/VII/Corbis.
Photo 11.2, page 284. AP Photo/Anthony Mitchell.
Photo 11.3, page 287. Coca-Cola is a registered trademark of the Coca-Cola Company. Permission for use granted by the company.
Photo 11.4, page 288. ©Paul Joseph/Wikimedia.
Photo 11.5, page 290. ©JasonHuen/Wikimedia.
Photo 11.6, page 292. N/A.
Photo 11.7, page 295. ©iStockphoto.com.

Part 4 Photo Essays

Photo Essay 4.1, page 306 (top). ©iStockphoto.com.
Photo Essay 4.2, page 306 (right). ©iStockphoto.com.
Photo Essay 4.3, page 306 (bottom left). William P. Gottlieb/Wikimedia.
Photo Essay 4.4, page 307 (left). ©iStockphoto.com.
Photo Essay 4.5, page 307 (right). ©Can Stock Photo Inc./jwolf29.

Chapter 12

Photo 12.1, page 312. AP Photo/Zhang Guofang.
Photo 12.2, page 322. Library of Congress.
Photo 12.3, page 323. Photo by Tomas Castelazo/Wikimedia.
Photo 12.4, page 330. Photo courtesy of Burleson County Chamber of Commerce.

Chapter 13

Photo 13.1, page 343. ©Can Stock Photo Inc./wico.
Photo 13.2, page 344. ©Can Stock Photo Inc. / Arvids.
Photo 13.3, page 347. Library of Congress.
Photo 13.4, page 355. http://www.regan.utexas.edu/archives/speeches/1984/103184c.htm.
Photo 13.5, page 358. *People en Español* cover. Copyright © 2002 Time Inc. All rights reserved.
Photo 13.6, page 361. N/A.
Photo 13.7, page 362. Tyson.

Chapter 14

Photo 14.1, page 371. ©Can Stock Photo Inc./ KarolinaL.
Photo 14.2, page 374. ©Jim Mahoney/Dallas Morning News/Corbis.
Photo 14.3, page 381. ©LEHTIKUVA/X00718/Reuters/Corbis.
Photo 14.4, page 384. ©iStockphoto.com.
Photo 14.5, page 387. Digital Vision/ Digital Vision/ Thinkstock.

INDEX

Abeele, M. V., 51
Aboriginal, 9–11, 281
Accent, 122–123
Acculturation, 316, 329–334, 384–386
Activity orientation, 209–211, 239
Adaptation, 316
Adaptation potential, 299
Adjustment, 316
Adler, P. S., 309
Adopters, 299
Adorno, T. W., 52, 90
Africa, languages, 5, 152
African-American, 52, 129
African "Eve," 5
Afrikaans, 152
Agger, B. 281
Al-Ashmawy, Sai'd, 232
Alaskan Native, 13
Albarran, A. B., 359
Allen, H. G., 159
Allen, Jim, 177
Allport, Gordon, 85, 88
al-Nasseri, Ahmed bin Khalid, 227
al-Sayyid, Ahmed Lutfi, 227
Amae, 177
American Indian, 13, 17, 44, 83–84, 90, 198
   languages, 160–161
   school mascots, 87
See also Indigenous cultures
American Indian Religious Freedom Act, 17
Amish, 17, 340–344
Amnesty International, 383
Andersen, K. E., 37
Andersen, P. A., 200
Anxiety, 82
Arab culture, 140–141, 225–246
   communication barriers, 242–246
Arabic, 140–141

Arab states, 272–273
Argentina
   immigration from Europe, 317–318
   immigration from Korea, 317
Argot, 367–368
Argyle, M., 119
Aristotle, 39, 41, 59
Arizonans for Official English v. Arizona, 158
Armstrong, N., 119, 120
Artifact, 285–286
Asian-Americans, 89–90
Assimilation, 316, 334, 347–348, 384–386
Assuming similarity instead of difference, 82–83
Asuncion-Lande, N., 140–141
Asylee, 309
Aurand, A. M., Jr., 341
Australia, 9–11, 152–153, 281
Authoritarian personality, 90
Axtell, R. E., 117, 142

Back, T.-H., 340
Baker, I., 100
Bank of America, 361
Barbarian, 6, 22
Barber, W., 50
Barbie dolls, 233, 296
Barer-Stein, T., 72
Barna, LaRay M., 81
Barnum, W., 374
Baron, D., 346
Barrett, Colleen, 375
Barriers to intercultural communication, 11, 44, 81–92, 129
Baseball, 177–178
Basque, 24, 344
Baum, G., 29

Belay, G. 35
Beltran, L. R. S., 298
Bennhold, K., 25
Berger, C. R., 81
Bergqvist, C., 262
Berlo, David, 42, 44
Berry, J. W., 332, 350
Bickerton, D., 146
Biculturalism, 311, 334
Bigelow, B., 199
Bilingual speakers, 136
Birke-Smith, K., 139
Black, G. 100
Blanchard, F. A., 54
Bolton, R., 380
Bond, Michael H., 188
Borchorst, A., 263
Border cultures, 6
Bosmajian, H. A., 22
Boucher, J. D., 83
Brazil
   immigration from Japan, 317
   immigration from Korea, 317
   immigration from the U.S., 318
Breakdowns in intercultural communication.
      See Barriers to intercultural communication.
Brettell, C. B., 249
Brislin, R. W., 12
British punk, 370–372
Brooks, David, 311
Brown, Mark, 145
Bruce, J., 276
Brundtland Commission, 31
Buchanan, Patrick J., 321
Buck, R., 107
Buddhism, 175
Budweiser, 296, 360–361
Burger King, 293–294
Burgoon, J. K., 108–109, 113

Busari, S., 151
Buss, D. M., 275

Caliph, 229
Calhoun, John C., Senator, 352
Campbell, B. G., 19
Canada, 153 *See also* Quebec.
Cann, Rebecca L., 5
Cant, 367
Carey, J. W., 41
Carliner, D., 321
Carroll, J. B., 136
Carson, Rachel, 38
Caucasian, 13, 19, 22
Cavalli-Sforza, L., 5, 19
Cell phones, 46–49, 360
Chance, N. A., 140
Chang, H.-C., 41
Change, 210–211, 343–344
Change agent, 298
    ethics, 299
Channel, 43, 45 *See also* Media
Chapman, M. 193
Chauncey, George Jr., 381
Chen, G.-M., 35, 36, 39
Cherry, C., 60
Chicano, 350
China, 39, 85, 93–104
    culture effect on perception,
        64, 66–67
    economic issues, 103
    face, 72
    food, 73–74
    free speech, 100
    harmony, 60
    human rights, 100
    Internet, 101–102
    language use, 97–98
    media, broadcast, 100–101
    migration, 96–97, 312–313
    one-child campaign, 266–267
    Shanghai Disneyland, 291
    women, 265–267
Chinese Culture Connection, 188
Chiu, L.-H., 64
Chomsky, Noam, 133, 135
Chronemics, 121–122
Chu, Godwin C., 39
Chyz, Y. J., 330
Citzenship policies, 313–316
Civilization, Western, 6

Clinton, Hillary, 102
Clothing, 125–126
Clough, M., 200, 220
Cobo, J. R. M.,
Coca-Cola, 287–289, 361
Cochtane, A., 38
Co-culture, 13–14
Code switching, 354
Cohen, M. N., 85
Cohen v. California, 54
Cole, M., 6
Collectivism, 169–172, 193, 201
Collier, M. J., 7, 13, 19, 122, 348
Collins, P. H., 369
Colonialism, 279–280
Coming out, 385
Communication, 39–44
    apprehension, 123
    Confucian perspectives, 39–41
    hate speech, 52
    language, 65, 133–162
    media 45–51
    mitigated speech, 183
    nonverbal, 107–129
    skills, 36
    Western perspectives, 41–44
Competition, 216
Conceptual equivalence, 143–145
Condit, C. M., 249
Conformity, 217–218
Confucian ethics, 189–190,
        269–270, 301
Confucian work dynamism, 188
Confucius, 39, 59, 73
Contact zone, 22–32, 279
Context, 44, 69–72
Convergence, 301
Cook, Captain James, 15,
        280–281, 386
Corporate cultures, 372–376
Costello, E. 87
Coulton, T. M., 179
Cowan, M., 142
Cowen, T., 26
Craig, Robert T., 39
Crawford, J., 154, 156, 158
Creole, 146–147
Crosby, F., 92
Cultural adaptation. *See*
    Acculturation
Cultural awareness, 36

Cultural hegemony, 286–287
Cultural icons, 285–297
Cultural identity, 7
Cultural imperialism, 282–285
Cultural invasion, 147
Cultural nearsightedness, 85
Cultural relativism, 84–85
Cultural studies, 11, 281
Culture, 5–11
Culture shock, 36, 309–311
Cultures within cultures, 11
    See also Subculture
Cyworld, 51

Damasio, Antonio, 5
Dannin, R., 229
Darwin, Charles, 107–108
Davidson, C. M., 236
Davin, D., 313
Davis, Angela, 362
Davis, Edmund Wade, 137
Deal, T. E., 372
Decoding, 43
Deetz, S., 60
    de la Garza, R., 351
    de la Zerda, N., 122
Demick, B., 102, 267
Deming, W. Edward, 300
De Mooij, M., 286, 301
Denning, M., 369
Deviant, 18
DeVito, J., 42
Dialects, 221
Diamond, J., 31
Diaspora, 337–338
Diffusion, 298–302
Discursive imperialism, 280
Disney, 289–291, 372–373
Dogs, 66–67
Doi, Takeo, 177
Domhoff, G. W., 185
Doty, R. L., 127
Downing, J. D. H., 357, 359
Doyle, J. A., 249
Dresser, N., 119
D'Souza, D., 198
Dubai, 230, 236–238
Duberman, Martin, 385
Dudley, M. K., 17
Duff-Brown, B., 139
Duncan, D. E., 121

Dunn, M., 133
Dyer, R., 20
Dynes, W., 381

Eastman, C., 354
Eck, D. L., 203
Ecoimperialism, 285
Economic class, 12
Education, 342
Efficiency, 210
Ehrlich, Paul, 38
Ekman, P., 107
Elliott, L., 285
Ellis Island, 323
Emerson, Ralph Waldo, 348
Emic, 197
    *Employment Division of Oregon
        v. Smith,* 17
Encoding, 43
English, 50, 148–161
Environmental ethics, 38
Environmental Performance
        Index, 191
Environmental sustainability,
        31–32, 102, 190–192
    Recycling symbol, 111–112
Environmental Sustainability
        Index, 190, 241
Epstein, S., 377
Equality, 216–217
Eskimo, 138–139
Esperanto, 147
Essoungou, A.-M., 47
Esty, D. C., 241
Ethics, 37–38
    change agent, 299
Ethnic and religious conflict, 24–25
Ethnic identity, 13
Ethnicity, 12–16
Ethnocentrism, 83–85
Ethnography, 11
Etic, 197
Euro, 27
Eurocentric ethnocentrism, 85
Euro Disney, 289–290
Europe,
    immigration to Western Europe,
        319–320
    migration to Argentina, 317–318
    migration to United States,
        322–328

European-American, 13
European Union, 27
Expatriate, 309
Experiential equivalence, 143

Face, 41, 72, 178, 301
Facebook, 47–50, 151, 244
Fackler, G. D., 360
Falwell, Jerry, 217
Families, 273–275
Feedback, 43–44
Fejes, F., 383
Femininity, 180–182
Feminist theory, 249
Feng shui, 126–127, 290
Ferguson, N., 197
Ferguson, W., 332
Fertility rate, 266
Field dependence, 61
Fischer, David Hackett, 198
Fishman, J. A., 138
Fitzpatrick, L., 267
Fong, M., 41
Food, 72–74
Ford Motor Company, 362
Foreign Service Act, 35
Foss, K. A., 249
Foster, R., 372
Fox, S., 360
*Fragante v. City and County of
        Honolulu,* 123
France, 29
Frank, T., 26
Franklin, Benjamin, 83–84
Freire, Paulo, 147
French (language), 153
French, P. 270
Friedman, G., 356
Fukuoka, Y., 92
Furnham, A., 309
Fuss, D., 377
Future orientation, 201

Gandhi, Mahatma, 285
Gao, G., 40
Garreau, J., 220
Gay, *See* sexual orientation.
Geary, D. C., 249
Geddes, R. W., 338
Gelassenheit, 341
Gender, 249

Gender Empowerment Measure,
        252–253
Gender equality, 201
Gender Inequality Index, 253
Gender-Related Development
        Index, 252–253
Gerber Baby Foods, 301–302
Gerbner, G., 349
German, 154–156
    Immigrants to United States,
        331–332
Germany, citizenship policy,
        313–314
Gerner, M., 311–312
Ghosh, B., 229
Gibson, C., 20
Gilbert, D., 12
Gillettte, J., 178
Gladwell, M., 183
Glendon, M. A., 214
Gonzalez, A., 351
Goodness, 212
Google, 50, 102, 376
Gordon, D. R., 60
Govorchin, G. G., 330
Grammatical-syntactical
        equivalence, 140, 143
Greece,
    Individual identity, 60–61
Greenberg, J., 52
Griffith, J. E., 355
Grimm, Jacob, 133
Grosjean, F., 156
Gross, Larry, 385
Guanxi, 41
Gudykunst, W. B., 81
Guernica, A., 350
Gypsy. *See* Roma

Haiek, J. R., 238
Haiman, F. S., 52
Hall, Edward, 35, 69–70, 109,
        114, 116, 122, 169
Hall, J. H., 220
Hallett, V., 386
Hallstein, L. O., 249
Hamilton, S. 83
Hampden-Turner, C., 193
Handlin, Oscar, 321
Haptics, 124–125
Harding, S., 369

Harper, R. G., 119
Harris, D., 385
Hate speech, 52
Hawai'i, 159–160, 280–281
Hayakawa, S. I., 44, 157–158
Hayden, T., 137
Hayes, Joseph J., 385
Hayes-Bautista, D. E., 355
Hayman, R. L., Jr., 20
Hebdige, Dick, 370–371
Hegemony, 286
Heidegger, M., 60
Heider, Fritz, 60
Herodotus, 6, 22
Heroes, 6
Hickson, M. L., III, 109
High context, 69–72, 169, 176
Hindi, 151
Hispanic, 22, 156, 350–362
Hmong, 17, 337–339
Hofstede, Geert, 6, 169–172,
    180–193, 201, 261, 265,
    275–276, 372, 380
Hoijer, Harry, 65, 138
Hollinger, D. A., 362
Holm, J. A., 146
Holson, L. M., 290
Homogeneity, 172, 176–179
Homophobia, 381–383
Homosexual, *See* sexual
    orientation.
Hong Kong, 96, 102
    Disneyland, 290–291
Hopi language, 136–138
Hostetler, J. A., 341
Hotz, R. L., 20
House, R. J., 201
Hu, H. C., 72
Hu, X. B., 313
Huffstutter, P. J., 341
Hui, K., 153
Hull, R. B., 205
Human activity, 209–211
Human being-nature orientation,
    202–209
Human couriers, 45
Human Development Index,
    251–252
Human nature orientation,
    212–213, 240

Human orientation, 201
Huntington, Samuel P., 102,
    202, 353
Hurstfield, J., 351
Husted, B. W., 191
Hyperindividualism, 214

Ichioka, Yuji, 89
Icon, 285
Idiomatic equivalence, 142
Imam, 229
Imhofe, J., 158
Immigration, 28–31, 316–329
Income, 184–185
India, 30, 150–151, 270–271
Indigenous cultures, 281–282,
    345–347
Individualism, 6, 40, 169–172,
    177–178, 190–191, 193, 201,
    212–214
Infante, D. A., 44
In-group/Out-group, 40
Ingle, S., 300
Inglehart, R., 203
Integration, 316, 334, 386
Intercultural communication,
    barriers to, 11, 44, 81–92, 129,
        242–246
    competence, 35–37
    defined, 9, 35
    media, 45–51
    ethics, 37–38
Intermediaries, 40, 45
International Covenant on Civil
    and Political Rights, 52
Internet, 49–54, 101–102,
    150–151, 360
Interpretation, 66–69
Iran, 225
Irish American, 92
Iroquois, 198
Isaacs, J., 281
Ishii, K., 62
Islam, 227–231
Israel, citizenship policy, 315–316
Ivins, Molly, 220
Iwama, H. F., 312

Jablonski, N., 19
Jackson, D. Z., 294

Jackson, R. L. II, 21
Jain, N. C., 123
Jandt, F. E., 22, 280
Japan, 27–28, 172–180, 268–269
    anxiety over speaking
        English, 82
    baseball, 177–178
    citizenship policy, 316
    culture effect on perception,
        61–62, 65
    earthquake, 179–180
    high context, 70–71
    instant ramen (icon), 286–287
    migration to Brazil and Peru, 317
    prejudice, 92
    quality circles, 300
    smile, 109
    tea ceremony, 70–71
    women, 268–269
Japanese language, 63–64
Jargon, 367
Johnson, R., 382
Johnston Pump Company, 67–69
Jones, S. E., 125
Jung, C. G., 69

Kale, D. W., 37
Kallen, Horace, 349
Katz, J., 377
Katz, J. H., 20
Keesing, R. M., 146
Kelleher, Herb, 373–374
Kennedy, John F., 35
KFC (Kentucky Fried Chicken), 295
Khoisan languages, 5
Kidd, J. K., 311
Kim, Min-Sun, 113
Kim, Y., 51
Kim, Young Yun, 35, 169, 316,
    329, 345, 348
Kinesics, 116–120
King, R. -D., 133
Kinney, M. V., 271
Kinver, M, 49
Kipling, Rudyard, 23
Kirkland, S. L., 52
Kissinger, H., 94, 104
Kitayama, S., 61
Kluckhohn, F. R., 202–218, 238
Knapp, M. L., 108, 110

Knighton, J., 172, 275
Kohls, L. R., 202
Kohn, G. C., 24
Kohn, M. L., 12
Koran, 230, 239
Korea, Republic of 27–28, 269–270
    communication, 39–40
    migration to Brazil and
        Argentina, 317
    prejudice, 92
Korean-American, 129
Korean language, 40–41, 183
Koreans in Russia, 340
Kraut, A. H., 325
Kraybill, D. B., 341
Krippendorff, K., 39
Kuhn, A. 98
!Kung San, 5
Kushner, Harold S., 213

Labov, W., 220
Landis, D., 310
Language, 65, 133–162
    Ababic, 140–141
    bilingual speakers, 136
    dialects, 221
    English, 50, 148–161
    Eskimo, 138–139
    Esperanto, 147
    Hindi, 151
    Honorific, 41, 183
    Hopi, 136–138
    Internet, 49, 150
    Japanese, 63–64
    Khoisan, 5
    Korean, 40–41, 183
    nationalism, 147–161
    Nushu, 250
    official, 154, 157–159
    origins, 5, 134–135
    othering, 22, 280–281, 377–381
    pidgin, 146
    Spanish, 156, 354
    tonal, 122
    translation, 50, 141–145
Lao-Tzu, 73
Laqueur, T., 249
Latino, 350. *See also* Hispanic
Lau v. Nichols, 156
Lazarus, Emma, 324

Lee, W. S., 142
Leeds-Hurwitz, W., 35
Le Play, F., 274
Lerner, Daniel, 298
Lesbian, *See* sexual orientation
Letter writing, 46
Levine, E. S., 355
Levy, G. D., 249
Lewis, B., 231
Liberman, K., 9–11
Ling, R., 46
Linguistic determinism, 137
Linguistic relativity, 138
Linnaeus, Carolus, 19
Lippmann, Walter, 85
Lipset, Seymour Martin, 203
Lipski, J., 354
Livingston, G., 360
Long-term orientation, 188–190
LoonLounge, 330
Lorde, A., 377
Losada, A., 279
Low context, 69–72, 169, 176
Luther, Martin, 215, 26
*Lyng v. Northwest Indian Cemetery
    Protection Association,* 17

Ma, R., 45, 72
Macao, 96
Macfarquhar, N., 380
MacGregor, S., 261
Mack, A., 62
Maddox, K. B., 21
Magnier, M., 180
Mäkinen, M., 48
    Malotki, Ekkehart, 138
    Maniere, Philippe, 29
Māori, 15–16, 125, 152–153, 159
Marcus, A., 185
Marginalization, 333, 337–339
Marketing and cultural identity,
    360–362
Marlboro, 296–297
Marriage, 275–276
Marshall, T., 313
Martin, J., 47
Masakazu, Y., 170
Masaru, Katzumie, 110
Mascots, American Indian, 87
Masculinity, 180–182, 191, 201

Masood, E., 231
Matawain, 233
Materialism, 207–209
Matthews, S., 135
Maurer, David, 367
Mayer, J. P., 199
McClelland, D. C., 202, 215
McCroskey, J. C., 108, 123
McDonald's, 26, 291–294, 372
McIntosh, Peggy, 21
McPhail, M. L., 21
McSweeney, B., 192
Mecca-Cola, 288
Media, 45–51
Media and cultural identity,
    357–360, 383–384
Media, Subgroup and values, 368
Mehrabian, A., 108, 112
Meier, M. S., 345
Melkote, S. 298
Melting pot, 348
Melton, J. Gordon, 204
Melville, Herman, 348
Mencken, H. L., 149
Mendes, Chico 31
Merchant, Carolyn, 206
Merriam, A. H., 140
Message, 43
    adapting, 301
Mexican-American, 351
Mexico, 85, 265
    instant ramen (Japanese icon),
        286–287
Micheltorena, Manuel, 329
Middle class, 12
Migration, 5, 27–31, 312–313
Miike, Y., 173
Mikkelsen, C., 346
Miller, D. H., 377
Miller, M. D., 250
Milne, J., 16
Minority, 13
Mirandé, A., 350
Mitigated speech, 182
Mixi, 51
Miyamoto, Y. 69
Modley, R., 110
Monochronic time, 121
Montepare, J. M., 21
Moore, Monica, 120

Morris, Desmond, 116–117
Mott, F. L., 84
Muhammad, 229
Multiculturalism, 349
Murdock, George P., 273
Muslim, 227–231
Mutability, 213
Myspace, 50
Myths, 7

Nafeesi, S., 233
Nakamura, H., 175
Nasr, S. H., 231
Nationalism, 147–161
Native American, 14
Nature, 204–206
Need for achievement, 202, 215
Nelson, C., 387
New Guinea, 302
New Zealand, 14–16, 152–153
Ng, S. H., 183
Nigeria, 282–283
Nisbett, R. E., 60–61, 65, 71, 86, 136–137
Noise, 43
Nonverbal communication, 107–129
    Design elements, 50
Nordenstreng, K., 283
Nordic countries, 261–263
Norway, 320
Nushu, 250

Oberg, Kalvero, 309
Obeyesekere, G., 280
Official language, 154, 157–159
Oil, 102, 232
Oleh, 315
Olesen, A., 103
Olfactics, 126–128
Oliver, R. T., 123
Omi, M., 20
Onishi, N., 28
Opinion leadership, 298
Orbe, M. P., 16, 345
Ordnung, 341
Oregon Department of Transportation, 31
Organization, 64–65
Orkut, 151

Ostler, N., 149
Othering, 22, 280–281, 377–381
Owens, K., 19

Paabo, S., 19
Pacanowsky, M. E., 372
Palestine, 226
Paralanguage, 122–123
Park, H., 191
Participant observer, 369
Particularism, 40
Passel, J., 351
Patterson, O., 214
Pavlidou, T. S., 47
Peace Corps, 35
Pedersen, P., 309
Penn, M. J., 197
People's Republic of China. See China
Pepsi, 288, 361
Perceiving, 62–69
Perception, 59–74
Personality strength 35–36
Peru, immigration from Japan, 317
Peters, T. J., 372
Pew Global Attitudes Project, 243, 378
Pew Hispanic Center, 354, 360
Pew Research Center, 23, 29
Pew Research Center for the People and the Press, 26
Pew Research Center Forum on Religion and Public Life, 203, 228, 320
Pfeil, U., 50
Pharr, S., 381
Phenomenological tradition, 39, 60
Philipsen, Gerry, 369
Physical appearance, 125–126
Piatt, B., 346
Pidgin, 146
Pluralism, 334
Plyler v. Doe, 322
Polychronic time, 122
Posse, A., 318
Postcolonial studies, 281
Postethnic cultures, 362–363

Power distance, 182–186, 191, 193, 201
Practicality, 210
Pratt, Mary 22, 279
Prejudice, 52–54, 90–93
Profiling, 87–88
Progress, 210–211
Proxemics, 114–116
Psychological adjustment, 36
Puenta, S., 354
Puerto Rico, 161
Putnam, L., 372
Putnam, R. E., 30

Quality circles, 300
Quebec, 16, 153, 288
Queer theory, 378
Queuing, 115–116
Quran. See Koran

Race, 19–21
Racial profiling, 87–88
Racism, 52–54
Radio, Spanish language, 358–359
Ramadan, 230
Rand, Ayn, 214
Rapaille, G. Clotaire, 209
Rationality, 212–213
Receiver, communication, 43
Receiver response, 40
Reciprocity, 40
Recycling symbol, 111–112
Redemptive analogy, 302
Reese, L., 370
Refugee, 309
Reid-Pharr, R., 378
Relation to nature, 202–209
Relational orientation, 213–218, 240–242
Religion, 175, 203, 205, 215, 227–231, 341
Religious Freedom Restoration Act, 17
Republic of China. See Taiwan
Reverse culture shock, 311
Rheingold, Howard, 342
Ricci, J., 386
Richardson, D., 302
Riggins, S. H., 22
Rituals, 6

Ritzer, G., 291–292, 294
Robbins, S. S., 186
Robertson, I., 73
Robinson, E., 20
Rodriguez, A., 358–359, 361
Rodriguez, Richard, 351
Roediger, D. R., 369
Rogers, E. M., 81, 298–299, 301
Rojas, R., 54
Rojjanaprapayon, W., 128,
    172, 182
Roma, 25, 91
Romaine, S. 146
Romero, D., 150
Ross, M. W., 380
Rotello, Gabriel, 385
Rothenberg, P. S., 90
Roy, A., 149
Rushing, Janice Hocker, 6
Russo, V., 382
Ryan, M. G., 122

Sabogal, F., 355
Said, Edward, 280–281
Sakamoto, N., 116
Samovar, L. A., 202, 204
Sandburg, Carl, 149
Sapir, Edward, 136, 138
Sapir-Whorf hypothesis,
    135–141, 367
Saudi Arabia, 232–236, 273
    culture effect on perception,
        68–69
    cultural patterns, 238–241
    relations with the United States,
        234–236
    women, 241
Sax, L. J., 209
Scheper-Hughes, N., 272
Schiller, H. I., 283–284
Schmid-Isler, S., 50
Schradie, J., 370
Schroeder, H. W., 69
Science, 205–207
Scollon, R., 40
Sechrest, L. 141
Sedano, M. V., 350
Segal, A. F., 214
Segall, Marshall, 61
Segregation, 22, 334, 347

Selection, 62–64
Self-motivation, 214–216
Semiotic tradition, 39
Sennett, R., 126
Sensing, 60–62
Separation, 334, 340–344,
    384–386
Sex ratio at birth, 255–256
Sexual orientation, 376–386
Shachtman, T., 342
Shaheen, J. G., 88, 246
Sharia, 234
Sherif, M., 18
Shiite, 231
Shin, H. B., 155, 354
Shinto, 175
Shioiri, T., 107
Shome, R., 280–281
Short message service (SMS), 48
Short-term orientation, 188–190
Shuter, R., 48, 119
Sierra Club, 356–357
Signs, 110–112
Sikh, 17
Silence, 123
The Silent Language, 35
Simmel, Georg, 81
Simmons, A. M., 340
Simons, D. J., 62
Singapore, 39, 188–190
Singh, N., 50
Skin color, 19–21
Slagle, A., 377
Slang, 367
Smith, Alfred G., 39, 113
Smith, C. A., 312
Smith, J. I., 229
Smith, R. R., 377
Smith, Ruth, 372
Smutkupt, S., 124, 128
Snyder, M., 89
Social class, 12
Social media, 46–48, 54, 151,
    330, 360, 370, 372, 384
Social networking, 49
Social network sites, 50–51
Social organization, 216–218
Socioeconomic status, 12
Sojourner, 309
Source, communication, 43

South Africa, 152
South Korea, 269–270 Also see:
    Korea, Republic of
Southwest Airlines, 373–375, 382
SPAM® (food), 296
Spanglish, 354
Spanish, 156, 354
Starbucks, 26
Stark, R., 212
*State of Wisconsin v. Jonas Yoder
    et al.,* 343–344
Stauffer, J., 323
Stavenhagen, R., 12
Steele, C. M., 89
Stereotypes, 85–90, 246
Steinfatt, T. M., 138
Stevenson, V., 149, 152, 153
Stewart, Edward C., 197
Stoneking, Mark, 5
Subculture, 12–17 *See also*
    Cultures within cultures
Subgroup, 17–19, 369–386
Sub-Saharan Africa, 271–272
Sugawara, Y., 82
Sunni, 231
Superstitions, 8–9
Sustainable development, 190
Sutherland, W. J., 137
Sweden, 29
Symbols, 6–7, 39, 110–112
Sypher, B. D., 372
Szalay, L. B., 143, 353

Taijfel, H. 62
Taiwan, 93–94, 98–99
Tanno, D. V., 22, 280, 350, 351
Taoism, 73
Taylor, D., 16
Tea ceremony, 70–71
Technology, 26, 205–207, 341
Tejano, 351
Telemundo, 359
Telephone, 46–49
Television, Spanish language, 359
Temporal orientation, 211–212
Territoriality, 126
Text messaging, 48
Thailand, 128–129, 172
Tharoor, S., 30
Third-culture kids, 311–312

Tibet, 99–100
Time, 121–122, 211–212
Time orientation, 211–212,
    239–240
Ting-Toomey, S., 45, 72, 348
Tobin, J., 43
Tocqueville, Alexis de, 199–200,
    204, 210–211, 214, 218
Todd, Emmanuel, 274–275
Tolson, J., 231
Translation, 50, 141–145
Triandis, H. C.,
Tribes, 12
Tsujimura, A., 176
Tung, Tran Minh, 338
Turner, Frederick Jackson, 199
Tutu, Archbishop Desmond, 53
Twitter, 47–48, 244, 330
Tylor, Sir Edward B., 6

Uncertainty avoidance,
    186–187, 201
Unicode, 50
United Nationals Global
    Compact, 297
United Nations
    Convention on the Elimination
        of All Forms of
        Discrimination Against
        Women, 25, 260
    Declaration on the Rights of
        Indigenous Peoples,
        282, 346
United Nations Development Fund
    for Women, 260–261
United Nations Development
    Programme, 31, 205, 228,
    239, 251–254, 257–258,
    264, 284
United Nations Environment
    Programme, 49
United States
    assimilation, 347–348
    attitudes toward, 26
    census, 20, 22–23
    citizenship policy, 321
    communication
        apprehension, 123
    communication barriers,
        242–246

culture effect on perception,
    61, 65
cultural icons, 287–297
cultural patterns, 197–221
    Hispanic, 350–362
    immigration, 30, 198–199,
        320–328, 340, 352–351
    integration, 349
    Japanese-American
        internment, 347
    language use, 154–161
    migration to Brazil, 318
    Muslims, 229
    prejudice, 92
    regions, 200, 219–221
    relations with China, 97–104
    relations with Saudi Arabia,
        234–236
    value orientation theory, 202–218
United States v. Sandoval, 90
Univision, 359
Useem, Ruth Hill, 311

Value orientation theory, 202–218
Values, 6, 354–356
Varnell, P., 386
Vidal, Gore, 353, 383
Vidal, J., 283
Vocabulary equivalence, 138–139,
    141–142
Von Humboldt, Wilhelm, 142

Wai, 128–129
Walker, S., 52
Walters, S. D., 386
Wang, X., 266
Warner, M., 377
Warschauer, M., 50
Wasserstrom, J. N., 100
Watson, Thomas J. Jr., 372
Wealth, 184–185
Weiner, M., 92
Weinstein, N., 55
Weller, A., 127
Wells, S., 5
Westbrook, R. B., 349
Western Europe
    immigration, 319–320
Western perspectives on
    communication, 41–44

Westernization, 173–174,
    245–246
Western Union, 330
Wexler, B. E., 22, 59
Whetmore, Edward J., 285
White, 13, 20–21, 52
White privilege, 21
Whorf, Benjamin L., 136
Whorfian thesis. *See* Sapir-Whorf
    hypothesis
Willis, D. B., 312
Wilson, Allan C., 5
Winter Sonata, 28
Wittgenstein, Ludwig, 64
Witt, S. D., 249
Women, 25–26, 206, 235–236,
    241–242, 249–273
Wong, D. F. K., 313
Wood, J., 249
Woodring, A. A., 172
Work, 210, 342
Working class, 12, 369–370
World Economic Forum,
    254–255, 265
World Commission on
    Environment and
    Development, 31
Worldview, 202–209, 238

Xhosa, 152

Yang, 73
Yep, G. A., 378
Yin, 73
Yon-sama, 28
York, J., 245
Young, B. B. C., 280
YouTube, 47–48, 54,
    102, 330
Yum, June, 39, 41, 54

Zagorin, P., 227
Zamenhof, Lazarus, 147
Zam Zam Cola, 288
Zelinsky, W., 199
Zenner, W., 12
Zhao, Y. H., 312
Zibin, Li, 313
Zuckerman, M. B., 95
Zulu, 152

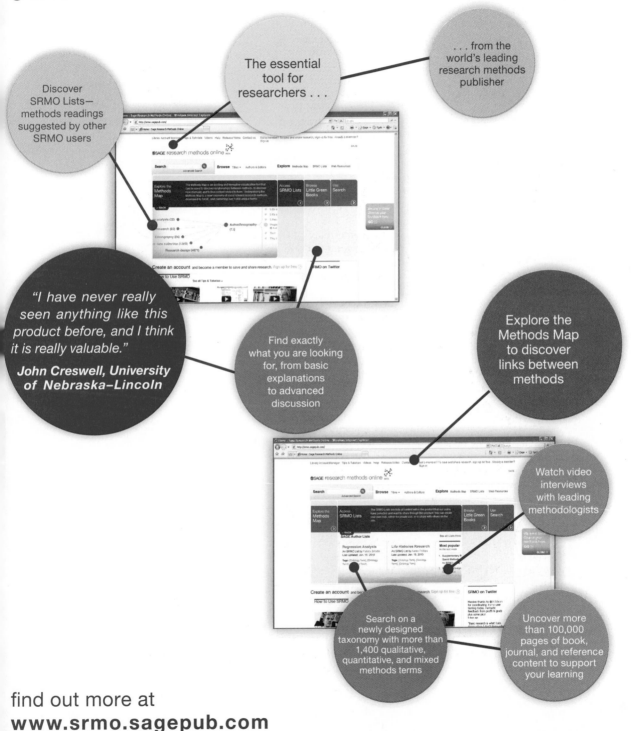